Tito
and His
Comrades

Tito *and His* Comrades

Jože Pirjevec

THE UNIVERSITY OF WISCONSIN PRESS

The University of Wisconsin Press
728 State Street, Suite 443
Madison, Wisconsin 53706
uwpress.wisc.edu

Printed in the United States of America

This book may be available in a digital edition.

Library of Congress Cataloging-in-Publication Data
Names: Pirjevec, Jože, 1940–, author.
Title: Tito and his comrades / Jože Pirjevec; foreword by Emily Greble.
Other titles: Tito in tovariši. English
Description: Madison, Wisconsin : The University of Wisconsin Press, [2018] | Translated into English by Jože Pirjevec. | Originally published as: Tito in tovarisi (Ljubljana: Cankarjeva zalozba, 2011). | Includes bibliographical references and index.
Identifiers: LCCN 2017044551 | ISBN 9780299317706 (cloth : alk. paper)
Subjects: LCSH: Tito, Josip Broz, 1892–1980. | Tito, Josip Broz, 1892–1980—Friends and associates. | Presidents—Yugoslavia—Biography. | Yugoslavia—History—1945–1980.
Classification: LCC DR1300 .P5713 2018 | DDC 949.702/3092 [B]—dc23
LC record available at https://lccn.loc.gov/2017044551

ISBN 9780299317744 (pbk.)

Contents

Foreword

Emily Greble

For three decades, Josip Broz Tito, the charismatic communist dictator of Yugoslavia, sailed the world in a majestic yacht, the *Galeb* (seagull). He entertained a motley crew of international celebrities, from Elizabeth Taylor and Richard Burton to Nikita Khrushchev and Indira Gandhi. Never one to kowtow to the expectations of the bipolar Cold War world, Tito made his boat an oasis of nonconformity. Under his rule, socialist Yugoslavia did things in its own way. Today, Tito's yacht lays abandoned in the port of Rijeka, Croatia. Its hull is rusted, its deck dilapidated. Much like the tangled legacy of Josip Broz Tito, the founding father and lifelong ruler of socialist Yugoslavia, locals have mixed feelings about the abandoned ship. It is a nostalgic vestige of the greatness of Tito's Yugoslavia, and yet an unforgiving reminder of the state's wrenching collapse in the 1990s and the undoing of his legacy.

It is not easy to write the history of the founding father of one's lost country. A prominent historian whose career crisscrossed the Cold War border between Yugoslavia and Italy, Jože Pirjevec is uniquely suited to do so. He studied in Trieste and Vienna, held important academic positions in both Italy and Slovenia, and is familiar with the region's many archives and the diverse historiographical approaches to Yugoslav history around the world. A prolific author, Pirjevec has written many highly regarded works on diverse subjects of Yugoslav history and has often been the first to lay the foundations of new avenues of research.

In crafting Tito's story, Pirjevec navigates a complex historiographical landscape. Tito's predominating story long belonged under the tutelage of the Yugoslav state. Starting in the Second World War, Tito began to actively shape his own legacy, a process he continued for the next few decades. Through interviews and several authorized biographies, he presented himself as a symbol of unity and strength. Under his military leadership, the multiethnic Partisan army drove the Nazis out of Yugoslavia. His political ingenuity led to the subsequent foundation of a formidable socialist state. In 1948, when Stalin and the Cominform broke ties with Yugoslavia, hoping to force the young country to bend to Soviet influence, Tito guided his country through a sequence of turbulent global alliances with grit, vision, and cunning, emerging by the 1960s as the leader of the powerful Non-Aligned Movement. These were the driving themes of Tito's story, which formed the centerpiece of predominantly hagiographic biographies in both Serbo-Croatian and English. These studies looked sympathetically upon the socialist experiment and credited Tito with its success, ignoring the dictator's role in the crimes communists committed under his rule.[1]

Tito's biography became closely entwined with Yugoslavia's foundational myths and its political legacy. In the aftermath of the Second World War, control of the past was essential to solidifying new regimes and helping societies heal from the traumas of war and genocide.[2] Governments closely monitored historical production, especially the public narrative of the war, and Yugoslav efforts echoed this pan-European process. As a country created amid Fascist occupation and international and civil war, socialist Yugoslavia's foundational myths emphasized two central concepts: "anti-Fascism" and "brotherhood and unity." These tropes highlighted the comradery of Yugoslavia's diverse populations who fought in the Partisan army, papering over the bitter rivalries and civil conflicts that had destabilized the region since the First World War, as well as the nationalist factions that collaborated with the Nazis or fought against the communists. Those who dissented in the early postwar years were branded as Fascists. To promote this singular historical narrative, the regime developed a cult of Partisan heroes through history books, posters, and newspapers; it also held public rallies and parades and built memorial complexes to fallen Partisan soldiers, which quickly became mandatory sites of pilgrimage for Yugoslav youths.[3] In Yugoslavia's story, Tito was the devoted father, his sons and daughters were the many diverse constituents of Yugoslavia. Occasional dissident literature, notably works by Tito's one-time communist comrade Milovan Djilas, complicated Tito's image by pointing out his more tactical and less benevolent acts.[4] But for the most part, after 1950, the Yugoslav and Western public were sympathetic to Tito. Captivating and gregarious, he was known as the man who beat the Nazis and defied Stalin, who collected exotic animals on an Adriatic island, and who socialized with movie stars and world leaders.

In the aftermath of Tito's death in 1980, historians began to challenge Yugoslavia's grand foundational narratives and the story of Tito himself. Within Yugoslavia, scholars documented crimes committed by Partisan soldiers during the Second World War and unearthed stories of communist repression. They also called attention to the falsities of historical production in the socialist era, encouraging critiques of Tito and the Yugoslav socialist project.[5] Even Tito's official biographer, Vladimir Dedijer, published a controversial volume that acknowledged the communists' darker past.[6] A renewed focus on human rights in Eastern Europe, inspired by the Helsinki Accords in 1975, placed Tito's legacy under a more critical international lens as well.[7]

Several prominent historians of Yugoslavia in the United States and the United Kingdom also rigorously reassessed key parts of Tito's narrative and Yugoslavia's foundational moment in the Second World War. Among the earliest works were Denison Rusinow and Sabrina Ramet's influential studies on the socialist Yugoslav state, which introduced readers to Tito's dilemmas of state-building and provided a nuanced analysis of the socialist political project.[8] Ivo Banac's seminal work on the Tito-Stalin split clarified the vicious factionalism in Yugoslavia's Communist Party and the ways that Tito, like other communist dictators, used purges, camps, and repression to solidify control.[9] Stevan K. Pavlowitch's biography of Tito, published just as the Yugoslav state collapsed, presented a more nuanced account of Tito's accomplishments and failures, introducing new questions for historians to consider when investigating Tito.[10] But the majority of Communist Party and secret police archives remained closed to foreign researchers well into the 1990s, leaving historians without the essential tools for answering these questions and providing revisions of the historical record. Many Western historians interested in Tito's life and career thus relied heavily on Allied documents; their prevailing interest, it seems, was to investigate Yugoslavia's place in the global history of the Second World War and the Cold War, rather than to understand the country's leader.[11]

Within the region, the unearthing of repressed histories took on a new character with the collapse of socialist Yugoslavia in 1991 and the subsequent foundation of seven new countries.[12] National leaders in Bosnia and Herzegovina, Croatia, Kosovo, Macedonia, Montenegro, Serbia, and Slovenia revised the stories of the Second World War and socialist Yugoslavia. Constructive historical reevaluations unfortunately served as components in new, uncompromising nationalist frameworks.[13] Whereas Yugoslav histories had emphasized how the Partisans crushed foreign Fascists and their domestic collaborators for the sake of unifying Yugoslavia, nationalists sought to reclaim the Second World War experience as a fight against communism. In these new national histories, Yugoslavia—and by extension, Tito—had foiled their national self-determination and sovereignty through harsh repression. Politicians actively engaged in the practice of historical rehabilitation. People who had been condemned by the Tito regime as war criminals were recast as popular national heroes.[14] The new states played a central role in this process, with courts overturning socialist courts' judgments and publicly condemning the process by which Tito's regime had prosecuted—or persecuted—alleged Fascist collaborators. In post-Yugoslav countries, anti-communism became the new moral high ground, with many politicians and historians seeking to draw moral equivalencies between the crimes of Tito and the crimes of the Fascists.[15] They believed that history had to be rewritten to serve their new national myths, and they employed the same tools as their socialist predecessors—propaganda, mythology, and public shaming—to do so.

In the late 1990s, as the wars ended and the archives opened, we began to see innovative new approaches to thinking about Yugoslavia as a twentieth-century phenomenon. Pirjevec was among the first of a group of prominent international scholars of Yugoslavia who grappled with Yugoslav history in toto.[16] But even more so than survey histories of Yugoslavia, new, rigorously researched monographs have provided critical foundations for the reexamination of Tito's biography. From detailed studies on politics and policing in interwar Yugoslavia to innovative histories on the complexities of the Second World War and the messy solidification of the socialist state, historians began to articulate a much more dynamic understanding of the context in which Tito came to political maturity, built a movement, and founded a state.[17] Recent works on everyday life in Tito's Yugoslavia and on Yugoslavia in the international system also shed new light on the connections between Tito the leader and the broader history of socialist Yugoslavia.[18]

In the shifting historiographical landscape of the 1990s and the first decade of the twenty-first century, a balanced biography of Tito proved elusive, and attempts tended to swing between hero-worship and vituperation.[19] In part, this may be due to the expansive topic and the number of archives involved in any thorough investigation of a political life that spanned from the Habsburg era to the late Cold War. But more than anything, the absence of critical analysis of Tito's story speaks to his colossal stature. Consider the profound challenge of revising the history and memory of not merely the founding father of one's late country, but of a myth, a hero, the closest thing to an embodied state.[20] Slowly, historians of the region have begun to excavate newly opened archives in an effort to map Tito's complex biography onto the region's contested history. The results are mixed: some avoid hyperbole by settling into quasi-encyclopedic accounts; others situate Tito in the nationalist narratives that have emerged since the fall of Yugoslavia.[21]

In *Tito and His Comrades*, Jože Pirjevec skillfully navigates the complex terrain of history and memory that Tito evokes, composing a biography that is both respectful to Tito's complicated legacy and sensitive to the emotionally charged questions of history that have fueled discord in the region. Originally written in Slovene, the book has been adeptly translated into English by the author himself; Noah Charney played a significant role in editing the manuscript. The book integrates numerous archival sources, an extensive secondary literature in Slovenian, Serbo-Croatian, Italian, German, Russian, and English, and local anecdotes to present the most comprehensive and circumspect English-language history of Tito to date. Pirjevec does not take sides, nor does he ask his readers to do so.

Pirjevec portrays Tito in his many venerable roles: political strategist, valiant marshal, global leader. Tito is the mastermind of the Yugoslav Partisan army, the man who mobilized the most extensive and successful resistance army during the Second World War. He is also the heretic who defied Stalin in 1948, breaking from the Eastern bloc and creating a different path to socialism. He is the visionary who modernized Yugoslavia, rebuffed Cold War divisions, and empowered smaller countries across the globe.

But, Pirjevec reminds us throughout the story, there were other Titos as well. Tito was a dogmatic ideologue driven by an unflinching faith in Marxist revolution. He was an outcast in the interwar Yugoslav Communist party, viewed at times as shady, untrustworthy, or precarious. Under his military command in the Second World War, the Partisans killed tens of thousands of enemy soldiers and their families during and after the war. As a communist dictator, Tito persecuted civilians who opposed him and deported political opponents to the infamous Yugoslav gulag of Goli Otok, a work camp perched on a barren, windy island in the Adriatic. He suppressed religious dissent with targeted executions and imprisonments, and he crushed nationalist opposition.

Unlike most biographies of Tito, which gloss over his formative years, Pirjevec analyzes Tito's life from his impoverished childhood in late Habsburg Croatia to his global leadership at the height of the Cold War. Set against the backdrop of European state-building and a global communist movement, the biography shows how Tito's ideology formed in response to his personal experiences in the Russian Revolution and civil war, Stalin's Soviet Union, and authoritarian interwar Yugoslavia. Pirjevec also draws connections between global political shifts and Tito's ideological development, so readers see how he came to understand the relationship between Yugoslav communism and other manifestations of socialism around the world, notably in the Third World. This background helps us to understand why Tito did not flinch when abandoned by Stalin and left to his own devices in 1948, and to make sense of the way Tito balanced authoritarianism with a more flexible approach to communist economic structures and culture. Rather than shy away from Tito's association with communism, Pirjevec embraces it, allowing this biography of Yugoslavia's leader to serve also as a reckoning with the Yugoslav state, its sociopolitical victories and failures, and its relationship to the international communist movement.

It is perhaps fitting that as Pirjevec's study hits the stands in the United States, the city of Rijeka is transforming Tito's timeworn yacht into a museum, a repository of history and memory. We can hope that it will be a place for locals and tourists alike to reflect upon Tito's legacy, to celebrate his diplomatic and domestic successes, and to critique the ideology and failures of a deceased state. Pirjevec provides us with the scholarly framework to do such memory work. Indeed, *Tito and His Comrades* goes beyond simple biography to serve also as a reevaluation of the history of socialist Yugoslavia.

Acknowledgments

For this edition of my book I have many to thank. First of all, Noah Charney, who took my own English translation and improved it, editing it with patience and skill. I would also like to thank Gwen Walker and her formidable team at the University of Wisconsin Press. Many thanks to Emily Greble, who agreed to write the foreword, and to Karolyn Close, who reread and bettered the text with intelligent care. Last but not least, Sabrina Ramet, who although busy with her own writing dedicated a great deal of attention to the manuscript and gave me some vital suggestions out of sheer kindness. After such an experience life is brighter.

Abbreviations

AVNOJ—Antifašističko veće narodnog oslobođenja Jugoslavije (Antifascist Council for the National Liberation of Yugoslavia)

CIA—Central Intelligence Agency

CC—Central Committee

Comintern—Communist International

CP—Communist Party

CPY—Yugoslav Communist Party

CPSU—Communist Party of the Soviet Union

ELAS—Ellinikós Laikós Apeleutherótikos Stratós (the Greek National Liberation Army)

FBI—Federal Bureau of Investigation

GDR—German Democratic Republic (East Germany)

IKKI—Ispolnitel'nyi komitet Kommunisticheskogo internationala (Executive Committee of the Comintern)

KGB—Komitet gosudarstvennoj bezopasnosti (Committee for State Security)

KOS—Kontraobaveštajna služba (military counterintelligence service)

KUNMZ—Kommunisticheskij Univerzitet Nacional'nyh Men'shinstv Zapada (Communist University for the Ethnic Minorities of the West)

LCY—League of Communists of Yugoslavia

NATO—North Atlantic Treaty Organization

NDH—Nezavisna država Hrvatska (Independent State of Croatia)

NKVD—Narodnyi kommissariat vnutrennykh del (People's Commissariat of Internal Affairs)

OGPU—Ob'edinennoe gosudarstvennoe politicheskoe upravlenie (Unified State Political Directorate)

OF—Osvobodilna fronta slovenskega naroda (Slovenian Liberation Front)

OSS—Office of Strategic Services

OZNA—Organizacija za zaščito naroda (Service for the Defense of the People)

PLO—Palestine Liberation Organization

SFRY—Socialist Federative Republic of Yugoslavia

SHS—Kraljevina Srbov, Hrvatov in Slovencev (Kingdom of Serbs, Croats, and Slovenes)

SKOJ—Savez Komunističke Omladine Jugoslavije (Union of Communist Youth of Yugoslavia)

SOE—Special Operations Executive

TASS—Telegrafnoe agentstvo Sovetskovo soiuza (Telegraph Agency of the Soviet Union)

UDBA—Uprava državne bezbednosti (State Security Administraion)

UN—United Nations

USSR—Union of Soviet Socialist Republics

ZAVNOH—Zemaljsko antifašističko veće narodnog oslobođenja Hrvatske (State Anti-fascist Council for the National Liberation of Croatia)

Tito
and His
Comrades

Introduction

> Nothing is more to be desired than that the people who were at the head of the active party, whether before the revolution in the secret societies or the press, or afterwards in official positions, should at long last be portrayed in the stark colours of a Rembrandt, in the full flush of life. Hitherto these personalities have never been depicted as they really were, but only in their official guise, with buskins on their feet and halos around their heads. All verisimilitude is lost in these idealised, Raphaelesque pictures.[1]

So wrote Marx and Engels, optimists who did not imagine that the revolution could fail, or that its protagonists could finish on the infamous column. Something similar happened to Tito, flattered during his lifetime and, after the disappearance of Yugoslavia, often demonized.

Let us try to depict him à la Rembrandt.

Tito's Eyes

From the moment he stepped onto the historical stage in 1928 due to his bold behavior in a courthouse in Zagreb that ended with him being thrown in jail as a communist, Tito's contemporaries, friends and enemies alike, would comment on his expressive eyes. Reporting on his 1928 trial, the Croatian newspaper *Novosti* wrote, "The features of his face call to mind steel. Through the pince-nez he wears, he stares with clear, cold eyes, but with energy and calm."[2]

In his short essay "Tito's Return in 1937," Miroslav Krleža, the Croatian poet, writer, and chronicler of provincial Yugoslavia and Croatia, recalled:

> I was seated in the twilight of my room, looking at the clouds . . . in this stillness, the bell rings . . . I get up and cross the flat . . . in front of the glass door there is a foreigner. . . . After nine years, Tito was like a shadow from the past. At the

> very beginning, I had the impression that he had not changed at all, but at the same time, that he had changed a lot. Six years of prison and three of exile have erased that ingenuous and immediate freshness from his face. Instead of a smiling youth, I saw a serious foreigner whose eyes, behind that pince-nez, seemed dark and stern.

Tito spent the entire night catching up with Krleža, the comrade who sensed in Tito an old friend, and someone who had been reborn, cast anew. Their dialogue lasted until dawn, as Krleža learned some of the details of Tito's adventurous life and revolutionary ideas. Tito told him of his homesickness, which one night after his return from Moscow compelled him to visit his native village, though he knew the risk he took in doing so, since he was an outlaw at the time. When he reached his father's home, he had the impression that nothing had changed in that faraway place since his last visit so many years ago, despite the great events that had changed the world in the meantime. "In the silent closeness of this lyrical monologue," Krleža continued, "Tito's voice changed and his blue, pigeon-like eyes darkened into an intense, metallic blue. 'Kumrovec is snoring, God damn it, but since when does everyone in this country snore!?' asked Tito with the rage, the violence with which, in our language, all the higher and lower divinities are thrown from the skies."[3]

Tito's eyes likewise impressed Milovan Djilas, one of his most fervent followers (and later opponents), when they met for the first time. "He was a man of mid-size, rather strong, lean. Lively, slightly nervous, but in control of himself. His face was hard, calm, but gentle, the eyes blue and benevolent."[4] The Serbian doctor and veteran of the Spanish Civil War (and later chief of the Partisan Sanitary Service), Gojko Nikoliš, wrote in his diary of his first meeting with Tito, in November 1941: "We met in a large and simply furnished room. . . . After my salute and report, I sized him up, immediately observing some of his traits, this man for whom we had waited so long and who would shape the fate of our fight. The first thing I noted were his blue, slightly veiled eyes, then his sculpted face, the face of an ideal worker, a worker who seemed to have stepped out of a Russian proletarian poster."[5] It is all well and good that Tito's collaborators and followers should find him charming, for his countrymen were already primed to admire him. Foreign politicians were likewise impressed, and similarly commented on his eyes with distinctive frequency. Fitzroy Maclean, chief of the British Military Mission to the Supreme Staff, described his first impression when he met Tito in 1943: "Tito was an imposing personality: he was fifty-two years old, physically strong—hair iron silver. His regular face, as sculptured in stone, was serious and tanned, wrinkles—resolute without appeal. Beneath the glare of his light blue eyes, nothing remained hidden. In him was concentrated the energy of a tiger ready to attack."[6] The ambassador of the Federal Republic of Germany, during his first meeting with Tito on the shores of Slovenia's Lake Bled in 1951, stressed in a dispatch back home that Tito was not physically similar to Hermann Göring at all, contrary to what Tito's detractors would have people believe. "He is mid-sized, not fat, but corpulent and very tough, nearly monolithic. His face is severe, not sallow at all, energetic without being brutal. Most impressive are his light blue eyes. They are very luminous, in contrast to his skin, which has been deeply tanned by the Brioni sun."[7]

Ten years later, during a journey to Africa, Tito's eyes troubled the Serbian writer Dobrica Ćosić, who accompanied him as a chronicler of his tour. "Rich expression of face," Ćosić wrote, "very sentimental, thoughtful, introverted. Sometimes menacing, serious, dangerous, sometimes joyful and benevolent, sometimes somnolent, as if thinking nostalgically of times past. But suddenly, in his green-blue eyes, there is menace, obstinacy, self-confidence. He does not show the fatigue that should accompany his age. I have never seen eyes like his."[8]

A member of a French delegation visiting Tito late in his career noted that Marshal Tito appeared quite old: "He was still in good physical shape, with a lively sense of humor. He ate and drank like Gargantua, and was always ready to smile. But as he is elderly, he was prone to forget things or to repeat them and to be somewhat oblivious. . . . He has elusive eyes, like all the Communists of the old generation. At the beginning, he looked down, in any case never at his interlocutor. But sometimes there came a direct look, and I would not like to be the enemy of a man with such eyes."[9] The first to observe just how dangerous Tito's eyes could seem was Louis Adamic, an American writer of Slovene origin who returned to his homeland in 1949 and described his numerous conversations with Tito in his book *The Eagle and the Roots*. Altogether they spoke for thirty hours, developing a friendly relationship that allowed Adamic to say many things that no one in Tito's entourage would have dared to mention. For example, he did not hide his critical attitude toward the marshal's "Bonapartism" and his penchant for uniforms. After a political meeting that ended in a thunderous applause, Adamic could not suppress his reservations. When Tito was leaving, he noticed that he was being observed. "Suddenly, with a flash in his eyes that wasn't all humor, he said: 'You know, *gospodine Adamicu* [Mister Adamic], I happen to be Commander-in-Chief of the Armed Forces.' So this is his retort to my criticism of his marshal's uniform."[10]

And finally there is the impression of Henry Kissinger, secretary of state to President Nixon: "Tito was a man whose eyes did not always smile with his face."[11] Did Kissinger know that the same had been said of Stalin?[12] Stalin instinctively felt how similar they were, and offered him a word of advice: "Why do you have eyes like a lynx? That is not good. You have to smile with your eyes. And then you drive a knife into their back."[13]

1

The Young Broz

World War One, Imprisonment, and His Rise in the Yugoslav Communist Party

1892–1939

Learning and Wandering

Josip Broz was born on 7 May 1892 (though he used to quote other dates as well)[1] as a subject of Franz Joseph in the village of Kumrovec, the district of Zagorje—"the land beyond the mountains"—on the border between the Banovina (vice-realm) of Croatia and the Duchy of Styria, in what is now Slovenia. Although both regions were part of the Habsburg monarchy, they differed in many ways. The Croatian side of the territory was part of the Kingdom of Hungary, while Styria belonged to the hereditary lands of the ruling dynasty. Franz Joseph was called emperor in Vienna, but king in Budapest. These were not just ceremonial distinctions, since after the establishment of the Dual Monarchy in 1867 two autonomous states were created, with only three key ministries shared between them (war, finance, and foreign affairs), plus of course the head of state himself—otherwise they were governed separately. Thanks to the industrial revolution, the Austrian half of the Double Monarchy experienced slow but steady development. The Hungarian part, however, lingered beneath the yoke of a conservative feudal class, alien to the social and ethnic problems that plagued the kingdom.

Had Josip Broz been born in the valley of Bistrica, just a few miles away from his village, at the home of his Slovene mother, Marija, then his destiny would likely have been very different indeed. The local priest would have almost certainly noted his intelligence and therefore sent him off to the renowned Bishop's College in Ljubljana. This would have opened two doors for him: that of the seminary or, if he was as diligent as he was capable of being, then the university—that is, if he could manage to escape "God's calling" (for his beloved mother dearly wished that he would become a priest). But since he was born in Croatia, where the Roman Catholic Church was less organized than its

Slovenian counterpart, no one took particular note of his cleverness, and so his education was not provided for. He wound up finishing only four years of primary school and two years at a mediocre secondary school for apprentices. Far from taking him under his wing, his local parson, a known drunkard, verbally and physically abused him when, at age twelve, he assisted the priest with his vestments for mass. Young Joža (the familiar version of Josip) never forgot this abuse, as he would later say, "Although I continued to go to Mass on Sundays because Mother wanted me to, I think I was through with the Church from then on."[2]

Josip grew up in appalling living conditions, although it was the norm for his time, place, and social status. His father owned just eight hectares of land, which was insufficient for the survival of the family. For this reason, Joža was sent early in his childhood to live for a number of years with his Slovene grandfather, who was a bit better off.[3] Joža's memories of his parental home were dark indeed. The house was shared with relatives, in addition to his many siblings, despite the fact that the home consisted of only two rooms, plus a common kitchen. Once, lying sick against the earthenware stove, the home's only source of heat, Joža overheard a neighbor predict to his mother that he would not live long. None of the children in the family had shoes, but they had to go outside, even in winter. They developed a trick: step into cow dung, which warmed up the feet and doubled as a temporary pair of winter shoes. The children were often hungry and undernourished. Joža used to ask his mother for an extra slice of bread when a friend of hers was visiting, knowing that she would likely feel obliged to give it to him in the presence of a guest. She did, but afterward she scolded him for having pulled such a trick and wept.[4]

Coming from a family "blessed" with fifteen children, eight of whom died at a tender age, he was obliged to start working to help support the family as soon as he reached puberty. His father, Franc, whom Tito described as being "black as a devil," was a heavy drinker who wound up selling the meager lands he owned and not for a wise investment. Tito had less than fond memories of him, and likewise of the peasants of his native region. "If they disagree with you," he used to say later, "they stay apart, with their hat brims pulled down on their foreheads and their hands in their pockets. They are passive and not very bright."[5] Despite this, he was fascinated by stories of the peasant uprisings that frequently broke out and ravaged the region during the second half of the sixteenth century. Likewise, he was captivated by the tragic death of Matija Gubec, the leader of one of these uprisings, who was crowned in Zagreb in 1573—but with a red hot iron ring. Later, Tito would even hang a large painting by Krsto Hegedušić on the wall of his study that depicted the rebel peasants at the Battle of Stubica, where they were finally defeated.[6]

Young Josip's initial plan was to become a tailor, as he liked elegant clothes. But the village schoolmaster, an authority for the local community, considered him a restless boy, not suited for a sedentary occupation. Josip first found work at an inn in Sušak, a nearby provincial town, but after a short time moved on to a local blacksmith's workshop, and then to another one in Zagreb, Croatia's capital. Perhaps the schoolmaster was right after all, because Josip did demonstrate a restlessness and refusal to stay put. The moment one apprenticeship ended, in 1910, he set off on a series of jobs that were really an excuse to travel in Croatia, Carniola, Bohemia, Bavaria, the Ruhr, and Upper Austria. At one point he even tried to emigrate to America, believing that he would become a millionaire if he could make it there, but he got only as far as Trieste. There his lack of funds would have landed him in trouble had it not been for a local branch of the Social Democrats who organized shelters for poor proletarians like him.[7] That same year, now back in Zagreb, he joined the metallurgical trade union, and the following year signed up for the Union of Socialist Youth, a sociopolitical fraternity through which he would become a member of the Social Democratic Party.[8] The prominent cultural figure and writer Miroslav Krleža, who knew Broz early on, described that time in fairly bleak terms: "Our youth was spent in those boring, grey streets of the lower city of Zagreb ... where the inns are poor and stinking, the shops smell of flour and dried cod, as does most of this gloomy province, and in ugly two-storied houses dwell grey, badly paid employees of a grey, dull Empire that is on its deathbed."[9]

In the autumn of 1913, Josip was drafted into the Austro-Hungarian army, quickly rising to the rank of sergeant major. By age twenty-one he was one of the youngest petty officers of the Imperial and Royal Army.[10] As a member of the patriotic sporting association Sokol (Falcon), he was an excellent sportsman in various disciplines: skiing, riding, fencing. His fencing prowess was so great that he nearly won an army-organized tournament, claiming later that he lost out in the end because he was a Croat and his opponent a Hungarian count.[11] Despite this, he never nourished hostile sentiments toward the Habsburg monarchy, always considering it an orderly state, although at that time he was already attracted to the idea of an independent Yugoslavia[12] capable of uniting Serbs, Croats, Montenegrins, and Slovenes under a single political entity. When Milovan Djilas, later one of Tito's closest associates, scornfully described the pre–World War One king of Montenegro, Nikola Petrović, as a "character from an operetta," Tito protested on his behalf: "No, no! We young folks considered him with sympathy. He had guts, he was a patriot, a Yugoslav."[13]

Nevertheless, he would always remain attached to his Croatian fatherland. In 1971, during a dramatic political power struggle with "liberal" party leaders in Zagreb, whom he deemed too weak in their approach to dealing with local nationalists, Tito said to Savka Dabčević-Kučar, the president of the League of the Communists of Croatia: "You suspect that I have no national feelings, that I do not feel that I am a Croat, since as a young worker I traveled the world and, in keeping with proletarian internationalism, I lost my patriotic consciousness. Yes, I am an internationalist, as every communist should be. But I am also a Croat!"[14]

The First World War

When the First World War broke out at the end of July 1914, Tito was sent to the Serbian front, where he served in August and September in the ranks of the Twenty-Fifth Infantry Regiment. He tried to hide this chapter of his life in order not to provoke negative feelings in Serbia. Soon he was dispatched to the Russian front in the Carpathian Mountains. Before this transfer, however, he spent a few nights behind bars at the fortress of Petervaradin, near Novi Sad (today in Serbia), charged with participating in anti-war propaganda. He considered these charges to have been a mistake made by overzealous military authorities.[15] In fact, at this early stage of the war, he does not seem to have harbored any pacifist sentiments. During the heavy fighting against the Russians in Eastern Galicia, where Broz was transferred in February 1915, he distinguished himself through bravery as the leader of a patrol and was recommended for decoration. The official description of the event is as follows: "The night of 17 and 18 March 1915, at the head of an infantry patrol [of four soldiers], he attacked an enemy group near old Krzwotuly, took eleven Russians prisoner and brought them to our quarters. This petty officer, who volunteers for every dangerous mission . . . has wrought disarray in the enemy ranks on several occasions."[16] These actions earned Broz a substantial bonus, since his commanders paid five krone for every gun taken in battle.[17] However, before he could collect his "little silver medal for valor," he was seriously wounded during an Easter Sunday clash against the so-called Wild Division of Circassian soldiers, who were renowned for their cruelty. The fight took place near the town of Okno, in the Bukovina region. Tito and his comrades first engaged a group of Russians who attacked them with greater numbers. Tito decided that his men should surrender, and he told them not to shoot. Then suddenly, a clutch of Circassians emerged *behind* them. "We did not even notice when they appeared, jumping our position," he recalled. He lifted his hands but, despite this, a Circassian attacked him with a two-meter lance. Instinctively, Tito defended himself, and he parried the lance with his bayonet. The fight was on. Tito, an excellent swordsman, could have killed him, but he did not want to. Just at the moment another Circassian, riding a huge dappled horse, struck him in his back, under the right armpit, with a lance. "I turned around and saw the wild grimace of this second Circassian, with his enormous eyes and heavy brows."[18] He fell to the ground. The last thing he noticed was a Russian soldier, who tried to prevent the assailant from dealing a mortal blow. He was taken prisoner, along with his entire battalion. When he came to, he was in the military hospital.[19]

Prisoner of War

While his name appeared in the list of war casualties suffered by the Habsburg army between 10 and 12 April 1915, it was the beginning of a new chapter in the life of Josip Broz. He was one of two million Austro-Hungarian prisoners scattered throughout the far-flung territory of the tsarist empire. For nearly a year, between May 1915 and March 1916, he was under treatment in a hospital that had been hurriedly opened in the Uspenskii Monastery on the Volga River. He was later transferred to a camp among Chuvash, near the city of Alatyr on the Sura River. There he became acquainted with the daughter of a local doctor and her friend, who used to pay visits to the prisoners of war. They brought him books and often invited him to their homes: "They kept insisting I should play the piano." So he learned.[20] He would have been freed had he enlisted in the volunteer corps organized by the Serbs among their Austro-Hungarian "compatriots" for the Dobrudja front, but he refused to return to combat along with seventy other comrades. As an officer, according to the Hague Convention, he was not obligated to do manual labor. Even so, he accepted the offer of a rich peasant in the village of Kalashevo, near Ardatov, to work in his flour mill. In the autumn of 1916 he was transferred with other prisoners to the Urals, and the town of Alatyr, not far from Ekaterinburg. There he worked on the railway as an interpreter and "elder" prisoner, or supervisor. In May of the following year, he was sent to the small station of Ergach, near Perm. After a run-in with the commander of the prison camp, he was arrested and beaten by three Cossacks with a knout (an event which he never forgot), prompting his escape.[21]

In the disorder following the February Revolution of 1917, he managed to reach Petrograd in early summer, traveling mostly on foot. Once there he hoped to find a job in the Putilov factories. He actually worked there for two or three days, and even had the chance to hear Lenin at a rally and to see the famous left-wing writer Maxim Gorky. He felt a deep veneration for Lenin throughout his lifetime, keeping his photo in his Belgrade office and a bronze bust on a shelf of his library.[22] When the Bolsheviks attempted to seize power on 13 July 1917, Broz took part in the demonstrations. When the police sent to quell the uprisings opened fire, luck was on his side: he first found shelter under the bridges of the Neva and later escaped to Finland, an autonomous principality of the former Russian Empire. However, he was arrested as a "dangerous Bolshevik" near Oulu and sent back to Petrograd, where he languished for three weeks in the dank cells of the Petropavlovsk Fortress.[23] Only when the local authorities established his identity did they decide to send him back to the Urals, but he managed to escape again before reaching Kungur, jumping from the train as it stopped at a station. Although one of his former guards, whom he met by chance, recognized him, he was able to hop onto a train for Siberia without a ticket and slip away. He was fortunate to choose a day when the conductors had other things on their mind—the day before, Lenin had taken power in Petrograd. It was an eventful journey, full of violence, since the soldiers traveling in the same direction rebelled against their officers, throwing them off the train.[24] When Broz reached Omsk, he joined the International Red Guard there and worked as a mechanic from autumn 1917 until summer 1918. It was still not clear who would win the civil war raging in Russia between the Reds and the Whites. In the village of Mikhailovka, not far from Omsk, where he was again working in a steam mill, he met Pelagiia D. Belousova (also known as Polka), a girl of thirteen or fourteen, who became his wife. This was the first of his five marriages, none of which featured a storybook ending.[25]

In 1918, he applied for Soviet citizenship and for membership in the Communist Party, but received neither. His personal dossier in the Comintern archives suggests that he was not accepted into the party because at the time there was no Yugoslav section. Shortly thereafter, Omsk was occupied by General Aleksander V. Kolchak's White Guards, who imprisoned all potential political adversaries. Broz found refuge in a Kirghiz *aul* (a fortified steppe village) fifty or sixty miles from the city, finding work on the farm of a rich peasant, Isaia Diaksenbaev. But Czech legionnaires, former Russian prisoners who collaborated with Kolchak, reached even these remote places. They wanted to arrest Broz, suspecting that he was in contact with the Omsk communists. It is not clear whether Diaksenbaev hid him or whether the villagers came to his aid by testifying that he was not a deserter but had been among them since 1915 as a prisoner of war. In any case, he succeeded in avoiding imprisonment as well as more fatal possibilities. The fact is that the Kirghiz liked him and considered him a brave young man, quick in his decisions and with an extraordinary feeling for animals.[26] This latter characteristic would remain with him throughout his life. The following episode is revealing: some friends gave him a gift of a falcon. He cared for it, fed and stroked it lovingly, and the bird learned to perch on his shoulder. When it grew up and spread its wings, Josip decided to free it. Two days later, the falcon returned and settled on his shoulder, calmly waiting to be fed. When sated, it flew away, to return once more two days later. It was only after the fourth time that the bird was not seen again. All those who heard this story said: "Every living being has to love a man like Broz."[27]

When the Red Army drove Kolchak's bands from Omsk in 1919, reestablishing rail communications with Petrograd, Josip decided to leave with Pelagiia, his wife. In Petrograd, where he remained for approximately three weeks, he received news of the creation of the Kingdom of Serbs, Croats, and Slovenes after the collapse of the Habsburg monarchy. When he read a newspaper article reporting that a revolution had broken out there—the news was false—he felt he had to participate. The Soviet authorities placed him at the head of the group of war prisoners from the former Austrian territories, now part of Yugoslavia, who were to be repatriated.[28] He returned home with them in September 1920, crossing the Baltic, but not without a serious incident in Vienna. Some Serb fellow travelers denounced him to the local Yugoslav diplomatic representatives as a communist. At the Austrian-Slovenian border in Maribor he was detained with his pregnant wife and kept in quarantine for a week. After this they were allowed to return to Broz's native village.[29]

Russia, and particularly Siberia, with its taigas (forested regions), moonshine, and horses, remained forever in his heart. He would come to know the land of the Soviets intimately, in all its enormous industrial and military might, and would retain a sentimental attachment to it even in his old age. In spite of disillusionment, doubts and conflicts, Tito was always convinced that "the socialist continent really exists, that it embraces one-sixth of the globe, that it represents the start of an unstoppable process."[30] When in 1952, at the very height of the conflict with Stalin, one of his generals began cursing the Soviet Union in vulgar terms, he reacted irritably: "Every wolf has his den that he never abandons. It is the same with me."[31] As Veljko Mićunović, one of his most important diplomats, said at the beginning of the seventies, Tito filed his last will and testament in Moscow since he had no faith in the people who surrounded him.[32]

Party Agitator

Returning home, tragic news awaited Josip Broz. His mother, whom he loved dearly in spite of the fact that she was a stern and austere woman, had been carried away by the Spanish flu two years earlier, a devastating epidemic that struck throughout Europe shortly after the First World War. As Polka remembered, he cried and later confessed, "It was the saddest day of my life."[33]

The country he returned to was completely different from the one he had left. The Austro-Hungarian monarchy had vanished, and a strange chimera had been created in its place: the Kingdom of Serbs, Croats, and Slovenes, in which the South Slavs were united under the scepter of the Karadjordjević Dynasty, regardless of their different cultural and historical heritage and their different economic and social development: the Serbs were Levantine and Orthodox, the Croats and Slovenes Central European and Catholic. Together with these three major ethnic groups, at least seventeen lesser minorities (Albanians, Hungarians, Germans, and others) lived in the Kingdom SHS (Kraljevina Srbov, Hrvatov in Slovencev; Kingdom of Serbs, Croats, and Slovenes), as it was known, along with Macedonians, Montenegrins, and Bosnian Muslims (whose ethnic identity was not recognized by Belgrade), making it the most heterogeneous state in Europe. At least 80 percent of the population lived in the countryside, where the conditions were often similar to if not worse than they had been under Turkish rule because of the terrible poverty in the wake of the war.[34]

For the ruling classes in Belgrade, it was obvious that such a complex and potentially conflict-ridden society could be dominated only with an iron fist, a policy they soon started to practice, banishing the recently founded Yugoslav Communist Party (CPY) in December 1920. It was a heavy blow for the party, pushed as it was into illegality: in 1920 it had sixty-five thousand members, in 1924 just 688.[35] Josip Broz was one of them, although he remained aloof from the factional fights initiated by the troopless generals who made up the CPY leadership. He was involved in trade union activity, in which the communists also participated. Although he was not very active politically, he was unable to avoid persecution, discrimination at work, even arrest and ill-treatment.[36] As before the war, he did not like to stay in the same place for too long. From Zagreb, he moved to Bjelovar in central Croatia, to the shipyards of Kraljevica on the Adriatic coast, to Veliko Trojstvo in Bilagora County, and to Serbia, where he found employment in the railway wagon factory at Smederovska Palanka. He even returned briefly to his first job, that of a waiter, which he soon lost because he spread communist propaganda among his colleagues.[37]

In 1926, he tried to join the local party cell in Belgrade. The left wing faction, which was strong in the capital, rejected him, for its leaders were highly suspicious of his critical attitude with regard to internecine party quarrels. As Tito later noted, "This infighting reached such dimensions that the honest communists were prevented from joining the party organizations. The leaders were interested only in retaining their positions . . . and the Comintern's financial aid. Actually, it was more than that, as it involved a regular monthly salary, much higher than the salary of ranking State bureaucrats. This too compelled me to enter the fight against the factions."[38] When he returned to Zagreb, Broz began working as the secretary of the Metallurgical Workers Union, as well as of the Union of Tanners and Leather Dressers. Later he joined the leadership of the Civic Committee of the CPY, in which he represented the middle line, hostile to both the left- and the right-wing factions. The former favored a federal organization of society and state, the latter a single centralized one, expressions of the different political cultures of Zagreb and Belgrade, which were tainted by a hostile antagonism between Serbs and Croats. As Miroslav Krleža wrote later, the discussion was entangled in the vicious circle of opposite beliefs: "It is impossible to solve the national question without democracy," or "Without the solution of the national question there is no real democracy."[39]

From the middle of the twenties, the Executive Committee of the Comintern (Ispolnitel'nyi komitet Kommunisticheskogo internationala; IKKI), controlled by Moscow, considered the Kingdom SHS an "artificial creature of Versailles" and a possible imperialist springboard for an attack against the Soviet Union. It had to be dismembered so that a Federation of Socialist Republics could be created on its ruins. In a resolution published in spring 1925, the CPY received the following instructions: "The party has to convince the working masses with all propaganda means at its disposal that the destruction of such a State is the only way to solve the national question. . . . As long as Yugoslavia does not disappear, no serious communist activity is possible. Hence, Yugoslavia has to be destroyed, with the help of all separatist forces present within it."[40] This is why the IKKI attacked the right-wing faction and its leader, Serb secretary general of the party Sima Marković, who was criticized by Stalin himself for his adverse stance toward Lenin's doctrine of national self-determination. He was expelled from the CPY in 1929. But the IKKI was also opposed to the left-wing faction, led by Rajko Ivanić, who considered peasants inevitable allies of the bourgeoisie and therefore enemies of the working class. In 1928, in an open letter to the members of the CPY, the Comintern described the conflict raging between both groups in these terms: "The vital questions of the proletarian struggle have been relegated to the last place; first place has been taken by a scholastic dispute that only nurtures the clashes between factions."[41]

Moscow's interference in the internal quarrels of the CPY exacerbated things. In this atmosphere the so-called "Zagreb line" prevailed, which asserted that it was necessary to go beyond the factions, since they were nothing but the skirmishes of intellectuals who should be replaced by workers at the head of the party. Tito remembered later, "We tried to find a way out of a difficult situation that the communist movement in Yugoslavia had to face. We knew that it was necessary above all to repair the party and to achieve its unity." Naturally, this proposition was risky, considering that the leadership was prone to inflict heavy sanctions on its critics, quickly claiming that they were "anti-party elements."[42]

In the midst of these discussions, Josip Broz succeeded—not without mocking opposition from those who considered him intellectually inferior—in attaining the post of secretary of the City Committee in Zagreb at the end of February 1928. The main candidate for this office had been Andrija Hebrang, a young Croat Jew employed in a bank, but he stepped down in favor of Broz, claiming that the secretary should be a laborer and not a clerk. The City Committee of Zagreb numbered approximately 180 members and was the most important communist group in the country; so prominent, in fact, that two months later its decisions were blessed even by the Comintern, which provided a morale boost for Broz. The emergence of the "Bolshevik line," aimed at creating a Leninist unity in the party and saving it from the "nightmare of the factions," called Broz and Hebrang to the attention of the police.[43] In 1927, Comrade Georgijević, as Broz was known in the party at the time, had already been jailed for seven months as a result of his revolutionary activity, and on 1 May 1928 he was arrested again because of a demonstration organized by communists in the Apollo cinema that was designed to disturb a social-democratic gathering there. He was particularly conspicuous among those shouting: "Death to social-patriots! Death to the servants of capitalism!" Along with several comrades, he was arrested and detained for fourteen days. At the time, the following notations were made to his personal file: "Height: 170 cm, Eyes: gray, Teeth: some lacking, Far-sighted, Wears glasses" and "Until now his behavior has been impeccable."[44] Obviously, they did not know much about him from the police in Zagreb. The following July and August he was arrested again, and this time charged with seditious activity against the regime. In fact, during that period the communists engaged in strikes, mass demonstrations, and riots in Zagreb, some of which cost human lives.[45]

The time for revolution seemed ripe after 20 June 1928, when the Belgrade Parliament was the site of a shooting by a Serb nationalist, a member of the ruling party. His victims were five Croat deputies, among them Stjepan Radić, the charismatic leader of the Croat Peasant Party, who died after several weeks of suffering. Following the directives of the Comintern, the CPY chose this critical period as suitable for action. Josip Broz and his comrades adhered to the party line with blind fanaticism, although they had little or no support among the masses.[46] Thanks to a tip from an informer, the police organized ambushes and on-the-spot investigations. Five days before Radić's death, on 4 August 1928, they arrested Broz, who was carrying a Browning revolver for which he had no license. In his "illegal" apartment they also found a basket full of ammunition and four WWI German bombs stashed beneath a pile of Marxist brochures under his bed (during the trial he declared that they had been planted there to frame him, but this was not true). "If I had had a 1 percent chance," Broz later told a friend, "I would have escaped and started shooting."[47]

He was arrested and beaten to force him to testify falsely against his comrades. He kept his mouth shut and decided to start a hunger strike in protest as he had done during an earlier detention in the rural town of Ogulin. His letter from the jail, in which he exaggerated the "tortures" to which he was subjected, was published on 24 August 1928 by the Comintern magazine *International Press Correspondence* under the title "A Cry from the Hell of Yugoslav Prisons."[48] At the beginning of November, he appeared before the court and was sentenced to five years imprisonment on the basis of a law prohibiting "all communist propaganda," after a trial known as the "bomb case." During the trial, Broz behaved as the Comintern expected of its members: "You have to aim for one thing only. Not the minimum penalty, but the prestige of the party, which you must strengthen in the eyes of the working masses."[49]

According to instructions, Broz bravely proclaimed himself not guilty, maintaining that he did not recognize the "bourgeois" tribunal, since it was an instrument of reactionary forces. "Long live the Communist Party! Long live the world revolution!" he shouted.[50] The local press, but also the Comintern, took note of his defiant attitude. Not everyone approved, however, for shortly afterward Avgust Cesarec, one of the most important left-wing intellectuals in Croatia, wrote in the party's illegally published paper *Proleter*: "If this young and morbidly ambitious communist becomes leader of the CPY, it will be a disaster."[51]

In Jail

After the trial, Broz remained in the Zagreb prison for several days. His comrades tried to arrange his escape with the help of a guard, sending him a metal file hidden in a round loaf of bread. Unnoticed, he succeeded in sawing through five of the six iron bars of the window of his cell. Just as he was beginning on the last bar, he was transferred to another cell and sent shortly afterwards to Lepoglava, in the Zagorje region—the site, since 1854, of the most important penitentiary in Croatia. The fate of the guard who had helped him was more tragic. Suspected by the authorities for his pro-communist sympathies, he escaped to the Soviet Union, where some years later he was accused of being a Yugoslav agent and condemned to death.[52] Broz's correct behavior and discipline soon earned him the esteem and affection of the comrades he met behind bars, first at Lepoglava, later in Maribor ("King Aleksandar's toughest pen") and in Ogulin.[53] There he began to study the Marxist and Leninist classics that the authorities were forced to tolerate as result of hunger strikes by the political convicts. With the help of their "criminal" mates they smuggled in the necessary literature, transforming the jails into Party schools. In this way, a new generation of revolutionary leaders was formed in these and other prisons of the Yugoslav kingdom. Josip Broz, Moša Pijade, Aleksandar Ranković, Milovan Djilas, and Edvard Kardelj all seriously studied the ideology, politics, economics, and military tactics that they considered necessary for the future revolution.[54] During the years spent in jail, which he remembered with amused levity, Broz became a professional revolutionary, as the authorities in Maribor noted. Under the blank space for his profession they wrote in his file: "criminal, communist."[55]

In spite of its obvious hardships, the prison probably saved Broz's life. On 6 January 1929, only a few days after he was sentenced, King Aleksandar dissolved parliament, abolished the constitution, and created a dictatorial regime under the premiership of General Petar Živković, one of his henchmen. The king and the prime minister were of the opinion that Yugoslavia (as the state was renamed) should be governed with an iron fist, without any pretense of parliamentary democracy. They acted accordingly, abolishing all political parties and declaring war on all forces of the opposition: Albanians in Kosovo, Macedonian separatists, Croat nationalists, both moderates and extremists (like the newly formed Ustaša), and, naturally, communists. During the years 1929 to 1931, the enemies of the regime were arrested en masse. Some hundred members of the CPY, the most staunch and pugnacious, were tortured to death in the terrible "Glavnjača" in Belgrade, or in other police stations scattered throughout the country, while the prisons of Lepoglava, Mitrovica, Maribor, Zenica, Niš, Požarevac, and Skopje bulged with their comrades, sentenced to prison terms with varying degrees of severity. Those who managed to survive the interrogations and were not simply shot in the back by policemen during an "attempt at escape" were lucky, since at least behind the bars they were comparatively safe.[56]

In Exile

In March 1934 Josip Broz, aged forty-two, was set free. He returned to his native Kumrovec, as the law required former prisoners to do, but shortly afterward he resumed his underground activities in Zagreb and Belovar. By order of the party, he emigrated in June to Austria with the task of improving contacts between the communists in Croatia and the Central Committee, which had been operating in Vienna since 1929 to keep clear of King Aleksandar's persecution. There the Austrian communists were still able to offer assistance to Yugoslav comrades. Under the guise of a tourist and carrying a card of the Croatian Alpine Club in his wallet, Broz illegally crossed the frontier near Tržič in north Slovenia. Once in Carinthia, he immediately found himself in trouble, because it was just then that the Nazis were attempting a putsch against the clero-fascist regime of Engelbert Dollfuss. When Broz finally managed to reach Vienna from Klagenfurt, he was beset upon by his comrades, "like bees to a honey pot," eager for news from the fatherland. In a coffeehouse, he met a bunch of grim-looking men who shocked him because of their aggressiveness and mutual hostility. He told them without mincing words that no real communist, of those he had met in or outside of prison, had any faith in the Central Committee of the CPY. Gorkić, the secretary general of the party, twirled his red moustache. "It did not become him," Tito later said, remembering the episode, "since it only set out his pallor." He assaulted Broz with vulgar insults.[57]

In spite of this less-than-friendly reception, on 1 August 1934 the "comrades" brought him into the Politburo, the party's executive body. At its Fourth Conference, organized in Ljubljana the following December, he was elected to the Central Committee (CC), although the reverse procedure would have been more logical.[58] He was sponsored by a young Croatian communist, Ivan Krajačić, nicknamed Stevo, with whom Broz would remain closely linked for life.[59] At the time, the leader of the party was Josip Čižinski, known under the pseudonym of Milan Gorkić, or Sommer, a thirty-year-old man of Slovak-Polish origin, born in Bosnia. He knew very little of the Yugoslav reality, since he had left the country in 1922 at the age of nineteen for Moscow, where he had worked in different Comintern offices. Being well connected with the NKVD (Narodnyi kommissariat vnutrennykh del; People's Commissariat of Internal Affairs) and those in "high Soviet circles" closed to ordinary mortals, he married a woman from this privileged class, the director of Moscow's famous Central Park of Culture and Leisure (later Gorky Park). Inevitably, Gorkić became a senior bureaucrat, being appointed secretary general of the CPY in 1932. Infatuated with himself and convinced that the communist movement in Yugoslavia was a "mess," he decided it needed a new leader able to impose order. He found himself at the head of a party with only three thousand enlisted members, the majority of whom were in prison or in exile. Among them there was no lack of provocateurs, spies, and police agents. This transformed the CPY into a viper's nest, where everybody suspected everybody else and denounced each other to the Cominform, knowing that in Moscow ears were attuned to every malevolent insinuation. Not surprisingly in the Comintern a joke circulated that two Yugoslavs represent three fractions, whose adherents hate and attack each other so much that they forget about the class enemy.[60]

Broz, aware that the internal life of the party had to be healed, wrote a report to the CC on 2 August 1934, stressing the need to overcome abstract ideological quarrels, strengthen ties with the working masses, and move on to action. This was the first document he signed with "Tito," a name not unusual in his native region.[61] Broz did not wish to stay in Vienna but hoped to move to Moscow, enroll in Lenin University, and meet up with his wife and son Žarko, born in 1924, who had fled to the Soviet Union after his arrest. Gorkić, however, had other plans for him. Two weeks after the report, he sent Broz home with the task of organizing the Party Congress for the region of Slovenia and the Fourth

National Conference. The first conference took place in September, at the summer residence of the bishop of Ljubljana, whose half-brother was a "fellow traveler" (a term widely used for Communist Party sympathizers).[62] The second, convened in December in the Slovenian capital and headed by Gorkić, was attended by eleven delegates but not by Broz. Gorkić used the explanation that for security reasons the organizers of the gathering should be banned from it. Tito would later consider this a hollow excuse used by the secretary general to get rid of him.[63] Both were important occasions, intended to overcome the sectarian policy of the past and to renew the party, linking it more organically with the environment in which it operated. To this end, the Central Committee made the decision, with the blessing of Moscow of course, to create autonomous parties in Slovenia, Croatia, and Macedonia under the aegis of the CPY.[64]

In September, Broz returned to Vienna, but Gorkić immediately sent him to Zagreb to discuss the organization of the Party Conference with Croat comrades. From the beginning, these assignments raised doubts in his mind, as he suspected that the secretary general was purposely exposing him to danger by entrusting him with clandestine tasks, even though he had only recently been released from prison. Although he could not criticize Gorkić's lifestyle, Broz considered him too confident toward the members of his entourage and, therefore, not suitable for this complicated position. Furthermore, the secretary general had no use for those who had grown up and become communists in Yugoslavia, confining them to bottom-rung positions to prevent them from getting access to the funds the Comintern assigned to the CPY. "I was truly disgusted," Tito said.[65] Wisely, however, he kept his mouth shut and at least outwardly maintained proper relations with the secretary general. Only years later did he confess to Louis Adamic what he really thought about Gorkić, observing that "his red hair and mustache were the reddest parts of him."[66]

At the end of 1934, in the wake of a continuing devastating economic crisis and a new shattering tragedy, Broz sent instructions from the Politburo to all Party cells and to the Union of Communist Youth of Yugoslavia (Savez Komunističke Omladine Jugoslavije; SKOJ) to organize an armed uprising in Yugoslavia. On 9 October, King Aleksandar I had been assassinated in Marseilles, at the very beginning of his official visit to France. He had just disembarked from his yacht when he was shot down by a Bulgaro-Macedonian assassin sent by Ante Pavelić, the leader of the Ustaša, the terrorist group that fought for a free Croatia and hoped that killing the monarch would also kill Yugoslavia. Convinced that the elimination of the hated Aleksandar was the beginning of the end of the despised Karadjordjević Dynasty, Broz had no qualms about recommending that the party's armed units join all other organizations that were also hostile to the regime, including the right-wing extremists.

This was the only way in which the monarchy could be overthrown.[67] However, these proposals bore no fruit, since after the violent death of his cousin Aleksandar, Prince Paul assumed the regency in the name of the new king, Petar II, who was only ten years old at the time, and managed to take control of the situation. The ill-conceived revolutionary proposal failed, demonstrating its hollowness, since the masses were not behind either the left- or the right-wing extremists. At the end of February 1935, Broz finally received permission to go to Moscow. He left on the advice of comrades in Zagreb, who thought that in the coming years the situation in Yugoslavia would become extremely dangerous, even more so than it had been during the years 1929–31. They therefore recommended that the best of their men who were not in prison should leave the country and go to the Soviet Union to be ideologically groomed for the inevitable upheaval.[68]

On the eve of his departure, Broz nearly fell into the hands of the Viennese police. He lived illegally in the apartment of an elderly Jewish landlady, whose daughter tried to commit suicide with gas. Broz saved her at the last moment, but when the gendarmes arrived, he barely managed to get away by taking advantage of the general chaos.[69]

In Moscow

Broz came to the country of the victorious proletariat where, he believed, "love, solidarity and sincerity"[70] reigned, with a presentation letter from Gorkić addressed to Vladimir Čopić, one of the founders of the CPY who worked as its representative at the Comintern. As Gorkić said, "He represents the best of our movement and shortly, in six or seven months, he will be called to cover leading positions in the CC."[71] Although Čopić saw a possible competitor in the newcomer, he found Broz a room in the Russian art nouveau Hotel Lux. Only the name still hinted at its former splendor; it was crowded with foreign communists seeking refuge in Moscow and was infested with rats, to say nothing of the stench from the common kitchens situated on every floor.[72] Broz's first task was to write his autobiography, as was the custom in the Comintern. He had to write it several times, so that the officials of the Cadre Department could compare the various versions and verify his trustworthiness.[73] Later, a certain Iakubovich, who was a representative of the OGPU (Ob'edinennoe gosudarstvennoe politicheskoe upravlenie; the Unified State Political Directorate, or security police), and a Bulgarian communist called Ivan Karaivanov had him write about the "characteristics" of the seven most important members of the CPY, including Gorkić. He carried out this assignment commendably, making an effort to be sincere, praising but also criticizing his comrades. He had no critique of Čopić, of course (although to tell the truth he considered him like a "gossipy old woman").[74] The latter rewarded him by proposing to send him for a short time to a "sanatorium" (what would today be called a spa) for party functionaries in Crimea. According to Nikita Bondarev, the historian who studied Broz's Moscow years, the sanatorium could also have been the Lubianka, the infamous seat of the Soviet secret police, where its agents tried to recruit promising new collaborators (or cadres, as officials were often called) by hook or by crook.[75]

On 21 May 1935, after Broz had returned, Karaivanov certified that "from the political point of view, Broz deserves trust."[76] This was also confirmed by Čopić and by the powerful director of the Cadre Department, the Bulgarian Georgi Damianov, alias Belov, although from the very beginning he did not like him. Later on, the Executive Committee of the Comintern suggested that the CC CPY propose the candidature of "Comrade Walter Friedrich"—Broz's new code name—as a "political referee" to the Balkan Department, led by the German communist Wilhelm Pieck. The CC CPY unanimously approved the proposal.[77]

At that time, the Comintern was headed by the legendary Georgi Dimitrov, the Bulgarian revolutionary who had been implicated in the arson of the Reichstag in Berlin but had been acquitted by German judges thanks to his brave and efficient defense. The newcomer soon entered his good graces. Although Broz did not excel in Marxist theory, he was considered a faithful communist, and one of the few Yugoslavs capable of practical work.[78] In spite of his lack of education, Broz (now known as Walter) was occasionally called to lecture at the Yugoslav section of the International Leninist School (Medžunarodnaja Leninskaja Škola) and at the Communist University for the Ethnic Minorities of the West (Kommunisticheskij Univerzitet Nacional'nyh Men'shinstv Zapada; KUNMZ). His experience at Lepoglava and in other prisons led him to believe that the CPY would be unable to overcome the crises that plagued it unless it succeeded in eliminating its internal struggles. But the situation he found in the Yugoslav colony in Moscow, which numbered around nine hundred persons, was similar to the one at home.[79] As he said later, he tried to avoid the "comrades" as much as possible, in part because he loved solitude, to which he had grown accustomed while behind bars, in part because he soon realized that in Moscow silence was golden, "Especially in rooms with a telephone."[80] It was taken for granted that telephones were bugged, so the less said, the better. He completely dedicated himself to his work, attending courses in management and conspiracy techniques as well as the famous Frunze Military Academy.[81] As he later wrote, "As far as possible I used this period for study; I went only from the Hotel Lux to the Comintern building and back. This is probably what saved me from Stalin's knife."[82] His cautious behavior is likewise noted in the memoirs of Ruth von Mayenburg, the wife of the Austrian communist, Ernst Fischer, about her stay at the Hotel Lux. "Tito moved along the long corridors like an invisible mouse. None of the neighbors paid attention to the silent comrade, who exchanged a word with hardly anybody, and went his own way. The Yugoslavs were in a conspiratorial world unto themselves, one that rarely allowed the foreign comrades to glance inside; even the Balkan section of the Comintern building, on the Mokhovaia, worked behind closed doors."[83]

Broz arrived in Moscow only three months after the assassination of Sergei M. Kirov (1 December 1934), leader of the Leningrad Communist Party, which offered Stalin a pretext for his purges of all possible "conspirators," especially the old Bolsheviks. It is not clear whether he was as naïve as his younger comrades in Yugoslavia who, from their domestic safety, believed every word proffered against these "traitors" by Andrei Vyshinskii, general prosecutor at the Moscow show trials, and considered everybody who dared to doubt a "class enemy" and a Trotskyist.[84] In any case, Walter managed to survive, although some of the things he wrote about his comrades were not in tune with information in possession of the NKVD (the secret police department that had absorbed the OGPU).[85] In the shadow of Stalin's terror Broz learned a great deal, especially about the mechanisms of revolution and power. In accepting Stalin's brutal practices (arbitrary arrests, torture, deportations, slave labor, murder) as a necessary tool for achieving the new social order, Broz compromised himself morally, at the same time drawing up the main guidelines of his life to come. This is how Milovan Djilas described Walter's metamorphosis at the beginning of his stay in Moscow: "The revolutionary Josip Broz . . . understood at that time that the institutions and revolutionary methods, although inseparable from the ideology, are even more important than the revolution."[86] His modest intellectual background kept Tito free from doubts, from skepticism, and from the need to confront problems critically. Savka Dabčević-Kučar, a prominent Croat communist and later Tito's opponent, even affirmed in her memoirs that he abandoned traditional values such as honesty, fidelity, friendship, and fair play, considering them just bourgeois "tinsel," in the name of communist morale, in its Machiavellian sense, in which the end justifies the means.[87] It is only fair, however, to counter this severe judgment with Tito's declaration, published in the monthly *Komunist* on 15 April 1959, that through the Comintern Stalin had done enormous damage to communism and "destroyed the revolutionary physiognomy of the Communists and created a kind of Communist-weakling."[88] The testimony of Edvard Kardelj, who in the mid-thirties collaborated with Walter in Moscow, is also pertinent, as it shows that the latter was not completely in tune with the Stalinist regime. According to

Kardelj, during the Great Terror Broz did everything in his power to save as many Yugoslav émigrés as possible, sending them home to work underground or to Spain, where the Civil War broke out in July 1936.[89] The Soviet Union decided to help the republican government against the right-wing generals, led by Francisco Franco, who had organized an armed revolt. Walter embraced this policy, convinced that Spain could be an excellent school for future Yugoslav military and political cadres, which indeed turned out to be the case. During WWII, no communist party had as many "Spaniards" in its ranks as the CPY. They were the ones who took the lead in the Partisan struggle.[90]

In July and August 1935 Walter participated in the Seventh World Congress of the Comintern, as secretary of the Yugoslav delegation and as a delegate with a consultative vote—a vote without full value, but merely an opportunity to express his opinion. In the multilingual form he had to compile on that occasion, he gave two names, "Tito" and "Rudi," in answer to the question about which pseudonym he was using in the party. With regards to the code name under which he was taking part in the congress, he answered "Walter Friedrich." Of the more than seventy pseudonyms he used during his life, Tito and Walter were the most important and frequent. He also gave his birth date as 1893 instead of 1892, and slightly stretched the truth when he said that his education was "primary, partially secondary." Describing himself as a "mechanic" from 1910 on was also an exaggeration. The photo attached to the questionnaire bears witness to the fact that he had not set foot in a factory for a long time, showing a young bespectacled man who looked more like a university lecturer than a manual laborer. At the congress he saw Stalin for the first time, but from afar and only briefly. He caught a glimpse of him when Stalin came to the sessions once or twice and stood behind a marble column: "Now you see me, now you don't," Tito later remembered mockingly.[91]

The Seventh Congress was important specifically because it changed the Comintern's political strategy. It was decided that the international revolutionary movement should abandon the belief that the communists had no political friends, not even among Western socialists and social democrats (accused of being "Social Fascists" because of their adherence to parliamentary democracy). Considering the Nazi threat, which began in Germany with Hitler's accession to power in 1933, the Soviet Union realized that it was no longer possible to march toward the splendid goals of communism without allies, who must be sought not only among the social democrats but also among Christian or even nationalist and conservative parties. Consequently, the Comintern implemented the policy of a "popular front," which encouraged the creation of a united bloc of anti-Fascist forces, in the hope that the Soviet Union would be preserved from the "reactionary" danger. In this perspective, Yugoslavia was also necessary for the defense of the proletariat's fatherland. No longer considered a link in the cordon sanitaire that the imperialists created to contain Bolshevism, Yugoslavia was thought of as a possible bulwark of the Soviet Union, together with other Central European and Balkan states, united against Hitler. Although the idea that the Karadjordjević Dynasty should be destroyed was still being discussed at the Fourth CPY Conference in December 1934, the Yugoslav communists immediately adopted the new political line. Their CC stated that while in principle it was in favor of national self-determination and the right of different South Slav nations to secede, "in view of the contemporary international situation" Yugoslavia should be kept alive. Any other policy would help "Fascism" with its war-mongering plans. The Politburo stressed this radical change in a circular letter sent to all the principal CPY organizations without causing any adverse reactions.[92] Nevertheless, many "comrades" continued to have reservations regarding Yugoslavia because of its centralistic structure based on Serb dominance. They would have preferred a federation or confederation of Southern Slav or Balkan Soviet republics.[93]

During the Seventh Congress, Walter was implicated in an unpleasant incident. In mid-August, the question arose as to who the new CPY representative in the Executive Committee of Comintern was to be. A group of delegates who arrived unexpectedly from Yugoslavia proposed Josip Broz for this prestigious post, even though he was a junior member of the CC. There was a heated discussion at the party summit, ending with the unanimous decision to back him. It was, however, only a maneuver, for Gorkić and his followers immediately protested to Dmitrii Manuilskii, Stalin's man at the Comintern, asserting that the election of Broz would strengthen "sectarianism" in the party. An angry Manuilskii, Gorkić's close friend, decided not to accept the decision of the Yugoslav delegation: "Since you have not chosen Gorkić, the only one trusted by the Comintern, we will not allow you to have a representative, but only a candidate, and this candidate will be Gorkić. Take it as a warning."[94] In communist nomenclature, a "candidate" was a member of a political body without full powers. This was one of the first signs of conflict between Broz and Gorkić, and of Moscow's low measure of esteem for the CPY. "I noticed at that time," Tito said later, "that something was wrong. Something was not working as it should. Dimitrov asked me at a certain point: 'Tell me, Walter, do you have party organizations?' I answered that we have them. Our party was judged in the same manner as the leadership in Vienna. And in Vienna they have shamefully quarreled among themselves."[95]

The Conflict with Gorkić and Work in the Underground

The split mentioned by Walter was the result of the policy Gorkić tried to implement after the Seventh Congress. In the new, relatively more liberal atmosphere in Yugoslavia after King Aleksandar's death, he thought the moment had come to forge an agreement with the other opposition forces. The elections of May 1935 brought good results, showing that these forces, first of all the Croat Peasant Party, were still alive and kicking. He was ready to enter into an alliance with socialists and form a common list at the next elections. The majority of the CC, however, rejected this idea, although the socialists accepted a radical program, opening the way for collaboration between the parties.[96]

Walter, in the meantime, licked the wounds Manuilskii had inflicted on his ego, and accompanied Yugoslav delegates on a long trip to the eastern regions of the Soviet Union at the end of August and in the first half of September. They visited large factories and kolkhozes, traveling as far as the Urals. They were greatly disappointed by the reality they encountered, by the appalling conditions of peasant and worker life, which they tried to justify in terms of the backwardness of pre-Bolshevik Russia and the enormous difficulties the Soviet regime had in coping with a hostile world. "My revolutionary duty compelled me not to criticize and not to support foreign propaganda against this country, being at that time the USSR, the only state where the revolution has been accomplished and where socialism should be built," mused Walter. "What I saw produced a great conflict within me, but I tried to excuse the Russian communists, considering that it was not possible to achieve everything in such a short time, although a fairly long period has passed since October 1917: more than seventeen years."[97]

Meanwhile, struggles between the CPY factions continued. At home in Yugoslavia, the police succeeded in capturing and interrogating several important communists (the party had been outlawed since 1920) who, under pressure, decided to collaborate, and this resulted in mass arrests in the winter of 1935–36. At a certain point, between 69 and 70 percent of all party members were behind bars and the party was nearly destroyed in Montenegro, Dalmatia, Croatia, Slavonia, Serbia, Macedonia, and Bosnia-Herzegovina.[98] Hopes for greater freedom, nurtured when Milan Stojadinović came to power in 1935, vanished quickly, fueling opposition to Gorkić in the party. In April 1936, Gorkić hastily convened the CC of the CPY, without informing the Comintern and without waiting for the arrival of its delegates from Moscow. This was considered an insult, and the fact that he was unable to implement the decisions of the Seventh Congress regarding the popular front was seen as a failure. At the

April session, the members of the CC voted a series of resolutions on the work of the party and its tactics, rejecting every possible dialogue with the socialists, thus further isolating Gorkić.[99] In this confused situation, the Comintern secretary created a "grand commission," charged with the task of preparing a report on the "Yugoslav question." At the commission's first session, Dimitrov harshly criticized the internal situation of the CPY, stressing the need "to find other structural forms to allow the Yugoslav party to have a positive attitude toward the questions that are open. We should not allow Yugoslavia to become a Fascist country."[100] The decisions taken at the April session of the CC CPY were annulled and, simultaneously, the Comintern decided to change the leadership of the party. They also approved efforts made by Gorkić to come to an agreement with the opposition forces at home, although at the same time the first doubts began to emerge about his ability to master the situation.[101]

In mid-March 1936, Walter left his employment at the Comintern for reasons not wholly clear, but probably in order to attend courses in guerilla warfare and espionage organized by the Cadres Department at the so-called "Partisan Academy" in Riazan in reaction to the Spanish Civil War. "The Spanish question," said Stalin, "is the question of all progressive mankind."[102] In order to block Francisco Franco's "counterrevolution," supported by Hitler, Mussolini, and the Vatican against the lawful republican government, Moscow decided to encourage the creation of International Brigades, military units consisting of volunteers from different countries who were to join the fight. Walter's task was to enroll volunteers in Yugoslavia, where he arrived in August 1936 in the guise of a well-dressed Austrian tourist.[103] At the end of the month he was back in Moscow, where he took part in discussions on the internal situation of the CPY. He also supplied information to the Cadre Department of the IKKI "on the members of the CC and candidate members," stressing their qualities, but without omitting critical remarks. He did not, however, accuse anyone of Trotskyism, which would have been deadly in the Moscow of that time. On the basis of proposals from its members, the commission, led by Dimitrov, decided on 19 September 1936 to transfer the operative leadership of the party to Yugoslavia, leaving only a small group abroad with the task of maintaining contacts with Moscow and working within the Yugoslav diaspora. Concerning the composition of the leadership, the secretary general asked Manuilskii to prepare a suitable proposal together with the Cadre Department.[104]

Nearly a week later, on 25 September 1936, the IKKI—this time Ercoli (whose real name was Palmiro Togliatti) was in the chair—discussed "the errors of our Yugoslav comrades" and named a special three-member commission to carry out further inquiries.[105] On 16 October, Walter wrote a long report criticizing the cadre policy of the leadership of his party, headed by Gorkić. Instead of putting trustworthy people in positions of responsibility, Gorkić chose people about whom only second-hand information was available. This was how careerists and provocateurs had infiltrated the ranks. Moreover, the CC did not remove those who were under threat of arrest soon enough and, consequently, when under "pressure" they betrayed their comrades. Among the culprits responsible, Walter mentioned first of all Gorkić himself, stating that he was too prone to trust people when they showed they were willing to collaborate. In order to right what had gone wrong, he proposed that no more than two members of the Politburo should be in charge of selecting the cadres. They should make sure that posts of responsibility were covered by mature comrades who were ideologically trustworthy and had experience in the field. All the older communists living in Moscow should therefore be sent home, since they were known to the masses and had contacts both with the Social Democrats and the "petit bourgeois" groups. They would be invaluable in the establishment of a common antifascist popular front. He went so far as to include in the list two comrades who had been expelled from the party, even daring to criticize the disorganization within the Comintern itself, and stated that matters that should have been confidential were widely known. Gorkić had proposed that in resturcturing the party two men be kept abroad. Walter opposed this, believing that one would be sufficient, for if two centers of power were formed, one at home and one in exile, they would hinder each other. Only Gorkić should stay abroad with a small technical staff and one comrade who was not a member of the CC. The latter should be in charge of the *Proleter*, the party organ. While this paper, Broz's first on organizational questions, was not without critical remarks regarding his comrades, it did not sound like a denunciation but rather an attempt to stress the shortcomings of Gorkić and Broz's own political experience. It was widely circulated among the IKKI leaders and confirmed their impression that Comrade Walter could be trusted.[106]

On 16 October 1936, the day this paper was delivered, Walter left for Vienna with a passport in the name of a Yugoslav subject called Ivan D. Kisić and $200 in his pocket.[107] Years later, he would remember Dimitrov and Pieck with gratitude, as they had helped him "to disappear from Moscow in time." Because of the Stalinist purges the situation there was becoming exceedingly dangerous. Especially terrible were those nights in the Hotel Lux when arrests were being made: "Women's cries, children's laments, to make one's hair stand on end."[108] In the Austrian capital he found the party in total disarray because some weeks before the police had succeeded in arresting almost the entire leadership. After a week, Walter continued his journey to Yugoslavia, this time with new duties that enlarged his field of action. His task was to lead, restructure, and strengthen the party organization and to continue to enlist volunteers for Spain.[109] At the beginning of December, he was once more in Vienna, together with Gorkić, who had returned from Moscow full of self-confidence. In spite of the criticism he has been subjected to, he had been confirmed secretary general of the party and now had the right to veto any decisions taken by the leadership at home or abroad. Until this point no one in the CPY had had such prerogatives. In addition, the Comintern expelled his left-wing adversaries from the CC and nominated new ones. One of the new nominees was Walter, but they also included Sreten Žujović, called Crni (the Dark One), a former soldier of the Foreign Legion, "so handsome that the women turned their heads after him," to quote Djilas, and Rodoljub Čolaković, Broz's former prison mate. Gorkić, aged thirty-three, was bursting with pride, since it was obvious that he had powerful patrons in Moscow.[110]

To Walter "it seemed strange" that Gorkić had the power of veto. This meant that he was able to define the party line and to seek whatever alliances he wished with the opposition in Yugoslavia. In fact, he did just that, hoping that the CPY would be able to take part in the town and district municipal elections in December 1936. Walter was charged with coming to an agreement with the socialists "at all costs" and was not to worry about the name with which the party would present itself to voters. Walter did not agree with Gorkić's contention, developed in several brochures, that it was necessary to join the opposition, even at the cost of the party's identity, especially since the socialists demanded that the Communist Party should renounce its clandestine structures. According to Broz, the situation was similar to that in Russia during the years 1907–14, when Mensheviks wanted to "liquidate" the clandestine party committees in order to find a common language with the liberals. Lenin had opposed this "liquidation."[111] By the end of 1936, Broz was of the same opinion as the father of the October Revolution. But he asked no questions and did not protest, happy enough to be sent by the Comintern to work in his own country: "I did not wish to say anything, since Gorkić had all the rights. I was just satisfied to go home."[112]

In mid-December 1936, he left Vienna with a false passport, but not the one Gorkić had given him. Nor did he take the route Gorkić had recommended, since "too often comrades to whom he had given a passport were arrested at the Yugoslav border."[113] Among other places, Walter visited Ljubljana, Zagreb, Belgrade, and Split, with the task of organizing a large expedition of volunteers to Spain. At the end of the year, while this work was in progress, he went to Prague in order to discuss the details with Gorkić. The secretary general informed him that the volunteers would be transported from the Dalmatian and Montenegrin coasts to Spain by steamship, that the trip would be organized by

Adolf Muck-Löwy, a candidate for the Politburo, and that the enrolment would be carried out from Belgrade by a Jewish woman from Latvia, Brana Voss-Nenad. Her way of campaigning differed completely from that of Walter. Whereas he insisted that the expedition be organized in strict secrecy, Brana Voss wanted to "publicize it as much as possible." The people she contacted were not those whom Walter trusted, provoking a furious quarrel between him and Gorkić.[114]

The task was difficult because police from half of Europe, including Yugoslavia, were trying to prevent the departure of volunteers for Spain. Gorkić did what he had promised: early in March 1937, he sent a steamship, *La Corse*, from Marseilles to the Yugoslav coast. It was to carry the enthusiastic volunteers who wanted to combat Fascism. Gorkić was certain that this would be a noteworthy action in the international endeavor to help Republican Spain, and that with it he would show the Comintern how efficient the CPY was under his leadership. However, the expedition was doomed from the start. Since the organizers had talked too much, the police were alerted and near Budva they stopped the ship, which had been rented for the huge sum of 750,000 francs. Nearly five hundred young men, mostly peasants, who had started the journey in an atmosphere of euphoria, ended up in jail. It was the largest arrest of left-wing sympathizers carried out by the Belgrade government to date. To make the catastrophe worse, Muck, who was arrested together with Brana Voss, confessed to the police everything he knew about the CPY, as Djilas said, "without even being touched." Thank God, he did not know anything about the new organization of the party.[115] In Moscow, Walter, together with Gorkić, was considered responsible for the failure of the expedition, and an avalanche of accusations threatened his life. Tito later scornfully related that it was Gorkić who enrolled Muck in the party leadership: "Imagine, he made a man who owned a coffeehouse in Budva a member of the CC, a man who was completely unknown to the party and had no qualifications: he was a petit bourgeois."[116]

~

Broz returned from the Soviet Union exhausted and restless. It was obvious, however, that he was relieved to be able to work underground once more in the "militarist and monarchic-fascist" Yugoslavia. Nevertheless, in spite of having experienced Stalin's terror in Moscow, where every night one could expect the "fatal knock on the door,"[117] he continued to believe in the Soviet brand of socialism, in the necessity of a merciless war against the "class enemy," considering it indispensable in destroying the capitalist world. His attitude was dictated, of course, by these beliefs, which he clung to with the fanaticism similar to that of a religious sect, but also by his personal ambitions for a career in an organization that, in his opinion, would dominate the world. This was a historical imperative, considering that capitalism, according to Marx's prophecy, was doomed and Fascism/Nazism was just one of its last and most aggressive manifestations.[118]

Less than ten years had passed since the 1928 trial when his photo had been published by all the newspapers and Walter had not changed all that much. He therefore decided to dye his hair black, although sometimes with less than perfect results in terms of functioning as a disguise. A year later during a trip to Belgrade, the young journalist Vladimir Dedijer, upon meeting him for the first time, called his attention to this. Broz nonchalantly answered: "You know, I was in a hurry, and besides I didn't have enough dye." Dedijer's mother considered the newcomer strange: "He seems dangerous. Look, he has French toothpaste and Czech soap!"[119] It was not only Broz's toiletries that were strange. His speech was even stranger, for he spoke Serbo-Croatian with a foreign accent that was difficult to identify. In addition to German and Russian, which he spoke more or less fluently, he also knew some Slovene, French, Czech, Hungarian, and Kirghiz. Later, he improved his English, which he had begun studying in jail, by reading *The Economist*.[120]

His linguistic ability, on the one hand, and his strange accent while speaking Serbo-Croat, on the other, caused doubts for years about his origins. Shortly before his death, America's National Security Agency published an expert analysis in its internal bulletin *Cryptologic Spectrum*, in which it was asserted that on the basis of phonologic and morphologic characteristics, Tito was not Josip Broz, but a Russian or a Pole who probably took over the latter's identity in the thirties.[121] Outlandish though it may sound, the only firm objection to this study, written by a specialist, is that no information about such a switch of identities exists in the Comintern documents regarding Josip Broz, where it should be. Even so, Moscow had no qualms about stirring up doubts about Tito's identity when it suited them. In 1948, for instance, when he was an outcast because of his quarrel with Stalin, Radio Moscow told the following story: the real Josip Broz fell in 1915 on the Russian front. His uniform and documents were taken by a deserter from the tsarist army, probably a "Jewish bourgeois," the son of an Odessa furrier. "As his father cheated customers, so this adventurer, who has seven different passports, today tries to cheat the working people of Yugoslavia."[122]

Provisional Leadership of the CPY and Tito's Role in the Spanish Civil War

From the Croatian capital, Broz organized regular meetings in Samobor, eighteen kilometers west of Zagreb, where there were no political police but only gendarmes who were not used to fighting against communists.[123] These meetings were attended mostly by young people who called him Stari—"the Old One." This nickname, used only by the comrades of the inner circle, was invented by two Belgrade students, Milovan Djilas, of a modest Montenegrin family, and Ivo Lola Ribar, son of a distinguished solicitor and politician from Zagreb who was also president of the Constitutional Assembly of the Kingdom SHS in 1921.[124] Ribar was charged by Broz with leading the SKOJ, the youth organization of the party, which had no secretary at the time, and swiftly became one of his most trusted colleagues. Between the three, a symbiosis developed that, as Djilas said, had the character of a "familiar blood bond."[125]

The dictatorship of King Aleksandar and the crises after his violent death induced many university students to join the CPY. They had not witnessed the factional struggles of the twenties and saw communism as the only way to change society. They unhesitatingly believed in Marxist doctrine and were undisturbed by the news of Stalin's terror in the Soviet Union, if they even noticed it. If they did, they hid it carefully. "Nobody was allowed to doubt openly," confessed Gojko Nikoliš much later.[126] With no hesitancy, these young intellectuals and utopian idealists found a charismatic leader in Broz. "The Old One is the most precious asset of our party," was the general opinion among them.[127] From contemporary reports it is known that Broz felt safer in the apartments found for him by the members of the SKOJ than in those put at his disposal by regular party members. In that period, the latter were often arrested by the police, which generally did not happen to young people.[128] Convinced that it was necessary to get rid of old sectarians and enroll fresh forces in the party, Broz contacted workers, artisans, students, people from various milieux. He was fortunate in choosing his collaborators. Apart from Milovan Djilas and Ivo Lola Ribar, a young Serb named Aleksandar (Leka, also Marko) Ranković, a tailor by profession who had just finished his military service, was among the first to join the team.[129] Slovene teacher Edvard Kardelj, whom Broz first met in Ljubljana in 1934 and later in Moscow, was among them too. Between those young men and the "Old One," a relationship of mutual confidence emerged, completely different from the conflicting and aggressive atmosphere so typical of the Comintern. Tito liked to say: "If somebody makes a mistake, find the right word for him, without destroying him. This creates trust."[130]

Among those ardent left-wing adherents Broz also found his new love: Herta Haas, a pretty student at the Zagreb School of Economics, born to German-speaking parents but from Slovenian Maribor. Through her, he entered into contact with the intellectual circles of the Croatian capital, where he met an aspiring solicitor, Vladimir (Vlatko) Velebit, one of his more important collaborators during the war and a diplomat after it.[131] With the help of these young communists or party sympathizers, Walter organized a series of strikes in the shipyards of Kraljevica and in the Trbovlje mines, which caused considerable worry to industrial circles in Yugoslavia. They spoke about him as a dangerous Comintern agent—a certain Brosz, son of a Czech Jew and a Hungarian woman, who had served in the Habsburg army during the war and had been a prisoner in Russia. This at least was what A. S. Howie, the Scottish director of the important Trepča mines in North Kosovo, told Rebecca West, the famous English writer and traveler, during her journey to Yugoslavia in the late thirties.[132]

Broz's efforts to create a new party organization—which even succeeded in infiltrating the royal court—were furiously opposed by the old guard of political prisoners. In Sremska Mitrovica prison, they had created a close-knit group of about 150 men who considered the CPY their fief and thought of themselves as an exclusive sect. It was probably the most efficient party cell at the time, as much for the number of its adherents as for their orthodoxy.[133] They were known as "Wahhabists," similar in their fanatical puritanism to Saudi Arabian fundamentalists. Beginning in 1934, their leader was a member of the CC, the thirty-seven-year-old Petko Miletić, called Šepo, who had a turbulent past. In 1919 he had supported the Hungarian Revolution of Béla Kun and after its failure tried to spark an insurrection in Yugoslavia. After living clandestinely in the Montenegrin woods for two years, he was captured by the police and imprisoned. Once free he went to Moscow where he enrolled in the party school. At his core, he remained a traditional Balkan rebel, with a minimum of ideological culture. In Moscow he strengthened his dogmatism, convinced that all means were allowed in the political struggle. At the beginning of the thirties he became a member of the CC CPY but in 1934 he was arrested once more. After enduring allegedly terrible interrogations and tortures, he was sentenced to several years in jail. "Petko" came to Sremska Mitrovica with the halo of a martyr; a hero and a real communist who had not confessed anything and had not signed any compromising documents. He was known as being inflexible, unwilling to collaborate with the "class enemy," and as a result his influence among the youth, in prison and out, was particularly strong.[134] His followers adored him, sang songs dedicated to him, and in Spain one of the International Brigades was named in his honor.[135] "They wanted action," Djilas wrote. "They sought a strong guide and it seemed that Petko Miletić was what they were looking for."[136] Petko soon began plotting against Broz, whom he considered a dangerous rival in the struggle for power.[137] Due to his popularity in the party and his good relations with Moscow, Petko succeeded in his intentions, as confirmed by an article published by *Rundschau*, the German paper of the Comintern, which reported that in prison Miletić was conducting a "Bolshevik" struggle against Trotskyists and was building "a new era in the party."[138]

In this tension-rife atmosphere, Broz insisted on putting his program into practice. First he decided to implement the decision of the Fourth CPY Conference, organized in Ljubljana in December 1934, by creating an autonomous Communist Party of Slovenia. This decision, approved by the Comintern, was based on the conviction that the Yugoslav Communist Party could not appeal to the popular masses if it ignored the burning question of ethnic relations. Although Gorkić had many doubts concerning the need to create separate national parties under the aegis of the CPY, the task was accomplished, according to Broz's directives, by Edvard Kardelj. On 18 April 1937, in the house of a local sacristan not far from the mining center of Trbovlje, he organized the First Congress of the Communist Party of Slovenia, which included no more than two hundred members.[139] On this occasion, Kardelj stressed that the Slovene bourgeoisie was not capable of defending the interests of the nation. It could offer, in the best case, cultural autonomy within the framework of Yugoslavia. But the national question was not just a question of culture and language. It could be solved only when the Slovenes received their own state in this greater body of Yugoslavia, including the right of self-determination and secession.[140] He remained faithful to this idea for his entire life.

The night of August 1–2, the Communist Party of Croatia was also founded in the woods near Samobor, at a meeting attended by seventeen delegates and in the presence of Broz. He also planned the creation of the Communist Party of Macedonia, which, however, was not founded until 1943. At a time when the Serbs were all-powerful in Yugoslavia, nobody thought about a Communist Party of Serbia. (Broz discussed this with his friend Josip Kopinič, trying to explain that Croats and Slovenes were oppressed by Belgrade's rule, whereas the Serbs were not. Kopinič objected, saying that the Serb masses were also oppressed and that sooner or later they would take revenge because of this discrimination).[141] Once in power, Tito considered this creation of national and autonomous communist parties to have been a mistake that undermined the very foundations of socialist Yugoslavia from the start, because it divided the Orthodox and Catholic parts of the country. But, as he said with resignation, quoting a popular saying from his native Zagorje: "It is useless to go to mass in the afternoon"[142] (mass was traditionally held in the morning). In any case, the creation of two "national" parties gave new impetus to the CPY, which underwent a significant renaissance.

At the end of March 1937, Broz left by train for Paris, where the political situation was better than in Vienna, because the Popular Front, a coalition of socialists, radicals, and communists, was in power there. This was why the members of the CC CPY decided to seek refuge in the French capital, followed by other prominent Yugoslav communists. When in the spring of 1938 Hitler annexed Austria to the Third Reich, three Slovenes also came to Paris: Boris Kidrič with his wife Zdenka, and Lovro Kuhar, a talented Carinthian writer known under the pseudonym Prežihov Voranc. He was given the management of the party's bookshop and under this cover acted as a middleman between communists scattered throughout Europe. They were a group of lively intellectuals, among whom Broz was probably less educated but certainly no less cultured, thanks to his great experience and his love for books.[143] They lived in modest apartments and met in coffeehouses and bistros, acting more like bohemians than professional revolutionaries. Between 1937 and 1938 Tito resided in different boroughs in Paris, first in a small hotel in the Latin Quarter. He could stay no longer than a month in the same arrondissement because that would mean registering with the police. Therefore, he often changed his address, generally remaining in the city's center.[144]

From home Broz brought "interesting and optimistic" news, as Gorkić wrote in a report to the Comintern. As an expert cadre, he was immediately sent to Central Europe to "liquidate" the technical apparatus the CPY had used in Vienna and Prague to publish newspapers, leaflets, and propaganda material. This mission accomplished, he returned to Yugoslavia at the end of April and went to Paris again in mid-May, leaving there at the beginning of June for Zagreb, always, of course, traveling with forged passports and under fake names. "It was a dangerous life," recalled Tito. "I came and went across different frontier posts in Yugoslavia, in order not to be remembered by the policemen."[145]

Something unexpected happened in the meantime. Invited by the Comintern and fearing the worst, Gorkić suddenly left for Moscow on 14 July 1937. There was no further word from him. "The mist swallowed him," as he used to say about comrades who disappeared into the dungeons of the NKVD.[146] Rumors had been circulating at the IKKI since the beginning of the year that the leadership of the CPY had made a lot of "stupid mistakes" for which it should be held accountable, especially the tragic expedition of Yugoslav volunteers to Spain. The young secretary general would have been pardoned for this had he not been caught in the machinery of internal NKVD infighting, which destroyed him. The call to Moscow did not presage anything good for Gorkić, whose own wife, when arrested, denounced him to the secret police. On 19 August it was his turn to be arrested on false accusations that he was a British spy and an enemy of the people. He was shot on 1 November 1937.[147] The Yugoslav diaspora in Paris, however, had no idea of what was going on, although rumor had it that "Gorkić was itching to be off."[148]

Because the CPY had been practically decapitated—Ivan Grzetić, the representative of the party at the Comintern, also disappeared—Rodoljub Čolaković and Sreten Žujović proposed to "Walter" that he assume leadership. Of all the members of the CC, he was best suited for this task, not only because of his critical attitude toward Gorkić but also because of his impeccable past and his working-class origins.[149] In mid-August Čolaković and Žujović urged him to come to Paris as soon as possible to explain to him what had happened. "This is all we need," was his sorrowful comment.[150] At first he hesitated to accept their proposal, since it was dangerous to do so without the Comintern's approval, then he agreed. As unofficial leader of the party, at the end of August he queried Moscow about Gorkić's silence and the lack of information forthcoming. When he received no answer, a month later he sent Pieck a telegram asking the same questions. Again no answer. Even worse, the Yugoslav communists in Paris found themselves in financial trouble because there was no money coming from the USSR. Walter's position was so precarious that he was unable to get a visa for the USSR from the Soviet diplomatic authorities.[151] After several weeks, in mid-December 1937, a letter came from Pieck with the news about Gorkić's fall and with an order for "Otto" (another of Broz's codenames) to see to the Yugoslav "branch" of the party. Shortly afterward, he was informed that Gorkić and his wife had been arrested on charges of espionage. This did not surprise him, because he had already suspected that the former secretary general—as his NKVD friends had confided—was a British spy, having spent a short time in an English prison some years before.[152] Walter did not pity him, considering him a "straw man," politically formed abroad, and therefore with no authority to represent the Yugoslav working masses. In Broz's opinion, Gorkić had acted systematically against the CPY, especially against those members who came—like Broz himself—from the proletarian class. He even suspected him of having plotted with Serb nationalists in order to "liquidate" the party. "In the country nobody knows him," he wrote about Gorkić to Dimitrov, "except for a few unimportant intellectuals."[153] He later told Louis Adamic that Gorkić "beyond a shadow of a doubt" had been at the service of King Aleksandar's regime and other dark forces, including the Jesuits. Only at the end of his life did Tito admit that "Gorkić was not a spy, as they accuse him."[154]

Along with the provisional leadership of the CPY in 1937–38, Walter was given another delicate task, about which little is known. According to Josip Kopinič, he had inherited the role of intermediary between the Soviet Union and Spain from Gorkić. This included contacts with the fourth section of the NKVD, which was charged with the repression of Trotskyists (i.e., anarchists, especially numerous in Catalonia). According to another document from the archive of the leading French communist Maurice Thorez, in Paris Broz headed a group of special agents including the Italian Vittorio Vidali, the Croat Ivan Krajačić, the Slavonian Ivan Srebrnjak, and the Bosnian Vlajko Begović, leader of the NKVD operative center in Albacete. All of them were "liquidators," as Stalin's killers were known.[155] This is the most obscure chapter in the life of Josip Broz. He himself confessed that he went to Madrid in 1936 or 1937, whereas the Swedish communist Gusti Stridsberg allegedly met him in Barcelona in 1938.[156] These trips involved summary inspections of Yugoslav volunteers in Spain but also, according to Dobrica Ćosić, a famous Serb writer and for some time Tito's intimate, "other activities, about which we as yet know nothing."[157] It seems that he wanted to join the International Brigades but was prevented from doing so by his comrades because his presence was important at home and in Paris.[158]

Did he participate in the "liquidations" of Trotskyists triggered in Spain by Soviet agents? It is still not clear whether Broz was one of "los Russos," as the Spanish called those who came to their country to fight in favor of the republic. In a letter sent to Foreign Minister Anthony Eden in May 1944, Edith Wedderburn, an Englishwoman involved in the Civil War, accused Broz of organizing special military tribunals in Barcelona that were charged with judging those who opposed the tyranny of the Soviet secret services. In another letter, sent the following day, Foreign Office diplomat M. E. Rose mentioned to Elizabeth Barker, who was active in British wartime propaganda, that word of crimes committed by Tito during the Spanish Civil War were circulating in London in the spring of 1944.[159] Fred Copeman, an English communist and a commander of the British brigade, later wrote in his memoirs that Broz, under the pseudonym Čapajev, led the Georgi Dimitrov brigade, composed of volunteers from Central Europe and the Balkans. However, Santiago Carillo, the longtime secretary general of the Spanish Communist Party, denied this.[160] In an interview with American journalist C. L. Sulzberger, André Malraux, the French novelist who fought in Spain on the side of the republic, spoke about an encounter with Broz there. And in June 1966, the Paris newspaper *L'Aurore* wrote that "Tito does not like to remember this period of his life, since his stay in Barcelona and Albacete at the end of 1936 coincided with the killings, committed by Soviet agents, of the most important Yugoslav communists."[161]

Until the Soviet secret service archives are opened, it is impossible to say how deeply Broz was implicated in the tragedy of the Spanish Civil War. In a report to the IKKI about the party's work, he distanced himself from the "liquidators," stressing that they led a sectarian struggle and had harmed the party. But which liquidators did he have in mind? Did this include those who acted on behalf of the NKVD? One of those, Ivan Krajačić (Stevo), was a lifelong close friend, probably not just out of mutual sympathy but out of a common murky past.[162] In 1948, when the split between Stalin and Tito occurred, during a dinner with Aleksandar Ranković, Svetozar Vukmanović (Tempo), and Krajačić—so goes the story by Vlado Dapčević—he said in anger: "Look how they attack us, although we have given them our best cadres. Even I have worked for the Ministry of State Security." When Krajačić gave him a kick, in order to warn him to shut up, Broz answered that he had nothing to hide, since the cadres mentioned were all seated at the table.[163]

Tito spoke fleetingly about his stay in Spain with Louis Adamic and with Vladimir Dedijer, who mentions it in his biography, published by *Life* magazine in 1952. By Tito's express desire, however, this information was omitted in a more complete version of this text, which appeared in a Serbo-Croatian edition.[164] The memory of Spain was obviously unpleasant for him, especially considering the testimony given by Leo Mates, a Croatian revolutionary of Jewish origin and, after the war, one of the most important Yugoslav diplomats. According to him, in Spain Broz did "dirty work" for the Soviet secret service, taking part in purges of its adversaries. As a communist he was obliged to assist them, but he considered it a sacred duty and an honorable task. Tito himself, in 1939 or 1940, indirectly confirmed this in Mates's home in Zagreb. As Mates recounts, during lunch he suddenly looked at Anka Butorac, a party activist seated at the table and said: "It was me who, in Spain, sent your comrade to die."[165] The "comrade" was Blagoje Parović, a famous Serb communist and potential rival for the leadership of the CPY, who had been in disgrace with Comintern and was killed on 6 July 1937 in a village near Madrid under questionable circumstances. In fact, he was ordered to go on a suicide mission and launch an impossible attack (though he may well have been shot from behind by an NKVD agent, as many whispered).[166]

The Fight against the "Parallel Center"

Gorkić's arrest threw a dark shadow on the CPY. The Yugoslav communists, especially those who happened to be in the Soviet Union or in Spain, were suspected en masse of being Trotskyists. It seemed that Trotskyism had taken root in the Russian and in particular in the Polish and the Yugoslav parties, which therefore were subjected to enormous pressure. While the Polish party was simply disbanded it appeared, as Gusti Stridsberg remembers, as if the Yugoslavs were suddenly the victims of a political epidemic. "German communists, above all, but also others, treated them like lepers."[167]

In this troubled situation, with the very survival of the party at stake, a "parallel center" was created among Yugoslav refugees in Paris by Ivo Marić, called Železar, a Dalmatian, and the Montenegrin Labud Kusovac, called Obarov, which was supported by the French Communist Party as well as some of the Comintern circles. Marić was in charge of contacts with Yugoslav economic émigrés abroad, while Kusovac represented the party in a committee for aid to Republican Spain. They made a proposal to Walter, suggesting he form a collective that would provisionally lead the party. In exchange, they asked him to get rid of all those "comrades" whom Gorkić had put in executive positions, especially Čolaković, Žujović, and Kuhar, who were allegedly the former secretary general's men. Although Walter sent Čolaković to Spain to meet the Yugoslav fighters and to report about them, this was not enough for Marić and Kusovac. In fact, he kept Žujović in France and appointed Kuhar as representative of the party in Paris and editor of its organ, *Proleter*.[168] In the past, both Marić and Kusovac had collaborated with Gorkić, but more recently they had quarreled with him. His "disappearance" offered them the chance to settle accounts with all those who were close to him. Walter, however, was not ready to accept their proposal, in part because the functionaries they mentioned had been chosen by the IKKI and also because he was unwilling to share power with anyone. He reminded Marić and Kusovac that in December 1936 Pieck had entrusted Gorkić with the leadership of the party abroad, whereas he was to have the leadership at home. Since Gorkić had been executed, the responsibility was his alone, as the only leader left. This made them suspect that Walter wanted to dominate the party and they accused him of behaving like an autocrat without any clear-cut mandate from the IKKI. From this point forward the members of the "parallel center" stopped following Broz's directives and tried to get in touch with Petko Miletić in the Sremska Mitrovica prison who, they felt, "was valuable for the party."[169] And as if this were not enough, they were joined by Ivan Srebrnjak (Antonov), an agent of Soviet military intelligence, who said that some of Broz's young collaborators, for instance Boris Kidrič and Ivo Lola Ribar, were from well-to-do bourgeois families, sons of notorious Freemasons, and therefore clearly in the service of the Yugoslav regime. Srebrnjak also called the attention of the IKKI to the romance Walter had in Moscow with a certain Elsa, a member of the German Communist Party, who was suspected of working for the Gestapo. He also affirmed that the young woman who brought party correspondence from Yugoslavia to Paris and back (obviously Herta Haas) was also a Gestapo spy. For all these reasons, Srebrnjak felt that Walter needed to explain himself, underscoring his resemblance to Gorkić and inviting the IKKI to disband the CPY.[170]

Broz responded to this offensive by counterattacking, increasing his fight against the "Trotskyists," "Fascists," and "spies" who surrounded him. At the beginning of 1938 he wrote an article entitled "Trotskyists: Agents of International Fascism," published by *Proleter* under the pseudonym T. T. He called attention to the fact that many Yugoslav antifascists, honest but poorly informed, did not believe in the proliferation of the new ideological plague: "They do not believe that the Trotskyists have fallen so low as to become a band of spies, killers, saboteurs and agents of Fascism." Broz invited his followers to be cautious and vigilant: "In the future the machinations of the Trotskyist bandits will collide head-on with the monolithic discipline and unity of our party."[171]

The most dangerous figure, with regards to this monolithism, was Petko Miletić. When the news came that Gorkić had fallen, in agreement with his Belgrade comrades Walter decided to inform Miletić and his former cellmate, Moša Pijade, about what had happened. He urged them to keep the information to themselves, so as not to demoralize the comrades in jail. Petko did not follow this advice, trying to use it as an occasion for "saving" the party and taking over its leadership. According to Rodoljub Čolaković, by November 1937 he already had plans to escape from prison in order to convene an extraordinary congress of the CPY, where the current "opportunistic" leadership would be changed for a "Bolshevik" one (it seems that to this end his followers were already digging a tunnel under the prison wall). These machinations seriously preoccupied young Broz's followers in Yugoslavia once they heard about them. Djilas and Ranković, who in the past had been under the sway of Miletić, but had renounced his "Wahhabism," immediately sent Ivo Lola Ribar to Paris to warn Broz of the danger, advising him to change the party leadership in the Sremska Mitrovica prison as soon as possible. As a result, he disbanded its committee, dominated by that "lord of the souls," Petko Miletić, and in its place named his old mentor and friend Moša Pijade as a provisional "commissioner."[172] This provoked a wave of protest among the prisoners, who accused Pijade of being "a bandit, a traitor, a Trotskyist." They were joined by the "parallel center" in Paris, where Pijade was considered an "opportunist" of the worst kind.[173] In spite of this adverse reaction, Broz's will prevailed: at the beginning of November 1937 he convened the CC CPY in order to condemn the "anti-party activity" of the faction in Sremska Mitrovica led by Petko Miletić. Accused of being a sectarian and opposing the line of the Comintern's Seventh Congress, Petko was obliged to renounce his post as party secretary in jail. This was just the start of his downfall. The "parallel center" tried to react, proclaiming that the party was without legitimate leadership and that Walter was a "usurper."[174] "I don't know what to say about Železar," commented Tito. "But he has done so much harm to our party that he must be either stupid or a traitor."[175] In the meantime, a ferocious struggle was raging between Miletić's followers and those of Pijade, who were growing more and more numerous. Many of the prisoners started to realize that the latter was the stronger, and therefore decided to "repent" and to "adapt" to the situation. It was a dramatic process in which Moša Pijade used every means possible to isolate, malign, and besmirch Petko and his group, accusing them of being homosexual, of having tried to poison him, and the like.[176]

~

At the end of March 1938, Nikolai P. Bogdanov, a member of the "Red Aid" (Medžunarodnaja Organizacija Pomošči Borcam Revolucii) and a Comintern envoy, came to Paris on his way to Spain. He got in contact with Kusovac and Marić, ignoring Walter altogether. This worried Walter, as it seemed that Moscow's sympathies were leaning toward the "parallel center" that had already started to build a "new team" and declined to obey the directives coming from the CC. Aware that he could strengthen his position only at home, where it was urgently necessary to shore up the CPY and halt the spread of sectarianism, Broz decided to take a bold and dangerous step. Without asking the Comintern's permission, he disbanded the leadership of the party in Paris and departed for Yugoslavia.[177] This was an utterly unusual move in the practice of the communist parties that depended on Moscow and was interpreted by Marić as his victory, since he proclaimed that Walter had "taken flight." Actually, this was the first time that Broz truly asserted his leadership and made an independent decision that showed that he was not ready to be a Soviet puppet. Also telling is a proclamation published as one of the last acts of the Paris CC that appeared on 12 May, in view of the crisis provoked by Hitler's annexation of Austria. It stressed the need to fight the Nazi menace with determination and to find allies, even including the bourgeois forces in power. For the first time, Walter and his comrades expressed their faith in Yugoslavia as a common homeland for Serbs, Croats, and Slovenes—three interdependent nations. It read in part: "Peoples of Yugoslavia, who all love democracy, who all love the fatherland and the country, all patriotic citizens, who do not wish to serve Fascist conquerors, unite!"[178] Broz affirmed that it was the right time to finally stop the "sectarians" who had paralyzed the party and develop a common direction in order to unite all the "healthy elements." The fact that at an April congress in Zagreb the Social Democrats and the representatives of the trade unions decided to collaborate with the communists within the framework of a Popular Front against Fascism and to abandon anti-Soviet propaganda was a sign that he had succeeded.[179]

At the time, Walter frequently met prisoners who had been released from Sremska Mitrovica, even if they were followers of Petko Miletić, to see whether it would be possible to include them in the party's activity.[180] At home, the new leadership was definitively installed with a CC of nine members. It had not yet been recognized by the Comintern, but nevertheless started to function. Included were comrades who had collaborated with him during the past year, with Djilas, Ranković, and Kardelj foremost. Except for Kardelj, none of the others had been in Moscow or were personally known there, and this allowed Broz to be a sort of intermediary between them and the Comintern.[181] Having abolished the leadership of the party abroad, stating that the "Parisians" had no right to meddle in its domestic affairs, he strengthened ties with provincial cells and gave them new impetus. The three regional centers of Belgrade, Zagreb, and Ljubljana, until then only sporadically in contact, began coordinating their activities. The newly instituted military committee made every effort to create task groups of those able to handle arms. The party developed a semi-clandestine editorial program, publishing newspapers, books, and pamphlets that were widely distributed and brought in some income.[182] Broz also insisted that the CPY be financially independent from Moscow. Psychologically, this was of great importance, for the communists could no longer be accused of being "in the pay of the Bolsheviks." He made this decision under the pressure of circumstances, given that the Comintern persevered in its decision not to send money, as if it had already decided to abolish the CPY. In a letter to Dimitrov on 1 March 1938 reporting on his activity, Walter wrote: "It is hard to work in such difficult times without any moral, political, or material help." But he optimistically concluded: "I understand the complexity of the situation and will do everything possible to save the 'firm,' and to accomplish the tasks awaiting us."[183]

The impact of this letter was widespread. On Dimitrov's initiative, it was circulated among the most important Comintern leaders, who had been discussing the future of the CPY since the beginning of the year. On 3 January 1938, the secretary of the IKKI named a special commission, consisting of Pieck, Manuilskii, and the eminent Bulgarian communist Vasil Kolarov, to study the question. They were charged with "examining the situation in the CPY, evaluating its cadres and preparing proposals regarding the renewal of the leadership and the work of the party at home."[184] In spite of a remark by Georgi Damianov (Belov) criticizing Walter for having "fled the revolution" in October 1917, the members of the commission agreed that he was the man best suited to lead the party and should therefore be summoned to Moscow. On 26 April 1938, Dimitrov laconically wrote on this document, "He can be called."[185] As soon as he was informed, Broz rushed to Paris, where he arrived on 14 July, sure that he would stay in France only for a short period, and that he already had the nomination as secretary general in his pocket. (As early as May 1938 he introduced himself as the secretary of the Central Committee to his future biographer Vladimir Dedijer, then still a student).[186] His Soviet visa was late in coming, however, and his stay in Paris was prolonged. This caused him a great deal of anxiety, both because he wanted to return to his work in Zagreb, and especially because he suspected that the delay was the result of enemy intrigues.

In fact, factional machinations were at their peak. Železar and Obarov accused Broz of being a Gorkić man and of continuing his Trotskyist policy because he refused to dismiss people from the old staff who were suspected of being police informers.[187] They intimated that the party was a "circus," that it lacked a real CC, that the Comintern trusted only them, and that "Georgi" would call them shortly to its leadership.[188] These assertions were not groundless, considering that, from the old CC, only Walter and Kuhar were not on the Comintern's blacklist. Not so Čolaković and Žujović, who were proclaimed "Gorkić's follower number 1" and "number 2," respectively, and who managed to stay alive only because they were not within the reach of the NKVD. As if all this were not enough, Broz risked being arrested since King George VI's official visit to Paris had increased police control. Under the influence of the "parallel center," the French comrades refused to find him a safe apartment.[189]

Walter was helped in this awkward situation by Josip Kopinič, called Vokšin, the Slovene he had met in 1935 in Moscow at the Communist University for the Ethnic Minorities of the West (KUNMZ). They apparently became friends not only because both were interested in Marxist doctrine but in women as well. Kopinič was a mysterious and adventurous figure. He had joined the CPY during his military service in the Yugoslav Royal Navy, where he had organized thirteen clandestine cells.[190] When, in 1934, he suspected imminent arrest, he fled to Moscow, where he began collaborating with the Soviet secret service. From the start of the Spanish Civil War he fought for the republic and was among the first five volunteers to join the International Brigades. He distinguished himself for his bravery, reaching the rank of corvette captain, and was sent to Paris as a member of the local Spanish mission.[191] With the help of a marquise who was a military attaché at the Spanish embassy, he found shelter for Broz in the former's mansion and, even more important, he promised to support him in Moscow. Broz gave him a letter for Dimitrov, with a desperate appeal to "Comrade Georgi" to do something and "save my family."[192] Kopinič delivered it, adding a letter of his own, the closing sentence of which testifies to how shaky Walter's fortunes in the Soviet Union were at that time: "I turn to you as a son to a father, begging you to give me an answer in regard to Comrade Walter. . . . You are my last hope, because all the others tell me, when I enquire, what should be done, that it is better not to ask too much."[193]

Although Dimitrov was favorably inclined toward Broz, he could do no more than advise Kopinič to get in touch with the Cadre Department of the

IKKI. Damianov (Belov), the arrogant leader of that department, brusquely declared that nothing could be done: "There are charges against Walter and until they are cleared I cannot intervene."[194] Kopinič was not disheartened. He returned to Dimitrov, trying to convince him to allow Walter to come to Moscow in order to exculpate himself. This time Dimitrov sent him to Božidar Maslarić (nicknamed Andreev), Manuilskii's substitute, who knew him well because they had fought together in Spain. More articulate than Damianov, he enumerated in detail the accusations leveled against Broz by his adversaries. First, there was the suspicion that he was, directly or indirectly, in the service of the Yugoslav police and the Gestapo. Since the Comintern was no longer financing the CPY's press, who was financing it? The guess was that it was probably the police. This was the only logical answer. Ivo Lola Ribar and Boris Kidrič were the sons of capitalists, therefore probable agents provocateurs. Even worse, Ribar's father had been president of the Yugoslav parliament when the decree outlawing the CPY was passed, and he was a Freemason. Not to mention Herta Haas, a German and a Gestapo spy. Such accusations were enough to put anyone into Lubianka, the NKVD prison in Moscow, if not before the execution squad. Kopinič, obstinate as he was, managed to pull through. Maslarić offered him the post of secretary general of the CPY, stressing that "we have faith only in you," but he declined and convinced him to let Walter come to Moscow.[195]

Back to the Soviet Union

Broz left Paris on 23 August 1938, flying to Stockholm and then to the Soviet capital, where he arrived the next day after an absence of nearly two years. One can imagine what his feelings were in view of the fact that between 1936 and 1937 eight hundred of the nine hundred Yugoslav communists living in the Soviet Union had been arrested together with their families. He felt like the last of the Mohicans, because it was unclear whether or not the CPY would be abolished.[196] "What was difficult?" he mused later. "To die in the Soviet Union under the accusation of being a counterrevolutionary. To die in Yugoslavia was not difficult. You knew that you would die as a revolutionary."[197]

On 24 August, he was at Comintern headquarters, where he was humiliated by having to wait for four hours before being allowed to enter the building.[198] He immediately had to defend himself before a commission of five members, among whom were three hostile Bulgarians who wanted him condemned because of the failure of the Budva expedition. They maintained that Petko Miletić should be named secretary general of the CPY and, if this were not feasible, a certain Captain Dimitrev, a Bulgarian who fought in Spain, should be nominated as commissar. Walter was to be "liquidated." Among other things, the commission felt that his lifestyle was not compatible with his income, which gave rise to suspicions that he was corrupt. The Soviet counterespionage agency also had a say in the inquiry, accusing him of Trotskyism. Broz saved himself, even if only by the skin of his teeth (and probably with Dimitrov pulling some strings), since it was evident that the charges against him were groundless.[199] A report Walter had presented on 23 September 1938 was also of help. It described in detail his relationship with people "who had been discovered to be saboteurs and enemies of our party," nine eminent Yugoslav communists, of whom seven had already been shot and two were still alive but on trial. Obviously he had nothing good to say about any of them, although later he maintained that he had been prudent because, as he had not worked with them, he did not know them well.[200] Manuilskii also spoke in his favor, and probably the powerful Mikhail Trilisser, called Moskvin, one of the leaders of the NKVD with whom Broz was acquainted. This came just in time, for at the end of November Moskvin fell victim to the Stalinist purge. According to Tito, this was the most difficult time of his life. "I was not sure," he said later, "whether I would be taken away one day. It was above all thanks to Dimitrov that I was not arrested. In fact, he trusted me, convinced that I should lead the party as secretary general."[201] In any case, it was a particularly distressing time, sketched as follows in a conversation with Dedijer: "Night at Karaivanov's. Some bottles of vodka. I am terribly afraid. Now I understand why, in the USSR, they drink so much. They drink because they are afraid."[202] Ivan Karaivanov, the Bulgarian Communist, collaborator with the NKVD, Broz's confidant and, naturally, a spy, wrote about that period: "He was extremely preoccupied. His eyes were full of tears. These were the days when Comrade Tito got his first grey hairs."[203]

Despite all this, he won the day. After this trying experience he was rehabilitated and on 17 September 1938 he was already taking part in an IKKI session where his report on the Yugoslav situation was discussed.[204] In his diary, Dimitrov wrote laconically: "In its main lines, the Yugoslav report is correct."[205] The demonstrations in support of Czechoslovakia organized by Yugoslav Communists at the end of September and beginning of October during the Czechoslovak crisis also played a part. In Belgrade and in Zagreb thousands of students paraded in the streets, shouting that they wanted to go to Czechoslovakia and fight Nazism. Many of them even went to Prague in order to enroll in the International Brigades and resist the aggression of the Third Reich. The Munich agreement between Adolf Hitler, Benito Mussolini, the French prime minister Édouard Daladier, and his British colleague Neville Chamberlain regarding the annexation of the Sudetenland to Germany was seen in Moscow as an anti-Soviet move, and this also worked in Walter's favor.[206]

But his tribulations were not yet over. In autumn 1938 he was asked, together with Vladimir Čopić and Kamilo Horvatin, to edit the Serbo-Croatian translation of the *History of the Communist Party of the Soviet Union (Bolsheviks)* recently published under Stalin's name. That meant that every word was sacred. This "brilliant synthesis," so it was said, had been written by the "universal genius."[207] Before the work was finished, on 3 November 1938, NKVD agents arrested Čopić. "They took him away," Walter was told by the cleaning woman of the Hotel Lux, where both were staying, "during the night." Čopić's important role during the Spanish Civil War at the head of the Anglo-American Abraham Lincoln brigade was of no importance. Kamilo Horvatin, accused of Trotskyism, also soon fell victim to the Stalinist purges. Since Walter was not willing to testify against him before the commission investigating the case, stating that in good conscience he could not say something he did not know, he was once more in trouble. This became even worse when the *Short Course* was published.[208] Marić, Kusovac, and their friends organized a new attack against him. In a series of letters sent to the IKKI, they accused Walter of having introduced Trotskyist formulations into the fourth chapter, which was dedicated to dialectic materialism, committing lèse-majesté against Stalin himself. They were joined by Dragan Müller, a Jew from Osijek, known in Moscow as Ozren, who was employed at the Innostranaia kniga (foreign book) publishing house. Because of those denunciations, Walter was once more hauled before a vigilance commission and managed to save his life a second time thanks again to Kopinič, who demonstrated the correctness of his editing, and thus his innocence.[209] Aleksandar Ranković was right when he later said: "If there had been no Kopinič, there would have been no Tito."[210]

To celebrate, Walter used the money he got from publishing the *History* to buy a ring with diamonds and an opal, which he greatly treasured. Even this threatened to ruin him, because a spy accused him of having bourgeois tastes. Was the accuser the "young Russian girl" with whom he lived in Moscow in 1938 and who wrote—as Kopinič says—reports about him every day?[211]

~

Important elections were held in Yugoslavia in the autumn of 1938. They were won by the prime minister, Milan Stojadinović, but only thanks to ballot rigging. It was clear that his regime would not last for long. Walter wanted to return home as soon as possible, considering that "the situation was vitally important for our country, and that everything should be done to achieve the victory of democratic forces."[212] But he was not permitted to leave. It was not until 26 December 1938, when he had refuted all the accusations that had poured in from Paris, Sremska Mitrovica, and from the Comintern itself, that

V. P. Kolarov wrote a report proposing to confirm the provisional leadership of the CPY, to restore financial help, and to order the magazine *Rundschau* not to publish anything without Walter's permission (this was clearly aimed at the "factions" in Paris and in Yugoslavia).[213] In spite of this favorable judgment, on 30 December he had a stormy discussion with Dimitrov, who took a critical view of the chaotic internal situation of the CPY, saying: "Your work is completely meaningless, it just won't do."[214] Since the secretary general had branded the leading Yugoslav communists as "sectarians," Broz included, in Dimitrov's opinion no permanent party leadership was possible at the moment, only a provisional one. Even so, at the end of this diatribe he charged Walter with carrying out the "final instructions" he had given: "The leadership (provisional) inside the country. A conference. Installment of a stable leadership. In Paris: a man for communications."[215]

But he did something more. Some days later, on 5 January 1939, he received Walter again, informing him that he had been nominated secretary general of the CC CPY, with the task of completely changing the old party structures. Dimitrov cautioned him: "You are the only one left. This is your last chance. Either you will be able to restore order or, as in Poland, everything will be disbanded. Everyone has been arrested. People for whom I would have put my hand in the fire."[216] In a note about this meeting, so decisive for his future, Broz modestly affirms that he was utterly surprised, because his ambitions were not that of being the leader of the party; he was mostly moved by the desire to save it from dissolution and transform it into a compact and revolutionary organism headed by a strong collective. Nevertheless, he accepted Dimitrov's nomination, promising: "We will clean the filth."[217] Dimitrov answered with a grimace: "Don't boast too soon."[218]

That same day, the IKKI secretariat also met and gave Walter a series of instructions on how to restructure the party and strengthen it politically. It recommended closing the ranks against the Fascist menace, uniting all democratic forces in a Popular Front, and above all keeping in mind the trade unions so as to have contact with the workers, the most important component of socialist life. This resolution was to serve as an outline for a letter that Broz would write and send to all members of the CPY.[219] However, there were still conflicting opinions about him. This is revealed in a note Manuilskii sent to Dimitrov two days later, on 7 January 1939, proposing that Walter be removed from the leadership of the party and given a "lower post" in consideration of the fact that he was at least partially responsible for the failed expedition of volunteers two years earlier.[220] His enemies in the Cadre Department acted immediately: a new commission was instituted to investigate the incident once more. Broz tried to blame it on adverse meteorological conditions, claiming that a storm delayed the arrival of the ship. The commission was not completely satisfied, as is evident from Damianov's (Belov's) remark in the final report: "Comrade Walter still does not recognize his responsibility for the failure of the expedition."[221] There were no other adverse consequences, aside from the fact that he was unable to get an exit visa from the Soviet Union. In the meantime, word started to circulate that Petko Miletić had arrived in Moscow with serious evidence to support the prosecution of Walter and that the NKVD would not allow him to go home. Dimitrov had to intervene personally with Lavrentii Beria, the minister for internal affairs, to finally get permission for Walter to leave.[222] Walter complained to Karaivanov about this new obstacle, who advised him to write directly to Stalin. His answer is revealing: "Better that Stalin ignores my existence."[223]

Head of the CPY

The Comintern appointed Walter secretary general of the CPY with the right of veto, which meant that he would always have the last word. Obviously this would have been impossible without the trust of Moscow, or if he had not been deemed to deserve the post.[224] Later, Tito proudly declared to Louis Adamic: "In Moscow, I was vetted in all possible ways. They had faith only in me."[225] In any case, it was a tumultuous process, which Tito described with understatement in a conversation with journalists: "It was neither easy nor simple." Rodoljub Čolaković wrote in his memoirs with more poignancy that it resembled a theatrical tragedy, "in which unbridled passions frothed and heads rolled as in Shakespeare."[226]

When he returned home, Broz immediately made his intended working methods plain. On the basis of his Soviet experience, he realized that the revolution would not be possible without a new party that was ideologically and organizationally centralized. By nature, he was a man of action and did not like empty discussions, interminable meetings, and repeated stock phrases, all of which had burdened the CPY for so long.[227] His circular letter, written on behalf of the Comintern, is revealing in its capacity to interpret correctly the policy of the Popular Front, while combining patriotic and social arguments. It read in part: "Considering the perils that threaten Yugoslavia, the main task of the CPY is to rise and organize all its peoples in the fight for the defense and integrity of the country against the aggression of German and Italian Fascists and their like. The conditions necessary for the realization of this task are the following: it is necessary to overthrow the present anti-popular Stojadinović government, and to constitute a national salvation government capable of organizing the defense of the state and resisting, without hesitation, Fascist aggression."[228]

Walter's long absence had given the sectarian groups a chance to catch their breath, since they were convinced he was already doomed. Even some comrades in Paris, Spain, and Canada started to waver. Dimitrov, however, intervened in his favor, asking the French Communist Party to back him in his struggle against his adversaries, which they did.[229] The CPY's close alignment with Moscow at that time is evident from a meeting of the provisional leadership on 15–18 March 1939, on the shores of Lake Bohinj in Slovenia. Kardelj, Djilas and Ivo Lola Ribar, among others, took part. Unanimously and "with joy"—as Walter wrote to Kuhar—they decided to expel from the party all Yugoslav communists recently arrested or killed in the Soviet Union as "Trotskyists" and "sectarians," as well as those who were causing trouble in Paris and at home (Marić, Kusovac, Miletić). This decision demonstrated that Walter, in spite of the fear he had had to cope with in Moscow, was not critical of Stalin's terror but accepted his ruthless methods. Not just his enemies but friends like Vladimir Čopić were among those expelled from the party.[230] When he returned from the USSR, Walter confided to his comrades that according to Dimitrov, in the recent purges the Soviet Union had at times "exaggerated" charges, but that in any case it was better to cut into healthy flesh in order to completely extirpate the "malignant tumor."[231] Evidently Broz agreed with this idea, since he implemented similar practices during his leadership, although in a less cruel way than that of Stalin. From the very start he could count on the solidarity of his collaborators: "We were proud to be faithful to Stalin," remembered Djilas, "and to be Bolsheviks of firm character. The highest ideal of the party was to be a Bolshevik, and for us, Stalin was the incarnation of Bolshevism."[232]

In 1939, Walter returned from Moscow firmly convinced that the party should be financially autonomous (largely through party membership fees). He was extremely satisfied when told that, in this regard, the CPY was finally independent from the Comintern. "This was the first emancipation," comments Djilas, "much more important than it seemed at the moment."[233] In truth, this was only partially the case, for in 1940 a false-bottomed suitcase came from Moscow with secret instructions and a respectable amount in US dollars.[234]

One of the most important successes achieved by the CPY during that period was the organization of communist youth (the SKOJ), in particular high school and university students. Once the distrust toward young people, long a feature of the party, disappeared, membership in the SKOJ increased, especially at the three Yugoslav universities where its activities were "legal." "In Belgrade alone ten thousand young people are studying at the university," wrote the British ambassador in his dispatch to the Foreign Office. "If more than half of these, perhaps even three-quarters, are Communist in their views, it is above all out of anxiety for their future; Yugoslavia has a cultured proletariat screaming for bread and work."[235] Consequently, the SKOJ became a party within the party, so to speak, with even more members than the CPY. The communist movement began to be an expression of protest for young intellectuals more than for the proletarian masses, who were not numerous and were certainly less radical. In Yugoslavia in 1939 there were about 730,000 workers, only half of whom were employed in factories.[236] The influx of new people into the CPY increased revenue, which Broz watched over himself, and the circle of sympathizers grew steadily. It is interesting to note that during the regular meetings of the party nobody discussed the internal situation in the Soviet Union, which was in the grip of Stalinist terror. It was as if nothing was happening there, neither good nor bad.[237]

In spite of the internal opposition Broz had to deal with, in the months after his return from Moscow he continued to strengthen his position, introducing an "iron discipline" into the party, as his comrades approvingly said. On 9 and 10 June 1939, in a village near Ljubljana, he convened a secret session of the most prominent members of the party from all over Yugoslavia. On that occasion sectarianism was condemned and the measures taken against Petko Miletić, as its most important exponent, were confirmed.[238]

Although Petko was banished from the CPY, he, Marić, and Kusovac continued plotting against Walter, trying to deny him the right to lead the party.[239] Marić and Kusovac even managed to convince Yugoslav émigrés in America to stop helping the CPY financially, claiming that it was now led by persons whose mandate had been revoked by the Comintern.[240] The most dangerous of all three for Walter was Miletić, who was released from jail in June 1939 and was then able to further develop his intrigues against his rival, first in Yugoslavia, then in Moscow. "Petko writes, writes . . ." recalled Tito later, referring to the stream of his denunciations, as if in a nightmare.[241] Apparently he had gathered a group of followers who had been expelled from the party in Montenegro, "poisoning them ideologically with his lies." When, at the end of September 1939, Djilas and his colleagues managed to get the original transcripts of Miletić's police interrogations, it appeared that he had not behaved as bravely as was generally believed. This material was promptly sent to the IKKI. Miletić reacted immediately, leaving for Istanbul where, thanks to his Bulgarian friends, the Soviet consulate gave him a visa for Moscow. He went there certain he would still have supporters at the Comintern who would defend him from the calumnies of "that vulgar scum," as Broz and his comrades were labeled.[242]

At the end of September, Broz also returned to the Soviet capital through Le Havre and Leningrad. He came at the invitation of the Comintern, where many still suspected him of Trotskyist inclinations. He was traveling on board the ship *Sibir* when he received news about two decisive events: first, the nonaggression pact between Germany and the Soviet Union, signed by the two foreign ministers, Ribbentrop and Molotov; then, when they entered the Baltic, about Hitler's attack on Poland.[243] What concerned Walter more than the beginning of the Second World War, however, was the hostility unleashed against him by Miletić. Once more Kopinić came to his aid, writing a fifty-page paper on Petko with the support of his old comrade-in-arms Maslarić (Andreev) and Manuilskii, who procured him access to all the relevant archives. In fact, it seems that as early as 1923, when he was first captured, Miletić had begun collaborating with the police and betraying his friends. This was why he was put in the Sremska Mitrovica jail—as an agent provocateur. Together with Djilas's material, Kopinić's memoir was so compromising and convincing that Miletić was arrested shortly afterward. On 21 September 1939, he was condemned to eight years of forced labor. He died at the end of January 1943 in one of Stalin's gulags, although some believe that he was still alive as late as 1971.[244] Walter met his mortal enemy only twice: the first time at the seat of the Comintern, where Petko could come and go as he pleased; the second on a Moscow bus. That time Petko had stood, immobile, holding the bus strap with his right hand. His dark and bony face seemed indifferent to everything, although from his clenched fist, a thread of blood trickled down, drop by drop.[245]

When Dimitrov informed him that Miletić had been arrested, Broz experienced one of the most gratifying moments of his life. He was on his way to the office of Damianov (Belov), the powerful Bulgarian who had supported Petko and had sponsored him for the leadership of CPY.[246] When he entered the room, Belov received him with bureaucratic haughtiness: "How do you do, Comrade Walter? Is there something new?"

"Nothing, nothing," was the answer. "Nothing in particular, the only thing I can think of is the arrest of Petko."

Damianov jumped to his feet, surprised and shaken. And for the next half hour he was unable to speak.[247]

2

World War Two and the Partisan Struggle

1939–1945

The Hitler-Stalin Pact and the Start of the Second World War

When the Second World War began on 1 September 1939 subsequent to Nazi aggression in Poland, with Great Britain and France deciding to come to its aid, Walter and his comrades saw these events as further proof of imperialist warmongering, which meant that the conflict "could not be a struggle of the working class."[1] When, the following 28 September, Germany and the Soviet Union signed an agreement of mutual friendship and common borders, they immediately conformed, blaming the "colonialist" forces and the "criminal policy of the English and French provocateurs" more than Germany's territorial ambitions.[2] On that occasion, Dmitrii Manuilskii convened a meeting of all the representatives of the communist parties present in Moscow, in which Broz took part. Manuilskii explained why the agreement with Germany was necessary, adding, however, that this was merely a political maneuver. Nothing kept the other parties, aside from the Soviets, from continuing their attacks on Fascism. He asked everyone present to write a proclamation to their own party that traced future lines of conduct in conformity with what he had said. With the exception of Broz, none of the representatives adhered to his request, afraid of saying something wrong. In his proclamation, he asserted that German and Italian Fascism, the worst enemy of progressive humanity, continued to be a threat to Yugoslavia. Manuilskii enthusiastically approved, adding that here was someone capable of thinking with his own head.[3] This attempt to distance the CPY from Soviet foreign policy was, however, only temporary. When the Soviet Union attacked Finland, Stalin's directive prevailed, according to which the fight against Fascism was not of primary importance, since what mattered most was the "class struggle" with the bourgeoisie. As Tito said later, "Just when Hitler's Army was changing the map of Europe, and the Fascist offensive was in full swing, a policy of this sort, which did not take national interests and the defense of independence into account, could be fatal."[4] It would have been even more fatal to him personally had he openly expressed his reservations at the time. He therefore adhered to "Stalin's wise peace policy," which had obliged Hitler to capitulate to the Soviet Union, "strong with its Army of invincible peasants and workers."[5] Consequently, Broz and his comrades applauded Stalin's behavior in the following months, when the Red Army "liberated millions from capitalist slavery in Belarus and the West Ukraine, in Bessarabia, Bukovina, Latvia, Estonia and Lithuania." In the Comintern paper, *Die Welt*, published in Stockholm, he wrote that the Yugoslavs had greeted these invasions with enthusiasm.[6]

At least in the case of leftist youth, he certainly did not exaggerate. As Hans Helm, chief of a police delegation to Yugoslavia, reported on 21 December 1939, the impact of communist activity on students was obvious. It was impossible to overlook the fact that the Molotov-Ribbentrop agreement had positive consequences for Germany, since communist propaganda was working in its favor. Anti-Nazi "excesses" had practically ceased in Yugoslavia, and instead the polemics were all directed against British and French imperialism. "Before the signing of the German-Russian Pact, the Yugoslav communists were the most passionate nationalists in Yugoslavia. The communist students of the Belgrade University formed volunteer battalions trained by army officers. After the Pact, these volunteers disappeared. Up to 23 August, the communists could hardly wait for the war to begin. Today they are pacifists *à outrance*."[7] At the end of November 1939, when the Soviet Union attacked Finland and was consequently banished from the League of Nations, there were pro-Russian demonstrations in Belgrade during which the students shouted: "It is better to die on the streets of Belgrade [fighting their own bourgeoisie] than on the Slovenian frontier [fighting the Germans]." In fact, they believed that "Hitler did not represent any threat to Yugoslavia." The British diplomats were convinced, as they wrote in a dispatch to the Foreign Office, that "beyond doubt German money and German agents are behind much of the Communist propaganda in this country." The communists were undoubtedly successful in exploiting the social question as well as the pan-Slav sentiments of the population.[8]

But this approach did not thrive everywhere or in every milieu, left wing though it might be. In Belgrade and in Ljubljana many were unprepared to swallow the Molotov-Ribbentrop Pact and the ensuing political conversion of the CPY; even less so in Zagreb, although there the communists kindled the fire of Croat nationalism and anti-Serb sentiments. While fighting for survival and power, Broz was also obliged during this period to cope with Croat leftist intellectuals who did not like Moscow's Socialist Realism in the arts, its involvement in the Spanish Civil War, and above all Stalin's terror with its farcical trials and Siberian gulags. The chief critic was Miroslav Krleža, nicknamed Fritz, the most famous writer in Croatia at the time, who knew a great deal about the Stalinist purges since he was acquainted with one of the "liquidators." When they met in Zagreb they conversed until dawn, although what they discussed is something that Krleža never told anyone. He said only that he had never heard a more demonic tale.[9]

Broz tried to overcome the so-called "conflict on the literary left." Before his departure for Moscow in August 1939, he met Krleža in an inn on the edge of Zagreb and tried to convince him that the party's authority should not be undermined. His interlocutor observed, during their discussion, the arrival of a highly suspicious group. "Now I had my first chance to see Tito in action," Krleža later said. "He is seated calmly and looks to the entrance, where several small steps lead to the garden. From his pocket, he takes his gun, puts it on the bench and says: 'In any case, I will resist. I cannot do otherwise, but you, jump over the fence and try to flee.' He gave me advice, which way I should go. In cold blood."[10]

But Miroslav Krleža and the intellectuals associated with his magazine *Pečat* (The seal) were not as easy to influence as the students in Belgrade. Considering the difficult international situation created by Hitler's aggressive policy, he was convinced that it was not wise to insist on a sterile radicalism. "He did not believe in the victory of the revolution," Tito explained later, "because he kept in mind the relationship of material forces. I said to him: 'It is true, what you are saying, but what is missing is the moral factor. The will and the consciousness of victory."[11]

The following autumn, when in Moscow, Broz tried more than once to convince Krleža and his friends to change their minds, but without success. In a report about the situation in Yugoslavia, written in September 1939, he observed, more in sorrow than in anger, that the "Trotskyists" active in the literary field were confusing the intelligentsia with their revisionism, and that the party was strenuously attempting to oppose them.[12] This policy was approved by the Comintern's leadership, which endorsed Broz's work in a session on 23 November.[13] Not everyone in that organization was appreciative, and the IKKI's approval did not stop them from plotting against him. Broz, who had come down with the flu, was unable to leave Moscow until 26 November 1939. (Many of his comrades in Yugoslavia already feared he was behind the bars of the NKVD).[14] On the eve of his departure his old chum Karaivanov counseled him not to return home by train via Prague, because of a possible assassination attempt, but to go via Turkey. Broz went to the railway station, boarded the train for Prague, descended by the opposite door and embarked on the train for Odessa.

He had come to the Soviet Union with a passport in the name of Tomašek, a Czech engineer, and he left as Spiridion Matas, a Canadian citizen of Greek origin.[15] Once in Istanbul, he remained there at length, since he did not deem it safe to travel with a passport with a Soviet exit visa. Nor did he have the Bulgarian or Yugoslav transit visas now requested by the authorities from subjects of the British Empire.[16] He asked his comrades at home to get him a new fake travel document, but something went unexpectedly wrong. "Both [Vladimir] Velebit and Herta [Haas]," Tito later recounted, "brought me passports so badly made that the first gendarme would have noticed they were not authentic, and would have arrested me." And not without a hint of malevolence toward Kardelj, he added: "Under the direction of Bevc (one of the latter's pseudonyms) we had such excellent technical service that we could have printed money. In spite of this, they sent me passports that were clearly forged, as if somebody wanted to get me into trouble."[17] In a letter sent years later to Kopinič, he was even more explicit: "In 1940, Kardelj wanted my head!" He suspected Kardelj/Bevc of conspiring against him because he was returning home endowed with full powers by the Comintern.[18] This reveals his habitual suspicious attitude, even toward his closest collaborators.

Broz only returned to Yugoslavia on 13 March 1940 with the document he had been given in Moscow.[19] So as not to raise doubts, he bought a first class ticket for the transatlantic ship *Rex*, which was leaving Genoa for New York in mid-March. At the Greek-Yugoslav border his passport, officially issued by the British consulate in Moscow, raised suspicions, but without serious consequences.[20] When in Zagreb, he got off the train to stretch his legs but did not, of course, continue the journey. His feeling of imminent danger was anything but unfounded, as confirmed some days later, when in the Corso coffeehouse he read in a newspaper that the British authorities in Gibraltar had blocked and checked an Italian ship in search of a suspect—almost certainly him. The ship was delayed for six hours, much to the annoyance of the passengers. "And in the meantime, I was sitting in Zagreb."[21]

He was furious when he returned to the Croat capital, suspecting that his comrades wanted to get rid of him, possibly even in favor of Petko Miletić. "I had the impression," Djilas writes in his memoirs, "that Tito, returning from Moscow, even suspected me of having helped Petko." There was a turbulent session of the CC, during which Broz vented his rage at having to wait so long for a decent passport in Istanbul. He already seemed to have resolved the problem with Kardelj, so now it was Djilas's turn to be accused. His explanation that the party's expert forger had been arrested, and therefore could not do his job, was of no interest to Tito. The accusations directed at Djilas made him so indignant that he did not even try to defend himself, and when at last he started to speak, he had tears in his eyes. "But when the session was over and I was still tense . . . he came to me and invited me for a stroll. Generally, he didn't come often to Zagreb, so as to avoid meeting anyone who knew him. But now he did it. He started to speak about commonplace matters, mostly about my private life and situation. From time to time he smiled mildly. In all this there was something human and warm, and when we separated I went happy as a child whose father has recognized that he has punished him unjustly, although he doesn't wish to admit it."[22]

In Zagreb, Broz and Krleža once more confronted each other. Krleža twice promised he would stop the propaganda against the Molotov-Ribbentrop Pact, but he did not keep his word. During the months when Broz was extremely busy strengthening the party and circulating its program among the masses, Herta Haas said that at least half his time was spent in discussions with Krleža and his friends.[23] Because he could not convince them, he branded them "Trotskyists" again and published a volume of essays edited by Vladimir Dedijer to refute their writings.[24]

Krleža was particularly critical of the Soviet Union, above all because he was hard-hit by the tragic fate of his acquaintances and friends, "who gave their life for Bolshevism and have been liquidated under their own banners."[25] Broz's answer to these moral considerations regarding Stalin's terror was: "What can we do in a situation like the present one, with the war knocking at our door? Upon whom can we rely? We have no other protector than the USSR, whether we like it or not."[26] But Krleža, believing that the revolution was "a suicide mission," did not change his mind. During the war he did not take part in the Partisan struggle, although Tito invited him to join on several occasions, convinced that as a "revisionist" he would be "butchered" if he ventured into the liberated territory.[27] Because of this attitude, Tito himself had some difficulty protecting the writer after the war, although he made peace with him. When, in August 1945, the writer came to Tito's residence, the White Palace in Belgrade, for the first time, he was received with marked coldness. Without offering to shake hands, Tito said sharply: "Sit down!" But after half an hour he invited him to lunch. Their comradeship, formed during the First World War in the same barracks, obviously survived.[28]

~

The change in the Muscovite political line also changed the attitude of the communists toward the internal situation in Yugoslavia. Prior to the signing of the Molotov-Ribbentrop Pact, they had tried to dialogue with all those forces that might accept collaboration. After August 1939 they looked at local events through a new ideological lens, in accordance with the Comintern's instructions that "Bolshevik vigilance and discipline" was to be strengthened.[29] In accordance with this, Broz was especially active in his attempts to extirpate "the malign tumor of our party" in Dalmatia, where "sectarian" elements were numerous. He uncompromisingly denounced them, urging his followers to boycott the culprits and not even greet them in the street.[30]

The agreement, reached in August 1939 by the new prime minister of the royal government, Dragiša Cvetković, with the leader of the Croat Peasant Party, Vlatko Maček, recognizing an autonomous Croatia within the boundaries of Yugoslavia, would probably have been approved by the communists earlier. In light of the new orthodoxy, however, it was seen as a pact between two bourgeoisies who were unable to solve the many national questions of the country, not to mention the other scourges that tormented it. With regards to foreign policy, Broz and his comrades feared that the new Cvetković-Maček coalition government would be dependent on Great Britain and France, which would allow them to involve Yugoslavia in their "imperialist war." Alternatively, as recommended by the Comintern, they favored an alliance between Yugoslavia and the Soviet Union, "which is the strongest enemy of the imperialist war and a guaranty for the independence and security of small countries."[31] That Stalin, in March 1940, had taken a big chunk of Finland's territory and was going to do the same with the Romanian province of Bessarabia did not bother any of the faithful, nor did Hitler's attack on Denmark and Norway.[32] In a report sent to Moscow at the end of May, Broz did not mention these events. Instead he spoke at length of pro-English and pro-French sentiments, which were "still unfortunately" widespread in Yugoslavia.[33]

When the Wehrmacht defeated France in the first half of June 1940, Broz argued that the moment had come to act in order to save Yugoslavia from the war. His policy, with its slogan "for peace, bread, and freedom," favored an alliance of Balkan states that would seek shelter from the German menace under the wings of the Soviet Union. The clandestine paper of the CPY, *Proleter*, considered this possibility in an article, although it asserted that the Yugoslavs would be wrong if they were counting solely on the help of the Red Army. It would come to their rescue, if they helped themselves. How? Evidently, with the creation of a popular government, as should be done according to Lenin's doctrine. The bourgeois revolution should be the first step to the proletarian one.[34]

The minutes of a session held on 15 September 1940 in the Comintern's archives tell an interesting story. On that occasion, the four main leaders of the Executive Committee of the Comintern (or IKKI), Wilhelm Pieck, Palmiro Togliatti, Klement Gottwald, and Dmitrii Manuilskii, discussed a verbal message sent by Broz through his special envoy, Nikola Petrović, an engineer from

Vojvodina.[35] In it he proposed organizing the fall of the Cvetković-Maček coalition, in order to replace it with a "truly popular government." To explain the need for this initiative, he drew attention to the tense situation in Yugoslavia and to the fact that the dismemberment of the country between Italy and Germany, under the auspices of the Yugoslav bourgeoisie, was a real danger. "A truly popular government," endorsed by workers and peasants, should prepare an armed resistance against its Fascist neighbors and their attempts to enslave the Yugoslav peoples.[36] Evidently Tito had become convinced that the Russian experience of 1917 could be repeated in Yugoslavia: first there would be a bourgeois-democratic revolution, the expression of liberally oriented middle classes. After that, power would be taken by the proletariat, or better by the Communist Party, as its vanguard.[37]

The IKKI session participants did not favor this proposal. The four leaders observed that the CPY was underestimating the forces of their adversary, and overestimating its own strength. In their opinion, Yugoslavia was not ready for a transformation such as the one that had taken place in Russia in 1917, since the CPY had little influence among the industrial workers and even less among the peasants. They warned against any premature action, because propitious domestic and international conditions were absent, and stressed that no one should cultivate the illusion that the Red Army would come to the aid of the proposed uprising. In this document, in which Broz was addressed as secretary general for the first time, Pieck, Gottwald, Togliatti, and Manuilskii did not limit themselves to warnings. In the second part of their "decision" they also indicated the political line to be followed by the party. It should oppose the Fascist plans regarding the dismemberment of Yugoslavia and favor those forces that would be ready to resist foreign aggression among the popular masses, the bourgeoisie, and the army. The decision read further: "If the Yugoslav State is divided into protectorates between Italy and Germany without a military struggle, the party has to organize the masses against the betrayal of the Yugoslav bourgeoisie and the violence of the imperialist powers." With this in mind, the CPY should elaborate appropriate military, political, economic, and national programs for the different ethnic regions of the country. "The party should use every means possible to collaborate with the petit bourgeois opposition, and also with social-democrats, in order to broaden and strengthen the front against the reaction, and to call the masses in defense of Yugoslav independence."[38]

The Fifth State Conference of the CPY

When he returned to Zagreb in March 1940, Broz decided to convene the party congress as soon as possible. In order to organize this important event properly—the last congress had been held in Dresden eleven years earlier—he started with a series of provincial conferences, which took place between May and September 1940. The general consensus of the fifteen hundred delegates was that the Party had grown ideologically and organizationally in the past few months. It gained the trust of broad sectors of the popular masses, becoming an important political force. It had 6,500 regular members, to whom an additional 17,800 members of SKOJ should be added. "This number," said Tito later, "would grow from month to month."[39]

Although the courier who brought the IKKI's message tried to convince Broz not to convene the Party Congress, maintaining that under the Cvetković-Maček police regime, it would be impossible to organize an assembly of more than one hundred people, he did not give up the idea. The only concession he was ready to make was that he did not call it a "congress" but rather a "conference." Between 19 and 23 October 1940, the Fifth "National" Conference of the CPY was convened at Dubrava, a suburb of Zagreb, where Tito hoped to pass unobserved. Money was not a problem, since the party had at its disposal some gold inherited from the independent trade unions.[40] It was necessary, however, to find a house large enough, with easy access in and out, and where a meeting hall could be fashioned by pulling down some walls. In addition, chairs and benches had to be bought, as well as equipment for the kitchen, food had to be procured and a second bathroom had to be installed. All this with the utmost discretion, so as not to alarm the neighbors. Even the delegates would not know the location—they were to come at night. Just one spy would have been enough to destroy the entire leadership of the CPY.[41] When it was suspected that a local woman might inform the police about the gathering, Broz did not hesitate: "I ordered Končar [leader of the Croatian CP] to kill her. That's what had to be done."[42] The danger did not come only from the police: the followers of Petko Miletić planned an attack against the conference. They failed because one of their gang informed the leadership of the CPY in time.[43]

The Conference adopted the Comintern's interpretation of the war as a conflict between two imperialist blocs and decided to oppose it, influencing the masses "from below" in order to organize them into a Popular Front.[44] In his introduction, Broz condemned "the pseudo-democracies of the English and French imperialists," stressing at the same time that "the Fascist powers were destroying the independence of one country after the other, and that Yugoslavia was increasingly threatened in a direct way."[45] It was necessary, in his opinion, to exploit the contemporary crises in order to bring about the revolution: "The imperialist bourgeoisie wish to end the war with a 'peace' founded on a new division of the world and on the oppression of the enslaved nations, worse than the old one. On the contrary, the working class, allied with peasants, now has the opportunity to destroy imperialism . . . and to abolish forever the imperialist wars."[46]

The CPY emerged from the Conference as a monolithic Stalinist party, convinced that a variety of opinions represented the worst of the worst: "sectarianism." It only appeared that its organs were elected democratically, since it was the secretary general who named the Central Committee (CC), which in turn nominated the other structures of the party.[47] The members of the CC and the seven members of the Politburo were confirmed on the basis of a list that was prepared in advance. Because of the conspiracy, their individual identities were to be indicated only vaguely, so that later it was difficult in some cases to establish who was who.[48] Generally they were young men in their twenties. As regards Tito, there was no doubt that he should be elected secretary general, since he had been anointed by Moscow. The result was the creation of a strong and disciplined party, appropriately compared by a British diplomat to the Jesuit order. This unintentionally echoed the words of Djilas, who described the CPY as a collective united in the comradeship, mutual love, and dedication characteristic of a primordial religious sect.[49] "A clandestine party like ours," boasted Kardelj, "did not exist anywhere. We have learned to trust each other."[50] And Tito was of the same opinion: "At that time, the results our party had achieved, what its possibilities were, and the enormous extent of these possibilities, were evident. The ranks had been purged of factions . . . of police spies. This gave us great moral satisfaction."[51] The judgment of Stane Kavčič, one of the cleverest representatives of "liberalism" in Slovenia during the sixties and seventies, was more restrained: "Tito became the effective head of the party, liquidating different ideological and political factions, reducing it to one. . . . He remained a vigilant guardian of this achievement."[52]

The CPY also turned to the Soviet Communist Party in modeling the privileges granted its leaders. Prior to Broz's return from Moscow, each of them received two thousand dinars a month, more or less the pay of a public school teacher. But since comrades called to posts of responsibility were better treated in the Soviet Union, he added one thousand dinars to the salary of every member of the Politburo and tripled his own. As a gift, the party gave him a vineyard near Zagreb, with which he increased his monthly income. He passed himself off as a wealthy engineer called Slavko Babić and bought a small villa with a garden in the suburbs of Zagreb. He wore elegant clothes and even had a chauffeured Ford, with the excuse that he had to live expensively in order to avoid police suspicion.[53]

Yugoslavia under Pressure and the Belgrade Putsch

Broz, Herta Haas, and other friends spent New Year's Eve 1941 in the company of Josip and Stella Kopinič, who had come from Moscow to Zagreb on behalf of the Comintern. "We are probably celebrating the last New Year's Day of old Yugoslavia," he said. "Hitler will not leave us in peace, therefore the situation will be difficult. But, we communists are used to it."[54]

How intensely he lived that historical moment is demonstrated by the article "Tactics and Strategy of Armed Revolt," which Broz wrote in March 1941 for a lecture cycle to be held at the party school. In it he exalted the proletarian revolution as the "supreme manifestation" of class struggle, which must begin at the critical moment when the "commotion of the masses" and the "swaying of the people" could be exploited to foment war against the bourgeoisie. What moment could be better than the crisis provoked by the probable impending attack of the Axis against Yugoslavia? An attack would be the ideal occasion to light the spark of a popular uprising. In the article, he stressed the need of the party, as the workers' avant-garde, to immediately take the initiative, to prepare the revolution in detail, and to organize combat units—the "iron fist" of the proletariat—in order to destroy or take control of the old administrative and military order. "The party should not allow the revolt to start spontaneously, without its organization and guidance."[55] Many years later, when asked how he had arrived at the idea for the partisan war that he predicted in this article, Tito answered that he had thought about it a great deal, and was thoroughly acquainted with the Marxist doctrine of the people at arms. He was inspired by Carl von Clausewitz but had also studied the history of the First World War, the October Revolution, the Chinese partisan struggle and the Spanish guerrilla war against Napoleon. But mostly he had, before his eyes, the recent Spanish Civil War as a warning regarding the errors to avoid and the examples to follow.[56]

~

At the beginning of 1941, Yugoslavia was in a terrible situation. Italy and Germany had it in their grip, since the Third Reich was allied with Hungary and Romania, and Mussolini had moved into Albania, occupying it in April 1939. With the intention of restoring the Roman Empire and transforming the Adriatic into a *mare nostrum*, Mussolini also planned to occupy Yugoslavia but was prevented from doing so by Hitler. In recent years Germany had spread its economic influence to the Balkans and the Führer did not want the Duce's ambition to compromise the supply of oil and other raw materials from the region. It was not easy to keep Mussolini at bay, however. On 28 October 1940, without informing his German ally, he attacked Northern Greece with nine divisions from Albania. Against all expectations, the Greek army reacted vigorously and by mid-November had liberated its territory and had begun to move into Albania. After a winter truce, in March 1941 the Italians launched a new offensive, again without success.[57] Prince Paul, regent of Yugoslavia, an Anglophile in his family ties and education, resisted the invitations from Berlin and Rome to join the Axis for as long as he could. In June 1940, in hopes of finding support, he even accepted diplomatic relations with the Soviet Union, although in the past the Karadjordjević family had considered it the country of the Antichrist. The following November, and then in January 1941, Moscow informed the Yugoslav government that it had asked Berlin not to extend its military action into the Balkans. It could do no more.[58]

When, in spring 1941, it became clear that Great Britain, the only country still opposing Germany, was unable to aid Prince Paul, he decided to join the Axis in order to save Yugoslavia from military occupation. The alliance offered by Hitler was, in fact, quite favorable, since it did not call on the Belgrade government to participate in the military efforts of the Wehrmacht or permit the transit of German troops through its territory. Prince Paul's hopes of sparing his people the horrors of the war did not last long. Following the example of Bulgaria, which joined the Axis on 1 March 1941, on 25 March Premier Cvetković and his foreign minister, Cincar Marković, signed a pact at the Belvedere Palace in Vienna. A fellow traveler who had access to press conferences in which Cincar Marković had briefed journalists on what to write informed the Politburo of the CPY about these secret maneuvers. Neither the capitulation of the government nor the mass revolt that exploded in Belgrade the next day under the auspices of nationalist circles and the Serb Orthodox Church came as a surprise.[59] The popular demonstrations, aimed at "saving the honor of Yugoslavia," were topped off by a military coup on the night of 26–27 March, which was staged by a group of aviation officers headed by General Dušan Simović and inspired by British agents active in Belgrade. Thereafter events developed quickly: King Petar, only seventeen years old, "took" power as a puppet of the military junta in order to give it the necessary legitimacy, while Prince Paul and his family were sent into exile.[60]

The day after the coup d'état of 27 March 1941, thanks to the good offices of a Montenegrin aviator, Tito flew from Zagreb to Belgrade in order to follow the course of events on the spot.[61] (The motor broke down and the plane almost crashed, which is probably why, thereafter, Tito never liked to fly). Upon meeting his Belgrade comrades, he observed that the pact between Yugoslavia and the Axis had failed. "War is inevitable. Our country will be attacked."[62] In a telegram sent to Moscow, he proposed that the communists organize a general revolt against probable German and Italian aggression, but also resist the attempts of the British to involve Yugoslavia on their side in the conflict, recommending instead "popular pressure on the new government to get it to denounce the Vienna pact and conclude an agreement of mutual aid with the Soviet Union."[63] This bellicose attitude alarmed Moscow, where fear of provoking Hitler was still very much alive. On 31 March 1941, the CPY was advised to avoid street demonstrations and possible clashes with the authorities. "Do not expose yourselves, do not allow yourselves to be seduced by enemy provocations. Do not expose the people's vanguard to repression and do not send them prematurely into the fire. The moment of the final fight with the class enemy has not yet arrived."[64]

Attack on Yugoslavia and the Call to the Uprising

Once installed, the Simović government did not know what to do. It attempted to pacify Hitler, proclaiming its fidelity to the recently signed pact. The Führer, however, did not accept the proffered olive branch. Infuriated, he ordered his generals to prepare for intervention in Yugoslavia, along with armed intervention in Greece, where the Italians had to be saved from catastrophe.[65]

Operation *Marita* was therefore joined by Operation *Strafgericht* (court martial), which began at dawn on 6 April 1941, Palm Sunday according to the Orthodox calendar. The friendship pact signed in Moscow between the Soviet government and the Yugoslav ambassador at 2:30 that morning, in the hope that it would deter German aggression, had no influence whatsoever on events. As Kardelj recalls, that day the communists were organizing impressive demonstrations in Belgrade, in celebration of the pact with Russia, but the Germans were quicker.[66] Their planes took off from Bulgaria and, without any declaration of war, violated Yugoslav air space and heavily bombed Belgrade, even though it had been declared an "open city." A few hours later, at Maribor (Slovenia), the Wehrmacht crossed the Austrian-Yugoslav border and moved in the direction of Zagreb. By 8 April 1941, units of the Second German Army were already in the streets of Belgrade. In the days that followed Yugoslavia was invaded, practically without resistance, by Italian, Hungarian, and Bulgarian troops, and dismembered according to Hitler's plans. On 10 April, the Independent State of Croatia (Nezavisna država Hrvatska; NDH) was declared under the leadership of the Ustaša *Poglavnik* (leader) Ante Pavelić, who returned from Italy, where his terrorist, fanatically nationalist gang were under Mussolini's protection. He extended his control over Bosnia-Herzegovina but ceded central Dalmatia to Italy, which also got the southern part of Slovenia, Ljubljana included. Germany occupied Lower Styria and Upper Carniola, and the Hungarians the region of Prekmurje. The Italians sent their troops into Montenegro and the greater part of Kosovo, annexing it to Albania. Central Serbia was under the control of the Germans as a protectorate, ruled by local Quislings (a term for collaborators in general, coined after a Norwegian politician, Vidkun Quisling, a prominent early collaborator). Vojvodina was given to the Hungarians and the greater part of Macedonia to the Bulgarians. The Yugoslav Army, considered strong and valiant, turned out to be completely unprepared to fight the invading forces. On 17 April 1941, General Kalafatović was forced to capitulate. Thousands of soldiers scattered in all directions, hoping to avoid capture. The Germans took 344,000 prisoners, mostly Serbs, whereas three hundred thousand men managed to escape.[67] At the same time, King Petar II and the majority of Simović's government followed Prince Paul into exile, seeking refuge first in Athens, where British forces were still present, then in Palestine and finally in London.

As Winston Churchill observed, with the 27 March putsch, the Yugoslav nation had found its soul but was unable to save its territory.[68] The Wehrmacht attack was an exemplary blitzkrieg, in the course of which the Germans were primarily interested in maintaining communication lines with Bulgaria, Greece, and Romania and in exploiting the chrome, bauxite, and copper mines that were important for their military industry.[69]

During these dramatic events, Tito was constantly in contact with Moscow. One of his more important successes in 1940 was the installation of a radio link between Zagreb and the Comintern, thanks to Josip Kopinič (who changed his nickname from Vokšin to Vazduhk, similar to the Russian word for "air") and Stella Panajotis-Bamjazidos, a Greek telegrapher trained in Moscow. The two had initially pretended they were married, but soon enough they actually were. Vlatko (Vladimir) Velebit found them a house near a wood on the outskirts of Zagreb in case they needed to escape. This was an unnecessary precaution as the transmitting apparatus, cleverly hidden in a bunker below stairs, was never discovered by either the Ustaše or the Germans. In addition to the CPY, seven other parties were linked to this clandestine center: the Italian, Swiss, Austrian, Hungarian, Slovak, Bulgarian, and Greek parties.[70] This was the beginning of an intense flow of communications, which grew to enormous dimensions, first through Vokšin and then also through radio transmitters at Tito's headquarters. During the war, Tito exchanged hundreds of telegrams with the Comintern and other Soviet services, unbeknownst even to his most intimate collaborators. He wrote them personally and saw to them with great care.[71] "At the Politburo sessions," Ranković later said, "he told us only what he considered opportune in the dispatches from Moscow or the Comintern. None of us has ever seen any of these telegrams. During the war, Tito would take off his boots before bed, put the telegrams in them, and put them back on." This lack of confidence in his comrades irritated Ranković. "What am I doing here? What is my responsibility, if the telegrams from Moscow are hidden from me?" Tito's sharp answer was: "I am the secretary general of the party. I have the right to decide what to tell you and the others."[72]

The sudden collapse of the Yugoslav Army surprised the communists, who also believed in the myth of the heroic Serb tradition, linked to their anti-Turk uprising at the beginning of the nineteenth century, and their opposition to the Austro-Hungarian armies during the First World War. In 1944, Djilas confessed to Manuilskii: "We made the mistake of thinking that the majority of the officers, together with the General Staff, would resist the Germans. It did not happen. Most of them surrendered."[73] The leaders of the CPY thought that Yugoslavia would resist for a month or more, giving them the opportunity to strengthen their military organization and to connect with sympathizers, who were numerous in the armed forces. In reality, the Wehrmacht encountered almost no obstacles to its advance: "There was no serious resistance; it was a triumphal march," said Djilas.[74]

At the session of the Croat CP on 8 April 1941, two days before the German troops entered Zagreb, Tito openly recognized the blunder regarding the Royal Army, highlighting the fact that during the dramatic events of the last two weeks the communists had not been very efficient, since they should have taken the initiative. After the aggression of the Axis and the occupation of the country, the question of what to do became urgent.[75] Since Stalin was still allied with Hitler, it was clear that room for maneuver was limited, as they could not act openly against the occupiers. However, they were convinced that the imperialist forces would soon give up the common fight and the time would come when the suicidal struggle of the European bourgeoisie could be exploited for the creation of the revolution, as Lenin had done during the First World War.[76]

On 10 April, when the Independent State of Croatia was proclaimed under Italian and German tutelage, Tito installed a military committee, which he headed, to give party members the necessary directives while the state was collapsing. They were to collect and hide light weapons, organize military committees in all major cities and provinces, create small fighting groups and commanding cadres, and try to convince the soldiers not to surrender but instead to go undercover with their arms.[77] On 15 April 1941, the CPY published a proclamation to the Yugoslav peoples in which it condemned the foreign aggression, the betrayal of the royal regime, and the spread of chauvinism and hatred between brothers, inviting the population "not to surrender in spirit." It read in part: "From this bloody imperialist war a new world will emerge. . . .

On the real independence of the Yugoslav peoples a new fraternal community will be built."[78]

No one else in Yugoslavia at that time used language of this sort. "I think that the proclamation of 15 April had historic significance," said Tito later, and with reason, "since in that critical moment the CPY indicated to the Yugoslav popular masses the real problems of society and the prospect of the fight against the Fascist occupier."[79]

The CPY did not reach the decision to fight without internal conflict, since it was not easy to decide whether it would be better to organize an armed revolt or limit themselves to sabotage. "Against the revolt," writes Kardelj, "there were not only large democratic circles and many leftist intellectuals, but also some of the communists. The prevailing thought was that the party and the resistance forces should concentrate mainly on the political struggle, combining it with sabotage. Many considered the attitude of those in the Party who were favorable to the idea of armed uprising to be an adventurous one that would help the Fascists destroy the people. . . . They opined that it was better to postpone the struggle until the final stage of the war and only then to call the proletariat to arms in order to take power. They were convinced that the 'right place for the revolution was not the woods but the cities.'"[80]

The day the royal government fled the country, Tito informed the Comintern that the CC CPY had decided to resist the occupier, strong as it might be.[81] In order to assess the situation created after 6 April, on 4 May 1941 he convened a series of meetings in Zagreb, attended only by Croats, some Serbs, and Slovenians, whereas the comrades from Montenegro and Bosnia-Herzegovina were absent due to difficulties traveling. Those from Macedonia, led by the local secretary, Metodij Šatorov, called Šarlo, decided to join the Bulgarian party, thus recognizing the dismemberment of the state. The disappearance of Yugoslavia was confirmed by Moscow shortly after, which severed diplomatic relations with the royal government in exile, informing the Yugoslav ambassador 8 May 1941 that the Soviet government did not foresee any juridical reason for the presence of the Yugoslav mission in USSR.[82] The discussions in Zagreb, however, refuted the dismemberment of the state and expressed the fear that the enmity between the Yugoslav peoples could be used both by the occupiers, in order to dominate them, and by the domestic bourgeoisie, prone to collaborate with the Axis. According to Tito and his followers, it was necessary to close ranks and under the leadership of the party begin the fight against the German, Italian, and other Fascists, but also against the English imperialists. On that occasion, Tito once more asserted that the moment to seize power had come, affirming that it was not correct to wait, as Marxist doctrine preached, for the democratic bourgeois revolution. The communists, he said, should organize themselves militarily, in order to affirm the dictatorship of the proletariat everywhere after the defeat of the occupying regimes.[83]

~

It was clearer to Tito than to Stalin, who was blind to reality, that the war would not be limited to the capitalist camp, but would also involve the USSR. Tito paid no attention to anything else in anticipation of this event, which would give him the chance to realize his revolutionary plans. To Leo Mates, with whom he shared living quarters, he seemed like a man who kept saying to himself: "I will, I can and I must be a leader."[84] He worked so fervently that he neglected the Croat communists that the Ban (viceroy) Ivan Šubašić had imprisoned in the castle of Kerestinec, and who had fallen into the hands of the Ustaša when they proclaimed the Independent State of Croatia. There were about a hundred of them, including eminent intellectuals. "In the chaos that reigned, when Pavelić's regime was not yet firmly in power, since it had no police and no army," says Vladimir Velebit in his memoirs, with a hint of reproach, "it would have been easy to save them."[85]

Since the situation was becoming dangerous in the NDH capital and it was clear that the communists had little hope of influencing the Croat masses, who were intoxicated by their newly acquired "sovereignty," the Politburo decided to move to Belgrade. There the Germans were still tolerant of the communists.[86] With regards to the Ustaše, no doubt remained as to the criminality of their proposals. After coming to power under Hitler's and Mussolini's tutelage, they mercilessly persecuted the Jews, "Gypsies," and especially Serbs, who constituted more than 30 percent of the entire population of the new "independent" state. This ethnic complexity was intolerable to Ante Pavelić, who was ready to consider the Bosnian Muslims, his new subjects, of "pure Croat blood," and treat them accordingly, but was determined to get rid of all "foreign" nationalities. Hence, he launched an extermination program against the hated Serbs, trying to massacre a third of them and deporting the survivors to Serbia or forcing their conversion from Orthodoxy to Catholicism. Should they convert, they could be considered pure (or nearly so) Croatians. This policy was immediately put into practice without any firm opposition by a Church that, under the spell of nationalism, refused to openly condemn it.[87]

Tito hurriedly abandoned Zagreb, without even waiting for the birth of his and Herta Haas's son.[88] He left on 23 May, a day before the frontier between NDH and Serbia closed. As he said later, he decided to go, not just because of the Ustaša but also because some of the Croat communists, believing in the alliance between Hitler and Stalin, were trying to come to an agreement with Pavelić in order to separate the CP of Croatia from the CPY.[89] In reply, he wrote an article for the party's newspaper published under the title: "Why Are We Still in the Framework of the CPY?"

> Since the imperialist bandits have occupied Yugoslavia and the "Independent" State of Croatia has been created, it is not clear to many of our comrades why our Croat Communist party is still in the framework of the Yugoslav Communist Party. . . . They say that we are against the liberty and the independence of the Croat people and in favor of a restoration of old Yugoslavia. . . . We communists do not recognize this occupation and dismemberment of the country, since it was not done according to the wish of the people, but with the violence of imperialist conquerors. . . . When, joining our forces, we will gain true liberty and independence, we will create fraternal relations, according to the interest of our peoples. Just as the people of the Soviet Union have done.[90]

Tito came to Belgrade under the name of Slavko Babić, a representative of Škoda, a Czech arms manufacturer, and found the Serb communists ready and willing to fight the occupying forces and their own bourgeoisie. As he told the Russian writer K. M. Simonov in October 1944, there was a reign of terror in the city. If you went out into the street after sunset, you risked being killed. Under pain of death, it was forbidden to lock the doors of your house: the Germans were allowed to enter where and when they wanted. For some weeks, he went to bed without taking off his clothes and with a gun under his pillow. "The only thing that, in those days, assured me, was the fact that I lived just four house numbers away from the residence of the Belgrade commander, General Schröder. Yes, this was a period when it was necessary to live and die thinking only about the future of the Country, and not for a moment of one's own future."[91] The atmosphere of those days was tellingly described by Djilas: "Patrols during the night, darkness and continuous shots from all over the city. The Jews with yellow ribbons, with fear and anger, hunger and death, somber faces of citizens, and young Germans, gay and arrogant, with prostitutes and cameras. Flights of airplanes toward Greece and Romania. First local newspapers at the service of the occupiers."[92]

At the end of April and again a month later, Tito tried to convince Moscow that the tempest was approaching, informing "Grandpa," as the Comintern was called, through the military attaché of the Soviet Embassy still open in Belgrade, that the German troops were advancing toward the frontiers of the Soviet Union, and that the Wehrmacht officers in Zagreb did not hide this fact. In contact with the local bourgeoisie, their generals were openly saying that they would enter Russia like a "knife into butter." *Nach Moskau* (To Moscow) was written on the tanks passing through Belgrade in the direction of Romania, openly declaring that their final destination was the Soviet capital.[93] From a telegram Tito sent to the Comintern on 31 May 1941, it is clear that he was planning an uprising to coincide with the attack on the Soviet Union. "We are organizing military units, instructing military cadres, preparing an armed revolt."[94] A leaflet distributed at the end of May by the communists among the German and Italian troops, warning them that the Führer was going to propel them into war with Russia, is also evidence of the inevitable clash.[95] Considering Stalin's hostile attitude toward all those who dared inform him about the imminent attack, it would have been strange if Tito's admonitions had been favorably accepted in Moscow. As Vladimir Bakarić wrote many years later: "In the apparatus of the Comintern (at least in its majority) there was a strong distrust against Comrade Tito." For them he was not "obedient" and "humble" enough, he was too "independent" and "full of his own ideas."[96]

However, a document in the archives of the Comintern shows that not everyone in Moscow was critical of him. Dated 29 May 1941, it mentions secret meetings in Zagreb and Belgrade between Broz and a Soviet agent, who reported as follows: the CPY had eight thousand members and thirty thousand adherents of the SKOJ, the youth branch of the party. Its organization was intact and ready to fight; the CC had a military committee and a committee for diversion activities. The party had arms and they were well hidden, but it needed about ten thousand dollars to complete its reserves of weapons. "Pray, transmit my greetings to the comrades and inform them that the tasks given to the Yugoslav Communist Party will be accomplished."[97] It must be said, however, that the urge to fight was not only nurtured by revolutionary ideals or by faith in the Soviet Union. As Koča Popović remembers, interpreting the thoughts of the masses: "There were also a lot of young people wishing to rebel."[98]

Uprising and Revolution

The persecutions of the Serbs unleashed by the Ustaša, as well as by the Hungarians in Vojvodina, the Muslims in Bosnia-Herzegovina, and the Albanians in Kosovo, resulted in a wave of refugees who tried to reach what remained of Serbia, or took to the woods, where they organized armed groups to defend themselves. In addition, groups of soldiers who decided not to accept defeat passively gathered around Royal Army officers who had escaped capture and continued the fight. The "Chetniks"—as the Serb rebels against the Turks had been called in past centuries—started to appear as early as April 1941 in some areas. In the mountains of Ravna Gora in western Serbia, a forty-nine-year-old colonel, Draža Mihailović, led a handful of men who intended to keep the embers of the country's independence alive and to recall King Petar II to his throne. It was the start of an impassioned, highly patriotic Serb Orthodox movement, which was, as one of its followers later admitted, rooted in a hatred of all other Yugoslav peoples, especially Croats and Muslims. It is clear, he added, that it was impossible to win the war with presuppositions of this sort. "Moreover, we built everything on the myths of the past and it is obvious that today this leads to defeat."[99]

Meanwhile, Stalin tried to do everything he could to stay in Hitler's graces. On the eve of Operation Barbarossa, the name given to the Nazi invasion of the Soviet Union, the Moscow press agency TASS (Telegrafnoe agentstvo Sovetskovo soiuza; Telegraph Agency of the Soviet Union) published an article stating that information regarding the great concentration of forces on the Soviet border was false. For Tito, the fact that there was no reaction on the part of the Germans was a signal that the attack was imminent.[100] The Nazi aggression against the Soviet Union on 22 June 1941 did not, therefore, come as a surprise to him, as it did to Stalin. The invasion of the "flowering Soviet garden," as Tito wrote on behalf of the CC CPY that same day, in a proclamation called "To Workers, Peasants and Citizens of Yugoslavia," required all proletarians to take arms in its defense.[101] This audacious, even reckless, decision was based on the fact that the communists had no doubts that the ruin of the capitalist world was imminent, that the Red Army would confront the Wehrmacht without difficulty, and that its victory was a question of weeks, at most months. They considered its catastrophic retreat as a brilliant tactical move on Stalin's part: indeed, what could happen to an army that had recently celebrated the construction of a million and one tanks?[102] "The Russians influenced all our aims, our strategy and tactics. We were convinced that 'If the Russians win, we will also win,'" Ranković recalled.[103] In Tito's inner circle, as well as among the masses, the rumor spread that the Russians would be parachuting into Yugoslavia at any moment, and that it was necessary to be ready and welcome them. When Djilas asked a comrade if the war would end quickly, and received the answer that it would be over before the year's end, he reacted angrily: "Hang yourself on a lamp post, it will be over in two months."[104] Faith in immediate Soviet help is eloquently revealed in a message sent from Tito to the Comintern at the end of June 1941: "We are preparing an armed revolt against the occupiers, since our people are ready to fight. Tell us, what do you think? We are short of arms. Can we get some quickly?"[105]

In the meantime, on 22 June 1941, Dimitrov asked Broz to do everything possible in favor of the "rightful struggle of the Soviet people." Well aware, however, of his radical leanings, he stressed on behalf of Stalin that, at the moment, the liberation from fascist oppression, and not the socialist revolution, should be his concern: "The whole party today is an instrument of war: today, every member of the party is mobilized as a red soldier."[106] "The real significance of this telegram," Tito told Dedijer:

> became clear only later. If we would do as Moscow wanted, we could never develop our insurrection. In our condition, this directive would signify the liquidation of the uprising even before it started. On 6 April, the old regime, with the king at its head, abandoned the Yugoslav peoples to the mercy of the conquerors, and what was left of the state's apparatus passed to the service of the occupiers. This demonstrated its fragility, abandoning the historic Yugoslav tradition of fighting for national independence, confirmed in 150 years by thirty-nine revolts and ten wars against foreign forces. In Yugoslavia, a popular revolt against the occupiers was unimaginable as it would not assure the people that they would be given a chance, after the war, to have a new truly patriotic government with an administration that was firm enough not to allow Yugoslavia, in spite of her natural riches, to resist colonization by the great powers, to hold fast against ethnic oppression, and to see that the majority of the people would no longer live in misery.[107]

~

From the very beginning of the liberation struggle, Tito's revolutionary proposals fanned the flames of his disagreement with Stalin, who refused to consider the fight with Hitler in ideological terms, considering it an aggression against Mother Russia and proclaiming it a "Great Patriotic War" (comparing it with the "patriotic war" against Napoleon nearly 150 years before). Tito realized that the only way to mobilize and unite the Yugoslav masses in a common uprising was to create a strong chain linked by different patriotisms—their ethnic loyalties were too divergent—with the messianic promise of a better life and justice after victory. It is significant that he ignored Dimitrov's message, and turned his attention to immediate practical tasks. The Politburo, called to session on 27 June 1941, transformed the Military Committee into the General Staff of the Partisan units for the National Liberation of Yugoslavia, naming Josip Broz its commander-in-chief. On 4 July, it decided to move from acts of sabotage to a general popular revolt. "There was enthusiasm and great joy," Tito later recalled.[108] And further: "At a time when fascism was dominating Europe, when no voice was heard aside from the CPSU [the Communist Party of the Soviet Union], the CPY raised the revolutionary banner, leading the working masses, the peoples and nationalities of Yugoslavia into a victorious fight of national liberation, of socialist revolution, honorably showing its revolutionary and internationalist spirit."[109]

On 4 July 1941, in order to light the spark of the revolt, the CC CPY sent twelve emissaries to different parts of the country, stressing "brotherhood and unity" and the equal dignity of all Yugoslav nations. For the communists, the ethnic question was primarily of tactical significance in their search for power, but they succeeded in exploiting it for their own ends, taking the Soviet experience as a model.[110] In Croatia, where love for the fatherland was stronger than party discipline, they met with an unexpected obstacle. With the Wehrmacht advancing in Belarus and the Ukraine, the communists assiduously listened to Radio Moscow, which said nothing about the war, speaking instead about life in the kolkhozes (collective farms) and about Stakhanovites (shock-workers whose performances were well above the norm).[111] Why in the world should the Croatian communists not believe that everything was in order on the Eastern front, and that the Red Army would be in Zagreb in two, or at most six weeks? Why should they not hail the breakup of Yugoslavia, which the Soviet Union had stopped recognizing on 8 May 1941? For nearly a month, Andrija Hebrang, leader of the Military Committee of the Croatian CP, could not decide whether or not it was opportune to fight the occupiers, as ordered by the Comintern and the CC CPY.[112] According to Vladimir Dedijer, Hebrang held talks with important people from the Ustaša regime with the aim of creating an independent Croatian party. It seems that, during a meeting in June, he even declared that the NDH was the realization of the secular dream of the Croatian people.[113]

In that moment of uncertainty Moscow condemned this "cowardly and treacherous" behavior through Dimitrov, who asked Kopinič to overthrow the leadership of the Croat party and take over so that sabotage activity against the Wehrmacht could begin as soon as possible.[114] However, Kopinič's attempts were unsuccessful, for they were opposed by the upper echelon of the Croat Party.[115] The consequences of the ensuing chaos were tragic. The Croats believed that it was essential to show that they were ready for action. On the night of 13–14 July, the Zagreb City Committee decided to organize a mass escape of prisoners still held captive in the castle of Kerestinec. A few days earlier, the Ustaša had shot three of them as hostages and threatened to kill others in case of further sabotage. According to Kopinič, it was better for the prisoners to fall fighting, during an attempt at escape, than to wait passively for death. The undertaking was so badly organized, however, that sixty-eight people, the flower of the Croat leftist intelligentsia, lost their lives.[116]

Tito immediately reacted to this failure by sending a commission of inquiry to Zagreb and, on 10 August, he summoned the Politburo to Belgrade. The entire Croat CC was reprimanded for "its indecision and lack of vigilance." A week later, Walter (the name he still used in contacts with Moscow) sent the Comintern a telegram, asking that "Valdes" (Kopinič's codename) be removed from his post, since the Kerestinec catastrophe was his fault. But in spite of the harshness of this denunciation—one of the most severe he ever wrote—"Grandpa" decided otherwise, stating that Kopinič should continue his mission.[117]

The communist call for resistance initially found greater response in Montenegro, where Milovan Djilas had been sent with the recommendation to be prudent. "The Italians are still strong and well-organized. They will crush you. Start with small operations," Tito ordered.[118] As it turned out, the Italians were not well organized and on 13 July 1941 their lax regime made the eruption of a general uprising possible, fostered by the wounded pride of the people and by their traditional pro-Russian leanings. In the course of a few days the entire country, aside from the major cities, was liberated with a facility that surprised even the communists, which suggested that the hour of revolution had struck. Djilas, the former "Wahhabist," intoxicated with success, also began to attack not only the foreign foes, but also the local "class enemies," thus fatally weakening the uprising.[119] The Italians reacted by laying waste to the countryside, with the help of Albanian and Muslim troops, and by mid-August had already regained control. Even worse for the communists was that the Montenegrins, frightened by the red terror (later euphemistically called "leftist errors"), turned their backs on them and began joining the Chetniks. Convinced that, in the second phase of the revolution, the "kulaks" (members of the peasant class who were better off) and their sons would betray them, Djilas and his comrades began shooting them, publishing a bulletin with the names of those killed with the addendum: "it continues."[120] Because of these excesses, on 22 October Tito decided to recall Djilas from Montenegro, accusing him of having badly organized the revolt. Djilas was not particularly worried, although he was nearly condemned to death, as were many others. Since he was a member of the leadership, he did not suffer any consequences. On the contrary, Tito entrusted him with the direction of *Borba*, the party's central publication which, after being banned in 1929, was once more being issued.[121]

After the attack on the Soviet Union, the Germans recalled their best troops from the Balkans. Only second-rate units remained in dismembered Yugoslavia. These units were necessary to keep control of the communication lines between Ljubljana, Zagreb, Belgrade, and Thessaloniki, which were essential in providing provisions for the Wehrmacht forces in Greece and North Africa. Their main task was to garrison the roads, the railways, the mines, and the largest industrial centers, paying little attention to the rest of the territory. In order to strengthen their grip over Serbia, the Germans immediately sought out and found the aid of local collaborators. At the end of August, they installed General Milan Nedić, one of the most prestigious officers of the former Royal Army, as head of the government in Belgrade. Once in power, Nedić organized a strong gendarmerie, established secret contacts with Draža Mihailović, and proposed that he and his men cross over into Bosnia to fight the Ustaša and their Muslim allies. In the meantime, he would destroy the communists in Serbia. The Germans, when informed, prohibited such initiatives, convinced, as Hitler had said, that the "treacherous Serb gang" should not be trusted. On 16 September, he ordered the Southeast Command of the Wehrmacht to "suppress with all necessary energy the rebel movement," meaning both the Chetniks and Tito's followers. In order to achieve this, he sent fresh troops to Serbia from Greece, France, and even from Russia.[122]

That same day, Tito left Belgrade with a false passport, issued in the name of one "engineer Petrović," a collaborationist. He was on his way to southwestern Serbia, where a "liberated" zone had been created by the first insurrectionary units, led by Sreten Žujović (the Black One), Koča Popović, and Petar Stambolić, all Spanish Civil War veterans. Elegantly clad, he departed from the central station in the company of two women, a German from Vojvodina, and an Orthodox priest. One of the women was Davorjanka Paunović (called Zdenka), his secretary and new lover.[123] The trip was adventurous. In the vicinity of Valjevo, where the party left the train, Tito first ran into a group of drunken Chetniks at an inn. They let him go only after he showed them a pass, issued by one of their *vojvods* (chieftains). Immediately thereafter, he met a Partisan unit that regarded him suspiciously, thinking he was a spy because of his distinguished appearance, foreign accent, and passport. They nearly shot him.[124]

A week later, on 26 and 27 September 1941, Tito convened about twenty collaborators in the village of Stolice. The decisions they made influenced the subsequent course of events. They agreed to organize a guerrilla-type resistance, avoiding head-on confrontations with the enemy, and to structure their units regionally, in accord with the ethnic variety of the country, but under a common Supreme Staff. Following the Russian example, the combatants were to be called "Partisans," and were to be led by political commissars as well as military officers. More important still, they decided to replace the old royal administration in the liberated areas with national liberation committees, which were to be an expression of the new power. As their symbol they chose the red star, that ancient magical pentagram, and the clenched fist as the Partisan salute, a symbol of solidarity, both made popular by the October Revolution.[125] Tito proved a good organizer of the uprising; he chose mostly the "Spaniards," former members of the International Brigades who had substantial fighting experience, to be commanders of the Partisan units. He also renounced the so-called "Comintern cadres," whose only merit was having spent time in Moscow.[126] As Koča Popović wrote: "In one word, he showed that he was able to fully grasp what needed to be done. . . . When the uprising started, he rapidly became the unquestioned leader; from the very beginning, he thought with his head, even though he decided to start the resistance only after the German attack against the Soviet Union."[127]

Tensions with Chetniks and the Užice Republic

The appearance of a rival resistance movement ready to help the Soviet Union in its struggle against Hitler, regardless of the sacrifice, compelled the Chetniks to better define their program and tactics. They declared themselves against a mindless fight with the Germans, in anticipation of a change in the fortunes of war, affirming that the "moment of decisive struggle had not yet come" and that it was necessary to save Serb blood and preserve the "biological substance of the race." Awaiting the right moment for the uprising—"when the day will come"—Mihailović decided to drastically limit any confrontation with the Germans for the time being. Nonetheless, in spite of this basic difference, at the very beginning the two groups were not prejudicially hostile to each other but even tried to coordinate their actions against the Wehrmacht and against the Ustaše in East Bosnia. The results of these attempts were, however, minimal, mostly because of the Chetniks' poor discipline and lack of pugnacity, as they considered themselves not yet ready to fight.[128]

Tito met Mihailović and his deputy, Dragiša Vasić, on 19 September 1941 in the village of Struganik, near Valjevo, on the slopes of Ravna Gora. But since they had opposite aims, they were unable to find a common understanding. Mihailović claimed the command of all the fighting forces for himself so he could have them passively wait for "better conditions" and so he would be able to reestablish the old royal regime after the war, whereas Tito was burning with impatience to continue an undertaking that had started so well. Above all, he was not ready to give up the liberation committees that were appearing in villages under his control, rightly considering them the basis of the new social order. In the end, they only managed to agree that Partisans and Chetniks would refrain from shooting each other.[129] However, Tito did not come away from this first meeting with a negative impression of Mihailović, as he later confessed to a group of friends: "You know, Draža was my weak spot." He found him a brave Serb officer of the old school, who could have been an ally if he had not been encouraged to fight the Partisans by the royal government in exile.[130]

Mihailović did not share those sentiments, suspecting Tito of being a Soviet agent of Russian origin. He was well aware what color the new regime would favor if the Partisans won. Indeed, the red flag with a hammer and sickle had been raised in the first free territory, around the town of Užice, a fairly important center of Yugoslav military industry, where Tito established his headquarters on 23 September. They also introduced a new salute: "Death to Fascism!" proposed by Tito, to which the answer, as suggested by Ranković, was "Freedom to the people!" Stalin's pictures and proletarian slogans appeared on the facades of the houses, while the hated gendarmes who had not run away in time or who did not join the new masters, as well as several wealthy local men, were "liquidated."[131]

It was estimated that, at that time, there were forty thousand Partisans in Serbia, while six hundred members of the party and two thousand members of SKOJ still lived in Belgrade.[132] "The peasants who brought food to Belgrade were the only link with the surrounding areas, since the Partisans had interrupted all communication with the capital. . . . The Partisan movement in Serbia was at its peak," wrote Kardelj in his memoirs, "the first Partisan patrols could be found only fifteen kilometers from Belgrade."[133] Tito was even more optimistic. At the beginning of October he communicated to Moscow: "the Partisan army in Yugoslavia has a hundred thousand men and about thirty thousand Chetniks, our allies." He renewed the request for arms, stressing the fact that he had several airports at his disposal where Soviet planes could land.[134]

The political and organizational experiences of the "Republic of Užice," which covered nineteen thousand square kilometers and counted about three hundred thousand inhabitants, gave the leaders of the CPY their first taste of power,[135] and the first occasion for them to apply it in a cruel way. When Živojin Pavlović, a former communist who rebelled against Stalin's bloody dictatorship by writing pamphlet entitled "Balance Sheet of the Soviet Thermidor" fell into their hands, they accused him of being a spy, then tortured and shot him.[136]

Naturally, Tito took up residence in the best building of the city, the National Bank, where he discovered a rich bounty in cash and silver.[137] He recalled that "at that time, 56 million was quite a haul. In those first days this was very useful, since it permitted us to avoid molesting the peasants, whereas the Chetniks robbed them wherever and whenever possible, without fighting. For instance, our unit crossed a village, the fruit was ripe, it was autumn, but nobody touched a plum or an apple. The peasants offered and were surprised that our men did not drink slivovitz. They brought out jugs of brandy and wine. But nobody was allowed to touch them. I prohibited the drinking of alcohol and the expropriation of the peasants, under penalty of death. The discipline was really exceptional."[138] In this army in formation, highly disciplined, nobody as yet wore a proper uniform, apart from the *šajkača*—the traditional Serb military cap, on which a red cloth star had been sewn. The only exception was Tito who, at the time, was already wearing a Soviet *pilotka*, a hat with an enameled five-pointed star with the hammer and sickle at its center.[139]

It was about this time that a new figure, Arso Jovanović, appeared on the scene as one of Tito's closest collaborators. He was a former lieutenant of the Royal Army, a Montenegrin who, thanks to his military experience, quickly became a member of the Supreme Staff and later chief of staff. According to Djilas, Arso's advice and suggestions more than once prevented Tito from making rash decisions.[140] However, Kardelj noted that he was "a typical officer of the old General Staff, unable to understand that the Partisan struggle was not a head-on battle."[141] For instance, on his orders a group of Montenegrin Partisans attacked the town of Pljevlja in the Sandžak region on 1 December 1941, which was defended by a strong Italian garrison. In spite of their bravery, the Montenegrins, who had tried to take Pljevlja by storm, suffered a disastrous defeat, with 203 casualties and 269 wounded. The General Staff of Montenegro consequently decided that Jovanović should be dismissed, but when one of his comrades, Peko Dapčević, came to the Supreme Staff with this news, Kardelj said to him: "By God, do not mention this to Tito, since he has already named him chief of staff." According to General Velimir Terzić, also a former army officer and one of the best Partisan commanders, this was a mistake. Eventually Tito realized it, although he stubbornly kept Jovanović at his side throughout most of the national liberation struggle.[142]

The Soviet press dedicated a great deal of attention to the uprising of the Yugoslav peoples: between the end of July 1941 and the end of the year, they published twenty-five articles on the events in Yugoslavia, generically referring to the rebels as "Partisans," including the Chetniks under this term, as if there were no distinction. This made Tito suspect that Kopinič had not transmitted all his telegrams to the Comintern.[143] The clashes that took place in Montenegro and Serbia during the summer of 1941 also drew the attention of London, where King Petar II and his government had arrived on 21 July. British official circles welcomed this handful of exiles, realizing very soon, however, that despite their shared misfortunes, a visceral hatred existed between the Serbs and Croats, which was further exacerbated by news regarding the Ustaša massacres. When more information about the Chetnik movement arrived, the Serbs became cocky, especially because the British did not hide their admiration for "small, brave Serbia," an impression left over from the First World War. It was a scenario that the British had hoped for since the beginning of the conflict: a guerrilla war would be organized and guided by their agents in the territories occupied by the Axis forces. With this in mind, immediately after France's capitulation in July 1940, a new agency was created on Churchill's initiative. It was called Special Operations Executive (SOE), and had the task of fomenting subversive activity against the "enemy overseas."[144] The main SOE headquarters in London was soon supported by a branch in Cairo that covered the Balkans and the Near East. In order to be better informed, on 20 September 1941 the SOE sent a mission called Bullseye to Montenegro and Serbia. It was led by Duane T. Hudson, a mining engineer from South Africa, who knew Yugoslavia well having worked there before the war. According to British documents, "Bill" Hudson was to head the Yugoslav resistance, which was seen in London as an aid to the Soviets in their mortal fight against Hitler.[145] Initially the Soviets were not opposed to this idea. In October 1941, their envoy to the UK, Ivan M. Maisky, proposed to Anthony Eden, the British foreign minister, that they coordinate their mutual assistance to the Yugoslav rebels. Winston Churchill's government agreed, hoping to unite the Chetniks and the Partisans in a common front, but knowing full well that it could offer them little aside from propaganda. It was the British who chose Mihailović as the movement's champion and created its myth.[146] The British press and the BBC, followed by the American media, presented him as a shining example for the whole of Europe, especially for countries under German occupation, of "how to fight and to die for the fatherland." In this context, it was of secondary importance that the heroic deeds so exalted had been done by Partisans, and not by Chetniks.[147] No one paid much attention to the Partisans, not even the Soviet government, which was incapable of sympathizing with a clearly revolutionary movement at a time when German troops were approaching Moscow. It is interesting to note that Radio Free Yugoslavia, organized by the Comintern on 11 November 1941 in Ufa in the Urals, did not broadcast any criticism of Mihailović, instead, as Tito indignantly noted, uncritically repeating news from the Western media, which turned him into a hero. According to the British, the Serb guerrillas were blocking six German divisions and many Italians in the Balkans. Through Kopinić in Moscow, Tito protested bitterly against this "terrible lie," but to no avail.[148]

The hopes of the British to forge an alliance between A/H31 (Mihailović's code cipher in SOE files) and Tito, with the help of the Soviets, did not last long.[149] Although Tito did not place much trust in the colonel or in his movement, after taking Užice he was ready to share the bounty, handing over fifteen thousand rifles and 5 million dinars.[150] In a conversation with Hudson, he confirmed that personally he did not nurture any grudge toward him, although he thought that the majority of his followers were a bunch of unworthy men. The negative traits of the Chetniks were, in his opinion, drunkenness, lack of discipline, outlawry, and violence against women. All were contrary to the Partisan ethics. He stressed, however, that he wanted to avoid any dispute with Mihailović who, if not ready to collaborate, should at least not hinder the Partisans.[151]

The two leaders met once again, the night of 26–27 October 1941, in the village of Brajići, on Suvobor Mountain, in order to hammer out an agreement based on thirteen points formulated by Tito. After spending the night in the same cottage, they reached a decision to help each other, but this treaty wasn't worth the paper it was written on. Tito refused Mihailović's request to extend his control over Užice, whereas Mihailović rejected the most important points of the proposed program: the creation of a common general staff and common supplying of Partisans and Chetniks, the establishment of a provisional government in the liberated territories, and the introduction of voluntary conscription.[152] Only two days later one of Mihailović's representatives met with some officers of the Wehrmacht and asked for weapons in order to fight the communist danger.[153]

A few days later, between 1 and 2 November 1941, a series of skirmishes between Chetniks and Partisans flared up near Užice and other localities under their control. This was the beginning of the civil war in Serbia, and in other territories where the two movements coexisted.[154] In his memoirs, Djilas affirms that he and his comrades were glad that hostilities had broken out. It resolved the question of how to deal with resistance forces considered class enemies by the communists.[155] Tito and his comrades, who were waiting for the start of hostilities, were sure that Mihailović had ordered the attacks on Hudson's suggestion. In other words, they believed the British were behind it. After a short stay in Užice, where Hudson arrived with Djilas from Montenegro, he went with two Serb officers, members of his mission, straight to the Chetnik headquarters in Ravna Gora. His radio-telegrapher, Veljko Dragišević, decided to stay with the Partisans, however, and paid dearly for this decision. He was suspected of being a British spy and shot, probably on the orders of Ranković or Tito. This shows how firm was their assumption—based on an ideological point of view—that the British were and would remain hostile to the Partisans. "I am sure," wrote Vladimir Dedijer in his diary, "that we have been attacked on the orders of the English and of the Yugoslav government (in exile). The bourgeoisie was not interested in freeing the people and, therefore, started the class struggle, this between the Serb bourgeoisie and proletarian forces. The Serb bourgeoisie, the most voracious of all, was the first to begin. One part of it bet on the German horse, the other on the English. But both were united against us."[156]

Since the alliance with the Soviets and the British required that they be treated with some regard, the Partisans did not attempt to annihilate the Chetniks, even when they surrounded Mihailović's headquarters.[157] The colonel hastened to affirm that the insurrectionary forces should not fight each other, declaring he was ready to accept a bilateral commission charged with verifying who was responsible for the recent incidents. For his part, as a sign of good will Tito released about a hundred Chetnik officers who had been taken prisoner.[158]

Later, in Čačak, not far from Užice, the delegations of the two parties met and agreed on a ceasefire but it did not last.[159] In the following days, tragic incidents happened one after the other: On 21 November a bomb with a timed detonator exploded in the vaults of the National Bank, where the Partisans had installed their munitions factory. There were between 120 and 160 victims. Tito, just a few meters from the explosion, barely managed to survive. It was the most terrifying experience of his life.[160] When, four days later, the Germans attacked Užice, Mihailović withdrew his proposal that Partisans and Chetniks fight side by side.[161]

In spite of Hudson's efforts to mediate, it was impossible to overcome this mutual hostility. The reason for the definitive split between Mihailović and Tito is to be found not only in their ideological, political, and strategic divergences but also in the colonel's firm belief he had been appointed by London as commander in chief of the Yugoslav resistance—not to mention the dramatic retaliations against the civilian population recently undertaken by the Wehrmacht, which stirred his heart and soul. In fact, at the Führer's request, on 16 September 1941, General Wilhelm Keitel, commander in chief of the German troops in the Balkans, ordered that one hundred Serbs be shot for every German soldier killed, and fifty for every wounded.[162] This ferocious reaction to Partisan and Chetnik sabotage was immediately put into practice, reaching its peak in the small town of Kragujevac on 21 and 23 October 1941, when 2300 hostages, among them students and teachers of a local high school, were gunned down.[163]

This and other atrocities left deep marks on Serb public opinion. As Hitler had hoped, the Serbs began to distance themselves from the Partisans, going so far as to denounce them to Nedić's gendarmes. The Germans, emboldened by the success of their policy, decided in mid-November to launch the so-called "first offensive" against both the Partisans and Chetniks.[164] At the end of the month, the Germans succeeded in driving the Partisans out of Serbia into the nearby Sandžak territory, where, because of the Italian occupation, the conditions were easier for the guerrillas. Vladimir Bakarić, the most prominent Croat communist leader after the war, later wrote, "The uprising in Serbia was heavily defeated and, if it had not been for Bosnia, Croatia and Slovenia, nothing would have been done."[165] Tito, however, did not fully acknowledge this tragic situation. A month after he lost more than a thousand combatants at Užice and Zlatibor, a mountain region in the western part of Serbia, he wrote to his Slovenian comrades: "Our troops are intact, nearly without losses. . . . The situation in Serbia is decidedly better."[166] Not until thirty years later did he confess: "I nearly lost my life at the crossroads between the villages of Zabučje and Ljubanja."[167]

The shared adversities did not reconcile Tito and Mihailović. In December, they resumed their fratricidal struggle, carrying it on until the end of the war. Meanwhile in Serbia, an uneasy peace was restored. According to a report by Blagoje Nešković, one of the leaders of the local CPY, only thirty-two Partisans remained alive by the end of the year.[168] It took a long time before the Partisan movement recovered, while many Chetniks joined Nedić's police forces, a move that offered the communists the opportunity to denounce them as traitors. The royal government in exile was of a different opinion: it proclaimed the Chetnik movement as its "Home Army," conferring the rank of general on Draža Mihailović on 7 December 1941, and including him in its team on 9 January 1942 as minister of war. Every Yugoslav subject who refused to recognize him as commander in chief would be guilty of high treason.[169]

The Crisis and the Development of the Civil War

The autumn offensive, which caused the fall of the "Soviet Republic of Užice," was a hard lesson for Tito, since it destroyed the illusion that the Partisan state had a solid base on which to build. In his attempt to show his military qualities to Hudson, who was in the town, he made the mistake of ordering one of his battalions to defend one of its access points at all costs, although it was obvious that it was impossible to block the advance of the enemy. The entire battalion was killed in an unequal clash with German tanks, creating the myth of a Partisan Thermopylae.[170] The remaining troops, who had underestimated the Wehrmacht's might, evacuated Užice at the last moment. Chaos and violence reigned as the Germans crushed the wounded Partisans with their tanks or shot them and threw them into the river. Dragojlo Dudić, the first president of the Committee for the National Liberation of Serbia, openly attacked Tito for having needlessly sacrificed so many lives.[171]

Apparently Tito had also retreated in such a rush that even his aide-de-camp lost track of him. He was lucky, however, for the Germans only chased his units as far as the banks of the river that demarcated the German and Italian zones of occupation.[172] The telegram Walter sent to "Grandpa" on 1 December 1941, in which he once more asked for military help, came to the attention of Stalin, his commissars for internal affairs, L. P. Beria, and for foreign affairs, V. M. Molotov, but remained unanswered.[173] At the time the Germans were just south of Moscow, the Soviet leaders obviously had other priorities. To many Partisans, the entire Yugoslav resistance seemed doomed as a result of the defeat at Užice. "We had no efficient defense," Kardelj affirmed, "and were hunting for isolated Partisans in order to block the Germans on the slopes of Zlatibor and give us at least enough time to evacuate the wounded."[174]

During a session of the Politburo convened in the village of Drenova in the Sandžak and attended by Kardelj, Ranković, Djilas, Žujović and Lola Ribar, in a moment of discouragement Tito offered his resignation—it is not clear whether from the post of commander in chief or secretary general or both. The proposal was rejected on the grounds that Moscow would interpret it as a sign of a split in the CPY. Ranković said that if Tito resigned, they should all resign. "During the war," he writes in his memoirs, "Tito was often subject to depression and was frequently demoralized . . . but he generally quickly grasped the situation, made rapid decisions and carried them out energetically."[175] Tito's ability to overcome depression and master the situation was also seen during this meeting, even though their position was in fact disastrous, since they had only 1500 combatants at their disposal. The Politburo members kept their revolutionary élan, but concluded that in light of recent events the revolt against the occupier had been transformed into a class struggle, with peasants and workers on one side and the bourgeoisie on the other. Certain that Hitler's military and political defeat was imminent—as confirmed by the recent success of the Red Army, which stopped the Germans outside of Moscow, marking the failure of Hitler's blitzkrieg—they concluded that the second stage of the revolution had come. They believed that the imperialists were well aware of this, which explained why Great Britain had not yet opened a second front in Europe, but was instead trying to unite the reactionary forces and launch them against the progressive revolutionary forces—as shown by the attack of the Chetniks on Užice. It was therefore necessary to continue the fight against the occupiers and to settle accounts with the class enemy—the bourgeoisie—at the same time.[176]

Due to these abstruse considerations, the news that as a result of Pearl Harbor the United States had entered the war as an ally of Great Britain and the Soviet Union had little impact. On 21 December 1941, Stalin's birthday, Tito created the First Proletarian Brigade (later called "division") in the village of Ruda. It was to be the spearhead of the national and social struggle. Since many Partisan units had gone over to the Chetniks, or had sought refuge in the woods near their villages, Tito and his comrades decided to form an armed group that could be trusted and committed on all fronts, wherever necessary. In Kardelj's words, "since we had splendid Serb proletarian forces, a parade was organized in preparation for the future brigade . . . when we were still in Sandžak. There had been a heavy snowfall and it was terribly cold, but the men, half naked and barefoot, exhausted by marches, marched in columns and sang with incredible enthusiasm."[177] Their banner was red with a hammer and sickle because, as Tito said, "those were the armed forces of the party."[178]

Peasants were not accepted into the First Proletarian Brigade, which consisted mostly of CPY and SKOJ members. It was to become the germ of a regular revolutionary army, unlike the Partisan units, which had a guerilla character.[179] According to Edvard Kardelj, this decision had an extraordinary influence on the further development of the resistance. "The appearance of the First Proletarian Brigade radically changed the political and military situation in Bosnia, compensating for the fall of Užice with new successes. There was also a long-term effect. The nucleus of a revolutionary army was born, capable in the following months of organizing widespread operations in Yugoslavia and of beginning to take on the enemy in frontal combat—especially in the final stages of war."[180]

Under the command of Koča Popović, scion of a Belgrade banking family and veteran of the Spanish Civil War, it became an excellent fighting body. Together with the Second Proletarian Brigade instituted some months later, it became the symbol of the revolutionary forces in Bosnia-Herzegovina, the region where the majority of Tito's troops fought over the following two years. Tito described the spirit that animated them at the 1 March 1942 ceremony to mark the founding of the Second Proletarian Brigade, proclaiming: "We will even open fire against our father, if he opposes the people."[181] As this really happened, Tito later remembered the horrors of the revolution with a certain embarrassment. At the same time, he was unable to hide his admiration for those capable of committing acts of this sort: "This is the real consciousness of the party."[182] However, it must be added that he did not participate directly in these atrocities. "He never himself signed anything that was compromising," Ranković observed later, not without reproach, "death sentences, burning of villages, everything dirty and bad, but he allowed others to do it. He was always conscious of his role in history and behaved in such a way as to be victorious, just and magnanimous."[183]

On 7–8 January 1942, Tito held a party council in the village of Ivančići, which decided to "give impulse to the revolution" and increase the class struggle. A document prepared for this occasion lays out the CPY's intention to change its tactics: "The policy of our party was clearly aimed at unifying the people in the fight against the occupier, regardless of ethnic, religious or political affiliations. Our adversaries, however, the pan-Serbian bourgeoisie and its representatives, gave priority to the future organization of the state, going so far as to openly collaborate against us with the occupier to preserve the old regime. They have imposed the class struggle on us and we accept it."[184]

After its flight from Serbia, the Supreme Staff found refuge in eastern Bosnia, nominally part of Ante Pavelić's Independent State of Croatia, in the mostly Muslim city of Foča, where it remained three months in spite of continual German air raids. There Tito was able to see with his own eyes what kind of

Yugoslavia Mihailović had planned. The corpses of Muslims, slaughtered by his Chetniks in revenge for their alliance with the Ustaše and their participation in atrocities against the Serb population, still drifted in the waters of the Drina.[185] The fact that the Ustaše were even worse than the Chetniks spoke in favor of his resistance movement, as the communists were the only ones who didn't fan national hatred but stressed "brotherhood and unity" among Yugoslav peoples. In the new Bosnian environment the movement recovered quickly, in spite of the terrible cold and hunger suffered by the Partisans. They ate mostly oat bread mixed with dried wild pears and, if they were fortunate, drank "horse tea," a thin, meager soup of boiled horse meat with no salt. "Since then," said Tito, "I don't even want to see pears."[186] He lost a great deal of weight during that period, even though he was privileged. He had his own cow for fresh milk and even his own cook.[187] That does not mean that he did not share the hardships of Partisan life. Josip Kopinič, who came to Foča from Zagreb, remembers that once they slept together under one blanket because of the extreme cold. "Do you have lice?" asked Tito. "No!" he replied. And Tito laughed: "Don't worry, you will have them soon. I have them, too."[188]

With Kopinič's assistance, a direct radio link with Moscow was organized on 7 February 1942. It was managed by Pavle Savić, a nuclear physicist and former assistant to Marie Curie—a "man of superior intelligence" according to those who knew him.[189] This new facility allowed Tito to be independent of Zagreb's clandestine radio center, which was reachable only through couriers, and to get in touch with the Comintern on a daily basis. At the end of February, on the twenty-fourth anniversary of the Red Army's establishment, Tito sent an enthusiastic congratulatory message, which was published by the newspaper *Kommunisticheskii Internatsional* and by the *War News*, the bulletin of the Soviet Embassy in London. This was the first time his name was mentioned in a Western country.[190] It was not until summer, however, that the leftist papers in Great Britain and the United States began receiving dispatches from Moscow with Tito's reports about clashes between Partisans and occupiers, showing that the assertions of the Yugoslav government in exile ascribing the successes in Yugoslavia "to the guerrilla forces of General Mihailović" were lies.[191]

After the Battle of Moscow, fortune started to turn in favor of the Soviets. With this Stalin's mood improved, and he began to pay attention to the Partisans in Yugoslavia, especially because the London government continued to ask him to force Tito to cooperate with Mihailović. "It seems," he said mockingly, "that the Yugoslav Partisans are quite efficient if the English ask us to help!" And when the royal government in exile reiterated the same request, he added: "They are not able to reach an agreement with the Partisan movement at home, and would like to subject it, with our help, to Mihailović, in order to suffocate it later. This is sewn with a white thread [obvious to everyone]. Those are shrewd but childish traps! Pity that, for the moment, we can just sympathize with the Partisans and are unable to offer them any practical help."[192]

In spite of these first signs of support there were also rebukes from Moscow. In February, the Comintern proposed sending a manifesto of endorsement to various resistance movements in Europe, particularly the French and Czechoslovaks. Tito enthusiastically agreed and drafted the text but shortly afterwards Moscow signaled that, all things considered, it would be better not to publish it, so as not to worry the royal government in exile, with which diplomatic relations were resumed even before Hitler's attack. At the beginning of March, the Comintern congratulated Broz for his successes, stressing however "that for now the basic, immediate task, above all others, is to unite all anti-Nazi movements, crush the invaders, and achieve national liberation." The Comintern therefore demanded that he not make trouble for the Soviet government in its relations with the Western allies. "Grandpa" wrote: "Do not consider your fight only from your own national standpoint, but also from the international standpoint of the British-American-Soviet coalition.[193] "A study of all the information you provide," Dimitrov wrote further, "gives the impression that the supporters of Great Britain and the Yugoslav government may be justified in suspecting the Partisan movement of acquiring a Communist character, and aiming at the Sovietization of Yugoslavia. Why, for example, did you need to form a special Proletarian Brigade?"[194] In short, "Grandpa" counseled Broz to radically review his policy, and to exploit all possible opportunities to organize a common popular front against Hitler and Mussolini. He also urged him to bear in mind that "the Soviet Union has treaty relations with the Yugoslavian king and government, and that taking an open stand against them would create new difficulties in the joint war effort."[195] Tito answered with a cable stressing that the IKKI had mistakenly interpreted his information. He was of the opinion that, while the supporters of the government in exile did not collaborate openly with the invaders, they did so in fact by aiding Nedić's forces, to which Mihailović had joined his Chetniks. The CC CPY had at its disposal documents that showed their treachery. He also requested that the CPSU send observers to the liberated territory, and a considerable quantity of arms and ammunition, for all those who wanted to fight the invader.[196] He was desperately and chronically short of weapons, which the Partisans were largely obliged to capture from their enemies, wresting them away with their bare hands. For a while, it seemed that Moscow would, in fact, send the requested help. Moša Pijade was dispatched to the Durmitor uplands in Montenegro to organize an airport where Soviet planes could land. He and his men waited for thirty-seven nights in cold and snow worthy of

Siberia, but no aircraft arrived. Although Dimitrov had repeatedly asked for help from Molotov, Beria, and Stalin, he was not successful. The most he could do was to send "recipes" for producing explosives at the end of May 1942.[197]

The rebuke from Moscow led to an interesting discussion between Tito and Moša Pijade. The latter expressed the opinion that the Comintern was probably right when it said that they had gone too far. Tito answered his two letters on this subject sharply, suggesting he stop "philosophizing" about the so-called "leftist deviations."[198] However, on 6 April, he convened the CC CPY where he himself called attention to such deviations (especially in eastern Herzegovina, Montenegro, Vojvodina, and Slovenia), which had assumed worrying dimensions. Some Serbian members of the party even argued that in the second phase of revolution all peasants, teachers, officers, and priests who had joined the Partisan movement would have to be killed. They too could be considered, at least potentially, as future enemies of the working people. In line with "Grandpa's" suggestions, Tito and his comrades opted for a new political line based on the Stalinist theory of a "patriotic war." Stalin considered the war with Germany not in ideological terms, Nazism against Bolshevism, but in national ones—Germany against Russia. This made him critical of Tito's idea to use the war for national liberation as a tool for the social revolution, which was taking the fight into ideological waters. "To prattle on about the world revolution," he said, "only favors Hitler and damages the union of all antifascist forces."[199] Therefore, the CC decided that, from then on, it would stress national liberation rather than class struggle. It also decided to change its attitude toward the British and toward the royal government in exile, with whom it would no longer quarrel about ideological matters, but only about the aid offered to the treacherous Chetniks. Naturally, this adherence to Moscow's directives did not imply a renunciation of the revolution, but only the recognition that, for the time being, it was more opportune to stress the patriotic nature of the uprising. This was necessary as even the most fervent "believers" now realized that there was no sense in waiting for the immediate intervention of the Red Army. The decision was crucial in giving impetus to the struggle, although in Montenegro, Herzegovina, and eastern Bosnia it was not easy to stop those who persevered in "leftist errors." In spite of it all, "from now on," wrote Djilas, "there were no essential changes with regard to the political and tactical line. In its fight with the occupier the revolution had found itself."[200]

In the middle of January, the Wehrmacht launched the so-called Second Offensive in eastern Bosnia against what they termed the "bandits," refusing them the status and guarantees to which regular combatants were entitled under international law. By the end of the month it was over, with great suffering. It was resumed the following spring, this time with the help of the Italians, with whom the Germans heatedly quarreled about whether it was right or wrong to use the Chetniks in the struggle with the communists. Hitler claimed that they too were nothing but outlaws with whom no collaboration was possible. General Mario Roatta, commander in chief of the Italian troops in the Balkans, was of the opinion that, for the time being, they should be used and discarded later when they were no longer needed. The discussion, which degenerated over the following months into a serious quarrel between Rome and Berlin, came to nothing. Although they agreed with the German objections, the Italians did not renounce Chetnik aid, considering them an essential ally in the fight against Tito's forces.[201]

Under the joint blows of the Germans, Italians, Ustaša, and Chetniks (there were attempts at collaboration even between the latter), the Partisan detachments vacillated. Tito tried to resist on the Serbian frontier, hoping to return to Serbia and defeat the locally popular Chetniks, which he believed was imperative in order to attain power.[202] However, in mid-May 1942, he lost his strongholds in the Foča area. The retreat from the town at the confluence of the Drina and Čehotina rivers, ordered on 10 May, was inevitable.

Because of the difficult situation in which they found themselves, many combatants deserted Tito's camp and joined Mihailović, whose prestige was growing thanks to the assistance of the Italians and the endorsement of the British. The Partisans reacted by shooting deserters and burning villages, but in so doing the civil war, which by now resembled a fratricidal massacre, gained in strength. In order to escape from his entanglements, in mid-June 1942 Tito reluctantly decided to move his forces to the Bosnian Krajina, stressing that it was necessary "to go west in order to return east."[203] He approached Croatia and Slovenia, where the resistance was quite successful at the time. The intensity of the outbreak of insurgent fighting in the province of Ljubljana in the spring of 1942 surprised "the occupiers," Kardelj noted, "but, it must be said, even ourselves a little."[204]

The decision to move the bulk of the Partisan forces to western Bosnia, where the Ustaše had committed some of their more heinous atrocities, was not easy, since many in the Supreme Staff were against it, instead advocating a return to Serbia. But Tito's orders were categorical, and this probably kept the resistance from breaking up.[205] "As the Red Army withdrew to the depths of Russia," Ranković recalled, "so we withdrew to the center of Yugoslavia."[206]

The "long march" of the bulk of the Partisan army (about 4,500 men) started on 22 June 1942 and lasted for three weeks, with continuous clashes with Germans, Italians, Chetniks, Ustaše, and their Muslim collaborators. Tito took advantage of the tensions between the Italians and the Germans, who jealously guarded their individual zones of occupation from their enemies but also from their allies. He planned his march toward the Bosnian Krajina, constantly moving from the Italian to the German zone, for he was well aware that the Wehrmacht and the Supersloda (as Roatta's army was called, with reference to Slovenia and Dalmatia, its original occupation areas) would be unable to coordinate a common action.[207] In spite of this, this period was, as Vladimir Dedijer remembers, "the most difficult of the initial months of our resistance. Draža Mihailović tried by every means, together with the occupier and with the support of the royal government in London, to destroy the National Liberation Movement."[208] Tito's bitterness is eloquently expressed in a dispatch that Dimitrov quoted in his diary on 24 May 1942:

> The Chetniks have enormous quantities of automatic weapons, mine-throwers and munitions. They forcibly mobilize the peasants, killing those who oppose them or transporting them to concentration camps in Albania. Our Partisan battalions are exhausted because of continuous clashes and, moreover, are without munitions. We had to recall our battalions from Montenegro, in order to prevent their complete annihilation. The people curse the London government which, through Draža Mihailović, is aiding the invader. On all sides people and fighting men are asking: "Why does the Soviet Union not send us aid, even if it is only automatic weapons and some ammunition?"[209]

Hebrang's Enigma

When the Axis forces attacked Yugoslavia, Ivan Srebrnjak (a.k.a. Antonov, the agent of GPU, the military branch of Soviet secret services) returned home from France in order to organize an "information point" for the Red Army in Zagreb. Tito had not forgiven that "viper" for his attempts to ruin him by tipping off Moscow during the struggle for the CPY leadership, and as revenge he urged "Grandpa" to relieve Srebrnjak of his post, asserting that the Party did not trust him. (Kopinič suspected him of being a Gestapo collaborator.) But this attempt did not succeed, since he had powerful patrons in Moscow. Some months later, in February 1942, the Ustaša arrested Srebrnjak and tortured him mercilessly until he "behaved badly," apparently talking "like an open book." Ivan Krajačić (Stevo) organized his assassination on Tito's behalf, in order to limit the damage he was doing. Because of his revelations, ten to fifteen people in Croatia, Bulgaria, Greece, and Italy had been arrested.[210]

One of these was Andrija Hebrang, called Fatty because of his resemblance to the famous Hollywood comedian, Fatty Arbuckle. He was captured in Srebrnjak's house, as they had been collaborators. (Why he did not find a better hiding place is a moot question.) For the Ustaše this was an important success, for Hebrang, after his release from Sremska Mitrovica prison in 1941, had become one of the leaders of the Communist Party in Croatia and, as such, was in contact with all the most important personalities of the National Liberation Movement. During a clash with the police, he was seriously wounded in his right eye and admitted to the hospital. Released from hospital, he was sent to jail, where he found himself in the hands of those who, only a short while before, had been his cellmates and with whom he had planned a common fight against the hated Belgrade regime. Because they respected him, the Ustaša leaders, according to his account, did not torture him (according to other sources, he was tortured violently). In any case, on 20 July 1942, he revealed Tito's identity, until then unknown to the occupiers, confessing that his name was Josip Broz. As the British historian William Deakin writes, Eugen Kvaternik, the interior minister of NDH, immediately informed Pavelić and together with the Germans they began plotting an audacious project: to infiltrate the CC CPY with their undercover agent. Hebrang was an ideal candidate, since he did not hide from his jailers his Croat patriotism or his critical attitude toward Tito's Communist Party, which was too "Yugoslav" for his taste. It is important to add, however, that Vladimir Velebit did not believe the story of Hebrang's treachery. If it were true, he wrote, "the police would have arrested both me and Kopinič, since we were both linked to the Comintern radio station. Hebrang was one of the few who knew about this activity."[211]

The right moment to establish a link between the Ustaša-German and the Partisan camps came on 3 August 1942, when Tito's units occupied the town of Livno in western Bosnia, valuable because of its bauxite mines (bauxite is an aluminum ore used almost exclusively in the military industry). They took prisoner, among others, a German technician named Hans Ott who worked for the Hansa Leichtmetall mining company, but who was also an agent of the German secret services.[212] When, after heavy fighting, the Partisans entered Livno, Ott lost no time in offering himself as a go-between with the Germans in order to arrange an exchange of prisoners. In mid-August he went to Zagreb where he started negotiations, moving in the next weeks between the Partisan Supreme Staff and the Croat capital. His most important interlocutors were Edmund Glaise von Horstenau, the Plenipotentiary General of the Wehrmacht in Croatia, and Siegfried Kasche, the ambassador of the Third Reich to Pavelić's government.[213]

After long negotiations, Andrija Hebrang was freed from the infamous Stara Gradiška concentration camp on 23 September 1942 with thirty other comrades in exchange for two Ustaša officers. Once in Partisan territory, he was neither "interrogated" by a special Party Commission, as would have been usual, nor debriefed about his experience in prison, but automatically reinstalled in his high office. Kopinič, who acquired copies of Fatty's interrogation files through his contacts with the Ustaša police, sent Tito dispatches regarding his "behavior" via Moscow. Tito, however, later denied he had received them.[214] (There was a suspicion that the Russians withheld these signals on Hebrang's treachery, planning to use the Partisan leader as a double agent at the party summit.) At the end of April 1943, Fatty was named secretary of the Croatian CC CP, succeeding Rado Končar, who had been killed by the Fascists at Šibenik on 24 May 1942. Later he was also co-opted into the Politburo of the CPY. At the Croatian headquarters he became the most influential member of a commission charged with interrogating the prisoners who had been exchanged for German or Ustaša officers. He was extremely severe, requesting the death penalty for those who had "sullied the banner of the party." Later, of course, this severity was interpreted as an attempt by Hebrang to get rid of possible witnesses to his agreement with the Ustaša.[215] As he had since 1928, he still felt equal to Tito, a dangerous conviction that he maintained almost to the end of his life.[216] As prominent Croat communist Jakov Blažević said, "in that period Andrija Hebrang was a great authority for us all, a famous convict who had spent twelve years in jail, learning a lot. He knew how to speak in a convincing manner, concise and with sentiment . . . like Stalin."[217]

The Formation of the Antifascist Council for the Liberation of Yugoslavia (AVNOJ)

The clashes that flared up in the spring of 1942 in Bosnia and Slovenia also had international repercussions. The Soviet Union, which had long ignored Tito's repeated requests to denounce Mihailović as traitor, finally decided to take action after a careful examination of the documents sent from Yugoslavia. As Dimitrov wrote in his diary, it was clear even from the Fascist press "that only our Partisans are fighting, whereas Mihailović, at best, remains in the mountains."[218] On 6 July 1942, Radio Free Yugoslavia broadcast an appeal by patriots from Montenegro, Sandžak, and Bocche di Cattaro, pointing to the Chetniks as collaborators and fomenters of civil war. The text of this document was published on 19 July by the Soviet news agency TASS and, in the following weeks, by the leftist press in Sweden and Great Britain and by *The Daily Worker* in New York. The famous writer and publicist Louis Adamic subsequently organized a widespread press campaign against Mihailović in America, in spite of the fact that on 24 July the White House spokesman hailed his fight as an "autonomous and altruistic will to win."[219]

Moscow's new policy was of considerable concern to the royal government in exile and to that of Britain. Thanks to different sources, especially the Ultra operation, which allowed British Intelligence to decipher Wehrmacht messages,

Churchill and his closest collaborators were aware of the fact that Mihailović was cooperating with the Italians. But they also knew that the Germans still considered him an enemy and therefore kept hoping that he would be able to take over leadership of the Yugoslav resistance. The condemnation from Moscow, being the first open attack against Mihailović, was therefore seen as a bad omen, especially because it was soon confirmed by the Soviet government. On 3 August 1942 the NKID (the People's Commissariat of Foreign Affairs) sent a diplomatic note to the Yugoslav minister, Dušan Simović, officially condemning the Chetnik leader.[220] Four days later, Ivan M. Maisky, the Soviet ambassador in London, did likewise, approaching the British foreign minister, Anthony Eden. The Yugoslav and British governments, suspecting that Stalin wanted to take over the Balkans, reacted vigorously in defense of Mihailović. Nevertheless, the British were not indifferent to the Muscovite note and, from August 1942 onward, started to pay closer attention to events in Yugoslavia, asking themselves whether the general was "playing a fair game" there.[221]

Between July and August 1942, the Italians moved an army of 120,000 men against the Partisans in the province of Ljubljana and succeeded, with the help of local collaborators, in inflicting a heavy blow on the Liberation Front. The "integral results" that Mussolini predicted at the start of the operation were not achieved, however, since the Partisans managed to organize their troops into a more or less regular army, as Tito had done in Bosnia. In spite of setbacks and retreats, they emerged in the eyes of foreign observers as the most vital force against the Axis in the Balkans. This was confirmed by the creation, in autumn 1942, of a free territory in Bosnian Krajina, Lika, and North Dalmatia, an area of forty-eight thousand square kilometers—larger than Switzerland, Belgium, or Holland—with 2 million inhabitants. The center of this vast area was the city of Bihać, taken by Tito's troops after intense fighting with the Ustaša on 4 November 1942, just in time for the twenty-fifth anniversary of the October Revolution. The booty was substantial, but even more important was the psychological effect of the victory, since it showed the public, at home and abroad, that the Partisan army was a force to be reckoned with. The collaboration between the Partisan shock troops in Bosnia and Dalmatia fueled a popular revolt that brought together fighters from Serbia, Montenegro, Bosnia, and the Adriatic coast.[222]

In London, where Churchill was already considering an attack against the "lower belly of Europe's crocodile," the question of whether Britain should continue to support Mihailović, or whether it would not be better to bet on the "Partisan horse," was becoming increasingly urgent. In order to spur the Chetnik leader into action, at the end of October the BBC mentioned Partisan activities together with Mihailović's, while the SOE invited him to prove his usefulness to the Allies by sabotaging the communication lines between Greece and Rommel's troops in North Africa. At a time when the Allied armies under the command of General Montgomery were starting an offensive against the Germans and Italians in the Libyan Desert, such sabotage would have been welcome. But Mihailović, still afraid of possible reprisals and their effect on his own authority, turned a deaf ear, compelling the British to officially ask on 5 November 1942 the Yugoslav government in exile to order its minister of war to attack the Belgrade-Thessaloniki railway. This attack never took place.[223]

Increasingly confident in his strength, at the end of 1942 Tito made a daring decision. On 1 November, he ordered the formation of regular armed forces, initially the two Proletarian divisions, and, some weeks later, a third.[224] He also convoked an Antifascist Council for the National Liberation of Yugoslavia (Antifašističko veće narodnog oslobođenja Jugoslavije; AVNOJ) in order to get its approval for the creation of a new government to replace the royal government in exile. He communicated his proposal to Moscow as early as August 1941, certain that he was in tune with "Grandpa's" recommendation to unite all the democratic forces active in the country in a common front. When he received news at the end of July 1941 that the Soviet Union had resumed diplomatic relations with the government in exile, he gave up the idea, but only for the time being, proposing it again the following year. In its answer, Moscow praised the Partisans highly, but also invited Broz to see the struggle within its larger international framework and to refrain from taking initiatives that could disturb Stalin's coalition with Churchill.[225] Grandpa was so worried about the possibility of Broz making rash decisions that he sent the same dispatch to Kardelj in Slovenia, asking him to curtail Broz's ambitions to become president of the National Liberation Committee (i.e., the new government). The Western Allies might interpret this as proof that a revolution, and not a patriotic war, was taking place in Yugoslavia.[226]

This compelled Tito to be prudent, but only in part. He renounced the idea of replacing the royal government, but not the Anti-Fascist Council, which had convened in Bihać on 26 and 27 November 1942. The delegates, few of whom were communists, had been chosen from a list prepared by Ranković and confirmed by the CC. They were mostly from Bosnia and Croatia, since the war prevented the Slovenians and the Macedonians from reaching Bihać. People from the Partisan ranks represented Serbia and Montenegro. The discussions at the council were full of pathos but lacking in substance, since everything had already been decided behind the scenes. Moscow's recommendation not to raise the question of the monarchy and not to oppose the government in exile was followed. However, the First AVNOJ, in which thirty-four delegates took part, proclaimed itself the highest political body of the Yugoslav peoples, electing an executive committee constituted by representatives of different ethnic groups (Serbs, Croats, Slovenes, etc.) and ideological orientations (communists, liberals, Christian-socialists, etc). While this body did not possess the formal status of a government, it was nevertheless the first sign that the Partisan movement aimed not only at liberating, but at ruling Yugoslavia.[227]

At the inauguration of the AVNOJ "people sang in the streets, crowded in front of the building where the council was in session, acclaiming the Supreme Staff, Comrade Tito, our valiant army. The streets were full of men and women in typical Bosnian Krajina and Lika dress. Some even came from distant villages, thirty to forty kilometers away, to be present at the great event."[228] "The First AVNOJ was entirely Tito's work," wrote Djilas, "he formulated all of the decisions taken."[229] It was not without significance that Tito did not mention Stalin in his inaugural address, although he praised and sent greetings to his Slav brothers, first of all to the Russians and to all the peoples of the Soviet Union.[230]

Tito signed the dispatch sent to Grandpa on 29 November 1942, informing him of the conclusions reached by the AVNOJ. He did so as Walter, as if he were still a Comintern agent, but formulated it in such a way that Stalin would grasp the subtleties of his message, in which he firmly stressed that his movement now had an army, popular representation, and a territory. Although the delegates hailed Stalin as the "great warlord and organizer of victory over Fascism," he was not satisfied by the events taking place in the Partisan camp. It is telling that the *Kommunisticheskii Internatsional* published the news about the First AVNOJ together with that of the Antifascist Women's Conference, as if both were of equal importance. This enraged and depressed Tito but did not divert him from the political direction he had chosen.[231]

Both the administrative apparatus that began being formed in the free territory and his lifestyle testified to this. In the period of the "Republic of Bihać," he began behaving like a head of state. He lived in a manor, surrounded by famous intellectuals, tolerating a cult of personality little different from that of Stalin. Branka Savić, who replaced her husband Pavle in the code office of the Supreme Staff, remembered later: "It seems to me that Comrade Tito changed at that time, or better his position and tasks changed. He was not just a man leading an army and military operations, nor only the head of a party, but a man who was forging a state. The atmosphere around him was solemn."[232] And Antun Augustinčić, a sculptor who in the past had done a bust of Pavelić, but later joined the Partisans, wrote: "In 1943, I noticed that it seemed more and more important to him that his clothes were clean and pressed, that he carried himself erect even when he was dead weary. In that very difficult period . . . he filed his finger nails daily . . . I think that, subconsciously, he developed the need for a bit of bravado, for personifying the pride of his ragged, half-starved army and the working people generally."[233] In the following months, his cult of personality spread rapidly: in 1944 the Party propagandists were instructed to always mention Tito's name along with that of Stalin. Tito was certainly very much aware of his importance and historical role.[234]

Operation Weiss

The increase in guerrilla warfare came as a disagreeable surprise to the Germans, who were convinced that the British would exploit it in order to organize a landing in the Balkans, and who were skeptical about the capacity of their Italian allies to defend the coast from Trieste to Corfu. As early as 24 September 1941, Joachim von Ribbentrop wrote in a note: "This area will be considered by England as a center of unrest, and the main base for a European moment of rebellion; and for English planes, submarines, explosives, English propaganda and intelligence. The need, therefore, arises for Italy and Germany to pacify the region and restore order."[235] In November 1942, Hitler received Pavelić at Vinnytsia, his general headquarters in Ukraine, and between 18 and 20 December he convened an Italo-German conference at Rastenburg in Eastern Prussia. Ribbentrop and Mussolini's foreign minister, Galeazzo Ciano, took part, together with military experts, to discuss how best to restore order in the Independent State of Croatia. On that occasion, Hitler reaffirmed his belief that a British landing in southeastern Europe was possible, expressing the opinion that such an event could have serious consequences, since it would induce the Turks to enter the war on the British side. He stressed, however, that the landing could not take place as long as the Axis powers held Rhodes, the Dodecanese Islands, Crete, Greece, Albania, Dalmatia, and its hinterland: "Everything depends on crushing all nationalist and Communist revolt there."[236] On that occasion, and in the subsequent meeting in Rome on 3 January 1943, the Axis decided to exploit the Chetniks in the fight against the communists and then to eliminate them. This was the only concession that the Führer made to the Italians, who insisted on keeping the Serb nationalists in their service. Resuming these discussions, General Alexander Löhr who, in August 1942 had been appointed commander in chief of the German Army Group Southeast, wrote in a memorandum, "The liberation of the hinterland must be completed—and by the end of March."[237]

When the fortunes of war turned against the Axis because of the Wehrmacht's defeat at Stalingrad, they initiated Operation Weiss, or the Fourth

Offensive as it was called by the Partisans, on 20 January 1943. It was to develop in three progressive phases: the first two aimed at the total destruction of "Tito's state" in Croatia, the third at the suppression of Mihailović's movement in Herzegovina and Montenegro.[238] Although Tito did not order a general mobilization in the "Republic of Bihać," after the successes of the Liberation Army and of the Partisan forces, young people had begun to flock to their units, so he was able to create a new "Dalmatian" division. According to the plans of the Supreme Staff, these forces would move the following spring to Montenegro and southern Serbia with the task of stirring up revolt in those regions and overcoming the local "counterrevolution." At the end of 1942, Tito sent his best troops in that direction, which appeared providential when he found himself in the midst of Operation Weiss. Although at that moment the weather conditions were adverse, with temperatures at -25°C, he had no other choice than to follow the bulk of his troops and order a retreat from Bosnian Krajina. Meanwhile he was confronted by a terrible dilemma: what to do with the nearly four thousand wounded scattered in the woods around Bihać? If he abandoned them, he could maneuver easily but their fate would be sealed. Since the occupiers did not recognize the Partisans as a military force but considered them "bandits," they would be shot when captured.[239] Therefore, Tito decided to take them along, in Velebit's words, hanging a millstone around his neck. The chaos was even worse because the local Serb and Muslim population—about fifty thousand people—fearing the Ustaša, fled with the Partisans, and Tito had no choice but to accept them, although he did not know how he would feed them.[240]

In the beginning of January, the Supreme Staff was already receiving information about the amassing enemy troops on the borders of the free territory. Although it expected the "Fourth Offensive," it made no attempts to resist or to inform the various branches of its apparatus, such as the health service, of its imminent arrival.[241] According to Djilas, Tito had no particular military capacities, although in an article written during the war and published by the Soviet newspaper *Voina i rabochii klass* (War and the working class) Djilas asserted the contrary. In that article he praised Tito so blatantly that the Soviet editor had to reproach him: "In the USSR we write in this way only about Stalin."[242] During the Fourth Offensive, especially during the battles on the Rama and Neretva rivers, Tito often changed his directives, with potentially fatal consequences. "The most human battle in history," the "battle for the wounded," the battle on the Rama and Neretva ended as well as it did not because of the ability of the commander in chief, as propaganda later proclaimed, but thanks to the inventiveness of the commanders of the individual units. They soon became aware of Tito's weak points and began adapting his orders to the circumstances, improving them as the situations changed.[243] However, it is only fair to agree with Koča Popović, who said that Tito had the gifts of an authentic leader: ability, courage, decisiveness, and imagination. "He was, so to say, a real wolf, or a condottiere, which is in my opinion his characteristic feature. He was able to find a way out of even the most complex situations, to destroy enemy resistance without thinking twice or foreseeing danger."[244]

At the start of the offensive, General Löhr said that he would establish peace in the country, if necessary the peace of the graveyard. He had 105,000 soldiers at his disposal, whereas Tito had only forty-four thousand. Although unlike Tito, Löhr had planes, tanks, and guns, he also had three weak points: the morale of his troops was low, the alliance with the Italians shaky, and the Partisans were motivated and able to adapt to unexpected conditions. At the beginning of the war, the German soldiers considered service in the Balkans preferable to that on the Russian front or in North Africa. After two years of fighting, this opinion changed. General Lothar Rendulic, who came to Croatia in 1943, wrote in his memoirs that after his arrival about a thousand men asked to be transferred to other fronts, even to the Eastern front, in order to escape the guerrilla war with the Partisans on the rugged Bosnian terrain. In addition, disagreements with the Italians, who were not at all convinced that strengthening German power in the Balkans would be to their advantage, intensified from one day to the next.[245]

In February 1943, Tito's units occupied Prozor, which was defended by the Italian Murgia Division, at the cost of a large number of casualties. This created a new problem for the Partisans, since despite the lack of vehicles and carriers, the wounded had to be evacuated. On 5 March, it was decided that the Partisan army should cross the Neretva in order to take refuge in the hills of northern Herzegovina and Montenegro. Tito planned to conquer the city of Konjic, which was still in the hands of the Italians, reach the paved road, and transport the sick and wounded to safety across a nearby bridge. At the same time, in order to secure his rear he ordered the destruction of all other bridges on the Neretva. As General Velimir Terzić wrote later, provoking Tito's ire, the destruction of the bridges was a mistake that resulted in heavy and unnecessary losses.[246]

The resistance of the Italians at Konjic was more resolute than foreseen and consequently the Partisans found themselves trapped with the Germans at their heels, and the only way out across another bridge near Jablanica. The bridge had collapsed into the river gorge but nevertheless still precariously connected the two banks. In this desperate situation, even more dangerous because of the presence on the other bank of numerous Chetniks and Italians, Tito was forced to order a retreat. The operation, celebrated later by regime propaganda as a "brilliant military trick," was successful. On 9 March 1943, the

Partisans started to transport the wounded and sick across the Neretva on wooden scaffolding laid on the iron structure of the former bridge. The twenty thousand Chetniks, mostly peasants forcibly enlisted, were unable to offer resistance to the Dalmatians and Serbians, who were armed to the teeth. They took flight, allowing six of Tito's battalions to cross the Neretva that same night. By the end of the following week, all the wounded, together with the bulk of the combat forces, were safe despite heavy losses. They were lucky the Germans did not follow them into Italian territory, as they were convinced that the Chetniks would destroy them.[247]

At that time Draža Mihailović suffered a heavy defeat that he would never get over. He invoked the help of the British, who, as Tito and his comrades suspected, had encouraged him to fight the Partisans. It seems that before the battle on the Neretva, the BBC broadcast a coded message, which the Partisan leaders interpreted as approving of Mihailović's collaboration with the Italians, the Ustaša, and even the Germans. "This was the largest coalition against the revolution formed during the war," wrote Vladimir Dedijer. Once it was clear that Mihailović had been defeated, the BBC commented sarcastically, quoting a Serb folk poem: "Military fortune is not decided by glittering arms, but by the hearts of the heroes."[248]

The Partisans destroyed Mihailović's plan to unify all the Serbs in Croatia, Dalmatia, and Bosnia-Herzegovina under his command. He abandoned them to their fate, seeking refuge with the greater part of his forces in Sandžak, and hoping to preserve at least Serbia from the Partisans.[249] As General Löhr admitted: "These skirmishes are proof of Mihailović's failings as a military commander."[250] "During the next critical six weeks," writes Deakin, "Tito's forces concentrated, with impunity, on carrying out the same task the Germans themselves had outlined in Operation Schwarz, the liquidation of the Mihailović movement, and for the same reasons—to control the hinterland of Herzegovina and Montenegro in anticipation of an Allied landing."[251]

The epic feats of the Fourth Offensive instilled in the combatants of the liberation movement some sorely needed pride and discredited the myth of German superiority. It also compelled the Western powers to consider the Partisans as possible allies.[252] "Tito on the Neretva," wrote Milovan Djilas, "was like a tiger in a cage, trying to find the weakest mesh in the net among the Italians and Chetniks, in order to enlarge it and allow Partisans to jump through in a furious storm."[253]

The March Negotiations

In order to have free rein with his most dangerous allies, the Chetniks (whom he considered potential British allies), Tito decided to renew contacts with the

Germans.[254] The exchange of a German major who had been taken prisoner offered an opportunity for him to propose a cease-fire, which was desperately needed in order to give him the breathing space to liquidate the Chetniks. At the time, he did not know that Operation Weiss had fizzled out and that the Germans were unwilling to pursue him across the Neretva. Before making this fateful decision, he called a meeting of his collaborators, at which Djilas asked: "And what will the Russians say?" Tito, who had already vaguely informed Grandpa of his intentions to contact the Germans, answered dryly: "They also think, first of all, of their people and army."[255]

On 11 March 1943, negotiations were arranged between the two parties in Gorni Vakuf, not far from Jajce. Milovan Djilas, Vlatko Velebit, and Koča Popović informed their Nazi counterparts that, for the time being, the national liberation forces did not intend to fight them, as shown by the fact that they only defended themselves when attacked. Their only aim was to destroy the Chetniks. The three also affirmed that their movement was completely independent, and that they had joined the Soviets only for propaganda reasons. If there was to be a British landing on the Dalmatian coast, the Partisans would oppose it while the Chetniks would not. On the contrary, the Chetniks were in contact with London, with the connivance of the Italians. Tito's delegates also wanted the Germans to recognize the Partisans as a "militant party," which would oblige them to respect the laws and customs of war, especially regarding the treatment of prisoners.[256]

The Germans behaved like gentlemen, praising Tito's combatants for their bravery and their treatment of prisoners. It seemed that an agreement was within arm's reach. To show his good will, Tito even ordered the Partisans in Slavonia to stop sabotaging the Zagreb Belgrade railway, as the Germans requested.[257] Referring to the aforementioned proposals, Siegfried Kasche sent a dispatch to Berlin on 17 March 1943, counseling "that the possibility should be seized, since the defection of this world-famous fighting force from our enemies would be very significant. Actually the bulk of Tito's Partisans are not Communist, and have in general committed no unusual excesses in fighting, in the treatment of prisoners and the population."[258]

In the days that followed, negotiations continued at Sarajevo and Zagreb, where Velebit and Djilas represented the Partisans. Kasche informed both the Croatian foreign minister and the Italian envoy, who were in agreement with him, that the possibility of a cease fire should be examined further. The Italian military were also greatly interested in a cease-fire with Tito. But on 29 March, the Berlin Foreign Ministry abruptly ordered that the talks be suspended. Two reasons were given: "not only mistrust of Tito's promises . . . but primarily the fear that the Italians would exploit the German agreements with him to make even closer agreements with the Chetniks."[259] Kasche tried to insist, noting that General Glaise von Horstenau favored a "political settlement" with the Partisans, but Ribbentrop replied: "The statements in your telegram of 17 April lead me to comment that we cannot, by clever tactics, play off the Chetniks and Partisans against each other, because it is matter of destroying both of them. Since we have succeeded in bringing the Duce round to our view that both the Chetniks and Partisans must be liquidated, we cannot now, on our part, agree to a move which is not altogether different from the Italian method of using the Chetniks against the Partisans."[260] Hitler was even more emphatic, wrongly convinced by his secret services that the Chetniks were as dangerous as the Partisans. He stated: "One does not negotiate with rebels; rebels must be shot!"[261]

With this, the political framework of the negotiations was exhausted, although Kasche tried to defend his point of view again, in August and September 1943, during his talks with Hitler. Hans Ott's role as a middleman continued until the end of the year, however, in spite of his obvious dependency on the German secret services and the Ustaša. He even tried to plan a kidnapping of Tito with the help of Spezialeinheiten. At the close of the war, he was arrested by the Yugoslav Service for the Defense of the People (Organizacija za zaščito naroda; OZNA) and thoroughly interrogated—so thoroughly that, after that, any trace of him was lost.[262]

Since a hagiographic image of the national liberation struggle had to be preserved, after the war the "March negotiations" long remained taboo, until Tito himself mentioned them on the occasion of the thirty-fifth anniversary of the Neretva battle. But even then he did not tell the whole truth, accusing Djilas, Popović, and Velebit of having misinterpreted his instructions. The first two were in disgrace at the time and could not reply. Velebit, who had gone on to a brilliant career in the UN European Economic Commission in Geneva, was indignant, but preferred to keep silent.[263]

In the dispatch of 30 March 1943, in which he informed Moscow about the exchange of prisoners, Broz mentioned that "the German envoy in Zagreb . . . wishes to meet me." Stalin, informed of this cable, immediately realized what was happening and instructed Grandpa to give Tito a real talking to. Dimitrov asked how it could be possible that the Yugoslavs, until then a heroic example to a subjugated Europe, could think of abandoning the fight with the enemy of the entire human race, adding: "I want an explanation."[264] But this time Tito was not ready to bow his head; without wavering, he answered that if they could not help him the Russians had no right to stop him. "That was the first time," Djilas commented later, "that a Politburo member—and it was Tito himself—so vehemently expressed any disagreement with the Soviets."[265]

Operation Schwarz

The ability of the Partisans to offer resistance to six German and four Italian divisions, in addition to consistent attacks by Chetnik forces, had notable significance in terms of politics, strategy, and morale. Among other things, it induced the Soviet Union to resume its pressure on the Yugoslav government in exile concerning its attitude toward Mihailović, which it did with a note dated 2 April 1943.[266] Interest in the Balkan area was also revived in British circles. Although they had long been deluded by the Serb nationalist movement, they began to realize that, in the case of an Allied landing in Sicily, the Yugoslav "Communist" rebels could play an important role, since they would be able to block substantial enemy forces on the eastern side of the Adriatic.

Meanwhile, Mihailović inadvertently did everything in his power to dig his own grave. In order to have a clear idea about his intentions and his operative capabilities, the British sent a mission to his headquarters led by Colonel William S. Bailey, one of their best experts on Yugoslavia and one of the leading SOE men. Relations between the two parties rapidly deteriorated, since Mihailović was angry at the British because he believed he had not received enough aid from them. On 28 February 1943, at a baptism in a Montenegrin village, having drunk too much *rakija*, he launched into a bitter tirade against the Allies, stressing that his enemies were the Partisans, the Ustaša, and the Muslims, in that order. He would fight them and only after their defeat would he turn against the Germans. As for the Italians, they were his only source of supplies and no pressure or menace would compel him to abandon them. This outburst, duly registered by Bailey, came to Churchill's attention, who reacted with a note of protest to the Yugoslav government, informing them that unless Mihailović changed his attitude toward the Italians and his Yugoslav compatriots, His Majesty's Government would be obliged to review its policy toward him and provide assistance to other resistance movements in Yugoslavia instead.[267] This warning was eloquent enough, although it did not reveal the fact that London had already begun to consider three possible moves in Yugoslavia: first, to force the Chetniks to collaborate with the Partisans, if necessary with Soviet help; second, to divide the country between the two enemy forces along the Ibar River in Serbia, allowing Mihailović to control the area to the east; or if this were not possible, then third, to transfer all their aid from Mihailović to Tito. The London branch of the SOE and the Foreign Office did not look on this last solution favorably since they knew that, in that case, the whole of Yugoslavia would be consigned to the communists. After long discussions, Churchill's request that above all it was necessary to support those who would "kill more Germans" prevailed.[268]

On 3 April 1943, Field Marshal Alfred Jodl signed an order entrusting General Alexander Löhr to begin a new operation against the Yugoslav rebels, called Schwarz. As Deakin describes it: "After the destruction of the Communist Tito State, the question arises of destroying an array of national 'Serbianism' under the leadership of Draža Mihailović, so as to have, in the event of an Allied landing in the Balkans, the hinterland cleared. Hitler and his generals were unaware that they were victims of a British hoax, aimed at convincing them, with forged documents, that the invasion was imminent."[269] The Germans planned Operation Schwarz with the Chetniks as the primary object, in full secrecy, so that even the Italians were not informed about it until the last moment, in mid-May, when the formidable military machine organized by Generals Alexander Löhr and Rudolf Lüters had already begun moving.[270] Lüters had at his disposal 127,000 men from the elite Edelweiss Division, transported for the occasion from the Caucasus, and the SS Division Prinz Eugen.[271] At dawn on 15 May 1943, he unleashed the attack, this time unhesitatingly entering the territory occupied by the outraged Italians. Since it was soon clear that the latter were protecting the Chetniks, at least those who did not run away, he was forced to change his initial plan and to attack the Partisans, "the only serious enemy."[272] He encircled the Supreme Staff and the bulk of its forces in the rugged mountainous area of Durmitor in northern Montenegro, between the Piva and Tara rivers. To his great surprise, Tito, who was still hoping for a cease-fire with the Germans, found himself besieged in a circle of fire, with his men, about four thousand of whom were wounded and sick, exposed to the attacks of the Luftwaffe, as well as Italian, Ustaša, and Bulgarian troops. Since he had never organized any real intelligence, it was not until 18 May 1943 that he came to the realization that a new offensive against him was in fact occurring. Moreover, the Germans were in possession of the codes used in communications between the Supreme Staff and the General Staffs of its divisions, and therefore had a pretty good idea of Tito's whereabouts. Their planes, and those of the Italians, regularly bombed the Supreme Staff and no one knew what to do in the ensuing general chaos.[273] The problem, what to do with the wounded, was once again pressing. Gojko Nikoliš, the chief of the Sanitary Department at the Supreme Staff, describes the situation critically and with bitterness: "The coolness, the optimism, the self-confidence, the faith in the final victory, the refusal to think that the situation could be critical for us, the trend to 'ignore the peril'—all those traits were an ideal to which the entire Partisan mentality was linked. But if such a mentality is not corrected by at least some critical thought, then your eyes are shut to reality. I think that also these details should be considered symptoms of the growing pains of a young revolutionary army."[274]

The only ray of light in this bleak picture came on the night of 27 to 28 May 1943, with the arrival of a British mission, parachuted in by the SOE in the Durmitor area to assess the real strength of the Partisan movement.[275] Tito considered the mission so important that he delayed his departure from Durmitor, although it was obvious that he urgently needed to leave if he wanted to escape the enemy's grip. Because of bad weather, the wait for an SOE airplane dragged out over three or four fatal days. According to General Terzić, the Partisans lost seven thousand fighters because of the delayed arrival of two British agents.[276]

The two leaders of Mission Typical, captains Bill Stuart and William (Bill) Deakin, could not have arrived at a more dangerous but also more favorable time to get an impression of the value of Tito's troops. After parachuting in, they immediately took part in a meeting in which it was decided to try a sally across Vučevo, Sutjeska, and Zelengora. Tito also ordered the hospital center to be moved in that direction, but this was easier said than done, since the Partisans had at their disposal only two or three hundred Italian prisoners, who were utterly exhausted, for the transportation of the more than two thousand sick and wounded. They also had only around a hundred horses.[277] Food was scarce and so it was no longer a question of the peaceful acquisition of victuals from the population, as Tito had ordered at the beginning of the revolt when he said he would not be at the head of a plundering army.[278] Consequently the inhabitants of the Piva plateau, already impoverished, began rebelling against the Partisans and siding with the Chetniks. On 3 June 1943, the Supreme Staff decided to divide the main operative group into two smaller units and to abandon those who were severely wounded, hiding them in the caves and rocks of Piva Canyon. Days of terror and chaos followed, when in the storm of fighting everything seemed lost. To top it all off, the Germans knew precisely where Tito was, thanks to the Italian prisoners who managed to escape while transporting the old and frail poet Vladimir Nazor. The Germans launched an attack on 9 June 1943. As Tito remembers, "They hammered us terribly, intensely, without interruption, they hammered the same points. They threw hundred-kilo bombs. And then machine-gun shells started to rain on us. The Germans were shooting from a mountain about five hundred meters away. I ordered the commander of the Fourth Brigade (he lost his life) to take this mountain with his men, because otherwise the brigades could not pass. The English with us watched him with fear and respect."[279]

In the course of the fighting on 9 June 1943, Tito was wounded in his left arm while trying to protect his head. His life was saved by his German Shepherd, Lux, who covered him when a bomb exploded near a fallen tree where he and his lover, Zdenka, had tried to find shelter.

> Lux lay by my head, the bulk of his body pressed close against one side of my face. He wasn't clean, he smelled to high heaven, and he was full of lice. Besides, he blocked my view. I had to lift my head to see what was going on. We were in a bad spot; many of the *drugovi* [comrades] near me were killed or wounded that day. I kept pushing Lux away. But it was no use; he settled himself almost on top of my head and wouldn't budge. He lay very still, unless I shoved him; and when I shoved him, his body simply fell back against my face, like a sack of grain, not quite full. I became impatient and angry, but there was no moving him; so I let him be. All at once, in the midst of the din, I felt a tremor ripple through Lux; then he was absolutely still. He stopped a piece of shrapnel that otherwise would have gone through my head.[280]

The explosion was fatal not only to the dog, but also to Captain Stuart and to Tito's bodyguard, a Spanish veteran, while Bill Deakin was wounded. "I was badly hurt," Tito remembered later. "This is the end, I thought." When he came to his senses, in the middle of the devastation his eye fell on a ravaged tree, on which a small bird was twittering in lament. "The explosion broke his little leg and wounded his wing . . . this tiny creature stood on only one leg, flapping its wing. I remember it vividly."[281] Two days later, some grenade fragments were removed from his arm, which had started to grow black and rigid. Two other fragments were not removed until 1947, when he had a hernia operation. He was the only commander in chief to be wounded in battle during the Second World War.[282]

During the Fifth Offensive, Tito had another one of most horrifying experiences of his life. "I was marching with my bodyguard, tired, keeping an eye on every move of the enemy. It was raining. I was holding a stick on which I was leaning. At a certain point, I stumbled in the dark and fell. My hands sank into something hard and flabby. There was a bad smell. I had fallen onto a decomposing corpse. I tried to clean my fingers in the rain and wet grass, but to no avail. The stench of death did not go away. Wherever I went, this terrible stench accompanied me."[283] And yet the hardships were not without funny moments, as Tito relates: "This happened when my arm was wounded. It was in bandages, whereas in the other one I had a stick, since I could not carry a machine gun. During the walk, we met an old woman. I said to her: 'Step aside, granny, and let the army pass.' She stopped and looked at me: 'What kind of a soldier are you, if you don't even have a gun.'"[284]

Those who happened to survive were saved from the encirclement on the night of 8–9 June 1943 by a sortie of the First Proletarian Division near Tjentište on the river Sutjeska. Koča Popović, without informing or asking for the approval of the Supreme Staff, created a gap in the ranks of the enemy—an action Tito never forgave, suspecting that Koča had tried to run away, abandoning him with the main body of the troops in the rout.[285] Later he demanded that Popović and his deputy, Žujović, be tried by a court-martial, which Ranković prevented.[286] The Battle of Sutjeska was an absolute massacre and a terrible suffering, as it resulted in seven thousand dead, including important Partisan commanders. The Germans claimed that about eleven thousand Partisans had fallen, and ten to twenty thousand had died from hunger and typhus fever. According to the German report, there were fifteen thousand losses among civilians, as well. Only three to four thousand combatants managed to escape from Durmitor, heading in the direction of Bosnia.[287] As Bill Deakin's assistant noted in his diary: "We succeeded during the night in passing through German lines, about one kilometer on one side and five hundred meters on the other. The circle was closed again only fifty minutes after our sortie."[288]

For a moment, the Germans were even convinced they had taken Tito prisoner, according to a telegram General Lüters sent to Hitler's High Command, asserting that "the last hour of his army has struck."[289] But shortly afterward it became clear that this was just wishful thinking.

The Change in British Policy

When they reached the woods of eastern Bosnia, it was finally clear that the Partisans were safe. Their morale of course was low, since news arrived from all sides about enormous losses of life, numerous commanders fallen, and massacres of the wounded and the sick.[290] The tragic experience, however, was not in vain, since as early as 4 July 1943 the British ambassador in Moscow informed the Soviet government that, from now on, Great Britain would assist *all* resistance forces in Yugoslavia, in other words, that it would send aid to Tito's Partisans.[291] The reports that Bill Deakin, Churchill's former research assistant, sent to Cairo were decisive in changing the prime minister's mind with regards to the Partisan movement, inducing him to send military aid to Tito on the condition that he would not use it against Mihailović. This new attitude, particularly welcome to the British military, was influenced by the fact that during Operation Schwarz the Germans had suffered about 2,500 casualties, an impressive number, including the losses among dead, wounded, and dispersed, "a remarkable feat . . . when one realizes that the Axis flew some 1,500 sorties and dropped over 1,000,000 lbs. of bombs."[292] The aid came quickly, in fact. On 25 June 1943 Allied planes had dropped explosives needed in the destruction of the Sarajevo-Brod railway. Shortly after the landing of English and American troops in Sicily on 10 July, dispatches of military material started to come regularly, among them also unnecessary items such as shoes that were all left-footed or food where there was an abundance of it and not where people were starving.

On account of their ideological blindness, the Partisan leaders interpreted this not as a sign of bureaucratic sloppiness, but as sabotage by the "perfidious Albion."[293] In any case, the aid that the Western Allies began parachuting in was of decisive psychological importance for their struggle, which began to be important on an international level and integrated into the strategic planning of the Anglo-American Supreme Staff for the Mediterranean. Tito and his comrades were not able to fully appreciate this fact, however, infatuated as they were by the Soviet Union and its Red Army, which they considered a model for their own. In 1941, they had begun introducing military ranks in their units, but now they started to respect them rigorously, offering salaries for the officers and developing an increasingly heavy administrative body, which widened the gap between the graduates and the simple soldiers.[294]

Five days after the landing in Sicily, on 15 July 1943, Tito convened a meeting of the Supreme Staff and the CC CPY in order to discuss the situation both in Italy and on the Eastern Front, where the Red Army was now on the offensive. Subsequent to his proposal, it was decided to move most of the troops into the Italian occupied areas so as to take all possible advantage of their imminent collapse, as well as to resist an eventual Anglo-American landing on the Dalmatian coast.[295] In August, the Partisans triumphantly entered Jajce, the medieval capital of Bosnia, where there was a Bogomil catacomb built by the Bosnian heretical sect before the Ottoman conquest, which could be used by the Supreme Staff as a bomb shelter in case of an attack by air. They were very proud of their victory, since this was the first time they had conquered a city of any importance for more than a few days. "Meanwhile," as Gojko Nikoliš wrote, "from the small coffee-houses, the old Muslim world observed us with oriental indifference, as if they were saying: here all possible forces and hordes have passed, but we, through the centuries, remain in the same spot."[296]

On 8 September 1943, Tito was informed by radio that Italy had capitulated. In Jajce, there was great enthusiasm and arms of all kinds were fired in celebration. While Tito shared in their joy, he was also indignant that the Allies had not informed him in advance about the signing of the armistice with the Italians, which would have enabled him to take full advantage of the new situation. In any case, his troops profited greatly from the Italian collapse. Over the following two weeks, they disarmed thirteen divisions, acquiring enough weapons for eighty thousand men, as well as military equipment and provisions.[297] For several days before the arrival of the Germans, they occupied the greater part of the territory previously held by the Italians. In the meantime, more and more promising news was coming from the Eastern Front. After the Red Army won the titanic Battle of Kursk in July, which was the largest tank battle in history, the Soviet offensive to the West became an avalanche. By mid-October, the

Russian soldiers were already "collecting the waters of the Dnieper in their helmets." They crossed this river, the largest in Ukraine and the third-largest in Europe, on 6 November, a date chosen in honor of the October Revolution, and liberated Kiev.[298]

In that same period, the Western Allies occupied Puglia in southern Italy, where they organized a base in Bari. This was to be important in furnishing provisions across the Adriatic to the Partisans and in evacuating their wounded, together with thousands of civilians, women, children, and the elderly. The connection between the Allies and Tito's Supreme Staff allowed the Slovenes and Croats from Venezia Giulia, enlisted by the Fascists in "special battalions" and confined as untrustworthy to southern Italy and to the islands, to join the Partisans. Together with compatriots who had fought as Italian soldiers in North Africa and had been taken prisoner by the Allies, they organized the so-called "Overseas Brigades" to fight for the freedom of their homeland. Through Bari alone, thirty thousand Slovene and Croat soldiers reached the Dalmatian coast in the following months.[299]

The belief that Germany's defeat was inevitable began to take hold among the general populace and encouraged volunteers to join the Partisans. Within a month of 8 September, Tito's troops had nearly doubled in size to three hundred thousand combatants. There were, however, serious problems as the recruits had little to no military training. The Italian soldiers who decided to continue to fight after the collapse of their army, although now for the Partisans against the Germans, were much more efficient. "Garibaldi" units took part valiantly in the resistance and were thus established among the Partisan ranks.

Frustrated by this turn of events, the Chetniks tried to make the best of a bad situation. In view of the fact that they still believed that the Communists were their only enemies, they sought an agreement with the Germans, who initially persisted in their hostility toward the Chetniks. Information about these propositions reached the British, lending strength to those in the London government who advocated breaking off relations with Mihailović.[300] The new chief of the British mission at Tito's Supreme Staff, Fitzroy Maclean, a diplomat, writer, and brigadier in His Majesty's Army, also supported the Partisans. He came to Bosnia in mid-September as a representative of General Henry Maitland Wilson, commander in chief of the Allied forces in the Mediterranean, arriving, like his predecessor, by parachute. The fact that this was an official mission implied at least a de facto recognition of the Partisan movement as an Allied force, whereas the previous mission headed by Deakin, who was only an SOE agent, was not at the same level. In an interview given years later, Maclean said that he had come to Yugoslavia with an "open" but not empty mind. In fact, during their first meeting, he was unable to resist Tito's charisma, automatically recalling Napoleon's famous phrase: "In war it is not the men, but the man who counts."[301] Whereas Tito and his comrades considered Deakin an anti-communist and a spy, having been sent by the SOE, they discovered a friend in Maclean, the Scottish aristocrat. Being an adventurer, he was immediately captivated by the Partisans' epic feats, seeing himself as a reincarnation of Lawrence of Arabia. It did not take him long to realize that the situation in Yugoslavia was completely different from what the British government and Allied military circles imagined it to be, and that the Foreign Office's plans of a possible arrangement between Mihailović and Tito were an illusion. After a stay of only two weeks, he decided to return to Cairo to report what he had seen, or believed he had seen, and to recommend that his superiors, as he wrote in a memorandum at the beginning of November, "stop the aid to Mihailović and . . . substantially improve their aid to the Partisans."[302]

In this "blockbuster" memorandum, Maclean did not go into whether Mihailović was personally responsible for collaborating with the enemy, but stressed his anti-Croat and reactionary politics, as well as his Serb chauvinism and his inability to unite the Yugoslav peoples and lead them against the occupiers. It reached London along with news about the changing attitude of the Germans toward the Chetniks due to their growing lack of manpower. On 1 November 1943, the Wehrmacht's Headquarters for Southeast Europe wrote a document asserting that the Partisans were extremely dangerous. As a result, the main task of the German forces would no longer be that of policing the Balkans in the eventuality of an Allied landing, but the destruction of Tito's troops. This obviously meant a change in their attitude toward the Chetniks, which was soon confirmed. On 22 November, the British decoded a message relating to an agreement between the German command and Mihailović's representative in Montenegro concerning an armistice in the territory east of Sarajevo aimed at coordinating forces in a common fight against the Partisans.[303]

Maclean's memorandum, and the information gathered by British Intelligence, had a decisive influence on Winston Churchill. At the Tehran Conference with Stalin and Franklin Delano Roosevelt at the end of November 1943, he declared that Tito had done much more against the Germans than Mihailović, and that the British intended to aid him in whatever way they could. He began speaking of a possible landing in the northern Adriatic, which would allow English and American troops to penetrate Central Europe. The Soviets pricked up their ears, although they did not, at the time, seem particularly interested in the Yugoslav question. The secret agreement reached in Tehran by the three statesmen pledged to support the Partisans by sending "supplies and equipment and also by commando operations." Roosevelt readily agreed, as he too had received favorable information regarding Tito from an agent of the Office of Strategic Services (OSS), the American intelligence service. Indeed, this agency had begun contacting Tito in the autumn of 1943 and sending him arms and supplies from Bari.[304]

Further Developments of the National Liberation Struggle and the First National Tensions

The tumultuous events during the spring and summer of 1943 also had significant consequences for Yugoslavia's domestic policy. It was evident that, in the interim, the foundations of the new state needed to be clearly stated, much more so than previously, at the First AVNOJ. The Communist Party leaders had no doubts that the new state should be completely different from the old one. In a moment of sincerity one of them, Svetozar Vukmanović, called Tempo, Tito's envoy to Madedonia and adjacent regions, confessed to his Greek comrades: "In Yugoslavia we will not allow the return of the old regime and 'free' elections. We have had too many victims to allow anything of the kind! We will not allow the Allied troops to enter our country. Only the forces that have triumphed over the occupiers have the right to convene elections, [and it is from them that] the new power should arise."[305] For his part, in 1942 Tito had published an article entitled "The Yugoslav National Question in the Light of the Liberation Struggle," in which he tried to reconcile the different historical traditions of the Southern Slav peoples and their diverging territorial interests with the promise of a federal system.[306] In this context, he proposed that the Politburo of the CPY deny the government in exile the right to speak on behalf of Yugoslavia, and to definitively take power. "Tito and all of us present at that session," wrote Kardelj, "were well aware that this decision would have provoked dissatisfaction and negative reactions from the governments of the great powers and that it could, in particular, have led to political complications between the Soviet Union and the West. . . . But at the time, the interests of the National Liberation Struggle and of the future of our peoples were more important to us than their possible reaction."[307]

In preparing the groundwork, the first thing to do was forge the instruments best suited to represent the people who would constitute the new federal body. Slovenia already had a Liberation Front. In Croatia, a special committee charged with convoking an Antifascist Assembly of National Liberation had been constituted on 17 March 1943. It met in the lake area of Plitvice on the thirteenth and fourteenth of June and proclaimed itself the highest political representative of the country. The ZAVNOH (Zemaljsko antifašističko veće narodnog oslobođenja Hrvatske; State Anti-fascist Council for the National Liberation of Croatia), the acronym by which it came to be known, presented itself as a coalition of different ethnic and political groups—Croat, Serb, and other national minorities in Croatia—but, like the OF (Osvobodilna fronta slovenskega naroda; Slovenian Liberation Front), it was merely an instrument of the Communist Party. The hegemonic role the party claimed for itself, discreetly but firmly, did not, however, mean that it was free of tension resulting from the personal ambitions of the various leaders or local patriotic allegiances. It is significant, for instance, that the decision the ZAVNOH took on 20 September 1943, proclaiming the annexation of Istria, Fiume, Zara, and former Italian islands to the Croatian "fatherland," disappointed Tito. While he accepted it, he felt that the Croat communists, led by Andrija Hebrang, had appropriated for themselves sovereign powers that rightly belonged to Yugoslavia as a common state. But such a state did not yet exist, since the Supreme Staff had little or no influence in the areas controlled by the ZAVNOH or the OF.[308] In any case, the nationalism of Hebrang, who had about fifty percent of all the Partisan forces under his command in the summers of 1942 and 1943, appeared increasingly reprehensible to the majority of the Politburo.[309]

Nor were the national aspirations of the Slovenes, which the propaganda of Yugoslav "brotherhood and unity" barely managed to mask, welcomed by Tito and his Serb and Montenegrin collaborators. They were cautious, however, for they were well aware that the Partisan struggle in Slovenia would have been impossible without its patriotic charge. When celebrating the fall of Italy and the renewed outbreak of resistance after September 8, organized at a National Council in Kočevje, the Liberation Front proclaimed the annexation of part of Venezia Giulia (as the Italians had renamed the former Austrian littoral) to Slovenia. No one protested, so as not to stir up Slovenian reservations regarding a reunion with Yugoslavia. There is no doubt, however, that in Tito's circle Slovene and Croat aspirations for autonomy were viewed with growing concern. This was clear as early as spring 1943, when Arso Jovanović and Ivo Lola Ribar returned from Slovenia with alarming information about the local situation. They even accused the Slovenian comrades of not operating in line with the strategic and revolutionary plans of the Supreme Staff.[310]

After August 1943, Tito had been planning to convoke the Second AVNOJ as a parliament of all Yugoslav peoples. Since Stalin had dissolved the Comintern on 13 May of that year in order to convince the Western Allies that the Soviet Union was no longer interested in a world revolution, Tito was free from past restrictions. He thus decided to implement his old proposal to create a government, based on popular power, that would create a communist regime outside of the borders of the Soviet Union.[311] Assemblies similar to those at Plitvice and Kočevje were also held in other regions: in Istria, Bosnian Krajina, Montenegro, Sandžak, Bosnia-Herzegovina, and even in Macedonia. Unlike in Slovenia and Croatia, where nationalism was a disturbing factor, Tito and Svetozar Vukmanović promoted it in Macedonia in order to strengthen the resistance, which was slow in gathering momentum. In 1941 and 1942, the efforts of the CPY to organize a Macedonian revolt against the Bulgarians repeatedly met with failure. Initially, the local population had hailed the occupation by the Bulgarian army with enthusiasm, happy to rid itself of the Serbian yoke. But it was soon clear that the Bulgarians had no intention of respecting their language and national identity. With regard to the exploitation of mines and local manpower, things under the new regime were no better than before. More important than the popular dissatisfaction with the occupiers was Moscow's decision in June 1941 to resume diplomatic relations with the Yugoslav government, prompting the Comintern to immediately annul its decision regarding the union of the Macedonian communists with the Bulgarian Worker's Party. They should return to the Yugoslav fold.[312]

During the war, the policy of the Bulgarian Worker's Party differed completely from that of the CPY. It refused to fight the domestic Nazi-friendly regime in order not to stir up a civil war and limited itself to anti-German propaganda pending the arrival of the Red Army. It accepted the Comintern's decision on Macedonia, which favored the CPY and its struggle against Fascism, but in practice it continued to act in favor of a passive resistance, affirming that in Bulgaria conditions were not yet ripe for an armed uprising. At the end of 1942, Tito decided to act: he sent one of his most energetic collaborators, Svetozar Vukmanović (Tempo) to Skopje, where he soon succeeded in organizing a nucleus of resistance in Macedonia (especially in the western part, which had been annexed to Albania by the Italians). He was less successful in the province of Kosovo, where the local Albanian population had never enjoyed such rights or well-being as it had under Italian domination. Mostly the Serbs and Montenegrins of the region, finding themselves in the unpleasant role of a minority, were responsive to Tempo's words and began joining his units, which, however, could only operate along the borders of Serb, Montenegrin, or Macedonian territory. After the collapse of Italy this situation remained unchanged. Kosovo was occupied by the Germans, who stirred up anti-Yugoslav hatred among the population by claiming that the Partisans were Russian and Serb agents who were determined to split up Greater Albania and enslave Kosovo again. This propaganda was not without effect. In order to defend themselves against Slav enemies, the Albanians organized a political and military movement called Balli Kombëtar, which succeeded in controlling the province until the end of the war.[313]

In spite of tensions between the Slavs and the Albanians in Kosovo and western Macedonia, the CPY established cordial relations with the communists in

Albania proper. In 1941, the CC of CPY sent an "instructor," Miladin Popović, to organize the local resistance. Once he was joined by Dušan Mugoša, they managed to constitute the Communist Party of Albania by incorporating scattered leftist groups. On 11 March 1943, the first pan-Albanian conference of the party was convened and Enver Hoxha was elected secretary general. On that occasion, they also decided to create a popular army modeled on the Yugoslav example. In the beginning, the communists collaborated with Balli Kombëtar but, at the end of 1942, the Yugoslavs cut all ties, fearing a movement that favored a united Albania that included Kosovo. The CPY and the CPA could not avoid taking into consideration the future of this province, but they barely touched on the question, since Tito, conscious of Serb sensibilities, declared that it would be dealt with only after the defeat of the Fascists.[314]

The indefatigable Tempo also kept an eye on the Greek communists who had in turn organized their own Partisan units, which fought successfully against the Italians and Germans. ELAS (Ellinikós Laikós Apeleutherótikos Stratós; the Greek National Liberation Army) had strongholds in Rumelia, Thessaly, Epirus, and in Aegean Macedonia although, like the Yugoslav Partisans, they had to cope with a competing bourgeois-leaning movement. ELAS was unable, however, to give the Greek resistance that revolutionary impetus their comrades had given to the resistance in Yugoslavia. The Greek communists—as Tempo observed rather indignantly in his memoirs—did not fight for power, but only wanted to expel the occupier, so that after the victory the people could freely decide their political future. To rectify these errors, Tempo proposed the creation of a General Staff for the Balkans that could coordinate the common struggle, including the Greeks and the Albanians. Since communications between Macedonia and the Supreme Staff were difficult, and there was no radio link until the end of October 1943, for a long time Tito lacked precise information as to what was going on in the south. The first reports on Tempo's activity did not reach him until mid-September. He then learned that the party in Macedonia had been purged of the (pro-Bulgarian) "factions," that a CC of the CP of Macedonia and a General Staff had been formed, and that the Partisan units numbered four hundred to five hundred combatants. In his dispatches, Tempo also spoke about the situation in Kosovo, stressing that the Albanians were hostile to the Serbs because of nationalist propaganda. Only eighty of the two hundred Partisans in the province were Albanians. Tito was less than enthusiastic about the idea of a general staff for the Balkans because, on one hand, he feared that the British, who had their agents in Greece, could exploit such a body in their favor and, on the other hand, he suspected that the Russians would not be happy. From the surviving documents, it is not clear whether Tito had consulted Moscow on the matter, but it is evident that prohibiting Tempo from pursuing this plan was in accordance with Stalin's policy.[315]

In extending his activity to the south, Tito was well aware that he could not speak in the name of Yugoslavia until he set foot in Serbia, which was still under the Germans. (Among 150,000 Partisans who were under Tito's direct command at the end of 1943, only two thousand were in eastern Yugoslavia, and they were in poor shape).[316] In October 1943, he decided the time had come to shift the focal point of military operations across the Drina, but this proposal was thwarted by a vigorous Wehrmacht offensive during the winter, an attempt to occupy the territory evacuated by the Italians. In Slovenia, Istria, Gorski Kotar, Dalmatia, Herzegovina, and Sandžak, heavy fighting raged for nearly three months between Partisan and German troops for control of the coast and the lines of communication with the hinterland. In Slovenia, the Wehrmacht could count on the Domobranci (Home Guards) as local collaborators in combat, while in Montenegro with the help of the Chetniks and the Albanians they organized a vast operation to block the passage of Partisans into Serbia, "this irreplaceable bulwark for the defense of the Balkans," as Hitler called it in one of his messages.[317]

The Second Session of AVNOJ

In spite of furious fighting, Tito and his comrades did not abandon their idea of convoking the Second AVNOJ. The preparatory work was done mostly by Edvard Kardelj, Boris Kidrič, and Moša Pijade, formerly Tito's cellmate in the royal jails and one of the most accomplished intellectuals in his circle. As in the previous year, the Politburo discussed and approved the decisions to be taken by the Second AVNOJ in advance. By the end of October it had already decided that the assembly would create a provisional government, proclaim the unity of the Yugoslav peoples within the framework of a federation, and forbid the king to return home until the people decided whether they wanted a monarchy or a republic. While making these decisions, they could not help but ask themselves what the Soviet reaction would be, since signs of Moscow's disapproval of their overly independent policy were becoming increasingly frequent.

By mid-September the Bulgarian communist Sterju Atanasov had arrived at the Supreme Staff. He was the first man from Moscow Tito had met in some time. He informed Tito that a conference was in preparation in the Soviet capital between the foreign ministers of the Great Powers. Fearing that Viacheslav Molotov, Anthony Eden, and Cordell Hull might take decisions at odds with his plans, on 12 October 1943 Broz sent Dimitrov a dispatch in which he stated explicitly that King Petar and his government could not return home.[318] In addition, he presented himself, although circumspectly, as the future leader of Yugoslavia, communicating that "in Slovenia and in Croatia they have proposed to the AVNOJ to elect me in the next session as president of the National Committee and the chief of the army." Modestly, he added that he did not agree: "I need your help to convince the comrades. In my opinion, this would not be favorably accepted abroad."[319] Naturally, he immediately got the "help" requested from Dimitrov, who declared that the nomination would not be "appropriate."[320]

Tito's reaction to this is significant: he decided that it was no longer necessary to inform the Russians "about everything," so as not to give them the chance to sabotage the AVNOJ before it started. During the following two weeks, he did not send detailed information about preparatory work, but did allow Atanasov to describe, in two dispatches, the situation in the Partisan ranks. "The Communist Party," the Bulgarian wrote, "is the only force capable of creating the new Yugoslav State."[321] In the message that Tito sent to Dimitrov on 26 November 1943, he refrained from mentioning the decision about the monarchy, as well as the "unexpected" proposal of the Slovenian delegation to give him the title of "marshal," the highest rank of the Red Army, until then unknown in Yugoslavia.[322] It is doubtful that this proposal was really spontaneous, since on 29 October Tito had already signed the diplomas of the Supreme Staff's officers school as "marshal."[323] When the title was offered to him officially, he blushed and asked in embarrassment: "Aren't you exaggerating? And what will the Russians say?" Kardelj and the others hastened to reassure him. If the Russians had their own marshals, why shouldn't Yugoslavia? When this topic came up for discussion in the assembly at the AVNOJ session, according to Djilas, there was "an enthusiastic and exhilirated unanimity" and no end to hysterical applause, cheering, hugs, and kisses.[324] The next day, 30 November 1943, the presidency of the AVNOJ published an official decree "in order to give well-deserved recognition to comrade Josip Broz-Tito, the Commander in Chief, for his brilliant leadership of the operations of the National Liberation Army and of the Partisan Detachments of Yugoslavia, and for his capability and decisiveness in shaping them into their present form."[325]

Kardelj eloquently described how relations with Moscow deteriorated: "First of all we decided not to inform Moscow about this, because we were convinced that they would be against it. We still believed they were revolutionaries, but for tactical reasons, we did not want to inform them. Throughout our National Liberation struggle, they subordinated their relations with us to their political goals, which were aimed at maintaining good contacts with the Americans and the British. They thought it would be better to sacrifice the revolution in Yugoslavia than to quarrel on its account with the English and the Americans. We knew well that we could not count on them, and that we had to leave the Russians aside if we wanted to succeed."[326]

As in Bihać during the First AVNOJ, in Jajce, too, the communist leadership did everything required to bend the assembly to its will. Every decision was taken unanimously, with applause, and without discussion.[327] The Federal Republic of Yugoslavia therefore took shape—although with different characteristics—in a manner similar to the way the Kingdom of Serbs, Croats, and Slovenes was created. Although the Second AVNOJ proclaimed itself "the highest representative of the people's sovereignty and of the united State of Yugoslavia," it was once more the expression of the will and the interests of a small group who were militarily powerful and therefore able to form the new state as it wished, without heeding its Muscovite patron. "The new power," wrote Djilas in his memoirs, "was characterized by its break with the old power and its infidelity toward our spiritual fathers."[328] In his inaugural speech, Tito forcefully denied that the national liberation struggle was "a communist thing, aimed at the Bolshevik transformation of the state." According to him, this was propaganda worthy of Joseph Goebbels, spread by the occupiers and the traitorous Quislings.[329] In line with this assertion, the Second AVNOJ did not make any decisions related to the future social and political order, although the fact that it presented itself as an "instrument of the revolution and of power," to quote Kardelj, showed in what direction Yugoslavia would go.[330] No delegates from Macedonia or Serbia were present in Jajce. The Slovenes and the Croats dominated, as shown by the election of Tito as president of the National Liberation Committee, which had the prerogatives of a government, and Ivan Ribar as president of the AVNOJ. In addition to Tito, two Slovenes played key roles in the session: Edvard Kardelj and Boris Kidrič, a failed university student but a gifted politician. As Bilandžić notes, the role played by Tito, Ribar, Kardelj, and Kidrič at the Second AVNOJ supported the Serb belief that a plot had been hatched against them thanks to the dictates of the Croats and Slovenes, their ideological and political enemies.[331] "The fact that the provisional Partisan government in Bosnia—Ribar, Tito—is recognized and in the good graces of all the Allied forces," reads a report sent at the end of December from the special police in Belgrade to Premier Nedić and his ministers, "and that it is a focus of interest of the whole world, has aroused confusion and preoccupation in Serb public opinion. It [the Serb people] has been abandoned by all, and its fate is in the hands of those—non-Serbs—who, until now, have caused so much suffering. After the war, it will be very difficult for the Serbs to get rid of the communist contamination and it is generally thought that there will even be an armed conflict before we free ourselves from these communist thugs."[332]

It is interesting to note that, after the Second AVNOJ, the Serb communists also feared that Serbia could lose its central role in the new Yugoslavia. At the same time, the Croats and the Slovenes doubted whether they would really be equal in the future federation. Tito sought to calm their anxieties, meeting separately with both delegations, and promising more than he was later able to carry out. Asked by General Jaka Avšič, a royal officer who joined the Partisans, whether the Slovenian Army would be allowed to use its native language as the language of command in its own territory, Tito promptly answered: "It is clear, completely clear, you are a Slovenian Army and therefore you should have your own language."[333] This promise was forgotten by 1945.

In spite of the exaltation that permeated it, there was a tragic overture to the Second AVNOJ. On the eve of its opening, news arrived that Ivo Lola Ribar had lost his life on 27 November 1943, in an air attack on the field of Glamoč, where he had been scheduled to leave for Cairo as head of a military mission to the Allied Command for the Mediterranean. This mission was of great importance for Tito, who wanted to emphasize his parity with the Western powers. As he said, "They a mission to us—we a mission to them."[334] When informed of Lola's death, he placed both hands on the table and said: "They have destroyed my pillar." He then had to manage one of the most difficult tasks of his life: to inform Ribar's father, old Ivan Ribar, whose wife had already been slaughtered by the Ustaše, that he has lost not only Lola, but also his older son, Ivica, who had recently fallen in battle. Ribar stood silent, then embraced him: "It is hard, this fight of ours."[335]

Rumors were circulating that Ivo Lola Ribar's death had been the result of betrayal. Vladimir Velebit, who was near him during the fatal attack, firmly denied this, stressing that it was a tragic accident. Tito, who as an old conspirator did not trust anyone, was of a different opinion.[336]

Tito and Kardelj only informed Moscow about the decisions of the Second AVNOJ when it was over. Their dispatch went unanswered. "Generally they reacted promptly," wrote the latter in a memoir, "but now they did not. They did not dare make a hurried decision, because they did not know how the whole affair would end."[337] Stalin, tormented during the war by fear of a separate peace between Germany and Great Britain, did not want to give the impression that he had revolutionary ambitions in the Balkans. He angrily commented on the Second AVNOJ, saying that it was a knife in the back of the Soviet Union. This was immediately conveyed to Veljko Vlahović, the representative of the CPY in Moscow. The "Boss," as Stalin was called by his collaborators, was disturbed not only because of the monarchy, since he tried to prevent any suspicions in the West for his support to such revolutionary decisions, but also because of the possible impression that Serb hegemony in Yugoslavia had been replaced by a Croat one. "Take into consideration," wrote Dimitrov to Tito, "that, in various British and American circles, people are speculating about this." This is why Radio Free Yugoslavia was compelled to keep silent about the AVNOJ for two weeks. Only when it was evident that American and British reactions were on the whole positive and that the Western media had reported favorably on Jajce, could it broadcast a communiqué of which the Soviet government would take notice.[338] "Only then," added Kardelj in the above quoted note, "did we get a telegram, in which they neither agreed, nor disagreed, but only gave generic advice."[339]

Churchill's Illusions

Tito was well aware of the favor Churchill had done him by not taking a hostile attitude toward the National Liberation Committee of Yugoslavia. "The Russians would not fight for us," he said some years later. "Because of his interests, Stalin would have left us alone. Churchill's attitude brought the Great Powers together and helped affirm us on the international level."[340] Consequently the royal government in exile became isolated in its protest against the "violence of the terrorist movement" (as they called the Partisans), which, in its opinion, did not represent the national, democratic, and social aspirations of the Yugoslav peoples, and was successful only because of the disgraceful support "of some Allied institutions." This thinly veiled criticism had no effect on Churchill, and he remained firm in his decisions to abandon the Chetniks and help the Partisans. On his return from the Tehran Conference, on 10 December 1943, he received King Petar and his prime minister, Božidar Purić, in Cairo, in order to inform them of the change in his policy regarding Tito and Mihailović. Purić tried to protest: "You cannot betray Serbia, your ally in 1914, in this way. For you only the English interests are important, the whole world and also history will judge you." "But Mihailović collaborates with the Germans," replied Churchill. "Can you prove it?" asked Purić. "No, I cannot," said Churchill, "but I am sure he is a collaborationist."[341]

Churchill was not being entirely honest when he said he had no proof of contacts between Mihailović and the Germans, for in fact he did. He himself affirmed in a dispatch sent to Eden on 2 February 1943, that he had acquired proof from Deakin and from British officers who were in the areas under Mihailović's control.[342] He had received proof mostly thanks to Ultra, a jealously guarded secret that could not be revealed to the Yugoslav premier. The fact that not even the British administrative and military apparatus at high levels had been informed that their intelligence service was routinely cracking coded Nazi communiqués (as well as bureaucratic inertia and Foreign Office skepticism) prevented the immediate implementation of the prime minister's policy—to abandon Mihailović, denounce him as a collaborationist, and recall British missions from Chetnik headquarters. Between 1943 and 1944, the British and Americans aided the Partisans yet continued their (frosty) relations with Mihailović. In the meantime, their planes had successfully prevented the Wehrmacht from occupying all the Dalmatian islands. The island of Vis, off the coast of Spalato, remained under the control of both the British and the Partisans. In December 1943, the military circles in Cairo decided to test Mihailović once more. The Allied command for the Middle East asked him to blow up two bridges in order to block the railway traffic between Belgrade and Thessaloniki. "In mid-January," Colonel Bailey, who was still at his headquarters, wrote in his memoirs, "it appeared obvious that the two bridges would never be mined."[343]

Under the pressure of the Sixth Offensive, unleashed by the Germans in Bosnia and in Sandžak on 6 January 1944, the Partisan leadership abandoned Jajce, where it had found refuge for 145 days. The Politburo decided to split into two groups: the first, with Kardelj, would go to Croatia; Tito and his political and military collaborators would remain in Bosnia. The new offensive was not as devastating as the previous two, but since it took place in the midst of winter, many Partisan units suffered greatly. The Supreme Staff was practically untouched, having found shelter in the small town of Drvar on the Unac River.[344] The town was practically in ruins and Tito therefore decided to stay in a grotto on the right bank of the river, in front of which a wooden cottage, fitted with three rooms, was erected. The grotto was on the slopes of Mount Gradina, about twenty meters above the surrounding plain, with a splendid view over the entire valley. It was reached by steep steps hewn out of the rock, and its walls were hung with parachute silk. Randolph Churchill, son of the British prime minister, who had been sent to Tito and who could be brilliant (when he was not drunk), wrote to his father in March 1944 with mocking irony: "His office is more like the love nest of an expensive prostitute than that of a Partisan leader."[345]

As the Germans, still fearing an Allied landing, were concentrated in Dalmatia to strengthen their position on the Adriatic coast, in Western Bosnia the situation was relatively calm, so that the newly promoted marshal found time for chess games with Ranković and Djilas, and for practicing in Cyrillic the signature of his name, TITO, which was so distinctive that after his death his faithful wore it as a golden pin. He also paid great attention to his clothing, ordering a uniform from a Slovenian tailor that was in keeping with his high rank. In spite of their primitive living conditions, the comrades maintained certain standards and as Djilas recounts did not, apart from Moša Pijade, use expletives. But, as Djilas, who had hated Moša Pijade since their time in jail together, sarcastically said, bad words were in his blood as a result of his Levantine spiritual and linguistic heritage.[346]

Tito—Šubašić

There seemed to be no end of good news. On 8 January 1944, Churchill informed Tito, as well as Stalin, that he would break off relations with Mihailović. The following day, Tito asked to be officially recognized, and informed Moscow thereof.[347] He could not restrain himself from telling his collaborators—and Dimitrov—that he was in contact with the British prime minister, who still wanted him to come to an agreement with King Petar II.[348] These were obviously purely illusory, since it was evident that the Karadjordjević dynasty was doomed. Stanoje Simić, the Yugoslav ambassador to Moscow, was also of this opinion and on 10 March 1944 terminated his relationship with the government in exile.[349] Fitzroy Maclean concurred—he had already written to London at the end of 1943 that the time had come to confront reality: "The Partisans are containing more enemy divisions than the combined British and American armies in Italy, and they will remain the rulers of Yugoslavia whatever we do."[350] Most important, however, was Stalin's decision to support Tito in his hostile attitude toward the monarchy. When he realized at the Tehran Conference that the English and the Americans would recognize the National Liberation Committee as a fait accompli, he radically changed his negative stance regarding the AVNOJ government and began acting, to quote Kardelj, "as if he recognized it."[351] A significant episode in this regard took place at the airport in Baku during his return from Iran. As Marshal A. E. Golovanov recalled, he was approached by the Boss and told that the Yugoslav Partisans were to be aided with weapons immediately and at any cost.[352] When, on 22 December 1943, Purić, the premier of the Yugoslav royal government, mentioned to the Soviet ambassador in Cairo, Nikolai V. Novikov, that he was ready to sign an agreement of friendship and collaboration with Moscow similar to the one signed recently by Stalin and Edvard Beneš, prime minister of the Czechoslovak government in exile, Novikov flatly refused. "I offered you 8 million Serbs," commented an outraged Purić, "but you do not want them."[353] Through Dimitrov, Stalin informed Broz on 9 February 1944 that both the royal government in Cairo and Mihailović had to be removed. The only legitimate power in Yugoslavia should be the AVNOJ and the National Liberation Committee headed by Tito. "If King Petar accepts these conditions, the AVNOJ will not refuse to collaborate with him. It is clear, however, that the question of the monarchy will be decided by the people after the liberation of Yugoslavia."[354] This letter was later sent by Tito to Churchill as if he himself were its author.[355]

The aforementioned dispatch from Moscow to the Supreme Staff was intercepted by British Intelligence, which gave Churchill a chance to see how close the collaboration was between Tito and Stalin.[356] Churchill, however, continued to believe that he would still have some degree of influence in Yugoslavia, thanks to his tactical skills. At the beginning of 1944 he wrote: "Our policy should be based on two factors: the Partisans will govern Yugoslavia. They are so important from the military point of view that we must offer them all aid, subjecting our political to our military preoccupations. It is questionable, therefore, whether we can still consider the monarchy as a connecting factor in Yugoslavia."[357] In mid-February, his government decided finally to halt formal relations with the Chetniks and ordered the British military personnel with Mihailović or his units to leave. On 22 February, Churchill gave a speech in the House of Commons in which he explained this change of policy, praising Tito as "an exceptional leader, glorious in the fight for liberty." He stressed that Great Britain had no intention of imposing the monarchy on the Yugoslav people, however, while abandoning Mihailović, it would not dissociate itself from King Petar.[358] In other words, Churchill promised military aid to Tito without recognizing him as the political representative of Yugoslavia, in hopes of creating a modus vivendi between the sovereign and the marshal. To justify his attachment to the king, he argued that the Serb peasants were hostile to Marxist doctrine and that they did not support the national liberation struggle. Only if Tito succeeded in reaching a compromise with Petar II could he unite all those who were hostile to the foreign occupiers.[359] Tito was clearly elated by Churchill's speech, although he did not agree with his last assertion. On the contrary, he affirmed that the Serb peasants were not at all in favor of the king. "You will see," he said, "when our forces reach Serbia."[360]

On 5 February 1944, the Soviet news agency TASS announced officially that the Soviet government had rejected the proposal by the Yugoslav government in exile regarding the agreement on postwar collaboration. This meant that it was openly casting its lot with the new Yugoslavia led by Tito.[361] Moscow did even more: it decided to establish relations with him, not just on a "clandestine" level, as had been the case until then, but to openly send a military mission to his headquarters in Bosnia. This decision was also made because the pro-German camp in Yugoslavia spread a rumor that the absence of a mission testified to the Soviet Union's disinterest in the Balkans. The mission came to Drvar on 23 February 1944 and was welcomed by the Partisans with enthusiasm, although it cannot be said that they were proud of the way in which the Russians arrived. They were not parachuted in like the British, but used gliders, with the excuse that their chief, General-Major Nikolai Vasilievich Korneev, was elderly and invalid (his left leg had been injured at Stalingrad). They were comforted, however, by the consideration that he had the highest rank among the other mission chiefs and was not accredited at the Supreme Staff, as the

English and Americans were, but at the AVNOJ.[362] For the Yugoslav communists, this was undoubtedly an important achievement. In spite of an initial coldness due to the formal behavior of the Soviets, a genuine comradeship soon emerged between them and the Yugoslavs. In honor of the newcomers, Tito organized a reception on 24 February, for the first time sporting his marshal uniform.[363] Two or three weeks after their arrival he told his collaborators, with embarrassment and pride, how Korneev, when drunk, embraced and kissed him, calling him "Oska, Oska," the Russian nickname for Josip.[364] In an interview given in April to Joseph Morton from the United Press—the first given to a foreign correspondent—he stressed the fact that there were no "pro-Soviet elements" in the Partisan movement, although it was actually quite the opposite.[365]

In the spring of 1944, Tito and his comrades found themselves in the pleasant situation of a girl courted by two suitors: the Russians and the British outdid each other in praising the success of the Partisans' guerilla tactics. According to the British, after the war a string of friendly monarchies should be established in the Mediterranean area, in Italy, Albania, Yugoslavia, and Greece. This project was dear to Churchill, not only because of his royalist sympathies but also because he was convinced that these monarchies would be an instrument of British domination in their respective countries. In short, Sir Winston, trusting his diplomatic ability, changed horses mid-race in Yugoslavia, sure he would emerge victorious and in indirect control. However, he found in Tito a worthy adversary who was able to dissimulate his intentions, to engage in dialogue without showing all his cards, and who was ever ready to exploit the increasingly available Allied supplies to strengthen his forces. Thanks to the stubbornness of the Serb members of the government in exile, Tito succeeded in postponing Churchill's request for talks about his collaboration with the king until late spring, a delay that gave him extra time to send his Partisan units to Serbia and reinforce the national liberation movement there. This significantly changed the balance of power in his favor.[366]

In hopes of reaching an agreement with Tito about the monarchy, in the first months of 1944 Churchill tried to convince King Petar II to repudiate Mihailović. This was not easy, since the Serb coterie surrounding the sovereign vehemently opposed such a move. The British prime minister was obviously not a man to allow his plans to be hindered by the "imbroglios of Serbian politics." He initially considered organizing a coup against the Chetnik leader, but abandoned this proposal when he realized there were no officers in Mihailović's camp capable of implementing one. "A pity," commented Eden, adding that in order to expel Mihailović, the Yugoslav government in exile had to be overthrown as soon as possible.[367] At the beginning of March 1944, Petar II returned from Cairo to London to celebrate his much-contested wedding to Princess Alexandra of Greece (according to Serb tradition, one should not marry in wartime.) At the time, both Churchill and his foreign minister tried to push him in their direction, initially with poor results. To strengthen British influence in Yugoslavia, Churchill reckoned above all on the aid in arms and food, which Tito desperately needed to feed a population that was on the verge of famine in many parts of the liberated territory. Serbia continued to play an important role in the prime minister's calculations as he was still convinced that it was hostile to the Partisans and that Tito had not accurately gauged the situation. The marshal had only a few thousand combatants across the river Ibar at his disposal, whereas Mihailović could count on almost twenty thousand men and forty-five thousand reservists, aside from Nedić's forces and other right-wing troops. From Churchill's point of view this was not necessarily unfavorable, for it offered him the possibility of executing a diplomatic and military maneuver that would bring the Serbs under Tito's banner, and Tito eventually under British influence. The main problem was finding a new president for the Yugoslav government acceptable both to the king and Tito, popular in Yugoslavia and especially in Serbia, and able to carry out the aforementioned delicate operation.[368]

It was not easy to find such a man, since all the Serb politicians in exile were followers of Mihailović and were unwilling to collaborate with the communists. In the end, Churchill had to accept a non-Serb candidate who was, however, favored by the Americans and by their secret services: Ivan Šubašić, the last ban of Croatia, loyal to the dynasty but also openly in favor of Tito and his movement. In May 1944, on Churchill's invitation, "the shepherd" (his code name) came to London from the United States, where he resided, to begin negotiations for the establishment of a new government. Petar II, excluded from this operation, obviously felt humiliated as Churchill had already announced the constitution of the new Yugoslav government in Parliament. Together with Purić he tried to resist, but abandoned by Roosevelt as well, was forced to surrender at the end of the month. A new government was thus created, anomalous in view of the fact that Šubašić held all ministerial posts, including that of Mihailović, who formally ceased to be minister of war by royal decree on 8 July 1944.[369]

Yugoslavia's position in postwar Europe was suddenly of immediate concern, as shown by Churchill's letter to Eden of 1 April 1944, in which he mentioned, with preoccupation, the "grandiose Soviet mission" sent to Tito, and Tito's decision to send his own military mission to Moscow.[370] While General Velimir Terzić was at its head, the most important personality was Milovan Djilas who, in his discussions with Molotov and Stalin, could not hide the Yugoslav leaders' infatuation with the Soviet Union. Furthermore, Djilas was sure that there would be words of praise in the Kremlin for a mission accomplished, and indeed there were. Stalin was even momentarily annoyed when Djilas asked him for a loan to pay for arms, hastening to assure him that it would be honored when the war was over. "You offend me. You shed your blood and think that I could take money for arms. I am not a trafficker, we are not traffickers!"[371] After his meeting with the Boss, Djilas came to the conclusion that the Yugoslav communists could count on Soviet aid, but that for opportunistic reasons they needed to maintain good relations with the Western Allies, although not without circumspection, since they were capable of hitting below the belt. Stalin hinted that the Yugoslavs should not even exclude the possibility of an Allied attempt to assassinate Tito. This was the beginning of a subtle game of politics between the Yugoslavs, the Soviets, and the British, whose objective was to gain political influence in the Balkans, leaning only on the conviction that the Germans had to be ousted first.[372]

The positive results of Djilas's meetings with Stalin and his top collaborators soon became apparent. On 22 April 1944, the Soviets communicated to the British that they would, from then on, collaborate more intensively with Tito. In agreement with the Allies, a Red Army base with ten transport aircraft was set up in Bari, so that supplies could be flown in for the National Liberation Army. They also sent medals and decorations to the leaders of the Yugoslav resistance, as if they were part of their military. Churchill, of course, kept a wary eye on events and began thinking about the division of spheres of influence in the Balkans.[373]

In Tito's Supreme Staff, these maneuvers were looked upon with growing concern, as evident proof of British imperialistic aims. The marshal remained calm and even subtly countered Churchill's argument that the Serbs did not support him. In an interview with British and American journalists, published by the *Times* on 16 May 1944, he stressed that his forces were composed of 44 percent Serbs, 30 percent Croats, 10 percent Slovenes, 5 percent Montenegrins, 2.5 percent Muslims, and 6 percent "others," including Italians. He neglected to say that most of the Serbs came from Bosnia-Herzegovina and Croatia and that, in Serbia proper, the results of his efforts to encourage the revolt were still modest, albeit growing.[374] He was heartened, however, by the fact that he could count on Russian support. In mid-April, he sent a dispatch to Moscow once more protesting the attitude of the Bulgarians and of Dimitrov himself toward the Macedonian question—they still persisted in considering Macedonia as part of greater Bulgaria. Stalin answered through General Korneev with a conciliatory letter, promising that he would not accept any decision regarding the question "without your agreement." In addition, he mapped out his vision of the postwar Balkans, stressing the pivotal role of Yugoslavia in southeastern Europe. Once the Germans had been eliminated, Yugoslavia was to ally itself with the Soviet Union, along with Bulgaria. The only point that Tito found hard to swallow was the affirmation that "in our plans, there is no Sovietization of Yugoslavia and Bulgaria."[375]

Operation Rösselsprung

In the spring of 1944, the valley of the Drvar was at the height of its splendor: sudden but brief storms blew in from the mountains, rays of light shone through the clouds, fresh water gushed from the rocks. The entire valley was green and full of flowers.[376] It was against this idyllic background that the Germans launched their attack, known as Operation Rösselsprung (knight's move), on 25 May 1944, Tito's official birthday (Tito had two birthdays—the real one, 7 May, and the official one, 25 May).[377] It had been organized by the Fifteenth Mountain Corps, in collaboration with infantry units from Bihać, Knin, and Livno, and its purpose was to destroy the leadership of the resistance. Hitler personally ordered the Wehrmacht to attempt a coup against Tito and his Supreme Staff. It was coordinated by a center that had been specifically established in Zagreb. The Germans prepared the operation in secret, planning to encircle Drvar and occupy it by dropping in paratroopers. A special "punitive battalion," manned by condemned officers, was employed, since it was clear that the descent was extremely risky, nearly suicidal—punitive battalions were assigned high-risk missions with the prospect of redeeming themselves through military heroism. They departed from the Zagreb airport, informed about their task only two hours in advance.[378] The assault, in which two thousand soldiers of the elite Prinz Eugen Division were also involved, took place so unexpectedly on a Sunday that it was nearly successful. Thanks to information that had begun filtering through in February, and because of the frequent Luftwaffe reconnaissance flights, the Supreme Staff had an inkling that something of the sort was in the air and, as early as April, had called in the First Proletarian Division, led by Koča Popović. When the Germans got wind of this, they decided to temporarily postpone the operation. Since nothing happened, Popović and his men returned to the battlefield. When the attack came, Tito had at his disposal only an escort battalion and the cadets of an officer school, altogether about eighty men. The cottage, built as it was over a waterfall in front of a cave, was far from ideal and Tito therefore decided to move to the nearby village of Bastasi, where he would be safe as the Germans were unaware of his move.[379] Certain that the danger had passed, on 24 May Tito returned to Drvar to participate in a dinner offered for members of the foreign military missions, including Churchill's son Randolph and General Dwight D. Eisenhower's personal envoy, Robert Crawford. He decided to pass the night in the grotto above the valley, intending to celebrate his birthday with Kardelj, who had recently returned from Slovenia, Zdenka, his secretary and lover, and other comrades of both sexes. This was where he was surprised at dawn by the German attack.[380]

Planes filled the sky of Drvar between six and seven in the morning. There were Dorniers, Stukas, biplanes and, for the first time, fighter planes. They bombed the town of Drvar for half an hour, after which transport planes came in low over the valley, nearly touching the rooftops and the trees. They dropped parachutists while gliders full of German soldiers, each with a photo of Tito in their pockets, landed in dizzying parabolas on the fields and meadows.[381]

At first the situation did not seem to be particularly alarming, since the Partisans were used to German bombing, but when, after the initial attack, parachutists and gliders landed near the cave where Tito and his comrades were hiding, it became serious. The first parachutists were killed, but others kept coming. Assault Group Panther, consisting of one hundred men, began advancing toward the local cemetery, convinced that the Supreme Staff was in the vicinity.[382]

When they discovered their blunder and realized that the main defense was around the cave, they started to machine-gun Tito's shelter, trapping the marshal and those with him. From the very beginning, Tito's comrades had advised him to leave while there was still time. Visibly shaken, he asked whether the parachutists had also occupied the mountain plateau above the valley. Since no one knew for certain, he refused to move, stressing that he had no intention of exposing himself to the German machine guns: "I don't want to fall into their hands!"[383] To make matters worse, Zdenka revealed their position with her hysterical cries, tempting some of the comrades, Ranković among them, to shoot her on the spot. Tito's new bloodhound, Tiger, also kept barking, and more than once his master was about to silence him permanently, but could not bring himself to pull the trigger.[384] In this tense situation the only one who kept calm was Ranković. He decided to leave the cave with Žujović and Arso Jovanović and organize a defense. Under fire, he reached the escort battalion and sent a courier to the officers school, ordering its cadets to fight. "We have no arms," was the answer, "but we shall do everything we can. We will take the arms from the enemy."[385]

The only way out of the cave was along the slope of the mountain, which was dangerously exposed to the attackers. Ranković climbed to the top without knowing what he would find there. He was lucky as it was not yet occupied by the Germans. In the meantime, the situation in the cave and in the cottage was going from bad to worse. Kardelj's bodyguard, who from time to time went to the door to peep out and see what was going on, paid for this temerity with his life: a bullet hit his temple, his blood covered the walls, and part of his brain flew into his cap. Tito ordered his escort to give him a coup de grâce. "Glory to Comrade Vlado," he said, kneeling near the body.[386] It was not until about eleven o'clock, when everything seemed lost, that Ranković managed to send a note through Žujović, advising Tito to climb to the top of the mountain, where there were no enemy units. Once back, Žujović noted Tito's bewilderment and drew his gun, shouting: "Come on out, you old coward! Do you want to surrender to the Germans and save your skin, you the commander in chief, and at the same time betray our fight?" He browbeat him into abandoning the shelter, calmed Zdenka as much as possible, and convinced her to come along.[387]

It was impossible to use the steep stairs leading to the cottage as they were continuously under fire. Žujović suggested making a hole in the wooden floor and lowering themselves with a rope to the bed of the stream that ran through the cave, and which turned into a small waterfall when it rained. At the time, the stream was dry and hidden from German fire. They braided silk parachute cords to make a rope that was strong enough to let them drop down nearly fifteen meters. They then turned left, climbing in the high noon heat toward the peak of the mountain. "The bed of the stream that we passed," Kardelj later recalled, "was full of rocks and was very uneven, offering good cover, but naturally we were more prudent in descending with the rope and taking the path, where we climbed up on all fours behind the bushes."[388] Because of his leg, injured since birth, Kardelj had at times to be carried piggy-back. Zdenka was in such a panic that she refused to cross the stream, in spite of Tito's curses when he tried to convince her to follow him. Finally, she listened.[389]

They had just left the cave when, at about 11:30, a new swarm of aircraft appeared. Parachutes filled the sky, but Tito's party was already safe. Crouching down, they moved from bush to bush along the slope, everyone taking a different path. Tito was so exhausted that he nearly fainted twice. Finally, everyone reached the plateau, although Kardelj and Ranković and the others were worried by the fact that Tito was the last to arrive.

They were all there. Ranković and Tito embraced with tears in their eyes. "Where are the foreign emissaries?" Tito asked. "Marko," as Ranković was known, assured him that the Russians were out of danger.[390] Meanwhile, the Partisan units, joined by the First Dalmatian Brigade, counterattacked so vigorously that the Germans found themselves in trouble. The Germans were saved from total defeat by a motorized column from Bihać that came to their aid.[391]

The German plan was evident: a combined airborne and ground assault would capture the commander in chief and then destroy the greater part of the Partisan army in the surrounding mountains. What they succeeded in getting, though, was Tito's jeep and his new marshal uniform, which was exhibited as a trophy at the arsenal in Vienna, where the young Broz had started his military service in Franz Josef's Imperial Army. The building was eventually bombed and the uniform perished in the flames.[392] They also took Randolph Churchill's and Vladimir Nazor's diaries, but that was all.[393] Hitler was furious when informed that Tito had not been captured. "It seems that the Führer is very angry and cries treason," Glaise von Horstenau wrote in his notes.[394]

Although they had escaped from Drvar, the members of the Supreme Staff were not yet safe. They made their way toward the Šar Mountains, where they met the members of the Allied missions. Since they had not been surrounded by the Germans, it was easier for them to withdraw to the plateau above the valley. The situation remained critical, for four enemy columns were heading toward Tito's refuge from different points. During the night, the Germans occupied the entire area, leaving only one path open by which the fugitives could escape the tanks of the Wehrmacht. The Russians lost their tempers, in part because one of them had been wounded and, in the resulting quarrel, General Korneev cursed Ranković, telling him that he would be held personally responsible if anything happened to the Soviet general and his mission.[395] He then demanded that he and his men be evacuated by one of the Soviet aircrafts at Bari. Ranković immediately embraced this idea and proposed that Tito go with the Russians to Italy. At first Tito would have nothing to do with this suggestion, but eventually gave in under pressure and agreed to have a call for help put through via the British radio station.[396]

What happened then, according to the Russian version of the events, is indicative of the lack of confidence they had in their Western allies. Aleksander S. Shornikov, the Soviet pilot and a famous champion who was to come to the aid of Tito and his companions, was informed by the British commander of the air base in Bari that a dispatch, allegedly sent by the Soviet mission, fixed the appointment for the night of 4–5 June. Korneev had previously told Shornikov via radio that it was supposed to be the night of 3–4 June on the field of Kupres, nearly a hundred kilometers from Drvar.[397]

Shornikov said nothing but simply informed the British commander, who was fluent in Russian as he was the son of a diplomat who had been attached to the British Embassy in Moscow, that he wanted to do a reconnaissance flight the night of 3–4 June. When permission for takeoff was granted, he left immediately and landed that same evening at the field of Kupres. This was just another sign of Soviet mistrust of the "perfidious Albion," which went back to December 1943 when Stalin, setting his sights on the Partisans, had begun alluding to a possible assassination of Tito by "foreign friends." "Do not forget," he said during his talk with Djilas, "that airplanes break up easily when in the air."[398] In February 1944, upon learning that Churchill had sent his son Randolph to Tito, he told Air Marshal Golovanov: "Consider that the sons of prime ministers are not parachuted in for nothing, and they don't go to foreign headquarters without precise goals." When the news came about the attack on Drvar, which he followed from hour to hour, he acidly commented: "I would like to know what is brewing. . . . Evidently little sons do not waste their time."[399]

The fact that the sky was full of Allied aircraft before the assault on Drvar, whereas there was no trace of them in the days around 25 May, abetted these suspicions, both his and those of the Yugoslavs, that a conspiracy was underway. Only three days later the English and American air forces took control of western Bosnia.[400] Meanwhile, in an audacious move on the night of 3–4 June, Shornikov landed from stormy skies on the improvised airstrip, demarcated by fires, where the members of the Supreme Staff and foreign missions were waiting for him. There was room for only twenty people on the small plane. In all this chaos, Tito still found time to shout to Žujović: "Crni, take care of my horse!" Žujović was not at all amused: "He worries about his horse and leaves us in this shit!"[401]

When they arrived in Bari Tito tried to avoid the British and sought hospitality in the Soviet barracks. After an animated discussion, Vlatko Velebit convinced him that he should not risk alienating the landlords and that he should take up residence in the villa assigned by them to the Yugoslav mission.[402] The fugitives were under such psychological pressure that they still suspected that the British might attempt to assassinate Tito. In reality, it was the Germans who had not given up the idea of killing him. After the failure of Operation Rösselsprung, they started to plan another operation called Theodor, this time counting on just one person, Andreas Engvird, a Nazi collaborator who had formerly fought in Spain and was a member of the Dutch Communist Party. With such a past, they figured he could easily approach Tito and eliminate him with a miniature bomb hidden in a fountain pen. Thanks to the vigilance of the Partisan secret services, which were by then well organized, this attempt also failed.[403]

The Tito-Churchill Meeting

Operation Rösselsprung was unable to destroy the bulk of Tito's army, thanks in part to the Western Allies, who launched more than a thousand air sorties against the German units in Yugoslavia from their Mediterranean bases. The price paid by the Partisans was, however, very high. The First and the Sixth Divisions, which were under particular pressure, suffered about six thousand casualties[404] while Tito and his collaborators were forced to seek refuge via Bari on the island of Vis, where they arrived on 7 June 1944. In view of the crisis of the Partisan movement, the Supreme Staff was obliged to accept the help of the British, who had transformed the Dalmatian island into a fortress. Their humiliation was such that for a long time they tried to hide Tito's flight, fearing the negative effect such news could have on the Partisan troops. The Politburo found shelter in a cave on the slopes of Hum, one of the island's highest mountains, while in the valley the British transformed the vineyards into an improvised airstrip, thus guaranteeing connections with Bari.[405] The retreat to the Dalmatian island was later explained by Kardelj in these terms: "We went to Vis because it was well fortified on the sea. . . . If we had stayed in Bosnia, we would have been subject to continuous attacks and cut off from the world for a month or two. That was the moment when the epicenter of our struggle passed into the field of foreign policy; therefore we wanted to move . . . from the embattled area, to be able to intervene directly in the international political situation surrounding us."[406] This, however, was an explanation given in hindsight.

British hospitality did not attenuate the hostility Tito and his comrades felt toward the Western Allies. The fact that the British and American missions had abandoned Drvar and sought a more secure place outside it on the eve of the German attack corroborated their worst suspicions. The British were unaware of that state of mind and were trying to exploit the "God-sent opportunity" offered by Tito's flight into their territory in order to arrange a meeting between him and Šubašić and unite the two Yugoslav camps. Although the landing in Normandy was imminent, Churchill and Eden spared no time or energy in achieving this aim.[407]

Thanks to their perseverance, but also thanks to Stalin's advice to the Yugoslavs not to refuse a dialogue with Šubašić, the latter arrived at Vis on 14 June 1944.[408] There he presented his optimistic and naïve proposals to Tito, Edvard Kardelj, Vladimir Bakarić, Ivan Ribnikar, and Josip Smodlaka, the "foreign minister" of the National Liberation Committee. He felt that the Partisan movement should recognize the royal government and participate with some of its exponents in order to create a truly representative body. First of all, Tito should replace Mihailović as minister of war. There were no Serbs at the negotiation table, which gave their nationalist supporters a chance to complain later that the meeting was an anti-Serb plot. In reality, this occasion showed the weakness of Šubašić and his Western patrons, which was further confirmed by substantial financial aid from the Soviet government, signed for by the Yugoslav military mission on 16 June 1944.[409] It was the first international treaty of the emerging state, highlighting the secondary importance of the document signed that same day on Vis concerning cooperation between the Partisans and the royal government in exile.[410] With the Tito-Šubašić agreement, the subject of much heated discussion in the weeks to come in the party circles, especially in Croatia and Slovenia, the royal government recognized the future federal organization of the state, condemned all collaboration with the occupiers, and invited all patriotic forces in Yugoslavia to unite in a common struggle.[411] Tito, however, declined to take part and allowed that only three politicians close to the Liberation movement could assume a ministerial post, but on a personal basis. More important, he stressed that the final decision on the monarchy, as decreed by the AVNOJ, would be settled after the war. In recognition of his status, he received a gift from Stalin: a new marshal's uniform similar to the Soviet counterpart, tailored according to the measurements Djilas had brought to Moscow. Even though the cap did not fit well, he nevertheless wore it proudly.[412]

Churchill, not at all happy with the Tito-Šubašić agreement, decided at that point to intervene personally. In a note sent to Eden in July 1944, he wrote that while he was certainly not going to change his policy toward Mihailović and Tito, he was determined to get something in exchange for the aid he had granted the latter. "Now, when he is secure on Vis, it is the best moment to let him know."[413] His son Randolph was more realistic. At the time, he wrote his father from Croatia: "There are two reasons why it is essential for British interests to support Marshal Tito and his Liberation movement: (a) they are the only Yugoslavs who are fighting the Germans; (b) whether we help Tito or not, after the war, he will be the master of Yugoslavia."[414]

Tito knew very well what it was that Churchill wanted: "He wanted to force us to accept the king," he said later, "the king would be like the Trojan horse, with whose help we would return, little by little, to the old system."[415] Initially, the British tried to organize a meeting between Tito and General Wilson to take place on 12 July 1944. However, two days before his departure Tito cancelled it with the excuse that his agreement with Šubašić had met with negative reactions in Yugoslavia and that the meeting could harm the liberation struggle and him personally. The British suspected that Moscow had a hand in this. They were right: Korneev counseled the marshal not to accept General Wilson's hospitality since he was only a military figure, whereas Tito was de facto head of state. In view of the British decision to reduce their aid to the Partisans as a result, shortly afterward he changed his mind, informing Maclean that he would go and meet the Allied commander in chief for the Mediterranean after all. But in the meantime, Churchill decided to see Tito himself, attracted by "this man from the people of modest origin who, thanks to his initiative, organizational skill and courage, managed to create from nothing a strong army."[416]

Tito came to the meeting, organized by the British in southern Italy, with the intention of blandishing him, hiding the revolutionary core of his movement as much as possible. It is interesting to note that Tito paid a great deal of attention to details, asking his generals on the peninsula to remove the red stripes from their trousers since they were too subversive a color. Despite this, he was not received by the "Allies" with much regard. While a cottage had been prepared for him, the members of his suite were put up in improvised quarters with a shed roof and separated one from the other by metal nets that resembled animal cages. General "Jumbo" Wilson, with his ruddy butcher-like face, treated his Yugoslav colleague with boorish arrogance. His attention wandered during their conversations, and he treated Tito as a subaltern and not as commander in chief of an Allied army. Tito managed to stay calm, reacting from time to time with a sardonic smile.[417] As Vlatko Velebit recalled, it was not only the Westerners who were responsible for this awkward atmosphere but also "our lack of trust, sometimes unjustified, our wildness and scarce education, not to mention our ignorance of social graces."[418]

The trip to Italy gave Tito the chance to meet Western personalities of the highest level for the first time, which was gratifying for him, although he was ill at ease. This is confirmed by an episode narrated by Robert Murphy, an American diplomat who became acquainted with Tito on his arrival in Caserta and immediately invited him to his villa for dinner. The marshal came in his heavy uniform, with bodyguards and with his interpreter, Olga Ninčić, daughter of the former Minister of Foreign Affairs for Kings Alexander and Petar II. The evening was hot and humid. Murphy proposed they take off their jackets, since the meeting was totally informal. "Is das erlaubt?" ("It is permitted?") asked Tito sheepishly, but was obviously happy to follow the example of his host.[419]

After talks with Wilson, Tito met General Harold Alexander, commander of the Allied forces in Italy, at Lake Bolsena. Alexander informed him that, if they occupied Trieste, the British would continue their offensive to Central Europe through Yugoslav territory. "We tried to oppose the arrival of their army in Yugoslavia," Kardelj recounted, "but Alexander insisted, stressing that he had to continue advancing toward Austria . . . and that he needed the Ljubljana-Maribor, Fiume-Zagreb corridor. . . . Following our discussions with Alexander, we concluded that the English wanted Slovenia and Croatia for themselves, and were ready to cede Bosnia and Serbia to the Russians."[420]

With these unpleasant considerations in mind, Tito decided, on 7 and 8 August, to take a tour of recently liberated Rome. His refusal to accept the

English offer of flying to the Italian capital, preferring a car with an armed escort, bears witness to how suspicious he was of his hosts. Even more than the British, however, he feared Ustaše or Chetnik émigrés and German agents, who were numerous in Rome. He even wanted to enter Saint Peter's Basilica in the company of his two heavily armed bodyguards, which Vatican security tried to prevent. A compromise was reached and the guards left their machine guns at the entrance. Tito himself was allowed to visit Saint Peter's tomb with his pistol belt. The visit was not without some minor incidents: in the basilica he was recognized by a priest who tried to approach him, apparently to show him some monuments. He was, of course, promptly blocked and sent away.[421] Despite it all, the marshal was pleasantly surprised by an enormous banner with the words "Evviva Tito" (Hurray for Tito) hung on the Coliseum. Pity though that he was not able to enjoy the delicacies of Italian cuisine; he did not dine in the hotel where he was lodged for fear of poison, eating mostly hard-boiled eggs.[422]

The meeting in Naples on 12 and 13 August between Churchill, in a light jacket, and Tito, in his "magnificent blue and gold uniform," more suitable to a Russian than a Mediterranean climate, was no more successful than those with Wilson and Alexander. The British prime minister, whose son Randolph had miraculously survived an air crash in Croatia, was emotionally stirred but also full of aristocratic irony, and not just with regard to Tito's attire and his excessive diffidence. He wrote later in his memoirs: "The Marshal, who was attended by two ferocious looking bodyguards, each carrying automatic pistols, wanted to bring them with him in case of treachery on our part. He was dissuaded from this with some difficulty, and proposed to bring them to guard him at dinner instead."[423] It seems, however, that although Tito was aware of Churchill's sarcastic attitude, he was touched by the fact that, when Churchill received him, there were tears in his eyes when he mentioned his son and said: "You are the first person from occupied Europe I have had the chance to meet." But he was also affected by Churchill's remark that he would like to come to Yugoslavia, if he were not too old and heavy to jump by parachute.[424] In spite of the skepticism of his comrades, Tito did not hide how much he appreciated Churchill's reception. Although he was not completely at ease during his debut in the highest international political circles, he did not lose his head and judiciously defended his interests. In general terms, the two agreed on a possible military collaboration in Istria in the North Adriatic Sea, which did not allay Churchill's suspicions that Tito wanted to avoid his meddling in Yugoslav affairs. In spite of the latter's assurances that he was not going to introduce Communism in Yugoslavia, his hostile attitude toward the monarchy was enough to support Churchill's worst predictions, corroborated by the Red Army's victorious advance in the Balkan and Danube area. It was clear that Stalin wanted to have a free hand in these territories, without regard to British interests. The prime minister told Tito openly that his government would oppose the confederation between Yugoslavia, Albania, and Greece that was being discussed in Moscow. His ideas concerning Yugoslav ambitions in the northern Adriatic, formally still part of Italy although occupied by the Germans, were quite clear. "He agreed that Istria should be ours, excluding Trieste," remembered Tito later. "He did not say that it would be given to the Italians, he said only that the Allies needed Trieste and Pula [an important naval base at the tip of Istrian peninsula] for their march toward Austria."[425]

The Flight from Vis

In order to propitiate Churchill, once back in Vis, on 17 August 1944, Tito published a declaration in which he wrote: "The National Liberation Movement of Yugoslavia is, in its essence, of the people, national and democratic. Therefore, I repeat again that the leadership of the National Liberation Movement has only one important goal—the struggle against the occupiers and their slaves, and the creation of a democratic and federal Yugoslavia, and not, as our enemies say, the affirmation of Communism."[426] Pressed by Churchill, King Petar II promulgated a decree at the end of August that recognized Tito as chief of the armed forces in Yugoslavia and that removed Mihailović, who rejected the decision, proclaiming that the sovereign had acted under duress, and ordered a general mobilization. This had no impact, however, in view of what was happening on the Eastern Front, where, in the two weeks between 23 August and 8 September 1944, the Red Army achieved decisive successes. At the end of August, in Romania, General Antonescu's pro-Nazi regime fell, and King Michael offered the Soviet Union and the Western Allies an armistice; a few days later, the Red Army reached Bucharest. On 5 September, the Soviet government declared war on Bulgaria, who did not even try to resist and, with a sudden volte-face, in turn declared war on Germany, yesterday's ally. In short, in fifteen days, the Red Army advanced five hundred kilometers, practically surrounding Serbia from the east and overturning the balance of power in the Balkans.[427]

In Bosnia, the Supreme Staff started to organize special divisions charged with liberating Serbia once and for all according to Tito's conviction that in order to strengthen his power, control of that region was an absolute priority: "There we have to settle the question of the structure of the state, the government in exile in London, and especially the question of the king."[428] An assault group crossed the Ibar River at the beginning of August, occupying the mountainous region of Kopaonik in central Serbia. On the twenty-fourth, the First Proletarian Division reached Zlatibor and advanced toward Užice and Požega. New brigades also formed in south Serbia and went on the offensive.[429] Heartened by this news, but mostly by the awareness that he could count on the Soviet Union, Tito expressed his belief that victory was near in a speech on 12 September 1944, after passing the First Dalmatian Brigade in review at Vis. On that occasion, he openly affirmed that Yugoslavia would not accept the northwestern frontiers that had been drawn up after 1918, but insisted upon new borders with Italy and Austria: "We don't want what belongs to others, we will not cede what is ours."[430]

He greeted the arrival of the Soviet troops on the eastern Yugoslav frontier with a manifesto, hailing "the great, long-awaited day," and making a drastic decision: he would go to Moscow, where he would coordinate the intervention of the Red Army in Serbia with Stalin, killing two birds with one stone. He would get control of those key territories for the domination of Yugoslavia and the triumph of the revolution. In this way, he would thwart the West's plan to create a Karadjordjević bulwark in Serbia.[431]

Meanwhile, the Americans, knowing that the Partisan units were blocking fifteen German divisions and at least one hundred thousand collaborationists in the Balkans, established their own autonomous contacts with the Supreme Staff in spring of 1944, cutting themselves loose from the British. Tito and William Donovan, director of the OSS, met secretly in August on the island of Capri in a friendly atmosphere as the latter too followed Churchill's decision to sever links with Mihailović.[432] Within the OSS, however, the understanding prevailed that it would be useful to maintain information groups in all the Yugoslav territories, including those under Mihailović's control. One of the reasons for this was that there were of a good number of American pilots who had participated in military actions in the skies of Bosnia and Serbia and had been shot down by the Germans but rescued by the Chetniks. Ambassador Robert Murphy and other top officials in Washington approved the implementation of this proposal. On 3 August 1944, a group of special soldiers was parachuted near the village of Pranjane, eighty kilometers from Belgrade, where Mihailović had gathered about 250 American pilots. A provisional airport was built with the help of the local population. Between 9 and 10 August the pilots were evacuated by C-47 planes, the beginning of an audacious rescue operation that continued until November. In addition, on 25 August the OSS sent another mission to the area under Mihailović's control. Their leader, Colonel Robert

McDowell, told the general that his only task was to collect military information and that his mission should not be considered in support of the Chetnik movement. Such, at least, was the official version. However, not long after his arrival, a leaflet began circulating in which Mihailović wrote: "The Allied American Government has sent [to our headquarters] delegates and personal representatives of President Roosevelt, the faithful friend of peace-loving people."[433] This was not mere propaganda, since McDowell was openly pro-Chetnik, convinced as he was that the arms sent to the Partisan communists would be used against the Serbs and, later, against the Western forces as well.[434]

When Tito was informed about this (from 1943 on, Ranković had his spies in Mihailović's General Staff) he was furious, although Donovan had informed him in advance about McDowell's mission. He ordered his units to cease their collaboration with American and British officers and to limit their freedom of movement and their intelligence activities. The British later managed to mitigate these harsh measures, but not the Americans, toward whom Tito remained very cool, considering them untrustworthy.[435] The Americans for their part did not trust him either, to which a dispatch sent by the local OSS agent from Tehran to Washington in June 1944 bears witness. Djilas, after leaving Moscow, stopped on his way home in the Iranian capital and while drunk told a group of Western officers some details about his conversations with Stalin. The Boss had confided in him that after the war he would sever his relations with the British and the Americans and that he was counting on Tito's fidelity.[436] President Roosevelt's decision not to answer two letters the marshal had sent him further aggravated matters. The latent hostility between the Yugoslavs and the Americans was eloquently expressed by William J. Donovan in a memo sent on 1 January 1945 to James V. Forrestal, the US defense secretary. In it, the chief of the OSS stated that in the future it would be necessary to spread the clandestine activity of his organization throughout Eastern Europe, considering that "those who are not with us, are against us." To give more weight to his words, he quoted a declaration by Tito published on 29 September in *The New York Times* that sounded like a prediction of imminent communist revolution in that area.[437]

It was within this framework of growing mutual suspicion between the Western and Eastern partners of the anti-Hitler coalition that Tito's trip, or rather his flight from Vis, took place. With the help of the Soviets, it was prepared in total secrecy by Ranković, head of the Service for the Defense of the People (OZNA), which had been instituted the preceding May as the Partisans' security agency. The British, who were controlling the airport, were told that Soviet pilots based in Bari had to practice nocturnal landings and that the island was the ideal place for this. They gave the necessary permission and for the next three or four nights watched the Soviet aircraft take off and land. When the Russian aviators had been sufficiently "trained," Tito left with them at three o'clock in the morning of 19 September 1944. His airplane took off without signaling, in the dark, with the head of Tito's inseparable companion, his dog Tiger, wrapped in a sack to silence his barking. Their distrust of the Allies was such that the aircraft with Tito on board was escorted by another plane that, on reaching Bosnia, flew in the opposite direction.[438] When a few days later the British realized that their illustrious guest had "levitated," to use Churchill's expression, they indignantly protested. But they had already lost control over the Yugoslav situation. As Kardelj contemptuously said: "In the end, Churchill has to continue behaving as a friend, because if he doesn't, the English would say that his politics in the Balkans was a failure. But in the meantime, the Russians are at Donji Miholjac" (a provincial town in Slavonia).[439]

To the subsequent reprimands from Fitzroy Maclean for having gone to Moscow without informing his British protectors, Tito answered defiantly: "Churchill doesn't tell me where and when to go."[440] Nor did his flight from Vis remain hidden from the Germans who, in spite of their hostile attitude toward the Partisans, commented with manifest Schadenfreude. During a meeting with his officers, Reichsführer SS Heinrich Himmler stated: "I wish to mention another example of fortitude, that of Herr Josip Broz. Unfortunately, he is our enemy. When we catch him, we will get rid of him immediately, I assure you. . . . But how I would like to have a dozen Titos in Germany. . . . He did not have anything. He was between the Russians, English and Americans, but he had the guts to make fun of the English and the Americans, and cover them with shit in a most ridiculous way. He is a Moscow man. He has never capitulated."[441]

Tito flew on a C-47, first to Marshal Fyodor I. Tolbukhin's headquarters in Craiova, Romania. He remained there for two days after a hair-raising trip, since it was necessary to fly over enemy lines. Then, on 21 September, he left for Moscow, where he was welcomed with respect. Discussions with Stalin followed, about which little is known, since they took place in private. From Tito's later revelations it is evident, however, that the two examined both military and political questions, but in a rather chilly atmosphere. "The principal reason," observed Tito, "was probably related to my telegrams during the war, especially the one that started with the words: 'If you cannot help us, don't obstruct us.' This was also confirmed by Dimitrov, whom I visited after my meeting with Stalin. Dimitrov said to me: 'Walter, Walter, the Boss was very angry because of that dispatch. . . . He was so angry that he stamped his foot on the floor.'"[442]

The Liberation of Belgrade

In spite of disagreements over the revolutionary enthusiasm of the liberation struggle, and in spite of Stalin's rudeness, "Walter" was honored in Moscow as no other foreign statesman or commander before. In fact, the Boss invited him to a meeting of the War Council, where Marshal Ivan D. Cherniakhovskii presented the offensive plans against Germany. Clearly, Stalin wanted to show him how powerful he was, but also how much he trusted him.[443]

Regarding the monarchy and the introduction of socialism in Yugoslavia, Stalin continued to preach caution, although he suggested that the king would not last long: "You need not restore him forever. Take him back temporarily; then you can stick a knife into his back at the suitable moment."[444] Tito, who in the past—to appease Churchill—had told Maclean he would be ready to accept Petar II as a pilot in his air force—which was training on a British base in Middle East—was momentarily piqued by this advice. He already saw himself as obliged to find a modus vivendi with the king. However, Stalin readily agreed to his request regarding Russian intervention in Serbia where the Red Army would enter as allies and not liberators. Their presence was, in any case, urgent in view of Hitler's order of 8 August 1944 that the Wehrmacht retreat from Greece and the Balkans through Serbia.[445] The agreement between Tito and Stalin, which also planned for an attack on Hungary from the south and was presented as a Yugoslav concession to the Soviets, was signed on 28 September and enforced immediately. As Tito wrote later, it was formulated in such a way as to let the Westerners know how they had to behave if they needed Yugoslav territory for their military operations. The agreement stated that the National Liberation Committees should continue to exist in the areas occupied by the Red Army, preserving control over the territory for the Partisan authorities. This decision was of great political value, with Moscow recognizing the administrative structure created by AVNOJ as a legitimate and sovereign interlocutor. "Now," Rodoljub Čolaković, the leading Bosnian Communist, wrote in his diary, "no Allied Army will be able to come to our country without the previous permission of the National Committee, if it wishes to continue being an ally."[446]

In order to coordinate the operation in which Bulgarian troops were also to take part at Stalin's request, on 5 October Tito returned to Craiova, where he remained until mid-month, while the Red Army was quickly advancing through Vojvodina in the direction of Belgrade. Some forty to fifty thousand Partisans were also moving in the same direction. In a bold move, Tito had thrown them into the jaws of the German forces so that they would fight side-by-side with the Russians and prevent their contact with the Chetniks, who were eager to welcome them with red flags.[447] On the eve of the final assault on the capital, he tried to convince Marshal Tolbukhin, commander in chief of the Third Ukraine Front, to allow his men to enter the city first. But Tolbukhin, who had lost 25,000 of his 414,000 soldiers in the battles for the liberation of Serbia, refused, only allowing the Partisans to climb on his tanks and enter Belgrade in this way on 20 October 1944, after six days of intense fighting. The event was celebrated in Moscow with a salvo of cannon fire. Five days later, Tito arrived in the capital aboard a small Soviet military boat.[448]

The intervention of the Red Army in Serbia radically changed the strategic situation in the Balkans, giving the Partisans the chance to confront the Germans and their allies as equals during the last battles for the liberation of Yugoslavia. Stalin contributed by providing the Yugoslav army with weapons and dispatching a group of experts who helped to organize a strong artillery and good aviation and tank units.[449]

In the dispatch he sent to the soldiers of the Third Ukrainian Front on the occasion of the liberation of Belgrade, Tito wrote: "Your blood and the blood of the combatants of the Yugoslav National Liberation Army, spilled in a common struggle against the enemy, will cement forever the brotherhood of the Yugoslav peoples with the peoples of the Soviet Union."[450] The reality behind this heavily pan-Slavic rhetoric was, however, quite different. The tensions that soon emerged between the Soviets and the Yugoslavs were not so much due to a question of prestige, but to the behavior of Tolbukhin's men. They considered Serbia a conquered territory, looting, killing civilians, and raping women. The worst episode took place in a suburb of Belgrade, where a Serb engineer invited a group of Russian soldiers to dinner. When they got drunk, one of them, a major, began molesting the wife of their host, mother of several children. Her husband tried to protect her, but was shut up in the bathroom while the woman was raped by seven soldiers. After this, the husband and wife hanged themselves. The event provoked a rush of indignation in Belgrade, forcing Tito to protest officially to General Korneev, who answered abruptly: "In the name of the Soviet government, I protest against such insinuations related to the Red Army." "The fact is," commented Djilas, who was present at the meeting, "that our enemies try to exploit similar incidents in their favor. They make unfavorable comparisons between the correct behavior of the British liaison officers attached to the Partisan forces, and the excesses of the Red Army."[451] At the end of October Tito brought up the question in a very bland letter to Stalin, stressing that this was his duty as a communist. He added that the Red Army was violating the agreements, according to which it promised to give the National Liberation Army all the booty taken in Belgrade. Of the five hundred trucks requisitioned, it had received only six. In addition, he asked for several thousand trucks for his army and provisions for the hungry cities. All Tito got back was a rude reply, in which Stalin maintained that there had been no agreement about "trophies," expressing surprise "that a few incidents and offences committed by individual officers and soldiers of the Red Army in Yugoslavia are generalized and extended to the whole of the Red Army."[452] From then on, his attitude toward Yugoslavia and the Partisan movement cooled markedly, as the offensive remarks he often repeated during subsequent meetings with its leaders showed: "Your combatants fight badly. They do not smell of gunpowder. Look at the Bulgarians, this is really an army in formation!"[453] In spite of the efforts of the Soviet commanders to hold their men at bay, the acts of violence toward the civilian population continued, as seen in a report sent from Belgrade by an American officer, a member of the OSS, at the end of December 1944, which reached President Roosevelt himself.[454]

But these quarrels could not dampen an alliance that had allowed the Partisans to be victorious over the Germans, their Serb collaborators, and the Chetniks, the most dangerous of all enemies. When the Russians entered Serbia, Mihailović had hoped to cooperate with them, sending appropriate orders to his units. In fact, during the war he was in constant contact with Moscow, which was also interested in engaging with his movement. According to his own testimony, this lasted until April 1945. The Russians were ready to accept his help during the fighting but as soon as it stopped they had no qualms about arresting the Chetniks and handing them over to Tito or deporting them to the Soviet Union. Given the situation, Mihailović could do nothing but withdraw with his remaining troops to Bosnia and the Sandžak, abandoning Serbia to the Partisans.[455] They lost no time in organizing and strengthening their power, with Soviet assistance, not only in Serbia but in the whole of the country. Local groups that had expressed their resistance autonomously during the struggle—particularly the Slovenes and Croats—had a heavy cloak of conformity thrown over them in order to connect them even more closely to the central power. Soviet "instructors" were sent, to quote a letter by Tito to Ranković, from "up there" tasked with coordinating the work of OZNA. It is difficult to escape the impression that Stalin was preaching a policy his men were not following in practice. He kept repeating to Kardelj, for instance, that "the Yugoslavs should absolutely not try revolutionary experiments and ape the Soviet regime" yet, in the meantime, his agents were teaching the Yugoslav comrades precisely that.[456] How useful this advice was is attested to by the success of the secret police in those areas where the new "people's" regime succeeded in installing itself. The first notable results were visible in Banat, the historic region between Serbia, Hungary, and Romania, where the local German ethnic minority was punished because of its mass adherence to Nazism during the war. Those among the

"*Schwaben*" (Swabians) who did not escape in the convoys organized by the SS were slaughtered, deported to the Soviet Union, or shut up in concentration camps and later, if they survived, expelled from the country. This ruthless reprisal was initially led by Tito himself, as shown by a dispatch to one of his generals: "Send me immediately . . . one of the best divisions, possibly Krajina's. I need it to purge Vršac of its German population. . . . Keep this order secret."[457] The same treatment would also have been applied to the Hungarian minority which had stained itself abundantly with Serb blood during the war, had Stalin not intervened in its favor, affirming that in any case Hungary would be socialist and that it was, therefore, not acceptable to poison mutual relations.[458] In subsequent years the authorities began to transfer populations from the mountainous areas of central Bosnia to the fertile plains cleared of the *Schwaben*. These populations had collaborated in great number in the Partisan struggle and, after the war, were strongly represented among Tito's officers. The initiative did not yield the expected results. A great deal of tension resulted from these migrations, as people with different traditions and mentalities now suddenly lived in the same area.[459]

It is difficult to say whether "the purge of foreign elements" that took place in Vojvodina could be considered the moment that the National Liberation Struggle transformed into the "revolution from above," to quote Stalin, referring to social change implemented by communist leaders, not the masses. The majority of this took place in the days following the conquest of Belgrade, where the Partisan troops entered with orders to shoot all of Nedić's followers on the spot.[460] The OZNA did not miss the chance for merciless revenge against the "enemies of the people" and collaborators, true or supposed, who during the war had hunted down the communists to the point that not a single "comrade" could be found when the Partisans entered the city. "It will never be known," wrote Pero Simić, "how many thousands [of people] in Serbia, Slovenia, Bosnia-Herzegovina and in other parts of Yugoslavia disappeared in the purges. There were twenty concentration and death camps in Belgrade alone."[461] Even worse was the situation in Kosovo, where the Albanians tried to oppose the "liberators" with arms. The popular uprising they organized was so successful that, in February 1945, Tito was obliged to proclaim a state of war in the province. About twelve hundred members of Balli Kombëtar, the nationalist, anti-Communist organization, joined by one thousand deserters, barricaded themselves in a mountain village, which was surrounded by the Forty-Second Army Division and completely destroyed. Stalin approved this policy although, at the same time, he asked Tito for amnesty for the Chetniks.[462]

The liberation of Belgrade, of northwestern Serbia, and of eastern Srem and Vojvodina made it possible to mobilize young men from the newly conquered territory into large military units. Previously, the divisions of the Yugoslav Army had some three thousand combatants each, but they now numbered ten thousand. It was therefore possible to create a broad front running from Kraljevo, Čačak, Užice, along the Drina, the Drava, and the Danube rivers, up to the Hungarian border and beyond, where Soviet and Bulgarian forces were sent. From a tactical point of view, the front was compact only in the Srem region, where heavy battles were fought with the Wehrmacht, which was withdrawing from the Balkans with eight hundred thousand men, together with three hundred thousand collaborationists. The Serb recruits, who had never before held a gun, were not trained to face such an avalanche of highly efficient men, even though it was clear that the fall of the Third Reich was near. Tito decided to resist the German withdrawal more for political than for military reasons, eager to show that he had a regular army at his disposal. The result was a slaughter never forgotten nor forgiven by the Serbs. The "butchery of the Serb youth,"[463] during which thirty-seven thousand young soldiers lost their lives in the course of 175 days, was described in a poignant passage by Gojko Nikoliš in his memoirs: "From the window of my office, between Nemanja and General Ždanov streets, I am observing lines of peasants with coffins on their shoulders. The old men and grandfathers are going to find their nephews and sons, brothers and brothers-in-law. They dig them up in the cemeteries of Srem around Vinkovci, Djakovo, Požega, Čazma. . . . Some of them are going up the Nemanja, others are returning. The coffins of galvanized tin are whitish on the shoulders of the old curved men. So for entire days, months, two years."[464]

~

Collaborationists in every region of Yugoslavia followed the events on the Eastern front as an announcement of the coming *Götterdämmerung*. In Slovenia, where in autumn 1944 there were eighteen thousand Domobranci (collaborationist Home Guards), who had been used by the SS as auxiliary troops, the collective feeling of defeat was eloquently expressed by a priest who, celebrating the funeral of a group of the fallen on 6 October, declared: "For the Slovenian people, it is better to die heroically than to live under the communist curse."[465] In the Independent State of Croatia, some leaders of the ruling regime had contacted the representatives of the Croat Peasant Party during the summer, hoping to save themselves with their aid. The plan was that they would stage a putsch to rid themselves of the Ustaše thugs and ally the Domobrani (members of the regular army) with the Chetniks, hoping that, in the meantime, the English and Americans would have landed in Dalmatia, saving them from communism. With the help of the Gestapo, Ante Pavelić reacted promptly and arrested the conspirators on 30 August 1944, which failed to bring the general discouragement that was spreading among his followers to a halt. When on 31 August and again on 22 November 1944 Tito proclaimed an amnesty for all collaborationists who had not committed war crimes, inviting them to join the Partisans, the Croat Domobrani (but not the Slovenian Domobranci and the Chetniks) began deserting en masse.[466]

The Tolstoy Conference and the Tito-Šubašić Agreement

While the conquest of Serbia was in full swing, a diplomatic struggle was raging in Moscow. The so-called Tolstoy Conference, attended by Stalin and Churchill, was held there from 9 to 18 October 1944. Churchill arrived in the Soviet capital fully aware of his weakness in the Balkan and Danube area.[467] As Harold Macmillan, the British minister resident in the Mediterranean, put it, "We cannot hide from ourselves that our military strategy, by concentrating all our efforts on the west of Europe, has deprived us of effective power in Romania, Bulgaria, Yugoslavia, Albania, Greece and hardly gives us sufficient strength to finish the Italian campaign. We must certainly do all we can by bluff, but it is no good using bluff so transparently that it is easily called."[468]

The deal Churchill proposed to Stalin with regard to the respective spheres of influence in the Balkans and in the Danube valley (for Yugoslavia, they would divide the country fifty-fifty, each controlling half) was just such a bluff.[469] The British prime minister was offering the Soviet dictator land that the Red Army had already conquered, or had at arm's reach, and asking for political influence in territories where—aside from Greece—British troops were not present. Stalin, not wanting to unnecessarily compromise his relations with the West, accepted this proposal, in accordance to his assertion to Churchill that he did not aim to carry out a Bolshevik revolution in Eastern Europe.[470] The Moscow "naughty document" had little influence on the development of events, however, and left few traces in the memory of British diplomats, considering that four years later no one at the Foreign Office could remember exactly what its terms were. The same cannot be said of the Yugoslavs. They were already beginning to suspect that something odd was going on behind the scenes by the end of April or beginning of May 1944, when in a moment of rage Randolph Churchill mentioned the division of spheres of influence between his father and "Uncle Joe."[471] The next November when Stalin himself confided to Kardelj the terms of the fifty-fifty agreement, the Yugoslav were furious, realizing they were the object of a bargain between the Great Powers. For many years they maintained the impression that the Big Three were forging secret pacts between them, detrimental to Yugoslav interests, and often quoted the fifty-fifty agreement as clear proof of the greed of the Great Powers, both east and west. The British, for their part, could not forget Tito's rude behavior on the occasion of his escape from Vis, despite the favorable development of the Moscow Conference. Their foreign minister, Anthony Eden, complained about this treacherous flight to Molotov, who tried to calm him down: "Tito is a peasant, who does not understand politics and loves secrecy. Therefore he does not inform anybody about his plans."[472]

~

The day the Tolstoy Conference began in Moscow, Tito sent a dispatch to Šubašić, inviting him to return home and form a common government. He decided to do this after nearly two months of hesitation, when he was finally sure of his position and knew that the Soviets would not approve of any further deterioration of his relations with the West. As soon as the negotiation between the two started, the question of the role the king should play in the formation of the government arose, since according to the law he was the one to name the prime minister. Tito, undoubtedly entitled to this office, was not prepared to accept it from his hands. Finally Velebit suggested a solution: during his residence abroad, Petar II would transmit his powers to a regency composed of three dignitaries. After complex discussions, on 1 November 1944, Tito and Šubašić signed a document that stated that the regents would be named by the king, but with the approval of the AVNOJ. This solution, and a solemn declaration that political pluralism would be respected in Yugoslavia, would give the new government the international recognition that was urgently needed as the end of the war was approaching. Once the agreement was reached, however, it was necessary to get the assent of the king and the Allied powers. This was not an easy task, considering that at the end of 1944 relations between Belgrade and London were deteriorating by the day.[473] The Soviets were not satisfied either, as they were concerned about the British reaction, since it was evident that the Tito-Šubašić agreement was a further blow against the monarchy. In order to soothe Churchill, they invited both Tito and Šubašić to Moscow at the end of November, hoping to restore the balance of forces in favor of Petar II.[474] The marshal was prudent enough to decline the invitation, sending Edvard Kardelj in his place. Although the latter was compelled to hear insults and scorn from the angry Boss, Tito did not renounce his proposal to transform Yugoslavia into a "Bolshevik" state. At home, he felt strong. "At the end of the war," he said later, "we had enormous revolutionary support, the class enemies were completely impotent. . . . It was so because we had a strong revolutionary base, never seen before in the whole world."[475] This attitude was why he was not ready to accept the Churchill-Stalin deal regarding their mutual influence in his country. When Stalin mentioned the fifty-fifty agreement to Kardelj and Šubašić, he added: "It means that we cannot do anything without them, and they cannot do anything without us." "This was for us a further admonition," commented Kardelj, "that we had to be independent in our decisions."[476]

~

In this difficult situation, the British once more dusted off their plan to land in the Balkans, a plan on which Churchill had been working hard for the past two years without being able to implement. The same thing happened this time, but the Yugoslavs were highly alarmed, especially because British troops sent to Greece at the beginning of October clashed on 3 December 1944 with the local Communist resistance in order to assure the return to the throne of King George II, the Hellenic monarch who, like Petar II, lived in exile under British tutelage during the war. Unlike Stalin, who followed an extremely prudent policy, Tito encouraged the Greek left to continue fighting and promised them military assistance.[477] In Belgrade, the bloody events in Athens strengthened the suspicion that Churchill was preparing a similar coup in Yugoslavia, repeating the imperialist attempt to suffocate the Bolshevik revolution in Russia after the First World War.[478]

King Petar II tried to take advantage of the growing crisis between the British and Tito, refusing to renounce to his sovereign rights. Churchill, however, with his conservative Tory royalism, although convinced he had nursed "a viper in his bosom," was realistic enough to understand that the only possibility to save at least a trace of the monarchy in Yugoslavia was to accept the regents.[479] It took the stubborn monarch two months to capitulate—because of his obstructionism, the regents were not named until 2 March 1945. At the Conference of Yalta, organized between 4 and 12 February, however, Stalin, Roosevelt, and Churchill decided that the Tito-Šubašić agreement should be implemented in Yugoslavia and that—pending the Constitutional Assembly—a provisional Parliament should be installed, composed of the members of the AVNOJ and those deputies who had been elected before the war and who had not compromised themselves by collaborating with the enemy.[480]

This decision was an attempt to strengthen the bourgeois forces who were foreign if not hostile to the resistance and Tito declared it to be "a real crime against Yugoslavia."[481] His anger was directed more against the Soviets than the British and the Americans, since he reproached them for having been too subservient to Roosevelt and Churchill and having neglected to inform him in advance about their Yalta deliberations. With the fourth-strongest army in Europe (eight hundred thousand men) at his disposal, he was increasingly confident of his importance, going so far as to offer the Allies a task force in their final assault on Berlin in order to be among the great victors.[482] This was why he protested officially to the new chief of the Soviet military mission, General K. V. Kiselev, stressing that from now on his attitude toward *all* the Allies would be the same. The rift deepened even further in March 1945, when the marshal constituted his provisional government. In addition to Šubašić, who was nominated minister of foreign affairs, among its thirty members there was also Milan Grol, leader of the Serb Democratic Party. According to Kardelj, he was "an autonomous and prestigious man, but a reactionary who did not agree with us on practically anything."[483] Tito included him in his cabinet in order to show his independence to Stalin and to satisfy Churchill. The Soviets, informed by the British about this surprising nomination, were furious as they had expected their candidate, the former royal ambassador in Moscow, Stanoje Simić, to be appointed instead. Aside from this, they considered the solemn declaration that the new government addressed to the international community to be "very wishy-washy." In a top secret letter sent on 11 March 1945 to Tito, Kardelj, and Hebrang, they observed that there was no mention in this document of the collaboration between the Slavic countries and no expression of gratitude toward the Soviet Union for the liberation of Serbia. The letter continued, "This silence cannot be helpful to democratic Yugoslavia." According to the Soviet government, these omissions were due "to pressure by Šubašić and Grol who, from the very beginning, had negatively influenced the line taken by democratic Yugoslavia."[484] Tito answered that the nomination of Grol was dictated with the conviction that his presence would tame "the reactionary Serb bloc," stressing that without such a decision the Westerners "would never recognize the new government." Even so, the incident preoccupied him considerably, as shown by a dispatch sent to Dimitrov and intercepted by the British. In it, he anxiously asked: "What is my relation with Filipov like?"[485]

Filipov, alias Stalin, reacted immediately in his brusque manner, answering that he did not agree with Tito's explanation. The same day, on 15 March 1945, the new premier hurriedly convened the Politburo members who made amends for their errors in a letter, promising that from now on they would ask Moscow for advice on everything, since Yugoslavia had only one choice: "to proceed in accordance with the Soviet Union and under its direction."[486] In spite of their humble repentance, a new incident soon followed: Tito organized a reception for the ambassadors of Great Britain and the United States, who had just arrived in Belgrade. The place of honor was given to the king of England's envoy, although Stalin's representative, Ivan V. Sadchikov, had arrived in Yugoslavia before him and according to protocol should have had precedence. Again, sounds of protest could be heard from the Kremlin.[487]

Churchill knew nothing of these disagreements. Convinced he had lost out in Yugoslavia, he quickly adapted his policy to the new situation. In a note sent to Eden on 11 March 1945, he wrote that from then on he would leave Tito to stew in his "bitter" Balkan sauce, and would turn his attentions to Italy in order to preserve it "from the Communist plague."[488] He had in mind, first of all, the strong Italian Communist Party in the north, and the danger of a territorial union between it and the CPY in the Julian March, the contested region at the head of the Adriatic. Tormented by this not at all groundless suspicion, he observed with worry the territorial demands of the new Yugoslavia in that ethnically mixed area, including Trieste, where the Slovenian Liberation Front had begun organizing a strong resistance movement in 1942. He was aware that, in such a contested territory, it was necessary to prevent any immediate contact between the Italian partisans and Tito's forces.[489]

While the threat of a serious conflict with the Western Allies had already appeared on the horizon and relations with Moscow were not at all idyllic, the main body of the Yugoslav troops was still fighting the forces of General Löhr, which were trying desperately to reach the Austrian border and surrender to the English. The last struggles took place in Southern Carinthia in mid-May, although peace had already reigned for a week in other parts of Europe. On 15 May the Third Army, under the command of General Kosta Nadj, succeeded in taking prisoner more than three hundred thousand soldiers—among them twelve Ustaša generals and Montenegrin Chetnik leaders—and about twenty thousand civilian fugitives.[490] The national liberation struggle was finished, but the civil war continued nearly everywhere in Yugoslav territory over the course of the following months and years, until all of the groups who resisted the victorious communist regime were completely liquidated.[491] Although its adversaries were mostly routed by 1947, the ethnic and ideological feuds sown before the war and sharpened in the course of the conflict would continue to smolder among the Yugoslav people, in spite of the official propaganda that celebrated the nearly mystical unity of the new state: "We are Tito's, Tito is ours!"[492]

Victory

Arriving in Belgrade on 27 October 1944, Tito immediately visited the royal palaces on Dedinje Hill on the right bank of Sava River, and ordered their restoration. This was a symbolic act, signaling the arrival of a new, revolutionary power. In fact, as Dušan Bilandžić wrote, the new proprietor, who installed himself in what was once the residence of the Karadjordjević dynasty, was a "shepherd" from Zagorje who was viewed with horror by more than just the Serb bourgeoisie.[493]

The royal residences were more neglected than ruined, with furnishings and interior decorations still intact. Tito chose the White Palace for himself, built by Prince Paul in a neoclassical style, but also kept the Old Palace, where King Aleksandar had lived, and the Aćević family's still-incomplete villa at 15 Romunska Street (later called Užička Street, in memory of the town where Tito had first tasted power). The Old Palace was reserved for important visitors and heads of state, while the White Palace was for work, and the villa, where prior to the liberation the German commander of Belgrade lived, served as a private residence. Later, Tito annexed still more properties in the neighborhood, creating a large, walled compound. He soon set to work on the residences at Dedinje, which swiftly become his principal dwellings in Belgrade. In the courtyard of the White Palace he erected a bronze statue of the horse he had ridden in the war and, alongside it he put a statue of Ivo Lola Ribar.[494] Although technically Tito had no right to these buildings—he was not president, just prime minister—he acted with such self-assurance that neither the regents nor the later president of the federal parliament (old father Ribar, who was also formally head of state) put up any resistance. Tito celebrated New Year's Eve 1945 as if the war had already been won, with an extravagant party at the White Palace. For the first time his comrades saw him dancing with ladies, most of whom had grenades or revolvers in their belts. The only bitter note came in the form of an anonymous greeting card from a monarchist bearing the insulting words: "How does it feel to be on foreign soil?"[495]

Tito finally abandoned Paul Karadjordjević's palace and never lived in it with any regularity, using it just as his office. He did not, however, hesitate to claim the spoils of the old rulers. When chests filled with gold and other precious objects were found in a basement, Tito used his skill as a former mechanic to easily crack them open by hand. His bodyguard, General Moma Djurić, suggested the riches be transferred to the National Bank, saying, "We don't need them." "Eh, Djurić, steady on—we'll have this, too," came Tito's reply.[496] He was forgetting his own words, published in the *Proleter* in May 1939: "The public work of a party member can't differ from his private life. For communists, this is crucial in winning the confidence of the masses."[497]

Tito: Hunter and Bon Vivant

The requisition of royal residences was not confined to Belgrade: Tito also took possession of other manors, castles, and hunting lodges used by the Karadjordjevićes before the war. He was generous to his collaborators, who were allowed to grab foreign properties and were often invited to parties, films, and billiard games, but mostly to go hunting. Before the war, Tito and his friends did not hunt, but after the war it became an obsession and an opportunity for "comrades" to reinforce their bond as part of the ruling elite. It became a ritual, with rigid rules: each member of the *nomenklatura* knew exactly when and what he or she could shoot, according to their importance. Only Tito could hunt as he pleased.[498]

Tito was a passionate hunter, proud of every kill. At the end of 1953, when the tension surrounding the international situation of Yugoslavia was at its peak because of the Trieste crisis, and Djilas had started to rebel, Tito was at Brdo Castle, suffering from rheumatism, but nonetheless obsessed by an enormous ibex in the Julian Alps. When informed that the beast had been spotted, he set out immediately to shoot it. Later, one of his guards wrote, "All through his stay in Slovenia, Tito waited for snow and for this news. He waited at least four years for that kill."[499] Toward the end of his life, in April 1974, he shot a bear whose skin was awarded First Prize by an international commission, which left Tito thrilled. When, on another occasion during a hunting party in the Carpathian Mountains, the Romanian dictator Nicolae Ceaușescu shot a bigger bear than the one Tito had shot, he was furious, muttering, "I would never do that to a guest!"[500]

Over time, more and more estates were requisitioned from prewar grandees. Since, unlike Lenin and Stalin, Tito had no authority in the area of Marxist doctrine, much of his aura as a leader was created by these shows of power and by the luxury of his lifestyle. Tito simply had an innate weakness for trinkets and possessions, and he could not hide it. In this amassing of goods and property, he was ably assisted by Ivan Krajačić, a.k.a. Stevo, a former NKVD agent who had similar tastes. Stevo's letters to Tito after the victory are revealing: "Dear Old One, I send you three belts and a golden snuffbox, but also two necklaces. You will be able to bring them as gifts when you go 'up there' [to Moscow]. The experts say this grey cloth is excellent, and I send three meters of it for a trench coat." And: "I send you also two golden cigarette boxes: one for a table, the other pocket-sized. The bigger one, in my opinion, would look handsome on your nightstand."[501] Tito "inherited" an armored Mercedes from either Ante Pavelić or General Löhr, was given cars by Stalin and Nikita Khrushchev, as well as by the Republic of Slovenia, which presented him with a Rolls-Royce, to mention just some of the vehicles in his possession. He had a plane, offered by the Soviets, a yacht called the *Galeb* (seagull), King Aleksandar's sailing boat, and an enormous collection of paintings, statues, carpets, and other artworks. The opulence of his life, like that of a Habsburg archduke, also changed Tito's appearance. During the war he looked like a bird of prey with his bony face and lean body. In the postwar period he quickly gained weight and came to resemble an avuncular godfather. "From a distance," wrote the Croat diplomat Bogdan Radica, who defected to the West, "he looks a good deal like [prewar Yugoslav premier Milan] Stojadinović. In Belgrade they call him Göring; in Zagreb, Titler."[502]

At first, Tito's salary was modest—mostly symbolic—in part because no one controlled how much the "court" (or *marshalat*, as it was called) spent. Not until in 1952, three weeks before his election to the presidency of the republic, did the Welfare Office finally formalize his work status. Taking into account the effective years of his employment, including his years of clandestine work and the war years, it recognized him as active from 26 May 1908 until 7 March 1945: a total of thirty-six years, nine months, and thirteen days. Article 220 of the Constitution of 1963, which was dedicated to the president of the republic, awarded him a generous forty thousand dinars per month, tax-free, for his work. Two years later, the Federal Assembly increased this sum to an enormous 550,000 dinars, which was again doubled very soon thereafter. From 1 January 1967 he received a further ten thousand dinars per month for entertainment expenses; a sum that was augmented by an extra thousand dinars monthly. As commander in chief he was also paid ten thousand dinars per month and, from 1956, the Municipal Provisions Office paid him a supplement for his two nephews, sons of Alexsander Broz, whom he raised in his home.[503]

For the building and maintenance of his residences, security, travel at home and abroad, and "other" expenses, there was a special fund financed by the state. The General Secreteriat, which paid the salaries of Tito and his staff, had no control over these expenses; they were managed by a Serb from Lika, General Milan Žeželj, a "people's hero" and commander of the guards who was twice wounded during the war and who, according to Louis Adamic, "worshiped" Tito.[504] Tito cost the state much more than King Aleksandar, who had had the most expensive civil list in the world aside from the emperor of Japan. Vladimir Popović, who in the early sixties oversaw Tito's expenses, stressed that the daily cost of his court amounted to more than a billion dinars.[505] In short: Tito loved luxury. The insignia on his cap was of pure gold, as were the objects on his desk. He wore a ring set with a five-carat diamond, and by way of explanation claimed he had bought it in Moscow before the war, in case its value should come in handy. In fact, as Djilas wrote, he lost that Moscow-bought ring during Operation Schwarz, having grown too thin for it to stay on his finger. The ring he wore after the war, and which was visible on the cover of *Life* magazine when his biography was published, had nothing to do with that "investment." He received it, at his request, as a gift from the Soviet government in the spring of 1946.[506]

Tito ordered himself a new marshal's uniform, working with a team of stylists to choose the most apt decorations. He wore it when he met his officers, but also on occasions when he wanted to cultivate army loyalty. When Vladimir Dedijer asked him why he was so fascinated with uniforms, he replied tartly that he would not wear them at all if Yugoslavs were intellectuals: "But, unluckily enough, they are mostly peasants, and you know how the cult of the uniform is widespread in the countryside. Every peasant dreams his son will be a public servant, especially one that can wear a uniform."[507] Tito changed his clothes three or four times a day, and sunbathed regularly to preserve his tan. Once in power he had dental work to fix his teeth, and at the end of the fifties he started to dye his hair, to the surprise of his admirers.

He also shook hands in a peculiar way, barely lifting his hand, so that others were obliged, spontaneously, to bow. As Savka Dabčević-Kučar observed, nobody could more clearly show you your place—with a mere glance or while shaking your hand in greeting—than Tito could. He was like this even with his more intimate colleagues, such as Bakarić and Kardelj.[508] "He communicated not just with words," Dabčević-Kučar noted, "but also with his facial expressions, his speech, his look, but mostly in the way he carried himself."[509] Not for a moment did he cease to be the secretary general of the party, the president of the republic, and the marshal, wrote Dobrica Ćosić.[510] From the Karadjordjevićes he inherited the tradition of becoming godfather to every ninth child born in a family, and at the racecourses, horses started appearing "from the Marshal's stables."[511] He persisted in the role of godfather for almost twenty years, but soon abandoned breeding horses: confidential reports he received from the secret police about his popularity perhaps alerted him to the fact that his showing off had gone too far. "The tendency towards excessive vulgar display shown by the more highly placed members of the regime is one of their least endearing characteristics," wrote the American consul in Zagreb in the mid-sixties. "The gap between the theory and practice of communism in this respect is perhaps resented more by the general public than any other aspect of the social system."[512] The situation was particularly repellent during the first years after the war, when the authorities introduced meager bonuses for food and clothing for the majority of the population, allowing a lucky few to obtain goods from special "diplomatic shops" that in the past they could only have dreamed of. In May 1944, for instance, Edvard Kardelj longed simply for a fountain pen, which was unobtainable in the woods. One year later, as one of the strongmen of the new regime, he was in a position to ask for much more.[513]

Tito was often away from Belgrade and regularly stayed near Lake Bled in Slovenia, where he passed the summer months to escape the oppressive heat of the capital. From 1947, however, his favorite residence was on the Istrian archipelago of Brioni, where he occupied the villas of the Habsburg and Italian aristocracy. At first he settled in the villa of the duke of Spoleto (later ceded to Kardelj when he decided to build another one that was better equipped for large receptions). He ordered the afforestation of the islands, transforming them—as the ambassador of the Federal Republic of Germany wrote in the early seventies—"from a modest property to their present form, bringing to mind the country estate of a Roman Emperor."[514] On seven hundred hectares, where about two hundred deer roamed, he built a luxurious hotel and a series of bungalows for prominent Yugoslav leaders and foreign guests. Royalty and film stars were among these guests, including Orson Welles, Sophia Loren, Gina Lollobrigida, Elizabeth Taylor, Richard Burton, and Yul Brynner. Tito had the beaches groomed, and even organized a private zoo for the exotic animals he received as gifts from Asian and African state presidents. On the islet of Vanga he built a personal cottage, where he liked to develop photos and produce wine, but where he mostly tinkered with carpentry or mechanics (he remained proud of his grasp of machines and engines). Of course he had a well-stocked cellar, where he liked to entertain his guests and—on occasion, for the most important visitors—find a bottle of wine from their birth year.[515]

According to a British ambassador, Brioni was thus transformed into an amalgam of Arcadia and the London Zoo.[516] During the years of Tito's rule, thousands of people worked for him, or protected him, in this artificial paradise. As one of his private doctors wrote, no contemporary monarch lived so lavishly. Some of the construction at Brioni was even carried out by prisoners of war; a fact that did not disturb Tito in the least: "Throughout history, all great things have been made by slaves."[517]

The "revolutionaries" of Tito's entourage did not oppose his extravagance, partly because they themselves quickly adjusted to the trappings of power, and partly out of fear of offending him. They too seized villas and riches formerly belonging to "enemies of the people," enjoying the good life as if they were making up for lost time. Later, they built more luxurious residences with the excuse that they were needed by Tito and had the army maintain them; in truth, they were for their own use. "They had all been voluntary servants of the party and its ideology," wrote Djilas, "and they were all alienated and powerless outside that clique: outside the power, the Utopia."[518] The population at large was mostly unaware of the opulence in which the leaders lived. But on one occasion, at the end of the sixties, when a film was shown on Tito's everyday life at Brioni, including his zoo, the general comment was that there "the animals are better cared for than this country's workers."[519]

3

The Postwar Period

Consolidation of Power and Confrontation with Stalin

1945–1953

During the final military operations of May 1945, Yugoslav armed forces captured 125,000 collaborators and 280,000 German soldiers, making a concerted effort to prevent Gestapo members from escaping.[1] Toward the end of 1944, Tito had twice promised amnesty to all collaborators who had fought with the Nazis but had not participated in war crimes if they agreed to join the Partisans. After his agreement with Šubašić, numerous Domobrani seized that opportunity, deserting the regular army of the Independent State of Croatia. However, as Šubašić had no influence in Serbia and Slovenia, Chetniks and other right-wing groups such as the Slovenian Domobranci failed to follow their example.[2] On 14 May 1945, Tito issued an order prohibiting the killing of prisoners, while those suspected of war crimes were to be put before military tribunals to be organized by both the Slovene and Croatian General Staffs. As early as 18 May, however, he abolished the autonomy of these bodies, annexing their units to the Yugoslav Army and thus putting them under his direct control: a decision informed partly by the threat of an armed conflict with the British and Americans on the Western borders, but accepted reluctantly, especially in Slovenia, where the population was very proud of its army.[3]

When, on 1 May 1945, Partisan forces liberated and occupied Trieste and Gorizia, with their mixed Italian and Slovene population, serious tensions arose between Belgrade and the Allies. The Allies demanded an unconditional Partisan withdrawal from this strategically important area in the north Adriatic, which Italy had annexed after the First World War after a dire diplomatic dispute with the newly created Yugoslav Kingdom. In order to strengthen their position in Italy and show that they would not allow "Communists" to "grab land" at their pleasure, the Americans and the British were ready to use force against Tito's units and to march all the way to Ljubljana, if necessary. The level of threat felt by Yugoslav leaders because of this sudden quarrel only confirmed their conviction that captured collaborators should not be treated as prisoners of war, but should be "liquidated" as soon as possible, since it was feared that they could switch sides and ally themselves with the Westerners in case of an armed clash. Approximately thirty thousand collaborators managed to make their way to southern Carinthia, hoping to find shelter with the British who occupied the region. But the British felt no mercy for the former vassals of Hitler despite their tensions with Tito and tricked them, saying they would be sent to safety in Italy, when in fact they were returned home, although it would have been difficult not to imagine the fate awaiting them there.[4] The massacre that followed was discussed several times in Tito's inner circle, including at a Belgrade meeting of the heads of OZNA chaired by Ranković in late December 1944. On that occasion they decided that all members of the Quisling units would be executed by special Partisan detachments, a decision most likely confirmed in Zagreb at a top-secret meeting between Tito and the senior army commanders who were reviewing military strategy.[5] When the British began to return prisoners in the second half of May 1945, a colonel came to Slovenia bearing a letter from Ranković, addressed to the local OZNA head, Matija Maček, saying that the "justification" should be carried out.[6]

The settling of scores was brutal: thousands of collaborators were shot in Slovenia, or forced on "death marches" to hurriedly organized concentration camps in other republics where they were to be interned. Few reached the camps alive.[7] The massacre, whose victims also included followers of Mihailović, Nedić, and Dimitrije Ljotić, descended into anarchy. According to some contemporaries, this disturbed Tito. Still, he stood firm on its necessity. On 26 May, speaking for the first time in the Slovenian capital, Ljubljana, before an enormous audience, he said of the enemy collaborators: "The hand of justice, the hand of our people's revenge, has already reached the majority of them, and only a small number of traitors managed to escape our country, under the protection of foreign supporters. This minority will never again see our majestic mountains and blooming meadows. And if they should see them again, it won't be for long."[8]

Tito never regretted the killings, which were carried out in secret (although of course they could not be completely hidden). On the contrary, he believed they were more than justified, especially when in 1948 he argued with the omnipotent Kremlin "Boss," Josef Dzhugashvili, known to all by his nickname, Stalin. In case of a probable Soviet invasion, these fiercely anti-regime men could join the aggressors. "Then," he said later, "there was no Soviet military attack against us, because Yugoslavia was unified and the country's various reactionary elements had been too weakened during the national liberation struggle to carry out any provocations."[9] And during a speech in Pula in 1956, he confessed: "We have won the revolution with blood, thanks to the help of the liberation army. We have radically cleansed our home."[10] Together with those who perpetrated it, he claimed that the massacre was morally justified, saying that the "death sentence" had been pronounced "by the people."[11] When Djilas asked what was happening, Tito—without denying the terrible bloodshed—requested that he not mention the topic again; and, finally, he brought the killing to a close ("We have to stop the massacres. Nobody fears the death penalty anymore").[12] On 3 August an amnesty was proclaimed, putting an end to the great butchery, but certainly not to the pursuit of those—Croats and Serbs especially—who were still in the woods in armed opposition to the regime.[13]

This merciless vendetta against the "counterrevolutionaries," which cost the lives of an unknown number of people (estimates vary between seventy thousand and one hundred thousand) was a taboo subject in Yugoslavia for years, nor was it spoken of in the West, since no one among the victors could be said to be free of acts of vengeance against the defeated enemies. It did receive praise from Stalin, which made the Yugoslav leaders proud. At a meeting with a Polish delegation, Stalin criticized the Warsaw authorities for their lenience toward the opposition and cited Marshal Tito as an example: "Tito is a smart kid. He has murdered all his opponents."[14]

The Division of Power

At the beginning of March 1945, the provisional government constituted by Tito had twenty-seven members. They included former political émigrés, the vice-president and minister of foreign affairs, Ivan Šubašić, and others, including Milan Grol, Juraj Šutej, and Sava Kosanović. In this way, he made it look as if the agreement between Churchill and Stalin about the division of power in the Balkans had been adhered to: an agreement to which Tito was bound, since international recognition of the new Yugoslavia depended on it. Naturally, though, the real power was in the hands of the CPY, or rather, of its Politburo, composed of ten members with an even more exclusive Secretariat (Tito, Kardelj, Ranković, and Djilas). Tellingly, Tito did not participate in government meetings, aside from special occasions or when he wanted to report on his trips abroad. The sessions, convened at infrequent, sometimes monthly intervals, were chaired by Kardelj or another vice-president, while Leo Mates, Tito's old collaborator, kept him informed as to what was said. Within the party, too, there were no fixed schedules: Tito gathered his most important comrades informally. His clear focus was on governing, not dealing with minutiae or formalities.[15]

Tito governed thanks to the support of the army, which was controlled by the party and was unswervingly loyal. The party (100,000 of whose 141,000 members were from the military) had at its disposal a network of committees that kept the masses under control.[16] In addition, there was OZNA, which fought enemies both internal and external. If claims from the time are to be believed, it was kept busy with the 826 hostile groups comprised of six thousand "terrorists" or armed opponents sent by American and British intelligence to Yugoslavia in the first two years after the war alone.[17] It has to be said, however, that the majority of the population believed in the values of the Popular Front, as organized and led by the CPY, and that any "bourgeois" forces were largely discredited and impotent. As Tito later affirmed, the Provisional Government created the illusion among the opposition and abroad that all was not yet lost, but those around him knew his plans very well: to quickly bring about a revolution, regardless of the West and its generous aid, which was offered—mostly by the United States—through the United Nations Relief and Rehabilitation Administration. "We marched toward the construction of socialism with a zeal never seen before," boasted Tito.[18]

The quartet on the top divided Yugoslavia into fiefdoms. Tito, who was the most powerful and a good twenty years older than the others, dominated everything, especially—with the help of Kardelj—the situation in Croatia. Slovenia was also Kardelj's region, while Ranković and Djilas were in charge of Serbia and Montenegro and, through their subordinates, also oversaw Macedonia, Kosovo, Vojvodina, and Bosnia-Herzegovina.[19] The division of power was also clear on another level: Kardelj supervised the social system and foreign policy; Ranković was in charge of internal matters; while propaganda, indoctrination, and controlling intellectual life were handed over to Djilas. Together with Tito, this group of men made all the important decisions and subsequently presented them to the Politburo, where they were rubber-stamped. Power at a lower level was exercised by young people, between fifteen and thirty years old, who fought as Partisans and were chosen because of their "revolutionary" zeal. They carried out their duties tentatively, often having no idea about the problems they were supposed to be dealing with. Most of them had very little education, as many had not completed their primary schooling. This generation would stay in office for the next thirty-five years and occasionally longer, until the collapse of Yugoslavia.[20]

Nationalization and Agrarian Reform

Yugoslavia also underwent radical social change during this period, thanks to the Politburo's decision to nationalize the means of production with all possible speed. Many opposed this step, seeing it as premature and fearing its negative impact on the regime's popular support. They felt it was unwise to be so hasty: better to nationalize each economic sector individually, one at a time. This view was echoed by Moscow, which was apprehensive about a possible worsening of

Yugoslavia's international standing. The peace conference where important decisions would be made about the Western borders and Trieste was imminent, and most of Yugoslavia's mines, factories, and large banks had been owned in the prewar years by British, French, or American companies. Thanks to this cautionary advice, Tito and his colleagues chose to delay nationalization until the end of 1946. Only then, when the decisions of the major powers about the borders with Italy had been made, did they promulgate a law nationalizing 90 percent of all enterprises, leaving just the smallest businesses in private hands.[21]

This move provoked outrage in the West, as well as a wave of compensation claims. At the same time the Politburo decided that nationalization would not affect landowners unless they held large estates. Tito and his comrades were determined that the collectivization of land would not have the same outcome that it had after the October Revolution in the Soviet Union, when the gentry as a class had been destroyed just so land could be handed over to the peasants. In Yugoslavia the nationalization of land would in fact displace the peasantry, as most plots of land were possessed by small land owners. This decision would turn out to be economically unsound and politically dangerous, destabilizing the alliance between the working masses and the peasants, and alienating from the regime precisely those social classes that had participated most passionately in the struggle for liberation.[22]

The Trieste Question

At the end of February 1945, Field Marshal Sir Harold Alexander, commander in chief of the Allied forces in the Mediterranean, came to Belgrade for talks with Tito about the cooperation of Partisan and Anglo and American forces in the western part of Venezia Giulia, as the Italians called the area around Trieste, which they had annexed after the First World War. The Yugoslavs now wanted it because it had been liberated by them and the rural population was Slovenian or Croat. Interested in the control of the region in order to preserve it for Italy, Alexander claimed that he needed it to assure communication between his troops in the Apennine Peninsula and in Austria, and asked for permission to have his forces occupy the entire strip of land along the former Italian and Yugoslav border. Marshal Tito accepted this request, on the condition that the civil administration already established there by the Partisans who had been fighting the Fascists and the Nazis from the start of the war and who enjoyed wide support among the Slav but partially also the Italian population, should remain under their control.[23] The final decision on Italy's eastern borders would be made by the peace conference. In 1951, Kardelj said that Alexander was "terribly intransigent" in his discussions with Tito, boosting the suspicions of his Belgrade interlocutors that he wanted to bring about the division of Yugoslavia, as Churchill and Stalin had agreed in October 1944: "Churchill wanted to come to

Ljubljana with his forces, so that even now they'd still be in charge. It wouldn't be us in power, but the Russians in Belgrade and the English in Zagreb."[24]

Immediately after Alexander departed, sure that "he could get from Tito what he wanted," on 2 March 1945 Tito ordered the formation of a new army—the fourth—in Bosnia-Herzegovina, whose task was to reach as soon as possible the Isonzo, the river near Gorizia considered by the Slovenians to be their natural Western border.[25] His agreement with the field marshal, as with Churchill a year before, had been purely tactical, hiding completely different political and strategic goals. On 5 April, he went to Moscow on his first official visit, where the Soviets received him with a level of pageantry reserved, until then, for the likes of Edvard Beneš and Charles de Gaulle. The pomp, in fact, was a little excessive: Tito was ill from the flight to Moscow, and upon arrival he struggled to make his inaugural speech.[26] On 13 April, in the presence of Stalin, he signed an agreement at the Kremlin with Molotov, similar to that between the Soviet Union and the Czechoslovak government in exile in 1943, consenting to twenty years of collaboration and friendship. But in 1945, in the new world emerging after Hitler's defeat and already marred by the East-West confrontation, this clearly meant that he was siding with the socialist bloc. The implications of this were clear in the United States and Great Britain, where the treaty was openly criticized, which contributed to even more strained relations between Yugoslavia and the two superpowers.[27] How much Tito wanted to strengthen his relations with the Soviets is revealed by a minor but significant fact; he chose Gustav Vlahov as his private secretary, a Macedonian who was educated in Moscow and became a high ranking officer of the NKVD during the war.

Tito brought Šubašić, and also had Djilas join him on the trip in a bid to smooth over ill-feeling caused by his remarks about the bad behavior of the Red Army during its stay in Yugoslavia that past autumn. Stalin, who on that occasion had been outraged, was ready to accept Djilas's explanation and his excuses, saying, "Why did you not write about all this? I had no idea. To me, the whole thing is forgotten."[28] The atmosphere thawed, as demonstrated by the toast Stalin raised at a banquet held in the Catherine Hall of the Kremlin Palace: no longer would he address Tito as "sir." He would call him "comrade." He invited the guests twice to dine in his dacha at Kuntsevo, but did not stop speaking contemptuously about the Yugoslav Army, which Tito found hard to swallow. "In the relationship between Tito and Stalin," wrote Djilas, "you could sense something amiss, something unsaid—as if there was a mutual dislike which they both had to hide."[29]

On 15 April 1945, the Soviet Army newspaper *Krasnaia zvezda* (The red star) published an interview with Tito, in which he stressed that "the Istrian population [in Venezia Giulia] wants to be annexed to Yugoslavia, and we are confident this will soon be accomplished."[30] During a meeting with Yugoslav officers who had participated in military and counterespionage courses in Moscow, he boldly described how his troops would march on Trieste, though he did not hide the fact that opposition from the Western allies was to be expected.[31] After two weeks in Russia, he returned home feeling sure of Stalin's support, as confirmed in a report given to the Politburo: "They welcomed us with open arms. The Soviet Union will help us by any means."[32] Knowing there was no time to lose, he ordered the local authorities in Slovenia and Croatia to take immediate power in the disputed region and to guard it against any possible advance by English and American troops—even if this meant an armed clash. Meanwhile, the Fourth Army was ordered to rush towards Trieste, the main port of Venezia Giulia, in order to occupy the area and to reach the Isonzo River before the Allies, who were racing there from the Italian peninsula.[33]

On 1 May 1945, the Fourth Army and the Ninth Corps of the Slovene Partisan forces entered Trieste and Gorizia, accomplishing a long-held dream of the Slovene nation. The English and Americans immediately requested their withdrawal, in accordance with the agreement made between Tito and Alexander. On 6 May, the Yugoslav government contacted the Soviets to secure their help. The answer that came from Moscow on 11 May was promising, but diplomatically ambiguous: "The Government of the Soviet Union will collaborate with all powers, so that Yugoslavia's just claims can be achieved peacefully."[34] But it was soon clear that this "collaboration" would not be simple, as relations between Belgrade and the West worsened further, and the issue acquired increased political significance. By banishing Yugoslavia from Trieste and Gorizia, Winston Churchill and Harry S Truman, the new president of the United States, sought to show Stalin that they would not allow his influence to creep over the demarcation line dividing Europe into two blocs. In a proclamation to the troops, Field Marshal Alexander went so far as to compare Tito with Hitler, Mussolini, and Imperial Japan, denouncing his "territorial aggression."[35]

In pursuit of their aim, Churchill and Truman even threatened armed intervention, which the Yugoslav leadership saw as an attempt to divide their country. The situation was also viewed seriously in Moscow, where Tito's stubbornness was not appreciated and where there were fears that it could lead to an armed confrontation with the West, something the Soviet Union was not ready for. It was true that Stalin saw a war with the capitalist world as inevitable; for example, he had spoken openly about future conflict with the West to Moša Pijade and other guests at his dacha in January 1945. But not an *immediate* conflict.[36] Stalin was convinced that the Yugoslavs deserved Trieste, as it had been annexed by the Italians after the First World War and used as a springboard for their aggression against the Balkans, causing great suffering. He said this quite clearly in his correspondence with Truman and Churchill, protesting against Alexander's reference to "territorial aggression."[37] To Tito, however, Stalin was equally frank: he was not ready to risk a third world war for the sake of an Adriatic port, and he demanded the withdrawal of Yugoslav troops within twenty-four hours. When Tito conveyed this order to Peko Dapčević, commander of the Fourth Army, he allegedly included the telegram from Stalin by way of explanation.[38] According to the testimony of Tito himself, Stalin even refused to answer his call when he tried to reach him by phone to get him to help. His secretary informed the marshal that the Boss was absent at the moment, but that he would contact him as soon as possible. Tito paced around his study the entire night waiting for the phone to ring. It did not.[39] The Yugoslavs felt betrayed by Stalin's behavior. This view was expressed by the marshal himself in his famous speech in Ljubljana on 26 May, where he subtly likened the Soviet Union to the Western imperialists and resumed his rhetoric of "the new Yugoslavia," which would no longer be an object for barter and bargain between the great powers. Stalin's reaction was swift and severe: he threated to make their dispute public and leave Tito to his fate. The marshal responded with a demeaning mea culpa: "He tried to apologize with fawning embarrassment," reported the Soviet ambassador Ivan V. Sadchikov, in a dispatch. "He claimed to have lost his head in Ljubljana because of the bad weather: 'During the speech there was a terrible hailstorm. The rain and hail beat my face and made me so nervous that I spoke rashly.'"[40]

On 9 June, the English and Americans and the Yugoslavs reached an agreement affirming the withdrawal of Partisan troops from the Western part of Venezia Giulia, and its division—until a final decision was reached about the Italian-Yugoslav border—into two zones: Zone A, with Trieste, to be administered by the Allied forces, and Zone B, encompassing the rest of the region, which would be overseen by the Yugoslav Army.[41]

The incident with Stalin had further implications. It brought to light the latent tension between Edvard Kardelj and Tito, triggered by the latter's autocratic style. Kardelj took advantage of Stalin's rebuff and revealed to the Soviet ambassador his own misgivings about Tito's behavior: Tito saw Yugoslavia as self-sufficient, needing no help from the revolutionary and socialist camp. Kardelj took quite the opposite view. Tito soon came to hear of this criticism but, according to Djilas, he never reproached Kardelj, despite being displeased. According to Vukmanović (Tempo), Kardelj was very nearly expelled from the party. Be that as it may, the resentment toward Kardelj lingered.[42]

In spite of the failure in Trieste, the Yugoslav Communists' influence on the masses in the late spring of 1945 flourished in a way that had not been seen before nor after: the people were even ready to "take the sky by storm"—as the Serb proverb goes—so convinced were they that their leaders could deliver them a better life.[43] As reflected in Tito's own words at the First Congress of the Communist Party of Serbia in May 1945, the leaders themselves were unsure how to move from the struggle for liberation to the next phase of the revolution—fostering socialism. Just one thing was clear: the need to ruthlessly eliminate those political groups and bourgeois figures who, while ready to collaborate with the communists, still hoped to preserve some autonomy, since Tito and his comrades were not disposed to tolerate any ideological dissent.[44] At the Potsdam Conference, convened by the three Great Powers at the end of July 1945, Churchill worried aloud that "Tito's administration has created a rigid regime, propped up by the political police, where the press is just as closely controlled as it is in Fascist states."[45] Stalin, though he too was worried by the marshal's radicalism, disagreed—mostly so as not to endorse Churchill's view. During a private dinner, Churchill reminded him of the Moscow agreement on Yugoslavia, stressing that the influence of the two superpowers was now no longer fifty-fifty, but more like ninety-ten; and not in Great Britain's favor. Stalin was of the opposite opinion, arguing that "the Soviet government often has no idea what Tito's government is up to," which confirmed his terse words at Yalta: "If you offer Tito advice, he sometimes replies with a kick."[46]

The Popular Federal Republic of Yugoslavia

Although bourgeois Serb and Croat politicians had in recent months been useful to show the Western allies that Yugoslavia was not wholly in the hands of Communists, Tito and his comrades now moved to get rid of them as their presence was no longer necessary. They isolated Grol, Šubašić, and other representatives of the prewar parties via their gradual expulsion from public life, and internal or external exile.[47] Tito's view was that "in such a country as this, burdened with the immense ballast of the past, with national hate at the highest pitch, we would have achieved nothing had we allowed different parties. What would be the meaning of forming them? The parties would be formed in Croatia, Serbia, Macedonia, Slovenia, Bosnia and Herzegovina, Montenegro and all these parties would fight on the line of nationality; a state with such parties would not be able to exist."[48]

When the 1945 electoral law was passed, the communists included in it a series of articles banning the opposition from participating effectively in elections and denying civil rights to all those who could be accused of having collaborated with the occupiers and other upstart regimes. "Collaboration," however, was open to interpretation. Although Tito and his followers felt they could count on 60 to 70 percent of the vote, they were taking no chances. They formed the Popular Front, a vast political movement dominated by the CPY, which incorporated the various middle-class parties while also depriving them of their autonomy. The presidency of the Front was assumed by Tito, with Sreten Žujović, "the Black One," as secretary general. Despite Washington's threat to halt economic aid if the elections for the Constitutional Assembly were not free, the poll results on 11 November surprised no one: the Popular Front, the only organization that took part in the race, achieved an absolute majority.[49] Those who had the right to vote, including women (for the first time) and minors who had fought in the Partisan ranks ("if they can carry a gun, they can vote too"), could do so via a rubber ball, because of widespread illiteracy. Voters could place the ball in the box belonging to the Popular Front, or in the "black" box of no party, a mechanism designed to "guarantee" freedom of choice. The Popular Front received 8,393,435 votes, while just 838,239 voters were bold enough to put their rubber ball in the box without political affiliation. It is known that many voters, especially soldiers, were transported by trucks from one polling station to another in order to vote multiple times. There was no independent control of the vote count.[50]

On the basis of this electoral result, the Constitutional Assembly was convened, comprising two chambers, one federal and one national. At its first session, on 29 November 1945, it issued a declaration that abolished the monarchy and announced the Popular Federal Republic of Yugoslavia. Tito often said that this was the happiest day of his life. The Assembly then began to discuss the new constitution, which was solemnly proclaimed on 31 January 1945, despite it being an exact copy of the Soviet constitution of 1936 (making it an object of mockery in Moscow).[51] The constitution guaranteed the six federal republics the right to self-determination and secession which, at the time, seemed just a formula, but which would prove important later on with the dissolution of Yugoslavia. The equality of all Yugoslav people was symbolically emphasized with the reading of the text in Serbian, Croatian, Slovenian, and Macedonian, but not in Albanian, despite the size of Albanian population in Kosovo.[52] The question which status should be granted to the Albanians in Yugoslavia caused fierce internal quarrels with Serbs, as Tito confessed in 1978 in one of his last interviews, with George W. Hoffman, an American professor of Austrian origin. In the end, Kosovo was declared, together with Vojvodina, an autonomous province of the Republic of Serbia, a decision that did not meet the requirements of the Albanians or the Serbs. Asked about his most difficult task in domestic political life, Tito answered, "Convincing the Serbs to accept the provinces of Vojvodina and Kosovo [within the framework of their republic]." He felt that Kosovo should be the seventh autonomous entity within the boundaries of Yugoslavia, along with Slovenia, Croatia, Bosnia-Herzegovina, Montenegro,

Serbia, and Macedonia. "But that was impossible," Tito continued. "The Serbs just wouldn't tolerate it."[53]

Before the constitution, but even more so after it, the country was hit with an avalanche of economic and social reforms. Tito was aware of how risky this was: upon offering Vlatko Velebit a prestigious post in the "Yellow House," as the Ministry of Foreign Affairs was called, Velebit claimed that he was entirely inexperienced for the task. Tito smiled: "None of us creating this State is aware of how challenging this is. We have to learn on the job."[54] But he was full of confidence in himself and his comrades, as shown by a message he sent proudly to Moscow in January 1946, claiming that during the last months after the war Yugoslavia had reached the same stage Russia had in the years 1917–21, during its own bloody civil war—a time of daring and radical social experiments.[55]

Church and State

Ideologically, alongside the doctrine of "War Communism," which was in many ways similar to the economic and political system that existed in Soviet Russia during its civil war, the authorities began to introduce "Socialist Realism," the official art form as expounded by Andrei Zhdanov in the Soviet Union. In Yugoslavia, it was put into action by Milovan Djilas, minister of agitprop (agitation and propaganda). He did it with such enthusiasm, said Kardelj, that "we were compelled to mitigate the consequences of his dogmatic radicalism. . . . He was a wild sectarian."[56] But in spite of this fanaticism, the leaders of the CPY continued their policy, implemented during the liberation struggle, of hiding the party from the masses, as if it were still underground. At the First Congress of the Communist Party of Serbia in the spring of 1945, delegates were warned not to speak about Tito's attendance or about his speech, in order not to harm his standing as a statesman. At the First Congress of Yugoslav Writers in November 1946, Tito failed to mention the Communist Party and its mission to reeducate intellectuals regarding the advantages of Marxism-Leninism. Even in the CPY's leading newspaper, *Borba*, and in its magazine, *Komunist*, it was difficult to find an article on the topic.[57] In spite of this, the comrades in power, though obsessed by "conspiracy," openly imitated Stalin's hardline approach to social transformation. Edvard Kocbek, a prominent Slovenian writer and leader of the Christian Socialists who had been on the executive team of the Liberation Front from the very beginning, lamented in his diary on 11 June 1946 that "the party has forgotten that we're in Europe; that it should respect the pluralism of life and spirit more than Russia does; that our revolution was different; that it behaves immorally. It forgets the aid of the Allies, sinks into worse and worse brutality and sterility, and provokes outrage (hate, violence, excesses) in the countryside."[58]

Against such a background, attacks against religion, especially the Catholic Church, were inevitable. These attacks were shaped by Tito's conviction that Yugoslavia's prewar frailty, its lack of national robustness, was caused by ethnic and religious conflict.[59] Alojzije Stepinac, the archbishop of Zagreb, who had been imprisoned after Tito's victory, was released on 2 June 1945, the same day that Tito met with representatives of the Croat clergy. In his discussions with them he bemoaned the clergy's behavior during the war, hoping that in future the church would be more independent of the Vatican—which was openly pro-Italian—while stressing that he too was a "Catholic."[60] This did not induce Stepinac to become more compliant, despite his meeting with the marshal a few days later, on 4 June. He remained defiant in the face of Tito's request for a Church more autonomous from the Pope, saying, "No Catholic can ignore the supreme authority of the Holy See—even if it costs him his life—or he isn't a Catholic at all."[61] A later decision by the bishops to openly protest against land reform, which affected their own vast holdings, led to a further worsening in relations, which the appointment of the new papal nuncio in Belgrade, the American bishop Joseph P. Hurley, did nothing to assuage. "Who is Tito?" Hurley wrote in his diary, venting his hostility toward socialist Yugoslavia and its leader: "A Ukrainian Jew?"[62] This escalating conflict with the Roman Catholic Church, the only organization capable of resisting the new regime, reached its climax with the trial of Stepinac, held in a blaze of publicity in the autumn of 1946, on charges related to his involvement with the Ustaša.[63] This was just one of many great show trials staged by the new regime against real enemies (such as Draža Mihailović), potential enemies (such as the leader of the Serb peasants, Dragoljub Jovanović), and, later, even against prominent members of the party. All the trials were carried out in pure Stalinist style.[64]

As in the Soviet Union of the thirties, so in Yugoslavia was there an obsessive hunt for all possible internal enemies. An omnipotent and oppressive bureaucracy took hold, spreading into every part of civic life. Koča Popović summed up the postwar years: "The party is rapidly becoming 'everything'—ideology again has absolute preeminence. When I say 'ideology,' I mean a doctrinaire attitude that prohibits every disagreement."[65] Yugoslavia still differed from the Soviet Union in its choice not to abolish the private property of small enterprises, especially within the agricultural sector, but what emerged was a chaotic economy that fell short of the leaders' ambitions to drive communism forward in Europe and to succeed Moscow as the vanguard of the revolution.[66]

According to Djilas, relationships within this vanguard, so solid during the Partisan period, began to deteriorate around two years after the war, not least because Tito started to behave increasingly as the charismatic overlord who would not engage in discussion, but had to be obeyed. "In a strange way, merely by changing the tone of his voice, or his facial expression, Tito could signal that his interlocutor had crossed the line—that there had been a transgression. He could listen attentively (or pretend to) and not interrupt, especially if someone was speaking succinctly, but sometimes he cut in with incredible sharpness, putting you right back in your place."[67] This change was also observed by Fitzroy Maclean when he returned to Yugoslavia in 1947. He reported to the Foreign Office that the marshal seemed detached from the everyday life of the common people with whom he had shared the difficulties and hardships of the Partisan struggle: he delegated authority to individuals not always worthy of his trust and gave the impression of not being completely aware of the situation at home and abroad. And he did not permit anyone near him who would dare to tell him an unpleasant truth.[68]

The Paris Peace Conference

At the gathering of the three great powers in Potsdam, the British accused Yugoslavia of contravening the Yalta agreements, which provoked objections from the Soviets.[69] In fact, despite the recent skirmishes between Tito and Stalin, in the lead-up to the Paris Peace Conference, the Soviets supported Yugoslavia's border claims against Italy and Austria. On 21 October 1946, Tito argued that the Soviet Union provided a "strong guarantee" of Yugoslav independence.[70] He was right: between the 1 and 26 December, a meeting was convened in Moscow, where the foreign ministers of the United Kindom and United States yielded to Molotov's pressure and agreed that, despite significant reservations with regard to Tito's regime, their governments would recognize the newborn Yugoslav Republic.[71]

London's recognition at the end of 1945, and Washington's in April 1946, did not mean, however, that the British and Americans would give Yugoslavia an easy time. President Truman put it plainly when he recommended that his newly appointed ambassador, Richard C. Patterson, adopt a "two-fisted, tough policy with Tito."[72] The Allies refused, for instance, to return the Yugoslav Danube fleet, which had been requisitioned by the Germans and transported to the Reich, or the gold reserves deposited in their banks by Prince Paul before the war.[73] Even worse, at the end of 1945 the British and American spy agencies joined forces with the help of émigrés and dissident cells in Slovenia and Croatia who were attempting to continue the fight against the Communists. This underground uprising reinforced the importance of UDBA (Uprava državne bezbednosti; State Security Administration), as OZNA was renamed in 1946. It became the regime's primary safeguard, playing an increasingly important role in the new order.[74]

The West's hostility toward Tito was articulated most powerfully by Churchill who, having been defeated by Labour at the polls, could now speak freely without diplomatic restraint. In Brussels in January 1946, he declared in a private conversation: "During the war I thought I could trust Tito. He promised me to observe the agreement he had concluded with Šubašić, but now I am well aware that I committed one of my biggest mistakes of the war."[75] The following April, during a tour of the United States, Churchill gave a speech at Westminster College in Missouri. In it he described the conditions prevailing in Europe after the war, using the famous metaphor of the iron curtain dividing the continent in two, from Stettin to Trieste. Stalin protested against those words, which foreshadowed the Cold War. Five days later, Tito declared that he agreed with the Boss.[76]

In the following months relations between the two blocs deteriorated rapidly, which affected the negotiations of the foreign ministers of the four great powers (now including France) about the new border between Yugoslavia and Italy. Yugoslavia asked that the frontier lie on the Isonzo River, but because the West considered this proof of Soviet territorial ambition, no one but Molotov agreed. In June 1946, after protracted discussions, a compromise was reached in Paris: Yugoslavia could have the valleys of Isonzo and Vipava and most of the Karst region, but not Gorizia. Along the gulf of Trieste, from Duino near Monfalcone to Novigrad in Istria, there would be a Free Territory of Trieste, which would take the city from Italy but close off Slovenia's access to the sea. When Kardelj, who was outraged by this outcome, which he felt was a national catastrophe, flung this compromise in Molotov's face, the Soviet foreign minister replied angrily, "But do you think every 'gubernia' can have its own sea?" This was taken by the Slovenians as a deliberate affront to their Republic, which Molotov considered a mere province.[77]

British and American hostility toward Tito's regime provoked more than two thousand incidents on its terrestrial and maritime borders in the first few years after the war. "Our Foreign Ministry," recalled Tito, "protested many times against this brutal violation of our sovereignty, but to no avail."[78] During the Paris discussions, Yugoslavia's air space was routinely invaded—in June 1946 alone there were around 170 non-authorized militarily flights—provoking Tito to take drastic action.[79] When the Paris Peace Conference opened its doors, he ordered his army to force American planes to land. The first time this manoeuver was successful but the second time, on 19 August 1946, the pilot refused to comply. The aircraft was attacked and, in the subsequent crash, two crew members died. There was hysterical outrage in the United States, prompting Washington to demand the release of the survivors who had been taken prisoner and payment of hefty compensation to the families of the dead.[80] This atmosphere, so strained that an armed conflict could not be ruled out, was worsened by America's decision to interfere in the trials of Stepinac and Mihailović (who had been captured via a plot on 13 March, tried in Belgrade in June, and then shot on 17 July). Diplomatic relations between the two countries were at their lowest ebb, but relations with the Soviets were also deteriorating, with the Yugoslavs accusing them of not advocating strongly enough for their interests at the Peace Conference. When the decision on the Free Territory of Trieste was announced, the Yugoslav delegates threatened to abandon Paris, saying they would refuse to sign the peace treaty with Italy. They backed down from this threat only under substantial pressure from both East and West.[81]

Their conviction that the Soviets did not fight vigorously enough for their cause triggered deep bitterness in Yugoslavia. "They considered it their right," Tito said later,

> not to tell us about foreign policy issues that directly affected us, which were fundamental to the interests of our country. During meetings of the foreign ministers in the spring of 1946 in Paris, when the Trieste question was discussed, Molotov spent the entire night before the final session debating with Kardelj, our representative, about the border, without telling him what was being proposed: in fact, the following day he agreed with the collective decision, despite it being so unjust to us. In a meeting of ministers in London, Molotov also accepted the proposition that Italy should pay reparation of $300 million: $200 million to the Soviet Union and $100 million to all the other States. He didn't mention this to us, even though we suffered more from the Italian occupation than any other member of the United Nations.[82]

On 3 July 1946, in protest against such treatment, Tito sent a dispatch to Stalin, denouncing the passivity of the Soviet delegation. He received a reassuring answer, even though the subsequent policy of the Soviet Union remained effectively unchanged.[83]

~

Before the Second World War, Yugoslavia was one of the most underdeveloped states in Europe. Its economy depended largely on foreign capital, which controlled nearly 50 percent of its industrial sector. About three hundred thousand people worked in the industrial sector, 2 percent of the population, whereas nearly 80 percent lived off the land. The peasantry had almost no equipment—in 1939 there were only 2,500 tractors in the entire country—which meant that productivity was as low as the standard of living. After the war the situation was even worse, due to widespread devastation.[84] Average per capita income did not exceed $60 annually, one of the lowest in Europe. In August 1945, the government introduced agrarian reform, cancelling the debts of peasants and recognizing their right to own 20–30 hectares of land. But this did not solve the problem of overcrowding in the countryside, or improve living conditions. Things worsened in autumn 1945, when the obligatory sale of agricultural produce was implemented in a bid to feed the cities and the army and to keep factories supplied with raw materials. Food and other goods were distributed to workers, employees, and specific categories of the poor through bonuses and ration cards.[85]

The AVNOJ decree of 21 December 1944 approved the confiscation of the property of the Third Reich and its citizens, along with the assets of war criminals, collaborators, and traitors. The law of 5 December 1946 nationalized large and medium businesses such as shops, banks, and transport companies. By the following year, the state sector encompassed 90 percent of all production. This meant, in the words of Vlatko Velebit, "that at least half of all the industry in the country was destroyed in just one ultra-Bolshevik decree . . . Tito, Kardelj and the other leaders were oblivious, and if they weren't, they didn't bother themselves about the power of private property and the extent to which it motivates productivity."[86] Following the Soviet model, a Five-Year Plan was announced for the years 1947–51 that forecast GNP growth of 193 percent and a fivefold increase in industrial and twofold increase in agricultural production. Unsurprisingly, its emphasis was on heavy industry. Initial post-liberation propaganda about "the people's democracy" was replaced with a new narrative focusing on the "construction of socialism" and its capacity to free the country from its semi-colonial past and transform it into an industrial powerhouse.[87] When a journalist asked Djilas, shortly before his death, whether the leaders had enough economic knowledge to achieve this immense task, he answered: "You know they didn't have much. It was based on Marxist doctrine, badly understood and accepted in the Stalinist variant. The knowledge of those who led the economy was simply miserable. Those economists whom we considered bourgeois did know something. They were here to help as experts, but at that time nobody cared for their opinions."[88]

Billions of "the people's money" was put into a forced, overambitious industrialization, but very little was invested wisely: most of the cash went into badly conceived, poorly realized projects that yielded mediocre results. The entire country was full of grand "socialist factories," built by highly competitive "Stakhanovite" workers or by so-called "youth brigades," filled mostly with students on their summer breaks, some of whom enrolled voluntarily, although most did not.[89] Living conditions became much worse even than in the prewar years; the population was malnourished (only partially fed by United Nations Relief and Rehabilitation Administration aid), and at the mercy of disease (particularly tuberculosis). In addition, the regime was suspicious of intellectuals and professionals who were included in the black list of "petit bourgeoisie" and were socially discriminated against. As Yugoslavia lacked the means with which to realize its Five-Year Plan, and could not rely on Western aid, the government reached a series of bilateral agreements securing credit and investment from the Soviet Union, Poland, and Czechoslovakia, which it hoped would provide the materials and expertise needed to construct key factories. In the period leading up to May 1948, trade with other socialist states constituted 51 percent of the entire foreign trade budget.[90] According to Yugoslavia's supreme leader, however, the future was bright: "The well-being of the people will improve markedly," promised Tito at the end of his speech presenting the Five-Year Plan to the Federal Assembly.[91]

The Exclusion of the CPY from the Cominform

As Kardelj said to Dedijer in June 1952, Tito and his comrades based their postwar policy on the presumption that the Soviet Union would be stronger if Yugoslavia was strong, "but, at the same time, we were never servile toward the Russians."[92] They failed to understand that Stalin would not tolerate such arrogance. Despite the decorations he lavished upon them, his fundamental dislike of the Yugoslavs surfaced every time he met them. And for every honor given, there was a (perhaps deliberate) provocation. In the autumn of 1944, Stalin awarded Tito the Medal of Suvorov while the king of Romania, who in 1941 had declared war on the Soviet Union, was given the more important Medal of Victory, an honor for which Tito had to wait until October 1945.[93]

The only meeting at which Stalin made no offensive comments about the Yugoslavs took place in Moscow between 27 May and 10 June 1946, during Tito's second official visit. When they discussed the question of the border with Italy, which was to be decided in Paris, Stalin committed to protecting Yugoslav interests and pretended, in his deceitful way, to be entirely sympathetic to their cause. After dinner in his dacha at Kuntsevo, he strolled with his guest in the garden, where suddenly he grabbed Tito around the waist, trying three times to lift him up.

"Are you healthy?"

"Yes, I am."

"Take good care of your health. It's essential to Europe."[94]

Tito and his comrades were elated, particularly when Stalin proposed a toast to their brotherhood. They were even more pleased when, some days later, at the funeral of M. I. Kalinin, the former Soviet head of state, Stalin invited Tito to join him in the guard of honor. After the ceremony in Red Square, Tito followed Stalin to the top of Lenin's mausoleum and realized that his health was, in fact, precarious. Stalin struggled up the stairs, pale and breathless, but tried to hide his panting. "I thought: God's breath, you're dying!"[95]

In June 1946, the Soviet government issued a press release announcing its plans to supply the Yugoslavs with arms, munitions, and other essentials via a long-term loan. In addition, the two countries reached an agreement on trade and substantial financial aid for Yugoslav industry.[96] Tito did not hide that he was wholly aligned with the Soviet bloc. When he met his generals, who had been trained at Moscow's military academies, he declared, "If the Red Army needs us to lead its march toward the English Channel, we'll be there tomorrow!"[97] On his return to Belgrade, he sent the following "modest" gifts of gratitude to the ladies of the Boss's entourage: for his daughter, Svetlana, a platinum watch with diamonds; to Molotov's wife, a gold watch with diamonds, and a gold bangle for his daughter; for the wife of Anastas Mikoyan, the minister of foreign trade, a gold watch by Patek Philippe; for the wife of Soviet Politburo member Zhdanov, another gold watch; for Beria's wife, a gold watch by Eterna.[98]

This friendly atmosphere did not last long: it was soon disrupted by Yugoslav discontent about the solution to the Trieste question, as decided by the Allies. When their foreign ministers agreed to the creation of the Free Territory of Trieste, Tito was outraged, and his fury was expressed in the aforementioned retaliation against American encroachment on Yugoslav airspace. The resulting attack was the worst military incident between the two blocs since the end of the Second World War. Molotov was appalled. "Don't you realize they have the atomic bomb?" he asked Kardelj, chief of the Yugoslav delegation in Paris. "Big deal," answered his secretary. "They have the atomic bomb, but we have the Partisan one."[99]

It is impossible to understand the 1948 split between Belgrade and Moscow without taking into account this overconfidence. As Koča Popović said: "During the war, Tito got so used to being autonomous—with his position, charisma and power—that he couldn't even consider being Stalin's subordinate again."[100] His relations with Moscow were a mix of love and suspicion, until it became obvious that Stalin wanted to subjugate Yugoslavia: for example, with the creation of common economic companies. The first of these was dedicated to mining, which the Soviets spun as a kind of collaboration, "respectful of Yugoslavia's prestige." In the end, just two transport companies were created: Justa, for air, and Juspad, for river transport.[101] Tito and his comrades at times attempted to oppose Stalin, and at other times bowed to the Kremlin's requests in order to maintain goodwill, but they always tried to stay in control. In 1947, on signing an agreement in which Moscow promised to invest $200 million in Yugoslavia, they were convinced their strategy had paid off.[102] Soon, however, they began to suspect that the Soviet Union was attempting to slow down the country's industrial development, exploiting it as a supplier of food and raw materials. They began to protest this policy, applied not only to Yugoslavia but to other "people's democracies," as the states under Soviet tutelage in Central and Eastern Europe were called. Discontent was restricted first to Tito's inner circle, but soon became widespread. The marshal remained careful but stubborn, engaged as he was in a difficult struggle with an ideology that he had up to that point believed in: the building of socialism under the Soviet flag.[103]

Savelii V. Burtakov, the Soviet "resident" embedded in Belgrade, reported back to the NKVD on "the Eagle" (Tito's code name): "Alongside his positive qualities—popularity, good looks, an expressive face, courage and willpower—the Eagle has the following flaws: lust for power, lack of modesty, arrogance, and insincerity. He sees himself as the supreme authority, prefers unquestioning obedience, and dislikes exchanges of views and criticism of his orders; he is irritable, hot-tempered and curt—and a poseur." According to Burtakov, Tito should not be wholly trusted in his dealings with London, "though he makes an outward show of his supposed hostility towards the Allies, particularly the British."[104]

Tito and Ranković, his spy master, in turn took a dim view of Burtakov, who become notorious for his habit of looting jewelry and other precious items requisitioned from Belgrade's wealthy families. At the end of the year he was replaced as chief advisor to OZNA by Arsen V. Tishkov, known by the Yugoslavs as Timofeev. But tensions with Tishkov soon arose, too, when his agents, who were spread all over the country, began to be criticized for their arrogant behavior. Their attempts to entice Yugoslavs into being their collaborators provoked even greater disapproval—among those approached by Timofeev's men was, in fact, a young woman who was one of Tito's cryptographers at the cipher office. When Ranković informed Tito of this incident, he exploded: "We will not tolerate a network of spies. Tell them that immediately."[105]

Balkan Plans

Even more serious disagreements came to a head in the second part of 1946, when a civil war erupted between the Greek government in Athens and communist units led by General Markos Vafeiades. Tito supported Vafeiades, considering it his Bolshevik duty, although Stalin did not feel the same way, having agreed with Churchill about the division of the Balkans and having ceded Greece to the British. After the war, Stalin was convinced that an armed confrontation with the West was inevitable, but he was realistic enough to remain mindful of the Soviet Union's weakness—and its lack of an atomic bomb.[106] For this reason, he was inclined to stay in favor with the West (for the time being, at least), keeping relations cordial and not provoking them any more than was wise. Tito had no such hesitation, determined as he was to transform Yugoslavia into the revolutionary center of all of Mediterranean Europe, including Greece,

Italy, and even Spain. He paid little attention to public opinion in the United States and Britain, which had opposed his territorial ambitions at the peace conference, even provoking them by shooting down an American airplane and providing military help to Greek insurgents. In spite of the prohibition of the United Nations, Belgrade secretly aided the Greek insurgents, which reinforced the Truman administration's suspicion that Tito was a mere executor of Stalin's policy in the Balkans. In December 1946, following a request from Washington, the United Nations formed a Special Inquiry Commission tasked with establishing whether neighboring "people's democracies"—primarily Yugoslavia—were indeed arming the rebels, as the Greek government claimed.[107]

Meanwhile, the British, who had given the shaky Greek "democracy" military support for some time, were unable to continue their commitment due to serious problems arising in India and Palestine. In March 1947, Truman declared that the United States would take up this role of helping legal governments who were threatened by "armed minorities or foreign pressure."[108] This became a cornerstone of American foreign policy, underpinned by their conviction that the containment of communism was essential. In the face of a Greek crisis, and fears that Stalin would increase pressure on Turkey, the presence of American naval forces in the Aegean Sea escalated conspicuously in the following months. As a consequence, Yugoslav leaders resumed talks with the Bulgarians about a federation, which had begun at Stalin's and Dimitrov's initiative back in October 1943.[109]

The idea of a federation was so appealing to the Yugoslavs that in January 1945 they had proposed a treaty between the two states. The Soviets were more circumspect, arguing that such an important decision would need detailed preparation and suggesting a twenty-year pact of friendship and collaboration first. This had to happen discreetly, as the new Yugoslavia had not yet received international recognition. "In the area of foreign policy," said Stalin, "we have to be careful. Our task is to build on the victories we've achieved."[110]

Problems quickly emerged, as the Yugoslavs wanted Bulgaria to enter their federation as its seventh republic, whereas the Bulgarians insisted that a dual state be formed, similar to the former Austria-Hungary. At first, Stalin was in favor of dualism but later agreed with the Yugoslavs, which the Bulgarians—to Dimitrov's dismay—humbly accepted.[111] The possibility was soon quashed, however, when the British protested, declaring that, as a defeated country, Bulgaria could not establish an independent foreign policy. They were convinced that a federation would strengthen the Soviet Union in the Balkans and influence the situation in Greece and Turkey. Stalin, who before the Yalta Conference was hesitant to cause unnecessary discord with the West, agreed, ordering an interruption of the talks.[112]

Tito also hoped to include in his federation the new "people's democracy" of Albania, which his government recognized on 28 April 1945. One of his cherished ideas was the creation of a great socialist entity in the Balkans, to which other "people's democracies" would be attracted. He was convinced that Yugoslavia could become a communist hub and that he could achieve socialism more swiftly than the Soviet Union. He also wanted to solve the Macedonian question, reuniting (under his command, naturally) the three parts of Macedonia—the Yugoslav "Vardar," the Bulgarian "Pirin," and the Greek "Aegean" regions of Macedonia, which had been torn apart on the eve of the First World War.[113] In June 1946, Tito and Dimitrov met in Moscow and agreed to resume discussion on the Bulgarian-Yugoslav federation as quickly as possible. Stalin agreed, convinced that together the two countries could play an important part in the region. They also spoke about this project during Kalinin's funeral, deciding to mobilize in earnest after Bulgaria had signed the peace treaty. When this happened at the beginning of 1947, it seemed there was no longer any impediment to the plan's realization, though the treaty would not come into force until 15 September.[114]

In July 1947, a meeting was held at Lake Bled, Slovenia, between Tito and Dimitrov, who had left Moscow and returned to Sofia to lead his country after the war. On August 1, in an atmosphere rich with Slavic sentiment, the two signed a historic protocol committing to close economic collaboration, including a common currency and joint customs services. It was to be kept secret, however, as Bulgaria had not yet formally regained full sovereignty. They even spoke of a possible union between Vardar and Pirin Macedonia, and of the Macedonian people's right to self-determination—including the people of Aegean littoral. During a confidential conversation, Dimitrov went so far as to declare, "We will create a better Federation than the Russians, because our culture is superior."[115] Meeting with Bulgarian journalists, Tito emphasized that "together with the Soviet Union, the Balkans will be a beacon, showing the way to solve ethnic and social problems." At a session of the CPY, he added that "Yugoslavia was the only true herald of 'revolutionary socialism.'"[116] Tito felt invincible, convinced that he could create a powerful state in the Balkans capable of achieving independence from the Soviet Union and destabilizing the way in which the three great powers had divided the European southeast.[117]

When Dimitrov told Stalin what had happened at Bled, his fury was instantaneous: he sent telegrams to both leaders, accusing them of having signed an indefinite pact of collaboration, and observing that this was a highly irregular kind of diplomacy. Most of all, he was troubled by the discovery that they had acted without consulting the Soviet Union and without waiting for the implementation of the peace treaty. In doing so, they had given the West an excuse to strengthen its presence in Greece and Turkey. "The Soviet Union is allied to Yugoslavia and Bulgaria. . . . The Soviet Government is obliged to declare, however, that it cannot accept responsibility for important international agreements made without its consultation."[118]

Tito tried to explain that the Yugoslav government had had no intention of presenting the Soviet leader with a fait accompli, declaring that he was ready to publish a retraction of the agreement, along with the Bulgarians. He did not do this, but on a visit to Sofia on 27 November he and Dimitrov signed a pact of friendship and collaboration that took into account Stalin's observations. They decided to postpone talks about a federation. At a press conference, however, Tito declared that the pact was necessary to defend the two countries from possible German aggression and from others, saying, "We are not only against German imperialism, but against all those who wish to question our sovereignty."[119] Was he alluding to the West or to the Soviets, too? According to a still partially classified 1948 CIA document, the latter seems more likely. Apparently the split between Stalin and Tito started to take shape in July 1947, when Soviet Marshal Tolbukhin asked the Belgrade government to hand over naval bases in Pula, Šibenik, and Boka Kotorska to the Red Army. The Soviets demanded that the Yugoslav authorities completely renounce their jurisdiction over these ports and allow the Soviets to build another near Ploče in central Dalmatia with Yugoslav material and labor. Although it was repeated at the beginning of 1948, Tito dismissed this request. He was well aware that conceding strategic points on the Adriatic coast would signal the end of Yugoslavia's sovereignty and threaten his personal security.[120]

It was mostly the Soviet ambassador, A. I. Lavrent'ev, who fueled doubts about the loyalty of the Yugoslav leaders in Moscow. His dispatches from Belgrade missed no opportunity to denounce their errors. For example, he criticized Tito's speech at the Second Congress of the Popular Front on 27 September 1947, in which the marshal spoke about the success of the "people's democracies," without saying a word about the decisive role the Soviet Union had played in their formation and development. What disturbed Lavrent'ev more was Tito's silence regarding the role the Red Army had played in Yugoslavia's liberation: "All these omissions are consequences of the fact that Tito views the liberation of Yugoslavia and its socioeconomic transformation from a local and national point of view, making his outlook narrow and jingoistic."[121]

In Moscow, where Tito's nationalism and his "Bonapartist" ambitions were followed attentively, a dim view was taken of such behavior, especially because, in all his speeches after 1945, he mentioned Marxism-Leninism just once. The watchdogs of the orthodoxy at the party's CC wrote, "Tito and the other leaders of the CPY do not mention Comrade Stalin in their declarations as the most important theorist of our times—a worthy successor to Marx, Engels and Lenin. In their speeches, there is no hint of the groundbreaking role played by the communist parties, especially of the All-Soviet Communist Party (Bolshevik). The glorious influence of the Soviet Union, the only country to have successfully built a communist society, and which nurtures all human progress, is ignored."[122]

The behavior of the CPY leaders, their "hostile" attitude toward the Soviet Union, and the scope of their ambition in the Balkans was testimony to the audacity of their foreign policy and their belief that Yugoslavia was special: that it existed outside of the framework of revolution and socialism. As early as the beginning of April 1945, Dimitrov wrote in his diary: "I received Tito in my city apartment. We spoke at length about the situation in Yugoslavia, about relations with the English and Americans, and about a possible union (or something like it) between Yugoslavia and Bulgaria. General impression: underappreciation of the complex reality and of the difficulties before us, very superior, prideful and overconfident, and his success has clearly gone to his head. Thus, when he speaks, everything seems fine."[123] In the eyes of Stalin and his circle, in short, Tito and his comrades were becoming a bunch of dull-minded nationalists, perilously close to betraying the socialist bloc led by the Soviet Union.[124]

While Tito forged his grand plans with complete disregard for Moscow, Stalin decided to create a bureau of information (Cominform), signaling that he wanted the European communist parties to unite and be ready to march at his order. As the United States was inaugurating its Marshall Plan and providing relief to Western Europe, Stalin felt this gathering of forces was urgent. To this end, he convened a secret meeting of delegates from the most important Eastern and Western European parties, held at Szklarska Poręba, near Wrocław in Poland. Tito, in a discussion with Stalin in April 1945, had already stressed the importance of organizing a body that could offer mutual advice among the European communist parties. Stalin had expressed no view on the proposal at that time; but the next year, when they met again, he suggested that the Yugoslavs take the initiative. Tito answered that he felt the French should issue the invitation, given their status. In the end, it was the Soviets themselves who organized the conference, preoccupied as they were with the "dollar imperialism" of the Americans.[125] During the meeting at Szklarska Poręba, Andrei A. Zhdanov expounded his theory of two opposing camps that would, sooner or later, clash in an armed struggle, and pleaded for all communists to band together: this political decisiveness in some way renewed the heritage of the Comintern in Europe.[126] On 5 October, when *Pravda* published news of the conference, Dimitrov, the former secretary general of that organization, wrote enthusiastically in his diary: "This assembly is our atomic bomb. . . . It is the best answer to the anti-communism of the American imperialists."[127]

Djilas and Kardelj came to the meeting in Szklarska Poręba as representatives of ideological orthodoxy, though they could not entirely dismiss what Tito had said in a speech to Croatian peasants: "We speak with England and America, but also with other countries, as equals. We won't let anyone treat us like a mere colony."[128] The general impression in Moscow was that those words were aimed at the Soviet Union. "On this occasion, too," the Kremlin's observers said, "the Yugoslav leaders will tell us that our objections are based on misinformation. But they should reread the *Borba* of 25 May 1945 [Tito's speech in Ljubljana], and the newspaper *Glas* of 28 August 1947 [his speech to the peasants]."[129] Stalin was convinced that Tito was following an anti-Soviet policy, and doing so at the precise moment when he should have been supporting the USSR as the only power able to prevent, for the time being, a third world war.

In the constitution of the Cominform, the CPY was mentioned first, probably in recognition of the fact that the idea had been raised by Tito two years previously.[130] Stalin himself decided to install the headquarters of the new organization and its magazine, entitled *For a Stable Peace: For the People's Democracy*, in Belgrade. Tito officially interpreted this as proof that his internal and international policy was right, proclaiming on 27 September, at the Second Congress of the Popular Front, that its experience was vitally important, not just at home but also "across our frontiers."[131] In private, however, he and other Yugoslav leaders were less than grateful for this honor, complaining behind the scenes that the CPSU intended to "exploit the Cominform as a means of control over other parties."[132]

Tito continued to strain Stalin's patience still further, until his behavior became completely untenable. He even pretended that he was going to buy modern weaponry for his army, though the Russians reminded him that Yugoslavia could not afford them (as one Soviet officer put it, "Why do you need a strong army? We're here!").[133] Stalin increasingly had the impression that he was dealing with a bunch of self-serving "Pharisees" in Belgrade who were ready to praise him in public and denigrate him in private, claiming that the Bolshevik party had degenerated, that the Soviet Union was no longer revolutionary but was dominated by chauvinism, and that it was eager to "economically enslave Yugoslavia."[134] A rumor went around Moscow that "this is not mere criticism anymore, but strategic backbiting meant to discredit the CPSU and humiliate the Soviet order."[135] Kardelj was not exaggerating when he said later that no socialist leader was as hated by Stalin as Tito. Moša Pijade gave an accurate assessment of their relations when he said that the 1948 split was a conflict between a regime with no revolutionary wind left in its sails and a young revolution, full of energy and enthusiasm.[136]

The final straw for Stalin was Tito's policy toward Albania, with whom Yugoslavia had signed a treaty of friendship and collaboration in the spring of 1946. Actually, Tito intended to transform Albania into a Yugoslav protectorate, something Stalin did not oppose. However, he was displeased that Tito tried to hinder direct contact between Tirana and Moscow, obstructing his authority. The Albanian leaders were subjected to so much pressure that one of them, Naku Spiro, committed suicide in protest against Yugoslav domination (this, at least, was the official line). Stalin responded with a message to Tito, asking him to send a senior comrade to Moscow, possibly Djilas, to discuss "the situation in Albania."[137]

At the beginning of January 1948, Djilas, along with Koča Popović (chief of the General Staff) and Mijalko Todorović (minister of military industry), departed by train for the Soviet capital. A few hours after his arrival, he was summoned to the Kremlin and a decidedly awkward meeting with Stalin. The Boss voiced no objection to Yugoslavia "swallowing" Albania—even demonstrating, with a crude gesture, how to go about it. He also invited Djilas to send Tito a telegram to this effect on behalf of the Soviet government; a telegram that the Montenegrin, alarmed by this odd request, formulated in such a vague way that it was never sent. After the "urgent" tête-à-tête and a tension-filled dinner at Stalin's dacha, the Yugoslav delegation was left to its own devices and encouraged to roam the museums, theaters, and monuments of Moscow and Leningrad.[138]

The turning point came only at the end of the month, when the question of the Balkan federation arose. The Yugoslavs had signed a treaty of friendship with the Bulgarians in November 1947 similar to the one already in place with Tirana. In the middle of January, Dimitrov presided over a comparable treaty in Bucharest with the Romanians. During his journey back to Sofia on 17 January 1948, he gave an interview to Western journalists in the saloon car of his train, expressing his view that the time would come when the people of Romania, Bulgaria, Yugoslavia, Albania, Czechoslovakia, Poland, Hungary, and Greece would unite in a federation or confederation.[139] This audacious proposal, so alarming to the West, was unwelcome to Tito and even more so to Stalin, confirming as it did his fears that he was being kept in the dark about plans that could only be useful to the British and American propaganda. He wrote a letter to Dimitrov expressing his disapproval and ordered *Pravda* to denounce his statement as "inappropriate and impulsive."[140] At the beginning of February he invited Tito and Dimitrov to the Kremlin to clear up, once and for all, the "misunderstandings" that had arisen between the three governments. In the telegram written by Molotov on his behalf, addressed to both statesmen, he said: "The unfortunate interview by Comrade Dimitrov has provoked discussion about the creation of an East European bloc in collaboration with the USSR. . . . The international press could present this as an anti-American and anti-British move by the USSR, smoothing the way for the most aggressive Anglo-American elements in their fight against the democratic forces in the USA and Great Britain."[141]

Stalin's concerns were further heightened by Tito's proposal to send a division to South Albania, which was under threat from Greece for helping the rebel communist forces. He would establish a Yugoslav military base in the town of Korça as a warning to the West not to play with fire.[142] Tito made this bold decision despite the fact that, in August 1947, Stalin had advised him to be prudent. In response to Tito's suggestion that the Greek Communist Party be invited to Szklarska Poręba, the Boss had replied that its presence would only aid the Anglo-American agenda. It was clear that the arrival of Yugoslav military units in South Albania, as requested in June 1946 by Enver Hoxha, the secretary general of the Albanian Communist Party, could trigger conflict not only between Yugoslav and Greek troops, but also with the "Anglo-Saxons" fighting in Epir for the government of Athens and possibly even with the Americans. This could easily transform the Cold War into a hot one, a challenge that Stalin could do without given his interest in finding, for now, a modus vivendi with the West.[143]

As Ambassador Lavrent'ev wrote on 21 January 1948, even worse was the fact that Tito had made his decision without informing Soviet military counselors in the Yugoslav Army. (Djilas later said that he and Kardelj were likewise unaware of this.) Enver Hoxha, who had lost all enthusiasm for Tito as his relations with Belgrade had cooled, hurried to inform Stalin. The latter responded that he "did not see any imminent threat of an attack against you by the Greek army." At the end of January, Molotov sent Tito a message saying that the "Anglo-Saxons" might interpret the arrival of Yugoslav troops as an occupation, and use it as a pretext to enter Albania. During a conversation with Lavrent'ev, Tito immediately declared his willingness to postpone or even cancel the planned deployment of troops. He warned, however, that if South Albania was invaded by the imperialists, the Soviet Union and Yugoslavia would both be forced to swallow this "pigswill."[144] In response, on 1 February, two telegrams came from Moscow in which Molotov noted angrily that this unduly independent behavior by the Yugoslav government was "anomalous" and intolerable. "It's clear that there are serious disagreements between our two governments on the matter of bilateral relations. To avoid any further misunderstandings, we must clear things up definitively."[145]

Dimitrov took up Stalin's invitation, leaving Sofia for Moscow, in secret, on 9 February. Tito, however, showed again that he understood with whom he was dealing. Since the hernia surgery he had undergone the previous year, he had harbored suspicions that the Boss wanted to be rid of him. At the time of his surgery, when disagreements between Belgrade and Moscow were multiplying, Tito tried to mollify Stalin by accepting his offer to send his very best surgeons—even though the operation was to be a minor one. A series of complications then arose, raising suspicions about the real intentions of the imported luminaries. After the operation, one of the surgeons announced that he had forgotten an instrument inside the patient and wanted to reopen the incision. Being seriously inebriated at the time, he was prevented from doing this but only after a furious quarrel. The tension was such that one of the doctors had a stroke and returned home in a coffin. To top it all, the nurse who accompanied them carried vials of poison with her. This, at least, is the version recounted by General Žeželj, the commander of the guard, and Tito's personal secretary, Gustav Vlahov.[146] According to the historian Roy Medvedev, Tito sent Stalin a letter of protest after this failed "attempt on his life."[147] This would appear to be backed up by an ironic letter sent to Tito by his friend Ivo Krajačić (Stevo) on 27 May 1951, some days after a second surgery, this time for pancreatic duct stones, which was carried out in utmost secrecy so that Stalin would not be informed about it: "We wish you all the best for your birthday, which we celebrate after your successful surgery—this time, without 'the best specialists in the world,' as the despotic Tsar would say."[148] Tito himself remembered later: "Stalin tried to kill me several times. With that surgery, too."[149]

In February 1948, to Stalin's fury, Tito claimed to be sick and sent Vladimir Bakarić and Edvard Kardelj to Moscow to support Djilas. As guests of the Soviet government they were installed in a villa, which was likely bugged, so they were careful what they said. Whispering in Kardelj's ear, Djilas told him of his bad feeling about Moscow, saying there was nothing more to be gained from the Soviets. Kardelj told him about Tito's aims for Albania. Their wariness about their hosts was obvious: in the hall of their villa, they kept a radio on day and night to obscure their conversations. When a Soviet attendant asked why, Djilas answered: "We love music. Kardelj, especially."[150]

On 10 February 1948, during another of the nightly gatherings with Stalin and the Bulgarians at the Kremlin, the Yugoslav troika was on the receiving end of a number of criticisms, which boiled down to this: "The matter with you is not your mistakes, but your opinion on issues, which is different from ours."[151] At stake were three key points: the Bled agreement on Yugoslav-Bulgarian federation, Dimitrov's interview, and above all, relations between Yugoslavia and Albania and the possible bearing this had on the Greek question. In Stalin's view, in all these instances the governments of Belgrade and Sofia had made foreign policy decisions without Soviet consent, but in which the Soviet Union, being an ally, was obliged to support. This was the heart of the matter:

Stalin complained that he was not willing to tolerate satellite countries acting bilaterally and even less willing to allow them to muddy the waters with the West without his agreement. "Everything Dimitrov or Tito says is reported abroad, as if we already knew about it."[152] The Kremlin meeting, which began at 10 p.m., was over by 11:45 p.m. Stalin, who reproached Dimitrov for behaving like a gossipy old woman—though he maintained a more respectful attitude toward the Yugoslavs—did not invite anyone to dinner.[153]

The next day, to avoid future misunderstandings, Dimitrov and Kardelj were asked to sign a bilateral agreement with the Soviet Union renouncing any claim to independent foreign policy and promising "to consult Moscow in all important international questions." Kardelj, who on 11 February was summoned to the Kremlin in the middle of the night to sign the document, tried to comfort himself with the thought that the Russians had essentially asked for something he was already doing. Still, he was so bewildered that he signed it in the wrong place, causing the entire document to be retyped and the ceremony repeated the following day.[154] Afterward, the Yugoslav delegation stayed in Moscow for two or three more days, during which it had discussions with Dimitrov, among others, on how to bring about the federation between their countries, as Stalin had requested at the Kremlin. Unlike the "mythical" confederation of all people's democracies that Dimitrov wanted, Stalin considered this "feasible and realistic."[155] Kardelj took part in talks with the Bulgarian leader, having already told Djilas when they left the Kremlin that on the basis of decisions taken by the Politburo CPY before his departure, a federation with the Bulgarians was out of the question: "Such a federation would allow Stalin to bring a Trojan horse into our camp." The Yugoslavs left the Soviet capital almost in secret. According to Kardelj, "They took us to Vnukovo airport at dawn, and unceremoniously made us board the plane."[156]

Meanwhile, ominous signs were coming one after the other. Even before the Yugoslav delegation returned from Moscow, news arrived from Bucharest that Tito's portrait had disappeared from shop windows. And from Tirana, the Yugoslav Embassy brought news that the Soviet chargé d'affaires had toasted Tito during a reception, but "only if what he does really strengthens the international democratic front." To make things even more uncomfortable, ten days later the Yugoslav minister of foreign trade, Bogdan Crnobrnja, was told in Moscow that discussions on the renewal of economic agreements between the two countries were postponed until the end of the year.[157]

When Djilas, Bakarić, and Kardelj returned home from Moscow on 19 February 1948, the Politburo was summoned, and Djilas reported back on their discussions with Stalin and other Soviet leaders. Tito did not seem bothered by the issue of foreign policy, still convinced that in that respect there were no major disagreements between the two governments. He spoke against the federation with Bulgaria but reserved most of his anger for the economic and military pressure Stalin obviously exerted on Yugoslavia. "It's not clear whether the USSR wants us to be a strong, armed state. The armament is a terrible weight [because of the huge expenses]. We have to count on our own forces first of all, correct the Five-Year Plan and develop the military sector. . . . Our Soviet comrades fan irrelevant problems and draw the wrong conclusions from them. We must follow our own path to strengthen the role of Yugoslavia in the world. This, in the end, is also in the interests of the USSR."[158]

This independence in the face of Stalin's policy was also stressed by Yugoslav leaders two days later, in a meeting between Tito, Kardelj, Djilas and Greek party functionaries, led by General Secretary Nikos Zachariadis. The Yugoslavs informed them that during the Kremlin discussions on 10 February, Stalin had voiced doubts about whether their revolt would be successful, but reassured the Greeks that they could count on Yugoslavia's ongoing support in the struggle for liberation. These were not mere words: On 10 March, the minister of foreign affairs, Stanoje Simić, informed Lavrent'ev that the Yugoslav Air Force was on standby for any "provocations by Monarcho-Fascist Greeks." Tito and his comrades also put pressure on the Albanians, asking them to convince the Boss that the intervention of Yugoslav troops in their country and its union with Yugoslavia was necessary. The dispatch sent by the Soviet ambassador to Moscow on 26 July 1947 seemed more accurate than ever: "It's probable that Tito is now considering an armed response to Greek military provocation."[159]

The Showdown with Hebrang and Žujović

The postponement of talks on the renewal of economic agtreements decided by Moscow was an enormous blow for the Yugoslav leaders, considering the first Five-Year Plan was based on the assumption of close collaboration between the Soviet Union and other bloc countries. Thus, on 1 March 1948, an expanded Politburo was convened in Tito's Belgrade villa, where Kardelj and Djilas again reported on their discussions with Stalin.[160] Everyone present was aghast, and Tito even proposed that he should resign as prime minister (according to Djilas, more to test their loyalty than anything else). Tito acknowledged that Yugoslav-Soviet relations had reached a dead end, as shown by Russia's attempts to subjugate Yugoslavia economically and compel it to unite with Bulgaria, which would strengthen the influence of the NKVD in the Balkans. He expressed the view that there had been an ideological shift within the CPSU that had introduced shades of "Great Russian chauvinism." Kardelj, Djilas, and other members of the Politburo agreed: "We are not pawns on a chess board."[161]

Djilas even argued that the CPSU was likely to "place enormous pressure on us, as the new Yugoslavia is becoming an important center of ideological dissent." The problem was this: How would socialism continue to develop? Through independence or via the expansion of the Soviet Union?[162] All agreed that it was essential to have a strong army to guarantee their ongoing sovereignty. "We will have to make great sacrifices for the military sector and its armaments," concluded Tito. "The words from [Moscow] offer us nothing. I believe we can maintain the army by ourselves."[163]

Only Žujović, "the Black One," was meaningfully silent. He was an intelligent man, of great political experience, who made the mistake of binding himself too closely to the Russians. (Suffice it to say that, in the years after the war, he visited Crimea five times for "health reasons"; this aroused suspicion, as comrades started to see him as too pro-Soviet.)[164] Since no one wanted to inflame relations with Russia, at the end of the meeting they decided that what had been said should be kept secret from the Soviet ambassador. But Žujović did not comply. Thanks to his tip-off, Lavrent'ev was able to send Moscow a detailed report of the meeting, relaying the assertion of General Ivan Gošnjak, among others, that Soviet policy was a hindrance to global revolution, as well as Tito's response to this statement: "It's true!" The dispatch went directly to Stalin, who asked Molotov to convey his thanks to Žujović for such precious information: "Your work is vital to the Soviet Union and the Yugoslav people, exposing as it does the 'wrong comrades' in the Yugoslav CC."[165]

On 9 March, Lavrent'ev sent another letter to Moscow, in which he described the views of Žujović and Bosnian premier Rodoljub Čolaković. They argued that it was possible to save Yugoslavia from the trap it was caught in only through the intervention of the CPSU, given that Tito held all the levers of power and brooked no opposition. On one side, they said, was the party elite, accustomed to total power; on the other side were those of inferior rank who were not organized and ideologically weak. According to Žujović, Tito could not prevent the integration of Yugoslavia with the Soviet Union, if such a plan could be devised. Knowing that for the time being the international situation would not allow it, however, he suggested that a party delegation should come from Moscow for frank and decisive discussions. If the Yugoslav leaders would not accept this, he was prepared to denounce them publicly. He also had other suspicions: Wasn't it possible that Tito was in secret contact with the British and Americans through his middleman, Vlatko Velebit?[166]

That same day, on 9 March 1948, Lavrent'ev informed Moscow that the Yugoslav government was denying him all information and ordering their secret services to close off access. The previous summer the decision had been made to deny sensitive data regarding the Five-Year Plan to *all* diplomatic representatives in Belgrade. It had not been implemented, however, for the Soviet trade attaché. In his letter Lavrent'ev wrote that now the Yugoslav government has changed its attitude. According to him, the fact that the Soviet Embassy had again been formally notified of this prohibition could mean only one thing: the Yugoslav government's attitude toward the Soviet Union had changed.[167] Two days later, on 11 March, Tito met with Lavrent'ev to tell him that his government could not understand why the Soviet Union refused to sign their trade agreement, despite regularly signing similar agreements with other countries. Tito also brought up other questions, such as the toast made by the Soviet diplomat in Tirana, though he tried to keep things amicable, saying that quarrels could happen in any family, even between brothers. Molotov answered from Moscow that reports about the toast had been misunderstood, if not entirely made up, and that the same thing could be said about the Soviet Union's refusal to sign the trade agreement. Meanwhile, Žujović continued to stoke the fire: in his discussions with Soviet diplomats he spoke about Tito, Kardelj, Ranković, and Djilas as "political zealots," ready to bring about socialism in Yugoslavia "their way." This was why they wanted to keep their distance from the Soviet Union and why they emphasized their criticism of it.[168]

Troubled by such reports, Stalin took an unforeseen step. On 19 March 1948, he ordered the head of the Soviet military mission in Yugoslavia to inform Koča Popović, the chief of the General Staff, that his government had decided to recall all military "counselors" from what was now a hostile environment. The next day the Soviet chargé d'affaires informed Tito that civil counselors had also been recalled, adding by way of explanation: "You do not listen to us!" Both kinds of counselors were, in fact, hugely unpopular, thanks to their superior attitude, enormous salaries, and attempts to plant informers in important military and economic positions. "They wanted to shape Yugoslavia according to their own views, introducing Soviet customs," Tito said later. "At a stroke, they wanted to transform us into a mere Russian gubernia outpost."[169] But the sudden departure of Soviet personnel was so sinister that it provoked concern. Tito sent two letters to Molotov in which he refuted accusations that the counselors had been treated with hostility and that Yugoslav bureaucrats had been reluctant to work with them. "We want the Soviet government to tell us frankly what the matter is—what, in its opinion, is preventing harmony between our two nations."[170]

Kardelj, for his part, tried to convince Molotov to allow at least those civil experts who were essential to the completion of Soviet-backed projects to remain in Yugoslavia. But to no avail: on 27 March, this group too was obliged to return home. That day Molotov informed Lavrent'ev that he had sent an envoy to Belgrade with a letter that should be forwarded immediately to the "relevant address." The letter had been written by Stalin and Molotov, "on behalf of" the CPSU, and was addressed to Tito and the CC of the CPY. It was bound to worsen the situation.[171] Based on a report prepared by the most senior party officials, entitled "On Anti-Marxist Tendencies among Leaders of the CPY in Internal and Foreign Policy," they accused Tito and his comrades of harboring hostility toward the Soviet Union and of openly expressing their intention to break away from it. "These anti-Soviet declarations are often masked by leftist assertions such as, 'In the Soviet Union, socialism is no longer revolutionary'; or, 'Only Yugoslavia is the true representative of revolutionary socialism.' Once upon a time, Trotsky used these tactics. What happened to his political career says it all."[172]

There was more. The arrogant Yugoslavs had committed (numerous) other sins: though the CPY was in power, it behaved as if it were not, hiding behind the Popular Front; the CPY did not respect internal democracy, allowing the majority of CC members to be co-opted rather than elected; instead of the party controlling all state structures, in keeping with Marxist doctrine, they were overseen by the Ministry for Internal Affairs. How could such an arrangement be considered Marxist-Leninist and Bolshevik? Moreover, there seemed to be no spirit of class struggle within the Yugoslav party, with the leadership apparently unable to stop capitalist elements gaining influence over the countryside and towns. This was revisionism as theorized by Eduard Bernstein, Georg von Vollmar, and Nikolai Bukharin. But what else could be expected from a party whose leaders included such dubious Marxists as Djilas, Vukmanović, and Ranković, and that tolerated having Vladimir Velebit in the Ministry of Foreign Affairs, even though everyone knew he was a British spy?[173]

Together with an assistant, Lavrent'ev delivered this letter to Tito at Villa Weiss, his Zagreb residence. The marshal received them coldly and did not ask them to sit down. On reading the first few lines of the letter, under the enquiring gaze of the diplomats, he felt as if he had been "struck by lightning," but he managed to control himself and retain his composure as he read on. After three or four minutes, he dismissed the ambassador, promising to answer as soon as he had had time to study the letter properly. He then rushed to the phone, summoned Kardelj, Djilas, and Ranković to Zagreb, and immediately began writing his reply, which was finished in under two hours.[174]

Stalin's letter included several well-founded accusations, but others that, if not false and unjust, were at least exaggerated. Among the most serious was Stalin's assertion that the party was not acting transparently and was using the Popular Front as a screen. In fact, the Yugoslavs saw the Front as a new kind of political organization, uniting the masses under the party's leadership and allowing it to put down deeper roots. They saw it as an original contribution to Marxism-Leninism, and offered it as a model to other people's democracies. In theory and in practice, however, the party *did* control the machinery of state. The communists shrouded themselves in mystery and hierarchy: nobody knew who was in the Politburo and the CC, and even the word communism was rarely used, though in doctrinal terms Yugoslavia was perhaps the most orthodox and "monolithic" of all the satellite states. That is why Stalin's criticism seemed so unjust: it failed to take into account the great lengths the regime had gone to in order to adhere as closely as possible to the Soviet model, and it did not acknowledge what they had already achieved. As Kardelj observed: "In his first letter, Stalin didn't offer the Yugoslav communists any choice. He played judge, while imagining that they would accept the role of the accused."[175]

Tito formulated a dignified and speedy answer by ignoring any of Stalin's well-founded accusations and rebutting those that were incorrect. He began by claiming that the Soviet leaders were misinformed and that they had a very odd view of the situation in Yugoslavia. He stressed that Stalin's letter had been a "terrible surprise," and took the opportunity to raise some issues of his own, for instance, the attempt on the part of Soviet secret services to turn Yugoslav citizens and entice them to spy, which undermined the leaders' authority. Appealing for mutual understanding and stressing the Soviet Union's interest in keeping the new Yugoslavia as strong as possible, since it was "chest to chest" with the capitalist world, Tito wrote that he would make one concession only: Velebit would be stripped of his post as deputy minister of foreign affairs and kept under strict surveillance.[176]

In addition to his effort to clarify and justify the situation in Yugoslavia, parts of Tito's letter went beyond the issues Stalin had raised, getting to the very crux of things. He knew that Stalin's ideological accusations were mere pretexts for weakening the CPY and subduing it to his will. The real problem, which Stalin had deftly side-stepped, came from the new reality of the post–Second World War landscape, in which there was not just one socialist state on the international stage, but several. This raised the delicate question of their mutual relations and how national sovereignty should be understood. Stalin considered sovereignty to be mostly theoretical, arguing—more with actions than words—that every people's democracy should fall into line with the Soviet Union. Tito, by contrast, believed that local circumstances and traditions should be respected, because socialism could be strong and productive only if it was deeply rooted in every single country. He expressed this at the beginning of his letter, saying openly: "As much as one must love the Soviet Union, the birthplace of socialism, one cannot love one's own socialist homeland less."[177]

Toward the end of the letter he developed this thought further, emphasizing that the experience of every country forging a "new democracy," where communists were in power, should be seen as a continuation of the October Revolution: something new in the revolutionary praxis of communism, but also perfectly in tune with the spirit of Marxism-Leninism. In this dynamic vision of socialist evolution, he assigned to the Soviet Union the responsibility to support those countries that were ideologically aligned with it, rather than meddling in their internal affairs. Only in this way could the revolution spread throughout the world.[178]

These were not new ideas for Tito: he had already expressed them at the 1945 Founding Congress of the Serbian Communist Party. On that occasion, he had said that in Yugoslavia the phases of bourgeois and socialist revolution were not clearly defined, and that the country would evolve toward socialism differently than the Soviet Union had. He also revealed that he had personally spoken about this with Stalin, and received assurances that it did not contradict Lenin's teachings. In 1948, however, this belief seemed so daring that it was refuted by Kardelj, Ranković, Kidrič, and Djilas—the faithful four whom Tito had summoned to Zagreb. On their arrival, they read both Stalin's letter and Tito's, concluding that the latter was too provocative and likely to cause further irritation. Djilas was the first to articulate his reservations, which were echoed by the others. Tito accepted them without opposition, though half-heartedly. He knew that he could not afford to bite off more than he could chew and isolate himself from his comrades: for the moment, it was essential to preserve the unity of the leadership. Although Stalin had not attacked him personally—nor would he do so later—it was clear that his position was vulnerable. When Djilas offered him his resignation, along with the other "dubious Marxists," Tito refused it without hesitation, even irritably: "Oh no! I know what they want—to destroy our Central Committee. You first, and then me!"[179]

It was decided that Tito's reply to Stalin should be approved by the plenum of the CC, which had last been convened in October 1940. Stalin's reproaches about the lack of democracy in the CPY had hit their mark. For the same reason, Tito also proposed that the Fifth Congress of the party be organized, since the last one had happened back in 1929. This self-correction was necessary both to mobilize the party and to show Stalin that the leadership was ready to accept his criticisms, where justified. Tito did not believe that such measures would appease Stalin, but his comrades thought otherwise: only Kardelj, perhaps, was able to see the reality of the situation. Although he continued to recognize Stalin as the supreme leader of the revolution, and felt the need to disagree with him was a personal tragedy, he was under no illusions. On the return journey to Belgrade, he told his comrades that relations with the Soviet

Union had been compromised irredeemably: "I know the Russians . . . I know their way of thinking. They'd call us Fascists if it would morally and politically justify a war against us. If they could, they'd destroy us by force."[180]

Tito convened the secret session of the CC on 12 April 1948, at ten o'clock in the morning in the library of the Old Palace. This was an unusual place for a party meeting, and Tito had chosen it in hopes that it had not been bugged by the Soviets. There was also little danger there of an attack by air or from the surrounding areas.[181] Tito approached the meeting with an acute understanding of its "fundamental importance." "Life has taught me," he explained, "that in situations like this, the most dangerous thing to do is not to have steady convictions, and to waver. In these situations, it's vital to act bravely and firmly."[182] After a few words of welcome, during which he outlined the recent disagreement with Stalin, he read the letter of 27 March, along with his own reply. At the end, he called the gathering's attention to one critical point: all the ideological accusations were just a smokescreen hiding the real issue, which was the relationship between the two countries. He also asked his comrades to voice their opinions on the "terrible lies" they had heard, and so as to remind them of their responsibilities, he said that minutes would be taken and passed on, if requested, to the CC of the CPSU. They had to make a firm choice between Tito and Stalin. There was nowhere to hide.[183]

With this, he opened the floor to a series of comments, some better articulated than others, some more emotionally charged. Kardelj noted that Yugoslavia had secured its freedom by itself, whereas Czechoslovakia and other people's democracies had been liberated by the Red Army. "We have fought for our liberty," he argued, "therefore we deserve to be respected." Djilas, who was always inclined to exaggerate, declared that having been accused by Stalin of Trotskyism, he had but one choice: suicide. However, all supported Tito's view: "We have the right to negotiate with the Soviet Union as equals." But when it was Žujović's turn, he became "pale and upset," and defended the Soviet position: "Comrades! I appeal to your revolutionary consciences. . . . What role will Yugoslavia have in the struggle with imperialism? I think our aim should be to unite Yugoslavia and the Soviet Union."[184] Of all those present, only Žujović—apart from the members of the Politburo—had known about Stalin's letter before the meeting, as he had been told about it by Lavrent'ev. On reading it, he expressed approval that the problems had been communicated "in such a resolute way," though he doubted it would do any good. He counseled the Soviets: "All efforts to improve relations will be obstructed. For this reason, the CPSU must keep intervening (in the internal life of the CPY)."[185]

Žujović's words at the CC meeting in the Old Palace heightened his comrades' suspicions that he was a Soviet informer. Further decisive evidence came to light on 6 April, when Djilas passed the Soviet Embassy and saw a car driven by "the Black One's" bearded driver. He informed Tito immediately, during a meeting also attended by Kardelj and Ranković, who had met to prepare for the next session of the CC in two days' time. At the Central Committee meeting, Žujović accused his comrades of seeing themselves as peers of the Soviet communists, after which Tito asked him: "And you, Black One? What have you been doing with the Soviet ambassador?" Žujović answered that he had gone to see Lavrent'ev in order to discuss his new car, to which Djilas commented scornfully: "A Yugoslav minister who kneels down before the Soviet ambassador for a car."[186] The dispute was interrupted when Žujović asked permission to leave because of his obligations at the Federal Assembly. Those present decided to adjourn the session to the following morning, after accepting Tito's proposal to put on the agenda "a discussion about the Black One" and his betrayal. No one slept much that night. The most important members of the leadership had a series of consultations and decided to put Andrija Hebrang on the dock, together with Žujović. Hebrang had quarreled with Tito because of his opposition to the Five-Year Plan, but also because of differing opinions regarding the border between the Republics of Croatia and Serbia. In March 1948, he had already been brought before a Party Commission, charged with a "sectarian attitude," and was under house arrest "because of his behavior in the [Ustaša] prison."[187] Now the suspicions about his treason during the war, which for a long time had been ignored, were suddenly discovered and used against him. Tito and his comrades came to the conviction that, if a purge was necessary, it might as well serve to get rid of both these potentially dangerous "representatives of the Soviet line."[188] They were not wrong, considering the huge esteem Hebrang enjoyed in Moscow. In his dossier in the Cominform archives, he is valued as a "proven, strong, to the idea, dedicated communist, great, true friend of our interests. He is ready to do everything possible for the USSR."[189]

During the session of 13 April, which was quieter than the previous one since the die had already been cast, Ranković informed the CC about the "Hebrang affair." He read a letter the latter had sent him in which he agreed with Stalin's accusations. Tito himself analyzed Fatty's sins, denouncing him as an element hostile to the party and to its line. Djilas followed suit, declaring that Žujović and Hebrang were the main supporters of the CPSU in Yugoslavia: an assertion also based on wiretapping intelligence.[190] In the introduction of Tito's letter to Stalin, subsequently edited by Kardelj, the two were presented differently, accused of being the principal culprits responsible for the tension between Moscow and Belgrade, having given faulty and biased information to Soviet agents in Yugoslavia who, for their part, had incorrectly informed the Kremlin.

Hence, the anti-party activity of a few isolated individuals lay at the origins of the "dispute," which could easily have been solved if the CPSU had only agreed to send one or two members of its CC to Yugoslavia to discuss the unresolved questions on the spot.[191] This suggestion, which implicitly recognized Moscow's supremacy, along with the designation of Hebrang and Žujović as scapegoats, was the only revision to the draft that Tito prepared. His argument about the right of every country to its own path to socialism was further weakened to coincide with the feelings of the majority of the CC, according to whom Stalin, in spite of his despotism and iniquity, embodied an entire ideology. Consequently, the discussion led by the most important party members on 12 and 13 April, and the letter sent to Moscow, spoke a different language. This incongruence was not perceived by most, who were happy to be able to offer two sacrificial victims in a Stalinist rite. They believed that getting rid of a few individuals would suffice to recover the lost harmony of a relationship that had been fatally compromised. As a symbolic gesture of their attachment to the Soviet Union, Jakov Blažević, one of the junior members of the CC, was sent to place a wreath on the tomb of the Russian soldiers who had fallen during the battle for Belgrade.[192]

At the session of 12 April, Tito declared: "Our revolution is just, our revolution does not devour its children."[193] But he then immediately began to violate this assertion. When, at the beginning of May, it was clear that all the bridges with Stalin had been burnt, the marshal decided to get rid of Hebrang and Žujović to further warn off other possible traitors. Although he had already been unmasked as a spy, after 13 April the "Black One" continued to stay in touch with Ambassador Lavrent'ev, to whom he had delivered all his notes in anticipation of his arrest. In fact, he was convinced that the Soviet Communist Party was the only real interpreter of Marxism-Leninism and that Stalin was its "guide and master."[194] Hebrang, who was of the same opinion, had not given the Soviets any information, as Stalin admitted in a letter of 4 May 1948, but he was more dangerous than Žujović because of his managerial skills and because of his popularity in Croatia. It was not difficult to imagine that he would replace Tito in case of a putsch, as was apparently planned.[195] In the abovementioned letter Hebrang sent the Politburo at the end of April, he included a detailed criticism of the CPY in line with Stalin's writing. Kardelj commented in his memoirs: "It was a sort of dissertation of a future chief."[196]

On 6 May 1948, Tito denounced Hebrang and Žujović in the Federal Assembly as elements harmful to the party and hostile to unity and to socialism. Consequently, they were removed from their ministerial posts. The following day, this news appeared in the press without further comment. On 9 May, the Zagreb newspaper *Vjesnik* announced that two new ministers for finance and for light industry had been sworn in.[197] That day a plenary session of the CC was convened, before which a commission charged with examining the activities and the political stances of Hebrang and Žujović read a report accusing them of having plotted before, during, and after the war against the party and the state. They were then stripped of all their offices.[198] A few days later, the general prosecutor ordered their arrest. Djilas writes that Tito decided this himself, without consulting his comrades. It would be ridiculous, said the marshal, if Yugoslavia were to fall into the hands of an "Ustaša" and a "Chetnik."[199] According to information gathered by the British ambassador, Sir Charles Peake, militiamen visited Hebrang's villa four times in one day, first abducting him, then his wife and children, and finally removing all the family belongings. The same must have happened to Žujović because, as the ambassador observed, his house was empty and guarded by the police.[200] Initially, the two were confined in a villa near Belgrade, but later were transferred to the main prison in the capital so that Stalin's agents would not have a chance to kidnap them. As Kardelj stated, this was the main preoccupation of the Yugoslav leadership: Hebrang and Žujović had been arrested, above all, because it was feared they would be taken out of the country by the Soviets and proclaimed the true representatives of the CPY.[201] Rodoljub Čolaković who, like Žujović, was in touch with the Soviet ambassador, was luckier. Prudent enough to engage in some "self-criticism" in time, he was not prosecuted but only deprived of his power and functions, becoming "a pale image of his name and prestige."[202]

Stalin was so upset by the arrest of the two that he immediately requested the engagement of Soviet observers in the judicial inquiry against them. Tito and his comrades refused, considering the proposal an unacceptable interference in Yugoslavia's internal affairs. Stalin replied at the beginning of June, threatening that he would consider them to be "criminal killers" if something serious were to happen to Hebrang and Žujović.[203] Subsequently, the Belgrade newspaper *Borba* published a Politburo decree announcing their expulsion from the party and accusing them of being enemies of the people, sectarian elements who had been plotting against the party since 1937. This was the start of their ordeal. They were subjected to ruthless interrogations. Žujović was accused of having been a follower of Gorkić (the secretary general of KPY who in 1937 was deposed and shot by the NKVD as a British spy), of having taken reckless military measures during the war, and of having implemented a policy after 1945 aimed at undermining the country's economic development.[204] In protest he went on a hunger strike but broke it off when they convinced him to write Tito a letter.[205] It is not known whether he received an answer. Hebrang behaved with more self-control. An agent who entered his cell while he was reading a book informed him, on Ranković's instructions, that he had been expelled from the party. Fatty did not react. "All right," he said, and that was all.[206] In his case, the inquisitors wanted to know primarily about his contacts with Pavelić's entourage in 1941 and about his behavior in the Ustaša prison in 1942. Since they needed to show him guilty, false documents were produced in order to incriminate him. They also accused him of having sabotaged the formulation and implementation of the Five-Year Plan. It seems that he was not maltreated until the end, although he was subjected to psychological pressure with the help of false witnesses.[207] His fate was sealed on 10 June 1949, when he was taken from the prison for an interrogation and did not return. The story of his death comes in different versions: officially, he hanged himself from a radiator in his cell. However, there were rumors that he was strangled with a belt and that Tito, Kardelj, Ranković, and Djilas had "accepted" his "liquidation" since the Croat leadership requested that he not be put on trial.[208] Tito's testimony, given some months before his death, is probably the most reliable: he was given a lethal injection.[209] Tito mentioned Hebrang's story in spring 1952, on the occasion of a dinner given for Randolph Churchill, lamenting his double treason, first to the Gestapo and later to the Soviets. However, he did not say that Hebrang was already dead at the time and responded to Churchill's request to see him, at least from afar, with a sharp: "No!" On 21 May, Randolph published an article about this conversation in *The Daily Telegraph* and four days later the Yugoslav authorities sent a communiqué officially announcing Hebrang's death.[210] Sreten Žujović was more fortunate. He confessed his sins and was released after two years of solitary confinement. Regime propaganda even used him for an unusual show. On Djilas's initiative, the rumor was spread that he had been tortured and killed in prison. When this news appeared in the Western media and there were furious protests in the East, a press conference was organized at which Žujović appeared in person to deny such "lies."[211]

During the spring of 1948, Tito continued to irritate Stalin with his autonomous foreign policy decisions. On 22 March, for instance, without consulting the Soviet Union, he answered a diplomatic note from the United States, Great Britain, and France regarding the Free Territory of Trieste (the three powers proposed its return to Italy). He thereby violated the agreement signed in Kremelj by Kardelj after an acrimonious meeting with Stalin on 10 February 1948, which then allowed Molotov to renounce any further collaboration with the Yugoslavs, who made excuses for their behavior and asked the Soviets not to cancel the agreement, but to no avail.[212] In a letter that Stalin and Molotov sent on 4 May 1948 in the name of the CC CPSU, they accused Tito and his comrades of the worst left- and right-wing deviations known to the Bolshevik doctrine, starting with Trotskyism and Bukharinism, so called after N. I. Bukharin, one of the most prominent of Stalin's victims among the old Bolsheviks, who was shot in 1938. His crime was having quarreled with Stalin because of his brutal policy regarding the collectivization of agriculture. In the Soviet Union, just one of the ideological left- and right-wing errors heaped upon the Yugoslav leaders would have been enough to put them in front of a firing squad. The fact that they challenged the admonitions coming from Moscow, Stalin and Molotov's letter continued, showed that they considered themselves as unblemished individuals "who see everything and understand everything."[213] It also warned that "the Yugoslav leaders should take note that retaining this attitude means renouncing all friendly relations with the Soviet Union, and betraying the united socialist front of the Soviet Union and the people's democratic republics. They should also take note that this meant depriving themselves of the right to demand material or any other assistance from the Soviet Union, because the Soviet Union can only aid its friends."[214]

Stalin did not limit himself to threats, rebukes, and derision, affirming that, without the intervention of the Red Army, the Yugoslav Communists would not have been any more successful than the Italian or the French Communists. (He reproached Tito and his comrades for behaving in a childish manner and considering themselves giants for whom "the sea reaches only to the knees."[215]) His correspondence with the Yugoslavs was conveyed to other leaders whose parties were members of the Cominform and to the Albanians, with the request that they take positions. Everybody, of course, was in agreement with the Boss, although they were aware that a war was being waged between two "Caesarisms," to quote Stella Blagoeva, daughter of the founder of the Bulgarian CP.[216] The first to react, and the most violent, was the secretary general of the Hungarian CP, Mátyás Rákosi, whereas the Pole Władysław Gomułka tried to mediate, but without success. Even Dimitrov—who, when passing through Belgrade on 18 April on his way to Prague had whispered to Djilas: "Hold fast"—quickly changed his opinion, declaring that Stalin's letter of 4 May was a "marvelous document."[217] This meant that the leaders of the CPY who had closed ranks around Tito had already been condemned, and their lives would have been at risk if they had accepted the invitation to come to the second session of the Cominform, in spite of the fact that, in their public declarations, they continued to express their loyalty toward Stalin. Although Stalin did not send his best wishes on 25 May, the marshal's birthday, three days later *Borba* wrote that "Tito was the Soviet Union's best friend" and that "his love for the first socialist country was the spark that lit the flame of love and faith of our peoples toward the Soviet State."[218] However, the leaders of the CPY refused to take part in the session of the Cominform, stating in a short message to Stalin on 17 May that they felt in a condition of "total inferiority."[219] In order to persuade them to come, Stalin sent Colonel Vasilii V. Moshetov to Belgrade.

He was a member of the CC CPSU and the NKVD and for years had been in charge of Yugoslav affairs. If he had any hopes of convincing Tito when he came, he departed under the unpleasant impression that the game was over. The marshal's words played a part, as did a curious coincidence: in his study, Tito had two portraits, one of Lenin and one of Stalin. A few minutes before Moshetov entered the room, Stalin's photo had fallen from the wall and was momentarily set on the floor. The Soviet emissary certainly would not have ignored this sacrilege and its hidden significance.[220]

Exclusion from the Cominform

On 19 June 1948, a dispatch came from Moscow, this time signed by Mikhail A. Suslov, the director of the Office of Foreign Policy at the CC CPSU, with the announcement that the Comintern would meet in Bucharest. If the Yugoslavs accepted the invitation, they were to send their delegates to the Romanian capital by June 21. There they were to contact Gheorghe Gheorghiu-Dej, the secretary general of the CPR, for information about where the meeting was to take place. The dispatch concluded: "We are expecting an immediate answer to Filipov (Stalin)."[221] The answer, already written, was sent the next day. It was a carefully crafted document in which the Yugoslav leaders sought to explain, once again to their comrades and judges, why they refused to take part in their assembly. They were prepared to collaborate with the Cominform, but noted that the problem on the agenda exclusively regarded a dispute between the CPY and the CPSU, a dispute that should be resolved on a bilateral level.[222] According to Djilas, Tito sent this communication directly, without submitting it to the CC for a final examination. Obviously, the marshal wanted to resolve the issue once and for all and had no intention of leaving any leeway for those who were uncertain and doubtful. He had other things to think about, as he was weighing the possibility of a Soviet invasion and seeing himself in the woods again, this time fighting the Red Army. During a walk with Djilas near the pond at Brdo Castle, he spoke about that possibility with an almost Greek sense of fate: "To fall in one's own country. At least the memory remains!"[223]

Meanwhile, in Bucharest, or rather in the royal castle nearby, the Cominform met to judge Tito and his comrades in absentia, according to Stalin's directives. The Yugoslavs were accused of revisionism and of imposing a "Turkish-type terror" on their country. In the resolution, drawn up by Palmiro Togliatti, "our best jurist," to quote Zhdanov, the "Yugoslav Communists worthy of the name" were invited to overthrow the leadership of the CPY and to replace it with a new one faithful to the ideals of the international proletariat.[224] Zhdanov even went so far as to declare: "We have information that Tito is an imperialist spy."[225] Aside from these absurd accusations, it must be noted, however, that the resolution blamed the Yugoslav leaders for a number of theoretical and practical sins, without touching on the international policy issues that were the origin of the Tito-Stalin split: the Bulgarian-Yugoslav federation, Belgrade's policy in Albania, and the Greek question. The text of the resolution was published in Prague by the newspaper *Rudé Právo* on June 28, Saint Vitus's Day, a fateful day in Serb history ever since their defeat on the Kosovo plain by the Turks in 1389. Tito received the text immediately thanks to the teleprinter, the new technological marvel recently installed at Brdo. It is said that while reading the long and verbose document he pounded the table with his fists while cursing Stalin. The following night, to calm himself, he took a gun, went to the garden, and began shooting the frogs to silence them. Shortly afterwards he suffered his first pancreatic attack.[226]

As Nikita S. Khrushchev said later, Stalin boasted at the time that all he had to do to get rid of Tito was to lift his little finger: he believed his agents, especially the Soviet representative at the Cominform, the philosopher Pavel J. Judin, who told him that his authority in Yugoslavia was undisputed and could not be opposed, especially not by "Marxist illiterates" such as Tito and his comrades.[227] It was a blunder that induced the Boss to make one of the worst mistakes of his life. He was convinced that he could destroy Tito in two months at the most, but his calculations were off because he failed to realize that Tito had at his disposal an army and police force that were loyal to him and not to Moscow. According to Stalin, the "leaders of the CPY were afraid to confess their treacherous and hypocritical attitude toward the CPSU to the Yugoslav people, who nourished a profound love and liking for the Soviet Union."[228] Actually, it was just the other way round: the leaders of the CPY published the Bucharest resolution and their answer to it, written by Djilas, in full. In it, they did not restrict themselves to confuting Stalin's accusations, but counterattacked, stressing the soundness of Tito's policy. The worst of injustices had been done to the party, to the working class and to the peoples of Yugoslavia, Djilas wrote, offering forces hostile to the socialist camp a formidable propaganda tool. The CC CPY denied any responsibility for the consequences that would follow, since it was the accusers who would have to bear the brunt.[229]

If Stalin deluded himself that he would find enough "healthy elements" among the Yugoslav Communists to be able to overthrow Belgrade's "political acrobats" and align Yugoslavia with the other satellites, he had made a fatal error, not realizing that the majority of the population would support Tito precisely to rid themselves of the Soviet influence. From 29 June on, it was clear that the marshal was the master of the situation. He was supported by all the government bodies and controlled the press and other media. In the capital, and in the rest of the country, life went on normally. The men in power displayed a supreme calm. On 30 June, Tito, who had been absent for a long time, reappeared in public, visiting the building site of the *New Belgrade*, one of the flagships of his regime. In order to stress the closeness of the Yugoslav peoples, he was accompanied by two Serb-Montenegrin generals, Svetozar Vukamanvić (Tempo) and Koča Popović, and by two Croat personalities, Vladimir Bakarić and Ivan Krajačić (Stevo). For the first time, he wore a civilian suit rather than one of his flashy uniforms: evidently, it was his way of showing the new face of the CPY. The youth brigades building the *New Belgrade* greeted him with great enthusiasm. Without special security measures, Tito passed among thousands of young people, speaking with them and asking them how the work was progressing.[230]

The quick, firm, and dignified Yugoslav answer to the Bucharest resolution gave London and Washington the impression that Tito would not follow the example of so many Communists, however brave and powerful, who in the past had shamefully recanted when accused of revisionism. According to Cecil King, the British chargé d'affaires in Belgrade, this was one of the most important events in the history of Communism. For the first time there appeared a chance that a "heresy" might develop that could count on having a territorial basis. Lev Trotsky, for instance, did not have at his disposal anything more than a villa in Mexico, nevertheless it had been deemed necessary to kill him with an ice pick. The consequences of opposition in a European country would be much worse, equal only to those uprisings in the distant past when the schism between Rome and Byzantium occurred.[231]

If the Bucharest resolution raised a storm of rumors, commentaries, and interpretations in the West, it created an even bigger surprise in the satellite countries and in circles close to the summit of power. As in Yugoslavia, so in other countries party discipline and the conspiratorial mentality did not allow the news of the Tito-Stalin split to spread very far, so that it did not reach those who had no right to know. The testimony of Wolfgang Leonhard, a young and promising functionary of the CC CP Germany in East Berlin, is significant. When the news of the excommunication came, he compared the main seat of the party to a beehive, even though Stalin had just decided to block the former capital—administered after the war by the victorious powers but located within the Soviet zone—isolating it from the West. The Cold War had reached one of its peaks. But so surprising was the expulsion of the CPY from the Cominform that practically everyone was talking about it rather than the blockade. When the Yugoslav answer came—which no satellite country newspaper dared to publish—the news was spread by the Voice of America and the BBC, causing even greater amazement. Tito's refusal to slavishly submit himself or recognize his errors had a profoundly subversive subtext, not just with regards to the abused system of criticism and self-criticism but to the entire Stalinist regime.[232]

Reading the accusations that Stalin heaped on the Yugoslavs, it is hard not to admit that some, although distorted, were not groundless. In reply to the charge that the CPY was "illegal," hiding itself behind the Popular Front, Tito and his comrades decided to come out into the open after years of conspiracy. At the end of July, the Fifth Congress of the Communist Party was convened with great pomp in the Palace of the Guards, not far from the marshal's residence. In Belgrade, it was even more significant that the people adorned the windows according to tradition, with carpets and bedcovers, testifying to a popular mood certainly not dictated by propaganda.[233]

Tito inaugurated the congress on 21 July with a five-hour speech, written by himself, that he succeeded in completing in spite of the sweltering weather, without showing fatigue and even gaining momentum during the reading. More than a "Policy Report" (as the paper was entitled), it was a detailed description of the party's difficult history from 1860 onward. Tito exalted its glorious past with its struggles and sacrifices, stressing the merits acquired during the war and the postwar reconstruction. He decidedly rejected the Cominform resolution as a "monstrous defamation, an attack on the unity of the party and incitement to civil war." He criticized neighboring countries for their hostile attitude toward Yugoslavia, and mocked the "great Marxists" who interpreted the doctrine dogmatically, forgetting that it should be a source for action. He finally reviewed Yugoslav foreign policy, confirming its alignment with the Soviet Union and stressing the unchanged will of the CPY to remain in good relations with the CPSU: "Till now, the CPY has honorably accomplished its historical mission, and I am profoundly convinced that it will do the same in future, achieving victory in the construction of socialism and remaining faithful to the teachings of Marx, Engels, Lenin and Stalin."[234]

The speech, often interrupted by cries and cheering, was broadcast and was listened to in every home, factory, street, and square in the country. It was accompanied by delirious applause, which reached its apex at the end of the congress when Tito closed in a loud voice by saying: "Hail to the Soviet Union, led by the genius Stalin!" although it was clear, that he had no intention of accepting his criticism.[235] Aleš Bebler, the deputy minister of foreign affairs, wrote in his memoirs: "He who has experienced this congress cannot compare it with any other. The entire hall, several thousand people, was outraged because of the incredible accusations and ready for a clear, firm reply, without compromises. There were so many cries, songs, bursts of applause, and shouting. As if we were a single man. When Tito appeared at the rostrum and when he was explicitly supported by somebody, there were endless cries: 'Tito-Party! Tito-Army! Tito-Central Committee!' The hall resounded with these slogans in its entire extent. New words were adapted to old Partisan songs: 'Comrade Tito, we swear never to depart from your road . . .' and 'The more the accusations and lies, the more Tito is dear to us and the more we love him.'"[236]

The Cominformists

After the Fifth Congress, which confirmed the leadership of the party, Stalin's fight with Tito acquired a new slant: clandestine brochures, published by the *Pravda* in Moscow, began to appear in Yugoslavia, spreading the contents of the secret correspondence of the past months. The promoters of this action evidently wanted to convince Yugoslav public opinion of the validity of the Soviet accusations but also to frighten the people. In fact, since March, rumors had been circulating that those who were in opposition to the Soviet Union would be killed on the spot or sent to Siberia when the "healthy forces" came into power.[237] Although at the congress only five of 2,323 delegates voted against Tito, and no opposition group emerged, the marshal and his comrades feared a pro-Stalinist uprising. For this reason, as well as to avoid a possible Soviet attack, they decided to organize Partisan units that would back up the army, since its cadres had been heavily Russified. After the war, seventeen Yugoslav generals and about six hundred officers and sub-officers had attended Soviet military academies. Stalin thought he would use them, allowing those surprised by the Bucharest resolution in the USSR to return home. Of course, the Yugoslav authorities accepted them with due distrust, and with reason: Soviet agents were discovered even among Tito's bodyguards, above all General Moma Djurević (called Val). According to Djilas, he organized a plot, discovered by the UDBA, in which the members of the Politburo were to be "liquidated" while they were playing billiards.[238]

In spite of the vigilance of the UDBA, which under Ranković's guidance became particularly energetic in suffocating any activity favorable to the Cominform, it was not long before the "healthy forces" appeared on the scene. The first was the former "Wahhabist," Radonja Golubović, Yugoslav ambassador in Bucharest. On 1 August 1948, he published a long letter in the journal *Scînteia*, which he had sent a few days earlier to the presidency of the Fifth Congress. He had been sure, he wrote, that the CPY would try to heal the fracture with the other communist parties caused by Belgrade's political line. But this did not happen, and "open terror reigns within the party. All those comrades who express—however shyly or harmlessly—their disagreement with the anti-Marxist and anti-Soviet attitude of the Central Committee of the CPY are being expelled from the party, compelled by various methods to recant or, if this fails, be thrown into jail." Golubović had no intention of following the leadership on the path to bourgeois perdition, at the end of which Yugoslavia would become a colony of Western imperialism. He stepped down from his ambassadorial post. This decision provoked a sensation and was a source of considerable embarrassment to the Belgrade authorities, since his j'accuse was reprinted by *Pravda* and the communist press throughout the world, but also by that of the West.[239]

The confirmation that a pro-Stalinist opposition existed, which the proclaimed official unity was unable to hide, came a few days later from Montenegro. In that republic, the majority in the local government changed from one day to the next. Without a word of explanation, the vice-president of the Montenegrin government, the president of the Control Commission, and the ministers of commerce, education, and industry, all of whom had been delegates to the recent Fifth Congress, resigned and were replaced by new people. But there were "slight deviations," as Aleš Bebler confided to Western journalists, even in the federal government. Seeds of resistance, more or less vigorous, were present everywhere, and there were even cases of old Partisans who returned to the woods in order to fight the new "Fascists." Not to mention the Yugoslav diplomats abroad, who used the occasion to take refuge under Moscow's wings.[240] Especially dangerous was the unrest among the army officers, many of whom were questioning the future of the People's Army since it had lost its role as the left wing of the Red Army. Among those seduced by the NKVD was Boško Čolić, Tito's first assistant, who had faithfully stayed by his side during and after the war. After the resolution, he hid a surveillance bug in the wall of the marshal's office. When discovered, he would have been condemned to death if Tito had not prevented it. He was sentenced to twenty years in prison and was pardoned after twelve years.[241] This was, of course, kept secret, but shortly thereafter there was another episode that had a vast echo. According to the official version, on the night between 12 and 13 August 1948, three high ranking army officers tried to cross the Romanian frontier illegally and take refuge in Bucharest. The most famous of the three was Arso Jovanović, former chief of Tito's Supreme Staff, who had allegedly tried to organize a military coup d'état after the Fifth Congress.[242]

Conditioned as he was by his rigid mentality and his training in the Royal Army, Arso was incapable of playing a constructive role in the Partisan ranks, as he had already demonstrated at the beginning of the war. He was a courageous and intelligent man, but with limited horizons, fanatically hostile to everything Western and a convinced Russophile. Tito, however, appreciated his military efficiency and often entrusted him with delicate assignments.[243] It was Jovanović, for instance, who, together with Žujović, led the Yugoslav delegation that welcomed the Soviet mission when it arrived at the Supreme Staff on 1 February 1944. In January of the following year, he accompanied Andrija Hebrang to Moscow, where he took part in important political and military discussions. But it was then that his psychological limits became evident. At a dinner with Stalin he lost control of his nerves when the Boss, as usual, began saying that the Bulgarian troops were better than the Yugoslav ones. This upset Jovanović so much that he began to shout hysterically, making hostile gestures toward the host. That same night, two colonels of the NKVD came to his residence, where they subjected him to an intense interrogation, accusing him of bad behavior in Stalin's presence. Allegedly, this was when they forced him to accept a collaboration with the NKVD.[244]

Because of this incident, Jovanović had to step down from his post as chief of staff in favor of Koča Popović, and was sent to the Voroshilov Academy in Moscow for a specialized course. There he became even more entangled in the NKVD's net because of a love affair with the daughter of a Soviet general (Jovanović was married and the puritanism of the war years was still current in the party). The affair was brought to the attention of the Yugoslav secret services. When he returned from Moscow, he was put before a board of enquiry. The former chief of staff considered this an affront and withdrew into himself. At a reception given by Tito for the top brass, he behaved like a "wet hen," to use the marshal's words.[245] Although he was still seen in the inner circle, it was clear that the Yugoslav leaders no longer trusted him completely. He was given a relatively modest post as director of the military academy, which disappointed him and hurt his pride. At the time of Žujović's and Hebrang's arrest, rumors linking his name to the two were circulating, but they stopped when Jovanović seemed to side with Tito after the Bucharest resolution. Like all army colonels and generals, he participated as a delegate in the Fifth Congress. This was his first public appearance after his return from the Soviet Union. Although he did not play a significant role, the assembly elected him to the commission entrusted with formulating the new program of the CPY.[246]

His failed attempt to flee, which ended with his death (if the official version is to be believed) provoked enormous clamor and curiosity. Rumors circulated that the adventure of the unfortunate general and his companions was part of a precise political plan orchestrated by Andrei Ja. Vyshinskii, a Soviet high diplomat, and Ana Pauker, the foreign minister of Romania, to undermine the stability of the Belgrade government. According to these suppositions, they had come to Belgrade not just to take part in the international Danube Conference, organized there in August 1948, but also to arrange the flight of various Yugoslav personalities to Romania. Once in Bucharest, they were to create a government in exile which, when recognized by the Soviet Union and by the satellites, would have all the necessary authority to incite the

Yugoslav Communists to rebel and eventually to ask for the "brotherly" help of the Eastern troops.[247]

The news of Jovanović's death was published by *Borba* on 18 August, the day the Danube Conference closed its doors, which served as marching orders from the Yugoslav authorities to Ana Pauker and Vyshinskii, who left Belgrade empty-handed. The reaction to this unexpected announcement was immediate and extremely violent, akin to the press campaign unleashed some weeks earlier on the occasion of an assassination attempt against Togliatti. On 20 August, the Romanian agency Ager Press wrote that Jovanović had been the victim of a "vile murder" and, in a note reprinted by all the newspapers, accused the "treacherous Tito-Ranković clique " of using "Hitler-type methods." Similar suppositions, which also circulated in Belgrade, came from other sides as well: in Hungary, the party secretary, Mátyás Rákosi, protested in hysterical tones against the terror instituted by the Yugoslav leaders, who were, in his words, killing the most sincere democrats and heroes of the liberation struggle: "Today in Yugoslavia the supporters of the Soviet Union and of the international proletariat are hunted like game."[248] Although the Soviet media stayed out of the press campaign, it nevertheless got even worse over the following days. On 24 August, the newspaper *Scînteia* published a long article by the former ambassador, Golubović, who branded the leaders of the CPY as a "band of assassins and criminals" who used Fascist methods worthy of Hitler, Mussolini, and Franco.[249]

Golubović's article was the last straw for the Yugoslav leaders. Until then they had tried to show that, notwithstanding the falling out between the Parties, they stood loyal to the socialist camp. In the polemics with the Cominform press, their newspapers simply replied to the attacks in a more or less defensive manner. However, because of the accusations that poured in from the Eastern capitals after Jovanović's death, the Belgrade government felt it was time to change their tune. It went on the offensive with an official note on 25 August to the Romanian Interior Ministry. The note declared the behavior of the highest Romanian leaders "unacceptable," starting with "lady" Ana Pauker, who openly dared to urge the Yugoslav Communists to overthrow Tito and his comrades. It was obvious that the relations between the two states would be gravely compromised as a result. Moreover, the disgraceful activity of the "instigators" weakened the position of Yugoslavia vis-à-vis the imperialist forces, strengthening their pressure on a socialist country. The following day, a similar note was sent to the Hungarian government, which was also particularly hostile toward Yugoslavia.[250] The implicit conclusion of the Belgrade government's argument was obvious: if the socialist front in the Balkans and Central Europe collapsed, Yugoslavia would certainly not be to blame.

Goli Otok

The title of *Borba*'s editorial on 21 August 1948, "Let's Intensify Vigilance to Reinforce the Party Ranks," announced a purge that would free the CPY of careerists and wavering and hostile elements. Words were soon followed by deeds. Ranković's repressive machine started to run at full speed, and being well-oiled because of the struggle with the Chetniks and Ustaša, it worked extremely well against real or supposed Cominformists. Hundreds of army officers and administrative officials, mostly old Communists, were imprisoned. Soon the arrests were so numerous that the courts were unable to cope with them. To overcome this difficulty, a decree was published in August instituting so-called "administrative conviction." It stated that persons dangerous to the state could be sentenced to two years of "work useful to society" (doubled if necessary) by a simple decision of the organs of public security. In fact, this punishment often lasted ten or as many as eighteen years.[251]

Tito made the decision to isolate the "Cominformists" without previous consultation with the CC and the Politburo because his Moscow experience had taught him how to deal with the "internal enemy." The order for the purge came suddenly, before the first "concentration camp" was ready to house the internees. It was announced by the marshal himself at the Second Congress of the CP of Croatia when he said in an ambiguous but menacing manner: "Comrades, there are two ways to convince somebody: the first is with words, then there is another one."[252] A suitable place for this other way was found by Ivan Krajačić (Stevo), who discovered Goli Otok, or Bald Island, in the Gulf of Quarner while he and the sculptor Antun Augustinčić were looking for high-quality marble. He mentioned this to Kardelj, who immediately saw the possibility of organizing a concentration camp in that desolate location. Tito agreed.[253] The operation was implemented in utmost secrecy, to the point that it was not known even to the chief of the General Staff, Koča Popović. Kardelj later tried to justify himself, saying, "If we had not organized such a camp, Stalin would have transformed all of Yugoslavia into a terrible gulag."[254] The regime introduced on Goli Otok, and in other similar places, was utterly brutal, as its aim was to destroy the personality and dignity of the internees who, according to their jailers, were to be "reeducated." They were often deprived of water and food and subjected to backbreaking work that was completely useless, even Sisyphean: they had to chip away stones and transport them from one place to another. According to the ancient Russian custom, the new arrivals had to pass between two rows of "older" prisoners, who beat them with fists and sticks. This was only the beginning of the terrible physical and psychological suffering that awaited them. To quote Vlado Dapčević, who endured the Goli Otok regime for years: "In no concentration camp were there similar torments. Not in the German nor Soviet camps, nor in the American ones in Korea, nor in the French ones in Algeria. . . . Nowhere."[255]

More than thirty thousand people, some of whom were guilty only of having expressed a critical remark about Tito and his comrades, others who were completely innocent, experienced the hell of Goli Otok and similar institutions. At the same time, there was no lack of fanatical Stalinists among the internees who could have been very dangerous to the regime in case of a Soviet military attack. Both found themselves in a desperate situation, without any judicial redress, completely cut off from their families and from the outside world, where they could return—or so they were promised—if they would denounce prison mates who persisted in their error, which frequently happened. It seems that the Yugoslav leadership, ready to see enemies everywhere, had no doubts about the regime installed on Goli Otok. Only later were there any relative afterthoughts, as shown by Tito's attempts to save some of his generals. Yet he was also quite aware of the existence in the army of "dissident elements." According to the chief political commissar, General Otmar Kreačić, 30 percent of officers in combat units were pro-Cominform.[256] There would have been even more if so many of the prewar Communists, schooled in Moscow and therefore loyal to Stalin, had not fallen during the liberation struggle. Tito confessed this to John F. Kennedy, then a young member of the United States House of Representatives, during his visit to Yugoslavia in January 1951.[257]

Collectivization of Agriculture

While it was possible to isolate the Cominformist "fifth column," it was not so easy to master the peasants, whom Tito and his comrades tried to coerce onto collective farms in an attempt to demonstrate to Stalin how wrong he was in accusing them of being followers of Bukharin and of being too lenient toward the kulaks. After the war, the new leaders followed a rather prudent policy in the countryside; for example, in 1946 by the "law on cooperatives" that stated that these were "voluntary economic enterprises of the working people."[258] In October 1947, Tito affirmed: "With regards to the rumors about the expropriation of land, tell the peasants that it is an outright lie. Nobody will take the land from them, because, for God's sake, to whom should we give it?"[259] In this he agreed with Stalin, who counseled the Yugoslavs to be prudent with the collectivization of agriculture, for it was "a difficult and perilous task."[260]

At the start of the following year, Tito was indignant because of some "excessive" measures taken in the countryside by the local authorities. To Jakov Blažević, newly nominated as minister of commerce, he recommended caution in dealing with the peasants, saying, "We should not unsettle them, because who will fight tomorrow, in case of a war?"[261] But when Moša Pijade wrote an article after the Bucharest resolution in 1948 in which he dared to tell the truth, namely that the peasants had been the main supporters of the "revolution" during the liberation struggle, he was heavily attacked and obliged to recant this heresy.[262] Among the few who were against excessively radical measures were Edvard Kardelj and Vladimir Bakarić, but their words had no effect, even though the former cited Lenin in support of his argument and was not opposed in principle to the "strengthening of socialism in the countryside." On the contrary, he favored it, but in a humane way, sure that the peasants themselves would realize sooner or later where their interests lay.[263] In the end, the heavy-handed method prevailed for reasons described by an Agitprop representative meeting with peasants in Šumadija, deepest Serbia: "Cursed kulaks, because of you Stalin attacked us!"[264] In short, the opinion prevailed that it was necessary to "deny with deeds" the Boss's accusations, firstly at the expense of the peasants, who had to be destroyed as a social class. They accomplished this with due speed. At the end of 1947 there were only 799 "collective cooperatives," whereas in January 1949 they already numbered 1,318 and the following December, 6,492.[265]

By June 1950, the regime controlled 22 percent of all the arable land, but the result of this policy was disastrous. From the very beginning, the peasants opposed collectivization, more or less passively, butchering their animals or hiding provisions, but also burning crops. The most dramatic event happened in the Cazin region of eastern Bosnia, where during the winter of 1948 an uprising erupted among local Muslims, many of whom had participated in the liberation struggle.[266] The authorities reacted to the opposition of the rural masses by promising those who had joined the cooperatives that they could leave after a three-year trial. But when this period expired, it was evident that the optimistic predictions of the party ideologists, according to whom the peasants would discover by themselves the "advantages" of the collective economy, were wrong. During the 1951 harvest, the number of those who wanted to leave grew steadily. And since the authorities reacted with propaganda against the "class enemies," and used all possible forms of pressure, the peasants let the crops rot in the fields.[267] Tito himself recognized that the behavior of the local authorities toward the rebel peasants was excessive: "We don't have a Siberia, but if we had, we would not hesitate to send people there."[268]

After such bitter experiences and because they feared a popular revolt, the authorities finally renounced forced collectivization at the beginning of the fifties, when Yugoslavia was on the brink of famine, due at least partly to drought. However, they remained suspicious of the countryside, which seriously hindered the development of a modernized agriculture. Not until 1956 did production in this sector reach the prewar level.[269] In many parts of the country the land was cultivated in a primitive way, with wooden ploughs and without chemical fertilizers. In 1960, after the 1 May festivities, Dušan Bilandžić, a young representative of the CP of Croatia, escorted an Italian delegation through Posavina, a fertile area between Belgrade and Banja Luka. Only horses, sometimes replaced by men, were pulling the ploughs in the fields. "Look, how they plough with the communist tractors," commented an Italian scornfully.[270]

In such conditions the peasants could not live from agriculture alone but had to find work in factories and in the building industry. Although after the war more than half of the population lived in the countryside, the state was compelled to import food, since the peasants did not produce enough for the market. Tito was aware of this and relinquished the idea of a more rational agriculture, albeit with difficulty, opting for methods acceptable to the peasants. He admitted that "we have destroyed by ourselves our biggest factory, the factory that produces food" and that "we have made a capital error following the Soviet way," regretting that the regime had not been able to organize the cooperatives with the necessary patience and more democratic means.[271] In November 1965, he confessed to Eleonore Staimer, ambassador of the German Democratic Republic in Belgrade, that the implementation of a socialist agriculture was an extremely difficult venture, "even more difficult than the revolution itself."[272]

Exacerbation of the Conflict with the Soviet Union

The Yugoslav leaders made an enormous mistake in thinking that they could get back into Stalin's good graces with land collectivization and the nationalization of small family businesses. On the contrary, at the end of 1948 the Boss reinforced the offensive against them by starting to persecute all those in the satellite countries who could be accused of being favorable to Tito. The first to fall was Władysław Gomułka, secretary general of the Polish Workers Party and deputy prime minister of the Warsaw government, who Stalin accused of bourgeois and nationalistic leanings. In reality, his major crime was that he had maintained his distance from the Bucharest resolution. He was arrested and condemned to a harsh prison sentence.[273]

Meanwhile, on 24 August 1948, Andrei A. Zhdanov, the most important interpreter of the Kremlin's political line after the Second World War, died suddenly. According to information collected by the French ambassador in Moscow, Yves Chataigneau, after his burial Tito contacted Stalin with a final invitation to overcome the resolution crisis. The same rumors also circulated in Belgrade, nurtured by the hope that the disappearance of the principal protagonist of the Bucharest excommunication would give the Boss a valid excuse to correct his policy. These illusions were shattered on 8 September 1948, with a long article published by *Pravda* entitled "Where Is the Nationalism of Tito's Clique Leading Yugoslavia?" It was a tirade that condemned the Belgrade leaders without appeal, denouncing them as ignoble, hypocritical, and hostile to Lenin's doctrine. Their proclaimed love of the Soviet Union was just a cheap stratagem to deceive the Yugoslav people. In reality, during the Fifth Congress, when the rhetorical phrases about Yugoslavia as part of the united anti-imperialist front were especially loud, "Tito's faction passed to the opposite camp, renouncing the alliance with the revolutionary international proletariat and preparing the ruin of the country."[274]

These tough words, the harshest ever used by the Soviet press, were signed "CEKA" in boldface capital letters. In Russian, but also in Serbian, this suggested the Central Committee, giving weight to the text. According to the experts at the British Embassy in Moscow, this article was characteristic of Stalin's style, with his taste for heavy irony and obsessive repetitions of the same ideas.[275] This did not escape the Belgrade leaders, who until this point had taken comfort in the relative silence of the Soviet press, which they considered a good omen for possible reconciliation. The *Pravda* article therefore came as an unwelcome surprise, as shown by the fact that it was not mentioned in the Yugoslav media. To make the attack even more offensive, in the same issue *Pravda* published a biography of Arso Jovanović, "recently killed in a barbaric way" and "dear to the memory of all those who have fought Fascism." The following day, the article was also published by the Soviet government newspaper *Izvestiia*, this time accompanied by a violent letter written by the fugitive general Krsto Popivoda. The Kremlin obviously wanted to stress with all its authority that nationalism was an unforgivable sin, and admonish not only the Yugoslavs but the other satellites as well that "internationalism," in the sense of absolute subjection to Moscow, was a categorical imperative.[276]

In the face of the attacks that came from all sides and pinpointed Tito as the main enemy of the proletariat worldwide, many thought that Stalin would try to get rid of him with violence. "Tito's assassination," wrote American diplomat Robert B. Reams on 5 September 1948, "is probably the most concrete political option for the Cominform." He added, however, that "in the first place, it would have been necessary to penetrate one of the most rigorous security systems in the world."[277] The Yugoslav authorities, knowing that such threats were anything but imaginary, took strict measures to guarantee the safety of the marshal and his closest collaborators. Tito, Kardelj, Ranković, and Djilas no longer appeared together in public, and each always had a heavily armed escort. When the marshal visited Zagreb at the beginning of September, he came with three armored trains equipped with machine guns as well as two light tanks.[278]

The Yugoslav leaders did not limit themselves to strengthening their defenses but also went on the offensive. On 18 September, for instance, Moša Pijade, Tito's intellectual mentor, published an article in *Borba* entitled "Giving Up the Facts for Dogma." It was a sensation because, for the first time, the old revolutionary attacked the CPSU with all his caustic irony, implicitly accusing it of reactionary tendencies. He reproached the Soviet politicians for being lost in a sea of dogmatic quotations and for being totally incapable of formulating the new ideas that the times demanded and that were urgently needed by the countries who were moving toward socialism. Pijade replied to the assertion that the laws regarding the transition from capitalism to socialism, discovered by Marx and Engels and implemented and developed by Lenin and Stalin, were obligatory for all, by saying that the conditions for the progress of socialism differed according to particular places and situations and that, therefore, every doctrinaire approach would be foreign to true Marxism-Leninism.[279]

An article that appeared in *Borba* on 2, 3, and 4 October, under the title "Once Again Speaking about Unjust and False Accusations," caused even more of a sensation. It was not signed, but this gave it special weight. Obviously such a text could never have been published if it had not been written by Tito himself, or at least approved by him. In fact, the marshal identified so much with the author that during a meeting with an American visitor he mentioned the article as if it were his. In reality, he simply gave a *placet* to what Djilas had written, not without initially expressing some doubts as to whether it was opportune to attack Stalin in person, thus destroying every illusion about his possible change of mind. But Djilas insisted, as he reports in his memoirs, stressing that it was public knowledge who was behind the anti-Yugoslav propaganda and that remaining silent on the subject caused great confusion in the party ranks. "All right," said Tito, "leave it as it is, we have spared Stalin much too long."[280] In the article, Djilas expressed thoughts he had been ruminating on and had discussed with Kardelj and Kidrič. He began by claiming a special role in the socialist camp for Yugoslavia, recalling that its liberation struggle was at the same time a revolution, with its climax the seizure of power by the working class. This gave the CPY the right to build socialism in its own way. Those Eastern bloc countries, including the Soviet Union, that accused the Yugoslav party of nationalism, consequently deviated from "real internationalism." Yugoslavia had no intention of joining the imperialist camp and isolating itself from the democratic socialist countries, but it was not ready to accept unfounded criticism and foreign attempts to isolate its leadership from the people. It also refuted the Soviet monopoly on the correct interpretation of Marxism, contesting Stalin's carapace of infallibility. Until then, the Yugoslav press had not mentioned the Boss, not because of any illusion harbored about his position in the controversy, but because it seemed inappropriate to argue with him since he had not personally entered the arena. Be that as it may, the party members knew what his ideas were: "Stalin is the greatest living authority, not only of the international workers movement, but of the entire democratic world. Nevertheless, in the struggle with the CPY he is not on the right side."[281]

The article was immediately recognized by Yugoslav public opinion and by foreign observers as a deliberate attempt to reshape Stalin's myth and an open recognition that the split was irreversible. "Yugoslav criticism of the infallible prophet of Moscow eliminates all possibilities for reconciliation, if there ever had been any," commented the American ambassador to the Kremlin.[282] In fact, as Djilas affirmed, it set off within Yugoslavia a reexamination of the Soviet system and marked the beginning of its detachment from the Soviet Union and its political practice based on lies and abuse of power. Against the vision of a society crystallized in orthodoxy, Djilas affirmed ethical and revolutionary values, remarking: "Authority is not everything, truth is above authority."[283] Sir Charles Peake soon realized the importance of the article, confirming that the underground struggle had at this point come out into the open: "Indeed the present stage of this quarrel may not unfitly be likened to a game of chess. Up to the present there has been little more than a wearisome movement of pawns, but now for the first time the queens have a sight of one another, and are beginning to move up. It would be rash indeed to predict the result of the game; all it seems safe to say at the moment is that Tito is unlikely to give up without a struggle."[284]

Tito was able to survive in part thanks to the prevailing opinion in Washington and London that his rebellion against Stalin was relevant for strategic as well as psychological and propagandistic reasons. "A new factor of fundamental importance surfaced in the international Communist movement subsequent to the fact that one of its members had successfully challenged the Kremlin," the analysts of the American State Department wrote. They compared Tito with Martin Luther and Henry VIII, hoping that his example would fatally shake the monolithic Soviet bloc. At the same time, they thought it essential for the East that the "Ljubljana gap" under Mount Nanos (the easiest passage from Pannonia to the Padania Plains), as well as the Dalmatian coast and the Vardar Valley near the Aegean, should be controlled by forces free from Soviet influence. This meant that Moscow would no longer be able to exercise immediate pressure on the Eastern Mediterranean and the Middle East.[285] On the basis of these considerations, the Americans and the British soon decided to support Tito and to free him from the grip of Stalin, who had tried to ruin him economically by severing Yugoslavian commercial and industrial ties with the Soviet bloc.

Tito was well aware of the strategic significance of his split with Stalin. "The Americans are not stupid," he said to Djilas during the summer of 1948, "they will not allow the Russians in these conditions to reach the Adriatic."[286] In affirming this, he overlooked some hotheads in the American secret services who thought the time had come to organize a Chetnik coup against his regime. In spite of warnings by Ambassador Cavendish W. Cannon not to play with fire, they sent a group of Serb parachutists to Yugoslavia in January 1949, whose task was to kindle a revolt and put King Petar II back on the throne. However, the UDBA immediately managed to halt the attempt, capturing and killing the Chetniks. The State Department was against such initiatives and suppressed them in order to prevent them from exerting a negative influence on the nascent dialogue between Tito and the leaders of the capitalist world.[287]

Obviously, it was not easy to accept Western help, especially as Tito feared opposition by the most orthodox members of CPY. When the effects of the economic boycott proclaimed by the Soviet Union and imposed by Stalin on the satellites began to be felt seriously, Tito had no hesitation. The fact that suddenly industrial machines and even gasoline stopped coming from the East gave him no choice. In August 1948, he had already accepted secret supplies of crude oil, which had until then come from Romania, from Zone A of the Free Territory of Trieste, administered by the English and Americans, although in mid-1949 he still had doubts as to whether it was opportune to accept the more substantial economic aid offered by Washington.[288]

Aleš Bebler, member of the Yugoslav delegation to the General Assembly of the UN, also contributed to the conviction in Western circles that the split between Moscow and Belgrade was definitive, and that Tito had abandoned every hope in a "descent of Stalin from the sky." On 5 October 1948, he had dinner with one of the most important Foreign Office diplomats, Secretary of State Hector McNeill. They had met the previous spring, when Bebler was in London for several weeks, a circumstance that favored their dialogue. McNeill prepared himself thoroughly for the meeting, reading the most important dispatches sent by Sir Charles Peake. He therefore knew the ambassador's arguments about the gradual evolution of the regime, and the need to support its detachment from Moscow, but to do so cautiously.[289] He was surprised, however, by the political realism and frankness of Bebler, who did not hide that he was extremely down with regards both to his government's internal difficulties and its international isolation, which had been particularly evident in Paris, where the Yugoslav delegation was treated with coldness both by the Eastern and the Western blocs.

But mostly he was preoccupied because of the economic situation of the country: the entire Five-year Plan was in jeopardy. It seemed that the Yugoslavs could count only on their irremovable determination. Whatever assistance the British could offer in such an emergency would be of vital importance.[290]

If Bebler had known that Guy Burgess, one of the Soviet "moles" in the Foreign Office, was McNeill's assistant, and that many documents relating to Yugoslavia ended up on Stalin's desk, he would probably have been less sincere and would consequently have impressed the British diplomats much less. When McNeill's report began circulating in the Foreign Office, confirmation came from Belgrade that Tito himself shared Bebler's opinion. During this period, he also had dinner with Eric Johnston, a representative of the American Motion Picture Corporation, who had come to Yugoslavia to sell Hollywood films. The marshal, who loved cinema, not only agreed to open Yugoslav society to Western mass culture, but also gave the American a frank interview. Johnston informed him from the start that he would share the discussion with the leader of the Republican Party, Thomas Dewey, and the marshal, knowing he was speaking to a vast audience, decided to lay his cards on the table. He stressed the fact that he had lived and would die a Communist, but he wanted to be master in his own house and Moscow had tried to deny him this right. In the present difficult situation, he urgently needed better trade relations with the West, which should not however ask him for political concessions, since that might alarm his followers. When Johnston asked him what his attitude would be in the case of war between the Soviet Union and the United States, Tito initially answered evasively but later, disavowing what he had always said about his unshakable loyalty to Moscow, replied that it would depend on who started the war.[291]

These two conversations made waves in diplomatic and government circles in Washington and London. The British foreign minister, Ernest Bevin, after reading McNeill's dispatch, noted on it that he would like to "talk policy" with his colleagues in charge of the Balkan sector. They concluded that it was important to assist Tito in his efforts to remain independent from Moscow. Bevin expressed this idea with a laconic but authoritative directive that later almost became a rallying cry, not just for the British but for the West in general: "Keep him afloat!"[292]

Stalin knew all this, informed not by Burgess alone but by another "mole," Donald Maclean, counselor to the British Embassy in Washington. The frequent reminders in the British and American documents that they should be considered top secret, therefore, had the opposite effect. As Anatoly S. Anikeev says, this may have prompted Stalin to take a more radical attitude toward Tito than initially envisaged.[293] One of the most significant and painful measures he took was the exclusion of Yugoslavia from the Council of Mutual Economic Assistance (COMECON), formed in Moscow at the beginning of January 1949. This made it easier to coordinate the economic boycott of the Belgrade rebels. When Kardelj, Yugoslavia's foreign minister since September 1948, protested and reminded the Soviet government of the numerous commercial treaties signed by his country with members of the new organization, all he got was a sarcastic answer from the Kremlin. Only those states that had an "honorable and friendly policy" in their mutual relations had the right to be part of COMECON.[294]

The prudent policy that Kardelj had tried to follow from September 1948 had no effect. At the beginning of October 1948, he sent Tito a dispatch from the UN General Assembly in Paris, where he wrote with proud satisfaction: "Marko Ristić (the Yugoslav ambassador in France) has declared that Yugoslavia [after the United States and the Soviet Union] is the third independent country at this session. In fact, he seems to be right. It is pathetic to see the Czechs and the Poles avoiding us in the corridors, but trying to contact our delegates in the restrooms in order to express their sympathy."[295] In contrast to these self-congratulatory words, however, he participated in discussions and voting in the Assembly in complete harmony with the Soviets, as he did not want to quarrel openly with them. At the same time, he felt ashamed that he said nothing about the split with Stalin.[296]

When the Americans and the British felt that Tito was able and willing to cope with the terrible Soviet pressure, they decided to organize a rescue operation, which in the following month moved from economic assistance to diplomatic support. They did not try to influence his political regime, asking only one favor: the closing of the border between Vardar and Aegean Macedonia and the ending of Yugoslav military aid to the Greek rebels.[297] They therefore sent Tito's old comrade-in-arms Fitzroy Maclean to Belgrade; the marshal promised him that he would review his policy in Greece, since the situation had changed drastically there because of the decision by the Greek Communists to side with Stalin. Consequently, the governments of Belgrade and Athens, for years fiercely hostile to each other, found themselves on the same side of the barricade.[298] On 10 June, Tito gave a speech in Pula in Istria, announcing that he would accept Western economic aid and would seal off the frontier with Greece. This was decisive for the outcome of the civil war in that country and, a few months later, the Greek Communists had to surrender. This led to the bitter recrimination by the secretary general of the local party, who claimed that they would never have started the uprising if they had foreseen Tito's treachery.[299] The Soviets took immediate revenge during the conference on the peace treaty with Austria, withdrawing their support of Yugoslavia's territorial claims in southern Carinthia and recognizing the border between the two states as final. Because of this "sell-out," a heated debate developed between Belgrade and Moscow that, according to the Western press, seemed to announce with its rancor the interruption of diplomatic relations.[300]

The note delivered by a Soviet Embassy official on 20 August 1949 at 4:15 a.m. to a janitor at the Ministry of Foreign Affairs in Belgrade seemed to be of a particularly menacing nature. This was the custom in case of a declaration of war. The Moscow government lodged a complaint against the arrest of Soviet citizens residing in Yugoslavia, the so-called "White Russians" who, after the October Revolution, found shelter in the Kingdom of Serbs, Croats, and Slovenes. During the Second World War, some of these refugees had been recruited by the Germans, while at the end of the war those who had neither escaped nor been shot had to accept Soviet citizenship, which was granted by Moscow without bothering to ask for Belgrade's consent. This generosity had a quid pro quo: in return the "White Russians" were to become Stalin's "fifth column" in Yugoslavia. When the split openly erupted, Tito was not inclined to ignore the activity of these "counterrevolutionary" elements. They became victims of Ranković's police, who began to arrest them in 1948. Moscow reacted promptly. The note of 20 August was the last and the most threatening in a series of diplomatic protests: it denied Yugoslavia the right to prosecute Soviet citizens, even if guilty, declaring that the Soviet government would defend them, adopting if needed "more efficient measures" than mere words.[301]

Kardelj and Bebler panicked. Not long before, the Soviet Union had recalled its ambassador, the young and plump Lavrent'ev, from Belgrade, without naming a successor, while news of troop movements in Hungary and Romania toward the Yugoslav border were more and more alarming, especially in view of rumors about the existence in neighboring countries of "international brigades" ready to march on Belgrade. Could "more efficient measures" be interpreted as the threat of an imminent armed attack? Kardelj immediately rang the French, British, and American ambassadors, inviting them to come to the ministry for consultations that evening. When Bebler reached Tito by phone at Brioni, where he was on vacation, the appointment was cancelled. The marshal ordered the two of them to keep calm and thus not play into the hands of the Soviets. He decided to prolong his sojourn on the Adriatic for a few more days and to return to Belgrade via Zagreb, as he had promised the Croats. In reality, he too was extremely worried, for it was clear that the 20 August note had been written by Stalin himself.[302]

Since he did not want to repeat the situation of April 1941, when the aggressors had been able to cut off the Belgrade government from the outside world, even before starting hostilities, Tito ordered the highest political and military personalities to move to Topola, in Šumadija. In the meantime, he began transferring food, arms, archives, and even entire industries into the center of the country.[303] He ordered Svetozar Vukmanović (Tempo) to organize Partisan units that would stay and fight in the occupied areas in case of invasion. The main army forces, about 275,000 men, were to withdraw to the massif stretching from Bosnia to the sea, since only there would it be possible to organize an efficient defense. Maximum efforts were dedicated to the army, which got 50 percent of the 1949 budget.[304]

After seriously thinking it over, Stalin abandoned the idea of military intervention in Yugoslavia. According to Nikolai A. Bulganin, full member of the Politburo and marshal of the Soviet Union, "he did not strike" mostly because of the opposition of the Red Army top brass, who were aware that such a move could degenerate into a third world war.[305] Tito and his comrades, however, did not know this: it was only later, in 1951, that Pietro Nenni, the leader of the Italian socialists, informed them that Stalin had confided to him that he was willing to use every possible means against the Yugoslavs, short of an armed attack. To this end, he organized a special general staff in Bucharest who were appointed to plan sabotage activity, border incidents, and troop movements, in order to keep the pressure constant. The Yugoslavs, exasperated and convinced that the attack could come at any moment, tried to strengthen their defenses, using methods both licit and illicit. They reacted to the economic boycott, which heavily undermined the country, by organizing a smuggling network, flagrantly violating international rules.[306] To stop the advance of the enemy on Belgrade, they prepared an audacious plan that envisaged the destruction of the Djerdap Dam on the Danube and the flooding of the Pannonian plain.[307] At the diplomatic level, they decided to denounce the aggressive policy of the Soviet Union in the UN General Assembly, distancing themselves from Russia for the first time in this forum. Kardelj's speech at the Assembly in September 1949 accused Moscow of hegemonic ambitions, and created shockwaves with the announcement that from then on, Yugoslavia would follow an "independent" foreign policy.[308] Since the Americans too feared an attack of the Soviet bloc against Yugoslavia, in October 1949 they decided to support its candidacy to a provisional seat on the Security Council. This maneuver was successful despite the furious opposition of the Soviet Union, which favored the candidacy of Czechoslovakia. Its representative, Andrei Vyshinskii, did everything possible to accomplish Stalin's will but remained isolated in the General Assembly. On 20 October 1949, Yugoslavia was called to participate in the Security Council for four years, which meant that it would be among the judges of the Soviet Union in case of military action. The Yugoslavs triumphed, hailing Kardelj upon his return from New York "as a Caesar."[309] The Americans and their allies celebrated too. Early in 1950, an American news-magazine reported that to official Washington, thanks to his split with Stalin, "Tito (still) is a son-of-a bitch but (now he is) our son-of-a-bitch."[310]

With this audacious policy of internationalizing the dispute with Stalin, Tito provoked hostile attacks by the "shining Muscovite leader." Beginning in 1948–49, a series of spectacular show trials were organized in the East European satellite countries against political personalities accused of "Titoism," who were then condemned to harsh prison sentences or death. In Poland, as previously mentioned, Władysław Gomułka was removed from office and was lucky enough "only" to be jailed and tortured. The Hungarian foreign minister, László Rajk, the Bulgarian leader, Traicho Kostov, and the Albanian, Koçi Xoxe, ended up before the firing squad or on the gallows. Their accusers spoke about terrible plots—entirely invented—organized with Tito before and during the war, which created an atmosphere of hysteria in their respective countries.[311] The "revelations" made during the Rajk process offered Soviet Deputy Minister of Foreign Affairs Andrei A. Gromyko the pretext to denounce, on 28 September 1949, the "Treaty of Friendship, Mutual Assistance and Postwar Collaboration," signed by Tito and Molotov in April 1945. At the end of October, the Yugoslav ambassador, Karlo Mrazović, was expelled from Moscow on accusations of "espionage" and the following month the same happened to the chargé d'affaires who took his place. Although diplomatic relations between the two countries were reduced to a minimum, they were not completely interrupted. All the satellites followed this example except Albania, with which Yugoslavia had severed all diplomatic ties.[312]

During its third session, held in Hungary between 16 and 19 November 1949, members of the Cominform, furious and knowing there was nothing they could do to destroy Tito and his comrades, denounced them as "fascists." The resolution formulated on that occasion by the delegates and published on the anniversary of the Second AVNOJ was eloquently entitled: "The Yugoslav Communist Party in the Grip of Assassins and Spies." It proclaimed: "The fight against Tito's clique is the international duty of all Communist and workers parties."[313] The delegates did not limit themselves to words. In the following years, ninety-eight training centers were organized in the Soviet Union and its satellite countries with the aim of sending "every hour of every day saboteurs to Yugoslavia."[314] The Yugoslav borders with the countries of the Soviet bloc were practically sealed off, save for the guerrilla groups that provoked continuous armed incidents. Between 1948 and 1953, there were 142 serious border clashes, in which six hundred enemy agents participated.[315] An especially dangerous center of this offensive was Trieste, where Stalin's henchman, Vittorio Vidali, organized a stronghold of propaganda and espionage. With the help of Italian and Slovene collaborators, Vidali engaged in feverish activity, trying to arrange a military coup in the Yugoslav fleet. The plan, foiled by the UDBA, was that his followers were to occupy the military base of Split and subsequently call for aid from the Soviet navy present in the Mediterranean.[316]

Tito and his comrades lived in an atmosphere of siege, as witnessed by Sir Charles Peake, who had a long conversation with the marshal at the end of November 1949. During the meeting, he could not help but be aware of his tension, although Tito tried to be cordial, as usual. The conversation took place in the Dedinje villa, where the walled-up windows bore witness to the gloomy environment in which Tito lived. He tried, however, to convince his guest that he felt positive about the future, affirming that a direct attack by Stalin was improbable as he was politically wiser than Hitler. But these considerations could not diminish Sir Charles's impression that Tito had a lot more on his mind than he was saying.[317]

In the Grip of the Cold War

The Yugoslavs were not inactive even in this climate of siege, but in October 1949 began to establish secret ties with the Americans, as attested to by Kardelj's meeting in New York with Allen Dulles, director of the recently instituted Central Intelligence Agency. In November of 1950, Vlatko Velebit concluded a formal agreement of collaboration with Frank Wisner, chief of the Office of Policy Coordination (OPC; i.e., of covert CIA operations), which had had an agent in Belgrade since 1948. In order to show their trustworthiness, the Yugoslavs gave the Americans a precious gift: a MIG-15, the newest Soviet fighter, which had experienced a forced landing not far from Zagreb during a spy mission because of a technical failure.[318] The Americans soon returned the favor: thanks to a tip-off from a White Russian, they were able to inform Tito that, from 1949 onward, all the secret documents related to the correspondence with Washington, and handwritten for safety's sake by Kardelj himself, had been transmitted to Moscow by the chief of the Personnel Office, a woman whose lover worked in the cipher room.[319] This shocking discovery had disastrous consequences: a special UDBA office was created on the fourth floor of the Ministry of Foreign Affairs, which in subsequent years allowed Ranković to control and monitor Yugoslav diplomacy.[320] According to Dedijer, Tito himself frequently met CIA functionaries in Belgrade and together they planned common policy. This did not escape the attention of the Soviets.[321] In the meantime, Tito's colleagues developed an intense propaganda plan directed at the Communist and socialist parties ready to side with them. This activity took place in Italy and France and, to a degree, in Belgium and in Germany, as well as in India and Indonesia. "Our contacts with the socialists are developing well," wrote Dedijer to Tito from Paris in December 1951, adding with excessive optimism: "This is a terrible blow for the Russians."[322]

In spite of the difficult situation in which he found himself, Tito was not willing to implement a foreign policy that was not in line with his convictions, even if that meant displeasing the West. In January 1950, Vietnamese communists fighting French colonial rule took possession of the north of the country, creating a government led by Ho Chi Minh in Hanoi. The French reacted and installed a puppet regime in Saigon. On 31 January, Stalin recognized the Hanoi government, followed by Tito who was at least wise enough to inform the Western diplomats of his intentions. Paris was furious, protesting and threatening to withdraw the aid promised to Yugoslavia. The US secretary of state, Dean Acheson, was also indignant, but his reproaches did not deter Tito, who declared that he was not prepared to barter his independence for Western economic help.[323] He took the same attitude in 1951 when he sided with Mohammad Mossadeq, who, trying to overthrow Shah Reza Pahlavi, rebelled against the exploitation of the Iranian oil fields by British and American companies. In making these decisions, the marshal paid no attention to his comrades, who doubted the expediency of such an uncompromising policy. "We can exchange goods and products, but not our conscience and our ideas," he declared in a speech at Užice on 18 February 1950.[324]

This anti-imperialist orientation did not produce any positive or encouraging reactions in Moscow, where Yugoslavia continued to be ostracized. Soviet propaganda at that time, as well as that of the satellites (especially the Hungarians and Romanians) tried to show that during the war Tito had not been at the head of the liberation struggle and the revolution and that his "clique" had falsified history. In this narrative Yugoslavia, as was true for the rest of the East-Central European countries, had been liberated thanks to the "moral and material aid of the Soviet armies." On behalf of the CC CPY, Moša Pijade replied to these calumnies with a series of articles based on the correspondence between Tito and "Grandpa" in 1942, laughing at Stalin's "generous" help at the start of the resistance. These articles, published by *Borba*, were translated at the end of the year into English to show the West how deep the roots of disagreement were between the CPY and the Soviet Union. In the meantime, however, the international situation had deteriorated to the point where any debate regarding the importance and seriousness of the Tito-Stalin split had become superfluous.[325]

The Korean War

At the end of June 1950, the Korean War broke out, a war with which Stalin wanted to test how far he could go in his confrontation with the West. After the Second World War, two states had been created on the Korean peninsula, one to the north under communist rule and one to the south under American tutelage. When North Korea treacherously attacked the South, there was a heated debate in the Security Council as to what measures to take. The United States favored armed intervention by the UN in defense of South Korea, intervention that the Soviets were unable to veto since they had boycotted the Security Council when it refused to recognize the communist government in Beijing as the legal representative of China. According to the Americans and their allies, it was Chiang Kai-Shek who was entitled to this role. Because of the absence of the Soviets, the American motion regarding South Korea was passed with Yugoslavia abstaining from the vote on 26 June 1950.[326] The Yugoslav representative, Aleš Bebler, informed his American colleagues that Belgrade understood their decision but because of their ideological dispute with Moscow, they could not approve the proposed resolution regarding intervention in Korea.[327] The Americans were rather annoyed and reminded Tito that without their help his country would not have had a seat on the Security Council. He replied that Moscow would interpret his agreement of the armed defense of Seoul as evident proof of his alliance with the West, and this could unleash an attack of the Soviet Union and its satellites on Yugoslavia. When Mao's China intervened in the Korean War in November 1950, he changed his mind and decided to support the United States. Mao's commitment to the aggression against South Korea generated suspicions in Belgrade that Moscow's allies might collaborate in an attack on the Balkans, as well. In Washington, too, there was a growing concern that an attack on Yugoslavia was a serious possibility, since it was obvious that the elimination of the Tito "heresy" would strengthen the Kremlin's strategic and political position on the Danube and in the Balkans. Aware of this, the marshal therefore supported the UN's (i.e., Washington's) action in Korea, stressing that, in case of a world war, he would not stay neutral, but would fight against the Red Army.[328]

The propagandistic activity of the Soviet bloc against Yugoslavia had two peaks, one in the spring and summer of 1950 and a lesser one in November of that same year during the first months of the Korean War. In a speech given in Prague on 6 May 1950, on the anniversary of the liberation of Czechoslovakia, Nikolai A. Bulganin, member of the Politburo of the CPSU, declared: "The Yugoslav people deserve a better fate, and the day when they will overthrow the Fascist Tito-Ranković clique is probably not far away."[329] Yugoslavia was greatly alarmed and worried about the possibility of Soviet aggression. A second moment of tension came the following November, when US President Harry S Truman presented Congress with a legislative proposal relating to aid for Yugoslavia. The Soviets reacted by saying that Yugoslavia was planning to attack its neighbors as a preventive measure, not only Albania but also Bulgaria and Romania.[330] Thanks to Djilas's testimony, we know that Tito and his circle actually considered this possibility. They also envisaged additional defensive measures, even examining the possibility of taking refuge with the bulk of the army abroad, evidently under the aegis of NATO. Meanwhile, a Partisan guerrilla war with 100,000 to 150,000 men would be waged in the country.[331] These fears were not groundless, since in January 1951 Stalin invited the defense ministers of the satellites to Moscow to discuss a possible invasion of Yugoslavia the following spring. He argued that if Hungary, Romania, Bulgaria, and Albania violated their borders at the same time, and the Red Army advanced from Czechoslovakia and Hungary toward the Ljubljana gap, Yugoslavia could be subjugated before the UN could intervene. Faced with a fait accompli, the West would not risk a third world war in order to defend Tito's regime. Marshal Zhukov was ordered to review the invasion plans made the year before and to organize an allied military action with forces three times stronger than those of Yugoslavia.[332] At his debriefing, a Hungarian air force officer who defected to the West in 1951 said that intense propaganda was in progress in his country's barracks to prepare the troops for war. Tito was described as America's "chained dog," just waiting for a signal to attack Hungary.[333]

The Clash of Arms

At the Politburo session on 4 December 1950, Tito judged the situation to be extremely serious. The Russians, he said, would use their "vassals" to attack Yugoslavia, since they were arming them in contravention of the Paris Peace Treaties, which prohibited Hungary and Bulgaria from having large armies. In order to denounce this military pressure, in the spring of 1951 he published a white paper to alert international public opinion of the danger to his country.[334] The repercussions of this denunciation, which was presented the following autumn at the UN General Assembly in Paris, were particularly evident among the delegates of the Asian, African, and Latin American countries, who were impressed by the Yugoslav determination to resist the pressure of a big power. Tito, aware that he could not do much without direct agreements with the Truman administration, decided after much hesitation to "take concrete measures to get arms from the United States."[335] He therefore sent a secret mission headed by Vlatko Velebit and Chief of Staff Koča Popović to Washington, where they found interlocutors quite willing to take their requests into consideration, in view of discussions that had been going on in US diplomatic and military circles since November 1949 on how to arm Yugoslavia as soon as possible.[336] The favorable atmosphere created between the two parties was enhanced by the Yugoslav willingness to accept American "suggestions" regarding the reorganization of the People's Army. Tito accepted Washington's request to deploy his best troops at the Ljubljana gap, thus reinforcing NATO defenses in northern Italy.[337]

The new relations with the West guaranteed a significant increase in economic and military aid to Yugoslavia, which began in July 1951 with a "tripartite" agreement between the United States, Great Britain, and France.[338] The Soviets denounced this as a betrayal of socialism: on 22 July, Molotov affirmed in Warsaw that Yugoslavia was in the clutches of spies and criminals, ready to sacrifice its own people to install capitalism. This accusation caused Tito to lose his temper. On 27 July, on the anniversary of the start of the Partisan resistance in Bosnia, he replied more harshly than he ever had before, not just defending the socialist character of his regime, but openly attacking Stalin's tyranny: "With what right does [Molotov] speak, he who is one of the most important leaders of a country where an unheard of genocide is happening, where entire nations are destroyed before the eyes of the whole world?"[339]

In another speech, Tito sang the praises of the United States, proclaiming them the world's only champion of liberty.[340] This paean did not, however, signify that the marshal had renounced his political autonomy on the strategic field, and when the Americans asked him to concentrate his army in defense of the Ljubljana gap and the Vardar Valley, he refused, stating that his duty was to defend the entire country, not just the areas important to the West.[341] In Washington, where the Truman administration wanted to include Yugoslavia organically in its military structure, such independence was not greeted favorably. The following summer the United States, Great Britain, and France sent Tito a document informing him that he would no longer get "free" economic aid. In a meeting with the American ambassador, George W. Allen, the marshal observed that he did not like the tone and the spirit of this communication, stressing that if this attitude did not change, Yugoslavia would renounce Western help, even if it meant it had to "tighten its belt."[342] He was able to react so firmly because he knew he had vast popular support. This was confirmed by a survey organized by the American and British embassies that showed how popular Tito was, even among those groups that opposed communism. The authority and energy that Tito displayed in moments of crisis strengthened the unity of the Yugoslav peoples, in spite of their many ethnic and ideological differences.[343]

At the beginning of the fifties, Washington seriously considered the inclusion of Yugoslavia in NATO. The Americans had no doubt Tito's soldiers would "cut a good figure" in case of a Soviet attack.[344] One of the reasons why this ideal was not implemented was because of Italian opposition, since the Rome government was not eager to have as a military partner a country with which it was at loggerheads over Trieste. In spite of secret conversations Tito held in August 1951 at Lake Bled with General Michael West, the top British officer in Austria, and the following October with Generals Joseph Collins and Earle E. Partridge, he did not support the idea either, sure that the presence of Western troops in his territory would have endangered his regime.[345] During a meeting with the US deputy secretary of state, he stated that he would remain aloof from any bloc so that in the event of a Cominform attack, the Yugoslav people would not blame their government for provoking the action.[346] A compromise was therefore found, the result of complex, sometimes tense diplomatic work. In November 1952, for instance, a meeting took place in Belgrade between General Thomas T. Handy, chief of a "tripartite" military delegation, and Peko Dapčević, chief of the General Staff. On that occasion, the Yugoslavs disclosed their strategic plans, although Handy was not ready to guarantee that the West would fight with them in case of a Soviet invasion, as previously promised. During a session of the CC on 22 November 1952, Tito commented angrily on this attitude, observing that "the West behaved as if we were a client state. They want to know our plans without giving something in return."[347]

In spite of temporary coldness, the Americans kept strengthening their cordon sanitaire against the Soviet bloc by providing the People's Army with two hundred F-84 jets, training Yugoslav pilots at their bases, and sending their military counselors to the country. The victory of the Republican Party in the presidential elections in 1952 and the entrance of General Dwight D. Eisenhower to the White House did not change the attitude of the United States toward Yugoslavia, as indicated by the visit Koča Popović paid to the future president on June 1951, when he was still the supreme allied commander of NATO (SACEUR). They understood each other perfectly.[348]

Meanwhile, at the beginning of 1951, Tito established secret contact with King Paul of Greece and his chief of General Staff, informing them that he was ready to collaborate with the Athens government in defense of the Balkans. Formal contacts with Premier Sophoklis Venizelos followed, which showed how far the marshal was ready to go in case of a Soviet attack. In order to mount a rear guard defense, the two states even began working out plans for a common military occupation of Albania and its partition between them. These discussions were welcomed by the Americans. In 1953 and 1954, the Eisenhower administration encouraged the formation of a Balkan alliance between Greece, Turkey—both members of NATO—and Yugoslavia.[349] Initiated by Britain, the three countries signed an "agreement of friendship" on 29 February 1953 in Ankara, with the aim of reinforcing the Eastern Mediterranean against the Soviets. Along with political consultations, the agreement also planned for coordination between their respective General Staffs. After Tito's official visits to Ankara and Athens in February and July 1954, Yugoslavia, Greece, and Turkey signed a pact of mutual aid in case of attack the following August at Lake Bled. It thus became part of that defense structure Washington was trying to consolidate in Southern Europe against the Soviet threat, and received the same guarantees as the NATO members, without subjecting the People's Army to its command.[350] "I do not know whether this pact will defend us," said Tito, when the consultations were still in progress, "but it is an admonition to Stalin not to do foolish things in the Balkans if he does not wish to set off the third world war."[351]

The Degeneration of the Trieste Question and Its Solution

American foreign policy aimed at making NATO's southern wing more compact achieved another important result in the same period: the "London Memorandum of Understanding," signed on 5 October 1954, which brought to an end the conflictual situation between Italy and Yugoslavia of past years. The solution to the thorny Trieste question that until then had hindered Belgrade's collaboration with the defensive structures of the West seemed to lay the foundations for the friendly coexistence of the two neighboring countries.[352]

Because of the dispute related to the Free Territory of Trieste, Tito had become increasingly hostile to Italy in the postwar years, accusing it of irredentist claims in the Eastern Adriatic. The dispute came to a head in mid-August 1953, when Alcide De Gasperi's government in Rome was replaced by Giuseppe Pella's, which was decidedly oriented to the right. In Pella's inauguration speech to the Italian parliament, he asked the Western Allies to implement the "Tripartite Note" of 18 March 1948, which invited the Soviet Union to review the peace treaty regarding Trieste. At that time, the United States, Great Britain, and France believed that the entire Free Territory of Trieste (FTT) should be returned to Italy. Between March 1948, when Yugoslavia was still part of the Soviet bloc, and August 1953, when it was de facto a part of the Western bloc, the situation had changed radically. For internal political reasons, however, the Italians were not ready to admit it. Once in power, Pella decided to move from words to deeds, ordering the deployment of three armored divisions and a parachute unit near Monfalcone and Gorizia on the border with the FTT and Yugoslavia. He did not inform NATO about this move, although he should have. Unbeknownst to the Allies, he gave a green light to Operation Delta, which planned for the occupation of Trieste by Italian troops. Since, in that case, a clash with Yugoslavia was probable, the Italian General Staff planned an even a larger maneuver, which was to involve the entire area ceded in 1947 to Yugoslavia by the peace treaty.[353]

Tito replied to this provocation with one of his best-known speeches. On 6 September 1953 he took part in a Partisan rally not far from the border near Gorizia commemorating the tenth anniversary of the Italian capitulation. In his dashing white admiral's uniform, he stressed that the Yugoslavs did not fear the Italian "heroes" and their "wooden swords."[354] These intentionally offensive words sparked a heated polemic that convinced the British and the Americans that the Trieste question would not be solved without their radical intervention. They therefore decided of their own volition to give Zone A, which they administered, to Italy, whereas Zone B would remain with Yugoslavia. The diplomatic representatives of Great Britain and the United States informed Pella and Tito about this drastic decision the same day, on 8 October 1953. The latter, when notified of the "Bipartite Note," kept calm, observing only that the Italians would not be satisfied with Zone A, but would continue in their irredentist claims: the "Bipartite Note" would not eliminate the existing tension between the two countries. Although he said goodbye to the two with a smile, he was furious at having had a fait accompli put before him without previous consultation. All the more so as Pella proclaimed the "Bipartite Note" a victory, whereas Tito felt it was a "kick in the shin," saying, "We cannot sell our country for their aid."[355] Under pressure from those who reproached him for the failure of his Western policy, and fearing loss of prestige, he reacted decisively. On 10 October in Leskovac, southern Serbia, he declared to an enormous crowd that Yugoslavia would defend its interests, if necessary, even with arms, and that he considered the "entrance of the Italians in Zone A as an act of war." The following day in Skopje, he specified that the moment the first Italian soldiers stepped into Zone A, the Yugoslav troops would do the same. If American aid depended on accepting the "Bipartite Note," Yugoslavia was ready to do without.[356] Meanwhile, in Belgrade and in other localities, demonstrations broke out, in part spontaneous, in part prearranged, with people shouting slogans: "Give us arms, we will go to Trieste!" or "We are ready to give our life, but not Trieste!" It was all accompanied by a bellicose press campaign that stirred up popular support, and by the marshal's decision to order ninety thousand reservists to be called up to reinforce the army along the Italian border.[357]

Winds of war started to blow along the border, preoccupying all parties involved. As in previous difficult situations, Tito once more took the initiative. On 25 October 1953, he sent a message to London and Washington via Fitzroy Maclean: he could not accept a diktat by the Allies because this would endanger his position at home. Therefore, he was forced to take a more radical line than he would have liked, which did not mean that he was not ready to compromise. He declared that he would accept a division of the contested area along the existing frontier between Zones A and B, provided that Yugoslavia would get a port near Trieste along with the territory already in its possession. Also, it would be helpful if the Allies declared that they would renounce support of any further Italian claim.[358] Secret talks on this basis began in London on 2 February 1954 between Yugoslav ambassador Vlatko Velebit, Foreign Office representative Geoffrey W. Harrison, and the American ambassador to Vienna, Llewellyn E. Thompson. They were the result of intense diplomatic consultations behind the scenes that had begun in mid-January on the premise that it was necessary to find a solution for the Yugoslavs that was better than the "Bipartite Note," but that was not worse for the Italians.[359] Discussions continued until September 1954, even requiring last-minute intervention by President Eisenhower. The main obstacle to an agreement regarded a minor revision of the frontier between Zones A and B in favor of Yugoslavia, which inflamed tempers. To calm them down, the president sent State Department Deputy Undersecretary for Political Affairs Robert Murphy, an old acquaintance of Tito's, to Belgrade and Rome. He arrived in Belgrade on 14 September 1954 and had immediate talks with Kardelj and Bebler, but without any results. In fact, Murphy tried to link the solution of the territorial controversy with the supply of wheat, which Yugoslavia needed badly. The answer was the usual one: "The marshal would prefer to tell his people that this year they will starve, rather than accept territorial losses in exchange for food."[360] Tito, flattered by Eisenhower's letter and the fact that he complimented him for his "statesmanlike" qualities, was more malleable. Although he stressed once again that the question was "dynamite" from the domestic point of view, in the end he accepted the territorial adjustments the Italians requested in spite of Kardelj's angry protests. On 18 September, Murphy left for Rome with proposals acceptable to the Italian government.[361]

By the end of September 1954, the agreement was complete in every detail, and was signed on 5 October at the Foreign Office in London. On that occasion, British foreign minister Anthony Eden said with satisfaction that it was "a public understanding achieved secretly." This was not completely true, since the text was accompanied by a series of confidential letters that were not published.[362] Above all, the character of the agreement remained in question, since it was an international treaty, although not classified as such. It did not abolish the FTT de jure, but only de facto. In short, it was an ambiguous document that did not eliminate Article 22 of the Paris Peace Treaty, but limited itself to transforming the "temporary" administration of the two Zones of the FTT from military to civil, replacing the Anglo-Americans in Zone A with the Italians. Tito was, by and large, satisfied with the memorandum, as is evident from his observation that, although the Slovenes and Kardelj had not imagined their request for the port city of Capodistria/Koper would be honored, "We fought firmly and have obtained the maximum. In this situation, Trieste lost all relevant significance for Italy, above all its strategic significance."[363]

About a month later, Svetozar Vukmanović left at the head of a delegation for Washington to set up negotiations regarding American aid. During the talks, he had an altercation with Ambassador Murphy that ended favorably for the Yugoslavs: in addition to the 400,000 tons of wheat already promised, they got another 450,000. They also established contacts with the International Bank for Reconstruction and Development, which promised to guarantee a loan for the modernization of Yugoslav agriculture and the reconstruction of its medium-term debts. Hence, it was clear that Washington was doing everything in its power to prevent the collapse of the Yugoslav economy.[364]

Stalin's Death and the Normalization of Relations with Moscow

The inclusion of Yugoslavia in the Western world would probably have continued if, on 5 March 1953, Stalin had not suffered a fatal stroke. He had persevered in his propaganda struggle against Tito until the end and it continued by force of inertia even after his death. After 1948, there were about forty important trials against the "Titoists" in the people's democracies, not to mention the thousands of lesser personalities persecuted, arrested, and deported because of their presumed pro-Yugoslav sympathies. In November 1952, a spectacular trial against secretary general of the Czechoslovak CP Rudolf Slánský, former foreign minister Vladimir Clementis, and other prominent figures accused of Titoism, espionage, and other invented crimes took place in Prague. They were declared guilty and were condemned to death or years in prison.[365]

As long as he lived, the Boss did not limit himself to persecuting the "Titoists" or staging incidents. As Soviet sources testify, he tried until the end of his days to assassinate his archenemy. According to an FBI report, as late as January 1953, Stalin had issued orders to eliminate Tito within three months. The report notes that "Croatians were being trained near Vienna to carry out the elimination," adding: "Two people are available to replace Tito."[366] Among the different assassination attempts planned by his agents, the most ingenuous were those in which Josef R. Grigulevich (Max) was implicated. As ambassador of Costa Rica in Italy and Yugoslavia (although actually one of the Soviet dictator's killers), he was able to approach Tito thanks to his diplomatic rank. At a secret meeting in Vienna with his superiors, Teodoro B. Castro—that was his cover name—proposed four different ways of assassinating the "vulture," as the former "eagle" was at that point called. The first one was quite bizarre, but feasible, because of the lethal weapons developed in Moscow by Laboratory 12 for "wet work," the name given to political assassination. During a reception, Grigulevich was to contaminate Tito with a spray containing pneumonic plague virus, though he himself would be vaccinated against it. The second method of assassination planned for an attack during the marshal's visit to London, at the reception in the Yugoslav Embassy to which "Castro" would be invited thanks to his "friend," Vlatko Velebit. He was to shoot the marshal and flee after tear-gassing the guests. A similar attempt could take place in Belgrade, during a meeting between Tito and the ambassadors accredited to Yugoslavia. According to the fourth variant, Max would offer the marshal a precious box which, when opened, would release a deadly gas (Grigulevich, of course, would have been protected by an antidote).[367]

On 1 March 1953, at a meeting that took place at midnight, KGB officers informed Stalin about Max's plans, but he was not totally convinced, feeling that the problem should be reconsidered and that it would be better to focus on internecine conflicts among the Yugoslav leaders to eliminate Tito. Evidently, he still preferred a killer in the marshal's inner circle.[368] With all probability, this KGB report was the last document Stalin read before he had a massive stroke at dawn the next day. As Roy Medvedev recounts, letters that were important for him personally were later found in a drawer of his desk, under a pile of newspapers. Among them was a message from Tito, who wrote that the Boss's hatchet men had tried to kill him by all possible means, without success. "If this does not stop," he wrote, "I will send just one man to Moscow, and it will not be necessary to send another one."[369] It will always remain a mystery whether this was only a threat—although Tito would not have issued a threat unless he were sure he could follow through—or, whether that piece of paper had something to do with Stalin's sudden death. It cannot be ignored that Lavrentii P. Beria, the bloodthirsty Soviet minister of internal affairs, had opposed the split with Tito and remained in secret contact with him after 1948.[370] They met for the first time in autumn 1944, during Tito's visit to Moscow, at one of Stalin's dinners in his dacha. Obliged to drink a lot because of the Russian obsession with toasts, Tito, who during the Partisan years rarely drank, felt sick and went outside to vomit. Suddenly a shadow appeared behind him. "Don't worry," said Beria, "it is just me, your friendly policeman."[371] Did they remain friends even after Tito's expulsion from the Cominform?

When Stalin was in a coma after his stroke, Beria did everything he could to prevent the doctors from helping him, since he was in disgrace and feared the terrible fate of his predecessors, Genrikh Iagoda and Nikolai Ezhov, both of whom had been shot in the thirties. Pavel Sudoplatov, the "wet work" specialist, was convinced that Stalin had been killed by Beria's agents, as was Stalin's own son.[372] When the news of the Boss's death came, Tito did not hide his relief, although he considered Stalin to have been an intelligent statesman in spite of his roughness and brutality. To a journalist who asked him how he had reacted to the news of dictator's death, he answered: "I got the news together with a dispatch that my dog Tiger was really sick. I was terribly distressed for Tiger. He was a marvelous dog."[373]

After Stalin's death, the international position of Yugoslavia took a decisive turn since, in the spring of 1953, Moscow began attempting to reconnect with Belgrade. The first sign of a thaw came at the Boss's funeral, when the deputy minister of foreign affairs, Jakov A. Malenkov, approached the Yugoslav chargé, Dragoj Djurić, the only Yugoslav present, and shook his hand in front of the entire diplomatic corps.[374] The Yugoslavs also made a move in this direction, deciding to send Deputy Foreign Minister Veljko Mićunović to the Soviet Embassy to express his condolences. Other promising signs of Moscow's willingness to resume a dialogue soon arrived through Finnish diplomats. On 29 April 1953 Molotov, the Soviet foreign minister, received the Yugoslav chargé d'affaires and spoke with him for ten minutes.[375]

In the traditional May 1 message of the CC CPSU, the ritual greetings to Yugoslav communists who had sided with Stalin after the 1948 split (called Cominformists) were missing and, a few days later, Soviet diplomats at the UN in New York approached Yugoslav colleagues, declaring that the Russians and the Yugoslavs were the most brave people in the world and hinting at possible contacts between the two countries, at least initially in the field of sport. Less than a month later, on 6 June, Molotov decided to restore diplomatic relations at the highest level, sending an ambassador to Belgrade.[376] Tito followed these moves with vigilant but suspicious attention, although he did not exclude the possibility of a rapprochement. In the spring of 1953, during his visit to London, he declared to the foreign press: "In Yugoslavia, we would be happy if one day [the Soviets] would recognize that they had behaved incorrectly toward our country. It would please us. We will wait and see."[377]

It was not necessary to wait long, considering the rapid development of events in Moscow and the satellite countries. Except for Poland, all of them normalized their diplomatic relations with Yugoslavia. There were modest trade exchanges, an agreement on Danube navigation was signed, and the border incidents and anti-Tito propaganda gradually ceased. On June 16, Beria and Premier Georgii M. Malenkov met to agree on a message to be sent via an agent to Ranković. It read in part: "I seize the opportunity, Comrade Ranković, to send you warm greetings from Comrade Beria, who remembers you well. Comrade Beria asks me to inform you, personally and strictly confidentially, that Malenkov, Beria and their friends would like a necessary and radical revision and improvement of relations between our countries. For this purpose,

Comrade Beria asks you to invite Comrade Tito to organize a closed meeting of plenipotentiaries, if you and Tito both agree. The meeting could take place in Moscow and, if you think that this is not feasible, in Belgrade. Comrade Beria guarantees that nobody will be informed about this discussion, besides Tito and yourself."[378]

This message never reached Ranković. The following day, Beria was arrested during a dramatic session of the CC CPSU, which is why this first attempt to normalize relations between Moscow and Belgrade saw no result. The former "comrades" of Stalin's hated henchman considered his greeting to Ranković as proof of his intent to enter into contracts with "imperialists" and attested to these fact that, in Molotov's words, he was "an agent, a class enemy." According to these accusations, Beria plotted to introduce a two-party system in the USSR, and in his attempt to acquire supreme power he sought the support of persons such as Churchill, Dulles, Tito, and Ranković.[379] Conjectures of this sort, which were obviously concocted to sully the chief of the NKVD as much as possible and justify his death sentence, did not have serious consequences for relations between the Soviet Union and Yugoslavia. On 23 September, Dobrije Vidic, Tito's new ambassador, came to the Soviet capital and began a skillful diplomatic action to improve mutual relations, but without ideological content for the time being. In Moscow, Tito was not yet considered a "comrade," as Beria would have liked, but a "mister." Since Belgrade knew nothing of Beria's failed attempt to renew contacts with Ranković, they were not saddened by his fall. On the contrary, forgetting the secret connections of past years, about which little is known, the marshal declared that his sudden and dramatic execution was "a progressive deed."[380]

During the second part of 1953 and 1954, internal struggles in the Kremlin continued unrelentingly. A real turning point in Soviet-Yugoslav relations did not take place until Nikita S. Khrushchev became secretary general of the CPSU. Although on the occasion of Stalin's seventieth birthday in 1949, Khrushchev had praised the Boss for his "mortal" fight against all kinds of revisionism, including the "gang of assassins and spies" in Yugoslavia,[381] as soon as he was firmly in the saddle he changed his opinion and became convinced of the need to revise the domestic and international policy of the Soviet Union as soon as possible, starting with the Yugoslavs. It was necessary to prevent them from completely adhering to the Western bloc, as their approach to NATO seemed to forebode. Without embarrassment or shame, he set up a policy similar to the one Beria had tried to realize some months earlier and which had cost him his life.[382]

The Thaw

It was not easy to implement this policy, since Soviet propaganda had long equated Tito's regime with the worst revisionism, and since, after 1949, ideological mutations took place in Yugoslavia that were incompatible with the Soviet system. Yugoslav leaders began to criticize Stalin's foreign policy even before the expulsion of the CPY from the Cominform, and increasing their criticism after its second session, when they stressed openly that it was "hegemonic" in that it aped the tsarist policy in the Balkans and had nothing to do with socialism. Kardelj eloquently compared Napoleon Bonaparte and Stalin: "The nations who hoped to be liberated by the French experienced a delusion similar to that experienced today by the peoples of Eastern Europe."[383] He was even more laconic when asked about the real reason for the excommunication of the CPY from the Cominform: "*Genghis Khan*."[384]

After taking the first step toward criticism of the Soviet system, the Yugoslavs did not wait long to take the next one and began to ask questions about the soundness of a regime where power was entirely in the hands of the party, whereas the working class had none. Convinced that this was an "Asian" deviation, they reread the classics, first of all Marx and Engels, but also the French utopian socialists. They thus discovered a "European way" to socialism, founded not on coercion and bureaucracy, but on a freely organized society. In it, every individual should be able to decide autonomously about the results of his work, thus favoring the development of a real democracy better than the bourgeois one. In nurturing these ideals, they recalled their experience of the liberation struggle, claiming that there are also "many specific traits useful for the revolutionary development of other countries" to be discovered. In a letter from 13 April 1948, sent to Moscow at the very start of the dispute with Stalin, they had written: "This does not mean that we place the role of the CPSU and the social system of the USSR in the background. On the contrary, we study and take as an example the Soviet system, but we are developing socialism in our country in a somewhat different way. . . . We do not do this to prove that our road is better than that taken by the Soviet Union, that we are inventing something new, but because this is forced upon us by our daily life."[385]

This was in 1948. The following year, they were more audacious in rejecting the Soviet model and yearning for a new path toward social development. After the traumatic experience of their schism, they realized that "centralism, positive during the revolution, could regress to conservative bureaucratic autocracy." Kardelj wrote: "We opposed these tendencies even before [the expulsion from Cominform], but not methodically and decisively enough. An analysis of the reasons that moved Stalin to attack the CPY taught us, however, that it was necessary to take drastic measures in the fight against the dangers to which the revolution was exposed."[386]

The need to confront Stalin on an ideological level was not immediately clear to Tito. Kardelj and Djilas had to convince him, stressing the need to take a critical attitude toward the Soviet regime, as it had features of state capitalism that should be condemned like any other form of capitalism. They were supported in this by Boris Kidrič, Vladimir Bakarić, and other comrades who had reached the conclusion that the split with Moscow was a consequence of the crises suffered by the USSR from the October Revolution onward and that this should be rejected. In condemning the bureaucratic inertia of the USSR they noted, however, that the CPY too was at risk of falling into the same trap. This was a peril to be avoided at any cost. Although their more pragmatic comrades—Tito and Ranković above all—were less interested in this reasoning, they too started to have doubts about the dogma they had so long believed in.[387]

The Soviets well knew that in spite of their "revisionism" the Yugoslav leaders remained Communists, and thus dialogue was possible. It was not easy, however, to mend fences, since hostility and distrust toward Moscow still reigned in Belgrade. In any case, these feelings gradually dissipated thanks to several conciliatory moves on the part of the Soviets. There was a lively discussion of the Yugoslav question in their Politburo, which resulted in Khrushchev's decision, on 31 May 1954, to send a personal letter to Tito. He evidently wanted to tell him that it was he who was now in charge in the Kremlin, although in the past he had been one of the lesser personalities in Stalin's circle. In the letter, he proposed a summit "in Moscow, in Yugoslavia, according to your wishes," trying at the same time to put the blame for the 1948 split on Beria, an "agent of imperialism," and his collaborators, as "new facts," recently discovered, bore witness. The other scapegoat, he said, should be Milovan Djilas, "a false Marxist, a man to whom the interests of Communism are foreign," who had in the meantime also been disgraced.[388]

Tito and those few comrades who were informed about this letter were taken by surprise, thinking at first that it was a propaganda move. At a time when the Trieste crisis was still ongoing and the signing of the Balkan Pact was imminent, it was not hard to imagine that Khrushchev wanted to obstruct Yugoslav relations with the West. Tito's tactics were, therefore, extremely prudent. He did not answer personally but, a month later, asked Edvard Kardelj to get in touch with the Soviet ambassador and inform him that Yugoslavia welcomed the initiative, but at the moment was not able to act because premature news of a dialogue with the Soviets could influence the Trieste negotiations. On 21 July 1954, during a reception in honor of the emperor of Ethiopia,

Haile Selassie, Kardelj did as requested. The reply came on 24 July, in which Khrushchev affirmed that he understood the delicate situation and hoped for a favorable resolution of the Trieste question.[389] When the solution seemed near, Tito answered with a long letter in the name of the Executive Committee (the new denomination of the Politburo) proclaiming his readiness to normalize relations between the two states. He ignored Khrushchev's proposal to reestablish party connections and refused to blame Beria and Djilas for what had happened. During a meeting with 250,000 people in attendance, Tito hinted about what was going on behind the scenes, mentioning the possibility of restoring collaboration with the East, not just on an economic but also on a political level. At the same time, he dictated the terms under which he was willing to negotiate: "The normalization should not be achieved blindly with kisses and hugs, as if nothing had happened. It cannot transform our policy and cannot influence our internal development, or our path to socialism. Normalization has to exclude every interference in internal affairs."[390]

Khrushchev replied on 23 September with a third letter, accepting Tito's request that first state relations should be improved, rather than those of the party. Regarding responsibility for the 1948 split, he declared that it was of secondary importance and that it was necessary to silence mutual hostile propaganda and look to the future. Three days later, on 27 September, he sent another letter full of good will while at the same time the CC of the CPSU decided to put a stop to the subversive activity of the Cominformists who had taken refuge in the Soviet Union and in other socialist countries. Their newspapers and Radio Free Yugoslavia, which was broadcast from Bucharest, were closed.[391] Soon Ambassador Volkov informed Tito that the author of the entry "Yugoslavia" in the *Great Soviet Encyclopedia*, who was guilty of having declared it a fascist country, had been arrested in Moscow. In public libraries, slanderous books on Tito disappeared, while on 20 October 1954 the press published a series of articles "on the gallant National Liberation Army, which liberated Belgrade with the help of the Red Army."[392]

On 16 November, the Yugoslavs signaled that they were ready to accept a summit meeting, stressing however that they would not return to the "camp" (as the Soviets called their bloc) and renounce their own path to socialism and foreign policy.[393] These negotiations were prompted by Khrushchev's need to strengthen his power at home as well as his hatred for Stalin and his admiration for Tito, who had succeeded in opposing him. On 25 May 1955, the new "Boss" came to Belgrade at the head of an important delegation. This was an audacious decision, which the Stalinist group in the Presidium, under Molotov's leadership, opposed, although it was not strong enough to block the formidable Nikita S. Khrushchev. The "friendly" warnings of his "comrades" and their "friendly" pats on the back were of no avail: "Be careful, keep your eyes open, they can even kill you there."[394]

Going to Belgrade, Khrushchev ventured to a country outside the Muscovite orbit for the first time, and meeting Western diplomats and journalists who were merciless in describing his clumsiness and that of his escorts, and their pale blue suits, poorly tailored and rumpled as soon as they were worn.[395] Even if he were not fully aware of it, with that journey he began to demolish Stalin's myth, completely dismantling the "cult of personality" at the Twentieth Congress of CPSU the following February. "For you, it was easy to be victorious (in the conflict with Stalin)," he told Tito, in a moment of sincerity. "You had at your disposal a state and forty divisions. If I had had even one battalion, I would have rebelled against him much earlier than 1948."[396]

The "pilgrimage to Canossa"—as the *New York Times* labeled that penitential journey, recalling the 1077 trip of Emperor Henry IV to the Tuscan castle where he was absolved by Pope Gregory VII, who had excommunicated him—was not a complete success. In fact, Khrushchev did not succeed in convincing Tito and his comrades to return to the fold, despite a meaningful admonition: "If the bourgeoisie were able to settle accounts with the USSR . . . it would also quickly settle them with Yugoslavia."[397] The Yugoslavs were aware of this. But they were ready to collaborate with the Soviet Union only as equals, to which the so-called Belgrade Declaration, signed on 2 June 1955 by the two delegations and bound to be a kind of Magna Carta of their future relations, bore witness.[398]

Self-Management

Even before this happened, the leaders of the CPY had worked out a socialist doctrine that, from Moscow's point of view, was wrong. Party ideologues in the Kremlin muttered that "they like to introduce themselves as 'theoreticians,' who are discovering 'new,' 'specific,' 'autonomous' ways of constructing a democratic Yugoslavia, and boasting that they were accelerating the development of Marxism-Leninism."[399] If, in the first postwar years, the most learned of Tito's comrades felt they were called on to interpret Marxism-Leninism creatively, even if they had to be prudent because of Stalin's supreme authority, after the expulsion from the Cominform they hesitated no longer. During 1949 and 1950 the idea of workers' councils and self-management was born, based on Marx's *Das Kapital* and the work of the French utopian socialists, who were the first to develop the doctrine of "free producers," but also on the basis of Lenin's "Soviets," the councils organized at the time of the October Revolution as political and governmental bodies.[400] Djilas recalled in his memoirs: "The original idea of self-management was mine. . . . I thought that the system should be simplified, that we should give over the factories to the workers and just collect taxes. Essentially as in the Western businesses, preserving however socialist relations. . . . I remember well being seated with Kardelj and Kidrič in the car before my villa. . . . It was raining and we spoke at length. I mentioned my idea about self-management, which could help us to simplify many things. They replied that it was too early, that the idea itself was not bad but premature. After two or three days Kidrič calls and says: 'This is really a good idea. It's feasible!' Kardelj too agreed and we started to work."[401]

In the late spring or early summer of 1949, during a visit to Split, where Tito was vacationing, Djilas, Kardelj, and Kidrič discussed this project with him. At first he reacted negatively, since he did not completely understand what they wanted to do. The idea of "self-management" was foreign to his experience, aside from which, as far as he knew, the Yugoslav proletariat was not mature enough for it. But when they explained that self-management could save them from the trap of Stalinism and could become a model for other countries as well, proving their point with quotations from Marx, he understood and became enthused. If the aim of the class struggle was to free the proletariat from its dependency on capital, it should also be freed from that of the state. "All right, let's do it and let's launch the idea with the slogan: 'the factories to the workers,'" he said.[402] They therefore decided to create a global plan based on the experience of the People's Councils, which had existed during the war in order to change the entire management of the "social means of production." The party initially introduced these measures in the fifteen most important factories and enterprises, with the purpose of reinforcing its position in the working class. In this way the embryos of the worker's councils, or similar organisms that seemed promising, began to take shape.[403]

The idea of a new economic and political policy went ahead at the leadership level, although it was at odds with the entire postwar, highly centralized administrative experience. At first it encountered many obstacles, both because of objective difficulties and because of strong resistance from the bureaucratic structures. As Kardelj remembers, "It was not easy, in the factories or in the unions, or in the party," where "ferocious opposition appeared on the part of those comrades who were against dogmatism, against the Cominform, but still nurtured centralist ideas. The first law on self-management was approved only the following year."[404]

Tito submitted "The Basic Law on the Administration of State Factories and Main Industrial Enterprises by Workers' Collectives" to a special session of the Federal Assembly on 27 June 1950. He said on that occasion: "The slogan 'factories to the workers, the land to the peasants' is not an abstract propagandistic slogan, but has a profound significance, as it reassumes the entire agenda of social relations in production—regarding the social property and the rights and the obligations of the working people—and therefore we must and can realize it, if we really want to build socialism."[405]

Bombastic declarations aside, this new economic policy never fully won the trust of the masses, primarily because of the discrepancy between theory and practice. Self-management required the worker to become a broad-minded manager with a developed "socialist consciousness," ready to dedicate time and energy to administrative activities in addition to the commitment to his job. In everyday reality, a conflict soon arose between ideological premises and the actual social, economic, and political conditions of the population. The Yugoslav theoreticians frequently spoke of the "initiative of the masses from below," which, according to them, had already been the main cause of victory during the liberation struggle. The self-managing experience was paralyzed from the beginning by widespread illiteracy or semiliteracy, economic backwardness and the general deficiencies of the society, and above all the determination of the party not to renounce its hegemonic mission. It is true that, with time, the regime mellowed, for instance permitting a choice between several candidates when elections were held, but this does not mean that the central role of the party in all aspects of society disappeared. Technological development required increasingly sophisticated management and expert cadres, which is why the ideal of an active role of the workers in the administration of the factories began to be increasingly inefficient. Self-management was in reality a political and ideological façade that concealed something quite different. In his diary toward the end of 1954 the great Serb writer Dobrica Ćosić criticized the fact that "the Workers' Councils have not yet improved production or the economy. . . . They allow more initiative, but also more absenteeism, more words, but little real democracy."[406] In spite of this unpromising start, self-management was later introduced at all levels of public life, from rural communities to the administrative summit, on the assumption that it epitomized the highest form of the people's power. When the sun was setting on Yugoslavia, Koča Popović wrote the truth: "An overall look shows, in my opinion, that we were not mature enough for real self-management. For instance, how can self-determination and widespread illiteracy or general ignorance, not only of common interests, but even of the most elementary hygienic norms, go hand in hand? When he built his theories, Kardelj perhaps had Slovenia in mind, certainly not Kosovo."[407]

He was right, since Kardelj was unable to understand and accept the complexity of Yugoslav society or, if he did, he started from the premise that "Slovenia should be acceptable to Yugoslavia, and Yugoslavia should be structured in a way that would be acceptable to Slovenia," since Slovenia was the most advanced of the republics and the one from which he hailed. "This vision of his," said Tito at the end of his life, referring to Kardelj's preoccupation with his tiny homeland, "says everything."[408]

The reforms, in addition to the military budget, required financial expenditures that exceeded the capacity of the Yugoslav economy. The population, especially the urban one, lived on the edge of poverty, which resulted in an increase in crime. The party theoreticians—Kardelj, Kidrič, Bakarić, Pijade, Djilas—were critical not only of the Soviet system, but also of the Yugoslav one and were conscious of the fact that after the split with Stalin they needed to strengthen the popularity of the regime among the masses, who were often hostile to Communism. They therefore decided to adopt more liberal economic measures, as well as social and cultural ones. On 1 January 1950, an amnesty for seven thousand political prisoners was proclaimed (excluding the Cominformists), restrictions for traveling abroad were loosened, and pressure on religious communities diminished. They also decided to review the Five-Year Plan, which originally presupposed forced industrialization. On 12 November 1950, Tito declared in an interview with a German press agency that the second Five-Year Plan would not be similar to the first one, stressing that the Yugoslav economy would be more oriented toward consumer goods, considering that "in the coming five years, we have to improve the standard of living."[409] He recognized that the nationalization of the small artisanal businesses had been a mistake, and announced that some of them would be given back to their owners. It did occur, although the real change happened with some delay. It was not until September 1955 that a new economic course was implemented, aimed at funneling investments from heavy to light industry, improving agriculture, and strengthening foreign economic relations.[410]

There were also significant changes in intellectual life. For instance, the authorities abandoned the Russification policy and as early as January 1950 published a decree that equated the study of Russian in schools with that of other foreign languages. Russian textbooks, especially those of the social sciences, were replaced and, in August of the same year, the CPY's party organ *Komunist* announced that Stalin's *History of the All-Union Communist Party (Bolshevik): Short Course* was no longer obligatory reading for party members. Other aspects of intellectual life, especially in the arts, changed as well. An exhibition by the painter Miodrag Popović opened that year in Belgrade on 23 September accompanied by a brochure in which the painter criticized all kinds of censorship. The newspaper of the Serb Popular Front commented that "some of Popović's statements are not correct, but nobody will deny his right to express them."[411] This liberalizing trend was confirmed by the Second Writers' Congress, convened in Ljubljana in October 1952. In his opening speech,

Miroslav Krleža launched the slogan "creative liberty." Although he lamented the detachment from social commitment of those who proclaimed that "revolutions come and go, lyric poetry remains," he also condemned those who thought that only "politically engaged" literature was legitimate. His speech is a typical example of the intellectual atmosphere found in Yugoslavia in the early fifties. The Agitprop Department was transformed into the Commission for Culture and Education, which controlled the media, schools, and cultural and artistic activity. Although preventive censorship was abolished, this did not include the duty to follow the party line for all those working in radio, publishing houses, and other cultural sectors. Nevertheless, Western influences began to increase in intellectual and artistic life. The authorities observed this ferment with a mixture of approval and apprehension, in fear that the intelligentsia would be seduced by bourgeois values. Thus it is no wonder that, before being delivered, Krleža's speech, with its opening and warning, had been checked and approved by Kardelj, Djilas, and even Tito himself.[412]

The Sixth Congress of the CPY

The secession from the Bolshevik concept was signaled most authoritatively by the Sixth Congress of the CPY, at which the Yugoslav Communists proclaimed themselves the only true heirs to Karl Marx, determined to create the first socialist country in the world.[413] After lively discussions among the quartet in power, the congress was convened in Zagreb on 2 November 1952, with all the pomp of similar assemblies. Indian and Indonesian socialists were invited to participate as guests of honor. Tito and his most influential comrades met with them on the eve of the congress. The minutes of their discussion are of interest because they show how far they went in their speculation, but also how separated they already were from one another, without being fully aware that this was the case. During the conversation, Tito stressed that the Popular Front was assuming a pronounced socialist character, going so far as to envision its promising future: "We will transform the Popular Front into a Socialist Alliance of the working people, which will contact other socialist parties and could, sooner or later, join the Socialist International." With 8 million members, it would have been one of the most numerous parties.

Tito continued:

> Another important topic for our internal life is the health of our party, and the development of the theory and practice of socialism, which are bound into the change of the name of the CPY to the Yugoslav League of Communists. This will have a new role and a new task at the current stage of our social development: it will have an increasingly didactic character. If we would proceed along the current

> line, we would move towards bureaucratization, in spite of efforts to avoid this: the party could not evolve from the agent of proletarian dictatorship into an instrument of education of the masses. Our Communists will not have privileges, will not have social functions only because they are party members. We want to avoid the Soviet practice that has transformed the party into a bureaucratic organism. Those two entities, the Socialist Alliance and the Communist League are in same way linked together and complete each other.[414]

Djilas went even further, speaking about democracy and the universal value of the Yugoslav experience, while Kardelj stressed that in Western Europe socialism could develop in different ways and through different parties, "even non-Communist ones." Tito held back this wave of audacious thought, recalling the importance of democratic centralism in the party, even if it aimed to be first an educator. This was the principle by which members took part in policy discussions at all levels, but once the party line was established, they had to follow it, in order to avoid internal squabbles. Remembering his own fight against the "factions" in the past, he added: "Without democratic centralism, there is no harmonious development."

Djilas observed that the democratic centralism so praised by Lenin was not his invention. The Jacobins (the members of the most influential and radical club of the French Revolution) had already practiced it, but the Russians had distorted it completely. When speaking about democratic centralism, one should distinguish between state and party: in the frame of the party it was acceptable, but at state level it would mean dictatorship. Tito corrected him: "In Russia there is no democratic centralism: there exists only bureaucratic centralism."[415]

The Sixth Congress reverberated with rhythmic hosannas in honor of the "hero Tito" and the other leaders, "not always because of heart's drive or conviction, but because of habit and ritual convention," as the Serb writer Dobrica Ćosić noted.[416] There was no lack of unanimity among the votes cast by the two thousand delegates. In spite of the watchful organization and direction, disturbed only by the unexpected public accusation from the secretary general of the federal government, Moma Djurić, that the president of the Serb Council had seduced his wife, the congress was a dynamic one: the Soviet Union was branded as having hegemonic appetites, betraying the October Revolution, renewing imperial tsarist policy, introducing serfdom in the countryside, and abandoning the workers to the mercy of a despotic bureaucracy. In his introduction, Tito repeated Kidrič's assertion about "state capitalism" in the Soviet Union and also criticized the theory of the "leading nation" in the USSR, which ensured the domination of Russians. He was echoing Kardelj, who had stressed the danger of this concept: "In a multiethnic state, the theory of the 'leading nation' means, in reality, subjugation, national oppression and economic exploitation of lesser peoples. . . . It is understandable that the non-Russians were opposed to such a theory and practice, and are still against it."[417]

On the basis of these discoveries, the Yugoslavs returned to Marx and Engels: they not only changed the name of the party to the "League of Communists," recalling their 1848 "Manifesto," but announced that they would decentralize state administration and transfer its duties to municipalities, which would be local administrative bodies on the model of the Paris Commune of 1871 (the first Communist experiment, albeit ephemeral, in history). In accordance with Lenin, they proclaimed the need for a progressive withering away of the state, asserting that, in regard to this, there were two doctrines. The first was a "theistic" one that betrayed the values of Marxist classics in trying to suffocate the personality of each citizen, and the liberty of the working class.[418] By contrast, the Yugoslav Communists declared themselves followers of an "atheist" doctrine, taking as a model Lenin's New Economic Policy, stressing the need to replace the highly centralized planned economy, as practiced in Stalin's Soviet Union, with a market economy. According to Boris Kidrič, one of the most influent economic theoreticians, in this way the producers could have all social property at their disposal and freely sell their products. In industry, commerce, and agriculture, self-managed committees would take on the role of free entrepreneurs. "A society that tries to suffocate the law of value," affirmed Kidrič, "goes directly toward Stalinism."[419]

Tito announced in his conversation with the Indian and Indonesian socialists that the LCY (League of Communists of Yugoslavia), as it would now be known, would be completely different from the old CPY. The power that had until then been exercised by the CPY would pass to the Socialist Alliance of Working People, as the leading organization of trade unions and other collectives, including the LCY itself, veteran's associations, youth associations, and others. The LCY should be an ideological center charged with influencing economic, political, and social life with reasoning and not with orders. This prediction did not become a reality: although the LCY was more liberal than any of the other Communist parties in power, it never did allow the Socialist Alliance to become a truly independent body, using it rather as the classic Leninist "transmission belt," for conveying the party line to society at large.[420]

The radical innovations of the Sixth Congress produced a lot of confusion in the party, since to many it was unclear what its future role should be. By contrast, these innovations reverberated internationally, especially in the East, where the Cominform newspaper quoted them as proof that "the Yugoslav Communists continued to sink into the quagmire of their revisionism."[421] Despite this, they did not deviate from their line: on 13 January 1953, they issued a series of amendments to the 1946 Constitution that confirmed the reforms they had adopted, further distancing Yugoslav society from the Soviet model, and exalting, above all, its "self-managed democracy." The new law foresaw two parliamentary chambers, a Federal Council and a Producers' Council (workers' representatives), which according to Kardelj would become "the instrument of class policy," whereas the old Nationalities Chamber would become just an appendix of the Federal Council. The supreme governing body, which from now on would be called the Executive Council, would have forty-three members, of whom thirty-seven were elected and six were nominated by the republics. Its president should be, at the same time, president of the federation and commander-in-chief of the army. This office was assumed, of course, by Tito, who formed a new government whose members were now called secretaries rather than ministers.[422] Cultured, refined, but arrogant, Koča Popović became secretary for foreign affairs. He traveled to London with Tito in this capacity on the marshal's first visit to the West, at Churchill's invitation, once the British prime minster had returned to power again after 1951. The two statesmen agreed upon a common defense policy, assuming that an attack on Yugoslavia would be part of a general attack in Europe.[423] As usual, Churchill summarized this with a sentence full of eminently quotable rhetoric: "If Yugoslavia, our ally, will be attacked, we will fight and die with you." Tito, for his part, assured Churchill that his country was part of the "free world," although this could not yet be loudly proclaimed.[424]

Slowing Down the Democratization

Tito went to Great Britain on his yacht, the *Galeb* (Seagull). The "good" news about Stalin's death reached him before he left Montenegrin waters. During the following months, this sudden event influenced his policy in a decisive way. According to Djilas, before Stalin's death he adopted the line proposed by his more intellectually daring comrades, but abandoned it after Stalin died as a burden and a threat to his own power. Even during the years of his tug-of-war with Stalinism, he reacted with irritation if someone in his circle displayed doubts about the socialist character of the Soviet Union and, consequently, about socialism in Yugoslavia. "Sometimes it seemed," Djilas affirmed, "that he played the prophetic role of a high priest to the schismatics."[425]

Yugoslav leaders, Tito above all, hoped that, after Stalin's death, a power struggle would erupt in the Kremlin that would lessen the pressure on their country. When this actually happened, Tito was quick to use the occasion to slow down the democratization process and to once again subject the party to his will. As time went on, he was less and less ready to recognize his faults and to collaborate with the West, and he began to apply pressure on the members of the CC who were dealing with the economy, pushing them to get rid of American aid as soon as possible. He considered it demeaning and limiting to Yugoslav freedom of action in foreign policy. "Without an autonomous foreign policy," he used to say, "there is no sovereignty."[426] Not to mention the fact that he had a fundamental suspicion of Western democracy, which guaranteed the personal freedom of the individual, allowing people to do what they wanted at the expense of society and to exploit a thousand others.[427] The sudden left-wing turn of the regime was evident especially in the agrarian sector. In order to address the discontent of the peasants, on 30 March 1953, three weeks after Stalin's death, the government issued a decree on the reorganization of rural cooperatives.[428] The decree announced the end of the ideological war on the countryside, allowing the abolishment of the collective cooperatives and the reestablishment of private property. Although the law stated that the peasants could leave the cooperatives the following autumn, there was an immediate stampede, which had the flavor of an open protest against the socialist regime. The liberalization process was halted shortly afterward, however, because of the violent opposition of local bureaucrats and landless peasants, numbering about one-hundred thousand, who saw in it an attack against their interests. Hence, on 22 May 1953 the government approved a series of supplementary measures that annulled any of the advantageous effects the abolition of collectivization might have produced. It was decided, in fact, that the cultivable land in possession of single families could not exceed ten hectares (twenty in the mountainous areas) and introduced a fiscal system that heavily penalized the wealthier peasants and preserved state control over the sale of some of their products. In this way, every possibility for the healthy economic development of the countryside was suffocated in its embryonic phase, fueling the masses' distrust of the regime.[429] The by-product of this was the halting of a larger democratization of public life, the development of the Socialist Alliance into an autonomous force, and the integration of capable individuals not affiliated with the party into the economic and administrative structure of the country.

In spite of this return to orthodoxy, the Yugoslavs favorably greeted the uprisings of workers that occurred in June and July 1953 in East Berlin, Pilsen, Ostrava, and elsewhere. On 8 July, Radio Zagreb broadcast a commentary proclaiming: "The unrest in East Berlin, suppressed in blood by Soviet tanks and police, the insurrections in Czechoslovakia and in Hungary, are not symptoms of a devious disease. The ice is broken for a while and is moving. . . . It is impossible to deny that the Yugoslav case has had an important psychological influence, showing that human beings can successfully oppose such a terrible despotism as the Soviet one."[430] At the same time, the leadership did not ignore the fact that the weakening of the Soviet Union would also weaken "our positions," as Tito said. "True," Kardelj replied, "we should not allow anyone to resolve the crisis in the Soviet Union, and in Eastern Countries, with anti-socialist methods."[431]

While they stressed the importance of their rebellion against Stalin as a precondition of the crisis in the Soviet bloc, the Yugoslav leaders had to cope with domestic crises caused by the metamorphosis of their own party after its exclusion from the Cominform. Even before Stalin's death, Tito called his comrades' attention to its weak cohesion and the lack of "democratic centralism" in its ranks.[432] He was right, since before the Sixth Congress (and even more so after it) the party had been radically transformed due to the abolition of social or any other criteria in recruiting new members. In 1948, the party numbered only seventy thousand individuals with higher education, whereas in 1954 it boasted 319,000, since all posts of responsibility were reserved for its members. During the same time, it experienced a large "purge," considering that, between 1950 and 1955, 123,000 members suffered disciplinary measures or were expelled.[433] This turbulent dynamic caused a lot of apprehension among the cadres, who saw their privileges at risk and hence reacted to the reforms with passive resistance or resigned pessimism. Consequently, at the end of 1952, the LCY lost about eighty thousand members. Even the party's daily newspaper, *Borba*, commented on the moodiness in the party in June 1953, while the Zagreb newspaper, *Napred*, complained: "The Communists are passive, the people are lazy. In some mass organizations [a network of trade unions, women, students, peasants, cultural organizations, necessary to mobilize popular support] less than half of the League's members are active. . . . Many Communists are apathetic."[434]

In reaction to this, Tito called a meeting of the CC on 16 and 17 June 1953 at Brioni, where he stressed the need to close ranks and free the LCY of any superfluous ballast. He criticized those who had betrayed party discipline by spreading "petit-bourgeois ideas about freedom and democracy" and at the same time failing to resist "foreign and anti-socialist influences." He sent a letter to all party organizations, in which he described the need to overcome every manifestation of apathy and expel "old members affected with bureaucratic tendencies, to develop an ideological and educational activity, and to silence all enemies."[435] It was clear that he rediscovered his penchant for discipline, one of his favorite words, and considered enemies not just those Communists who were still weary of the recent reforms, but also those who were lured by decadent Western culture. They all should be reeducated or rendered harmless. According to Djilas, this meant that Tito began distancing himself from opposition to the Soviet brand of Communism, and tried to block the democratization process and to bring the party back to the old secure path of Leninism-Stalinism.

All the while, Tito awaited the improvement of relations with Moscow, as Kardelj confided to Djilas, during their return trip from Brioni.[436]

Djilas Falls

After the Brioni plenum, Djilas began to feel the urgent need to distance himself from Tito, in order not to be eclipsed by the splendor and shadow of his power. In his urge to go along the path of the Western-style democracy, recently discovered during his trips to New York and London, and particularly through his contacts with the exponents of British Labour, he was as intransigent as he had been in the past when he was, to quote Miroslav Krleža, a "Stalinist dervish."[437] As Djilas himself put it: "The preoccupation with my fate prevented me from continuing to glorify Tito's personality, and to consider infallible what I have learned from him."[438] In his absorption with his private ideological mutation, he lost touch with reality and did not realize that the regime gained strength and cohesion from Tito's charisma, which radiated its influence out to the popular masses, even those who were basically anti-Communist, for they saw Tito, after the split with Stalin, as the guardian of their national interests. Djilas was convinced that the will to restore bureaucratic power had triumphed at Brioni, and he felt the need to confront it in the name of his ideas, inspired by hope in the progressive withering away, not only of the state, but also of the party. He had already written an article on the possible degeneration of the party entitled "Class or Caste," published in the Belgrade magazine *Svedočanstva* (Testimony). In it, he affirmed that a new bureaucratic class, or caste, had emerged in the Soviet Union that obstructed the development of society.[439] There was just a short step from a critical stance toward this Soviet reality to a critical stance toward the situation in Yugoslavia.

Tito tried to save him. He noticed the increasingly reserved attitude of "Djido," as he was called, revealed, for example, in his reluctance to come to Brioni on vacation, instead coming only when he had to on party business. Tito offered to build a villa for him on the archipelago and reproached him from having "isolated himself from our collective."[440] But Djilas was increasingly intolerant of the marshal's paternalism and his tendency to identify himself with the LCY and the state, for instance calling the CC to meet wherever he happened to be, regardless of the inconvenience to others. "Why should I go to his feet to Brioni?" he once asked, expressing his anger in conversation with his new, young wife, the ambitious and socially aggressive Štefica Barić.[441]

In the autumn of 1953, Tito was seriously preoccupied with the Trieste crisis. Nevertheless, he found time to meet Djilas and discuss his ideological dilemmas. They met on 9 October in the White Palace, where Tito gently told him, but not without a veiled invitation to be prudent: "You write well. You should write more about the bourgeoisie, which is strong and self-conscious. And you should write for the young—the young are the most important. At this point, the time for democracy is not ripe. The dictatorship is still necessary!"[442] Djilas, long convinced that the weak and modest Yugoslav bourgeoisie was innocuous, was bewildered. He had the impression that Tito was not yet free from his old mental framework and that he needed to hear about other dangers and problems: about Leninism-Stalinism in a Yugoslav disguise, about the party and its reform. Djilas did not reply immediately but later he entered the fray with the passion of someone who is sure that nothing unpleasant could happen to him. In those days, did Tito not come to dinner at his home with his new wife, Jovanka, and was she not friends with Djilas's own wife? And had he not been charged to write the speech that Tito would deliver on the Yugoslav national holiday, 29 November, the tenth anniversary of AVNOJ? Did he not sit on Tito's right side at that solemn occasion?[443]

Djilas laid out his thoughts in eighteen articles overall. The first appeared on 11 October in *Borba*, the official publication of the LCY, and was entitled "The New Contents." In a discussion with Dedijer at the beginning of the month he affirmed that compromises were necessary in political life, saying: "The most important thing is that our development continues. We should not surpass the consciousness of the masses."[444] Some days after this somber reflection that it was important to consider the maturity of the people in forming one's political line, he sketched out a completely different discourse. In the *Borba* article, he covertly polemicized with Tito, arguing that the enemy of socialism was not only the bourgeoisie but also the bureaucracy, particularly the party bureaucracy, which continuously violated and took advantage of the laws while trying to rule under the cloak of ideology. To justify its existence and be faithful to its dogmas, the bureaucracy fabricated new enemies.[445] Invited by a "comrade" to indicate possible solutions, on 29 November Djilas listed the measures needed to fight the bureaucratic apparatus, stressing, however, that these were his personal opinions and were not supported by any "forum." In his opinion, the roots of "bureaucracy" were to be found in the fact that the party was waging a war against the bourgeoisie on an ideological basis, and not on a legal one. The fight against the "class enemy" should instead develop through legal measures. The task of state organs of repression and vigilance (the courts, the UDBA, the police) was not to exacerbate the class struggle but to apply the law. These organs should be free from all party interference, because otherwise they could not avoid becoming instruments of antidemocratic repression.[446]

Djilas developed his thoughts even more explicitly in the article entitled "Subjective Forces," published in *Borba* on 27 December 1953. According to him, in Yugoslavia, socialist and revolutionary conscience was strong with regards to problems that were no longer present, such as nationalization, unity of the country, and its defense. Those problems encountered daily, which were related to the class struggle, the implementation of law, the role of the administration and political and social organizations, and cultural freedom and criticism of "bureaucracy," remained unresolved. "Today we can see social consciousness even outside the official and Communist organizations," he wrote. "Yes, outside them and in spite of so many bureaus and Communist functionaries. We can find these so-called 'subjective forces' not only among the Communists and workers with developed class consciousness, but among all those who want an independent, socialist and democratic Yugoslavia."[447] In an article that appeared in *Borba* on 19 December, he even declared that "today, no party or group, and even less a class, can express the objective needs of society. Nobody can claim the right to direct the action of the productive forces [working people], without paralyzing and oppressing them."[448]

These affirmations found a vast echo in public opinion, not just in bourgeois circles but also in the party, especially in the middle ranks, where people were immediately eager to engage in "self-criticism," (part of the Communist fashion, to show how in line they were.) In Djilas's writings they saw the prelude to a prudent but inevitable democratization of the regime, presumably with Tito's blessing. Evidently Djilas had hit the mark, articulating the general malaise. It is interesting, in this context, that *Borba*, in its Letters to the Editor, published only favorable opinions on his writing. It was Djilas who called attention to criticism of his work, stressing in the article of 24 December that there had been four main objections: he was simply a philosopher and therefore a stranger to reality; he wrote only in order to make a good impression abroad; he departed from dialectical materialism and Leninism; and he played into the hands of reactionaries who took advantage of his writing in order to denigrate the party and the state institutions. In reply to these critics, he declared that his meditations surely were neither completely correct nor original. He had hoped to emphasize topical questions and start a discussion dictated by the objective development of contemporary society. After all, new ideas were never mass ideas. This inevitably precipitated a clash between new ideas, such as the ones being denounced today as "anarchic," "petit bourgeois," and "Western," and the old ideas, which were criticized as "bureaucratic," "Stalinist," and "dogmatic."[449]

The article "League or Party" caused quite a stir. It was published in *Borba* on 4 January 1954, a day after Djilas's election to the presidency of the Federal Assembly. In it, Djilas called attention to the transformation of the party between the Fifth (1948) and the Sixth (1952) Congresses, a transformation imposed by circumstances. In his view, such radical changes were no longer necessary, since the statutes voted on by the Sixth Congress were flexible enough to allow for the emergence of new organizational forms. He added, however: "Today the crisis of form and substance of political and ideological work is much deeper. The growing freedom in the economy is on a collision course with old relations and old visions. We now have to discuss this whole organizational and ideological system of ours, and about the future apparatus—it is a fundamental transformation."[450]

Djilas described as ridiculous the accusation leveled against him that he wished to disband the party. He only wanted to reorganize it, since the LCY was not the old party anymore; it did not have all the power in its hands and it was not homogeneous in its membership, since it embraced not just a Communist vanguard, but a good portion of the popular masses. Especially after the war, the party had become more and more populated by peasants, who presumed that they could assure themselves of its privileges. The old prerevolutionary and revolutionary party did not exist anymore; all that was left was its heritage. "Therefore," he wrote, "today the work in grassroots organizations . . . in the party apparatus is not only fruitless, but even paralyzes the creative activity of Communists, their fight for democracy and their real contribution to political and public life. . . . For this reason, the Communists have no need to solve the current political problems outside the Socialist Alliance."

What remained, then, for the grassroots organizations of the LCY? To choose the functionaries and delegates and, even more important, to reconsider ideology. But this should not be carried out in secret, but openly, with all those who were interested. "The contemporary League of Communists of Yugoslavia should, therefore, 'extinguish' itself as a classical party, whereas the voluntary discipline of true Communists should be strengthened," Djilas said. Gradually, the LCY would become a solid ideological nucleus that would operate beside the Socialist Alliance, just as "the Communist walks beside the citizen."[451]

Djilas's writing aroused the interest of Western diplomats and journalists who dedicated much attention to his reflections, considering them the most significant event in Yugoslavia after the Cominform split. This "bourgeois" backing did not help him.[452] His friend General Peko Dapčević was the first to signal how precarious his position was. At the close of the year, he met Tito at Lake Bled in Slovenia. When he returned to Belgrade, he alerted Djilas that the "Old One" was furious indeed. This was later confirmed by Kardelj and a heated discussion followed during which Djilas expressed ideas more daring than ever before: he asserted that Tito was supporting the bureaucratic apparatus and that, sooner or later, a clash with him would be unavoidable, saying "Tito is ready for a museum." He forecast the coming of a new socialist party that would stand side by side with the LCY, and nearly spoke in favor of a two-party system. Later he softened these positions but the words had been uttered. Kardelj was induced to believe (or to hope) that he would not repeat them and decided not to mention them to Tito, although his duty called him to do so.[453] On 24 December, reading *Borba*, he was alarmed to discover that Djilas had remained deaf to his admonitions; in an article entitled "The Answer," Djilas informed readers that his ideas had been criticized and that, therefore, he had to reply. He rejected the reproach that he was merely an abstract philosopher and stressed that, on the contrary, he wanted to "abandon the unreal world of the elected and predestined few, and immerse himself, as much as possible, into the real world of simple working people." He would not defend himself from the suspicion that he was a heretic: his heresy was "magnificent," and every Communist should be honored to share it. For his part, he was not ready to accept second-hand Stalinist dogmas as ultimate truth. The way he was being criticized testified eloquently enough to the character of his adversaries, who were "without principles, Stalinist, bureaucratic, pseudo-democratic."[454]

Meanwhile, Tito read his articles and realized that Djido, beyond his verbosity and abstruse reasoning, "attacked the LCY . . . tried to liquidate it, undermine the discipline."[455] This judgment was known to many in his circle, which is why, in the following days, Djilas discovered that a menacing void was developing around him, although some comrades continued to encourage him to go on with his writings. At the New Year's party organized by the federal government, Vukmanović (Tempo) told him: "Djido, do not sprinkle ashes on your head. I will stay with you till the end."[456]

The final two articles, which appeared in *Borba* on 1 and 4 January 1954, were dedicated to the Marxist doctrine regarding the withering away of the state, and also mentioned the withering away of the party. Djilas affirmed that in the future neither the merits acquired during the liberation struggle nor adherence to Communism would have any importance, but only what each person would be able to create through his work. As such, he counseled the LCY to get rid of all opportunists and careerists and rely instead on the idealists. "Today, the movement is feasible only in democratic and not revolutionary forms, whereas it is possible to preserve the soul of the revolution only in real freedom. . . . The Leninist form of party and State is obsolete."[457]

By the end of 1953, the impetuous Montenegrin understood that he was unable to follow Tito anymore, although in the past he had maintained that no force could separate them. He topped off his series of writings with an essay published in the magazine he had recently founded, *Nova Misao* (New thought), giving it a provocative title: "Anatomy of a Moral." Although he was aware of Tito's anger and was invited to Brdo Castle to clarify the situation, he made clear in a telephone conversation with Ranković that he refused to "throw himself at the monarch's feet."[458] On the contrary, he hurried feverishly to publish his text, convinced that he must accomplish his mission. "With his articles," said Stane Kavčič, one of the most prominent Slovene Communists of the postwar generation, "Djilas firstly and suddenly opened many questions related to socialism and democracy, but unluckily enough, in a way that did more harm than good."[459]

This is true especially for "Anatomy of a Moral," written nearly by chance in order to fill some empty space in the magazine created when Joža Vilfan, chief of Tito's secretariat, informed him that he would not contribute a promised article on state capitalism. In his article Djilas attacked "the false class morale" of the power elite without pity, reproaching it for having sullied itself with all possible bourgeois sins. He accused his comrades of having behaved like an exclusive caste and isolating themselves from those who had "recently joined the party." However, his main targets were the wives of the highest leaders, who would not accept a beautiful young woman into their circle, even though she had recently married a "people's hero," the highest honor a Partisan could receive. In Belgrade, rumor had it that he meant the charming actress who was married to General Dapčević, although Jovanka, Tito's consort, was sure that Djilas had her in mind. The pamphlet was an attack against the women at the highest level of the party who were too open to be acceptable. This angered the women who had created an exclusive, although informal, club of ex-Partisans, who had fought alongside their husbands and considered this a badge of exclusive merit. They spoke with contempt about younger women who tried to enter their group through marriage, wondering: "Where were these girls in short skirts when the trees were bursting because of the cold?"[460]

This attitude was denounced with sarcasm by Djilas, who mocked "all those exalted women [who] came from semi-peasant backgrounds and were semi-educated," and who seemed to think that they could "grab and hoard deluxe furniture and works of art" because of their war-time services. "Tasteless, of course, but by means of which they satisfied their primitive instincts of greed and imagined puffed-up notions of their social status, with all the pretentiousness and omniscience of the ignorant."[461] Consequently, protests came from the powerful Antifascist Women's Association, and arose in many domestic discussions, which hastened Djilas's fall. In fact, Tito interpreted the article as trying to discredit him and his inner group, which Djilas accused of no longer living up to its revolutionary task. This was not far from the truth, since the marshal had definitely closed himself off into an environment populated by a select few, given that among the 135 members of the CC, only five entered the party during the war, whereas all the others had been members since the days of the Comintern.[462]

When Tito summoned him at the beginning of January 1954 to have him clarify his position in the presence of Kardelj and Ranković, Djido was accused right from the start of having criticized even Marxist classics (texts by Marx, Engels, Lenin), claiming that they were not always right. Tito was aghast: "Are you ready to say this publicly?"

Djilas answered, "At any moment, and gladly."

"You are not the same anymore," said Tito, before requiring him to renounce the presidency of the Federal Assembly.[463]

Djilas tried to defend himself by recalling his attachment to Tito, the articles where he sang his praises, and those in which, polemicizing with the Soviets, he claimed the core values of his policy. It was to no avail. This does not mean that Djido's discharge was not painful for the marshal, as well as for Kardelj and Ranković. When, during the meeting, he asked for a cup of coffee, saying that he did not sleep at night, Tito remarked: "And others cannot sleep either."[464]

On 7 January, the Norwegian ambassador to Belgrade invited Djilas to visit Scandinavia, together with Tito's biographer, Vladimir Dedijer. Djilas accepted the invitation. But on 10 January, *Borba* published a statement by the Executive Committee of the CC asserting that Djilas's articles, especially "Anatomy of a Moral," had provoked a great deal of worry among members of the LCY, considering his high office. It read in part: "The articles by Comrade Milovan Djilas are the result of his own opinions, contrasting with those of the Executive Committee, with the spirit of decisions of the Sixth Congress and of the Second Plenum. He has published them without warning the comrades of the Executive Committee about the ideas that he intended to put forth and, indeed, he ignored admonitions by comrades, after the appearance of the first series, regarding the damage he could cause to the development of the LCY and the construction of socialist democracy in our country."[465]

That same day, a public showdown started with the appearance in the press of some critical notes by Boris Ziherl, one of the more orthodox Slovene theoreticians. In Belgrade, it was rumored that Djido was a "Trotskyist," which upset him greatly. Dedijer, who at that time spent every evening with him, described how he moved around his office, troubled, pale and slimmed down, with eyes bulging out; how he brandished the pistol with a silver grip, a gift from General Korneev; how he threatened to kill his slanderers and immediately after that his wife and newborn son.[466]

The End of the Yugoslav "Quartet"

After his expulsion from the Executive Committee on 13 January 1954, Djilas wrote a letter to Tito to "tell him some things related to our private relations, after seventeen years of common work." He apologized for the "Anatomy of a

Moral" article, claiming that it did not refer to Tito, who "unfortunately had to live as he lived," nor to his wife, Jovanka. "Often I have had some tiffs with you, always nervous but short, partly because of my wild temperament; but never have I done so in disingenuously. . . . I had no opportunity to say this in another way. Djido."[467]

If Djilas hoped to soften Tito with this mea culpa and to preserve at least his post in the Central Committee, he was wrong. This was so despite warnings from one of Yugoslavia's best friends and supporters, the Austrian ambassador Walter Wodak, who observed that the regime was facing a delicate test in its relations with the West. Three days after Djilas's expulsion from the Executive Committee, on 16 January 1954, an extraordinary plenum of the CC was summoned to discuss his "affair." The initiative was Tito's, who charged Kardelj and Ranković with its implementation. Djilas was not informed, only learning about the session, in which 108 delegates took part, from newspapers.[468] This was a bitter surprise for him, since he had hoped to overcome the rift with Tito and his comrades without public discussion and without too much damage to his career. He nurtured the illusion that he might remain in politics and might still be able, although in a limited way, to further develop his theories. He was aware that he had done a "stupid thing" in publishing what amounted to libel in *Nova Misao*. "I am a man-child . . . I am not a statesman. If I led the country, it would be a disaster," he said.[469]

A year before, Tito had gotten rid of Blagoje Nešković, the strong man of Serb politics, by isolating him from his comrades (Djilas, Ranković and the others), accusing him of Cominformist leanings, and removing him from power. He would use the same tactics this time.[470] Before the CC session, he had a series of conversations with those members whom he suspected of sympathizing with Djilas. Invoking the unity of the party, and stressing the damage done to the country, he managed to line them up on his side—except for Dedijer.[471] At the plenum, which met in Belgrade in a tense atmosphere and was broadcast live on the radio, Tito was first to speak. He dwelled on the dangers of Djilas's writings, as they undermined party discipline, which threatened the existence of the state. According to him, Djilas was preaching an abstract democracy, which was an end in itself and a call for anarchy.[472] Djilas took the floor after him, pale from fatigue and concern, in order to defend his theories without pretending, however, that the others would share them. "My main fault was that I have exposed my ideas without discussing them before with comrades," he said, "certain that the moment had come, when it would be acceptable to articulate them publicly, regardless of the official line."[473] Kardelj, charged to examine Djilas's thought from a theoretical point of view, accused him of following the worst "revisionism," introduced into Marxist doctrine at the end of the nineteenth century by the German Social Democrat Eduard Bernstein. It seems that in saying so he was not embarrassed by the fact that Stalin had also mentioned Bernstein when he had indicted Tito and his comrades with identical accusations in his first letter during the spring of 1948. Djilas's assurance that he had never read Bernstein fell on deaf ears. Kardelj challenged his criticism of the LCY, stressing its importance, but in a new light: he presented the party as a necessary tool in the fight for socialism and democracy in Yugoslavia.[474] "Possibly he was a worse heretic than Djilas," Dedijer later commented, "but he was more subtle and flexible. He was even able to draw back and to camouflage. . . . He knew how to make concessions, but defend the essential."[475]

Djilas felt Kardelj's words were a stab in the back, since in the previous months they had seen or at least called each other every day, and not just for work, but for reasons of common ideological understanding. Kardelj, however, was too pragmatic to overlook the precipice his friend was heading toward and had grown prudent and reserved toward him. He liked him for his "wild frankness," for his readiness to say anything "that goes through his head." But he understood that in his "limitless ambition" and in the abstractness of his thought he overrated the democratic process in Yugoslavia, and he was not ready to follow him down this drain.[476] When he decided to take sides against him, after establishing Tito's position, he even argued that Djido had temporarily gone insane. In his speech, he also revealed that he had heard him speak about the possibility of two socialist parties in competition with each other. He did not say, however, that one of these would be opposed to the marshal.[477]

Tito, who was well aware of the real issue at stake, went even further, branding Djilas a "class enemy." In Yugoslavia, he said, it was not possible to "liquidate" the party, because only the party was responsible for the implementation of the revolution, and it surely was not an outdated piece of junk. All present agreed with him, even Svetozar Vukmanović (Tempo), although he did so with tears in his eyes. Moša Pijade, who according to Kardelj was an opportunistic demagogue who had not been able to stand Djido ever since their time in jail together, even referred to "Anatomy of a Moral" as "political pornography." "From one moment to the next, he amassed all his malevolence, dumping it on me," remembered Djilas.[478]

The only one who defended Djido—aside from his ex-wife, Mitra Mitrović—was Vladimir Dedijer. Crying and totally confused, he stressed that the incriminating articles had been avidly read by the members of the CC, the same people who were now condemning him, saying, "He only tried to put our opinions into a systematic order." Djilas himself sought distance from Dedijer's intervention, saying that it was full of emotional, not political arguments. He did not know that Dedijer took his side not so much out of friendship, but to show him that he was not a coward, which Djido had once accused him of being during the war, in the presence of Tito.[479] This at least was his later explanation.

Djilas, "the best orator of the Partisan revolution," was not able to reply to his accusers properly. He followed Kardelj's advice to engage in an act of penitence, entangling himself in an incoherent round of self-criticism and partially repudiating his ideas. As he confessed later, during the plenum he discovered a kernel of masochism within himself, thinking: "Let's let things get weird and see how bad it gets." In the end, he was completely lost, and "roamed from room to room, as if he was trying to find help and counsel about what to do."[480] Although he carried out the "final heroic act of a Communist," abdicating his convictions and his honor, following the example of Stalin's victims, Tito remained unmoved. Quite the opposite, since the marshal admired the audacious, even if they were his adversaries. With his moral "suicide," Djilas had devalued himself in Tito's eyes. In regard to Djido's self-criticism, he said: "We will see how sincere it is," albeit without hiding his displeasure. Speaking with foreign journalists he declared that political death was the worst thing that could happen to a former protégé.[481]

Djilas was not accused of "sectarianism," since Tito was convinced that "there is nothing organized" afoot.[482] For this reason, he was not expelled from the LCY, although he was banned from the CC and punished with the "final admonition" which, in the Communist world, gave the culprit a chance to mend fences as a simple member of the party. After all, Tito did not want to appear to Western public opinion as one who executed repressive measures, similar to the Soviets. After the experience of Andrija Hebrang and the Cominformists, as Djilas wrote later, Tito understood that it was not necessary to physically eliminate his enemies but only politically, according to the slogan: "Don't knock the head off, just knock them on the head."[483] A ferocious press campaign followed, orchestrated from on high, which did not cool down even after Djilas's confession of his errors and his declaration that he felt "as if his soul was liberated from the devil."[484] A commission led by Vladimir Bakarić stripped him of all his public offices on 20 January 1954, whereupon he stepped down as president of the Federal Assembly. The following day, voters from Pančevo asked Dedijer to renounce his parliamentary seat, too. Even Dedijer's doctor was not willing to see him, despite his having had an epileptic attack, the consequence of a head injury during the war. When Tito was informed, he sent him his own physician. But this was the only act of mercy on the part of the two men.[485]

The presidency of the Federal Assembly went to Djila's adversary, Moša Pijade, while in the Executive Committee his place was co-opted by the Slovene,

Miha Marinko, and the Serb, Petar Stambolić, strengthening the orthodox wing. During Djilas's ordeal Montenegrin students, who were numerous in Belgrade and who supported him, published and disseminated leaflets in defense of his ideas. The authorities arrested a few dozen of them and, just to be on the safe side, transferred some Montenegrin officers from the capital to other garrisons.[486] Despite being completely innocent, Peko Dapčević, husband of the young actress mentioned by Djilas in "Anatomy of a Moral," lost his post as chief of the General Staff and had to settle for an appointment in the federal government. But the targets were not just Montenegrins: a major part of the Belgrade intellectual élite, who saw Djilas as their idol, was spitting mad, feeling that they had been up there with him in the dock. "The Communists have taken the freedom from themselves first of all, then from all others. This is the great tragedy of our existence. The revolution has become a religion. . . . The party's bureaucracy fears everybody who thinks," Dobrica Ćosić wrote. His friend, the well-known writer Oskar Davičo, was so upset he even considered suicide.[487]

Meanwhile, a modest "purge" was carried out, the most eminent victim of which was Dušan Dimić, member of the CC of Croatia and director of the magazine *Napijed* (Forward). The majority of those party members who had only recently cheered Djilas hurried to proclaim that the Central Committee's decision was entirely justified and logical from a political point of view. Djilas and Dedijer were informed, on 30 January, that they were not allowed to go abroad, which is why they did not end up visiting Scandinavia.[488]

It has to be said, however, that former comrades, including Tito and Ranković, were still ready to dialogue with Djilas, but he refused their offer, having decided to break not just with them, but also with the regime.[489] In making this decision he was not hindered by the fact that he had lost his ministerial salary, that he had a family, and that his only income—220,000 dinars—came from his ill-fated articles. (The sum was not modest at all, considering that an average salary was about nine thousand dinars per month). At first he gave this money to a library in Nikšić, a Montenegrin town where he went to school, but it was returned since the "dirty money of a traitor" was not welcome. "My mother, a wise Montenegrin peasant, commented: 'God bless them, otherwise we would be broke,'" Djilas later said.[490]

Two months later and subject to strict police surveillance, he decided to abandon the LCY. According to Dedijer, "A Slovene woman, his main supporter in that Republic . . . spat in his face when he humbly came to a meeting of the party's cell in the exclusive neighborhood where he still lived."[491] Djilas reacted with all the ardor of his temper: some days later he went to the villa of Marija Vilfan, wife of Tito's chief secretary, who presided over the cell where the incident took place. He rang the bell and the door was opened by thirteen-year-old Jernej, one of Vilfan's sons. "Give your mom this," Djido said, and handed him his party card.[492]

The Victory of the Right

On 22 December 1954, the *London Times*'s Belgrade correspondent published an interview with Dedijer in which he mentioned the pressures he had been subjected to because of his loyalty to Djilas.[493] In the same period, shortly before Tito's trip to India and Burma, Djilas gave an interview to the correspondent from the *New York Times* in which he criticized domestic and foreign Yugoslav policy, stressing that it was led by reactionaries and demanding freedom of speech and the introduction of a two-party system. Consequently, Kardelj attacked the two at the Congress of the LC of Bosnia-Herzegovina in his capacity as a substitute for Tito during his absence. According to him, they were failed politicians and tools of enemy forces who were hoping to return to power. Dedijer tried to react, calling foreign correspondents to a press conference at his home, but when they came UDBA agents prevented them from entering the building. Only days later, on 24 December, he was indicted, together with Djilas. Both hired lawyer Ivo Politeo, who had defended Broz in 1928, Archbishop Stepinac, and various Ustaša chiefs after the war. After a final hearing, partially behind closed doors, though described as fair by Politeo, they were condemned to rather light punishments: Djilas to a year and a half in prison, Dedijer to six months, both with commuted sentences. If they did not do anything illicit, Djilas within three years and the Dedijer within two, they would not be jailed. It was clear that the authorities did not want to give much weight to the affair, as Belgrade diplomatic circles observed, not without relief, in order not to provoke unpleasant polemics in the West.[494]

Djilas remarked with enthusiasm on the outcome of the trial. "This sentence is marvelous," he said to friends (and of course also to the UDBA). "This was Tito's decision, which increases his prestige in the country and abroad. I am nicely surprised by our democratic systẹm . . . I expected at least one or two years of rigorous imprisonment." He also affirmed that he would respect the verdict and would no longer meddle in politics.[495] But his rebel temper, which inclined towards martyrdom, did not allow him to make good on those promises. He continued to provoke and to give explosive interviews, and also to write articles and heretical books. His pamphlet, *The New Class* (1957), was highly successful and was translated into different languages and distributed, with the help of the CIA, in numerous countries. With this and with the following *Conversations with Stalin* (1962), he earned quite a bit of money, but paid a high price, since between December 1956 and the end of 1966 he was condemned to nine years in jail. He served them in Sremska Mitrovica, where he had been imprisoned during the reigns of both Aleksandar and Petar Karadjordjević.[496] Once released, he continued to provoke, which often exasperated Tito and tempted him, toward the end of his life, to imprison him again. That he did not is likely due to British Conservative Party leader Margaret Thatcher's advice: in December 1977 she told him that Djilas was more dangerous in jail than free.[497] She was right, since the persecution he was subject to damaged the image of Yugoslavia abroad and upset the honeymoon with the European social democrats that the country had enjoyed until the mid-fifties thanks to the reform activity of the LCY.[498]

Tito, Partisan supreme commander (TBM VIII 9 FO)

Josip Broz among workers in Kamnik (TBM VI 4 FO)

Josip Broz on the front, World War One (TBM VI 6 FO)

Josip Broz with his first wife, Pelagiia Denisova Belousova, and their son, Žarko, 1920s (TBM V 5 FO)

Josip Broz police photo, Zagreb, May 1928 (TBM VI 13 FO)

Forged Canadian passport (TBM VII 2 FO)

A 1943 "wanted poster" published in Cyrillic by the Germans offering a reward for Tito's arrest (TBM VIII 15 FO)

Tito and Koča Popović, 1944 (TBM VIII 8 FO)

Ivan Šubašić, Winston Churchill and Tito, August 1944 (TBM VIII 28 FO)

Viacheslav Molotov, Joseph Stalin, and Tito, Moscow, April 1945 (TBM X 5 FO)

Davorjanka Paunović (*right*) (TBM V 6 FO)

Herta Hass
(TBM V 7 FO)

Georgi Dimitrov and Tito, 1955 (TBM X 2 FO)

Nikita Khrushchev and Tito, 1955 (TBM X 20 FO)

Ernesto "Che" Guevara and Tito, summer 1959 (TBM XI 5 FO)

John F. Kennedy and Tito, October 1963 (TBM X 29 FO)

Elizabeth Taylor and Richard Burton with Tito and Jovanka, Brioni, 1971 (TBM IV 16 FO)

Tito and Queen Elizabeth, 1972 (TBM IV 20 FO)

Tito and Yasser Arafat, 1970s (TBM XV 46 FO)

Tito and Henry Kissinger, 1974 (TBM XV 48 FO)

Tito and Jovanka (TBM IV 9 FO)

4

The Presidential Years

Creating the Non-Aligned Movement, the Search for "Socialism with a Human Face," and the Struggle for Unity in Yugoslavia

1953–1973

After Djilas's fall, it was Kardelj who cultivated contacts with Western social democrats. He was eager to dialogue with the most progressive politicians and theoreticians, especially in Scandinavia. Aleš Bebler, the deputy minister of foreign affairs, well understood Kardelj's aspirations when he said to the West German ambassador in October 1952: "Yugoslavia is a European country and considers itself part of Western Europe, not just for geographic reasons, but also because of the spiritual and cultural character of the population. This is often forgotten abroad, since Yugoslav communism is considered akin to the Soviet version."[1]

In the autumn of 1954 Kardelj and Vladimir Bakarić visited Germany, Sweden, Norway, Denmark, and France in place of Djilas and Dedijer, meeting local social-democratic leaders. On 8 October, Kardelj gave a speech in Oslo about socialist democracy in Yugoslavia in which he reaffirmed what he had already said at the Sixth Congress, namely that elements of socialism could be found in capitalist countries, just as capitalist elements may be found in socialist ones. According to him, the ideology preached by the Soviets that conservative and progressive worlds were concentrated within the Eastern and Western blocs respectively was untenable. This rejection of a Manichean vision of contemporary reality, split between light and dark, and even more the affirmation that without democracy there was no socialism, provoked an enormous outcry in Moscow. This was largely because from the war years the Soviets suspected Kardelj to be opposed to an intimate collaboration with them, instead believing he favored an equidistant position of Yugoslavia between the great powers. The principal ideologue in the Kremlin, Mikhail A. Suslov, commenting on the Oslo speech, wrote that Kardelj "was not a communist, nor a Marxist-Leninist, but a Social Democrat."[2] From Suslov's point of view, Kardelj was a traitor to communist doctrine as preached by Moscow, which was based on the conviction that capitalism and socialism were antithetical realities. This negative judgment would remain: Kardelj was put on the black list of Soviet enemies and was constantly monitored in all he did and wrote. His speech was disliked by many in Belgrade too, where after Stalin's death unfavorable comments about the Sixth Congress's reform program could be heard, and even requests that "all this rubbish should be liquidated."[3]

Kardelj was unsuccessful in his attempt to court European social democratic leaders during his trip to Scandinavia, Germany, and France. They were interested in a collaboration with Yugoslavia but were not ready to recognize the Socialist Alliance of Working People as one of their members, asserting that it was impossible to accept an organization that was opposed to political pluralism and whose unions renounced to the right to strike.[4] The fact that they were denied inclusion in the Socialist International was profoundly disappointing for Yugoslav leaders, who were just beginning to have significant successes abroad. For instance they had overcome the Trieste crisis, settling for a policy of collaboration with Italy. They had put the split provoked by Stalin behind them, largely thanks to Moscow's initiative. With the "Belgrade Declaration," signed on 1 June 1955 after intense and dramatic discussions with Khrushchev, they had a document that was potentially important for the entire communist camp. It recognized Yugoslavia's right to build socialism in its own way, in harmony with its specific needs. This was a victory for Tito's belief that every socialist country was sovereign, although it did not signify that all friction between Moscow and Belgrade had been eliminated. By making verbal concessions on sovereignty, Khrushchev had hoped during his "Canossa pilgrimage" to induce the Yugoslavs to return to the "camp" and join the Warsaw Pact, the recently instituted military alliance. But, as Tito said, he and his comrades were not ready to discuss a reinstatement of Muscovite hegemony from "the Adriatic to Japan."[5] This, Khrushchev later said, "kindled an explosive spark in our relations."[6] Invited by the latter to liven up the farewell reception, famous opera singer Galina Vishnevskaya vividly illustrated in her memoirs the atmosphere that prevailed at the close of the Soviet visit to Belgrade. When Comrade Khrushchev, already tipsy, started to dance, Tito did not follow his example.[7]

The Discovery of Non-Alignment

Khrushchev's pilgrimage to Canossa resulted in Tito's victory thanks to the self-confidence he had acquired some months earlier during his trip to India and Burma. The Indian prime minister, Jawaharlal Nehru, and the Burmese prime minister, U Nu, were much more sophisticated interlocutors than Comrade Nikita who, to quote the American ambassador James W. Riddleberger, gave the Yugoslav political elite the impression of a "country cousin." And the British ambassador added in his dispatch to the Foreign Office that thanks to the Russian guests, the Yugoslavs had become aware of their own "Western" character as compared to "'rigid, old-fashioned, uninformed Soviet thinking,' reporting their feeling that the Soviet delegation was composed of 'uncouth second-raters,' and that Tito stood head and shoulders above any of them."[8] The Yugoslavs could not ignore the differences that had developed between them and the Soviets after Stalin had excommunicated them, and the gap between their political ideas grew. They were not only shocked by Khrushchev's speech at the Belgrade airport, in which he violated previous agreements and once again sought to blame Beria and Djilas for everything that had gone wrong, but also by his boasting that World War I had brought communism to Russia, World War II had added Eastern Europe and China, and World War III would see it spread throughout the world.[9] The Yugoslavs had stopped thinking in terms of world war, and did not consider a military confrontation between the blocs at all inevitable. They were aiming instead at peaceful coexistence and at a non-aligned policy (as independence from both West and East was to be called).[10]

The Yugoslavs had begun showing an interest in Asia even before the split with Stalin, trying to establish links with local communist parties. At the beginning of 1948, Tito sent Vladimir Dedijer and Radovan Zogović, a Montenegrin poet and Agitprop official, to Calcutta as delegates to the Second Congress of the Indian CP. They were tasked with contacting Mao Zedong, who was still fighting for power in China, as well as members of the anti-colonial liberation movement in Indonesia.[11] After the independence of India and Indonesia and the victory of the Kuomintang in China, Belgrade's interest in the area increased and acquired new substance as a result of the struggle with Stalin. As early as June 1948 the Chinese had aligned themselves with the Soviet Union, which meant that it was impossible to have a dialogue with them despite Belgrade's recognition of the communist government in Beijing on 5 October 1948. Yugoslav diplomats had new input regarding their interest in Asia once they joined the Security Council in autumn 1949. There they cultivated friendly relations with the Indians, who were also new members of that body, as shown by their frequently concordant voting on important issues such as the Korean War.[12] Krishna Menon, India's representative in the Security Council, even proposed to his Yugoslav colleague, Aleš Bebler, that Yugoslavia should open a window onto Europe for India, and India would do the same for Yugoslavia in Asia. Both states established diplomatic relations, setting up their respective missions in New Delhi and Belgrade. The first Yugoslav ambassador, Josip Djerdja, once installed, did not try to get in touch with the local communists, who were under Moscow's spell, but with socialists and the ruling Congress Party. He was soon attracted by Nehru's idea of a "third force" between the blocs, and his critical attitude both toward Western imperialism and toward the Soviet brand of socialism. Djerdja registered with pleasure that the Indian newspapers followed the Peace Conference organized in July 1950 in Zagreb with interest—it was the first attempt taken by Tito's regime to affirm its newly discovered political autonomy on an international level. The prestigious *New Delhi Chronicle* published an editorial saying that Yugoslavia had emerged after the split with Stalin politically and economically stronger than it was before. It could be said with good reason, the article asserted, that Yugoslavia was the only independent country in the world.[13]

The friendly attitude of Indian elites toward Yugoslavia, and the observation that the Asian masses had a general hostility toward Europeans, suggested a daring idea to Djerdja: Yugoslavia could find allies among the countries of the Third World, which was in the process of emerging from the grip of colonialism, if it were able to implement a new relationship with them based on mutual respect. When he returned home in the fall of 1951, at the end of his mission, he mentioned these thoughts to his colleagues, and they were favorably received. "This is interesting," said Kardelj at a Ministry of Foreign Affairs daily meeting. "Let's go to Tito." He rung him on a special telephone and agreed on a time to meet, which was followed by an exchange of thoughts without concrete results.[14] Initially Tito was not enthusiastic about the proposal of seeking allies in the Third World, agreeing with Koča Popović that it was not a good idea to secure friends among these "paupers." Popović, who in 1953 succeeded Edvard Kardelj as foreign secretary, looked instead to Finland and its neutrality, hoping for a similar international position for Yugoslavia.[15] Kardelj, too, was reserved toward the idea of a collaboration with the "feudal lords" who often were in power in the Third World, but later became attracted by the idea under the influence of his deputy, Aleš Bebler, who appreciated Nehru's independent foreign policy, which was already labeled "non-aligned." The Slovene leader developed it further, in spite of the skeptical attitude of his colleagues: "Once again he has discovered a toy; let it be, none of this will come to pass anyway."[16]

Only in later years did the marshal pay more attention to India and to Nehru's policy, which aimed to create a link between the former colonies of Asia and Africa. This idea found expression in the so-called Doctrine of Bandung, the Indonesian town where representatives of the newly emancipated countries met in April 1955 to create a movement of mutual collaboration. Tito quickly understood the revolutionary significance of this project. He recognized that thanks to his history of rebellion against both Hitler and Stalin, he could become a spokesman for the Third World, which no longer wished to remain a plaything of the great powers, but had yet to participate in a constructive way in the discussion about war and peace, and especially about the distribution of resources.[17] On 23 June 1954, he told Edwin Kretzmann, first secretary of the American Embassy in Belgrade, as an explanation for his future policy: "The small frog does not jump into the pond, but engages in dialogue with the bigger frogs, in order to get the best of both worlds."[18]

The first step was in July 1953: a private visit of the Indian vice-president and famous philosopher and religious scholar, Sir Sarvepalli Radhakrishnan, crowned an intense flow of Indian political and cultural personalities to Yugoslavia in the previous months. The official press communiqué of his talks with Tito stressed the excellent relationship between the two countries, declaring that "in sincere pursuit of world peace, India and Yugoslavia represent today an example and encouragement for the realization of friendly relations among all countries in the world, and a significant factor for overcoming the perils of war."[19]

In August 1954, a delegation of the UN General Assembly led by Vijaya Lakshmi Pandit, Nehru's sister, came to Yugoslavia, where they visited various republics and held talks with eminent politicians, including Tito. At the end of the journey, she unexpectedly handed the marshal a formal invitation to visit India.[20] Tito lost no time, and on 30 November set out at the head of numerous dignitaries, including Foreign Secretary Koča Popović, Interior Secretary Aleksandar Ranković, his chief of personal security, General Milan Žeželj, and the former ambassador to New Delhi, Joža Vilfan, now chief of his secretariat. Many in government circles were opposed to this journey, maintaining that the cost would not justify the expected results. Tito, however, was of the opinion that it was not possible to achieve great things without running the risk: "I thought of it like this: by God, what are we to do? We are living together. A good, peaceful coexistence. But this is a passive attitude. In order to survive, an active coexistence is needed. Therefore, in order to improve world relations, it is necessary for countries that are not linked to blocs to struggle together. And this is a revolutionary action."[21]

Tito was the first European head of state to visit India after its independence, and he was treated like royalty. Like Nehru, he stressed in his public speeches the importance of coexistence as an antidote to nuclear war. In his words, coexistence should be based on a rejection of the bloc policy, which did not mean a retreat into passive neutrality. On the contrary, India and Yugoslavia wanted to actively participate in the building of peace in a divided world.[22]

On 21 December 1954, Tito gave an important speech to the Indian parliament in which he developed his thoughts about a non-aligned policy. He started by listing the four main dangers of the contemporary world: inequality between nations and states, interference of great powers in the internal affairs of third-world countries, division of the world into spheres of influence, and colonialism. He confirmed his belief that non-aligned states should close ranks on a global level, and admonished those who had liberated themselves from colonialism not to be bewitched by Muscovite sirens. If they wanted economic emancipation from their former masters, they had to strengthen their mutual collaboration. He finished by hailing the "active coexistence" that would be able to create a new equilibrium in the world.[23]

Tito was aware of just how audacious his policy was, as shown by an informal conversation he had with his comrades and journalists on a train after his visit to Calcutta: "What could small Yugoslavia do alone, without being backed up by a great country? So we try to find allies. This is the aim of our trip. Otherwise, why go so far? Certainly not to go hunting tigers." This was his reply to the insinuation made by a newspaper that he had only come to India to hunt tigers—which he had, but armed only with a camera.[24]

Tito returned from India and Burma conscious that Yugoslavia had new political possibilities far beyond mere European dimensions. After his return, he spoke his mind in a speech at the Zagreb railway station, where he was welcomed by a large crowd. Feeling a favorable wind in his sails, he proclaimed: "We know that today we have numerous friends in Asia, that our country enjoys enormous prestige there. Our people have earned this respect with their fight, with their work."[25] This kind of boasting declaration, which further exalted the right of colonial countries to be independent, was not accepted with enthusiasm in the West. The more so since it was accompanied by Tito's pledge in Rangoon to supply the Burmese army with weapons. The president of the Commission for International Affairs in the US Senate, Walter George, warned Tito that he risked losing Washington's aid if he insisted on this path.[26] These more or less veiled threats did not deter the marshal, all the more so since Nehru was ready to collaborate with him, especially when he realized how respectfully the Yugoslav president was treated by the Soviets. During a visit to New Delhi, Anastas Mikoyan, a member of the Politburo, spoke in flattering terms about Tito, stressing that he had helped the Soviets to understand India. This impressed Nehru very much: the following day, he informed the Yugoslav ambassador that he would accept Tito's invitation and visit Brioni.[27]

On 18 and 19 July 1956, the leader of the world's biggest democracy took part in a meeting with Tito and Egyptian president Gamal Abdel Nasser that ended with a declaration that was destined to become the cornerstone of what would become known as the non-aligned policy. This policy effectively challenged the reigning division of the world into two opposite blocs, which had long been a source of fear and international tension. As the Ministry of Foreign Affairs in Bonn observed, with this move Tito left the European and communist spheres, where he had been active, in order to assume a political role of global dimensions.[28]

Moscow Declaration

Khrushchev's journey to Belgrade in May 1955 was of great importance to subsequent events in the Soviet Union. As the Soviet leader recognized in his memoirs, it was only after his conversations with Tito in Yugoslavia that he fully understood how wrong Stalin's policy had been.[29] In the Presidium of the Supreme Soviet of the Soviet Union, to which he submitted a report, a discussion developed that proved decisive to the destruction of Stalin's myth. It was Mikoyan who expressed the essential idea about this, noting that if Beria was not culpable for the split with the Yugoslavs, then it was necessary to target "others."[30] This was the start of the demolition of the "cult of personality," which peaked the night of 24–25 February of the following year at the Twentieth Congress of the CPSU, which had been convened in Moscow with the telling slogan: "Back to Lenin." In harmony with this program, Khrushchev denounced Stalin in his "secret speech," affirming, among other things, that the conflict between the Soviet Union and Yugoslavia was not Yugoslavia's fault. The real culprit was Stalin, who had completely lost any contact with reality. "It will be enough that I move my little finger and Tito will not exist anymore," Stalin had allegedly said before excluding the CPY from Cominform. "But this did not happen," said Khrushchev. "Although Stalin moved not only his little finger, but everything he was able to move, Tito did not fall. Why? Because . . . he had his country and his people behind him, formed in the arduous school of freedom and struggle for independence, people who supported their leaders."[31] This bold affirmation opened new possibilities for cooperation between Moscow and Belgrade. The LCY did not send a delegation to the congress, but Tito wrote a letter of greeting to his "Soviet comrades," in which he barely hid his contentment.[32] Slobodan Stanković, a collaborator on Radio Free Europe, the American propaganda radio station, affirmed that reading the newspapers and magazines of this period it was clear that the Yugoslav leaders were in seventh heaven: "In their eyes, Marshal Tito was a genius since, as the leader of a small country, he had been brave enough to successfully confront a giant. The Biblical story about David and Goliath was often quoted."[33]

Tito's letter to the Twentieth Congress was the first public answer from the Yugoslav side to Khrushchev's proposal to resume party and state relations. This seemed logical, since Nikita Sergeevich Khrushchev had meanwhile accepted the idea that communism could be attained not only through revolutionary but also parliamentary means, and that war was not the only way to solve the problems of the contemporary world.[34] The conditions ripened for Tito's visit to the Soviet Union, for which the two parties were preparing with a series of telling moves. In the summer of 1954, a Yugoslav parliamentary delegation of ten members from the CC and a member of the Executive Committee of the LCY came to Moscow. A commercial agreement followed, signed on 1 September and aimed at doubling trade between the two countries. At the same time, there was also an increase in Yugoslav trade with the Soviet satellite countries.[35] In February 1956, the Twentieth Congress CPSU approved a motion that recommended improving "friendship and collaboration with the fraternal peoples of the Yugoslav people's federation," and shortly afterward the Kremlin granted Yugoslavia fairly favorable financial loans.[36] It was rumored that Dobrije Vidic, Tito's ambassador in Moscow, had contacts with his American colleague that were too close, so at the beginning of March 1956 Tito recalled him, replacing him with Montenegrin Veljko Mićunović, at that time deputy secretary of foreign affairs and the "number two man in the Yugoslav secret services."[37] At the valedictory lunch organized for Vidic, Khrushchev took a booklet from his breast pocket and handed it to the ambassador: "Give this to Comrade Tito, he will read it with interest. To my mind, you Yugoslavs could not write better." It was the speech in which he had denounced Stalin. Tito was much impressed by this gesture, which strengthened his conviction that the administrative structure of the Soviet Union would be healed once and for all.[38] On 17 April, the Soviets decided to disband the Cominform, tacitly accepting the Yugoslav assertion that the organization had become anachronistic. In May, the two countries signed a treaty of collaboration and at the end of the month Tito recognized, in his own way, that the cult of personality in Yugoslavia was also outdated: he proposed that his birthday should no longer be celebrated on 25 May, but replaced instead by "Youth Day." Increasingly, he also spoke of the need to better relations not just between states but also between parties, in spite of the promises he had given to some leading comrades during Khrushchev's trip to Belgrade that this would not happen. On 2 June, after a triumphal journey through Romania and Moldavia, he finally arrived in the Soviet capital with a large entourage and his wife, Jovanka, who was abroad as first lady for the first time. At the railway station, where he was greeted by all the Soviet leaders, led by Khrushchev, he was welcomed with a large sign that read: LONG LIVE COMRADE TITO AND HIS CLIQUE.[39] (This pejorative term was used so often by the Soviet propaganda that it had lost its original meaning.)

The same day, Molotov, who had opposed the rehabilitation of the Yugoslav heretics, had to step down as minister of foreign affairs, an eloquent sign that Khrushchev wanted to receive Tito as a prodigal son. In fact, he was greeted with a solemnity not seen since the October Revolution. In Stalingrad and Kiev, he was hailed by several hundred thousand people, in Leningrad more than a million. The sincere enthusiasm of the masses, attracted by Tito's informal but gentlemanly behavior and by Jovanka's Paris-style elegance, created an excited atmosphere that involved even the seasoned and cynical Soviet leaders.[40] As Ambassador Veljko Mićunović wrote, Kliment Voroshilov, Nikolai Bulganin, Anastas Mikoyan, Lazar Kaganovich, and even Viacheslav Molotov competed, under Khrushchev's direction, to condemn Stalin's policy toward Yugoslavia as firmly as possible. However, although Khrushchev, trying to please his guests, stated publicly that "the Republic of Yugoslavia, too, builds socialism with success," this did not mean that he was ready to go along with their wishes. On the contrary, during a mass meeting at the Dinamo football stadium, where he and Tito spoke on 19 June, he endeavored to create the impression that Yugoslavia had returned to the "socialist camp" and its "monolithic unity." Tito hurried to correct him, stressing that he had no intention of relinquishing his autonomy and reaffirming that "our way is different from yours."[41]

Tito's intention was to top off his visit with the "Declaration," which would recognize not just the equality of the CPSU and CPY but of all other communist parties.[42] The Soviets, who had already refused these proposals in Belgrade, did not agree. They wanted to persuade the Yugoslavs that "ideological unity" among the parties was needed, which meant, in other words, that the LCY should join the fold. Khrushchev and his comrades were convinced that Yugoslavia's adherence would improve relations between other socialist countries and strengthen their own position in the Kremlin. As much as Tito desired to support Comrade Nikita against the Stalinist forces that were still active in the Soviet Union and in the popular democracies, he could not accept such proposals, nor the concept of a "camp," as it recalled Stalin's dictatorship and was "an obsolete form of organization."[43] An excited and sometimes sour discussion was sparked between the Soviet and Yugoslav delegations, which ended just an hour before the final ceremony. It was clear that the failure of the talks would reveal Khrushchev's frailty in a moment when the political situation in Poland and Hungary was menacing.[44] In the end, the Moscow Declaration, signed on 20 June 1956 in Saint George's Hall in the Kremlin, appeared to be a compromise, recognizing the equality of socialist states and mutual non-interference in internal affairs, and accepting "the variety of socialist development in the spirit of the internationalist principles of Marxism-Leninism." However, it did not explicitly state the equality of *all* parties, which is what Tito and his comrades had had in mind. Nevertheless, it was an extraordinary concession, and potentially dangerous for the Soviets. As Khrushchev said: "It would not be possible to grant to others what has been granted to the Yugoslavs."[45]

Uprisings in Poland and Hungary

When the Yugoslav delegation left Moscow, the Soviets immediately let it be known that they were not ready to abdicate their guiding role in the socialist camp. Even before Tito returned to Belgrade, on 22 and 23 June 1956, Khrushchev had gathered the top satellite leaders, totally ignoring the Moscow Declaration that had been so recently signed. "And nobody," wrote an indignant Veljko Mićunović in his diary, "had any objection or question."[46] If this way of working did not displease the Soviet vassals, since it confirmed the status quo and, with this, their power, it was not so with the Eastern European peoples, who had understood Tito's visit as a "third Russian revolution" bound to improve their living conditions. Tito had not yet left the Soviet Union when clashes occurred between workers and police in Poznań, Poland, on 28 and 29 June, which took on the characteristics of an uprising. This dramatic event weakened Khrushchev's position at home, encouraging those who disagreed with his policy. Proclamations about "international proletarian solidarity" and about the need to close ranks against "capitalist machinations" appeared in the press.[47]

Westerners were not able to see the link between the rehabilitation of Yugoslavia and Polish events. The fact that the Yugoslavs endorsed the Soviet interpretation of Poznań as the result of foreign reactionary meddling strengthened their conviction that there was a fundamental understanding between Tito and Khrushchev against the West.[48] In Washington, London, and other capitals of the "free world," Tito's entente cordiale with the Soviets caused worried disputes and debates. An amendment to a law about foreign aid from which Yugoslavia was excluded, discussed in the Senate on 29 June, indicated the hostile climate developing against him in the United States. The law was rejected, but the amount of aid to Yugoslavia was halved, and President Eisenhower was charged to bestow this aid only if he was certain that this was in the interest of the United States. Tito was alarmed by this news because if this attitude prevailed, he risked losing other kinds of American support too, such as the grain supplies that were essential for his regime. He sent Eisenhower a secret letter, in which he assured him that he considered the president's friendship more important than American aid. During a meeting with Ambassador Riddleberger, he pointed out that his policy of good relations with the socialist countries would help to free them from Stalinism by showing them that it was possible to have a different stance than that dictated by Moscow.[49] Those sweet words had some effect on the short-term decisions of the president, but did not eliminate further moments of tension between the two countries, tensions that were constant in their complex relationship. The fact that Yugoslavia received arms worth $717 million during the period of 1951–56, and worth only $16 million during the period of 1956–63, is telling.[50]

As much as he tried to calm Western apprehensions, Tito continued to reproach them for not understanding the new situation created in the Soviet Union was due to his influence. "The devil is sometimes not as black as painted," he told the American ambassador.[51] The drive to be a bearer of new values in international relations pushed him to intensify his contacts with African and Asian countries, but also to act against Stalinist remnants in the satellite states. In Poland, he supported Gomułka in his endeavors to bring about reform. In Albania, he conspired against Enver Hoxha, in Bulgaria he tried to overthrow Valko Velev Červenko, in Romania he aided the adversaries of Gheorghiu-Dej. His hostility was directed mostly toward the political leadership in Hungary, where he tried to undermine the dictatorship of Mátyás Rákosi, his old enemy, and replace him with Imre Nagy, who had served a long prison sentence for "Titoism."[52] His efforts to free Hungarians from the "Stalinist nightmare" were only partially successful, since the Soviets decided in mid-July to remove Rákosi from power and replace him with Ernő Gerő, a Stalinist of the first rank. However, they did accept Tito's request to posthumously rehabilitate László Rajk, the former foreign minister who had been condemned to death in 1948, and in whose honor a solemn funeral was organized in Budapest. This was greeted in Belgrade as an important sign of de-Stalinization.[53]

On 3 September the Soviet leaders reacted to the impetuous ferment in Poland and Hungary with a confidential letter to members of the CPSU and to satellite parties, distancing themselves from "national communism" and from the two documents solemnly signed in 1955 and 1956 with the Yugoslavs, who were criticized as opportunists because of their "pro-Western" policy. Further, they stressed that the title "communist-Leninist," given to Tito by Bulganin that past June during a toast, was at least premature (Khrushchev even requested a disciplinary admonition against Bulganin for honoring Tito in such a way).[54] The Yugoslavs were soon informed about the letter and acquired a secret bulletin containing Khrushchev's conversation with Bulgarian top leaders via their intelligence service. On that occasion, the secretary general of the CPSU affirmed the need to lure Tito into the socialist camp by all possible means, after which "we will throttle him."[55] The Soviet and satellite press began blowing anti-Yugoslav trumpets again, while in Belgrade the authorities began to prosecute some of the Cominformists who had recently returned home from the "camp." All this failed to thwart the impetuous Khrushchev from making an unexpected decision: although in the grip of domestic opposition, he announced his plan for an "informal visit" to Yugoslavia, obviously in order to get Tito's support. He still hoped for his return to the fold.[56]

The conversations between the two started on 19 September at Brioni and on the Belje estate, and after eight days continued at Yalta where, in spite of Kardelj's objections, Tito went "hunting." They stayed there until 5 October, meeting Gerő, the freshly installed Hungarian party leader, who was also vacationing in Crimea "by chance." Their long, and at times heated, discussions did not solve the open questions but brought them closer on a personal level, and so were not completely fruitless. Tito did not allow himself to be dragged into the "camp," but promised to normalize relations with the satellites and to support the man whom the Soviets wanted in power in Budapest.[57] Consequently, Ernő Gerő received an official invitation to visit Belgrade in the hope that this would strengthen his position in Hungary. In mid-October he came to the Yugoslav capital at a head of a delegation that included János Kádár. Unlike Gerő who, according to Tito, was unaware of the dramatic situation he was in, Kádár made a good impression: after the Hungarians left, the marshal told his colleagues that he appreciated Kádár's realism and calm.[58]

The pilgrimage to visit his former enemy did not help Gerő: on 23 October 1956, a demonstration took place in Budapest, brought about by the events in Poland, where two days earlier the "Titoist" Gomułka had come to power.[59] At first it seemed that the situation could be kept under control, so on 30 October the Soviet government published a declaration in which it proclaimed that from that point onward relations with the satellite countries would be constructed according to new theoretical and practical principles. It recognized perfect equality with them, stressed the inviolability of their borders, national independence, sovereignty, and non-interference in their internal affairs, and even hinted at a withdrawal of troops from Poland, Hungary, and Romania.[60] This move came too late: the Hungarian demonstrations developed into an uprising that the police and the Red Army, summoned by Gerő, could not control. The Soviets decided at that point to abandon that apparatchik, so hated by the people, replacing him with Imre Nagy as president of the government and with János Kádár at the head of the party.[61] Furthermore, Anastas Mikoyan, who hurried from Moscow to Budapest, promised a quick withdrawal of Soviet troops from Hungary in order to calm enflamed spirits. Tito, very much preoccupied by the turn of events, sent a letter to the Hungarian Worker's Party on 29 October endorsing the new leadership and inviting the "working people" not to lose faith in socialism, and not to be swayed by "reactionary" elements.[62]

The Hungarian Revolution

Events took another turn. In Hungary, upset by the popular uprising, bourgeois and even right-wing parties reappeared, and the newspapers were full of anti-communist slogans. In Budapest, a statue of Stalin was destroyed for the first time in Eastern Europe and there was an open hunt for communists, with policemen as the primary target—in some cases they were lynched.[63] From the West, Radio Free Europe stirred up the rebels, whereas in Moscow, where what was going on was interpreted as a manifest intention to upset the international equilibrium created in Europe after the Second World War, the press began speaking about "counterrevolution."

On 31 October 1956, Imre Nagy decided to restore democracy, declared the withdrawal of his country from the Warsaw Pact, and proclaimed its neutrality in the naïve hope that it might convince Moscow to grant it a status similar to that enjoyed by Austria. The Soviet leaders, who knew that yielding would mean the end of their hegemony in Eastern Europe (and their own power), decided that same day to intervene with force. This proposal was favored because a French-British-Israeli attack against Egypt, where Nasser had nationalized the Suez channel, prevented the West from intervening effectively in the Hungarian tragedy. Before taking such a risky step, Khrushchev wanted to be sure about the agreement of all the "brotherly" parties, including the Yugoslavs. Since Tito declined to come to Moscow, Khrushchev went incognito to Brioni on 2 November, escorted by Molotov.[64] In spite of a turbulent journey due to bad weather, he conferred the following night for ten hours with Tito and other Yugoslav leaders, who were seriously alarmed by the events in Hungary, and were even ready to intervene with their own troops to prevent the collapse of socialism there, which could negatively affect the entire Danube-Balkan area. As early as 30 October, Tito had admonished Nagy not to allow the international reactionary forces to foment turmoil in Hungary, but he was not ready to listen.[65] Unlike the Poles, who dared to disagree with Khrushchev's bellicose intentions, the Yugoslav marshal approved the deployment of the Red Army in a neighboring country without hesitation. He asked, however, that the new government be led by Kádár who, in his opinion, was more apt to realize the necessary reforms than Ferenc Münnich, the Soviet candidate. In order to get Khrushchev's approval, he offered his help him get rid of Nagy and his collaborators, proposing political asylum for them in the Yugoslav Embassy.[66]

Subsequent events developed according to the scenario established in Moscow: on 3 November 1956, Kádár (who two days before had fled Budapest to the Soviet zone with the purpose of creating a new government) invited the

Russians to smother the "counterrevolution." That same night, the Red Army moved into action. The rebels tried desperately to resist, but the following morning Khrushchev was able to send Tito an exultant dispatch: "Hurry, hurry, hurry, our troops are in Budapest!"[67] On 5 November, Tanjug (Telegrafska Agencija Nove Jugoslavije), the Yugoslav press agency, supported the bloody Soviet intervention, since it had been dictated by the need to "save socialism."[68]

At dawn on 4 November, Nagy asked for political asylum at the Yugoslav Embassy, in the company of numerous collaborators and their families, fifty-two people in all. However, in the following days he resolutely refused the Soviet diktat, conveyed to him by his hosts, to renounce his premiership. At this point, an unforeseen quarrel erupted between Tito and Khrushchev: Tito asked the Kremlin to allow Nagy to live freely in Budapest or to give him safe-conduct to travel to Yugoslavia. Khrushchev, considering Nagy a traitor who should be punished, gave the marshal an unpleasant choice: if he consigned the rebel and his followers to Kádár, the collaboration agreement reached between them in September would be valid; however, if he insisted on saving the reprobates, he would be denounced as a supporter of this Hungarian "counterrevolution."[69] In order to give more weight to his words, he moved Soviet tanks to the Slovenian-Hungarian border, in the Mura region, and surrounded the Yugoslav Embassy in Budapest with troops. A Soviet soldier even opened fire, shooting a Yugoslav diplomat who was seated at his desk.[70] Tito's indignation at these provocations was further strengthened by Enver Hoxha's article, published by the official Tirana newspaper, *Zeri i Popullit* (People's voice), in which the Albanian leader attacked fiercely "the new forms of socialism" that should be put on the "scrap heap of international opportunism." Obviously he had Yugoslavia in mind. The article was republished by *Pravda* and in this way achieved particular resonance.[71]

The reply soon followed. On 11 November, in the Istrian town of Pula, Tito gave a speech for LCY activists in which he condemned the first Soviet intervention, the one that took place following Gerő's invitation, as a "catastrophe," since in that moment popular fury could still have been channeled in the right direction. The second intervention, although bad, was to be considered a lesser evil, since it aimed to prevent the chaos of civil war and counterrevolution in Hungary, thus saving the world from a possible major conflict between the blocs. In part contradicting this assertion, he reconfirmed his firm opposition to every foreign intervention in the internal affairs of other states, stressing that the Hungarian tragedy had been caused by Stalinist practices still alive in the Soviet Union and in the majority of the satellite countries, saying: "They understood where the main cause of all these difficulties lay and at the Twentieth Congress they condemned Stalin's acts and his policy up to then, but they mistakenly made the whole matter a question of the personality cult and not a question of the system. . . . What they have sown since 1948, now is reaped: they have sown wind and are reaping a tempest."[72]

Although at Pula Tito had mentioned "certain Stalinist elements" in the Soviet Union opposed to Khrushchev's policy, and expressed the hope that these elements would not prevail, his speech, more disapproval than absolution, sent Nikita on a rampage. Khrushchev was well aware that in suffocating the Hungarian revolt he had also saved Tito's regime. During a reception in the Kremlin on 17 November 1956, he attacked Ambassador Mićunović, vehemently reproaching him with Tito's accusation of Stalinism, "as if here nothing had happened. Who does all this aid, if not our enemies?"[73] The "normalization" between the Yugoslavs and the Soviets seemed to have failed miserably. The press orchestrated violent anti-Yugoslav polemics, accompanied as a counterpoint by a heated correspondence between Moscow and Belgrade. "It is possible to trace in his speech," wrote the Soviet agency TASS, commenting on Tito's words, "declarations which contrast in form and content with the principles of proletarian internationalism and international worker solidarity."[74] The Soviet ambassador in Belgrade, Nikolai P. Firiubin, arrived at dinner with the marshal with a pile of anti-Soviet books that had been published in Yugoslavia in recent years. In a dispatch sent to Moscow on 21 November, he examined the principal lines of Tito's foreign policy, stressing that he and his comrades had started an open attack on the social and economic regime of the Soviet Union aimed at damaging its relations with the "people's democracies," in the hope that they would choose the "Yugoslav way."[75]

This quarrel decided Nagy's fate. On 22 November, he left the Yugoslav Embassy with his entourage, thanks to Kádár's promise of safe-conduct, which had been negotiated by Tito and Kardelj. Just as they were embarking on a military bus that was to bring them home, at about 6 p.m., they were arrested, since Khrushchev and his counselors thought that it would be too dangerous to leave them free. They decided therefore to grant them "asylum" in Romania.[76] The Yugoslavs reacted energetically to save face, insisting on radical changes to the political system not only in Hungary, but also in other socialist countries. An important speech given by Kardelj at the Federal Assembly on 7 December 1956 contained several echoes of Djilas's thought, even though he was on trial at that moment. In particular, it contained the assertion that a bureaucratic class had asserted itself in Soviet society at the cost of the working class. This caste, Kardelj said, called itself communist but governed in a despotic way, hindering progress and the affirmation of a new reality in social relations: "If a party does not understand this, it can well boast with communism and Marxism-Leninism, recalling its historic role as a guide. In reality, it will be an obstacle to the development of socialism. If it persists in this behavior, it can even become a reactionary force. To think that a party will guarantee the progressive and democratic role of its power only by declaring itself communist is a gross error of the anti-Marxist type."[77]

The Soviets did not overlook the affinity between Kardelj's and Djilas's ways of thinking, which is why, on 19 December, they wrote in *Pravda* that the latter's three-year prison sentence surely did not testify in favor of "mister" Kardelj, but rather showed how fragile the ground was on which his "revisionist" theories stood. They did not say, however, that the difference between Djilas and Kardelj was substantial: whereas in an article published in America the former had proclaimed the Hungarian revolt as the "beginning of the end of communism generally," the latter remained faithful to communism—albeit a Yugoslav style—as he was trying to implement it.[78] Khrushchev was particularly hurt by the speech of the Slovene "self-proclaimed ideologue of communist heresy," as *Pravda* labeled him, finding in it a scornful allusion to himself. When some days later he received Ambassador Veljko Mićunović, the latter observed a corncob on his desk, beside Kardelj's speech. "You think that I do not understand whom Kardelj had in mind, when he spoke about communist leaders capable of thinking only about corn," he cried, banging his fist on the table.[79]

The Hungarian events left the Yugoslavs totally isolated in the socialist camp, where Titoism, seen as the root of all evil, lost every attraction. Belgrade's relation with the West was likewise unfriendly. Tito's firm condemnation of the French and British adventure in Egypt—more critical than his attitude toward the Soviet intervention in Hungary—confirmed doubts in London, Paris, and Washington about his equidistance between the two blocs. On their end, the Yugoslavs tried to keep the polemics with Moscow on an ideological level, in harmony with the New Year's interview that Tito gave to *Borba* stating the need to distinguish relations between parties and states.[80] But they were not fortunate in this endeavor. Convinced that Yugoslav "national communism" undermined the unity of the Eastern bloc, in February 1957 the Soviets moved from words to deeds, freezing a loan of nearly $100 million that they, together with the German Democratic Republic (GDR; East Germany), had promised to Belgrade. In April, with the assistance of Budapest, Tirana, and Sofia, they reopened the delicate question of national minorities in Yugoslavia, which increased the threat of new border tensions with the neighboring states, whose minorities (and they were many) lived under Tito's rule. János Kádár even compared "national communism," meaning the Yugoslavs, of course, to Fascism, while the Albanians renewed their verbal offensive of the years 1949–52 by hinting at irredentist claims on Kosovo.[81] In Yugoslavia, the fear of a possible Soviet invasion flared again, activating the idea of popular defense. In addition to the military, the UDBA (Uprava državne bezbednosti; the State Security Administration) began gearing up for enemy occupation, organizing a web of agents who would stay behind and engage in subversive activity when needed.[82] This tense atmosphere was mitigated, however, by Tito himself, who on 10 April publicly asked the press to back off the attacks against the Soviets. This goodwill gesture provoked a new thaw between Moscow and Belgrade, although not without occasional polemical outbursts. In April, when Enver Hoxha, the marshal's main foe, visited Moscow, Khrushchev too declared that the polemics between the Soviet bloc and Yugoslavia must end. In May, *Pravda* dedicated a few paltry lines to the sudden death of Moša Pijade, but at the end of the month the Soviet leaders sent Tito their best wishes for his sixty-fifth birthday. Meanwhile, the news came that a circular letter had been transmitted to the satellite parties, inviting them to improve their relations with Yugoslavia despite their ideological differences. A trip to Moscow by the secretary for national defense, Ivan Gošnjak, followed, which seemed promising.[83] The thaw was consolidated in July 1957, when unexpected news came about the fall of Malenkov, Kaganovich, Molotov, and Dmitrii Shepilov, the "anti-party group" who had tried to overthrow Khrushchev. The fall from power of personalities who, in concert with Stalin, had managed anti-Yugoslav policy after 1948, was greeted in Belgrade with favor. It was clear that Khrushchev's victory strengthened the reformist forces and opened new space for dialogue.[84] This interpretation was proven correct as early as 16 July, when the Soviets—after a "private" journey to Crimea undertaken by Kardelj and Ranković—confirmed the promised loans for the construction of an aluminum plant in Montenegro, which was to be cofinanced by the GDR. This project had been discussed in 1947 by Kardelj and Stalin but was never realized because of the 1948 split. The Yugoslavs considered it very important, certain that it would improve their military industry and at the same time restore the economy of that underdeveloped republic.[85] Consequently, Tito proposed a secret meeting with Khrushchev on the Danube in order to resolve, in private, the questions that were still open. But at the last moment Tito changed his mind, opting instead for a public rendezvous in Bucharest. On 1 and 2 August the two statesmen, with their colleagues, met at Snagovo, not far from the Romanian capital, in the former royal castle where the infamous Cominform Resolution that had expelled Tito from the fold had been formulated in June 1948. During their exchange of views, the Yugoslavs claimed that socialism "should step out from the antechamber of Henry VIII, Ivan the Terrible and the papal Inquisition" stressing, however, their readiness to better mutual relations. The conversations finished with kisses and hugs.[86] The ambiguous press communiqué, published at the end of the meeting, was read with interest, especially in Western countries. The Central Intelligence

Agency and the intelligence organizations within the Department of State, the army, the navy, the air force, and the Joint Chiefs of Staff concurred that the Yugoslavs and the Soviets had reached an agreement whereby the first would support Moscow on an international level, and the second would recognize, in return, the Yugoslav path to socialism.[87]

The following autumn showed that these suppositions were not groundless. Tito himself, in an article published by the magazine *Foreign Affairs*, displayed his faith in the supposed pacifism of Soviet policy, making it clear that the major danger for world peace was represented by the West.[88] In consequence, in September 1957, a Polish delegation led by Władysław Gomułka visited Yugoslavia. On that occasion, Tito recognized the contested Oder-Neisse line as the final border between Poland and Germany and, in addition, made an important ideological concession, mentioning "proletarian internationalism" as a basis for relations between socialist states and parties. With this he renounced the belief that he had professed until then, that this concept was just a smoke screen that hid Soviet hegemonic tendencies. He even went so far as to recognize the "guiding role" of the Soviet Union at a gala dinner in honor of his guests.[89]

Meanwhile, a rumor started to circulate in the embassies of Belgrade that during the Bucharest meeting Tito had promised Khrushchev that he would establish diplomatic relations with East Germany, although he was aware of just how risky a move that was.[90] In order to prevent the international recognition of this Soviet satellite, Walter Hallstein, secretary of state at the Ministry of Foreign Affairs of the Federal Republic of Germany (West Germany) formulated a "doctrine" stating that the government in Bonn would not maintain diplomatic relations with states that recognized the GDR. This was meant to stress that West Germany did not recognize East Germany as a sovereign state based on the people's free will, but saw it as a mere Soviet puppet. Yugoslavia had been collaborating with the GDR on political and economic levels since 1954, but not as closely as with West Germany.[91] Tito had concerned himself for quite some time with the question of German reunification, one of the burning issues of the Cold War era, proposing to achieve it through a confederation that would respect the "administrative autonomy" of the two states created by the victors after the war. As it became obvious that this was just wishful thinking, on 15 October 1957 he decided to recognize the GDR in spite of objections by his closest advisers, starting with Foreign Secretary Koča Popović, who worried about the reaction of "our Western friends."[92] In order not to lose face, West Germany reacted immediately by severing diplomatic relations with Belgrade on 19 October, considering this a "hard lesson." Indeed it was, as the Yugoslavs, in spite of the warnings, did not expect such a reaction. If the Federal Republic had been put in a similar position by other states, the East Germans would gain and Bonn would exclude itself from countries that were of great interest.[93] Of course, it was widely reported internationally and was not without consequences. Tito hoped that his example would be followed by Third World countries, India above all. Nehru, however, was angry because Tito had misinformed him as to the true nature of the Hungarian revolt by denying its popular character, and because he had not been consulted in advance about his intention to recognize East Germany. Nehru refused to follow Tito's example and recognize East Germany, thus initiating a period of cool relations between the two countries.[94] The United States, for its part, further limited military aid to Belgrade, openly expressing their disappointment at the marshal's foreign policy, and cancelling his official visit to Washington, which had already been planned. To highlight his independence, Tito decided in December 1957 that from that moment on he would not accept "gratis" American arms. The following year, at his request, Washington ceased military although not economic aid, recalling its military assistance staff—about sixty members—who in recent years had collaborated with the People's Army, in spite of occasional disagreements, to prepare an effective defense against a possible Soviet attack.[95] On the occasion of his farewell visit to the foreign secretary, Ambassador Riddleberger correctly noted that "an epoch in Yugoslav-American relations was ending, and a new one was opening up."[96]

The Moscow Conference

Despite Tito's recognition of the GDR, the Soviets did not hold him in much regard at the time. Only two weeks after the marshal's decision to ignore the "Hallstein doctrine," Khrushchev suddenly rid himself of the legendary Marshal Georgii Zhukov, the conqueror of Berlin and the Soviet defense minister after Stalin's death. He was among Nikita's main supporters in the struggle for power, having had a key role in the overthrow of Beria and in the recent demolition of the "anti-party group." There was even talk of a "Khrushchev-Zhukov team" that would dominate the Moscow political scene. This was an eventuality that the Yugoslavs favored, as they were convinced that Zhukov could control the unpredictable and wanton Khrushchev who, even at the Bucharest meeting, affirmed that it would have been a "different tune" if Zhukov had sided with Molotov and Malenkov.[97] Two months later Khrushchev sacked Zhukov with the accusation of "Bonapartism" even before his return from an official visit to Yugoslavia and Albania. Tito was offended that Khrushchev had sent him to the Balkans to prepare favorable ground for Zhukov's dismissal from the party and the army. It was evident that Khrushchev had tried to strengthen his power by making a fool of him, whereas he, in discussions with his Soviet colleague, had declared his readiness to share some American military secrets of which he was aware.[98] Just as this affront was taking place, one hundred thousand copies of a booklet were published by Enver Hoxha in Moscow, attacking the "treacherous role" of Yugoslav revisionism. These unforeseen low blows forced the Yugoslavs to reexamine their foreign policy. Edvard Kardelj, vice-president of the federal government, was sent to Greece to restore links with Athens in case of the need to reanimate the Balkan Pact, which had never been implemented after being signed because of Yugoslavia's new international interests, and because of the conflict between Greece and Turkey over Cyprus.[99]

Three days after the publication of Hoxha's libelous booklet, on 29 October 1957, Tito suffered a sudden "attack of lumbago" so as to avoid taking part in the Moscow Conference, which had been organized for the fortieth anniversary of the "Great October Revolution," and to which all the communist parties in the world had been invited.[100] This included the LCY, whose leaders prudently asked in advance how the conference would unfold. "They answered us," Kardelj said, "that it would just be a consultation about experiences and forms of action, and that the eventual final document would stress the need for peace and coexistence." But when the draft of this document emerged in October, it appeared clear that the Soviets wanted to confirm their dogmatic interpretation of socialist solidarity and of the "camp," headed by the USSR. This was unacceptable to the Yugoslavs.[101]

At the celebrations organized between 3 and 9 November 1957, the Yugoslav delegation was led not by Tito, but by Kardelj and Ranković, much to Khrushchev's dismay, as he had planned to appear in public with the Yugoslav marshal and Mao Zedong at his side.[102] He had intended to use the occasion to stage a "council of communist and workers' parties of the socialist countries," so that after the Hungarian catastrophe the guiding role of the CPSU would be confirmed by a common declaration that would support the fundamental principles of "socialist development" as dictated by the Soviet experience. To this effect, he tried to convince Kardelj to abandon his reservations about that document by inviting the Yugoslav delegation to dinner in a Moscow suburb. On this occasion, a lively discussion flared up, during which Khrushchev accused the Yugoslavs of being reluctant because of fear of the Americans. "You need America's aid, the grain, you have forgotten Marxism," he said. "You are drifting away from socialism, if you have not done so already. . . . We were certain we had reached an agreement on everything in Bucharest. But now I see I have blundered. I'm afraid to appear before the Soviet people and the party and openly confess that I have been hoodwinked by the Yugoslavs."[103]

According to the other twelve delegations who signed the declaration, the reason for the Yugoslav refusal must be found in their evaluation of forces in the world, which was foreign to Marxism-Leninism, and their underestimation of the imperialist threat, especially the American one. The Yugoslav position, according to which the existence of two military blocs was responsible for international tensions, was not acceptable, since the Warsaw Pact safeguarded the successes of socialism and should be seen as a fundamental factor in the maintenance of peace. By contrast, NATO was a tool for stirring up imperialist conflicts. It was clear, they affirmed, that the Yugoslav "comrades," in evaluating the global situation, did not start from class positions. Their view of peaceful coexistence was far from a Leninist conception, since they did not take into account the need for ideological engagement. The Yugoslavs believed that the socialist forces in the world were strong and, therefore, did not have to be organized in order to triumph. This meant that they focused on the spontaneous workers' movement, opposing the Marxist-Leninist doctrine of a coordinated struggle. In short, they wanted to sit on two chairs at the same time, renouncing in practice or, more accurately, harming the most powerful weapon the proletariat had at its disposal.[104]

The Yugoslavs, together with the delegates of the other sixty-three communist and worker's parties present in Moscow, signed a Peace Manifesto on 19 November, although this did not calm the Soviets. On that occasion, Kardelj gave a speech that was warmly accepted by all but which did not change Khrushchev's hostility toward him. This attitude provoked the Slovene so much that he collapsed on his way back, when he was near Bucharest.[105] He returned from Moscow utterly upset, but determined to elaborate his political thought further. The Ninth Plenum, convened on 7 December 1957 at Brioni, also supported him in this. The participants unanimously approved the behavior of their delegation to Moscow, though stressing that the difference of opinions should not hinder "fraternal collaboration" between communist parties and states. But this was easier said than done.[106]

The Trbovlje Strike

Meanwhile, other storm clouds appeared on the horizon. It was not possible to ignore the ethnic conflict beginning to reappear among Croats and Serbs. In Croatia, the term "Serbo-communism" circulated, which expressed the popular opinion that the Serbs had reaped the greatest advantages from the regime. At the same time, the Serbs, Montenegrins, Bosniaks, and Macedonians felt discriminated against, as their standard of living was lower than that of the Croats or Slovenes. Even in influential party and intellectual circles, there were complaints about the privileges enjoyed by Slovenia and Croatia because of their relative well-being.[107] Dobrica Ćosić, a member of the Serb League of Communists and Ranković's favorite, often wrote about this, stressing that the Croatian and Slovenian "comrades" were sabotaging the development of the Serb regions. In 1954, he noted in his diary: "Everything is very expensive. Life is increasingly difficult. Belgrade is nearly without electricity. The power breaks down too often. From ministers to the retired, all are complaining about the bad crops. Everyone is unsatisfied. Everyone hates the Slovenes."[108]

Slovenia was obliged to yield 10 percent of its GNP to the federal government and the growing dissatisfaction manifested itself on 13 January 1958 when the first big strike since the war broke out in the mining center of Trbovlje, which had traditionally been a "red" district. Like their fathers who had protested violently against Belgrade in 1924, four thousand miners "crossed arms," refusing to work and asking for better salaries. They took the authorities by surprise, compelling them to confront an unforeseen question: How was it possible to strike in a state where the proletariat was in power? Even more embarrassing was the observation that the communists were totally isolated among the workers, since no party member was elected to the Agitation Committee organized by the strikers. Miha Marinko, one of the most prominent men in the Slovenian League of Communists, born in Trbovlje, tried to calm the waters, but his arrival in a Mercedes irritated the miners so much that he barely saved his own skin. It seemed that the strike would also spread to other industrial centers of the republic, since couriers had been arrested with messages from the Agitation Committee that invited the worker collectives to join the protest.[109] The Slovenian leadership considered the situation very serious. Edvard Kardelj, who at first tried to hide what was going on from Tito, saw the strike as a personal defeat. At the Ljubljana plenum on 24 January 1958, he compared the events in Trbovlje with those in Hungary, stressing that "only by chance was it not necessary to intervene with arms." Unlike the Hungarians, the miners had not allowed themselves to be influenced by "openly counter-revolutionary slogans," although that might yet happen. If the strike did degenerate into a protest against the regime, the authorities should use force. "I have to say," Kardelj went on, "that we were ready to use it, and without hesitation, if somebody had dared to raise his hand against the achievements of our working people."[110] Matija Maček, chief of the Slovenian UDBA, was more drastic, brutally affirming that there was "no need to use the troops. Give them wine and then into the cave with them!" The writer Bojan Štih, outraged by these words, which were a reminder of the fate of postwar massacre victims, protested by buying a helmet and a pickaxe and parading around with them in the center of Ljubljana. He ended up in jail.[111]

However, good sense prevailed among the politicians. They sent their delegates to Trbovlje, headed by Ljubljana's vice-president of the Executive Council,

Stane Kavčič, who set up a dialogue with the strikers and yielded to their demands: the price of coal was increased and subsequently their pay was improved. Kavčič later wrote that the Slovenian ideologues received a lesson "that was not without positive influence, and the further development of policy."[112] Although Tito branded the strike as the fruit of "imperialist forces" and "hostile elements," it is telling that the CC LCY, in a secret session on 6 February 1958, got to the core of the problem, the relationship between the center and the periphery, asking how to regulate the connection between party and society. Whereas Tito required "administrative [i.e., punitive] measures," the Slovenians wanted liberal political tactics, as outlined by the Sixth Congress, that asked the LCY not to rule with an iron fist but to guide and to show the right direction by soft, democratic means. As Kardelj observed, after 1952 a "slowdown began, the bureaucratic tendencies were strengthened (again) on all levels, while the party lost its ideological function." Because of these conflicting opinions, a quarrel flared up within the Yugoslav leadership for the first time. It did not have immediate traumatic consequences, but foreshadowed further disagreements that were doomed to last until Tito's death and beyond, until the collapse of Yugoslavia.[113] Kardelj did not speak without reason, conscious that Djilas's defeat in 1954 had been his defeat as well and that after Djilas's disappearance, the LCY had undergone a moral and psychological regression, rediscovering the need for the "discipline" Tito held so dear. In that period, the following warning could be heard at a party session: "From now on, comrades, we have to be alert and keep our eyes open, even when we read the writings of Comrade Kardelj."[114] Like Djilas, for many he too stank of heresy.

On 17 February 1958, the CC LCY sent a letter to all party members that summarized its discussions and confronted the political crises of the system. With arguments not dissimilar to those made by Djilas, it condemned the corruption of the League's functionaries, embroiled as they were in bureaucracy and privileges, and recognized for the first time the presence of nationalist, even chauvinist tendencies in Yugoslavia. However, it hushed up the principal problem, that of the relations between the republics and the federal center.[115] The letter reverberated among the members. "It is the most revolutionary document of this type since the party came to power," commented Dobrica Ćosić, adding prudently that "the letter will stay an anemic bit of propaganda if it is not followed by laws, administrative measures, state control, but above all by a free and unreserved critique by the press and public opinion. The stick will again hit only the average man."[116]

The Seventh Congress of the CPY

Beginning in February 1957, the Yugoslav politicians began preparing a new party program, after the old one had been abolished at the Sixth Congress in

Zagreb. The new one would be ratified by the subsequent congress, which was to convene in Ljubljana in November 1957. However, at the last moment it was postponed to the following April because of concerns raised in Kardelj's circle about the close relationship that seemed to appear between Khrushchev and Tito. Only when Tito cancelled his trip to Moscow did the tensions settle, allowing Kardelj to go on with his work. After Stalin's death he was more than ever convinced that Yugoslavia could act in a creative way on an international level thanks to its prestige and influence. "The Soviet leaders have suffered a total defeat," he noted. "We showed not only that we are right, but that we are able to rebel, too."[117] Soon, however, as a result of the Djilas affair, but also because of the events in Poland and Hungary, things drew to a standstill. Aleksandar Ranković took advantage of these dramatic events to strengthen his influence, which was already strong thanks to the UDBA's successes in its fight against Cominformists. The consequence was a slowdown of the democratization process that had started in the early fifties and a return to centralism. After the recent quarrel with Khrushchev, Kardelj began once more to hope that the time for reforms was ripe and therefore poured himself into the preparatory work for the Sixth Congress.[118] In this, he was assisted by a large group of experts, intellectuals, and party functionaries. Although physically he was not in the best shape, he elaborated on his ideas for a year while listening to Beethoven, in the intoxicated conviction that he could create a utopia. "But," he confided to his collaborators, "the peculiarity of a utopia is that it sooner or later becomes reality."[119]

On Tito's initiative, the program draft was sent to all "fraternal" parties, with the invitation to comment upon and improve it. It was more a courtesy than a real willingness to enter into a dialogue, this being obvious in the fundamental disparity between the text and Soviet doctrine. When Veljko Mićunović showed it to the CPSU's ideologue, M. A. Suslov, guardian of orthodoxy and sworn enemy of Yugoslav revisionists, a lively dispute ignited.[120] Subsequently, the Moscow Politburo began to suspect that Tito nurtured the ambition to take on the leading role in international communism, and that he was throwing down the gauntlet to the CPSU. As a sign of protest, it canceled its delegation's participation in the congress while Khrushchev dispatched a personal letter to the marshal, trying to induce him to strike some of the program's most radical points. The Poles turned up, sending two of their representatives to Belgrade. "Do not create difficulties for us, because the Russians will protest," they admonished, proposing adjustments that would distort the "heart" of the text. Tito allowed some formal changes, but not decisive ones, and not designed to calm the Soviets.[121]

During this time Khrushchev strengthened his position, taking on the presidency of the government on 28 March 1958, in addition to the presidency of the party, and enjoyed enormous prestige at home and abroad thanks to the recent successes in space discovery. He was not ready to swallow "Titoism," as presented by Kardelj, nor to accept his criticism of "hegemonism" and "Stalinism," nor his belief that the main goal for a communist society should be to function without any state and party. There was nothing in the LCY's program that the Yugoslavs had not already said, but since it was proposed during a passionate anti-revisionist campaign in the Soviet Union and was proclaimed as the only path to socialism, Khrushchev felt it necessary to react. Some days before the Seventh Congress, in the April issue of the Moscow magazine *Kommunist*, a critical article appeared in which three important ideologues accused the LCY of having distanced itself too much from "the theory and practice of Marxism-Leninism," and of having tried to undermine the unity of the communist parties and socialist countries. "The heroic Yugoslav peoples," they wrote, "who have spilled so much blood for freedom and justice, in order to build their life on a socialist basis, deserve a better fate. Do not lead them along isolated and confused byways to the great goal—to communism and socialism—but only by one common and bright road."[122] According to CIA analysts, "not since Stalin expelled Tito from the Cominform in 1948 has Moscow so forcefully declared that Tito must change his basic dogma before he can again be considered acceptable in Moscow's eyes."[123]

In mid-March, the Yugoslavs presented the program to the public, as well as the objections to it, breaking from the Bucharest agreement, which bound them not to make known their mutual disputes with the Soviets. In a text published over the course of ten articles, Kardelj, in his own fussy and convoluted style, elaborated on his vision of socialism and international relations as it had evolved in the awareness of the Yugoslav leaders, above all his own, during the last decade. It emphasized equality between all states and parties, refused all "bureaucratic tendencies" in the frame of the social body, exalted self-managing socialism, predicted the withering away of the state, and affirmed that even the dictatorship of the proletariat was transient. The Moscow dogma that communist parties should head up all progressive movements, and that socialism could be achieved only by and through the Soviets, was branded by Kardelj as wrong from a theoretical point of view, as well as harmful. Influenced by his Scandinavian experience, he reached the conclusion that socialism was to be found not only in the Soviet bloc, nor only in Yugoslavia, but was widespread everywhere, even in capitalist countries. (In private he even confessed that in Sweden there was "more socialism" than in Yugoslavia).[124] In short, the program denied the communists their monopoly over socialist practice and action, opening the door to collaboration with all "progressive" forces. This principle introduced a new dynamic into their mutual relations in which there was no place for a supreme arbiter. At the congress, Kardelj declared: "In the fight for the unity and collaboration of the workers' movement, we cannot ignore the ideological fight against opportunism, reformism, dogmatism, revisionism. In harmony with this, we will firmly resist every attempt to meddle in our internal affairs, and the influence of foreign ideologies. Without such a fight, unity would signify the suppression of revolutionary and socialist perspectives, the imposition of disorientation, of passivity, of conservatism."[125]

In foreign policy, his program proclaimed that bloc logic was the greatest danger to peace, and equated the fight for the national freedom of subjected peoples to the class struggle of the proletariat against the bourgeoisie. It condemned the division of the world into spheres of influence, and rejected both Western imperialism and Eastern hegemonic tendencies, even stating that it was not possible to exclude the possibility of the exploitation of one socialist state by another and armed clashes between them.[126] It continued: "It obviously goes without saying that we are sympathetic to all communist parties in questions regarding the development of socialist progress, the strengthening of workers' movements. The LCY has always been faithful to great revolutionary ideas of proletarian internationalism. To the other Marxist parties, we are also bound by the idea of Marxism and Leninism. The LCY's program foresees, however, that such collaboration should be based on absolute free will and equality, recognizing that every party has the exclusive right to judge the ideological and tactical utility of this or that decision."[127]

Kardelj went even further, stressing not just the party's autonomy, but also the fundamental autonomy of every human being. If fact, he reached the conclusion that "socialism could not subject anyone's personal happiness to 'superior aims,' since this was in itself the greater good." This affirmation seemed so radical that it was struck twice from the program's draft. In the end, Kardelj kept it in but was compelled to balance it with the phrase: "However, no one has the right to affirm his personal interest to the detriment of the common interest."[128] In spite of Tito's opposition, he was able to crown the LCY's program with an even more daring assertion, a paraphrase of Marx and Lenin, according to whom everything in existence could be criticized: "Nothing that has been created is so sacred that it could not be overthrown."[129]

Khrushchev was not furious just because of such thoughts, but also because of Tito's inaugural address, in which he warmly thanked the United States for its aid, above all grain, barely mentioning the loans promised by the Soviet Union, which at about $285 million were far from modest.[130] Moreover, the fact that the Yugoslav leaders reproached the Soviets for their past errors, even mentioning the prewar pact with Hitler, was so outrageous that the "camp's" ambassadors, present as observers at the congress, left the hall in protest (apart from the Polish ambassador, who claimed to have fallen asleep). Two days after the conclusion of the congress, on 28 April 1958, *Pravda* published a stinging editorial that did not mention Yugoslavia, only "revisionism" as a trend that should be fought against. On 4 May an even bolder attack against "Yugoslav anti-Marxists" came from Beijing, an article published by the ideological organ of the Chinese CC, *Hongqi* (Red banner), and reprinted in *Pravda*. In the following months, the Soviets and their satellites fueled poisonous polemics against revisionist Yugoslavia, which they accused of selling out Marx's ideology for money. They asserted that the Yugoslavs' program proposed an alternative to the Moscow Declaration, signed in November 1957 by twelve communist parties. Renouncing the doctrine of "two camps"—socialist and capitalist—and replacing it with the thesis of two equally dangerous blocs—Eastern and Western—they were accused of having lowered the socialist countries to the level of capitalist and imperialist ones. On 5 June 1958 in Sofia, at the Bulgarian CP Congress, Khrushchev aggressively condemned the LCY's program, reproaching Tito and his comrades for having been corrupted by "Western imperialists." He also mentioned that they had supported the "Hungarian counterrevolution," and stressed that the exclusion of the CPY from the Cominform was entirely deserved, saying: "We will declare war against all those who, by their deeds, weaken the unity of the communist and workers' parties, who weaken the camp of socialist countries, which is growing greater and greater."[131]

Tito did not keep silent, but on 15 June proclaimed from Labin in Istria: "Comrade Khrushchev often repeats that socialism cannot be built with American wheat. I think it can be done by anyone who knows how to do it, while a person who doesn't know how to do it cannot build socialism, even with his own wheat. Khrushchev says we live on charity received from the imperialist countries. . . . What moral right have those who attack us to rebuke us about American aid and loans when Khrushchev himself has just tried to conclude an economic agreement with America?"[132]

Only two days later, on 17 June 1958, another hit below the belt came from the Soviet side with news that Imre Nagy and three other comrades had been condemned to death and shot. The Hungarian government's press release stated that the executed leader had, in the past, asked for and been granted political asylum in the Yugoslav embassy, from which he instructed his followers to foment armed uprisings, strikes, and clandestine subversive activity. The Yugoslavs, accused between the lines of having tolerated such "counterrevolutionary" intrigues, reacted with a strongly worded diplomatic note, reminding the Hungarians of the agreement between the two governments in 1956, which should have guaranteed immunity to Nagy and his entourage. In protest, Tito sent Khrushchev a private letter, which was also issued to all LCY organizations. Further, at the beginning of 1959, a white paper was published in which the Belgrade government publicly revealed the copious documentation on the case.[133] Nagy's ghost, said Khrushchev's son Sergei, was forever present between Tito and his father.[134]

A month later, on 12 July, Khrushchev described Yugoslav communists as "parasites," accusing them of getting American aid as a prize for their attempt to destroy the socialist bloc.[135] Although in Sofia he stressed that the relations between Yugoslavia and the Soviet bloc countries at the state level should not be hindered, he soon decided to cancel the promised loans. This sealed the fate of the aluminum plant in Montenegro that would have improved the industrialization of the republic. The GDR also joined the boycott, which the Yugoslavs considered a rotten thing to do, given the price they had paid for their diplomatic recognition.[136]

At the time, the Yugoslav press unanimously celebrated the results of the Seventh Congress, stressing the importance of self-managed socialism and their non-aligned policy. It hailed beyond measure the achievements of the country, affirming that it was the victim of malevolent slander and exalting Tito.[137] Some months before the Ljubljana congress, but also after it, the rumor circulated that the sixty-five-year-old marshal would renounce the leadership of the government and party, keeping only the presidency of the federation. His successors would be Ranković, as secretary general of the LCY, and Kardelj, as head of the Federal Council. Moscow's offensive buried these projects—if they ever had any substance—convincing Tito that any change could be risky.[138] In Yugoslavia, memories of the "fifty-fifty" agreement between Churchill and Stalin started to resurface, as did the conviction that a division of the country among the great powers was still a current option.[139]

Chinese Polemics with Tito

In the manifesto published in 1958 by the CC CPSU to mark the anniversary of the October Revolution, Yugoslavia was not mentioned among the states that were building socialism. The LCY was also not invited to the Twenty-First Congress of the CPSU, organized in 1959.[140] In spite of this acrimony, the conviction prevailed in Moscow that it was opportune to preserve normal relations, at least at the state level, even if those at the party level had been practically severed. Economic, cultural, and scientific cooperation between the two countries was not compromised.[141] The Bulgarians and Albanians, who saw the Yugoslavs as their main enemies because of border frictions, took a harder line against "Titoist revisionism." As the Belgrade newspaper *Politika* wrote on 17 September 1958, the Albanians openly incited their nationals in Kosovo to rebel against Tito's regime. According to *Politika*, Albania instigated this "wretched and uncivilized business," and its leader, Enver Hoxha, exceeded the "vulgarity" that had been typical of him in the past.[142]

Nobody in Yugoslavia was surprised by Albanian and Bulgarian hostility, whereas China's attitude proved painful. Since establishing diplomatic relations on 11 February 1955, the collaboration with Beijing had always been without polemics, even cordial. As early as 1948, Tito and his comrades saw Mao Zedong as their natural ally against big brother Moscow. The conviction that the Chinese communists had achieved revolution with their own forces against Stalin's will, as had the Yugoslavs, seemed to justify this belief. This hope soon appeared illusory, since it became apparent that the Chinese stood unwaveringly with the Boss.[143] After 1955, however, they changed, openly recognizing that their attitude toward the Yugoslavs had been wrong. Commenting on Khrushchev's penitential visit to Belgrade that year, Mao Zedong declared at a reception: "My congratulations to Tito for the victory of his principles. The Belgrade Declaration [which recognized Yugoslavia's right to its path to socialism] is the most important document created as yet in the workers movement." Mao's closest collaborator, Zhou Enlai, said to the Yugoslav ambassador in India during an official visit: "We must be friends, and we will be."[144] The Hungarian and Polish uprisings against domestic Stalinism in 1956 seemed to offer the occasion to implement this proposal. Mao Zedong and other leaders of the Chinese CP, preoccupied about what had happened and aware of the need to preserve the unity of the socialist camp, promoted a communist world conference and proposed that Tito might join the initiative. Tito was weary of such summits and was not enthusiastic about the idea, which was abandoned, only to be resumed in 1957 by Khrushchev on the occasion of fortieth anniversary of the October Revolution. It was now undoubtedly a different conference from the one that Mao had envisioned.[145] During the Moscow meeting, Mao was cordial toward the Yugoslav delegation, led not by Tito but by Kardelj and Ranković, and stressed the similarity between the LCY and the Chinese Communist Party in their relations with the Soviets. "We differ from you only because you have whiskers and we don't," Mao said to Kardelj jokingly.[146] Kardelj agreed, noting that, paradoxically, the two really successful communist revolutions, Chinese and Yugoslav, had both been accomplished against Stalin's will: "He wished that the countries of revolution should remain dependent on the Soviet Union, knowing well that every revolution brings with it the desire for national independence."[147]

At the start of 1958, the two countries signed a commercial protocol, providing for a volume of trade amounting to $19.6 million.[148] When shortly thereafter the Seventh Congress made the heretical statement that renounced the idea of an inevitable clash between the capitalist and the socialist world and recommended that the Western and the Eastern blocs should be abolished to prevent a nuclear war, the Chinese took a stand. They accused the Yugoslavs of having repudiated the revolution and the proletarian dictatorship and reproached them for having elevated their unorthodox thoughts to a doctrinal level.[149] Hence a battle flared up in the press in which the Chinese newspaper *Hongqi* accused the Yugoslav leaders, starting with Tito, of being "agents of imperialism."[150] A freezing of diplomatic relations followed, including the recall of the Chinese ambassador from Belgrade and the Yugoslav ambassador from Beijing. This was only a smoke screen, behind which were hidden much more serious tensions between Khrushchev and Mao, although at that point they did not wish to express them openly. After the blow that the Soviet Union had suffered because of the Hungarian Revolution, Beijing wanted to affirm its status in the communist world by formulating an orthodox ideological line different from that of Moscow, which was aimed at a dialogue with the West. This sparked an impotent fury in the Kremlin.

Kardelj was aware of the rift between the two parties as early as the celebrations in the Soviet capital in November 1957, warning the comrades that "in the international proletarian movement, a fight has started between the Chinese and Russians for ideological primacy."[151] No one in Belgrade could have imagined, however, that the struggle would assume such a bizarre form. The two powers, at least initially, did not quarrel openly with each other but preferred to choose their own separate scapegoats as objects of their anger. The Chinese assigned this unpleasant role to the Yugoslavs, above all to Tito, whom they branded as a "traitor to socialism" and a "capitalist lackey."[152] The Soviets, for their part, chose Albania, which had of late become a puppet state of Beijing in the Balkans. The Yugoslavs, versed as they were in ideological battles, immediately recognized what was going on and, as Belgrade's ambassador in Beijing Vladimir Popović said, they were not willing to "kneel down" and sheepishly accept Chinese insults.[153]

The polemics peaked on 6 November 1959, when the world's eighty-one communist and workers' parties met in Moscow during another celebration of the October Revolution. On that occasion they tried to overcome the latent conflict between Beijing and Moscow with a unanimous condemnation of Yugoslav "international opportunism." They agreed that by stubbornly clinging to their revisionist ideas, the LCY leaders were edging away from Marxism-Leninism, allowing their country to become subject to American imperialism, and ultimately setting it against the socialist camp.[154] The only ones who were in any way sympathetic to the Yugoslavs were the Poles, though they also considered Tito and his comrades to be "idiots, unable to hide their thoughts."[155]

Commenting on the thaw that seemed to establish a new connection between Moscow and Washington at the close of the fifties, Tito affirmed in Zagreb in mid-December 1959 that due to technological progress there now existed a nuclear threat that could destroy humanity, and that could not have been foreseen by Marx and Lenin. Because of this, humanity had entered a "new epoch" in which peaceful development was a necessity. The problems that states had to confront were no longer linked to peace and war, but to international cooperation and economic competition.[156] The newspaper *Hongqi* criticized him on 16 April with these words: "Thus, this renegade completely writes off the problem of class contradictions and class struggle in the world, trying to deny the Marxist-Leninists' consistent analysis of our epoch as the epoch of imperialism and proletarian revolution, and of victory of socialism and communism. In Tito's new epoch, there really is no imperialism, no proletarian revolution, and of course, no theory and policy for proletarian revolution and dictatorship. The fundamental focal points of class contradictions and class struggles in our epoch are not to be found: the fundamental questions of Leninism are absent; in fact, there is no Leninism."[157]

In order to answer these tirades and the frequent Chinese theme of the inevitability of an armed confrontation with imperialism, Kardelj hastily wrote an essay on behalf of the CC LCY entitled "Socialism and War," which was published in August 1960. The Slovenian ideologue had nothing good to say about Soviet hegemonic ambitions, stressing that a conflict between socialist countries in which the aggressor aimed to impose its own interpretation of socialism would perforce have "a reactionary meaning," since it would fatally harm socialism. By aggressor he meant the Soviets, of course. In confronting the question of the inevitability of war with the West, however, he sided with Khrushchev, contesting the Chinese opinion that imperialism was just a paper tiger, not to be feared. On the contrary, everything should be done to prevent an armed conflict between the blocs of socialism and capitalism in order to avoid Armageddon.[158] General Hsiao Hua, deputy director of the political office of the Chinese Army, replied in *Renmin Ribao* (*The People's Daily*) on 4 June 1960: "Nothing could be more wrong than the thought that the aggressive nature of imperialism has disappeared, and that the possibility of a global war against the socialist camp does not exist anymore."[159]

Maybe because they were both condemned by the Chinese for the same sin, that is, their eagerness to do business with the West, Tito and Khrushchev, who were both in New York the following September taking part in the Fifteenth General Assembly of the UN, resumed their dialogue against all odds. They met several times, and decided to put an end to their polemics. "We fully come to terms," said Khrushchev, following his two-hour meeting with Tito, "as our viewpoints coincide or are very close."[160] These words were addressed to the Americans but more importantly to the Chinese, with whom the Soviets were nearing a final break. It was evident that Khrushchev was sending them a direct message: the foreign policy of the Soviet bloc was his domain, regardless of Beijing's attitude. He would decide with whom he would remain on good terms. The Chinese answered with pique, naturally in their own way—by once again haranguing Tito, that "running dog of imperialism."[161]

In February 1961, there was another outburst at the Congress of the Albanian CP in Tirana. Enver Hoxha, who was unquestionably Mao's ally, vengefully accused the Yugoslavs of having a "metaphysical ideology" that led directly to revisionism and, worse, opportunism, and mentioned the Moscow Declaration signed by Khrushchev and Tito in 1956 as the source of all evil. Recognizing the Yugoslav right to build socialism their way, the Declaration had destroyed the monolithic view of Marxist dogma. An acute tension once more built up between the two states, accompanied by armed incidents on the border that led once again to the severance of diplomatic relations.[162]

In the West, the reaction to these polemics was different. There, Yugoslavia was an object of great interest and was encouraged to persist in its courageous attitude. When Tito's new ambassador to Washington, Marko Nikezić, visited the White House in October 1958, President Eisenhower affirmed in his welcoming speech that his administration had observed Yugoslavia's firmness against the Soviet Union with respect and approval. Since Tito had been successful in opposing Soviet influence, he could continue to count on American aid to ensure the well-being of his country.[163] The following December, in response to Yugoslavia's request for a loan, the American authorities discussed how to implement a new aid program for Tito's regime. A year later, in confirmation of the important role that this Balkan rebel nation had for American foreign policy, a $15 million loan was granted for the construction of a hydroelectric plant near Dubrovnik.[164] In exchange, the Belgrade government ordered its newspaper to stop attacking the West, especially the United States, Great Britain, and France.[165]

The "Peace Journey" to Asia and Africa

After 1958, in the name of the "active coexistence" preached by Tito, Yugoslavia further developed its relations with Africa and Asia, Latin America, and Scandinavia. Given the polemics with the Soviets, Chinese, and with the West because of Yugoslavia's recognition of the GDR, the country needed to show that it was not isolated. To this end, Marshal Tito traveled to Asia and Africa, but numerous other delegations and politicians also visited friendly countries in Europe or overseas (Kardelj, for instance, went to Denmark, Norway, and

Sweden in 1958). On 1 December 1958, Tito sailed on board his yacht, the *Galeb*, for a round trip that included Indonesia, Burma, India, Ceylon, Ethiopia, Sudan, the United Arab Republic (Egypt and Syria), and Greece. As the West German ambassador in New Delhi wrote, his "unofficial" visit to the Indian capital on 14–16 January was greeted with particular warmth. It was clear that Nehru greatly valued his guest's opinion regarding relations with Moscow, and that a close friendship had developed between the two countries. The Yugoslav statesman enjoyed enormous respect and exercised extraordinary influence for his resolute anticolonialist stance, not just in India but also in other Asian and African countries, especially Algeria, where they were fighting for their independence from France.

Tito's and his wife's visit to Ceylon was marked by royal grandeur. The Yugoslav ambassador was able to arrange for the marshal the same treatment reserved some years earlier for Queen Elizabeth II of England. (It is a pity that Tito did not enjoy the local cuisine.) He was received with similar pomp in Indonesia, at the court of Ethiopia's emperor, Haile Selassie, and later in Sudan and in Egypt. Only in Burma was the hospitality not as friendly and lavish as had been anticipated.[166]

Because of the great deal of preparation needed, the number of the people involved, the quantity of baggage, the receptions, the hunting parties, and so on, this Afro-Asian trip was exceedingly pompous in nature, recalling Napoleonic expeditions. In Yugoslavia, naturally no one dared to grumble aloud. However, Dobrica Ćosić wrote in his diary: "Tito, this great statesman and fighter, had neither the force nor the wisdom to save his political triumph from regal and absolutist temptations, ruining his modern ideas regarding peace and the survival of civilization from conflicts and struggles of opposing blocs with feudal behavior, with operettas, parades, costumes and a circus of ships, aircraft and court trash."[167]

In August 1957 during a visit to Romania, Tito promised Khrushchev that he would use his influence in Asia and Africa to further the common interests of the socialist camp. Because of the ideological attacks he had suffered in recent years, however, he did the opposite: everywhere he went, he tried to convince his interlocutors to be wary of the Soviet Union and China, offering them a detailed report of his own recent experiences. If in Moscow they pretended not to hear, in Beijing they considered such behavior proof of Yugoslav connivance with the "imperialist aggressors." By contrast, his information was accepted and valued in London and Washington. The State Department commented that in this role as critic of Soviet and Chinese aggressiveness, Tito was more important than if he had been a member of the Western alliance.[168] They would not have been so satisfied had they known that Tito had started his "great peace journey" with a load of arms and munitions hidden in the hold of the *Galeb* and its escort boat. This arsenal was not intended for Indonesia, the first stopover of the journey, but for the Algerian Liberation Front, to which Indonesian leader Sukarno would pass it on with the help of the Egyptians. In fact, the French regularly inspected Yugoslav ships bound for Algeria after having discovered their smuggling activities on behalf of the rebel movement in 1957. At one point they intercepted a Yugoslav freighter off Oran carrying 150 tons of arms.[169]

The Economic Reform

After having visited several cities and villages, a French Communist Party delegation that came to Yugoslavia in 1957 stated that the population's standard of living was very low, even lower than in other socialist countries.[170] The situation improved in subsequent years, mostly thanks to an increase of industrial production where the conditions were favorable, especially in the northern republics of Slovenia and Croatia. Compared to prewar industrial output, it increased sixfold, while the GNP grew threefold compared to 1952. This stimulated a lively per capita consumption compared to the misery of the first postwar decade. Meanwhile, however, the gap grew between the developed republics, Slovenia and Croatia, and those that produced raw materials and energy using mines and hydrological sources. As a result, there was a constant migration from the south to the northwest. Remarkable differences in the standard of living also appeared between the industrialized areas and the agrarian ones, where the land was divided into numerous private plots, each one too small to feed the peasants who worked it (only 16 percent of the cultivable land was controlled by the state). Because of this, and also because of the authorities' persistent attitude of suspicion toward their own peasantry, conditioned by ideological prejudices, Yugoslavia was compelled for a long time to import food, especially grain (about a million tons yearly). This rapidly increased its foreign debt, given that the trade gap grew constantly, reaching nearly a billion US dollars by the end of the fifties.[171] Nineteen fifty-nine was the first year that they did not need to import wheat, thanks to a good harvest. (Tito also decided not to import wheat that year for political reasons, in order to answer Khrushchev's accusations that he was begging for grain from the imperialists.)[172] Under these conditions, it would be difficult to say that the population achieved an awareness of socialist solidarity: on the contrary, the "developed" were not at all pleased that they were obliged to assist their "underdeveloped" countrymen. They did not refuse to aid the less developed areas (Montenegro, Kosovo, Macedonia, some parts of Bosnia-Herzegovina, but also Serbia and even parts of Croatia), but asked that investments should be applied carefully, to augment the productivity of the country so that their money would not end up in a bottomless pit.[173]

These problems were not addressed openly, since the slogan about "brotherhood and unity" was still paramount. Nobody dared to say that self-management was not implemented according to official propaganda, given that the workers did not have the role in the factories guaranteed them by law. Because of the workers' scarce or nonexistent managerial skills, the last word mostly fell to factory managers, whose appointments had more to do with their party affiliation than their competence.[174] For years, Tito and his comrades had ignored the contradictions and shortcomings of their regime, lulling themselves into the conviction that it was the best in the world. At the Second Plenum, on 18 and 19 November 1959, they asserted enthusiastically: "Our development is growing three or four times as fast as that of the most advanced Eastern countries . . . and it is faster than that of the Western Countries." In his final speech, Tito reiterated that "the whole world speaks today about Yugoslavia's successes regarding industrialization and agriculture. . . . It is essential to keep the prestige we have achieved, and to show the correctness of our path to socialism."[175] It was soon clear, however, that the situation was not so rosy. The dissatisfaction of the population, especially of those who were younger and more intellectually aware, smoldered under the surface, reappearing openly only a year after Trbovlje, in mid-May 1959, during a protest organized by students in Zagreb. It started at noon in the university canteen as a reaction to the bad food: the students began to trash the room and then spilled out into the street, heading toward the city center. They raised banners with sarcastic slogans: *Long live Tito—we need bread! Long live Bakarić—we are hungry!* The demonstration, joined by some thousand people, was blocked by the UDBA and the police, who managed to divert it onto side streets, preventing the crowd from reaching the main square in front of the National Theater. Some ninety people were injured and there was one fatality. Many protesters were arrested and driven away in trucks. Calm was restored only at 5 p.m. The following day, Zagreb newspapers scarcely mentioned the incident, whereas the Belgrade papers ignored it altogether. The mini-revolt preoccupied the leadership, who were not used to street protests, and prompted them to immediately improve the economic conditions of the students by offering them grants, although they were ready to use the force if necessary.[176] When, during a session of the University Committee, the political organization of that institution, Vladimir Bakarić, Croatia's strongman, was asked how to calm down the youth, he answered: "Easy, we will compel them to disband with fire hoses." And when he heard the reply: "What if they will not relent?" he cynically retorted, as if it were completely normal: "Then with tanks."[177]

Along with the disappointment of the young, who grew ever more estranged from the party, and of the working masses, there was also the dissatisfaction of the bourgeoisie, which had started to reappear as a social stratum after the repressions of the postwar years The reason for this was the economic stagnation at the end of the decade, which the authorities tried to overcome with loans that resulted in massive foreign debts, triggering inflation. This temporarily created the illusion of a higher standard of living, but inevitably led the country into chaos when the bubble burst, the loans ran out, and the debts had to be repaid.[178] The situation was so tense that it was discussed at the Second Plenum, on 18 and 19 November 1959, in contradiction with its optimistic assertions. On that occasion Tito openly dealt with the problem regarding aid to the republics and branded every opposition to this aid as "localism." He also more or less plainly denounced the autonomist tendencies of the Croatian and Slovenian leaders. Even more explicit was Ranković, who stressed on 1 December at the Serb industrial center Kraljevo that it was urgent to enhance the underdeveloped areas, not just for economic, but also for political reasons: "This development is the first prerequisite for the unity and brotherhood of our people, because only in this way can a perfect political and material equality be possible."[179]

According to rumors circulating in Belgrade at that time, relations between Tito and Kardelj were increasingly tense because of foreign policy, but even more so because of internal issues. The older and more dogmatic cadres frequently complained that they were fed up with Kardelj's "show of democracy."[180] In the background of this malaise were the economic and national interests of the Slovenes, who felt uncomfortable in Yugoslavia because of their central European heritage, which was so different from the heritage of those who lived in areas ruled for centuries by Turks. In November, at the Second Plenum, Tito spoke mostly to the Slovenians when he observed that "national chauvinism" was present even within that group. He had Kardelj particularly in mind when he said: "Nobody here has the right to impose his opinion upon the majority. And if this majority decides something, it should be carried out. If someone is not ready to do this, he cannot be a member of the Central Committee."[181]

The object of discussion was the railway line connecting Belgrade to Bar, on the Montenegrin coast. The Serbians and Montenegrins believed the line would boost the economic development of their republics but it was obstructed by the Slovenes because of the enormous costs involved, which would be paid mostly by them.[182] As the CIA observed, a split started to appear in the LCY between "liberal" and "conservative" forces. The "liberals" wanted the democratization of the party, the spread of self-management, administrative decentralization on both political and economic levels, the affirmation of confederal principles, the strengthening of the autonomy of each republic, and the improvement of relations with the West. The "conservatives" were opposed to the democratization of the party, supporting economic and administrative centralism in a more robust federation and deeper ties with the Soviet Union. They believed that as LCY members they had right to a privileged position compared to those who were not, and were therefore opposed to everything that could threaten their status.[183]

Since the Five-Year Plan for the period 1957–61 had been accomplished a year in advance, this gave impetus to those who wanted an economic reform to transform Yugoslavia into a politically stable state. CIA analysts were convinced that this would be possible. In a paper dated 23 May 1961 they wrote: "It is in the economic sphere that the Yugoslavs have departed most notably from the practices followed by the other communist states. In the past decade, the regime has successfully freed itself from a whole series of obsessions inherited from the Stalinist period: that planning and administration must be completely centralized; that the peasants must be forced into collective farming; that heavy industry must be developed at any cost, preferably via very large investment projects; that the economy must be insulated from the influence of world markets. In giving up these dogmas, Belgrade has experimented cautiously, gradually coming to adopt a distinctive type of mixed socialism which combines state ownership and planning with many of the characteristics of a market economy. This approach, made possible in part by continuous Western assistance, has been singularly successful."[184]

The developments of the late fifties gave encouragement to those who considered the economy too dependent on the state. Tax revenues allowed for the accumulation of resources with which the state financed a general investment fund in order to aid factories and enterprises that needed financial aid for their survival, and that were obviously engaged in a fierce competition to get a piece of the pie. This competition intensified with more and more frequent statements by reform minded politicians that the "working class, being the owner of the means of production, has the right to decide by itself about the distribution of the earnings."[185] The factories, therefore, should dispose autonomously of their money, and thus would acquire momentum for their growth thanks to reduced pressure from the state. Yugoslav leaders began speaking about economic reform at the November 1959 plenum, stressing that it was urgent to increase industrial production and rationalize the bureaucracy's control over the economy. In some cases this would even have justified dismissals and tighter control of the workers. At the plenum Kardelj affirmed that production would rise only if workers had to queue to get a job at the factories. To those who reproached such "capitalist methods," he replied that sometimes even capitalism had something good and that there were "sensible people" among the capitalists who knew what was right and what was wrong.[186]

The following year Tito declared that there had been an additional increase in industrial production when submitting the new Five-Year Plan on 26 December 1960 at the Federal Assembly. This success was due, he said, to self-management, thanks to which, in the last three years, the GNP had risen 13 percent. Actually, this result was achieved thanks to modernization of the factories, to Western financial aid, and to the comparably low starting point of Yugoslav industry. But the press celebrated this as the world's most significant economic achievement, comparing it especially to the relative GNP in the Soviet bloc, where no country could claim similar growth.[187] Tito grew bolder in his aims and projects. He first spoke about the need to build a nuclear power station, and then even fantasized about nuclear-powered ships, as he was certain that Yugoslavia was on the threshold of an economic and technological boom. He saw it as a supplier of industrial and agricultural products to countries of the Soviet bloc and the Third World. In short, the general conditions of the economy seemed favorable to the decentralization of the state's role in the distribution of income and investment funds. This policy was warmly supported by the trade unions, headed by the dynamic and politically ambitious Svetozar Vukmanović (Tempo), which tirelessly hoped for a renewal of social and economic relations, asking for more self-management that too often existed only on paper. They highlighted the need to address the material interests of workers, because only in this way would it be possible to increase productivity. It was in fact the case that workers were not particularly keen on working harder or better, since the state took the greater part of their earnings from them in the form of exorbitant taxes. As the Croatian historian Dušan Bilandžić wrote, the system was structured so as to favor mediocre collectives, protecting them and exploiting those who excelled.[188]

Party leaders tried to react to discrepancies present in economic life by regulating the relations between the state and the factories regarding the distribution of income. In January 1960, the Federal Assembly issued a series of decrees on this subject in a bid to control consumer prices and to revitalize the banking and financial sector. A monetary reform plan was likewise launched, which envisaged the abolition of different exchange rates for the Yugoslav dinar, introducing a single rate for foreign trade and devaluating the currency. All this was to be carried out with the help of the International Monetary Fund, the United States, West Germany (with which economic relations had resumed) and Great Britain.[189] The state renounced its control of factories and commercial firms, granting them full economic autonomy, which, according to critics, was a bit too capitalistic for comfort. Kardelj, however, was optimistic: speaking with journalists he stressed that in the short run the reform would probably worsen the standard of living, but would create the basis for healthy price regulation connected to increased productivity, giving fresh impetus to the economy.[190]

Kardelj versus Ranković: Succession Fight

At the beginning of February 1961, there was a plenum featuring a lively discussion about the future development of the nation. The conservatives protested about the "vulgar economic logic" of the advocates of reform, mostly attacking Kardelj as a supporter of capitalist tendencies. He replied at the Second Plenum of the Socialist Alliance of Working People, affirming that the free market in Yugoslavia was not akin to the capitalist market, which was anarchic, without a plan. "Our market is affected by the plan," he noted, "and, in a certain sense, does not only complete it, but becomes its instrument."[191] To control some "excesses" in the setting of prices, salaries, and places of work, Kardelj announced administrative measures, thus showing his belief that policies should maintain control over the economy. His ideas prevailed. In an interview published in *Komunist* on 2 February 1961, one of his collaborators, Avdo Humo, president of the Committee for Social Planning, described the Yugoslav system in this way: in the Soviet bloc, the state is owner of the means of production, which signifies that the workers are its employees; in the capitalist system, private individuals are entrepreneurs and there workers depend on them; only in Yugoslavia are the working people also the entrepreneurs, which means that the dependent relationship is abolished. The basis of this new system is self-management, which functions thanks to workers and their councils. Until the advent of communism, where every individual has everything needed at his or her disposal, it was necessary to respect the Marxist principle as formulated by Stalin and Trotsky: "To each according to his contribution."[192]

Over the course of two successive sessions, the Federal Assembly adopted thirty-two laws regarding economic reform, which were ratified by the Executive Committee on 23 February 1961. These changes were accepted favorably in Slovenia, and partially in Croatia, Serbia, and Bosnia-Herzegovina, where the economy was healthy. However, the representatives of the underdeveloped areas in Macedonia and Montenegro did not hide their skepticism.[193] They were right, because in the following months it became obvious that the difficulties were greater than expected and it would not be possible to eliminate the disparity in prices between different republics nor avoid inflation. Not to mention the fact that economic anarchy appeared due to the passive resistance of workers and of the state and party apparatus in those environments where the reform was not welcomed. Some factories used the occasion to raise wages, especially for managers, thus worsening social relations from within. This was further exacerbated because many factories, especially in Bosnia-Herzegovina,

Montenegro, and Macedonia, began firing workers in the name of efficiency.[194] The trade deficit with the West and the East, but especially with the Soviet Union, increased. Yugoslavia was obliged to import half a million tons of wheat from the United States once again, since it was not able to feed the population because of alternating droughts and flooding.[195]

It was whispered that there were two opposing groups in the top ranks of government. The conservative group, headed by Ranković, did not favor the reform or the development of self-management, asserting that due to said reform, the LCY isolated itself from the Soviet Union and other socialist countries. The other, which had formed around Kardelj and Vukmanović (Tempo), was determined in its commitment to pursue reforms to improve democracy and strengthen relations with the West. In addition, the conflict between Kardelj and Ranković over Tito's succession, which had begun with the elimination of Djilas as a contender, if not before, became more and more explicit. As early as the beginning of the fifties, when Kardelj was minister of foreign affairs, Ranković tried to obstruct him by systematically refusing his candidates for ambassadorial posts on the pretext that they were unreliable: in 1952, he accepted only five of 150 names proposed by Kardelj, thus humiliating him.[196] Since Kardelj was the main proponent of the reforms, whereas Ranković opposed them, it was inevitable that groups of progressive "technocrats" and conservative "apparatchiks," or devotees to party bureaucracy, coalesced around them. These factions had, perforce, ethnic connotations: since the reformists wished for growing decentralization, whereas the dogmatists defended centralism, the former were supported by the developed republics of Slovenia and Croatia, while the others were backed by Serbia, Montenegro, and partially, Macedonia. Of course, in this game it was not without significance that Kardelj was a Slovene and Ranković a Serb.[197] Tito was extremely worried about this conflict, well aware that he was "unable to find a common language with my closest aides."[198] Nevertheless, he took advantage of their discord to reinforce his own power.[199]

The Trip to Africa

After the Seventh Congress, Tito invested a great deal of energy nurturing relationships with African and Asian countries, convinced that it would be possible to coordinate the development of the Yugoslav economy with that of the Third World. To this end, the Belgrade government set up a wide-ranging aid program for "developing countries" (in all, more than $11 billion would be invested), based on the exchange of its products for raw materials. Yugoslav experts collaborated on the construction of harbors, industrial plants, and geological research in these countries, developing a foothold in their economic life. Cultural relations also flourished, with hundreds of African and Asian students attending Yugoslav universities thanks to scholarships.[200]

Returning from his three-month journey to Indonesia, Burma, India, Ceylon, Ethiopia, Sudan, Egypt, Syria, and Greece, Tito was hailed triumphantly in Belgrade. About three hundred thousand people, from workers to schoolchildren, were conveyed by buses or trucks to flank the motorcade.[201] This "success" strengthened his conviction that the non-aligned countries should collaborate with the great powers to solve the burning issues of the contemporary world. In an international atmosphere marked by rising tensions, when more or less open threats of nuclear conflict were coming out of Washington and Moscow, he considered this sort of collective effort to preserve peace extremely urgent. When the summit between Khrushchev and Eisenhower failed miserably in May 1960 after the Soviet decision to shoot down an American spy aircraft, Tito blamed the United States for the breakdown. At the same time, he asked for a more active role in international relations for non-aligned countries and for the United Nations, stressing that it was not possible to leave the responsibility for the fate of the world to the great powers. He expressed this idea a month later in a press release at the close of Nasser's visit to Yugoslavia, and reiterated it at the Fifteenth General Assembly of the UN, when he met leaders from Egypt, India, Indonesia, and Ghana. On that occasion, they addressed an appeal to Eisenhower and Khrushchev, inviting them to resume mutual contact and together solve the world's current problems.[202] For the first time, the Non-Aligned Movement passed from words to action. Tito was radiant.[203]

Although worried about the effect that vaccinations against tropical diseases could have on his health, at the end of February 1961 Tito embarked on another trip, this time to Africa, which had been hastily organized to beat Khrushchev to the draw. In the spring of that year, Khrushchev in turn had decided to visit several countries on the African continent.[204] At the start of Tito's journey, he received information about the brutal assassination of Patrice Lumumba, the heart of the mutiny against Belgian colonial rule in Congo. Tito, who was on the side of the rebels in their fight against colonialism, started to think about a stronger future policy than he had initially intended. Outraged over Lumumba's fate (he had been shot, dismembered, and dissolved in acid by his enemies), he declared that this was "the worst crime of contemporary history," and that his death was to be ascribed mostly to the UN and its secretary general, Dag Hammerskjöld, who was guilty of not having protected Lumumba sufficiently. In Tito's view it was urgent to summon a meeting of "neutral" (non-aligned) countries in Cairo as soon as possible: "Call Abdel

[Nasser]. Send a telegram to Sukarno. . . . Only the small non-aligned countries can fight for peace. It is necessary to block these [imperialist] nuts. Set the world against them, isolate them."[205] Thus the idea of the Non-Aligned Conference took shape, at which the member states would come up with a strategy to confront colonialism and prevent war between the great powers. He also needed to persuade Nehru who, according to Tito, could not act because of India's debts with the West and because of reactionary forces he had to cope with in New Delhi. "But," Tito argued, "we have to help him free himself from the mess he is in."[206]

Tito started his journey to Africa with an entourage of about 1,400 people, among them forty musicians and folk singers. The yacht *Galeb*, which he boarded with his wife Jovanka and his collaborators, was escorted by three warships. The tour lasted seventy-two days, from 15 February to 22 April, reaching Ghana, Togo, Liberia, and Guinea—and from there by land to Mali—then Morocco and Tunisia. The last and most important stop was in Egypt, although this was an "unofficial" visit. At every stop Tito informed his hosts about his negative experiences with Moscow, warning them not to tie themselves exclusively to them. He even stressed that his relations with the West were more correct and balanced than with the Russians. Furthermore, he presented Yugoslavia as an example to be followed, since it was independent from the blocs. He found sympathetic listeners, particularly in Ghana and Guinea, which were led by two outstanding anticolonialist fighters.[207] The president of Ghana, Kwame Nkrumah, said: "He is the most realistic of the contemporary statesmen. No one has understood Africa better than he. And we, too, have understood him."[208]

This was an epochal event since, for the first time in history a European statesman had come to the Africans as to equals, approaching them without paternalism and without sparing criticism for the colonial powers. Rodoljub Čolakovic wrote in his diary that Tito was aware of the psychological effect of his visit. On his return, he spoke in his inner circle "about the African peoples, about their attitude toward the white man, and especially the white man called Tito."[209]

The trip was, however, not without incident: for example, once, during a distribution of luxury gifts, there was such a frenzy that Tito exclaimed in despair: "Everybody take what he wants."[210] The final statements in discussion with local leaders, prepared of course in advance, were adapted to the political and social conditions of every country, though always stressing the value of collaboration and equality among nations, and condemning colonialism and neocolonialism. The main idea presented by the Yugoslav theoreticians was the assertion that, beyond ideologies, the gap between the developed North and the underdeveloped South was the worst danger to world peace. Kardelj especially supported this idea, analyzing it in dialogue with the Swedish economist Gunnar Myrdal, but Tito also endorsed it in an interview with the *London Daily Herald* by urging systematic aid for poor countries, "because this is the first and most critical condition for the well-being of the entire world."[211]

At Cairo, Tito met Nasser for the ninth time and proposed organizing the Non-Aligned Conference, which he had already discussed with Nkrumah, Sukarno, and Nehru the previous autumn in New York.[212] During an excursion on the Nile Tito tried to convince his host that Nehru also supported the idea, although the Indian prime minister was in fact skeptical, fearing the emergence of a "third bloc" along with the two already in existence. Veljko Mićunović, Tito's diplomatic counselor, reminded him of the Indian prime minister's reserved attitude and the marshal reacted furiously, stressing that Nehru sooner or later would give his assent. He took this correction as an embarrassing offence, as it implied that he was lying in front of his host. When they were alone, he rebuked Mićunović for his insolence, since he had exposed Tito stretching the truth. It seems that he had never before been in such an unpleasant situation, and was so exasperated that he was unable to choke back tears when telling General Žeželj how he had been humiliated in Nasser's presence.[213] Mićunović had not only dared to contradict him in front of the Egyptian leader, but in the later confrontation he did not hide his disagreement with the marshal's despotic behavior and with Jovanka's meddling in political affairs, about which he felt she was ignorant. He even reproached Tito for behaving like an oriental satrap. "What you are doing costs our country a lot," he said. "It is such a waste that I am ashamed to be involved in it."[214] A terrible verbal confrontation followed, a quarrel that was only the tip of the iceberg. Actually, during the long journey aboard the *Galeb*, a frosty atmosphere arose between Tito and his comrades, between Tito and Jovanka, and between the arrogant first lady and the members of the entourage, who were horrified by the atmosphere in which they found themselves, one worthy of a Byzantine court due to the autocratic behavior of the presidential couple. Because of these reproaches, Tito experienced moments of deep psychological unease, which caused him to cut off all contact with his entourage from time to time. Dobrica Ćosić, invited to take part in the journey in order to describe it, preferred to keep silent. But the impressions he noted in his diary are frightening: "Tito and his comrades have disappointed me so much that I became sick. On the *Galeb*, I realized that the LCY leadership, starting with Tito, is a monarchic oligarchy, morally corrupt and without any satiation of its thirst for power."[215]

When he got back, Tito asked that Mićunović, Leo Mates, chief of his cabinet, and Lazar Koliševski, one of the most important Macedonian politicians, with whom he had also quarreled, should be punished. The three escaped by the skin of their teeth, mostly thanks to the peaceful intervention of Ranković, although they were banished, for a certain period, from the court. Mates lost his secretarial assignment, and even Ranković did not come out unscathed. Tito and Jovanka did not forgive him for having sided against them with the three "reprobates" and arguing against the punitive measures they had wanted to impose.[216] For Tito, the experience on board the *Galeb* was so traumatic that he began thinking about his retirement from public life. In fact, when the secretary of the Socialist Alliance came to Brioni for consultations, he mentioned the possibility of a collective presidency, which would take his place at the head of the federation.[217]

The First Non-Aligned Conference

The idea of a Non-Aligned Conference, aimed to "heal the UN," took root in spite of incidents and dissent. To what extent it was urgent to transform the movement of the countries that existed beyond the American and Soviet blocs into an efficient peace instrument was confirmed the very day Tito arrived in Egypt. On 17 April news came that a group of Cuban émigrés, organized by the CIA, had disembarked in the Bay of Pigs and tried without success to overthrow Fidel Castro's regime. Nehru decided to join the conference, hoping to prevent it from growing too radical. On 21 April in Alexandria, Tito and Nasser signed a letter inviting the heads of twelve countries to take part in a "summit" that would convene before the autumn plenary session of the UN General Assembly. From 5–13 June, a preliminary conference was held in Cairo, where the diplomats of twenty-one African and Asian states, plus Yugoslavia, prepared the agenda of the meeting. It was not without discussion and disagreement, since it was not easy to define such concepts as "neutrality," "non-alignment," and "independence."[218] The easiest decision was the one made to convene the conference on 1 September 1961 in Belgrade. This was a great success for Tito, since Yugoslavia, the only European country present (except Cyprus), found itself at the head of a movement that encompassed more than a third of humanity, a quarter of the seats at the UN General Assembly, and claimed to be the "conscience of the world." However, in comparison with the Western or Eastern bloc, this movement did not have much political or military weight. This is the probable reason why neither Washington nor Moscow objected to the conference; they were in agreement on at least on one point, satisfied as they were that Mao's China was not invited. Only France objected to the conference, since the Algerian Liberation Front was included among the eighteen participating anticolonialist movements, as an official representative of Algeria, stubbornly thought of in Paris as merely a French *department*. Charles de Gaulle, the only protagonist of the Second World War who never wanted to meet the Yugoslav marshal—likely because of Draža Mihailović's shooting—decided to recall his ambassador from Belgrade in protest.[219]

Meanwhile, a serious international crisis erupted, caused by the decision of the German Democratic Republic to separate East Berlin from the West by throwing up a wall to block the flight of its citizens from one side to the other. Before the start of the conference, Tito informed the American ambassador, George F. Kennan, that he disapproved of Washington's policy in Germany, making it understood, however, that at the summit he would refrain from saying something that could exacerbate international tension.[220] President Eisenhower reacted with a personal message approving the Belgrade encounter. Just when the delegations had started to assemble, things took a dark turn, after Khrushchev's decision to resume nuclear testing in the atmosphere. Although he had ceased such tests as a show of good will, he now wished to flex his muscles once more. The Soviets announced that they were ready to explode a hydrogen bomb in the archipelago of Novaya Zemlya, which with its seventy-five megatons would surpass all the nuclear experiments done until then. The Soviet ambassador informed Tito about this on 31 August, at the Belgrade airport.[221] The next day, the marshal opened the conference with a formal inaugural speech. After another meeting with the ambassador (which caused him to be late to the session on September 3) he spoke again, this time more boldly. In fact, Khrushchev had asked him to support his decision about the enormous "Tsar-bomb." Hence, at the last moment, Tito introduced some phrases into his written text that practically adopted the arguments put forward by the Soviets to justify their experiment. Instead of condemning it, as the majority of the participants of the summit would have wished, he only expressed some doubts about the moment chosen for the test and shared his hope that a "World Atomic Conference" would be organized in which non-nuclear countries would also take part. He also defended Soviet policy in Berlin and energetically attacked the West for its attitude toward the German issue.[222] To an outraged Ambassador Kennan, who felt betrayed, the Yugoslav diplomats later confessed that the marshal had done this to support Khrushchev against his (unspecified) internal "opponents."[223] It is doubtful, however, that Tito's comrades were convinced of this justification, considering that Secretary of Foreign Affairs Koča Popović was surprised by the marshal's offhand words and furious for not having been informed in advance.[224]

The attendees at the conference were not shy about high-sounding declarations of principles, among them speaking out on the fight against colonialism, neo-colonialism, and imperialism. They were incapable, however, of proposing any constructive initiatives for the solution to these world problems.[225] Tito's request that the UN should organize a global summit on international economic development, especially regarding the relations between the developed North and the less-developed South, resulted in a series of initiatives by the non-aligned that did not yield significant results. His idea about a "new mutual economic order" that would help former colonial countries financially did not take off as it found no support in either Washington or Moscow. The most the conference was able to do was to send an invitation to Khrushchev and to the newly elected US president, John F. Kennedy, to "start discussing the peaceful solution of contemporary issues," since the "key to peace and war" was in their hands.[226] The meeting was marked by a simmering disagreement between the Yugoslavs and some of the participants, starting with Nehru. Whereas the Yugoslavs wished for a solid organization that could participate in the international political arena, others like Nehru were more interested in loose discussions about important global issues, hoping to be able to mediate between the great powers. How "friendly" the atmosphere was at the first meeting of the non-aligned—a term that Tito avoided for a long time, preferring "non-engaged"—is shown by the Yugoslav decision to secretly bug all the residences of the foreign guests under the auspices of a particular operation called "Peace," authorized by the marshal himself.[227]

The most delicate question confronted by the non-aligned was that of Germany. Tito and Popović did everything possible to make sure that the conference would recognize the existence of two German states, but to no avail, because of the pressure exerted by the West on India and the countries under its influence.[228] Nevertheless, in the end Yugoslavia was successful in burnishing its image, thanks to its ability to organize such a complex diplomatic gathering. From that moment on, Tito gained the status of a world statesman, which he tried to exploit in internal policy too, as his contacts with the Third World were unpopular among the masses, who tended to prefer the West, which they perceived as less alien and more advanced. Answering his critics, who of course never dared to speak loudly, he often stated that an array of small, independent republics could never wield more influence than a federal Yugoslavia, as he had created. This proved his case.[229] However, his "comprehension" of the Soviet nuclear test aroused much indignation in the West, and raised questions concerning Yugoslavia's relations with both blocs.[230] No one suspected that the explanation given by the Yugoslav diplomats to Kennan could have some basis in truth, because no one knew the real balance of power beyond the Kremlin walls as well as the marshal. As early as February 1961, during his trip to Africa, he had said about Khrushchev: "He is the best man

Russia has today. The most progressive. . . . I am trying to help him, because I am sure that he will never be favorable to war."[231]

Kardelj in Disgrace with Tito

During the Non-Aligned Conference, Kardelj remained in the shadows, as he was in disgrace with Tito. In the past, he had spoken with admiration about the marshal: "In Tito's character," he had said, "there is something profoundly human. He can be violent, harsh, but this is a manifestation of fleeting sentiments."[232] In 1952, on the occasion of Tito's sixtieth birthday, he sent him the following greeting card: "Your sixty years—with all that you have given to our party and our country, in its yearning for a better future—are a reason for pride, not just for you but for all of us who, under your guidance, have fought and won for socialism, and who respect and love you as the soul and body of this fight."[233]

This paean had been written when Kardelj was still considered his natural successor. Among the Yugoslav communists the opinion spread that the he was second only to Tito. The Slovenian ideologue was so sure of this that during a visit to London at the end of 1945 he introduced himself to the secretary general of the British Communist Party as the "vice-president." In short, he did not have to fight for power, since everybody knew that he already had it.[234]

"This conviction," said Vladimir Dedijer in an interview on the occasion of Kardelj's death, "lasted till 1954, when new pretenders appeared who hoped to put on Tito's cloak after his departure."[235] First among them was Aleksandar Ranković. The new power relationships started to appear in the period when relations with Stalin's successors had been established, and Tito had begun making decisions without asking the opinion of his comrades. Kardelj was ready to review his critical attitude toward the Soviet Union and Stalin himself, whose policy, in his opinion, was not entirely negative. In spite of everything, thanks to Stalin, something of the October Revolution had remained alive. This historical judgment could not, however, mitigate his preoccupation with the excessive impetus given by Tito to his dialogue with the Russians.[236]

In his memoirs, Kardelj wrote that during the Belgrade discussions in 1955 the Yugoslavs refused every proposal regarding new forms of the international proletarian movement under Soviet aegis advanced by Khrushchev. He added: "For who knows what reason, [Khrushchev] has discovered in me the fiercest adversary to Yugoslavia's return to the socialist camp, and the stronger supporter of the non-aligned policy. In reality, our entire leadership, without exception, thought in this way, but Khrushchev kept attacking me, trying even to sow discord in our ranks. And he continued this policy, although without success."[237]

It is questionable whether this last sentence was completely honest. From other sources, we know that the first disagreements between Tito and Kardelj regarding the suitable attitude to assume toward the Soviets appeared in the mid-fifties. Kardelj and his circle thought that Tito was under the spell of the Muscovite sirens, and therefore they instructed Slovenia's former UDBA chief, Matija Maček, Tito's friend, to call on him to be more cautious. When Tito arrived at Brdo Castle for a vacation, Maček—an iron-fisted man who mistrusted Russians—performed this delicate task. A heated discussion followed, which according to Maček nevertheless ended on a promising note.[238]

During the Yugoslav delegation's journey to the Soviet Union in June 1956, Kardelj reaffirmed his discontent over the renewal of relations between the LCY and the CPSU sponsored by the marshal. He shared Koča Popović's opinion that the Moscow Declaration (between parties) derogated the positive principles of the earlier Belgrade Declaration, which dealt with the relations between states. He was also convinced that the unrepentant Stalinists prevailed in the Soviet Union, especially regarding internal policy, administration, and the security services.[239] Even the Western diplomats noticed that something was wrong, observing how neglected Slovenia was on important occasions. It was noticeable, for instance, that Kardelj was systematically relegated to the background in the edited photomontages of the most important leaders published by the press, and that in common sessions of the two parties, or during ceremonies, protocol assigned him a makeshift role. It was not just a case of discrimination in terms of protocol, but also of disagreements that were probably quite cutting if it is true that in the summer of 1956 Tito suggested to Ranković that they "liquidate" Kardelj, since he could no longer bear his protests regarding relations with the Soviets. After his return from Moscow at the beginning of August, Tito invited the UDBA chief to a dinner at Oplonac, a Karadjordjević estate where the marshal had not been for a long time. During a walk in the woods, he confessed that it was not possible to collaborate with Kardelj any longer: "He defies me at every step. He does not discuss anything with me. Pepca [Kardelj's wife] plots against me and Jovanka. Let's convene a plenum of the CC. Out of the party, either me or him!"[240]

Although he shared Tito's critical attitude, Ranković thought that the "liquidation" of Kardelj could be harmful, believing that they should not give too much importance to stances that could not damage the marshal's authority. He noted, moreover, that the Djilas case was still fresh, and that new friction at the top could have negative repercussions in both country and party. This annoyed the marshal, who decided to skip the dinner. "We drank our coffee and returned to Belgrade," wrote Dobrica Ćosić, quoting Ranković.[241] In his memoirs the latter tells more or less the same story, except the conclusion, where he asserted: "He told me then, for the first time, that Kardelj was an incorrigible nationalist, and that he would create a lot of trouble. In the end, he accepted my proposal [to subject Kardelj to strict surveillance], which is why we spent the rest of the day pleasurably. I was happy."[242] Happy because he had calmed Tito, or because he thought that he had rid himself of a dangerous rival?

American diplomats and secret services noticed the tensions within the Yugoslav leadership, and also the fact that in 1956 Kardelj had affirmed that some Yugoslav politicians (i.e., Tito) had gone too far in their uncritical sympathies for the Soviet bloc. They said that Kardelj, backed by the Slovenian and part of the Croatian CC, had tried to oppose the extent of the rapprochement with Moscow by stressing that the most developed republics in Yugoslavia would not accept such a policy.[243] The disagreement was nurtured by Ranković's agents, who told Tito what his principal collaborators said about him in private—Kardelj had been bugged since 1947—and this contributed to the cool relations between them. Contact became more and more sporadic culminating in an eight month period in the early sixties in which they did not speak to one another.[244]

At the end of 1956, the relations between the two saw a temporary improvement because of the Hungarian crisis, which showed how right Kardelj had been in counseling prudence in dealing with the Russians. Nevertheless, the rift soon reappeared. In 1957, for instance, Kardelj highlighted the ethnic question, which Tito considered obsolete, predicting the imminent formation of the "Yugoslav nation," something that never really occurred.[245] After Djilas's fall, Kardelj became preoccupied with the centralizing trend in the country, and worked to oppose this, although in an "Aesopian" way, as the East Europeans say, only revealing his thoughts in an oblique manner. He republished an essay that had appeared before the war under the pseudonym Sperans under the title "The Development of the Slovene National Question," and added a long preface in which he affirmed that socialist Yugoslavia could not and would not become a melting pot of the American or Soviet kind. In his opinion, Yugoslavia could be acceptable for the Slovenes "today and in this moment," but not necessarily in the future, when he imagined that the state might split into new political bodies (which, of course, it did). In a discussion with Dobrica Ćosić, he even said that the Yugoslav idea of a common nation could not be an ethnic concept; "It can only be a socio-political category, which means a socialist one."[246]

Because of Kardelj's role in the party, nobody had the guts to contradict him, especially because Tito had decided not to react. Actually, Tito had wanted to prohibit the publication of the essay, but on the advice of Ranković, he did not.[247] The essay was received, however, in a hostile silence that meant that the national struggle would be deferred for some years. It became manifest in 1961, when in the Zagreb magazine *Telegram* Dobrica Ćosić called attention to the ever more strained relations between the republics, affirming that "vampire nationalism" should be overcome with their abolition. "Sorry, What Did You Say?" was the title of the answer by one of the most brilliant Slovene intellectuals, Dušan Pirjevec, who attacked "the centralist leeches" with all the heat of his impetuous character (and not without Kardelj's approval), thus starting a polemic that openly confronted the national problem in Yugoslavia.[248]

Ranković's Bullet

The failure of the "new economic order," as the reform was called, provoked consternation among the power elite, which, in harmony with its ideological dogma, was sure that the socialist economy could not experience crisis and breakdown. It also provided the opportunity to settle accounts with Kardelj. His political life seemed to be hanging by a thread and his work was totally discredited, so much so that a study group preparing new reforms under his guidance was disbanded.[249] Kardelj had certainly lost his battle, and his life was even in danger. In fact, he had been seriously wounded at the end of January 1961 during a hunt in Srem, in the woods between Croatia and Serbia. He was "mistakenly" hit by Jovan Veselinov, a Serb politician close to Ranković, who was known to be a bad shot. The details of the incident were not revealed to the public, which was informed only that Kardelj had been hurt by the recoil from his own rifle shot. In his circle a different version of the incident was spread: that day they had hunted rabbits and pheasant using shotguns, whereas he was wounded by a bullet suitable for boar-hunting. The bullet penetrated his cranial wall at the top of the cerebellum, which convinced Kardelj that Ranković had ordered his liquidation. His wife Pepca was sure that the instigator was even higher, whispering to acquaintances: "Edo and I, we are living under an iron heel. Sooner or later Tito will send us to jail." She even said to Bakarić, with whom she was in confidence: "He will kill us all."[250]

After a stay in the hospital, Kardelj decided to go with his family to London for June and July 1961, ostensibly "to learn English." It was a voluntary exile, about which even Tito had not been informed. According to the Yugoslav secret services he intended to emigrate or if not, then to retire to Ljubljana and teach Marxism at the local university. Although the *Observer* and the *Times* wrote that the Slovenian politician's stay was not as innocent as it seemed, the Foreign Office did not listen. The British diplomats limited themselves to wondering how it was possible that, at such a demanding moment, on the eve of the Non-Aligned Conference, the Belgrade regime could do without one of its more prominent men.[251] In the British capital Kardelj consulted the best local specialists, who advised against an operation, noting that the bullet was just a few millimeters from his brain and that surgery could result in facial paralysis.

According to them, he had been saved by a miracle: it happened in one in ten thousand cases. "Ranković's bullet" remained in Kardelj's skull, and was removed only during the autopsy after his death, seventeen years later.[252]

Someone who was not troubled by Kardelj's flight was Ranković, who evidently wanted him completely isolated. For instance, he refused to allow him to participate some months later in the solemn celebrations of the twentieth anniversary of the "Užice Republic." Ranković turned down his request to be invited, suggesting dryly to him that he should "rest." (In that period the UDBA suspected that he and his wife were collaborating with the CIA). Bakarić was among those who could not resign themselves to Kardelj's retirement, as he was well aware that he would lose a precious ally. He did all he could to convince him to return home and to remain politically active.[253] The rumors that circulated abroad and in Yugoslavia about the hunting accident disturbed Tito, who staged a photo opportunity in order to quiet them. At the end of August, after his return, Kardelj was obliged to go hunting chamois in the Julian Alps with Veselinov and Ranković. The picture of the three "comrades" appeared the next day on the front page of *Delo*, the main Ljubljana newspaper.[254] But Kardelj's troubles continued: in that period a large part of his archive disappeared, transported in four trucks to a place never revealed, apparently by the UDBA.[255] By contrast, the Slovenian leadership answered to the disgrace of its point man by closing ranks and organizing a mass demonstration in his favor in the main square of Ljubljana. The event planners were told by the leading representatives of the Slovene League of Communists that the "centralist forces" had tried to liquidate Kardelj as the principal exponent of self-management: "Therefore we have to support him as much as possible." The demonstration was an enormous success: the crowd filled not just the square but also the adjacent streets.[256]

The March 1962 Plenum

The Third Plenum, on 27 November 1961, ended with the affirmation that too much democracy was an obstacle to the building of socialism, therefore the control of investments, industrial planning, wages, and trade was reinstated to "stabilize" the situation and restore the guiding role of the party. Kardelj's proposal to strengthen the Socialist Alliance of Working People, a parallel organization to the party that had been established in 1952 with the aim of enrolling non-party members and thereby allowing the masses to participate in political life, was rejected. The ideas of the 1952 Sixth Congress were also criticized, particularly those regarding the progressive disappearance of the state and the party. The most prominent supporters of the reforms, many Slovenes among them, were removed from the federal administration, and Tito began to associate himself with the dogmas of the defense secretary, Ivan Gošnjak, the Croatian interior secretary, Ivan Krajačić (Stevo), and the president of the Federal Assembly, Petar Stambolić. For thirty-eight months he ruled with their help alone, without convoking any higher party body. The danger of a return to the old political beliefs encouraged some Yugoslav economists to draw up a so-called "yellow paper" and later a "white paper," in order to show the Marxists in power that even in socialism there could be periods of development or recession, and to stress that the reform was not successful because it was not bold enough. The arguments of economists had little impact, especially in light of the infighting between liberals and conservatives at the top of the party. The apple of discord was the draft for the 1962 plan, which met with strong opposition in Slovenia and Croatia, since it favored the central administration and its economic hegemony. In December 1961, the Slovenian members of the Producers Council, one of the parliamentary chambers, left the session in protest while in the Federal chamber the vice-president of the Ljubljana Assembly voted against the legislative proposal in a move that had no precedent in postwar Yugoslavia.[257]

In spite of the difficulties and hostility he had to cope with, after a long period of work with his collaborators Kardelj finished the draft of the new constitution. When Ranković had the opportunity to read it, he discovered that the republics were given not just fictitious but real powers, which he considered unacceptable. He immediately contacted Tito to express his disapproval. Tito agreed with him, saying, "This cannot go on." The following day the marshal called Ranković: "If things are going to go on this way, I will resign." "It is not necessary," Ranković replied. "We will call the CC plenum and we will work this out there."[258]

Between 14 and 16 March 1962 an extraordinary and secret session of the Executive Committee of the LCY was organized, attended by the entire political elite, although the topic to be discussed was unknown. Unexpectedly, a document on corruption among the most important functionaries of different republics was presented, which also pointed out an increase in cases of local nationalism. In his speech, Tito noted that "sometimes decentralization manifests the characteristics of a disintegration," insisting on a strict respect for democratic centralism as defined by Lenin. "One wonders whether this state of ours is capable of resisting destruction. . . . Is it able to survive or not?"[259] This was the start of a fierce discussion that developed into a clash between those wanting further development of self-management and the defenders of "state-ism." The latter gained the upper hand, whereas the standard bearers of "republicanism," the Slovenes above all, found themselves accused of promoting "petit bourgeois anarchy."[260] Ranković argued for curbing self-management, bringing order to the state apparatus, reinforcing the role of the party in public life, strengthening the ideological struggle and opposing liberal tendencies, especially regarding investments, which reformers thought should not only solve social problems in underdeveloped areas, but also generate profits. His opponents naturally tried to defend themselves, starting with Kardelj, who reiterated his opinion: the experiment carried out to date was important not just for the Yugoslav people. Every surrender of self-management would jeopardize "the fundamental problem of socialist development in the world," and would be an acknowledgement that "there is no exit from the Stalinist dead end."[261]

Since they were well aware of how important this discussion was, Ranković and his minions decided to record it secretly in order to use it at the moment of Tito's succession to show how much the "liberals" had strayed from his path. The tapes should be used—or at least this was the conviction of Stane Kavčič and Miko Tripalo, two rising stars in Slovenia and Croatia—to block those who opposed the seizure of power by "Comrade Marko," a.k.a. Ranković a.k.a. Leka.[262] In this murky atmosphere, the Executive Committee of the LCY decided to ask all the republican leaders to take a stand on the questions under discussion and to inform the top-level politicians about their opinions in writing. Since they could count on the support of the majority (Vladimir Bakarić and the Croatian CP prudently kept silent), Tito and Ranković wanted to remove Kardelj from public life with this maneuver, or at least diminish his influence by shunting self-management to the sidelines. They did not take into account the support Kardelj enjoyed in Slovenia, where his "clan" dominated the scene and where he had the approval of public opinion in its fight against Belgrade centralism.[263]

The session of the CC of the Slovenian CP, organized on 29 and 30 March 1962, consequently condemned every attempt at centralizing. The Slovenian politicians, although well aware of the risks they were taking, did not hide their conviction that the "Old One has not been in the know about what was going on in the country for five years," suggesting that he was not able to govern anymore.[264] Tito's and Ranković's reaction to this challenge was swift: on 3 April they convened a new session of the Executive Committee in Belgrade, where Kardelj, frightened by the radicalism of his fellow Slovenes, accused them of having worsened his position. The Slovenians, headed by old Maček and young Kavčič, stressed that there were questions of capital importance at stake on which it was not possible to yield.[265] The following discussion did not bring clarification or an explicit victory to either side, although the conservatives came out ahead. During the debate, Kardelj remained isolated and exposed to Tito's and Gošnjak's criticisms. He was so upset that he was unable to reply: he kept silent, with tears in his eyes. This saved him, as perhaps did his final declaration of loyalty to the marshal: "The greatness of our party lies in the fact that it is headed by Tito: he is a genius, always capable of saving us in moments of crisis. I am sure that he will also save the moment now."[266]

On 3 April, the Executive Committee sent all party members a letter asking them to "put their ranks into order" and calling their attention to "unhealthy liberalism," but also to frequent manifestations of "chauvinism, nationalism, localism and various bureaucratic and petit bourgeois ideas." This was aimed at the Slovenians, who were accused of being barely interested in Yugoslavia and worrying mostly about their own republic.[267] The most eloquent sign of the clash that continued to tear apart the Yugoslav leadership was the decision to postpone the presentation of the new constitution that had been worked on by Kardelj for six months. The Federal Assembly extended its mandate for a year and reorganized some important economic sectors: it drastically limited imports, tightened up penal legislation and on 19 April established a network of commissions tasked with equalizing the income of different enterprises, in contrast to the doctrine of self-management. The slogan of the day was: "We have to fight against the deformity of society."[268]

The Split Speech

In order to explain to the people what was going on, Tito gave an important speech on 6 May 1962 at the inauguration of a hydroelectric station at Split, in Dalmatia. To an audience of 150,000, he spoke about the crisis in the LCY, stressing that the communists must resume the leading role in the country, which had been lost because of their "carelessness." Skirting the issue of the democratization of Yugoslav society, the marshal criticized unplanned industrialization, corruption, and social differences, which had recently spread because of the liberal climate and republican "localisms." He condemned those who threatened to strike in order to solve economic problems, railed against every nationalism and chauvinism, and pointed the finger at the intellectuals, especially "bourgeois writers," who were responsible for this mess.[269]

The Split speech, seen in the liberal circles as a return to Stalinism, attracted widespread public attention. Tito received an avalanche of letters with endorsements by citizens and requests for a purge of public life. Many of the party and state leaders, on the contrary, observed that "Tito has spoken severely, but this is not important. Certainly he did not mean what he said, and everything will be resolved shortly."[270] Kardelj was of a different opinion, perceiving the speech as directed against him and against Slovenia, and therefore persisted in his fight against centralism. "This enraged me," said Tito later, "and therefore our relations cooled off."[271] And there was not just the question of their mutual relations. There had been many past disagreements among the "comrades," but these had always been overcome. Now the split was final. Ranković said: "We all knew this, but we did not mention it. From where had all this come? Our contacts became so sporadic that we met only at party sessions, on official occasions, sometimes to hunt, but only when it was obligatory to go. As the nature of these meetings was mandatory, there was ill-will on all sides, great difficulty bearing each other, often verbal clashes."[272]

Tito's speech provoked turbulent discussions in Yugoslavia, which sounded—to quote Ranković—like an explicit repudiation of all particularisms, localisms, and exaltations of nationalism. Commissions were created to investigate the existence and the extent of illicit wealth in private hands, and measures were taken against embezzlement and economic offences, which in many enterprises provoked a real paralysis, since nobody was brave enough to make any decisions. The private sector was particularly under pressure, since the authorities obliged several artisans to close their businesses, and even aired the possibility of a new collectivization of land. The marshal himself remained struck by the wave of dogmatism that seemed to flood the country, so much so that he moderated his words some weeks later, stressing that he had no intention of setting off a "witch hunt."[273] These afterthoughts did not have much influence on the conservatives, who were on the crest of a wave and did not hide how they proposed to implement "brotherhood and unity." As the ambassador of East Germany—an arch-communist—observed with satisfaction, Tito's criticism entailed a progressive renewal of central planning. She noted, "The Yugoslav comrades openly recognize that they made great mistakes after 1950."[274] The entire concept of "integral self-management," so desired by Kardelj, seemed in peril. Just when he and Bakarić were ready to enact the new constitution, the "centralization of decentralization" called their project into question, a project on which they had been working since December 1960. The first draft, which featured enhanced self-management as well as envisioning the possibility of opposition within the framework of the party, should have been completed by the end of 1961. Because of the authoritarian turn of events, it was radically reworked in the following months. As Tito himself confided in 1962 to Adlai Stevenson, the American ambassador to the UN, only 10 percent survived from the original text. The rewritten version was presented to the public on 20 and 21 September 1962, just at the moment Tito was attempting to convince the most important Slovenian politicians to help him get rid of Kardelj. Stane Kavčič blocked this maneuver, stressing resolutely that there was no Tito-Kardelj conflict, but only a disagreement between Tito and Slovenia.[275]

The Approach to Moscow

Together with these dramatic internal events, there was an improvement of relations with Moscow that encouraged Tito, Ranković, and Gošnjak to propose striking the denunciation of Soviet hegemony from the LCY program. Thanks to the opposition of liberals like the Macedonian Lazar Koliševski, this initiative, however, was dropped.[276] The process of rapprochement between the two parties and states was topped off by Tito's visit to the Soviet Union from 3 to 20 December 1962. The composition of the Yugoslav delegation spoke eloquently about the power relationships in Belgrade: Ranković was included but not Kardelj, nor was Foreign Secretary Koča Popović. Popović had long asserted that to see in the USSR the "principal support of socialism" was wrong and that the "dogma of the international proletarian movement" was fatal.[277] Tito did not share his opinion, and talked at length with Khrushchev about the Yugoslav crisis, agreeing that now was the time to distance Kardelj from public life. The consonance between the Soviets and their guests was also shown by Tito's criticism upon his return of the decadent Western influence on literature and the arts in Yugoslavia, and even more by Ranković's speech in a plant in Kiev on 22 December, where he spoke about "the world working class, under the guidance of the Soviet Union."[278] This was the first time since Yugoslavia's expulsion from the Cominform that a Yugoslav politician had expressed such ideas, which provoked amazement from the hosts and concern from the liberals at home, not to mention reactions from the West. Since his words were later published by the Belgrade newspaper, *Politika*, it was evident that they were not a simple lapse in judgement.[279]

Only three days after the departure of the Yugoslav delegation to Moscow, on 16 December 1962, Kardelj went to Indonesia, where he spoke in a diametrically opposed manner. Influenced by the "useful and important discussions" that he had had a month before with the Swedish prime minister, Tage Erlander, he repeated the statement of the Seventh Congress of the LCY, and of the Non-Aligned Conference, stressing Yugoslavia's commitment to the fight against colonialism. At the same time, he attacked "hegemonism," presenting it as a contemporary form of imperialism. The anti-Soviet bias of this discourse was evident.[280] The Russian protests moved Tito to instruct Ranković to send Kardelj a telegram in which his opinions were criticized with the threat of an official reprimand from the party. As a consequence, a furious quarrel erupted between Kardelj and Ranković at the CC session on 27 December 1962 that was not limited to foreign policy, but touched upon problems regarding the further development of Yugoslav society. In protest, the Slovene practically withdrew from public life, preserving just two more or less representative functions: membership in the Council of the Federation and in the LCY presidency.[281] In spite of all obstacles, in the spring of 1963 he finished his work on the constitution. He was inadvertently aided by an article that had appeared in *Pravda* on 10 February of that year, which spoke about Yugoslav orthodoxy in such a panegyric way as to provoke worried conjectures as to its hidden significance among many in Belgrade. Did it imply that the LCY was returning to the fold? Without omitting that there were some leaders in the LCY who opposed Tito, thus departing from the "class positions of Marxism-Leninism," the CPSU organ stood up for Yugoslavia against Chinese attacks, stressing its closeness with the Soviet system.[282]

That pronouncement sounded more like an official declaration than a mere newspaper editorial, particularly because it ended with the appeal, "Proletarians of all countries, unite!" This was a phrase used by the Soviets in important documents. Although the Yugoslav correspondents in Moscow noticed this, in their reports they stressed only those passages that were palatable to the Yugoslav public. This renewed friendship with the Soviet Union was, according to them, completely in harmony with the non-aligned policy and self-management. The truth was otherwise, since the text in its entirety supported Khrushchev's stance about the unity of the "socialist camp."[283] Political commentator Slobodan Stanković, who was also the Yugoslav expert at Radio Free Europe, dedicated a detailed analysis to these events, in which he wondered whether the *Pravda* statements could not be seen as a proof of Tito's estrangement from his "particular path to socialism," from non-alignment and friendship with the West. He took comfort, however, stressing that all was not lost since there were still politicians in Yugoslavia who were opposed to a close understanding with Moscow.[284] He was right. At the beginning of 1963, as Koča Popović wrote in his diary, suspicions among the top level of Yugoslav politicians were awoken about a possible "parallel policy" developed by Ranković, which induced the Executive Committee of the LCY to dedicate their first session to that question. Referring to the Kiev speech, Stane Kavčič affirmed that in that period "Comrade Marko was a follower of a Soviet-type socialism," declaring contentiously that "Yugoslavia could not exist without a Scandinavian-style socialism."[285] Even more decisive was the attitude of some Serb leaders who were beginning to have doubts about Ranković's succession after Tito's retirement. Even the conservative Petar Stambolić maintained that "in Serbia we saw him as a considerable burden. I remember a conversation with Milentije Popović in 1963. We both agreed that it would be disgraceful if Ranković should take Tito's place. It has to be remembered that, in that period, everything was linked to the Russians, and we were very afraid we might once more be absorbed into their bloc. . . . It is necessary to frame the Ranković case in this context."[286]

These considerations remained limited to the power elite, but strengthened those who worried about conservative tendencies and wanted to oppose them. This increasingly hostile climate, which continued to build did not inspire

Ranković to act with the necessary prudence.[287] In his declarations, Tito also started to move closer to the reformist forces gathered around Kardelj, Bakarić, and their associates, and this was decisive. The result of the marshal's gradual passage from one camp to the other was the new constitution, adopted on 7 April 1963, in which the country assumed the name of the Socialist Federative Republic of Yugoslavia (SFRY). It appeared to be a temporary compromise. On the one hand it confirmed the role of the party in Yugoslav society, but on the other hand it preserved the basic point of the Ljubljana congress and its program: the pledge to self-management.[288]

Ranković's Pyrrhic Victory

Ranković, pulling the strings as organizational secretary of the party since 1940, was at first unaware how perilous Kardelj's maneuver to isolate him truly was: he did not consider the lofty words important, trusting his power to influence all appointments of any importance. These appointments were not made on the basis of a candidate's real value, but on the judgment of the secret services. In spite of his enormous authority, Ranković tried to further strengthen his position, vying for the office of state vice-president as a reward for his acceptance of the constitution. He received it at the last moment, at Tito's explicit request.[289]

Kardelj was furious. He did not have to read the *Washington Post*, which named Ranković as the recognized successor, to be aware of his perilous situation. "Ranković now is second to Tito in both party and government," wrote the CIA agents, "and his erstwhile competitor, Kardelj, has slipped after a prolonged period of political eclipse; many of the government functions he previously exercised will now be handled by Ranković. Thus Tito has been able to do what Khrushchev has not—to establish a clear heir apparent."[290]

They did not take into account that the marshal was not ready to relinquish control over the country, or to allow personalities too similar to his own into his entourage. Neither did they consider his wife, Jovanka, who was unwilling to tolerate anyone too authoritative at the court.[291]

Tito's first maneuvers against Ranković were prudent. Rumors reverberated, for instance, around Tito's decision in 1963 to fire the chief of the military counterintelligence service (Kontraobaveštajna služba; KOS), General Jefto Šašić, one of Ranković's friends. On the advice of Ivan Krajačić (Stevo, the Croatian éminence grise), his post was taken over by another Croat, Ivan Mišković, who until then had led the military police. Mišković's hands were notoriously blood-stained: after the 1945 victory, he had been involved as chief of the People's Defense Corps of Yugoslavia (Korpus Narodne Odbrane Jugoslavije) of the Third Army, and was responsible for the massacres of the Ustaša and Domobrani.[292]

At the beginning of 1965, an unexpected change also took place in the position of federal secretary for internal affairs. Vojislav Lukić, who led that department as Ranković's man, was forced to resign after only two years in favor of Milan Mišković, with the excuse that "the comrades in Serbia needed him [Lukić]." He was appointed organizational secretary of the Executive Committee of the Serb League of Communists, which meant an obvious loss of power. This change of cadres created an unheard of situation, in that for the first time there were two siblings at the head of the secret services, both military and civil—the brothers Mišković, neither under Ranković's control.[293]

Social and National Tensions

In spite of a disastrous earthquake in Skopje, which required rebuilding the city at great expense, the economic situation improved in 1963. In the first five months of that year, industrial production grew by 14 percent compared to the same period in the year prior, exports experienced constant growth, and the harvest was good.[294] But in 1964 the economy stalled again, so the authorities had to temporarily block imports and to apply for funding from the International Monetary Fund. The country was still mostly underdeveloped, with average productivity and salaries among the lowest in Europe. The workers were dissatisfied and started to strike, especially in Slovenia and Croatia, where public opinion overwhelmingly held that it was not possible to ask for any more sacrifices of the population. Tito himself, in a speech at Niš on 7 March, affirmed that living standards and development should go hand in hand, and that it was necessary to take into account individual needs in elaborating new economic plans. In spite of the opposition of Petar Stambolić, the president of the federal government, the Fourth Plenum of the LCY on 17 March 1964 decided to remove the economy from state control once again, and to condemn "bureaucratism" and redefine the role of the party. The plenum concluded, "Lead from inside, not outside or from above." By mid-April, the Federal Assembly had approved a resolution regarding further economic development with the support of the trade unions. Since the administrative measures taken until that point had not yielded satisfactory results, it was necessary to pass to a radical reform related to the distribution of incomes that would give individual enterprises sufficient room to maneuver.[295]

In an atmosphere strained by a revival of national polemics between Belgrade and Zagreb, preparations were made for the Eighth Congress of the LCY. The last one had been held in Ljubljana in 1958. According to the statute, the next congress should be organized five years later, but because of issues that had developed in the meantime, it had been postponed by a year and a half. Everyone involved was convinced of its importance, as it was evident that at the congress self-management would either be extended or simply demagogically confirmed. In the latter case, said Najdan Pašić, director of the Institute of Social Sciences, self-management would begin to shrink, remaining only a theory on paper and not applied in real life. The congress, continued Pašić, was going to be "paradoxical," because its task would be to create a more active party and, at the same time, to reduce its interference in the administration of economic and government affairs. It was necessary to give substance to the proposals formulated up to that point, which suggested that the party should play a guiding and not a controlling role in society.[296] These opinions, widespread in intellectual circles, stimulated a lively discussion in which Kardelj and Vukmanović (Tempo) took part as proponents of the liberalization against Petar Stambolić and numerous functionaries who mostly represented the underdeveloped republics. It was clear at the Fourth Plenum on March 1964 that the balance of power was such that neither faction would automatically get the upper hand.[297]

When the Eighth Congress finally took place in Belgrade from 7–13 December 1964 after months of internal debates, it became a forum where the most important topics, both economic and national, were openly discussed.[298] Tito, who after the turbulent plenum in March 1962 had tolerated the split between the liberals and conservatives, even trying to play them off one another to strengthen his regime, unexpectedly sided with Kardelj and his group at this congress. According to Ranković, since 1963 he had been influenced by the Slovenes and the Croats: "He is a turncoat. He did not even try to dissimulate. He has set up internal and state politics in a confederative way."[299] "During 1963 and 1964," observed an incensed Ranković, "Tito was constantly fawned over in Slovenia. Hunting lodges were built for him, hunts and parties were organized. . . . The Slovenes coordinated their policy with the Croats. He was surrounded by Stevo Krajačić, by Krleža and Bakarić, trying to keep him away from the Belgrade comrades. . . . In 1964, he was away from Belgrade for ten months, at Brioni, at Brdo, near Kranj, in different localities in Slovenia and Croatia."[300]

At the Eighth Congress, organized by Kardelj and his colleagues, Tito unexpectedly dealt with the key issues of the country, which in the past had not been discussed on such important occasions.[301] Although as usual he spoke extemporaneously and without any particular élan, he was quite explicit: he recognized that "chauvinist elements, a legacy of the old Yugoslavia, were still smoldering under the surface" and were present everywhere "in cultural life, the economy, in research and in the historiography." At the same time, he condemned the bureaucratic tendencies of those who tried to ignore the role of the republics and of the provinces. He attacked "administrative and centralizing methods," blaming the supporters for an "artificial" single Yugoslav nation.

The fact that he enrolled at the congress as a "Croat" for the first time was significant.[302]

Ranković, who had been informed in advance that "vampire nationalism" would be condemned at the congress, tried to protest to Tito, stressing that this move would ruin Yugoslavia. Such ill-will was created between them that they stopped communicating for two months. Ranković also tried unsuccessfully to convince Kardelj to condemn not only federal centralism, but also the "state-ism" of the republics, which in his opinion was equally damaging to the Yugoslav idea.[303] In the discussion that followed Tito's speech, the awareness emerged that the different ethnic groups of the country were in different phases of development, something that had never been formulated in such an explicit way. Kardelj articulated one of the key pronouncements on this issue when he stressed in his paper the right of every nation to live according to the results of its work.[304] This assertion, which accepted the discrepancy between the republics and was repeated in the final resolution, rejected the idea of a single Yugoslav people as an expression of bureaucratic centralism. In a proposal by Stane Kavčič, with which Dobrica Ćosić disagreed, the final resolution of the Eighth Congress affirmed that "every nation had the right to dispose of the surplus of its work. This right was not subject to the will of the state. The federal government was only a coordinator of the development and economic policy of the individual republics."[305]

In order to stress the importance of autonomy in the internal life of the LCY as well, it was decided that from then on the Congresses of the Republic Leagues should be organized before and not after the federal one, as had been usual. This meant that the local leaders would not be merely executors of a preordained political line but could influence its formulation. The only disagreement came from Ranković, since in his speech at the congress he stressed the importance of "democratic centralism," both in the party and in the state. He pointed out that factions were building up in the LCY that questioned its role in society. Although he was not in tune with Tito and the comrades, his report was approved "unanimously," and with the obligatory "frenzied" applause.[306] It was clear that the reform announced at the Eighth Congress could not be implemented without a decline in his power and from that moment on his fate appeared sealed.

One of the most important events of the Eighth Congress was the election of a new Central Committee of 155 members, with the unanimous confirmation of Tito as its secretary general. The same day, an enlarged Executive Committee was elected, composed of nineteen rather than thirteen members, as in the past. The two deputy secretaries of the League, Aleksandar Ranković and Edvard Kardelj, were joined by a third, Veljko Vlahović, who was more popular in the party than they.[307] The election of this triumvirate put to rest the rumors that had persisted over the prior few weeks in Belgrade that Tito might resign as secretary general of the LCY and settle for the party's presidency. He spoke about his plans for the future at the press conference on 13 December, saying that he felt fit enough (and indeed looked it) to continue leading the party.[308]

Another Economic Reform

Tito described the new reform envisaged by the Eighth Congress as a cut into the social tissue, "as a surgery," and everyone was aware that it would not be painless.[309] In fact, it was not just a correction of the system, but a comprehensive plan that would take several years to implement. The Yugoslav leaders dealt with the errors of the past, aiming to change not just the economy but also the political and ideological structure of both party and state. They were not building on sand, since after the war the country had experienced notable progress and modernization. The income per capita had reached five hundred American dollars (still modest, but better than ever before), the infrastructure was more or less sound, and the earnings from tourism approached 100 million dollars a year. Yugoslavia had a foreign debt of a $1.2 billion, but its industry was growing rapidly; like Japan, it was one of the fastest growing economies. This favored progressive urbanization and the influx of peasants into the proletarian masses, which gave the young a chance to escape traditional country life and discover the world. "This was such a leap," wrote Dušan Bilandžić, "that it did not happen for centuries."[310]

Between 23 and 24 July 1965, the Federal Assembly approved thirty laws on economic reform. Departing from the practice of communist states, Tito decentralized the authority for decision-making, introduced "market socialism," and started replacing party hacks with professional managers. The proposed goals concerned an increase in production, technological modernization, reduction of costs, and the viability of enterprises in the hope of reaching international markets with Yugoslav products. For this purpose, it was decided that enterprises could dispose of 70 percent of their earnings as they saw fit. The government also wanted a quick improvement in balance of payments, fiscal consolidation, and debt reduction, and counted on the help of the United States, Great Britain, France, Italy, and the Soviet Union for assistance.[311] The dinar was devalued with the intention of achieving convertibility and increasing exports.[312] For Yugoslavia to do this was a bold, unprecedented move. The state subvention was abolished and, at the same time, import duties were increased by 20 percent. Considerable importance was attached to tourism, so borders were opened and visas eliminated in spite of a lot of internal opposition.[313]

There was also substantial opposition to the initiative having to do with small private enterprises, which were no longer encumbered by high taxation, as they had been in the past. In the West, the reform was greeted with favor, given that Yugoslavia accepted the laws of the market and was the only socialist state to allow foreign investments.[314] In order to sustain Tito's regime, in November 1965 the Americans signed an agreement with the Belgrade government to deliver seven hundred thousand tons of wheat, worth $46 million, with the promise not to claim any payment for the next two years.[315] At that moment, nobody considered the negative aspects of the reform, including the fact that the two more developed northern republics, Slovenia and Croatia, would benefit from it (since they had advanced economies as compared to the other republics and were therefore keen to enter Western markets), whereas the rest of the country would stand by and watch.

The reform started at the end of July 1965 in the hope of stabilizing the economy and improving the living standards of the population. The result, however, was an increase in the price of consumer goods. Inflation, already present, began to spike. And since the subventions for rent, electricity, gas, and public transport were abolished, these services saw a considerable increase in price.[316] What happened in practice once again demonstrated that implementing the reform was more difficult than first thought: there were limited means for the modernization of production, and the administrative cadres were not flexible enough to adopt the new rules of the market.[317] The authorities resorted to severe restrictions on loans, but this provoked the collapse of economic growth and an upward spiral of unemployment. Tito, Kardelj, Bakarić, and other leaders tried to convince the people that these were just temporary difficulties and that reform was essential for the advancement of society, but without much success, especially in Serbia and in other less developed areas.[318] What worried them most—and this was not the first time Tito had lamented about this—was the fact that opposition to the reform did not come primarily from the masses but from the most prominent politicians. Many reacted with passive resistance to this radical change in the way of thinking, hoping that the "capitalist experiment" would fail. Stane Kavčič, the secretary of the Slovenian League, highlighted the differences of opinion among prominent communists in an article published by *Borba* on 2 November 1965 entitled "Wrong Observations by Some Communists." He argued with those who wanted to give state authority to the party and were unable to understand it was necessary to reshape the role of politics in the economy in order to assert the laws of the market.[319]

Dissatisfaction with the new line was especially manifest in Serbia and Montenegro, where passive resistance was joined by an open boycott. The protests were based on ideological premises, but also on concrete interests. At issue was the fear that the central bureaucracy and the secret services (largely made up of Serbs and Montenegrins) would lose control of the country. Ranković, considered the guardian of the Bolshevik tradition, became the catalyst of this apprehension. As a result he was increasingly isolated among those at the top of the party, and often quarreled with Tito. Ranković was aware of this and became edgy: his trembling hands, his furtive snatched glances, and his drinking habits betrayed him. When Vladimir Dedijer dropped by after seven years of absence to ask what was new, Ranković answered laughing: "Vlado, I will end up as a scribe at Vrška Čupa" (in the mountains on the border with Bulgaria, which meant the end of the world).[320]

Meanwhile, Tito lived in paranoid fear of his "comrades," who he believed intercepted his conversations, robbed him, and plotted attempts on his life. "Suspicion of everybody was in his nature. Innervated his character," Ranković later wrote. In the first part of the sixties Tito was at loggerheads with three chiefs from his cabinet, and even with Milan Žeželj, his bodyguard, who was faithful as a dog but hostile to Jovanka and her growing despotism at the court. On the basis of the groundless suspicion that she zealously nurtured, Tito required Ranković to arrest these people, interrogate them, put them on trial, and condemn them. "Leka" tried to calm him in vain, instead drawing his anger.[321] In 1964 something worse happened: Slobodan Penezić (Krcun), president of the Serb government, fell into disgrace. One of Ranković's minions, known for having arrested Draža Mihailović in 1946, Penezić was often too outspoken, for example when he declared that the stability of Yugoslavia depended on an agreement between Serbs and Croats: "We control the federal police, they the army, and everything is O.K."[322] But on another occasion he went too far. During a railway journey to Zagreb, already tipsy, he said to the marshal: "Old One, you should not be worried as long as we Serbs are loyal to you. But if you lose us, your Croats and Slovenes will not save you."[323] Tito did not ignore these threatening words, even more so since Jovanka had been trying to convince him that the Serbs had constituted a danger to him for some time. He asked Ranković to open a party investigation about "Krcun," at the beginning of November 1964. In December, Penezić, who used to say about himself that he had "arms bloodied to the shoulders," had a fatal road accident. He was forty-six.[324] According to one version, a mysterious liquid corroded the front tire of his car. According to another, the axle broke, while according to a third the driver lost control of the vehicle, crashing into a tree.[325] Although Penezić had saved his life during the Battle of Sutjeska, Tito did not attend the funeral, preferring to receive a Hollywood star at Brdo.[326]

Ranković's Fall

In September 1965, Vladimir Bakarić was back on the political scene after a long sick leave. With Kardelj, who admired him "for his deep theoretical spirit" and for his "highly developed political sense" he visited a Zagreb expo fair, the country's most important. As both were interested in creating a modern and democratic state, naturally within the limits of the socialist regime, they had a series of discussions that led to the subsequent fall of Ranković.[327] In the context of this reform policy, and also with the conviction that Western aid would disappear if the Yugoslav economy did not recover, Kardelj openly analyzed the contemporary problems of society, proposing a radical transformation. To everyone's surprise, at the session of the Executive Committee of the LCY on 12 and 13 November 1965 he resumed speaking about Yugoslavia in a way that could be considered bold and unprejudiced: "After all, I will tell you, comrades, that we are not united because of Yugoslavia, but because of socialism. And if we will not understand that it is socialism that unites Yugoslavia, nothing else can unite it."[328] According to Kardelj, three different political currents existed in the country: the Slovenian and Croat, which was interested in ample autonomy for the republics; the centralist, represented by the underdeveloped republics; and the hegemonic, especially strong in Serbia. The latter was the most authoritative and was the most likely to prevail when the old leaders eventually disappeared. In order to prevent this danger it was necessary to transform the state, as far as possible, into a forum where the different republics could coordinate their interests. Although this idea foresaw two guardians of the socialist order, the LCY and the army, it appeared too daring to the party leaders, as it assigned to the state only the function of a "technical instrument"—as in a confederation—appointed to mediate between the parties. As a result it was not developed further, which does not mean that Kardelj abandoned the idea.[329]

These problems remained unresolved, increasing the fracture between the "liberals" and the "conservatives" who, according to a CIA informant, did everything possible to boycott the reform.[330] The resistance was spearheaded by Ranković, who Kardelj respected for his contributions as one of the most prominent leaders of the party and its secret services and for the firmness of his thought and his organizational capacities. However, at the moment when new social and political rules needed to be established in the country, Ranković became a liability because of two traits of his character: "The inclination to overrate coercive means and the use of state discipline, which led the LCY down the path of centralism, of coteries, of pragmatic decisions without any sensitivity toward national issues."[331] For these reasons, Ranković had to be removed.

In Belgrade at the end of 1965, the rumors that Ranković would assume power before Tito's death grew louder.[332] This was also confirmed by telegrams sent to some ambassadors abroad, where it was written that the health of the marshal was not good (he had the flu) and that changes were ahead.[333] Tito, who in the past had nurtured friendly feelings toward "Leka," suspected that he was anxious to replace him, and for a long time could not decide what to do. As he confessed later, this was also because he had to wait until the balance of power in the party and the army were in his favor.[334] This happened between 1965 and 1966. Shortly after Christmas, Ranković resigned from the presidency of the influential Veterans Association, which he had led for decades. This was significant, as was the CC of the Slovenian League's contemporaneous criticism of the UDBA (or the Service for National Security, as it had been recently renamed), asking for the limitation of its powers, a proposal shared by the Macedonians who, like the Slovenes and Croats, were terrified of Serb nationalism.[335]

Public opinion in Belgrade saw things differently. Although in the past the Serbs hated Ranković because he had masterminded the arrest of Draža Mihailović, they now adored him, seeing in him a protector of their interests. When he drove through the city center, pedestrians applauded him, shouting "Leka, Leka," or sometimes "Leka for president."[336] This and much more reached Tito's ears. But what was critical for Ranković was his weakness in the Serbian League, since a liberal trend had increased within it from May 1965 onward, opposing internal "enemy elements."[337] By mid-March 1966, this progressive group exploited a session of the local CC in order to condemn the hostile attitude of the leading politicians of the republic toward the reforms, stressing that they should be removed in favor of younger cadres. During the discussion the liberals said that the past errors of the Serb leadership had caused the resurgence of "nationalist phenomena" in the republic and also among neighboring ethnic groups.[338] The warnings against nationalism were constantly repeated in the following weeks, culminating on "Youth Day" on 25 May, when Tito himself mentioned them in his speech, referring obviously to the situation in Serbia.[339]

Into this atmosphere of intrigue, tension, and uncertainty Bakarić appeared. He had lauded the UDBA on the twentieth anniversary of its foundation in 1964, thus emphasizing its connection with the people and the party.[340] Two years later, he took a completely different position, using his ability to operate behind the scenes. With Tito's consent, in a series of speeches he criticized the prevailing climate of suspicion in Yugoslav society, and with this implicitly Ranković. At the beginning of March, he gave an interview to *Borba* in which he condemned the nationalism and chauvinism that had spread not just among intellectuals but also among the workers and the young. Self-critically, he recognized that he had avoided dealing with the issue in the past, convinced that the time was not ripe for overcoming such wrongs, but he added that "it is clear that I made a mistake in ignoring the problem."[341] During the first half of 1966, Ranković seemed still steadfast, in spite of the menacing storm on the horizon. At the end of March Tito sent him to the Soviet Union at the helm of a delegation that took part in the Twenty-Third Congress of the CPSU. "Comrade Marko," who in 1964 had approved close collaboration between the secret services of the two countries, was received cordially and treated like a head of state. During a dinner attended by Kremlin leadership, one of the members of the Yugoslav delegation toasted "the future young president of the Socialist Federative Republic."[342] It was even said that Ranković had discussed Tito's physical decline with the Soviets, which he later denied.[343] In mid-May he visited Poland as a guest of the local workers' party. On that occasion there were no lack of rumors: it was said that in Warsaw he met secretly with Suslov, the éminence grise of the CPSU, which seemed to announce a coup d'état.[344] Tito, who was informed in detail, adopted a frosty attitude toward him. When during a reception a group of young people started to sing a song about the heroic deeds of "Comrade Marko," somebody asked him: "Comrade Tito, how it is possible that this is sung?" The marshal did not answer, but left immediately.[345]

The Plot

Tito's minion, Ivan Krajačić (Stevo), the prewar agent of the NKVD and Soviet "executioner," played an important role in the plot organized against Ranković.[346] He had a special position at the court because of his past, but also because the marshal feared or was in debt to him for reasons that were unclear. (The story goes that in 1948 Krajačić was tasked by Stalin to kill Tito. Tito, alerted by West German intelligence, invited him on a lonely drive and, during a stop, challenged him to shoot. Comrade Stevo did not.)[347] Krajačić always had the final say about Tito's security and could behave in Tito's presence with complete liberty, even raising his voice, which others were obviously not allowed to do.[348] In addition to Stevo, Federal Secretary for Internal Affairs Milan Mišković and his brother Ivan, chief of military intelligence, were also part of the plot. Later, Ranković remembered that Krajačić, the Croatian "Rasputin," invited him several times "to go hunting, where an accident could happen."[349] But since "Comrade Marko" always prudently declined such invitations, they had to get rid of him in a different way. It was not clear until the very end, however, as Kardelj confessed to his friends, whether Tito would support the liberal or the conservative faction, and who would be put in the dock: him or Ranković.[350]

Kardelj was not directly involved in the plot, since he had withdrawn to Slovenia for "health reasons."[351] This does not mean he did not know about it or that he disapproved of it. Some months after Ranković's fall, he confided in the American political scientist Fred Werner Neal that the Executive Committee had acted against "Comrade Marko" as a body, adding that the UDBA agents had developed a feverish workload in the months prior. With interceptions, recordings of conversations, and even open threats, they tried to convince high officials to boycott the reform, especially the rule about the "rotation" introduced by the Eighth Congress. According to this measure, decided on to prevent the creation of "baronies," no official could occupy the same post for more than two years. The system would begin with the elections to be held in May 1967, in view of which a special commission for the identification of candidates already existed. After the elections a radical administrative turnover would take place—about thirty thousand high officials would be replaced—in part because no one could occupy both party and state posts at the same time. Tito was exempted from these regulations, of course, but Ranković was not, although he also was not ready to renounce the vice-presidency of the SFRY and his appointments in the LCY.[352]

Neither Kardelj nor Bakarić could accept this idea, however, and Tito certainly could not, aware as he was that the Serbs, under the leadership of a strongman, could impose their hegemony on the entire country.[353] In his discussion with Neal, Kardelj was charitable toward Ranković, although it was known that at this point they were no longer on speaking terms. He recognized that "Comrade Marko" was not personally responsible for the UDBA's abuses, and blamed the leadership itself for leaving him too long in charge of the secret police: "We should have given him other jobs to do."[354] Tito was less indulgent, because in the past he had trusted him to such an extent that in 1948 he installed a direct phone line between his residence and Ranković's, in case of emergencies. But now, after receiving new information about bugs in his own residence, Tito convinced himself that "Marko" had plotted against him and acted accordingly.[355]

Edo Brajnik, the Slovenian deputy secretary of internal affairs, started the chain of events. At the request of the leadership of his republic, he sent a letter to Tito on 15 June 1966 asking for the convocation of the Executive Committee with just one item on the agenda: "The question of state security."[356] Its members met the next day at the marshal's Belgrade residence, where they were informed of the investigation by two Croat police experts whom Krajačić had secretly sent to the capital to examine the homes of Tito and other prominent individuals. As "Comrade Stevo" said, the two had done well in discovering, among other things, that bugs had been installed in the private apartments of the president, and even in his bedroom, which were connected to "Leka's" nearby villa.[357]

Ranković only became aware of the mess he was in during the Executive Committee session, to which he had been invited just an hour before. While his colleagues had been informed in detail about the matter under discussion, he had been kept in dark.[358] On that occasion, Tito announced that the UDBA had also spied on Kardelj and other leaders, stressing that a similar police system "has in the past cost the Soviet Union 15 million lives," referring to the Stalinist terror.[359] (He forgot to say that on different occasions he had been the one to give the order to install bugs in his residence, and in those of his comrades, and that Kardelj had done the same in his office).[360] The members of the Executive Committee, Ranković included, agreed that such methods should stop, although Ranković expressed doubts about the veracity of the accusations. In response, Tito proposed the formation of a commission, headed by the Macedonian Krste Crvenkovski, charged with an overview of the security department and its methods. In order to be as authoritative as possible, it was composed of six members, one for each republic. At the same time, he suggested the creation of another "technical" commission, which in fact already existed, though he wished to grant it official status.[361] Ranković offered to resign from all his posts, stressing that he felt responsible for the UDBA's activity. Although the session was short, he returned home worn out, perfectly conscious that he was the victim of a plot. To his wife, who came to meet him, he said: "It's all over because of some stupid interceptions" (a euphemism for bugging), adding under his breath: "If they even existed."[362]

The party and state commission finished its work on 20 June 1966, submitting the results to the Executive Committee. It was not considered appropriate to query Ranković, even though he had asked Crvenkovski to allow his voice to be heard. Crvenkovski was asked not to interrogate Ranković, since the marshal wanted to speak to him personally. Those who were interviewed were at first cleverly reticent, it being obvious—as Miko Tripalo, one of the members of the commission, said—that "amateurs," as he and his colleagues were, could not cope with professional policemen.[363] Initially, they all tried to defend Ranković and Stefanović (Ćeća), the UDBA chief, later deciding to sacrifice the latter to save "Comrade Marko." It was only when a safe was found at the Department of Foreign Affairs containing files with intelligence reports about numerous ambassadors and secretaries of state, which were filled with Ranković's and Stefanović's notes, did the first confessions started to pour in. Tripalo wrote: "Something was clear pretty soon. The security service had a powerful position in society and depended on a small group of officials. It would be difficult to say that Ranković was preparing a coup against Tito, nearer to the truth was that he was getting ready to succeed Tito smoothly when he died."[364]

The Crvenkovski Commission concluded that the security service had done good work, especially during the split with Stalin, but after the introduction of self-management it was unable to resist the temptation to place itself above society. Wanting to be "one of the key factors in the policy process," it tried to control not only the party and the state, but also a series of economic enterprises, in order to direct investments. It became "more or less a monopoly of some individuals while its leader, Aleksandar Ranković (a.k.a. Marko a.k.a. Leka), acquired a political significance similar to the CC of the LCY."[365] The discussion of this document in the Executive Committee moved those present to attack Ranković because of his presumed intentions when it came to the fight for succession, and to speak—as he said—"like gossipy women," repeating rumors spread by some of the wives of highly placed people stemming "from imaginary fears over the fate of their husbands."[366] Pepca Kardelj took a prominent role in this hostile chatter. More lenient toward "Comrade Marko" was Kardelj himself. At the end of June, he met him by chance in the elevator of the CC palace in Belgrade.

"Do you really think," asked Ranković, "that I was taping Tito?"

"I don't believe it. You know well, however, that Tito is obsessed with the fear of being killed by Serbs," Kardelj replied.

"I did not know this," said Ranković.

"Marko, but you should know this," reproached Kardelj.[367]

At its session on 20 June 1966, the Executive Committee decided to convene the Fourth Plenum on 1 July at Brioni, where the Crvenkovski Commission would present its final report. The defense secretary, Ivan Gošnjak, did not agree with this way of proceeding against Ranković; although they were not friends, a bond existed between them because they were both hardliners. He thought that it was unfair to ascribe all of Yugoslavia's problems to Ranković alone. He proposed to Tito the forced retirement of all the "historical cadres," and the constitution of a new leadership. The marshal accepted the suggestion, but later distanced himself from it.[368] Gošnjak did not give up: on 25 June, he organized a meeting between Tito and Ranković in which the marshal tried to convince Leka of the possibility of future collaboration. Saying this—Leka later told his wife—Tito automatically put on his sunglasses to hide his eyes. He could not, however, refrain from reproaching Marko for the bad company with which he had lately surrounded himself—those spreading rumors that Tito was ailing and needed drugs to go on.[369]

The action attempted against Ranković was risky: the UDBA had weapons and tanks at its disposal. Since the army and its secret service, KOS, rallied around the marshal, Ranković did not have much leeway, even if he had wanted to organize a coup d'état, which many who were party to the plot considered possible. In any case, they battened down the hatches, posting guards at all the radio and TV stations in mid-June and mobilizing the police. In doing so, they used mostly Slovenes and Croats, since the Serbs were considered unreliable.[370] The situation was so tense that the General Staff organized Tito's secret departure from Belgrade because, according to confidential information, there was a danger of his being kidnapped. (According to another version, he was escorted to Brioni by Krajačić in his Mercedes along back roads.)[371] The archipelago, which in summer was full of select guests, was on that occasion nearly empty because, apart from army and police units, there were only members of the CC. The tension of the time is well expressed by Krajačić's letter to Tito on 1 July 1966. Normally his handwriting was quite regular, but on that occasion he wrote nervously, so that some words are illegible. From the context it is clear, however, that Comrade Stevo had been in touch with Bakarić and Mišković, and that the latter was ready "to do everything necessary to clarify the situation, because those who surround you are treacherous, so we need to solve this."[372]

When they disembarked at Brioni, the members of the CC were given the material related to the discussion for the following day. Most of it was published later, but not the so-called "documentation," which was supposed to be returned and which contained information on the intercepted communications and the names of those involved.[373] Ranković, the last one to learn of the gravity of his position, only became aware of it late at night when he received the papers prepared for the discussion. The file contained new accusations never before mentioned. He was so shaken that he felt sick. It was later ascertained that he had suffered a mild stroke, about which the doctor who had been called informed no one, not even the patient himself.[374]

At the session of the Fourth Plenum, Tito started with self-criticism for not having dealt with the accumulated problems before, as he had been aware of them since March 1962. He accused Ranković and his deputy, Stefanović, of having tolerated the illegal activity of the UDBA group, which had tried to seize power and hinder the development of the self-managed democracy. To this end, he had been spied on and manipulated, and been given partial or even false information. As he described it: "This is a sectarian struggle for power, a factious one."[375]

During the turbulent CC session, which lasted several hours, Ranković was physically destroyed, feverish, and with a strong pain in his chest. As one of those present relates, he appeared more like a coatrack than a living man.[376] He tried, however, to address the floor immediately after Tito and Crvenkovski. At first he read a written declaration which contained no reply to the accusations against him. Although he admitted that the UDBA methods had been "dirty," he did not recognize them as his own, since for some time he had not led the service directly. He denied being a Serb nationalist but was interrupted by hostile shouts. During a break, Gošnjak took pity on him and suggested that he leave, since he would not be able to endure the rest. But he refused, saying that he wanted to hear what they would say about him to the end.[377]

At the end of the discussion, however, he had a psychological breakdown. He recognized his moral and political responsibility for the faults committed, although without servility. He promised that he would oppose as well as he were able all those who would try to turn him against the LCY, denying forcefully that he been informed about specific UDBA machinations or that he had plotted against Tito.[378] He told him, standing face to face, that "If at the 1962 plenum the Slovenians saved Kardelj, I am happy for the unity of the state, that the Serbs did not save me." And further: "It will not be difficult, Old One, to get rid of me, but in Yugoslavia there will be a deluge after me."[379] Tito chose to ignore this ominous prophecy. He closed the session with relief, thanking the members of the CC and stressing that everything went better than expected. He even praised Ranković for his "good behavior."[380]

For the Yugoslav public, who were in the dark about party infighting, the Brioni plenum had a shattering effect. In Slovenia the reaction was restrained, whereas the Croats were elated, stressing that "there would be no return to the past."[381] They saw in Ranković not just the symbol of the police dictatorship, but also as a guardian of Serbian interests and the desire to keep Serbia as the leading republic.[382] Serbia was shocked, the majority being convinced that they had lost their point man at a decisive moment when the question of succession was pressing. The general mood was expressed three days before the Brioni plenum by Dobrica Ćosić in a letter to the marshal in which he inquired about the reasons for the "scandalous" case, convinced that it had anti-Serb implications. His protest remained private, however, and had just one consequence: that the relations between Tito and the famous writer were severed, pushing him to be increasingly critical of the "Brioni regime."[383] Ćosić expressed the sentiments of those Serbs who believed in the Yugoslav ideal, provided that it coincided with the values and interests of their nation. In this sense he was dangerous, since because of his fame and popularity it was not considered appropriate to "liquidate" him.[384]

On 14 July, the Federal Assembly examined Ranković's request to be relieved of his office as vice-president of the republic. Since he had applied for a twenty-day leave "for health reasons," the session was held in his absence. The procedure was quick, lasting just ten minutes. The president of the assembly, Edvard Kardelj, read the resignation and, since nobody took the floor, it was accepted. Moving on to the second point of the agenda, he announced that thirty-six deputies had proposed Koča Popović as the new vice-president. This motion was received with applause, although the latter had not been politically active since 1964, when he ceased to be the secretary for foreign affairs.[385] His designation was a balm for the wounded pride of the Serbs, although nobody had any illusions that this isolated intellectual could have any decisive influence. "While Tito exists and he is the leader, the LCY will be what it is: an amorphous Stalinism, liberalized and conformist," wrote Dobrica Ćosić.[386]

The downfall of Ranković triggered a large purge in the UDBA and the party, especially in Serbia and Montenegro. The purge spread to Slovenia and Croatia, as well, although the secret services in the two republics had always been in the hands of the local political elites.[387] Thousands of officials were arrested, condemned to jail, expelled from the party, or dismissed. The LCY committees at every level competed to openly denounce the corruption and the abuses of the services, declaring that such crookedness would now finally end. The newspapers were full of hypocritical questions, like "how it was possible?" or polemics over "our version of Stalinism" and revelations about the illicit activities of the UDBA. Among other misdeeds, it was discovered that in Croatia alone the secret police had amassed 2 million files, which meant that nearly every adult had one.[388] The worst crimes of the postwar period, including the massacres of the collaborationists and the outrages perpetrated against the peasants and the Cominformists, were not, however, mentioned. "They were not discussed," wrote a friend of Ranković, "because it was not possible for them to wash their hands like Pontius Pilate."[389]

The Croats used the occasion to get rid of their "Rasputin," Ivan Krajačić (Stevo), who had been the main organizer of Ranković's downfall. He provided the pretext for his own removal on 3 July 1966, at the inaugural ceremony of a huge monument in memory of Ustaša victims at the Jasenovac concentration camp. After the official ceremony he entered the banquet hall, where party grandees from each of the republics were assembled and, in a state of euphoria over his recent triumph, he began shouting at the Serb delegation: "Out of here, Chetniks! Here rest honorable Croats. We have built this concentration camp for you Serbs! For Chetniks and Gypsies! We have killed too few here!"[390] Tito was shocked and outraged when informed. Krajačić was expelled from the Croatian Central Committee and other offices because of "bad health," which did not, however, mean that he had fallen from grace. For his birthday on 28 August 1966, he was awarded a high state honor and was warmly greeted by Jovanka and Tito himself.[391]

The Reorganization of the UDBA and the Liberalization of the LCY

At the end of July 1966, a commission of twenty members was created, which was instructed to reform the Service for National Security. As Milan Mišković, the federal secretary for internal affairs, said in several interviews, its task was to define the role of this body within the self-managed system, and to reestablish public control over it.[392] De facto, everything remained as before: although it was divided between the six republics, the UDBA continued to observe all those who attracted its attention, sending the results of this activity to Belgrade, where the confidential material kept accruing.[393]

More important than this commission was the one established to rejuvenate the LCY. It had forty members and began work with great flourish on 15 July 1966. Its main task was to reshape the party administration so that it did not end up in the hands of a single individual again. Mijalko Todorović, its president and a supporter of Kardelj's, declared to the press that the "LCY had, in recent years, been lagging behind the general development of our society," and had even "hampered instead of promoted the development of our society at many points." The Fourth Plenum, in his opinion, had extended action for further development or direct democracy and self-management to areas "which have so far been closed or not opened far enough" and admitted that one of those areas was LCY itself.[394] In October, a new plenum would be convened to approve the work of the commission and to decide whether it was necessary to organize an extraordinary congress.

The members of the Todorović Commission began tackling the problem with zeal. The Slovenian, Mitja Ribičič, even questioned the principle of democratic centralism, while his Macedonian colleague Krste Crvenkovski ventured to predict the disappearance of the LCY in the near future, asserting that the country was on the eve of a "non-party democracy." With their collaborators, they wanted to "cut off the head" of those who were close to Ranković's faction, and to distribute power in the LCY to prevent its concentration in the hands of the few. They believed that the ability to decide and the means to govern should pass from four secretaries and the Executive Committee to the entire CC, which had until then been an "amorphous body" without any real influence.[395] A cold shower came on 1 September in the form of a speech by Tito, in which he distanced himself from this way of thinking, refused every hint that the LCY might disappear and repeated the Leninist vision of party cadres, subjected to military discipline.[396]

At the Fifth Plenum, convened on 4 October, the participants agreed upon a formal but not substantial reorganization of the League. It was clear that the old guard held on to its power, since Tito himself "irritatedly" demanded that the LCY must have the right to establish the political line and to apply it directly, if necessary.[397] The democratization process had come to nothing. In his closing speech, the marshal expressed his astonishment at the dissatisfaction over the outcome of the plenum, which was conveyed by Koča Popović in an interview that *Politika* planned to publish on 29 November 1966, a public holiday. In it, the vice-president of the republic affirmed that "the task assigned to the party is more difficult than to govern with the help of police or military discipline, like some South American general. To do this, ideas are not necessary. But if we want to build socialism and implement it, we have to confront a much more demanding task."[398]

Tito did not like this opinion nor the interview. Although the paper had already been printed, it was never distributed.

Ranković's Pardon and the Seventh Plenum of the CC

On 9 December 1966, the Federal Assembly confirmed the decision by the Executive Committee asserting that Aleksandar Ranković had been involved in anti-constitutional activity and had worked against the aims of the socialist society.[399] At the end of the year, however, Tito decided not to prosecute Comrade Marko or another eighteen of his collaborators out of respect for Serb public opinion, but also because much of the evidence against them was shaky.[400] At the top of the party the opinion prevailed that the "sins" ascribed to Ranković should be considered a struggle for power, rather than criminal activity. After having been pardoned, Leka retired to private life. Apart from a short memo about his "shameful exclusion from the party and political life," which remained secret for a long time, he did nothing that could seem compromising or bothersome to the regime.[401] Nevertheless, he lived under police surveillance, which from time to time warned him to beware of possible Ustaše assassination attempts. He did not take the threat seriously, nor did he hide his low opinion of Tito. He compared him to Joseph Fouché, the ominous minister of police under Napoleon, quoting a French writer who had described his personality in this way: "He is a total traitor, because the treachery is not his aim or tactical decision, but his essence. . . . During my life, I have never met somebody who could be more egotistical and more mistrustful of the others. . . . With time, with years, he trusted the people around him less and less. . . . How often he said: arrest, judge, condemn, kick out, remove from a high post to a lower one."[402]

At the beginning of July 1967, the Seventh Plenum of the LCY was convened in Belgrade. It focused on the recent Arab-Israeli War and the military coup in Greece, but also on internal problems related to the reorganization of the party. Characteristic of the new atmosphere, which was critical of the strong influence of the secret services and somewhat more liberal, was the sharp criticism of Tito's decision to allow the Soviets to use Yugoslav air space to send military aid to Egypt, and of his decision to give a large number of tanks to Nasser.[403] Moreover, without informing the Executive Committee the marshal took part in two meetings of the Warsaw Pact, in Moscow and Budapest. During these meetings he agreed with Soviet policy in the Middle East, and on his own initiative broke off diplomatic relations with Israel, the creation of which he had supported twenty years before.[404] This decision, arbitrary and contrary to the sympathies of public opinion, caused an outcry: ten of the most important party members met confidentially and agreed that Tito could not remain head of state if he continued to maintain friendly connections with the Soviet Union, since such a policy was harmful to the interests of the country. Kardelj, Bakarić, and Koča Popović called for his resignation and only General Gošnjak defended him.[405] Among the party *nomenklatura* it was openly said that "the Old One did not understand the contemporary situation," that he had "a persecution complex" and did not know "what he was saying and doing."[406] Tito, of course, did not allow himself to be intimidated: he threatened to address the Federal Assembly if the "comrades" criticized him further, well aware that in such a case he would have the upper hand because of his charisma and authority.[407]

Beyond this dramatic discussion, the Seventh Plenum buried the ambitions of those who had wanted to overhaul the party, forcing them to recognize Tito's continued guiding role. "Democratic centralism," said Mijalko Todorović, one of the spokespersons of the reformers, "is subject to new conditions but is still the valid, fundamental principle of every coordinated activity."[408] "It seems evident," noted the highly orthodox East German ambassador, Eleonore Staimer, with satisfaction, "that Todorović and his allies have not been able to impose the liberal line. . . . As regards the internal problems of the SFRY, the plenum has shown that the positive forces, with Tito at their head, are still capable of asserting themselves."[409] The first secretary of the Soviet Embassy in Belgrade added in August 1967 that the expression "the reorganization of the LCY" promised much more than was carried out. Regarding the basic questions of democratic centralism, the role of the working class and of the class struggle, "healthy opinions" had prevailed.[410]

This defeat did not prevent Todorović and his group from continuing to criticize Tito's autocracy, forcing him into a complex set of political maneuvers. As a Croat and in order not to be accused by the Serbs of a coup d'état because of Ranković's removal, the marshal assumed a compliant attitude toward them. In the following years, Serbia received, 80 percent of all state investments (the new Djerdap Dam, the Belgrade-Bar railroad line, infrastructure in the capital), in addition to important political functions. Even so, Tito was not able to capture the sympathies of the liberal-inspired Serb leaders who had recently come to power with these concessions. They were convinced they were dealing with a dogmatic Bolshevik, an autocrat who was ready to do business with the

Russians. Fearing the return of Yugoslavia to the Soviet fold and its orthodoxy, they tried to neutralize him with maneuvers that were more or less successful. After Indonesian dictator Sukarno lost power, but conserved his post as nominal head of state, some in Belgrade said, "let's *Sukarnize* Tito." Many Slovenes agreed with the Serbs, above all Kardelj, as did Lazar Koliševski, for years the leading proponent of the Macedonians. In this atmosphere Stane Kavčič attempted to deprive the marshal of control of the army, which he had always had on a string thanks to General Gošnjak. But the initiative was fruitless.[411]

The Croats, convinced that they would be able to exploit Tito's political weakness for their own aims, took an entirely different approach. The newly elected president of the Croat League of Communists, Savka Dabčević-Kučar, said to her inner circle: "If Tito supports us, we will win."[412] It is evident that the other republics did not want to have a strong personality at the helm of the party and state, whereas Croatia wanted to invest in the marshal, provoking resentment in Belgrade and Ljubljana. In the two capitals, the Croats were bluntly accused of supporting an autocrat and preserving his power.[413]

The "Young Guard"

As correctly observed by the American ambassador to Belgrade, Charles E. Elbrick, Ranković's fall shattered the structure of power relations among the six republics that had been forged during the Second World War and carefully nurtured and built thereafter. In his opinion, the decisions of the Fourth Plenum also dealt a major blow to the "brotherhood and unity" principle that had hitherto cemented cohesion among party members. He further noted: "Probably the immediate result of all this will be an increase in tensions among nationalities, as each component a party and nationality of Yugoslavia, availing itself of new opportunities, presses its own interests which may not necessarily be the same as general Yugoslav interests or which may more likely be in conflict with those of other Republics."[414]

Elbrick's prophecy was soon realized as reformist groups emerged in the three main republics—a "national" one in Croatia, a "liberal" one in Serbia, and a "technocratic" one in Slovenia. They wanted to modernize every field of social life while complying with local traditions. Their supporters were middle-aged people who had established themselves in the LCY thanks to its partial restructuring. The League was transformed into a federal body made up of nine relatively autonomous entities: six of which were republican while two at a slightly lower level were provincial and one was military. Apart from the latter, which was still under the control of the old Partisans, the *homines novi* in Belgrade, Zagreb, and Ljubljana, but also in Skopje, did not contribute to the weakening of the centrifugal tendencies present in the country as Tito may have hoped, but in fact had the opposite effect. The CIA experts affirmed, "Although the trend toward further decentralization is probably irreversible, progress will not be smooth, and change in Yugoslavia will continue to be accompanied by dissension over the structure and role of the party and government, over the nationalities problem, and over the speed with which market forces will be introduced into the economy."[415]

These observations did not consider, however, the "old guard" who watched over everything and everyone, and did not have any intention of abdicating their "guiding role," especially when they realized they were under threat from the "young guard" who had filled the power vacuum left by Ranković. This was especially true for Tito. During a session in which some representatives of the "young guard" engaged in the discussion with particular vigor, he sent a note to Kardelj that read: "They want to replace us."[416]

The Economic Crisis and the Guest Worker

The "young guard" engaged in the renewal of society with a great deal of optimism. Evaluating the period 1965–70, Stane Kavčič, one of its members, asserted: "It was a radical showdown with our Stalinism in almost all sectors—we moved in a direction that would quickly bring us to a more developed democracy and economy—on this basis, we could progressively get rid of our material and ideological backwardness."[417]

And he added:

> Such social transformations obviously brought to light many contradictions and burning issues, but also many dangers. A more developed market economy demanded more knowledge: the role of the experts and managers took on new significance, causing, however, the emergence of technocracy. More democracy in the party and in society fostered more ideas and opinions, toward which more tolerance was needed. Liberalism was discovered, and it became evident that the economic, political and social interests of the republics were divergent, thus came a new nationalistic wave. It was not possible to solve these contradictions the old Cominform way, namely with discipline, repression and the hammer. Indeed, issues should be overcome with more democracy, tolerance and dialogue in the LCY. Even those who thought otherwise should enjoy civil rights in the party and society.[418]

In Croatia, a young economics lecturer at Zagreb University, Savka Dabčević-Kučar, rose up from the ranks. After Ranković it was she who, in a session of the CC of the Croat League, attacked the leadership and its privileges with the most force: "The party cannot escape its responsibility for past events," she said.[419] With the help of Vladimir Bakarić, who was envious of Miko Tripalo, the most intelligent "new man," Dabčević-Kučar was elected to the presidency of the CC of the Croatian CP at the end of May 1969.[420] Her way of doing politics, for instance renouncing stale verbal stereotypes, was immediately noticed by Miroslav Krleža. After a speech, he approached her with a compliment: "You would like to bring Europe into the party."[421] The same could be said for her colleagues in other republics: Marko Nikezić and Latinka Perović in Serbia, Stane Kavčič and his group in Slovenia, Krste Crvenkovski and Slavko Miloslavleski in Macedonia. Among them, the most important were the Serb liberals, who saw in Ranković's fall the chance to create a modern Serbia, democratic and free from the suspicion that it wanted to rule all of Yugoslavia.[422]

In the decades following the war, Yugoslav society underwent radical changes: in 1946 there were no more than 642,000 workers and employees, with 80 percent of the population comprised of peasants, half of them illiterate. At the end of the sixties, those who worked in industry and in the tertiary sector were 4 million strong, and peasants had shrunk to 50 percent of the population. The number of students jumped in the same period from 16,000 to 200,000. Nevertheless, Yugoslavia lingered behind Europe, registering for instance a GNP of only $860 per capita for 1970, a figure similar to Greece, but inferior to Romania and Bulgaria, not to mention Italy, which had double the GNP. The greater threat to Yugoslavia's development was the existing disparity between different republics, which continued to grow instead of diminishing: that same year, the GNP per capita in Slovenia was $1550, whereas in Kosovo, the Serb province populated mostly by Albanians, considered the most underdeveloped area in the country, it was one-fifth of that.[423]

The economic reforms were intended to gradually insert the country into Western markets. In 1970, for instance, only 25 percent of foreign trade was oriented toward the Soviet bloc, while 57 percent was conducted with the European community and 6 percent with the United States, the rest going to the Third World. During the first two years after their introduction, the reforms seemed bound for success, but it later became clear that the interface between the market and the planned economy did not yield the expected results. The president of the Federal Council, Boris Kraigher, one of the main architects of the reorganization, came to understand this at the end of 1966, a month before his death in what appeared to be a freak car crash. The following year, leaders such as Edvard Kardelj and Vladimir Bakarić likewise let go of the illusion of possible success.[424] Industrial production began to stagnate, causing unemployment. At the start of 1968, 327,000 workers were out of a job. To these nearly 750,000 should be added, those who emigrated "temporarily" abroad (as the authorities liked to say, implying that they would inevitably return home), to

France, Austria, and Sweden, but especially West Germany. Among them there were many Albanians from Kosovo and Bosnians, but as the Croats were most numerous of all, the phenomenon began to acquire a political dimension. In fact, in the West the Croat *Gastarbeiter* (a German term for a worker who comes from abroad) met the Ustaša diaspora, which launched the fiercely nationalist and anti-Tito Croatian Liberation Movement (Hrvatski oslobodilački pokret) after the war.[425]

The generation that had fought during the resistance and had acquired positions of power after the victory was unable to cope with the challenges of the times. Its most eminent representatives frequently affirmed that if in the past it had been necessary to combat the bureaucrats, today it was necessary to fight the technocrats, since both pursued the same goal: to usurp power in the name of the working class. The "old ones," Tito at their head, naturally felt that they had been designated to defend the proletariat and to govern in its name. During a discussion with the representatives of Bosnia-Herzegovina on 24 May 1968, the marshal affirmed this explicitly: "Our league of communists has to have a political line; it has to be not just an adviser, but a protagonist in the economic, cultural and every other sphere of development."[426]

Strengthening Ties with the Soviet Union

During the sixties Tito's international prestige grew progressively. After the success of the first Non-Aligned Conference, in Belgrade in September 1961, he managed to overcome his disagreement with Moscow. To everyone's surprise, Khrushchev let it be known that he had rehabilitated Yugoslavia at the Twenty-Second Congress of the CPSU at the end of October, at the same time he had Stalin's body removed from Lenin's mausoleum.[427] "The critics of so-called 'Yugoslav revisionism' appeared in a new light," the East Germans commented sheepishly.[428] The change of climate between the two countries suggested to Ambassador George Kennan this bitter consideration: "It seems . . . to be a sad truth that if the Soviet leaders were only to cast one inviting smile in this direction, Uncle Sam, with all his bouquets and food baskets, would be promptly forgotten by Tito, and some of those who are now his closest advisers, and they would almost swoon in their eagerness to bask in this eastern sunshine, I shudder to think."[429]

In April 1962, Soviet foreign minister Andrei A. Gromyko came to Belgrade on an official visit. This was followed by a visit from the president of the Supreme Soviet, Leonid I. Brezhnev, in September and October, and on Khrushchev's invitation, a "work permit" for Tito to come to Moscow the following December.[430] When he returned home, he affirmed that the Soviet leaders were ready for more constructive relations with Yugoslavia, and sent a document in the name of the LCY to all party organs, inviting them to "take people's minds off anti-Sovietism."[431] This attitude was also affected by Tito's growing preoccupation with America's aggressive policy in Middle and Far East. In his opinion, the United States was exploiting the lack of cohesion of the communist bloc, shaken as it was by Mao's "cultural revolution."[432] In this context, Tito was convinced that he could become a leader of international standing: he opposed Chinese ideological and military aggressiveness (due to his close ties with India the conflict between Beijing and New Delhi on the Tibetan border was of great concern to him), but also the American imperialism that found its expression in the Vietnam War.[433]

Khrushchev's visit between 20 August and 3 September 1963 was emblematic of the reciprocal exchange of courtesies between the two statesmen.[434] Tito, who loved to stress his independence from the rest of the communist bloc, rediscovered the role of Yugoslavia in the "international workers movement." In polemics with Western neocolonialism, he therefore tried to forge alliances with "progressive" forces in Africa, Asia, and Latin America.[435] When the Cuban Missile Crisis broke out in October 1962 due to the discovery of Soviet missiles on the island, followed by John F. Kennedy's ultimatum to Khrushchev to remove them, Tito did not hide his sympathies for the Soviet position, although he tried to mediate between Moscow and Washington. He stressed that American unilateral actions could hinder world peace and tried to solve the quarrel between the two superpowers in the context of the United Nations, where the non-aligned nations were a strong presence. In this sense, he appealed not just to the Americans but also to the Soviets, warning Khrushchev with the utmost seriousness—as George Kennan wrote—to be careful not to fall into Fidel Castro's trap.[436] His reserved attitude toward the United States was further strengthened by his experience in autumn 1963, when President Kennedy invited him to Washington for an unofficial visit at the end of his tour in Latin America—the first of a socialist head of state.[437] Although the White House made every effort to welcome him with open arms, violent protests were organized by Croat, Serb, and Albanian immigrants, who went berserk because after WWII they had been protected by the Americans, who preferred to ignore the fact that there were war criminals among them.[438] Tito had to cancel a planned trip to California with the excuse of a sudden flu, but he could not avoid a traumatic experience in New York. A hostile crowd besieged the Waldorf Astoria Hotel, where he and his entourage were staying, and it seems that he eluded an assassination attempt by a hair's breadth.[439]

Although the UN General Assembly gave him a standing ovation, he returned home embittered and convinced that the Chetniks, the Ustaše, and Albanian extremists were able to vilify him because they had the tacit support of the American security services.[440] When news came about Kennedy's assassination a month later, a Romanian delegation headed by Gheorghe Gheorghiu-Dej was visiting Belgrade. Gheorghiu-Dej later related that he and Tito spent the entire night discussing the possible consequences of the president's violent death and the future prospects of the United States.[441] Tito did not believe that the blame should be put on an unstable Lee Harvey Oswald, but that Kennedy was the victim of a military operation. In a discussion with the East German ambassador, Eleonore Staimer, who was an old acquaintance from Moscow, he affirmed that during his recent journey to the States what had happened to the president could have easily happened to him, and that the true killer would never be found, as he would be protected by influential people in the Pentagon. "I was a soldier too," he told Madame Staimer, "and therefore I know very well that with a gun like that, which was found after the assassination attempt, it is impossible to shoot three times back-to-back with such precision at a quickly moving car."[442]

Believing that American foreign policy was harmful to world peace, in the sixties Tito tried to block the "reactionary forces" and to create a broad "peace front." This would include the non-aligned countries, the majority of the socialist countries, the Third World national liberation movements, the progressive forces in the capitalist arena, and even some Western states critical of Washington's policy, such as France. He was sure that such a front could operate with success in the United Nations, where the balance tipped against the United States. The primary objective of this coalition would be to isolate the US and China and to force them by persistent pressure to pursue a more moderate policy.[443]

In order to curtail Beijing's influence on the leaders of the non-aligned countries, most of all Sukarno, who considered war a legitimate means in the struggle against the rich, in mid-April 1965 Tito visited Algiers, where the Chinese premier, Zhou Enlai, had been shortly before him. Westerners believed that the marshal was trying to secure a role on the international scene beyond his capacity for action, but nevertheless they were not hostile to his policy of peaceful coexistence.[444] They were much less inclined toward his anti-imperialist opinions, which he was not shy about sharing. In May 1964, the twentieth anniversary of victory in the Second World War, he compared American policy in Vietnam, Congo, and Cuba to that of Mussolini and Hitler before the war and their "diabolical plan to enslave the whole world." He particularly condemned the carpet-bombing of North Vietnam (operation Rolling Thunder) which, in his opinion, offended everyone, especially those who had similar experiences during the Second World War.[445]

These bold stances were not ignored in Washington, where Tito's opinion counted. At the end of 1965, President Lyndon B. Johnson sent Ambassador-at-Large W. Averell Harriman to Brioni with the task of consulting Tito about a possible way out of the Vietnamese imbroglio. The marshal did not hide his position: the first step would be to convince Hanoi to come to peace talks, the United States should stop bombarding North Vietnam. Moreover, they would do well to favor the formation of a "mixed" government in Saigon between the bourgeois forces and the Vietcong similar to the one he had formed with Šubašić after the war.[446] Washington did not follow this advice, but this did not hinder the Johnson administration from continuing cordial relations with Tito and supporting his economic reform financially.[447] His separate path to socialism, which disturbed Moscow greatly, was of paramount importance to the Americans because it differed from that of their Soviet nemesis.

The North Vietnam government was not particularly enthusiastic about the Yugoslav marshal's pacifist initiatives. In mid-June 1966, the Hanoi press agency condemned his efforts to reach a political solution to the crisis: "Tito cannot hide his servile attitude toward the American imperialists. It is public knowledge that he tries to sell, at all costs, the outdated merchandise of the peace talks produced by his patrons." Reportedly Tito was hurt by these attacks, especially because Ho Chi-Minh added personal criticisms to discredit him: he alleged that the marshal was an imperialist lackey used to a luxurious, even regal life.[448]

The Arab-Israeli War

Ho Chi Minh was right about Tito's passion for luxury, but he was wrong about the honesty of his anti-imperialism. For instance, he vigorously condemned the military coup in Greece organized in April 1967 by a group of right-wing colonels, with American assent. Tito believed that this maneuver was part of a new NATO strategy based on the concept of a "preemptive strike" against communism—although Greece was a constitutional monarchy, it did have a strong communist party. He also reacted firmly on the occasion of the Arab-Israeli War (or Six-Day War), in June 1967 which he believed could not have been possible without Washington's support of Tel Aviv. Because of his close contacts with Nasser, he favored the Arab cause, which did not prevent him from trying to mediate between Egypt and Israel.[449] When the war ended in disaster for Egypt, Jordan, and Syria, with Israel occupying vast territories, Tito did not give up: he formulated a five-point peace plan. The first and most important two points called for the withdrawal of Israeli troops to the border as it had been on 5 June, when the conflict had begun, providing in exchange international security guaranteed by the troops of the great powers and by the UN. To this end, he sent ambassadors to Washington, Moscow, London, and Paris and went personally with Kardelj to Cairo to try to convince Nasser to recognize Israel, although without success.[450] If nothing else, he received the support of Pope Paul VI and much credit from the patriarch of Constantinople, Athenagoras: "I have read your peace plan for the Middle East and I conserved it in my archive as an important testimony. . . . I would like to tell you that you are a real fighter for world peace. One day, the good seed planted in the hearts and souls of the people will bear fruit."[451]

The 1968 Student Revolt

In the middle of January 1968, the Serb liberals succeeded in a purge of their League of Communists. The Control Commission expelled about four hundred members, not just because of late payment of fees or absence from party meetings or similar transgressions, as they had been told, but because of their opposition to reforms.[452] This showed how much Serb society was divided, and how many different trends were present in it, from chauvinists to the radical left. The tensions that smoldered under the surface gave rise in 1968 to a student revolt, which was provoked by a brawl between students and young workers over admission to a musical performance. The police intervened in a brutal manner, sparking further disorder. It was an explosion of youth anger due in part to the difficulties of finding jobs, a situation worsened by the economic reform.[453]

In May, under the influence of the French, students in Belgrade rebelled with leftist slogans, renaming their alma mater "Red University Karl Marx." Many of them were under the influence of the philosophical magazine *Praxis*, which had been edited by a group of university professors from Belgrade and Zagreb since 1964. The magazine also enjoyed high prestige abroad, thanks to its summer school on the island of Korčula. It proved to be a vitriolic critic of the Yugoslav system, expanding on Marxian thought about the alienation of man, who is divided between the reality of the situation and his creative possibilities. In this context, it asserted that self-management could not be fully established until it became entwined with the authoritarian and hierarchical structures of the party and state, and this would require radical change to the regime. Although the magazine was temporarily suspended in April 1968 because of this "petit bourgeois" idea criticized by Tito himself, two months later the extension of its influence appeared obvious. The Belgrade students rebelled against the status quo, proclaiming their adherence to "true socialism," symbolized by an enormous picture of the marshal during the Partisan war, which was hung on the façade of their university. "Tito the hero" was in this way opposed to "Tito the bourgeois," whose dismissal they dared to demand.[454] The protest movement also spread to other Yugoslav universities, but its epicenter remained in the capital where, in addition leftist views, it was possible to hear the perspectives of centralists, Yugoslavs, and pan-Serbians (the *terminus technicus* to describe the idea that all Serbs throughout the Balkans should live in the same state).[455] Before Ranković's fall, the SFRY had been dominated by the Serb bureaucracy, but afterward they began losing power. The future bureaucrats could not ignore this, trying at the same time to acquire the support of the working masses to give weight to their protest.

The revolt of fifty thousand students unleashed a wave of panic at the top of the party. On 9 June 1968, the presidency and the executive committee of the CC were convened in Belgrade, where Tito did not hesitate to criticize the young, stressing the damage the protests were causing to the international prestige of the country. Kardelj supported him and even suggested using the army against the protesters.[456] This was not necessary, however, thanks to Tito's charisma: that same day he gave a televised speech and with conciliatory words, he recognized the value of the "positive dissatisfaction" of the students, promising that he would personally try to solve their problems. "If I am not capable of doing this," he said, "in that event, I should no longer be where I am."[457] At the end of his broadcast he made a very different comment off the record according to the Belgrade television director: "This is what happens, comrades, when some monkeys are not arrested in time."[458]

His tactical move had a cathartic effect: the students calmed down immediately, convinced that they had obtained what they had asked for. This was an illusion, because Tito not only did not keep his promises, but began harboring ill-will toward the "petit bourgeois" and liberal groups that found sanctuary at the universities.[459] The principal victim of the June events was the reform process, since the old guard began to fear the excessive liberty it had unleashed. When, in June 1969, they realized that they had been deceived, the students of the Faculty of Philosophy in Belgrade tried to renew their protest against the regime, but they remained isolated. The party magazine, *Komunist*, attacked the "radical opposition" at the university with hostility, comparing the editors of their paper, *Student*, to the Ustaše and the Chetniks.[460] "There is no hope," commented Dobrica Ćosić bitterly. "Everything will collapse in chaos, blood, tyranny, disintegration."[461]

Relations with the Soviet Union and the Satellites

Between 1964 and 1965, Tito received or visited every East European socialist leader with the exception of Enver Hoxha and Bulgarian premier Todor Zhivkov, thus further normalizing his relations with the Soviet bloc. In mid-October

1964, he was unpleasantly surprised by the sudden demise of Khrushchev, with whom he had kept on good terms over the previous two years, even taking on the role of mediator between the Soviet secretary and the Romanian leadership in its aspirations for autonomy. He especially valued Khrushchev's willingness to listen to the interlocutors, to think about what had been said, and sometimes even change his own mind. For a long time he had not been sure whether the new Kremlin leaders, starting with Leonid I. Brezhnev, would be worthy of filling his shoes.[462] When he visited Moscow, Minsk, and Siberia again between 18 June and 1 July 1965, he managed to establish a good relationship with the "troika" at the head of the USSR, who conferred the greatest of honors upon him: on the route from the airport to the Kremlin, he was greeted by an enormous crowd and once there he was installed at the Great Palace, its main entrance opened for the first time to a foreign statesman.[463]

Flattered by such attentions, in Sverdlovsk Tito declared that in case of war Yugoslavia would fight "side by side" with the Soviet Union. These words did not surprise the Westerners who, thanks to intelligence sources, were well acquainted with this line of thinking, but they were unpleasantly struck by the fact that such sentiments had been uttered publicly.[464] Back in Belgrade, Tito stressed that his views had been "identical or extremely close" to the Russian viewpoint on the problems discussed. This was mostly due to the increasing extremism of Chinese opposition to both Titoism and Soviet communism. Not surprisingly, wrote the British ambassador in Moscow in his dispatch, the Chinese were quick to attack Tito's reception in the Soviet Union and to proclaim that it proved all that they had been saying about both parties.[465]

In 1966, Ranković's fall troubled the cordial atmosphere between Belgrade and Moscow, since the Soviets were at least initially concerned about the reforms of the LCY, considering them without precedence in the history of socialism. They wondered whether Tito "was still controlling the situation," although they did notice that Yugoslavia did not try to hinder their efforts to form a coalition of the entire international communist movement. They were ready to take a tolerant attitude toward the changes underway, considering them internal questions that could not harm the "camp."[466] In this spirit Brezhnev visited Yugoslavia in 1966 for the first time as secretary general of the CPSU, and the following year Tito took part in the celebrations of the fiftieth anniversary of the October Revolution.[467]

The Prague Spring

At the end of 1967, when signs of a political thaw began appearing in Czechoslovakia, the Yugoslav leaders supported the "new course" with open sympathy, considering it necessary for socialism in that country. Returning from Japan, Mongolia, and Iran, Tito unwillingly took part in a secret meeting convened by Brezhnev in Moscow between 28 and 30 April 1968, to consult the leaders of the Warsaw Pact on how to respond to events in Czechoslovakia, where the leadership was attempting to modernize the country under the slogan "socialism with a human face." In practice, this meant a version of socialism closer to Yugoslavia's than to the Soviet Union's. On that occasion, a heated debate arose between the secretary general of the CPSU and the marshal, who expressed the opinion that the use of force would have "catastrophic" effects. In saying this, he intentionally used the same language that he had used ten years earlier, after the Hungarian Revolution. "Why do you Yugoslavs so fear the word 'intervention?'" asked Brezhnev. "Should we wait until they start to hang communists in Czechoslovakia, like in Hungary in 1956? History will not forgive us if we will remain idle in the face of anti-communist forces, watching the funeral of socialism without reacting. . . . Take care, Broz," he added menacingly, "that something like what's happening in Czechoslovakia does not happen in your house!" Tito responded to this last remark angrily, stressing that the situation in Yugoslavia was completely different, since he had settled with the enemies of the revolution at the time of the resistance. With regard to the threat to socialism in Czechoslovakia, he recalled that in his youth he had worked in the factories of that country and knew its proletariat well. He was certain that it would be able to hold off its enemies and to defend the achievements of socialism. They needed to trust Alexander Dubček, the secretary general of the Czechoslovak party, and the local intelligentsia, which was always on the side of the communists.[468]

In spite of this exchange of opinions, which did not promise anything good, Tito returned to Belgrade hoping that the Soviets would not use force to solve their differences with the Czechoslovaks.[469] Convinced that "the Prague Spring" would be a "passage to a superior form of socialism," he tried to organize a meeting with Dubček to show the socialist world that every country had a right to its diversity.[470] The Ninth Plenum, convened on 16 July, affirmed that the working class and other Czechoslovak socialist and progressive forces were called to judge the situation in their country for themselves, without foreign intervention, and to solve their own problems.[471] Kardelj followed the events with great interest, stressing that the Yugoslavs should not be overtaken by the innovations happening in Czechoslovakia. Soon, however, he began wondering how the excessive radicalization of the Prague Spring would end up. Together with many party "liberals," he was of the opinion that the system could be reformed "from above" by the party itself and not "from below" by the people.[472]

Tito, too, feared the resurgence of anti-socialist elements in Czechoslovakia. At Brezhnev's urging, he visited Prague from 9–11 August 1968 to persuade Dubček and his collaborators not to skip steps in their frenzy to reform. At a press conference, however, he supported the democratization process in the country and therefore was hailed triumphantly by the population. In the following days, together with the Romanian president, Nicolae Ceaușescu, he did everything he could to prevent the Warsaw Pact from intervening against the Czechoslovakian heretics. To this end, he contacted Brezhnev, Kádár, and other socialist leaders, who assured him that no intervention should be feared.[473] These words were bound to be refuted in the days that followed.

August 1968

The Warsaw Pact forces, the Romanians aside, entered Czechoslovakia on 21 August 1968 to fight the "counterrevolution" in the name of international solidarity. This "defense of the results of socialism" was seen in Yugoslavia as a warning of a possible invasion on their own soil. During the following two days, the federal government and the Central Committee of the League of Communists of Yugoslavia firmly condemned the military intervention as an "aggression," an "occupation," and a "brutal interference in internal Czechoslovak affairs." The five countries involved, especially the Soviet Union, were reproached by the Yugoslavs for having tried to stop the development of socialism in Czechoslovakia. Tito declared that it was absurd to speak about a "counterrevolution" because no such thing existed, as he himself had been able to see during his visit to Prague.[474] For him, the intervention of the Warsaw Pact was a heavy blow since in recent years he had often maintained that Western distrust of the Soviet Union was the result of imperialist propaganda. He lamented, "Where possible, I tried to contradict this opinion, but now, everything has been destroyed."[475] In a TV appearance, he did not hide his disillusion: "Foreign military units coming into Czechoslovakia, without the invitation and approval of the legitimate government, worried us very much. With this, the sovereignty of a socialist state has been trampled, and all the socialist and progressive forces of the world have suffered a heavy blow."[476]

The failure of Czechoslovakia's "socialism with a human face" created a strong impression in Yugoslavia, which had followed the Prague Spring with interest and sympathy. The Soviet Union, accused of neo-Stalinism and Russian chauvinism, was the subject of popular protests and a hostile press campaign. Moscow and other capitals of the Warsaw Pact countries responded that the Yugoslavs, in their anti-Soviet outbursts, were completely in tune with the West and with Chinese. These menacing accusations prompted Tito and his comrades to prepare the population for a possible armed attack. Their fear increased after the Russian ambassador, Ivan A. Benediktov, handed over a diplomatic note on 30 August, in which the Soviet leaders criticized Yugoslavia for its anti-Soviet and anti-socialist activity.[477] At that point, the army was put on red alert and a partial mobilization was ordered. Bulwarks along the frontiers with Hungary and Bulgaria were strengthened, and the airports were equipped to prevent enemy planes from landing. In the cities, air raid drills began.[478]

In autumn 1968, the situation deteriorated further as a result of a declaration made by Brezhnev, who asserted that the interests of the socialist commonwealth were more important than the sovereignty of individual countries. On 26 September, *Pravda* stated: "Every communist party is responsible not only to its own people, but to all socialist countries, to the entire communist movement. He who forgets this, stressing only the autonomy of the different communist parties, is the prey of egotism and is estranged from his international obligations."[479] For the Yugoslavs, this new "doctrine" had a sinister sound: it was obvious it was directed toward them. Even though the Soviet ambassador affirmed in a conversation with Tito that it did not concern Yugoslavia, the marshal was not consoled, especially because the Soviets refused his request to make these assurances public.[480]

As during his quarrel with Stalin, Tito had to seek help in the West. The American president, Lyndon B. Johnson, spoke clearly in favor of Yugoslav independence and integrity, dispatching the under secretary of state, Nicholas deBelleville Katzenbach, to Belgrade. Even De Gaulle received Tito's envoy—after a ten day wait—and was impressed by the Yugoslav decision to resist an eventual Soviet attack. During the conversation, the French president dozed off for a moment, but as soon as he grasped the spirit of what was being said, he opened his eyes and shouted, "What have you said?" The ambassador repeated his words. "But this is fantastic . . . fundamental! Today Tito is the only man in Europe able to react this way," the old soldier exclaimed, banging his fist on the table.[481]

During a NATO ministerial meeting in mid-November 1968, a press release was sent out warning the Soviet Union that "any Soviet intervention directly or indirectly affecting the situation in Europe or in the Mediterranean would create an international crisis with grave consequences." It was clear that the United States and its allies had in mind the so-called "gray zones," those not covered by NATO, and were concerned over the fate of Yugoslavia, Finland, Austria, and, in a somewhat different context, Romania as well. In harmony with the foreign secretary, the Yugoslav press initially hailed the declaration but recanted after some days of reflection, declaring it unwelcome and unnecessary. However, behind the scenes Tito continued to have consultations with the West, which showed its readiness to collaborate with Yugoslavia. Military agreements were established with Italy and the ex-partners of the Balkan Pact, Turkey and Greece (although in the latter the right-wing colonels were still in power). It was clear that NATO would not tolerate Soviet military expansion into the Adriatic, which undoubtedly comforted the Yugoslavs.[482]

At the end of the year, the fear of possible Soviet intervention gradually decreased. Tito commented on the NATO declaration about the "gray zones" with aloofness, affirming that his country did not feel threatened, and was not ready to seek shelter under the umbrella of this or that superpower.[483] At the same time, the Yugoslav press progressively ceased attacks against the socialist camp and more and more frequently underlined the willingness to preserve good economic, scientific, and cultural relations. At Jajce, on the occasion of the twenty-fifth anniversary of the Second AVNOJ, Tito mentioned the Prague events only fleetingly, revealing his intention to reopen a dialogue with Moscow.[484] During a meeting with journalists, he even declared that it was necessary "to favor collaboration" with the USSR, "in spite of different points of view."[485] This tactical move, which was criticized in Slovenia and Belgrade in particular, was not groundless. Tito was invited to mend fences with the Russians by Italian and French communists, but he was also motivated by economic interests: about 30 percent of Yugoslav foreign exchange was linked to the Soviet bloc. After having repressed the Prague Spring, the Soviets stopped the delivery of arms that the Yugoslavs had already paid for. Following the conciliatory speech in Jajce, an agreement was reached that increased the commercial interchange between the two countries by 16 percent. The same happened in relations with the satellites, which was of no little importance to Yugoslavia considering that its products did not have an easy outlet to Western markets.[486]

The Reorganization of the Army

On 11 February 1969, the Yugoslav Federal Assembly voted in the law on territorial defense with a fast-track procedure, establishing a force that would organize guerrilla resistance in areas that the regular armed forces (228,000 men) could not defend in case of enemy occupation. This idea of a popular defense was formulated as early as the fifties and sixties, on the basis of the Partisan experience, when it appeared clear that Yugoslavia could not resist the forces of the Soviet bloc or of NATO head on.[487] This meant that, in case of war, Yugoslavia would lose a significant part of its territory, although armed resistance could be carried on in the areas occupied by enemy forces. The territorial defense organization tried to recruit the entire population, between the ages of seventeen and sixty-five, without distinction as to gender and without regard to cost, which would be absorbed by all six republics and municipal administrations. It was also joined by the civil defense, which was able to mobilize another

3 million citizens against the enemy.[488] In short, at that time no European country was as actively involved in the preparation for national defense as was Yugoslavia, where even kindergarten children were taught to reach air-raid shelters. Military expenses rose steeply, reaching 5–6 percent of the annual GNP, since the government believed that it had as much to fear from its Eastern "big brother" as from NATO.[489]

In August 1968, when fear of a Soviet attack was at its peak, the top Yugoslav leaders met secretly on the islet of Vanga, Tito's private Brioni refuge. On that occasion, General Ivan Gošnjak, secretary of defense, was heavily criticized for his pro-Soviet attitude and accused of being ready to "open the frontiers to the Warsaw Pact troops."[490] After this session, Kardelj returned to Ljubljana and with great satisfaction announced to the local political elite that the idea of the "people in arms" had prevailed and that, in case of war, the resistance would not only be carried out by the regular army, but also by Partisan units organized autonomously in each republic. According to the testimony of his son, Matija Maček, the "iron man" of the local secret services, was so happy that he hopped around like a child. The Slovenes were elated, since they had not yet overcome the shock experienced in 1945 when Tito had compelled their own Partisan forces to join the Yugoslav People's Army (Jugoslovanska ljudska armija). The territorial defense plan was greeted with satisfaction in Slovenia and in Croatia: it offered them the chance to build their republican armed forces alongside the standing army that was controlled mostly by the Serbs.[491]

By contrast, the institution of the territorial defense was disliked by many military leaders, starting with Ivan Gošnjak, who raised doubts about its efficacy and was convinced that it would undermine the prestige of the Yugoslav National Army.[492] After Ranković's fall, it seemed that Gošnjak had reached the peak of his power and influence. He had an excellent working relationship with Tito, especially in opposing self-management in the armed forces, which Kardelj would have liked. But not a year passed before the rug was pulled out from under him: he was often criticized for appointing only likeable officers, often without the approval of the Executive Committee.[493] Gošnjak interpreted the nationalistic outburst after the Fourth Plenum as a consequence of Tito's refusal to follow his advice to completely renew the country's leadership and get rid of "historical cadres," which he saw as Tito's fatal mistake. The marshal, who was aware of these criticisms, was offended. Consequently, their relations rapidly deteriorated so much as to induce Gošnjak to use insulting epithets—"that dog" for instance—when speaking about Tito.[494] Although he remained deputy commander in chief, in June 1967 he was replaced as National Defense Secretary by the Serb Nikola Ljubičić who, in addition to having saved Tito at the end of 1941 from an Italian ambush, had only one quality: he knew how to obey. These changes could not clear the air of the tension and intrigues that dominated the army, where nationalism gained a foothold, worrying those officers from the original Partisan core who still nurtured "Yugoslav" ideals. Because of these internal frictions, 38 generals and 2,400 officers were removed from active duty in 1968. At the same time, the structure of the LCY in the army was reshaped to connect it more organically with the sociopolitical reality of the country.[495]

The Strengthening of Nationalisms

In the second half of the sixties, the national question escalated throughout the country. As early as autumn 1966, the Slovenes and Macedonians made their voices heard, lobbying for their languages to be used in federal institutions as dictated by the constitution.[496] Between the end of 1966 and the beginning of 1967 a conflict between Bulgaria and Macedonia flared up, initially involving the historians of both countries: the Macedonians accused their neighbors of practicing an oppressive policy toward members of the Macedonian minority living in the Pirin Valley. The government in Sofia turned a deaf ear to their request to grant this minority administrative autonomy, even denying the existence of a Macedonian ethnicity within its borders. Over the following two years the polemics grew more and more strident and did not cool down until Tito's death.[497] Ever since the end of the war, in order to reinforce their national identity, the Macedonians had been attempting to establish an autocephalous Church (functioning independently of a higher authority), the traditional sign of statehood in the Orthodox world. This aspiration could not be realized while Ranković was in power, since he was a protector of the Serb Church, which also included the eparchies in Macedonia. It was not until a year after his fall, on 18 June 1967, that Macedonians received the assent of the communist authorities to elect their own patriarch. The Serbian Orthodox Church opposed this with all its might, stressing that this was a blow to the Yugoslav ideal but without result. It could only refuse to recognize the autocephaly of the Macedonian Church, as it was not recognized by the ecumenical patriarch of Constantinople.[498]

Tito observed the rise of nationalist feelings within all the Yugoslav republics with concern. At the Fourth Plenum, in February 1967, he declared openly that he would not tolerate "the spreading of subversive slogans, national intolerance, and chauvinism, as sometimes happens in our schools, or other spheres of our public life."[499] In spite of this warning, a linguistic quarrel exploded the following month between Serbs and Croats, which appeared to be a greater problem than the Serb-Macedonian ecclesiastical conflict. The origins of the quarrel went back to 1954 when the representatives of two cultural associations, the Serb and Croat Matica (matrix), met in Novi Sad on behalf of the party. There they reached an agreement that confirmed the existence of a common Serbo-Croat or Croato-Serbian language, with two regional variations and two alphabets: the Latin and the Cyrillic. In the ensuing years it appeared, however, that in the common lexical area (Serbia, Croatia, Bosnia-Herzegovina, and Montenegro), the Serb version grew stronger than the Croat one as it was favored for administrative and military purposes. The Croats did not consider it adequate compensation that the Latin alphabet had undermined the Cyrillic one (it was even used in Serbia). Croats began to proclaim themselves victims of Serbian hegemonic tendencies that aimed to dissolve their language and culture in the name of Yugoslav unity.[500]

On the initiative of eminent members of the Yugoslav Academy of Sciences and Arts, located in Zagreb, and with the assent of Vladimir Bakarić, on 16 March 1967, a "Declaration on the Name and Status of the Croat Language" was published, signed by representatives of eighteen cultural institutions and by Miroslav Krleža himself. After the eclipse of Djilas, he was one of the most prominent intellectuals in Tito's entourage—as Maxim Gorky was to Lenin—and enjoyed great prestige. On this occasion, however, he did not take the precaution of consulting the marshal before signing. In the "Declaration," the Croat intellectuals proposed a constitutional amendment that would recognize the separation of the two languages.[501] A serious scandal followed: the Serbs were so upset that they asked for the arrest of the promoters (Bakarić prevented this but did not fight openly for the signatories' cause and abandoned them to their fate).[502] In response to Croat requests, the Belgrade writer Antonije Isaković, together with other intellectuals, published a "Proposal for Reflection" full of chauvinist ideas, stressing among other things that separate schools for children of Serb origin should be opened in Croatia.[503] Krleža was the principal target of the attacks, accused of being "a bulwark of Great Croatia."[504] In order to defuse the situation, at Tito's suggestion he resigned from the CC of the Croat League of Communists. The same evening the marshal invited him to dinner at Brioni, and the writer—whose motto was "Save the head at any cost!"—accepted gladly.[505]

After Ranković's fall, the Serbs were in crisis, not just because of the Croats, but even more because of the Muslims from Kosovo and Bosnia-Herzegovina. The Bosniaks were Slavs by origin but had converted to Islam centuries ago as a consequence of the Ottoman conquest. After the Second World War it took a long time before they were allowed to profess their nationality, since the authorities barely tolerated their religious identity. Only in January 1968 were they officially recognized as one of the constituent peoples of the federation—

a decision, as the Belgrade rumor mill had it, undertaken because Tito wanted to please the Arabs. The exasperated Serbs were sure that the move was aimed to weaken the Orthodox presence in the Balkans; the marshal, they said, wanted to bring back the old Comintern order as a way to destroy Yugoslavia.[506] These suspicions were fostered by the policy carried out in Kosovo towards the mostly Muslim Albanians (population about a million) after the fall of Ranković, which was less repressive than the one implemented by the UDBA in 1945. The more tolerant atmosphere could not appease the Kosovo Albanians, who after decades under a police regime wanted to emancipate themselves from Belgrade. On 27 November 1968, just before the Albanian and likewise the Yugoslav national holiday, student demonstrations erupted in Prishtina and in other cities of the province, which gave rise to a popular revolt that spread to Albanian areas in western Macedonia the following month.[507] The protesters carried banners with slogans such as: "We want a constitution; Long live Hoxha, We want union with Albania."[508] The Yugoslavs attributed the organization of the revolt to Tirana and decided to suppress it with violence. Subsequently, vast administrative reforms were instituted that favored the "Shiptars" (as the Albanians were derogatorily called), but that only temporarily calmed the situation without truly satisfying anybody. It certainly did not satisfy the Albanians, who saw themselves as being in a sort of colonial dependence on Belgrade, nor the Serbs, who considered Kosovo the cradle of their nation and were well aware of their hate: "We have given them their own administrators, a university, the Albanian flag, their language—but they want more. . . . The Albanians should be told that we will defend Kosovo, even with tanks, if necessary."[509]

In Serbia, a nationalistic surge was evident during Christmas 1968, which was celebrated with more vehemence than it had been seen since 1941. "With the Orthodox faith, we confirm our Serb identity," wrote Dobrica Ćosić, noting that the populace, disillusioned with the Yugoslav ideal of all southern Slavs living in a single state, was discovering the concept of Greater Serbia. In his opinion, this was necessary to save the Serbs from chauvinist Croat policy and from Slovenian economic hegemony, the aim of which was to reduce Serbia to a colony.[510]

Executive Bureau

The authorities tried to overcome these tensions with the liberalization of the system. Although liberalization had been discussed since 1967, it ground to a halt because of growing inflation and other difficulties caused by the failure of economic reform.[511] It gathered momentum at the end of 1968, when a series of constitutional amendments were voted in that recognized equality between the Yugoslav "nations" (Serbs, Croats, Bosniaks, Macedonians, Slovenes, Montenegrins) and the "nationalities," as the ethnic minorities were called (Albanians, Hungarians, Italians, etc.). In this context, the rights of the autonomous provinces—Vojvodina and Kosovo—were clearly defined within the framework of the Serb Republic, as were the relations between the federation and the republics, which saw their legislative and economic powers enlarged. One of the most important amendments prescribed equal rights for all the languages and alphabets of the country: this meant that, in Tito's Yugoslavia, eleven languages were officially recognized.[512]

Moreover, the reform of the party should also be mentioned, in which the traditionally rigid and highly centralized "cell" structure was replaced by less formal gatherings called "conferences," in order to democratize the country's political life. On the initiative of Lazar Koliševski, and with Tito's assent, the "old couch potatoes" were retired, officials whose merits were mostly connected to the liberation struggle and postwar reconstruction. After nearly a quarter of century in power, they were replaced by younger and more learned cadres. The new retirees were, however, only in their fifties or even forties and prone to personal dramas. "When I was left without any function [at fifty-five years old]," wrote Svetozar Vukmanović (Tempo) to Tito with bitterness, "I was practically blocked from working [in the political field]." He was one of the most illustrious victims of the "purge" because he had become a burden thanks to his constant requests to give the trade unions, which he headed, a greater voice in the formulation of policy.[513]

The Ninth Congress of the LCY was held between 12 and 15 March 1969, on the occasion of the fiftieth anniversary of revolutionary activity in Yugoslavia. It was not attended by any party from the Soviet bloc, apart from the Romanian one. Tito felt this boycott was a personal affront and in turn he did not take part in the International Communists Conference in Moscow between 6 and 19 June. However, twenty-five Western socialist and social-democratic parties did participate in the congress; it was the first communist gathering to include so many delegations of the moderate left since the communists and social democrats split following WWI. Moreover, the Ninth Congress was significant because it adopted a new statute for the LCY and for the first time dealt openly with the question of relations between the developed and underdeveloped nations in Yugoslavia. It also affirmed that the leagues of different republics were autonomous, which meant that the federal principle was also introduced into the party and with it, the right to dissent. Observing that businesses could spend only 6 percent of their earnings, the congress also recognized that self-management remained more of a concept on paper than a practical reality, and stressed that it should be strengthened. This suggestion was questioned by many economists, businessmen, and technocrats, however—some of them proposed drastic measures, such as the closure of 30 percent of the factories and the concentration of production in the healthy ones. The party theoreticians prevailed, having no intention of harming the sacred principles of self-management while at the same time ignoring the incompatibility between the ideals proclaimed and the actual presence of a political-state authoritarian apparatus led by them.[514]

As a counterweight to the decentralization of the LCY and its separation from the state and economy (the communists claimed to control the economy only ideologically, without meddling in day-to-day affairs), a new supreme body was created, tasked with directing the whole political structure.[515] In the days leading up to the congress Tito fought a dramatic battle when some of his comrades, in particular Kardelj, tried to depose him from one of his most important offices and install Mijalko Todorović as secretary general of the party. In order to block this maneuver, he chose a drastic and daring move: he decided tout court to abolish this function, and substitute it with an Executive Bureau with fourteen members—two for every republic and one for each province—which would operate as a collective body, since every member would preside over it for two months. "The delegates," Bilandžić related, "jumped for joy when Tito presented his decision."[516] They believed that with this he was saving Yugoslavia and the LCY from fragmentation, and intended to collect "the best and the brightest" from every republic and province in Belgrade to create a strong power core. Exactly the opposite was true: as with Versailles at the time of Louis XIV, the Yugoslav grandees were concentrated in the capital, the better to control them. With this decision, said Latinka Perović, Tito "buried" not just Todorović, but all the preeminent party personalities in an amorphous agency that he remained outside of.[517]

The Motorway Affair

The summer of 1969 was dramatic. Ustaša émigrés planted two bombs in Belgrade, although they failed in a parallel attempt to kill the chief of the Yugoslav mission in Berlin. Fear spread over the country, which overshadowed the renewal of its diplomatic relations with West Germany without causing them to break off, as the Croat extremists most likely wanted.[518]

Normalization between the two countries was possible thanks to the rise to power of a center-left government in Bonn, where the social-democrat Willy Brandt was called to head the Ministry of Foreign Affairs. One of the first moves of his *Ostpolitik* was the resumption of diplomatic ties with Yugoslavia, after ten years of tensions due to Tito's recognition of East Germany. West German diplomacy was forced to abandon the "Hallstein doctrine,"[519] as it was evident that overcoming the dispute with Yugoslavia was a prerequisite for dialogue with other socialist countries, which in turn had regular diplomatic relations with Pankow (the Berlin suburb where the East German government had its seat).[520] Since economic relations were never interrupted but in fact had continued to develop, the operation was successful, creating an atmosphere of mutual confidence that went beyond the personal sympathy between Tito and Brandt. In contrast with Konrad Adenauer, long-time chancellor of West Germany, who considered Tito "a common bandit,"[521] the new foreign minister thought that the marshal, despite his feudal way of life, was worthy of much respect because of his political rebelliousness against Hitler and Stalin as well as his efforts to create a new Yugoslavia, which was "in the interest of the Mediterranean." He valued his foreign policy even more since, according to Brandt, it had a positive influence, not only on the Third World, but also on the neutral countries of Europe.[522] Herbert Wehner, a leading West German politician who had known Broz from the time of the Hotel Lux and was grateful to him for a friendly gesture in those difficult times, said at a banquet organized in honor of a Yugoslav delegation in 1971: "We agree on so many points that it is better not to mention them, so that we and you will not be harmed. You will not find a better and a more careful observer of your path than we social-democrats on this side of divided Germany."[523] In this atmosphere the Soviet Union proposed the organization of a conference on security; cooperation in Europe was discussed, which, according to Tito and Brandt, should not result in a confrontation between the two blocs, but offer a chance to assert their positions to each other and to neutral and non-aligned countries.[524]

The summer of 1969 saw the "motorway affair" blow up in Slovenia: the Ljubljana government found the courage to oppose the federal government. The Slovenian population had long been in turmoil as a result of their unsatisfactory condition: they wanted a better lifestyle, which the reforms were unable to guarantee, and more political freedom, which the self-government policy had promised but not delivered. The Ljubljana government planned a motorway running from the Austrian border to Gorizia in Italy, aiming to link Slovenia with Central and Western Europe and boost its economy. In advocating their proposal, the Slovenians pointed out that more than 94 percent of the tourist traffic passed through their republic but, in spite of this, they received from the federal fund just three-quarters of a percent of the funds available during the period of 1956–69. The financing of the motorway seemed resolved: the necessary means would be provided partially by the republic itself, partially by the International Bank for Reconstruction and Development, a UN agency.[525] Ljubljana's indignation was unrestrained when the news suddenly came at the end of July that the federal government, headed by Mitja Ribičič, a Slovenian, had channeled the funds already granted into Serbian road projects of secondary economic importance. Following the principle that something should be given to every republic (Slovenia had already received an allocation for a section of the motorway), this decision was made after the World Bank had asked the government to choose the most pertinent of the numerous proposals.[526] The fact that the federal government discussed such an important issue without informing Ljubljana added fuel to the controversy, as the Slovenians were convinced that they had been cheated. After an extraordinary session, Kavčič and his colleagues sent a harsh letter of protest to Ribičič, asking him to examine their request again, and expressing the intention to discuss the issue in the Ljubljana parliament. Meanwhile voices were raised in the forty municipal assemblies involved but also in the factories and squares, some of them tinged with separatism.[527] "The motorway affair," wrote Kavčič in his diary, "was the first great revolt of those in Slovenia who wanted to continue the economic reform, who desired more real and less postured democracy, and the strengthening of the republic's independence."[528] They had no luck; because of the violent reaction, the conflict assumed dimensions that overflowed the limits of the controversy and became a matter of principle: what was the relationship between the republics and the federation? And to what extent could the latter make decisions, transcending their local interests, dictated by reasons that went beyond the economic? Ribičič, from his perspective, asserted that the revolt of his compatriots was unacceptable because if he gave in to their pressure he would have to give in to anyone who applied pressure, thus jeopardizing economic stability. According to him, this was a "mass movement against the federation." Since the issue was put in these terms, Tito and Kardelj, who had at first asked him to make concessions to Kavčič, changed their opinion so that the so-called "order party" (those who wanted more discipline) could not accuse them of promoting the disintegration of state unity. At a session of the LCY, they declared the behavior of the Slovenian government unacceptable, nationalistic, and indicative of technocratic bureaucrats. "A democratic state unable to oppose pressure from below," said Kardelj, "cannot remain democratic." He agreed with Tito that it might be necessary to adopt anti-democratic means to guarantee order if this practice continued.[529]

The *Maspok*

The clash between the "old guard" and the new liberal forces that took power in Zagreb, Belgrade, and Ljubljana was essentially a fight for succession: a fight Tito was aware of and skillfully exploited to preserve his role. Among the young, the most bellicose were those from Zagreb, who encouraged the popular masses to support their aspiration for greater autonomy in Croatia, motivated by the psychological need to be rid of the discrimination felt by the Croats after the war, because of the crimes of the Ustaša (the Serbs were convinced that the responsibility for the Ustaša was a collective one). The Croats wanted a radical transformation of the SFRY, which would guarantee the republics internal autonomy and full transparency in their relations with the central government, especially with regard to economics. "The *maspok* [*masovni pokret*; mass movement]," said Miko Tripalo, "tried to establish new democratic relations between the party and the working class, the party and the vast strata of citizens, between thoughtful action and spontaneous movement, but also the popular supervision of the party and its functionaries."[530]

Tito favored the rise to power of the new personalities. Under pressure from Belgrade government circles, the marshal hoped to carry out the so-called "federalization of the federation" with the help of the Croats, and to transform Yugoslavia into a community of more autonomous entities, weakening the Serbs and assuring for himself the role of arbiter-for-life.[531] He was convinced that in Serbia they plotted against him, and with typical senile paranoia often lamented that he was without any support. In reality, he could count on General Ljubičić, chief of the army, on the secretary for internal affairs, Radovan Stijačić, and on General Ivan Mišković, chief of military intelligence. There was also the Croat "young guard." Tito nurtured a great sympathy for Miko Tripalo and Pero Pirker, another member of the Zagreb power group. He was attracted by their joyful and youthful company, and their irreverent kind of fun that defied social convention, including dirty jokes that nobody else would dare to tell in his presence. Later he said that he had considered the possibility of making Tripalo his heir.[532]

The Croat liberals could count on the support of Vladimir Bakarić, who since the thirties had been one of Tito's most influential collaborators and confidants. After 1945, but especially after the fall of Hebrang, he became a sort of viceroy in Croatia, loyally carrying out instructions from Belgrade. His followers affirmed, half-seriously, that it was always prudent to observe which direction Bakarić went, because he never chose the wrong track. Bakarić did not govern with an iron fist, and never betrayed his bourgeois origins, but tried to be courteous in his relations with people. At the start of their collaboration, Savka Dabčević-Kučar noted in her diary that, at the seat of the CC, Bakarić was the only one who used to knock on the door before entering.[533]

After masterminding Ranković's fall, Bakarić joined the young leaders who rose to power in Croatia, watching their backs, but without taking any risks until the end of 1969. On 13 December of that year, he gave a speech to a party group, in which he refuted the accusations about the revival of Croat nationalism coming from Belgrade. The first to speak was a Dalmatian, Miloš Žanko, vice-president of the Federal Assembly and member of the Croat CC who, in February 1969, began crying wolf, evidently in concert with conservative groups that wanted to create a political crisis in Croatia.[534] Between 17 and 23 November, *Borba* published a series of his articles under the provocative title "In this

Nationalist Madness There Lies a Method." Žanko's anger was especially fired by an essay in the magazine *Kritika* written by poet Vladimir Gotovac, who described the situation in Croatia within the framework of the federation as "dirty, crazy, furious, irrational, ridiculous, grotesque, tragic and stupid."[535] In his answer Žanko settled scores with the "nationalist and reactionary tendencies" establishing themselves in Zagreb under the auspices of the "Matica Hrvatska" (Croat matrix) association, several newspapers, and the Catholic Church. He reproached local political leaders for being unable to shut down "vampire Croat nationalism," and instead supporting it. According to Dabčević-Kučar, it had never before happened that an entire legally elected republican leadership would be attacked so openly.[536]

The Serb nationalists saw in Žanko's articles a light shining in the twilight of the Yugoslav ideal.[537] The Croat leaders were of a different opinion, determined to use the occasion to show their rejection of Belgrade's centralism. Bakarić and Savka Dabčević-Kučar convened the Tenth Plenum of the Croat League of Communists on 15 January 1970, at which they condemned nationalism, but even more the centralism that, in their opinion, concealed the hegemonic appetites of the "more deserving nation" (as they ironically called Serbia).[538] This "historic" plenum elicited an enthusiastic spark in Croatia that created an understanding between the communists and the masses for the first time since the war. In Belgrade, it was interpreted differently, as a declaration of an ideological war against Serbia, as a moment of truth when the "Yugoslav mask" fell away.[539] This was not just the opinion of the conservatives, but also of the liberals, who were convinced that the Croat leadership was unilaterally handling problems that should be solved as a group. As they did not want to rekindle the argument, they prudently decided to keep quiet for the time being.[540]

The daring sortie of the Zagreb liberals, welcomed in Slovenia, resulted in a series of meetings and discussions in the Croat League, where the line taken at the Tenth Plenum was widely shared. This could not have been possible without the approval of the highest leaders, including Tito. The polemic against centralism acquired economic and social dimensions thanks to a series of publications that attacked the enormous accumulation of capital in Belgrade banks and enterprises due, according to the critics, to an unjust financial system that allegedly favored an "oligarchy" that was controlling the state economy to the detriment of the "direct producers," self-management, and the republics. The economist Šime Djodan even proclaimed that socialist Croatia was worse off than it had been under Emperor Franz Joseph.[541]

According to a 1967 law, Yugoslav enterprises that exported abroad or earned hard currency thanks to tourism could not freely dispose of their income. The factories, for instance, could keep only 7 percent of their earnings, whereas the hotels and catering companies kept just 15 percent. The rest went to the central banks in Belgrade, from where it flowed through different channels to several large financial institutions that dominated the Yugoslav market and the entire import system.[542] Add to this a scandalous distribution regime for hard currency that favored a sort of black market in which the direct producers had to buy back, in case of need, the money they had earned themselves. The Croatian and the Slovenian economies were the most closely linked to the West and had brought in large amounts of money, above all thanks to tourism. This mechanism caused great frustration among the people, who were convinced they were being robbed by their own government. The Croats became more and more insistent on having a so-called "third nationalization," which would allow the self-managed organizations to administer whatever capital they acquired. And this, so they said, would boost the economy of the entire federation.[543]

The Croatian requests were initially supported by Edvard Kardelj who had spent a great deal of time working on constitutional amendments to curb the power of the central administration and strengthen the economic and political rights of the republics.[544] In a session called on 8 July 1970 to discuss these questions, he declared that it did not matter to him whether Yugoslavia was a federation, a commonwealth of states, or a confederation: the most important thing was agreement between the different nations about their common interests. This should be handled by the Federal Assembly, all the rest should be left to the republics.[545] The following October, he published his third proposal on constitutional amendments, presenting it as a new institutional pact. In his view, sovereignty lay with the republics, while the federation should only take care of defense, foreign policy, and the unity of the socioeconomic system. But these tasks, as well as the appointment of federal officials who were in charge of implementing them, should be achieved in agreement with the leadership of the republics.[546]

At the same time, Tito and Kardelj decided to establish a presidency of the SFRY that would be able to lead the country after the marshal's passing. Tito spoke about this in public during a televised meeting with the Zagreb LCY on 21 September 1970. He announced the creation of a collective body that would function as head of state, although it was clear that he had no intention of relinquishing control. He spoke off the cuff, without notes, appearing fresh and alert, demonstrating his mastery of the situation.[547] His calls for harmony were unsuccessful, however, not just in Croatia but also in Serbia, where discontent was spreading because of the planned constitutional amendments, some of which would guarantee substantial autonomy to Kosovo and Vojvodina, the two provinces of the republic. In Belgrade, people were saying that the constitution should not be changed continually, and that important issues like those under discussion should not be resolved in an improvised way. At the same time, they feared the reinforcement of self-management, because—as Marko Nikezić and Latinka Perović said in a discussion with Kardelj—Serbia was still in *opanke* (the traditional footwear) and could not be modernized without the help of managers and technocrats.[548]

In addition, the Serbo-Croat linguistic dispute fired up again in 1971 because it was impossible to come to an agreement about the publication of a common dictionary. When the project became bogged down in disagreements, the "Matica Srpska" (Serb matrix) issued a declaration on January 10 accusing their Croat "sister" of filibustering. The Croats responded ten days later in an abrasive manner, reproaching the Serbs for denying the "individuality and the cultural and national unity of the Croat language," and announcing that their matrix would publish its own dictionary, without the Serb contribution.[549] This polemic caused quite a stir in the media, as did the election of the vice-rector of Zagreb University. According to the new academic statutes approved after the 1968 uprising, the candidate to that position should be chosen by the University Senate composed of professors, assistants, and students. The party organization of the university named its own candidate, but the Senate decided to elect Ivan Zvonimir Čičak, a twenty-five year-old student of literature and theology known for his nationalistic positions and fiery temper. The Croat leadership, while not enthusiastic, approved this appointment since it was reached in a democratic way.[550]

The watchword was "democracy," which was also affirmed by the most important personalities of the federation, who met under Tito's chairmanship at the end of 1970 at Brioni to discuss the constitutional amendments that would replace a third of the old norms.[551] The leaders gave their blessing to an ample administrative and economic pluralism that would encourage the establishment of a democracy able to represent all the ethnic and regional diversities of Yugoslavia. In the context of this broad approach to innovation the so-called "proletarian amendments" stand out. Kardelj considered them to be "extremely important and revolutionary," because they would give the workers the possibility of governing the entire production process. "In the relation of mutual dependence and common responsibility," the self-managers should be able to administer and to have at their disposal the entire income generated by their work. "Only such an economic condition can guarantee their governing role in the framework of political power."[552]

The Serb liberals (Marko Nikezić, Latinka Perović, Mirko Čanadović) played a decisive role in this renewal process, because they did not bet on the nationalist card.[553] Rather, they opposed the conservative current out of the conviction that Serbia should no longer be the "Yugoslav Piedmont,"[554] but should aim at development and an equal dialogue with other republics. Matko Nikezić, president of the CC of the Serb CP, competent and able, but arrogant, summarized this conviction with the formula of "clear agreements," asking that every republic be able to cover its own bills independently. This was a bold move, since it meant that Serbia renounced its position as the embryonic cell of the country, settling for the status of just one the federal state entities.[555]

D-day for the renewal was to be 17 April 1971, the last day of Tito's presidency of the SFRY. Based on his speech in Zagreb in September of the previous year, it seemed he was ready to accept the title of "honorary president," delegating his authority and duties to a collective presidency manned by representatives of the republics. It was evident, as recorded in a CIA document, that Yugoslav leaders wanted to insert the procedure for his succession into the constitutional norms to avoid any chaos at the moment of Tito's departure from the political scene. On 13 February 1971, Edvard Kardelj, head of the coordination commission for the reform, published a press release declaring that this could not be implemented, because the time was not yet ripe. He made it clear that the Yugoslav leaders would not tolerate any diminution of central power, which was also confirmed by the Federal Assembly's decision to extend Tito's presidential mandate until the end of August. It was widely believed in the upper echelon that it was not sensible to allow free reign at a moment when Croatia and Serbia were in a state of agitation.[556]

The Ustaša Migration

Meanwhile, Yugoslavia was in turmoil over a plot against the Croat leaders, who were accused of being traitors and collaborators of the Ustaša organizations in West Germany and elsewhere. Until the mid-sixties these opposition groups had not played a significant role, remaining fairly isolated. Things changed drastically when the Yugoslav authorities opened the borders with the 1965 reform and allowed workers to find jobs abroad. The majority of these workers went to the BRD (Bundesrepublik Deutschland, or West Germany) where, in 1970, there were already about half a million immigrant workers. There they came into contact with political refugees, of whom at least six thousand were involved in Chetnik and even more belligerent Ustaša groups. Under the slogan "Independent Croatia," these émigré goups promoted a fiery proselytism, trying to bring the compatriots who had come to Germany for economic reasons into their orbit. This worried the Belgrade authorities, especially at the end of the sixties and beginning of the seventies, when the Ustaše increased their terrorist activities. Since the protest to the Bonn government had little effect, the UDBA started to infiltrate these groups, so much so that it was aware of 90 percent of their plans. It was also implicated in the "liquidations" of those who caused too much trouble.[557]

This murky atmosphere was exploited by "centralist forces" in a plot to force the resignation of Miko Tripalo and Savka Dabčević-Kučar, as well as Vladimir Bakarić. The conspirators spread rumors that the Croat leaders were secretly in touch with Munich-based Branko Jelić, the chief of the Ustaša migration, and that they were preparing Croatia's secession from the federation "after Tito." According to information from the Romanian intelligence agency, the Securitate (Departamentul Securităţii Statului), the Jelić group nurtured pro-Soviet sympathies and was under KGB protection.[558] And its paper, *Hrvatska država* (The Croat state), affirmed in February–March 1971 that the Warsaw Pact would defend the independence of Croatia and recognize it with a status similar to that of Finland.[559]

The Croat leaders were furious at these rumors: they tried to curb their indignation in their public utterances, but not behind the scenes, and expected a formal inquiry from Tito to discover who was plotting against them. The marshal named a commission headed by Stane Dolanc, a former officer in military intelligence who had moved up the ladder over the past two years thanks to family connections, from secretary of the Communist University Committee in Ljubljana to secretary of the Executive Bureau of the CC. On 23 March 1971, the Dolanc Commission reached its conclusions. According to the commission, some functionaries of the state security service were so involved in the Jelić organization that it was impossible to distinguish which action was whose. All the conspiracy threads seemed to converge at the secretariat of foreign affairs, headed by a member of the liberal current, Miko Tepavac. Although, in this way, Tepavac, being responsible for that department, was indirectly involved in the affair, the Serb leaders tried to stay calm, convinced that the plot had been born neither in Zagreb nor in Belgrade, but at Brioni, under the supervision of Tito himself.[560]

In contrast the Croats, convinced that the Serbs were trying to diminish the importance of the affair, lost their heads. Although the Executive Bureau decided that the Dolanc Report should be confidential, the Croat CC published it anyway, on 6 April 1971, provoking outraged cries in Croatia and Serbia, obviously for different reasons. Miko Tepavac threatened to resign, while the declarations by Miko Tripalo, the Croat member of the Executive Bureau, were, according to the British consul in Zagreb, "breathtaking for their irresponsibility."[561] This already tense atmosphere was further inflamed by the news of an atrocious Ustaša attempt against the ambassador in Stockholm, the Montenegrin Vladimir Rolović (a former OZNA colonel), on 16 April 1971. In Serbia and Montenegro a hue and cry was raised against the Croats, further amplified by two Ustaša terrorist attacks at a railroad station and a cinema in Belgrade. It was even said that the KOS (military counterintelligence service) had discovered a list of 450 Serb individuals in Croatia whom the local nationalists intended to liquidate.[562]

To clear the air, Tito convened the plenum of the enlarged presidency of the LCY from 28 to 30 April 1971, the seventeenth since its foundation, which was to prove tumultuous. During a preliminary conversation with Tripalo, the marshal said that the situation was extremely serious, that there was danger of a counterrevolution, and that he would not behave as had Dubček, the ill-fated leader of the Prague Spring, but would restore order with the army if necessary.[563] During the session, the Croats were forced to listen to numerous reproaches because of their tolerant attitude toward "chauvinist elements," as were the Serbs, because of their reservations regarding the constitutional amendments. The most dramatic moment came when an assistant approached Tito and whispered something in his ear. Unusually for him, the marshal interrupted the discussion and left the room. When he returned, he informed the puzzled gathering that he had received a call from Brezhnev, who wanted to be informed about what was going on, and who was ready to offer his "fraternal" assistance.[564] Tito assured the participants in the meeting that he rejected such proposals, stressing that the problems would be resolved by the Yugoslav party itself. His words were met, however, by a hostile silence and interpreted as a tactical move designed to put pressure on the plenum so that it would give in to his will.[565]

In any case, perhaps even thanks to this episode, a compromise was reached. In the final statement, which was full of the usual, sometimes abstruse rhetoric, one thing was clear: that "foreign subversive elements" had tried to exploit the difficulties of Yugoslavia by relying on "internal enemies of the country." The attempt to discredit the Croat leadership was part of this plan, but no organs of the federal administration were involved. In short, it seemed that the Croats and the Serbs were both satisfied.[566] Before the final session Tito confessed that he was mostly in agreement with the Croats. After having listened to their laments about how Croatia was discriminated against, he rose from his armchair, visibly shaken, and hand on heart said with a grave voice: "Here I feel that you are right. But you are lacking political wisdom."[567]

Vladimir Bakarić, who was often compared to the Buddha because of his inscrutable behavior, also understood at the time that Savka Dabčević-Kučar, Miko Tripalo, and their collaborators lacked "political wisdom." At the end of April 1971, maybe even before, he had begun to distance himself from them, aware that his younger colleagues were unable to cope with this Croat nationalism, which would burn itself out. Later, in a private meeting, Tito observed that "Bakarić was not used to engaging in battles already lost." He was, as Kardelj also recognized, an insuperable master in assessing the political situation. (And he probably knew that Savka Dabčević-Kučar and her group had been controlled by the KOS for the last two years).[568] During a tour in Croatia, Bakarić began pouring oil onto the troubled waters, stressing that the adjective "national" should not be used for the Croat republic, and in this way recognizing the rights of the large and powerful Serb minority in the republic. In the provincial town of Tounj, he assumed an openly critical attitude toward the ruling trio in Zagreb (Savka Dabčević-Kučar, Miko Tripalo, and Pero Pirker) for the first time. He was severely reprimanded and compelled to defend himself for being too indulgent toward the advocates of recentralization.[569]

The Start of the Showdown

At the second Self-Management Congress, held in Sarajevo between 5 and 8 May 1971, Kardelj played the lead role. It appeared clear that Croatia could expect hard times ahead. In his introduction, the Slovene admonished the republics not to use the autonomy granted to them by the constitutional amendments to favor local chauvinist tendencies. He too, like Bakarić, had distanced himself from the Croat "young guard." Savka Dabčević-Kučar, seated in the first row, did not join the general applause that greeted this assertion. She was still shocked by a discussion with Kardelj in Ljubljana in April when he told her clearly: "I would prefer to see Russian tanks in the streets rather than anything that would endanger the achievements of the revolution, because of your policy à la Dubček."[570] He took for granted that every step toward mass democracy in Yugoslavia would necessarily bring "the victory of the counterrevolution."[571]

During the Sarajevo congress, it was not only the Croats who stood indicted, but also the Serbs. In Belgrade, opposition to the constitutional amendments was growing, as was a hostile attitude toward Tito. His critics affirmed that, at a moment when ample autonomy was offered to the republics and the two provinces, "our main task is to defend the rights of the Serb people, a large portion of whom [about 40 percent] live outside Serbia." This foreshadowed the destruction of Yugoslavia. A university professor even dared to declare that Tito should not run for the presidency of the federation again.[572] In addition, Mijalko Todorović, one of the most prominent members of the Serb political elite, said during a stay at the Yugoslav embassy in Moscow: "Tito is growing old. He will not last for long." Those words were immediately transmitted to the marshal, who reacted furiously.[573] Brezhnev, who had a specific channel of communication with Tito, admonished him to watch out for the Croats, who wanted to separate from Yugoslavia, but even more to watch out for the Serbs and the Bosnians, who wanted to overthrow him.[574]

It was significant for the political climate of the moment that in his speech at the Sarajevo congress, Tito had attacked "some retired generals," accusing them of plotting against him and of maintaining relations with the Russians with the intention of inviting them to intervene in Yugoslavia. Never before had he so openly criticized the army, and his words had an explosive effect. During the night of 8 May 1971, at a secret meeting with high-level personalities (Bakarić, Kardelj, Ljubičić, and Milentije and Koča Popović), he was even more blunt: he spoke about spies and putschists at the top of the Serb League of Communists, stressing that not only should some generals be arrested, but also Ranković, their crony. He did not stop there, but reproached Mijalko Todorović, who had recently dared foretell his death in Moscow, saying that he was the main instigator for the counterrevolution in Belgrade and asserting: "I know it. They plot against me!" He asked for the expulsion of Todorović from the party, accusing him of acting as an intermediary between the Serbs and the Russians. "In Belgrade, they say that I am an empty gun," Tito complained. "But I am not, and am looking forward to demonstrating this on somebody."[575]

This attack against prominent politicians who represented Serbia in the highest organs of the federation and the league was also directed at Kardelj and Bakarić. As noted by Latinka Perović, the secretary of the Serbian LC, it was an attack on those who had tried to free Yugoslavia from Stalinist socialism. Although the party leaders saw Tito as a hindrance to the development of society, they were conscious that he represented a bulwark against the Soviet Union, and therefore did not oppose him.[576] This, however, was not enough for the marshal. Milentije Popović was very close to Mijalko Todorović and called his friend immediately to inform him what was going on. They agreed to meet the following day at the Delegates Club in Belgrade. While they were meeting Popović received a dispatch in which Tito confirmed his accusations against them both. He was so upset that he had a stroke and died on the spot.[577]

Some four weeks after the Seventeenth Plenum, on 2 June 1971, a new plenum convened in Belgrade, tasked with examining the results of the decisions made at Brioni. Against all odds, the participants deemed the domestic political situation positive, and reached a sort of ceasefire, stating that they would no longer broadcast their disagreements. "Everybody should make a clean sweep of his own house," as Marko Nikezić said. Regarding the constitutional amendments, they decided to approve them as soon as possible, "in the spirit of Brioni," and planned a timetable that foresaw a vote at the Federal Assembly that same month, and the election of the state president and the new collective presidency the next. Thereafter a new federal council would be installed, and its members would be named.[578]

At that moment, Tito hoped to find an ally in Miko Tripalo. During the session of the Executive Bureau, on 15 June 1971, he invited him to a private meeting, promising him "a future he could not dream of" (i.e., the succession) if he would help him mend the situation in Croatia. Tripalo answered that he could not abdicate his principles and his loyalty to the fatherland, Croatia. Tito commented that the problem of Croatia was the Serb minority, whereupon Tripalo answered polemically that, in Croatia, the problem was not the Serbs, but the Croats. They separated without an agreement.[579] In Zagreb, where statements circulated such as "Tito, I'll spit in your face if you won't wear the Ustaša uniform," or "Until now we have drunk Dalmatian wine, now we will drink Serb blood," the leaders tried to hold off the nationalist euphoria of the popular masses.[580] When he met Savka Dabčević-Kučar and other important local politicians at his Zagreb residence on 4 July, Tito repeated his threats regarding the use of the army if they refused to act themselves: "It is better that the People's Army restores order . . . rather than the Russians."[581] The Croat leadership was caught in a triple bind: on the left they were attacked by the "Praxis" group, who asserted that the self-managed experiment had failed because it was not radical enough; while the nationalist students, united around "Vice-Rector" Čičak, announced a "hot autumn" of protest against the expulsion from the university of two "patriotic" and overly loquacious professors. Then there was Tito, the most dangerous of all.[582]

The Constitutional Amendments

The summer of 1971 saw the completion of the constitutional amendments, after much hard work coordinated by Kardelj. He had abandoned his long-cherished idea of building a Yugoslav society based on a myriad of communes—akin to the Paris Commune of 1871—preferring to stick with the republics and the two provinces as constitutive entities. On 30 June the Federal Assembly approved a radical reform of the federal structure, introducing confederal elements for the first time. Statehood was granted to the six republics, based on the sovereignty of their nations. A new body was also established, the Collective Presidency, composed of three representatives of each republic and two from each province, with rotating leaders. Thus no one could assure for himself a decisive role at the head of Yugoslavia. This, at least, was the initial idea, which Tito also shared, as he wanted a structure at the top of the state that would allow him to retire, as he said, "when I would like to."[583] However, since it was decided, mostly at the request of the Croats and Bosnians, that the marshal would stay at the head of the presidency and that only the vice-president would be elected every year, it was clear that, for the moment, he was not ready to abandon power.[584] In his public speeches, he declared that he was unhappy as a result: "Instead of being relieved of too many duties," he seemed to lament, "they have assigned even more to me. But it will be a temporary obligation."[585] He was in fact offered the presidency for life, which he refused, stressing that he would fill the post of head of state as long as he was able to perform it with dignity, perhaps a year or a little bit more, while the new institution developed the ability to function properly. It was expedient to name this sui generis office a "presidency without limitation of mandate."[586] The constitutional amendments prohibited the accumulation of state and party offices, but this did not apply to Tito, who remained president of both the SFRY and the LCY. This was yet another confirmation of his autocracy and provoked outrage in the Serb public, which accused him ever more openly of being too compliant toward the Croats. He visited the Belgrade National Theater on 3 July 1971 to celebrate its centenary, and for the first time since the war nobody rose to applaud him when he arrived.[587]

The Croat leaders welcomed the constitutional reforms as a great victory, seeing them as a starting point for the achievement of their economic aspirations. In their euphoria they hurried to introduce offices that had been taken away from the federal government and given to the administration of the republic, as suggested by intellectuals of the "Matica" and Zagreb University. Meanwhile, the Serb minority in Croatia, which constituted about 15 percent of the population and had not forgotten the horrors of the Ustaša regime, began to make its voice heard. Its representatives, who were numerous in the veterans' association and its cultural organization, Prosvjeta (Instruction), criticized the climate created in the republic and asked to be protected, both on cultural and socioeconomic levels. In fact, they had been experiencing discrimination when seeking employment.[588]

The Belgrade press followed the plight of the Serb minority with great attention and sympathy. It put Savka Dabčević-Kučar and her collaborators on trial, accusing them of being anti-Serb and anti-Yugoslav, asserting that they were destroying the state and that perhaps they were even in the service of an unnamed but well-known "foreign enemy."[589] It is true that the Serb leaders were not tempted by the sirens of nationalism, and on the contrary tried to begin a dialogue with the Croats, believing that this policy would bear fruit. But there was no response from the Croatian side.[590]

That fateful 1971 visit Tito made to Zagreb at the beginning of September showed, in an emblematic fashion, how uncertain he was as to how best to move forward. At the airport he was met by a guard of honor, which first played the national anthem but then also the Croatian anthem, which had not been heard in public since the days of the Ustaša. The marshal, surprised, made a step to move on but then stood at attention. In the capital, where they celebrated the newly recovered sovereignty awarded by the constitutional amendments, he was welcomed jubilantly. The population took to the streets and squares, cheering him with enthusiasm when he strolled through the city center in the company of local leaders.[591] By the end of his tour in the republic, he had mellowed dramatically in his attitude toward the *maspok* (mass movement), and became convinced, probably under Krleža's influence, that it was just a popular movement and not at all dangerous. During a gala dinner for two hundred guests at the Hotel Esplanade, he declared unexpectedly that the doomsayers of Croat nationalism were groundless: "Now, when we have established, with the amendments, the premises for a final solution to the national question, granting every republic the dignity of the state, we have not disintegrated our society, socialist Yugoslavia, but on the contrary, we have strengthened the unity on a new basis, as it should be in a multinational reality. This is what we want. Here in Croatia I have seen a lot and learned a lot. The next time, I will know how to correctly evaluate certain information and certain words," he said, referring to the bugbear of Croatian nationalism.[592]

The speech, broadcast on TV, was greeted with delirious applause, but not by all.[593] Those who had begun distancing themselves from the Zagreb leaders, or even to criticize them, were in shock: Bakarić's face was gray and sweaty, Kardelj was furious, and so was Jovanka.[594] It is possible to argue over just how sincere Tito was, and how much this was a tactical move on the eve of a meeting with Brezhnev and Richard Nixon to show that Yugoslavia was not in crisis, as the foreign press had declared.[595] The Serbs, however, were outraged at his words, convinced that Tito was trying to curry favor with the Croats in order to balance his unpopularity in Belgrade. So it was that a campaign of hostile propaganda was begun against him. It was said that he was the "gravedigger of Yugoslavia," that a civil war was imminent, that the army would be fatally involved, that Russian intervention was inevitable.[596] Tito tried to mitigate the unfavorable impression kindled by his words, affirming during a meeting with reserve officers a month later that he did not feel connected to his Croat origins because of the crimes of the Ustaša. This did not contribute to his popularity in Zagreb, where people were saying that posterity would never forgive him for the massacre of 140,000 Croats, most of them innocent, which Tito had ordered at the end of the war. It seems that he changed his tune after being informed that once the Esplanade dinner was over Savka Dabčević-Kučar exulted: "We have duped that old fart again!" This was overheard by a "bird"—as Vladimir Dedijer said—and the next morning the report was on his table.[597] It was the "blackbird," as the military counterintelligence service, or KOS, was called.

Richard Nixon in Yugoslavia

After the invasion of Czechoslovakia, Tito's attempts to get confirmation from the Soviets regarding Khrushchev's assurances that Yugoslavia had a right to its independence and to follow an autonomous path to socialism remained fruitless for a long time. During Foreign Minister Andrei Gromyko's visit to Belgrade in September 1969, and Mitja Ribičič's visit to Moscow in July 1970, Soviet leaders were not willing to publicly declare that the "Brezhnev doctrine" about limited sovereignty did not also refer to the Yugoslavs.[598] As Latinka Perović writes, quoting recent Russian research, after the intervention of the Warsaw Pact in Prague, the Soviet Union could not allow the success of economic reform in Yugoslavia. This would signify that socialism with a human face was possible, though the Soviets rejected any version of socialism that differed from their own.[599] The danger of a Muscovite intervention was ever present. In this situation, the marshal was obliged to follow a double political line: on one side, he attempted to hang on to the characteristic features of the Soviet model, based on the guiding role of the LCY (which preserved his power), on the other, he tried to bring to bear the international prestige he had earned in his relations with Moscow. After the deaths of Nehru and Nasser, the marshal was the only founding father of the Non-Aligned Movement left, and he felt that it was his duty to cultivate and strengthen it, not least because it assured him a prominent role on the international stage and guaranteed a certain measure of security to his country. Between 26 January and 27 February, he visited Tanzania, Zambia, Ethiopia, Kenya, Sudan, Egypt, and Libya. The result of this tour was the Third Conference of the Non-Aligned the following September in Lusaka, the capital of Zambia, which Tito had spent much time planning to give new impetus to the movement; he even tried to convince French president Charles de Gaulle to attend.[600] After the events in Prague, the movement faced a moment of grave crisis, since Tito's Arab friends did not share his urgency to condemn the intervention of the Warsaw Pact troops in Czechoslovakia and ignored his hint that a third non-aligned summit be convened to consider the problem. In Lusaka, however, the marshal succeeded in resolving the disagreements of the previous years, laying the foundations for an executive body capable of assuring constant, coordinated, and efficient activity for the non-aligned. At least temporarily, the movement experienced a golden period, and became more present and influential in the international arena.[601]

At the same time, Tito succeeded in renewing contact with China, even though over the previous ten years Beijing had not missed a chance to argue with the "Yugoslav arch-reactionaries." In May 1968, the Chinese press hurled invectives at Tito because of his adverse opinion of their "cultural revolution."[602] After the outburst ebbed, however, diplomatic relations were resumed thanks to the marshal's endeavors, but also those of Mao Zedong and Zhou Enlai (Mao's number two), since all three were convinced that Moscow constituted a danger to their respective countries. The Chinese ambassador, Seng Tao, was surprised that when presenting his credentials Tito received him without the usual austere protocol, instead holding a cordial interview of more than an hour, although the ceremony should have lasted just ten minutes or so. Besides the renewal of trade (ratified by a protocol in March 1969), the most evident results of this approach were the reopening of a dialogue with Tirana and a trip by the secretary of foreign affairs, Miko Tepavac, to Beijing in April 1971.[603]

Between the end of September and the beginning of October 1970, Tito's international prestige was also demonstrated by a visit from Richard Nixon, the first American president to come to Yugoslavia.[604] Although during his discussions with Nixon and his secretary of state, Henry Kissinger, the marshal did not hide his disapproval of American policy in Vietnam, of its military support of Israel, or of the presence of the American seventh fleet in the Mediterranean, the fact that he was able to speak frankly with his guests demonstrated the status of Yugoslavia in the contemporary world. On their end, the Americans declared their respect for "Titoism," which in their opinion symbolized the possibility of a pluralistic development of socialism, and contributed in a decisive way to the equilibrium of forces in Europe, especially thanks to the non-aligned policy.[605] This was not just politeness, as shown by Nixon's decision to visit Tito's birthplace, Kumrovec, and the following episode. At one point the marshal said to his guest: "You are a great president, but you will be even greater if you end the Vietnam War!" Nixon, who used to take note of the important things he heard, took a booklet from his jacket and wrote down those words.[606]

At the beginning of the seventies, Tito undertook a series of journeys to Western Europe. Before the autumn of 1970, he had visited only four countries in this area and these trips were widely separated in time. In fact, Ranković had instructed his men in Foreign Affairs to do everything possible to prevent him from traveling to the West. Nevertheless, in October 1970 he made an official tour of Belgium, Luxemburg, West Germany, Holland, and France, all members of NATO and the European Common Market. The only difficulty concerned Italy, although the Yugoslavs counted especially on this visit and had been planning a close military collaboration with the government in Rome since the suppression of the Prague Spring.[607] Although the border between the two states, established in 1947 and 1954, was "the most open in Europe," as Yugoslav propaganda proclaimed, Italy continued to insist on the question of sovereignty in Zone B of the former Free Territory of Trieste. This troubled the Yugoslavs, who had to cope with Bulgaria on their Eastern border, which continued to raise the Macedonian question. According to Sofia, "Yugoslav Macedonia" was an artificial construct, given that its population was historically and linguistically of Bulgarian origin. The Belgrade authorities were convinced that the Italian position regarding Zone B did not have any support in NATO, but they were also convinced that Sofia could not have conducted its irredentist policy without Moscow's assent. Consequently they considered Bulgaria the most dangerous satellite neighbor.[608] To stress the integrity of the borders drawn in Europe after the Second World War, they believed it necessary to solve the frontier quarrel with Italy as soon as possible. After a period of coldness in 1967, confidential discussions developed between Belgrade and Rome at the end of the decade, which the Italian right boycotted, forcing the shaky coalition government in Rome to back away from the nearly completed settlement. In December 1970 mutual relations were so tense as to induce Tito, on the eve of his visit to Rome, to cancel it altogether. In any case, in the following months, the diplomatic dialogue was resumed, and the foreign ministers managed to arrange Tito's visit to Rome in March 1971, though this did not resolve the controversy about Zone B.[609]

Tito and the Holy See

The most memorable event of Tito's journey to Italy was his meeting with Pope Paul VI: it marked the first time that the president of a socialist state had entered the apostolic palaces. Relations between the Holy See and Belgrade had been very tense from 1946 on because of the political trial of the archbishop of Zagreb, Alojzije Stepinac, which was carried out in spite of Tito's doubts as to its necessity. Accused of having cooperated with the Ustaša during and after the war, Stepinac, who declined the offer to go into exile, was sentenced to sixteen years of hard labor. Relations deteriorated further in 1952, when Pope Pius XII elevated Stepinac to the rank of cardinal, causing Belgrade to break diplomatic relations with the Vatican.[610] Tito could not understand why the pope had decided to take this openly hostile decision at a time when he was mortally endangered by Stalin, especially as he had been careful enough to release Stepinac from prison in 1951, confining him instead to his native village. This act of mercy did not satisfy the Catholic Church. In the eyes of believers all over the world, the cardinal remained a victim of Tito's regime. This stirred up feelings against Yugoslavia especially in the United States, where Stepinac was considered a martyr. Only after his death in 1960 and his burial in Zagreb Cathedral did relations improve. The fact that Tito permitted this in spite of the opposition of Croat party leaders did not go unnoticed in the Vatican. The successor of Pius XII, John XXIII, renewed dialogue shortly after the beginning of his pontificate, recognizing the postwar changes in Yugoslavia and distancing himself from the Ustaša diaspora. When Tito visited Latin America, the pope even tried to convince the local bishops not to take an openly hostile attitude toward him. In spite of the opposition of some influential circles in the Roman Curia and in the Serb Orthodox Church, John XXIII's successor, Paul VI, signed a Memorandum of Understanding with Yugoslavia after secret talks with Belgrade in 1966 and established diplomatic relations in 1970. In fact, the Vatican saw in Yugoslavia a model of cooperation between the Church and the State that could also be applied in other communist countries.[611] For his part, Tito too made symbolic gestures toward the Catholic Church, for instance visiting the Charterhouse of Pleterje in Slovenia with his wife Jovanka in 1964, and the following year sponsoring a law on religious communities that guaranteed more rights to believers.[612] After 1966, he had contacts through reserved channels with Paul VI, exchanging opinions on the most controversial international issues. Pope Paul VI was so impressed by Tito's statesmanship and his ability as mediator that he considered him one of the world's most eminent defenders of peace. This was underlined in his words of greeting on the occasion of the marshal's visit to the Vatican, during which the excommunication proclaimed by Pius XII against all the Catholics implicated in the Stepinac trial (which included Tito) was obviously forgotten. The pope praised his efforts to build better and more fruitful relations "between peoples and continents," stressing that the collaboration of Yugoslavia and the Holy See had already yielded promising results in this field.[613] The attention lavished on Tito's visit was evident from the moment he arrived in Rome, given that he was welcomed at the airport not just by Italian dignitaries, but also by Vatican representatives—a historical first. The secretary of state, Cardinal Jean-Marie Villot, declared that Yugoslavia was fortunate to have Tito, while Cardinal Eugène Tisserant added that "Tito was the pride of the Yugoslav peoples," and that "if other countries had a Tito, there would be world peace."[614] The pope received him on 28 March—the day that other communist leaders were gathering in Moscow for the Twenty-Fourth Soviet Party Congress—and held a conversation with him for two hours, which in itself was significant.[615] At the congress, Brezhnev only mentioned Yugoslavia in a single sentence, including it among the socialist countries, as if it were within the sphere of Soviet influence. But the efforts of Tito and his collaborators to oppose such pretensions were not in vain, as shown by his visit to the Vatican.[616]

Brezhnev in Belgrade, Tito in the USA

Believing it necessary to "keep Yugoslavia afloat," the West was not stingy in its economic and political aid. The political aid consisted mostly of more or less explicit declarations that NATO would not allow the extension of Soviet influence to the Adriatic coast.[617] Due to inflation, the foreign trade deficit, and growing unemployment in the late sixties and early seventies, Tito's regime was in trouble again. In order to move forward they asked for a loan of $600 million from the International Monetary Fund, the United States, and some Western European countries. The loan was granted. In Washington, however, the authorities presumed that because the economic situation was so shaky other pressing requests for help should be expected in the near future.[618]

In spite of the feverish activity displayed after 1968 at the international level among the non-aligned, China, and the West, the Yugoslavs repeatedly emphasized that their policy was not anti-Soviet. The result was an improvement in the dialogue between Belgrade and Moscow at the beginning of the seventies following a period of severe strain. When, in the summer of 1971, the news came that Tito had been officially invited to the United States—the first president of a communist state to receive such an invitation—Brezhnev hurried to Belgrade on his own initiative. Between 22 and 25 September, for the first time in three and a half years, the Soviets and the Yugoslavs had a direct contact at the highest level, laying their cards on the table. This included a talk of seven hours between the two leaders during a hunt at the game reserve at Karadjordjevo (which generated suppositions, suspicions, and fears that Tito had a soft spot for the Soviet Union and would promise too much to Brezhnev).[619] After a lively exchange of opinions, at the close of this "unofficial and friendly visit" Brezhnev published a statement that Tito had long been asking for. In it, he confirmed the validity of the Belgrade Declaration with which Khrushchev had recognized Yugoslavia's right to follow its own path to socialism in 1955. In exchange, Tito promised to regulate the internal situation of the country and furthermore allowed that "socialist internationalism" was mentioned in their joint statement, as well as the "bonds between the communist parties in the world."[620] The marshal certainly did not delude himself into thinking that the Soviets had renounced their hegemonic objectives, and declared that Brezhnev's assurances were "words, words, words." But he accepted them as a truce, a welcome one, even more so since the Soviets had promised a loan of $600 million.[621]

At the end of October 1971, Tito visited the United States as a "mediator"—to quote his words—between the two great powers, the US and the USSR.[622] It was an opportunity to extract a press communiqué from the Americans in which they declared inseparable the peace and the security of the "entirety of Europe." Never before had the US engaged in such explicit support of Yugoslav independence, further characterizing non-alignment as an "important factor" that "contributed considerably to the solution of world problems" and to the "development of international relations."[623] Not to mention the compliments Tito enjoyed from the American authorities, starting with Nixon, who recalled in his toast at the gala dinner that they met in the same room of the White House that had hosted Winston Churchill, Charles de Gaulle, Adenauer, Nehru, and Sukarno. "The people mentioned were at the helm of States bigger than Yugoslavia . . . but nobody met, as a Head of State and government, as many world leaders as the President Tito. It means that he who is fortunate enough to engage in discussion with him discusses with somebody who is better informed about the entire world than any world leader."[624] Tito was received in grand style, as reported by the *Evening Star*, but also with exceptional security measures. The *Washington Post* defined him as "a legendary leader" who enjoyed the open admiration of President Nixon, and was in tune with a changing world and its new political constellations. The *Baltimore Sun* stressed that he had managed to overcome domestic and international conflicts with his "conciliatory" ability, and that he was the spokesman for a policy aimed at reducing international tensions, a man whose advice and help were sought by many.[625]

To this positive, although overly optimistic assessment, it should be added that Tito's journeys in the West were also economically fruitful: Yugoslavia received nearly a billion dollars in soft loans in support of his stabilization program.[626]

The Calm before the Storm

In October 1971, the Yugoslav army and territorial defense, more than sixty thousand men in all, carried out impressive military maneuvers at the Plitvice Lakes in Croatia referred to as "Freedom '71," and were held concurrently with Soviet-Hungarian military maneuvers. The purpose was to demonstrate to what extent the armed forces were ready to defend the country and its social system.[627] Although in conversations with Croat leaders Tito continued to accuse some of his collaborators as well as high party and state personalities of being "agents of the foreign secret services," the domestic situation was relatively quiet by Yugoslav standards.[628] Frane Barbieri, editor of the influential Belgrade magazine *NIN* (an acronym for weekly information review) affirmed in mid-November that the constitutional reform had made it possible to resolve the Serb-Croat quarrel. Thus a thorn in the side of internal political development appeared to have been removed, since the "reform has taken the material basis of its power to the federal bureaucracy, leaving just as much as is possessed by the republics and the autonomous provinces, as voluntarily delegated to the central power."[629]

In reality, it was just the calm before the storm, which erupted in Zagreb a week before the Yugoslav national holiday (which fell on 29 November). The unrest followed a student strike in support of Croat economic and political demands. The protesters joyfully welcomed "the changes of the socioeconomic order and the promotion of the republic to a sovereign national state of the

Croat people." They called for a seat at the United Nations and a representative at the World Bank to enter into direct discussions for a new loan. They also stressed the need to create a national bank and an autonomous army but, above all, to keep hard currency earned in Croatia in its own coffers.[630] "They behave like a monkey in the jungle," remarked Miroslav Krleža. "They went up to the top of the tree and are shouting so much that they do not realize how the fire licks their asses."[631] Tito was informed of these requests during his journey in the United States. He was outraged, convinced that the Croat leaders should have been able to control what was going on.[632]

The students sent telegrams both to him and to the Croat leaders, assuring their loyalty without dispelling the suspicion that the strike was a counterrevolutionary action steered from abroad. It was not clear by whom: some pointed to the Ustaše émigrés, others to the Belgrade secret services who were committed to compromising the Croat leadership. The latter distanced itself from the students, while at the same time declaring that it understood the "impatience of the young."[633] Attempts by Savka Dabčević-Kučar and her colleagues to convince the protesters to keep calm fell on deaf ears, which gave the impression that this was a maneuver to mask their intention to use the demonstrations for their own ends. The decision of the Croat League of Communists to interrupt relations with the party organs at the federal level confirmed these suspicions.[634]

Although the student movement did not have significant dimensions, and it had already started to die down by the end of the month, Tito used the opportunity to get rid of the Croat liberals. In Belgrade it was whispered that he decided on this after having been advised that "Savka Dabčević-Kučar and Miko Tripelo" wanted to depose him.[635] At the end of November he interrupted a trip to Romania and returned home in haste, probably encouraged by a meeting with General Ljubičić, who informed him that the members of the Veteran's League, not just in Serbia, but also in Croatia and in other republics, were troubled because of his indecision. He made it clear that Tito's role as chief of state and of the army was in danger: "Either you, or them," said Ljubičić.[636] In response to this open threat, Tito convoked an emergency session, inviting "the Croat comrades" to Karadjordjevo, his cherished hunting lodge. He had a long discussion with the delegation on 30 November, which lasted twenty consecutive hours. This was unusual for him, since he did not like long meetings. The confrontation did not escalate dramatically, but the tension was underlined by the armed guards who surrounded the building. According to Tito, there were only a few hundred chauvinists in Croatia, but they had managed to create a mass movement, which was intolerable. Evidently there was too much democracy in the republic: "I have always said that there is no democracy for the class enemy."[637]

From Tito's point of view the meeting with the Croats did not end satisfactorily, because of the nineteen members of the delegation, only Vladimir Bakarić and seven others rallied behind him, whereas the majority supported Savka Dabčević-Kučar and Miko Tripalo and were not ready to bow. For this reason, the discussion continued on 1 and 2 December within the framework of the enlarged presidency of the League of Communists, chaired by Stane Dolanc. This time, Tito was more aggressive. He asserted that the goal of the *maspok* was to eliminate the Socialist Alliance of Working People and to gradually transform the party into a nationalistic organization. "Are we not far from national-socialism," he asked, "and edging closer to Nazi ideals?"[638] He concluded the session with a speech widely reported in the media condemning the Zagreb power elite and accusing it of insufficient vigilance, superficiality, and rotten liberalism with harmful consequences. In his opinion, the Croat communists' plan of action was unclear and foreign to the decisions of the Ninth Congress of the LCY, as shown by the dramatic increase in *maspok*. There was a danger that criminal proletarian elements, nationalists, chauvinists, dogmatists, and "the devil knows who else" would be drawn to such a movement. He called the attention of those present to the foreign support that such enemy forces could count on, having the Ustaša in mind, but also the Eastern and Western secret services. He condemned the Croat press for writing in an unconstitutional and illegal way, and he blamed "Matica Hrvatska" in particular for its seditious activities that had turned out to be extremely troublesome. More in sorrow than anger, Tito leveled the severe criticism that the Croat leadership in the past had been ineffective, as shown by the inability of their members to self-criticize.[639]

Tito was rebuked on that occasion too: in his contribution to the discussion, Kardelj reproached him for having supported the leaders of *maspok* for too long, and asserted that he was jointly responsible for the situation created in Croatia. But these words were not recorded.[640]

The marshal's speech was broadcast that same day on radio and TV, and was approved of almost unanimously. The only ones who tried to defend the Croats were the Serb liberals, headed by Latinka Perović and Marko Nikezić, as they had become conscious (although too late, as Savka Dabčević-Kučar observed in her memoirs) that they would be the next victims. In fact, they had already quarreled violently with Tito during a confidential meeting in May when he had voiced the supposition that an atmosphere hostile to him was spreading in Belgrade.[641]

Toward dusk on 2 December, Tito received Savka Dabčević-Kučar, Miko Tripalo, and their collaborators, to find out if they were ready to accept the decisions of the enlarged presidency. The two flatly refused, stressing that they needed to discuss this in Croatia before they gave a definitive answer. Tito rejected that argument and told them openly that the rebels would bear the consequences for their resistance. Savka, increasingly stubborn, attacked him: "Comrade Tito, beware what you are doing, the entire Croat working class is with us, the entire Croat nation." Tito looked at her and answered calmly: "Savka, you are utterly wrong."[642] In spite of this menacing attitude, the marshal tried to save Miko Tripalo. When the Executive Bureau was convened in Belgrade on 8 December in order to resume the discussion of the Croat crisis, Tito called Savka Dabčević-Kučar and Pero Pirker and asked them to resign from the CC of the Croat League. At the same time he invited Tripalo, who he very much liked, to meet him and tried to induce him to go on with his work, but he refused, saying: "I am responsible. I consider myself responsible for the policy we have followed."[643]

To fill the gap created by the removal of the disgraced leaders, people were called in "who would obey," as Vladimir Bakarić commented bluntly.[644] The presidency of the CC of the Croat LC was entrusted to the party ideologue, Milka Planinc, who—it was maliciously rumored—had taken part in the postwar massacres as political commissar, while the position of secretary was given to the journalist Josip Vrhovec, another inflexible doctrinaire. The old UDBA man and former federal secretary for internal affairs, Milan Mišković, took Tripalo's place in the Executive Bureau. With such lackluster yes-men in place, the real power was taken by the local conservative groups such as the Serb-dominated League of Veterans, and the security apparatus, which had grown so strong that by the mid-seventies Vladimir Bakarić himself felt compelled to admonish the party to beware of what was going on.[645]

After Ranković's fall, the "liquidation" of the Zagreb liberals was the most dramatic event of Tito's Yugoslavia. With it, he asserted himself as the undisputed ruler of the local political scene, proving that a communist regime could not function without an iron fist.[646] This was also demonstrated by the state of siege imposed on Zagreb, which was occupied by large numbers of police. Although the student dormitories were isolated to prevent possible incidents, the following days saw sporadic clashes between policemen and youths gathered in the Square of the Republic shouting "Savka-Tripalo."[647] Meanwhile, trials began that followed a precise choreography determined by Tito: the judges should not comply with the law "like a drunk at the stake."[648] The arrested students were given sentences of four to eight months in prison. The worst befell the representatives of the *maspok*, who were accused of having tried to overthrow the socialist order. According to Savka Dabčević-Kučar, the purge involved about seventy thousand people, including those who were expelled from the party or fired from their jobs. In intellectual circles a widespread panic set in, mixed with desperation over the fate of the Croat nation, which was put on trial for the second time as the weakest link in the Yugoslav chain.[649] "In Croatia, the population withdrew into a sort of internal exile," wrote the West German ambassador, "everywhere depression and lethargy reigns."[650]

The Fight against the Managers

From the start of the economic reform, Tito did not miss any occasion to warn against the danger of bureaucrats and technocrats. In 1969, in a speech held in Sarajevo, he reproached the managers for wanting a monopoly position in society and for relegating "direct producers" (a term for self-managed workers) to the role of employees.[651] Over the two years following the showdown with the Croats, he further accentuated this point. Actually, it was less about ideology and more about a power struggle, since Tito and his circle knew well that the "managers" were superseding the party in the workers' organizations, which had in the past been manageable thanks to those party members who, although small in number, were loyal. It was becoming increasingly difficult to implement the party line within the administrative structures of independent enterprises such as industries, banks, and business, where what mattered was education and competence. The danger was described by Edvard Kardelj when he observed that the LCY was at risk of "separating itself from its base, and becoming a meaningless addition to the bureaucracy, dominated by managers."[652]

The two speeches with which Tito deposed the Croat liberals became obligatory reading in all LCY organs. On such occasions, it was stressed that the main deviation of the fallen leaders should be seen in their estrangement from Marxism-Leninism, in the nullification of the guiding role of the party and the working class, in the lack of a firm hand, and in a general ideological anarchy.[653] It was increasingly said that the idea of the party that guides, rather than the party that controls, which had been popular during the last twenty years, appeared to be ineffective. Tito had reached the conclusion that the party should be firmly in control of the self-managing and decentralized society if it were to survive, and therefore asked for more power for the central organs and more discipline, declaring himself ready to implement all this with force when necessary. To this end, a special "Action Program" was put forward, which would assure the control of the workers over the investments, uproot corruption, and free the party from all "foreign bodies."[654]

The Second Conference of the LCY was called to give the green light to this offensive. It had an extraordinary character, the equivalent of a party congress. It was convened in Belgrade between 25 and 27 January 1972 to make, as Tito said, "a clean break." The top of the party was recentralized and the Executive Bureau was restructured and reduced from fifteen to eight members. The "great leaders"—Kardelj, Vlahović, Todorović, and Crvenkovski—were removed, and secondary personalities were incorporated to stress the importance of Tito's role.[655] At first, the conference condemned the laissez-faire policy that had threatened to remove control over the economy from the party, reducing it to a spare tire. On trial were mostly the banks and the export enterprises accused of accumulating capital to the detriment of the workers and enriching themselves with the fruits of their labor. This was, in essence, the opinion already developed by the Croat leaders, although in a national rather than a class variation. Tito, Kardelj, and Dolanc used those beliefs to challenge the concept of a company based on profit and competition with arguments totally foreign to economic logic, proposing to replace that concept with a new structure, "the organization of associated labor," based on proletarian solidarity. Tito closed the conference stressing the need to strengthen the LCY "as the most conscious power in our society, able to cope with everything that challenges it."[656]

This reasoning was opposed by the Serb and Slovene liberals, who emphasized the need to continue the reform and emancipate the economy from the party's tutelage. In particular, they warned that there was the danger of a "concentration of power" at the political top (which they wished to avoid), implying that the conservative forces were the main obstacle to development. Their weakness, however, was that they relied on the managers; this "new class" speculated in real estate, amassing substantial wealth, hording some of it in banks, and blowing the rest of it on fancy and conspicuous villas on the Dalmatian coast.[657] Among the managers corruption reigned supreme, since many had transferred funds abroad (an estimated $4 billion worth) on behalf of their enterprises to create companies that they would own, although they were created with money that was not theirs. These operations, which the managers justified by the need to improve Yugoslav industry, gave rise to all types of embezzlement and "dirty" dealings. The "socialist market economy," less controlled in many respects than the capitalist one, inevitably resulted in less discipline and theft on a level unknown in Yugoslavia since the time of the Karadjordjevićes. Enterprises took on debt without hesitation, creating an enormous foreign trade imbalance and the worst inflation in Europe.[658] Not coincidentally, sensing the danger from 1971 onwards, more than 130 managers cut their ties in Yugoslavia to manage "their own" companies abroad, beyond the reach of the domestic authorities. This, of course, provided the conservatives with an opportunity to pose as the guardians of morality and progress.

The Ustaša Terror

On 5 April 1972, *Vjesnik* published a rare interview with General Ivan Mišković, secretary to the Security Council of the SFRY presidency, in which he drew attention to the dangers that threatened the country from the right and the left.[659] The emphasis was on the right, since some of those Croats who had migrated were increasingly convinced that the time was ripe for a blow against Tito's regime. In West Germany the movement was so strong that the Jelić group was even able to organize subversive training sessions.[660] The end of January 1972 saw an attack against a Yugoslav plane shortly after takeoff in Prague. The explosion of a bomb on a train near Zagreb followed.[661] But this was only the start: at the end of June, nineteen young Ustaše, coming mostly from Australia, illegally crossed the Austro-Yugoslav border near Maribor, where they hijacked a truck and drove themselves to Bosnia, near Bugojno, in hopes of sparking an insurgency among the local Croat population. A struggle of some weeks with the Yugoslav armed forces followed, which ended with thirteen dead and fifteen wounded. Contrary to the terrorists' expectations, the people did not offer them any help and they quickly ran out of food and water and, in the end, were forced to eat wild herbs and fruits. The peasants informed security forces about their movements, actively contributing to the elimination of the group. Although the police and the army killed or captured the ill-advised and inexperienced Ustaša, the event had a traumatic effect on those in power, all the more so as it was part of a larger offensive unleashed against the regime by Croat émigrés.[662] As Tito confided to party activists in Croatia in the spring of 1972, they had even tried to use biological weapons: an extremist coming from Australia allegedly contaminated water and food in Kosovo and in Vojvodina with a deadly bacteria. "The biological, chemical and psychological war has begun," said the marshal. "The enemy action will increase, especially during tourist season."[663] He was right: the Croat émigrés had determined that Yugoslavia was being saved from bankruptcy mostly by the influx of nearly $2 billion a year in tourism. It was therefore necessary to frighten the foreign visitors away. How? Planting mines on the popular Adriatic beaches, in order to detonate them at the most crowded times, was the grim answer. Fortunately, these plans were frustrated by the security services.[664]

The tension created by these events came to a head when the news spread that the Italians had discovered a helicopter near Udine (northeast Italy) that the Ustaša planned to use to kidnap Tito while he was on holiday at Brioni. In spite of being advised to return to Belgrade, the marshal remained on the archipelago where security was extremely tight. Koča Popović, who liked spearfishing at night, almost lost his life from having failed to hear the "halt" of a sentinel.[665] As for Tito, his working routine stalled: officially he was on leave and nearly all his external communication was interrupted.[666] In this emergency situation, the Yugoslav authorities contacted some Western governments, first Australia, in order to get their support against the Ustaša.[667] They feared that after Tito's death the two superpowers—the Soviet Union and the

USA—would try to exploit the Croat opposition to strengthen their influence in the country. In Belgrade no one doubted that the political émigrés enjoyed the support of right-wing Western circles, but in the corridors of power they also spoke openly of Muscovite help. The party leadership did not want to make it a casus belli, but in contacts with foreign diplomats they did not hide their belief that the Ustaša and other extremists were manipulated by "mighty foreign secret services."[668]

The Liquidation of the Serb Liberals

During this period, Tito felt as though he had returned to his youth, when he fought against the factions in the old CPY. On 21 April 1972, during a meeting at Kumrovec with some veterans, he said that he had always overcome problems with sectarians, in 1937 and even earlier in 1928, and he would do so now.[669] It was clear that he did not have in mind just the Croats, since he also said that he was not satisfied at all with what was going on in the other republics. He was thinking first of all about Serbia, although it was not possible to accuse the local group in power of nationalist deviances. During his leadership of the Serb LC Marko Nikezić had been careful about his behavior, but also excessively optimistic, as he was compelled to recognize later: "I thought that it was obligatory to proceed in harmony with Tito, since it was useful. I thought that he could go a lot further on the path of democracy, being untouchable. I wanted to see him as a protector of our development. I believed that, under his umbrella, it would be possible to take further steps and reach a more modern reality."[670]

Although in a dispatch from the beginning of 1972 British ambassador Douglas L. Stewart described him as one of most intelligent and wise rulers Serbia had ever had, Nikezić was late in understanding how wrong he was about Tito.[671] The marshal was now dominated by a fixed idea, as confirmed by a statement from "a private conversation" with a British interlocutor: "It's hell to govern Yugoslavia. But I never forgot the words that Churchill told me in Italy [in August 1944] that, at the right time, what counts is power, and power again, and power once and for all."[672]

The action against Nikezić and his "excellent team" started in March 1972, when Tito received a "confidential and personal" report about Serbia from his informers. It said that over the last two years he had been the object of direct or indirect criticism from the highest representatives of the republic, who worked against the party line regarding a "further consolidation of our sociopolitical system." The Serb leaders were opposed to Tito's vision of the "class struggle," and disapproved of his attitude toward the Croat liberals, believing that such methods could not be useful in solving the problems confronting the country. They also maintained that his stress on the unity of the LCY meant that he wanted a Stalinist party. They criticized "democratic centralism" and proclaimed that "somebody" wanted to have a party that would be able to command.[673]

To clear up any misunderstanding, Tito convened a meeting on 11 April at Brioni with Marko Nikezić, Latinka Perović, and their collaborators, who attempted to soothe him. He was only partially satisfied, inviting them to show with facts their capacity to confront "enemy elements" in Serbia. Consequently, trials were held in Belgrade against students accused of "Trotskyism," against a university professor suspected of being a nationalist, but in particular against the Serb literary cooperative, one of the most prestigious institutions in Serbia. Its management, headed by Dobrica Ćosić, was compelled to resign. This test of loyalty toward Tito could not, however, save Nikezić and his friends. As Dobrica Ćosić said, "In the boat, sailing on the Yugoslav sea, they tried to save themselves from the crocodile, throwing slaves into its open maw."[674] But in vain.

In July 1972, an open split developed between the liberals and their adversaries, led by Draža Marković, a member of the collective presidency of the federation and Tito's crony.[675] These adversaries believed that Marko Nikezić, Latinka Perović, and their colleagues had taken too tolerant an attitude toward Croatia and had favored the establishment of an overly democratic regime in Serbia, compromising its "guiding role" in case of Tito's "departure." As a result, they should be removed as soon as possible so they could not continue their wrongheaded policy aimed at finding agreements with other republics, even with the Kosovo Albanians, to the detriment of the nation. The clash was resolved, however, in favor of the liberals, who held the majority in the party.[676] In spite of their victory, Tito, backed by Kardelj and Bakarić, continued to plot against them. During a visit to the Soviet Union in June 1972, when he was awarded the Lenin Prize and the field marshal baton of the Red Army for his eightieth birthday (he was the only foreign statesmen to be so honored), Brezhnev complimented him on the firmness shown in Croatia. Tito replied: "I have not finished yet: the main task awaits me in Serbia."[677]

After that "summer rest," when he lived nearly cloistered for fear of being kidnapped, Tito gave a speech in Prijedor on 10 September, the thirtieth anniversary of the Battle of Kozara, where Germans had massacred Partisans in a mountainous region of Bosnia. In it he made clear just who the enemies of the working class were: the nationalists, the technocrats, the profiteers, and the university professors who corrupted the young with Western ideas.[678] The experience of Ustaša terrorism had evidently strengthened his hostile attitude toward the West, convincing him that a return to Marxist orthodoxy was urgently needed for the good of Yugoslavia. The next stage was a session of the Executive Bureau on 18 September 1972, where Stane Dolanc proposed that they send party members a circular letter in order to point out the main problems of the moment and invite them to close ranks.[679] The marshal, persuaded since his youth that the "Bolshevik avant-garde" was indispensable for the construction of socialism, accepted the proposal, allowing Dolanc to snap into action: on 19 September 1972 in Split, he gave a speech that had a long echo and was published three days later by the Belgrade press. "Tonton," as Koča Popović mockingly called him because of his obesity, declared before his Dalmatian audience: "Without a united communist party, there would be no Yugoslavia, considering its historical, economic and cultural differences. This means it is necessary to strengthen the party with a purge at all levels, changing penal legislation to save the results of the revolution, if necessary also with administrative sanctions."[680]

These words, full of obscure threats, were even published by Moscow's *Pravda*,[681] and were followed by the "letter" that Tito and Dolanc sent to all the members of the LCY, but which remained unknown to the larger public. It confirmed the necessity to strengthen cohesion, the ability to act quickly, and the efficiency of the League, which should return to being a "revolutionary organization."[682]

In an interview for the Zagreb newspaper *Vjesnik*, given to a well-known journalist, Dara Janeković, Tito stressed that Yugoslavia needed an avant-garde party in which there would be no room for careerists devoid of any connection to socialism. He criticized the democratization of the regime introduced in 1952 by the Sixth Congress, underlining that communists were obliged to operate in a disciplined and unitary manner. "He who is a communist is a soldier," he said. "As long as the revolution is in progress, he is a soldier of the revolution."[683] A week later Tito convened an informal gathering of prominent members of the Serb party, also inviting the army chiefs. The discussion lasted from Wednesday the ninth to Monday the twelfth of October. This unusual and exceptional session of seventy-three people was organized on the marshal's behalf by Draža Marković, president of the Serb parliament and a leading conservative, with the aim of isolating Nikezić and his followers, who still controlled the institutional organs of the Serb LC.[684] A heated debate arose between the "healthy forces" and the liberal leaders, in which Tito himself took part. He stressed that "we have been too fascinated by democracy," although he was not able to convince the majority of those present of his views. On the contrary, at the end of the first session, the unthinkable happened: the marshal was outnumbered, although Marko Nikezić and Latinka Perović did not defend themselves very effectively. By Friday night, they had triumphed. Dušan Bilandžić wrote in his diary: "There was celebration in Belgrade. Tito is defeated."[685]

Certainly, Tito was not a good orator. According to the Serb writer Ivan Ivanji, who assisted him when he had guests from Germany, he was "the best bad speaker in the world."[686] He liked to improvise and therefore his arguments often lacked logic. He loved platitudes, empty words, popular sayings. The editors of his speeches had their hands full trying to make them publishable by purging them of syntax errors and colorful metaphors.[687] When things became serious, however, as in the middle of a political fight, he was able to organize his thoughts in a meaningful and logical sequence. His speech against the Serb liberals, says Djilas, was supremely coherent and rhetorically accomplished.[688] After the weekend the session was resumed, he presented himself as the champion of Yugoslavia, which was threatened by the wrongheaded policy of the Serb liberals: "The moment has come when we have to get rid of what troubles our people, our working people."[689] He was especially hard on the financial oligarchy, together with the politicians who favored it, reproaching them for not having set "the banks, export, foreign and wholesale trade" on their feet. This had long been the principal criticism of other republics with regard to Serbia, which Tito endorsed, since in his opinion this could have negative consequences for the entire country in the long run. The "gang of villains," to quote Draža Marković, was branded as "anarcho-liberal," elitist, and technocratic: it favored the concentration of capital in Belgrade and neglected the class struggle, as well as tolerating attacks against Tito himself, especially from the universities.[690] Swamped by these accusations, Marko Nikezić and Latinka Perović resigned all their state and party offices on 21 October.[691] Their fall signified the defeat of the "European" school of thought (as opposed to the traditional, based on myths and nationalism), which had been present over the previous two centuries in the political and intellectual life of Serbia, although it had generally not been strong enough to assert itself. The consequences for Serbia and Yugoslavia were serious, even more than those caused by the elimination of their Croat fellow sufferers. "Yugoslav liberalism," lamented the *Economist*, "has been thrown out of the window."[692] In fact, the defeat of the "most educated part of Serb society" opened the floodgates to the "Levantine" school of thought, xenophobic and closed in its myths, unable to pull the nation from its economic and civil backwardness, the consequence of five centuries of Ottoman rule.

The purge carried out in the name of "strengthening unity" was neither short nor easy. It was applied ruthlessly, regardless of who was involved, although Tito knew that he was sacrificing capable people. On 12 November, Koča Popović, in protest against this "palace coup," surrendered his office as a member of the collective presidency of the federation. In the following months more than five thousand (some say as many as twelve) personalities from political, economic, and cultural life were hounded from their posts and replaced by mediocre and practically unknown careerists.[693] Meanwhile, in businesses and institutions, a "tidal wave of primitivism" mounted—as one of the victims, the director of the Belgrade TV station, described it—encouraged by the most incompetent and inefficient employees and workers, who tried to take advantage of the restoration of the "dictatorship of the proletariat."[694] Among the intellectuals there was no lack of opportunists, causing Draža Marković to comment bitterly: "How weak and fragile are our cultural coryphaeuses! They come down like a house of cards as soon as our forces get their act together. . . . It is ridiculous and sad at the same time."[695]

After the Serb "anarcho-liberals" were deposed—with no regret from the masses, since they had stubbornly opposed nationalism—it was the turn of the Slovenes. In Ljubljana the purge was less spectacular because Tito did not participate in it himself, instead letting his local vassals handle it. The main target was Stane Kavčič, president of the Slovenian Executive Council, who was said to have been guilty of paying scarce attention to the working people and to favoring the middle classes. According to his adversaries, he had tried to integrate Slovenia into Western Europe with the help of neighboring countries of Italy and Austria as well as Bavaria; overlooked relations with the non-aligned; and provoked an unstable situation in his domestic strategic area that would not be tolerated in the long run by the Soviets. His faults were not limited to these: he had on his conscience the "motorway affair," separatist tendencies, and the goal of restructuring the economy in order to apply market laws and even introduce joint-stock companies. To quote Kardelj, who was envious of him because of his popularity, under Kavčič Slovenia was governed by approximately seventy directors who had eliminated the LCY from society. He added. "We were near the collapse of self-management and of socialism."[696]

The "Old Guard" Rules

Important party personalities in Bosnia-Herzegovina, Vojvodina, and Macedonia met the same fate in the following weeks. Tito and his cronies exploited the fall of so many illustrious heads and shifted the blame for Yugoslavia's societal problems onto them, including inflation, corruption, unregulated foreign debt, mindless investments, all kinds of illegality, and social inequality, as if the guillotine had not been manipulated by people who had been in power for decades. Thus with a proper coup d'état, the reformatory process started seven years before was discarded. According to Dušan Bilandžić, this was also a personal tragedy for the top leaders: they had kicked off the democratization of society, but when this undermined the regime and threatened their power, they abruptly ended the process with the excuse that it was necessary to save the system of self-management and to prevent civil war and avoid Soviet military intervention. Actually, frightened by the chaotic liberalization of the economy, of society, and of policy, they found a comfortable shelter under the shield of ideological orthodoxy. As Kavčič wrote in a passionate closing speech, in this way they brought an end to a period when the generation of revolutionaries met that of their sons, who wanted to implement a more modern conception of policy and society. The "old guard," unable to accept the new values, rebelled and won thanks to Tito's authority, unseating the generation of sons and associating themselves instead with the generation of grandsons, who had not taken part in the Partisan war but had been trained to obey in party-run schools. Thus the operation was completed: "The old guard rules, the middle guard keeps quiet, and the young ones administer."[697] On another note, Kavčič added this bitter consideration: "The Bolshevik system has won. The new ideological content that was needed was provided by Kardelj and Bakarić, the political authority by Tito. I think that the progressive role of the troika defaulted just in that time, because of their backward-looking attitude toward current problems. Here begins the dawn of the gods and with it, the great crisis of our society. In its time, something similar happened during the French Revolution, in the Russian and Chinese ones."[698]

Slogans and concepts in use for the last twenty years disappeared from the party lexicon: "withering away of the state," "relegation of the party from power," "democratization of society."[699] To testify to the assertion of the most orthodox brand of Marxism, the old values were seen as relevant again: "democratic centralism," "dictatorship of the proletariat," "union of thought and action," "ideological monolithism," "planned economy." The CC reiterated the need to rediscover the Bolshevik soul of the party, believing that only in this way would it be possible to improve relations with the working class, with which the "vanguard" in power was more and more out of touch. In recent years workers had begun deserting the party en masse, resorting to strikes in order to strengthen their requests and showing their opinion of the system of self-management. Tito and his entourage believed, however, that everything would be resolved if they could lay the blame for their defeat on those who had not repudiated reformist ideas and who had bet on the middle class, which had profited the most by them. In giving more weight to professionalism than to party loyalty, the liberals had in fact favored the technical and managerial intelligentsia, a group that it was now easy to accuse of being the standard-bearers of "bourgeois" values and errors. It was said that the strengthening of "techno-bureaucratic trends" in enterprises had robbed the workers of their rights, transforming self-management into a farce. This course had to change to allow the proletariat to regain power. The slogan of the day was ethical and political "suitability," a rediscovered dogma and a prerequisite for all those who aimed to achieve a position in the party or state administration. "It is a euphemism to say 'class and party membership,'" Dobrica Ćosić commented indignantly, as one of the relatively few famous intellectuals unafraid to protest.[700]

While Tito celebrated his eightieth birthday, behind these revolutionary slogans lurked the inevitable succession struggle so full of intrigue as to cause Serb liberal Zdravko Vuković to call to mind the biblical admonishment: sow the wind and reap the whirlwind. He lamented that the final result "will be terrible and devastating for Yugoslav socialist society and for self-management—it will be conservative, full of pan-Serbian nationalism, the enemy of self-management and socialism."[701] Tito naturally explained the coup d'état in a different way. According to him, there was the danger of civil war, which he was set on preventing with his army, if necessary, and without intervention of the Soviets.[702] Was this not an excuse to conceal his thirst of power? Aleksandar Ranković's description of Tito's mentality, written after he was "retired," sounds quite convincing: "For him, political crises were a necessity, which became in time an obsession: he seemed to enjoy having power over others. He never doubted his success, no matter how dirty, lurid, or how well or poorly the devised crisis was planned."[703]

5

The Later Years

Yugoslavia in Economic and Political Crisis

1973–1980

After the suicide of his only son, Borut, on New Year's Eve 1972, Kardelj retired to private life for several months, seeking refuge in alcohol. The Ninth Congress of the LCY (27–29 May 1974) provided the necessary impetus to work on the formulation of the fourth Yugoslav Constitution since the war, which gave him the illusion that he might exert some influence on events. As Stane Kavčič said, Kardelj was a sensible man, attracted to democracy and humanitarian ideals. Aware that the defeat of the liberal elite and the following purge could have adverse consequences since it was not supported by public opinion (especially in Slovenia and Croatia), Kardelj tried to find an escape from this dead end. "He tried to give to democracy and to our 'socialism with a human face' more than was taken away," believing that he might find a solution in the new constitutional law that he had been working on the basis of his Bolshevik and Proudhonian ideas.[1] He was sure that self-management was a "socialist category, born out of the fight with the bureaucratism of the state and an economic apparatus typical of the Soviet Union." He believed that this clash between "socialist self-management" and "technocratic Stalinism" had produced a "new revolutionary phase": the constitution he was working on would define and complete its characteristic features and traits. Its aim should be a conflict-free system in which the proletariat and the entirety of the working class would be able to implement their leadership in society. As Kardelj said: "The constitution is born of man, from his authentic interests and needs, but also from interpersonal relations, which develop on the basis of mutual rights and obligations, and not on the basis of relations between the individual and the state." From his point of view, the question transcended the internal structure of Yugoslavia, and concerned the very essence of socialism in its universal dimensions and meanings.[2]

"Kardelj wanted to be, first of all, a theoretician," noted Stane Kavčič. "He wanted to handle the practice and to steer it according to theory. For him, theory had a religious connotation—a Marxist religion—whose principal origin was not Lenin and the October Revolution but the Paris Commune and the visions of Marx and Engels. Especially in the last years of his life, he believed that history had tasked him with laying the theoretical and practical foundation for the realization of the ideas of classical Marxism."[3]

While he was seeking an ideal society he used the real one as a laboratory for his experiments, regardless of the scandal, intrigue, and corruption into which it was drawn. In doing so, he failed to consider the economic backwardness of Yugoslavia, the intellectual modesty of its cadres, and the mood of the popular masses, who found themselves in the unpleasant role of guinea pigs. He certainly did not have the sort of doubts that are to be found in the diary of historian Dušan Bilandžić from early 1973: "I wonder if it is possible to realize a new social system, different from the rest of the world, in a small and backward country, considering that enormous economic communities, with several million consumers, are being developed. The world's history cannot develop in a small state, unless it is an embryo of a global process."[4]

Kardelj's projects were even more unpalatable to Serb nationalists than they were to intellectuals of Bilandžić's caliber. In Belgrade, many observed with intolerance the "mighty troika" at the top, composed of Kardelj, Bakarić, and the Bosnian pasha, Branko Mikulić, who were able to influence the aging Tito and to appoint people of their liking into key positions in the state and party. Kardelj, in particular, was reproached for having imposed Mitja Ribičič as federal vice-premier. This was seen by the Serbs as a clear sign of the Slovenes attempting to tip the scales at the moment of impending succession. As Niko Kavčič, one of the keenest observers of the contemporary Yugoslav scene said, the Serb nationalists bore the ideological muzzle Kardelj tried to impose on them with increased intolerance.[5]

The 1974 Constitution

According to Djilas, in the seventies Tito repressed all the currents of renewal that appeared on the political scene, seeking support among the old social forces and in the simple, unchanging formulas of his youth. Party, class, and monolithic ideology were again the watchwords. Partially because of his old age, and partially because of automatic Stalinist reflexes, the marshal was not brave enough to ally with the liberal generation, choosing what he knew best and what he considered safer: bureaucracy.[6]

Kardelj, by contrast, still believed in the possibility of creating conditions in Yugoslavia that could guarantee the survival of the regime and its development to the full implementation of the revolution begun during the Partisan years. To this end, he created an enormous theoretical structure, aware that the Soviet

Union—although hostile to self-management and non-alignment—would tolerate the Yugoslav path to socialism as long as it was interested in mitigating the tensions in a divided Europe.[7] It was therefore necessary to take advantage of the propitious moment and to promulgate the new constitution as quickly as possible, to guarantee the establishment of the most progressive and just society in the world, rather than the "technocratic bureaucracy" of the Stalinist brand. Such a society, he believed, could not be easily demolished, even in the event of a grave internal or international crisis. It is a pity, however, as Savka Dabčević-Kučar said, that Kardelj "fought for a democracy whose origin, aim and criterion was his and his alone."[8] He believed that the popular masses should not be trusted but should be led and directed from above.

Kardelj did everything possible to explain to citizens the aims and substance of the constitution as well as the new concepts he was introducing into the political lexicon. He appeared at least eight times on TV, offering long explanatory accounts (although they were not very successful because of his verbosity). As the Czechoslovak ambassador in Belgrade noted, "Kardelj was not loved by the working class, since his theories were too sophisticated and obscure."[9] "If he had not been so intolerably long-winded in his speeches and writings," states a profile prepared by the British Embassy on the leading personalities in Yugoslavia, "he might well have been recognized as a political theoretician of major international standing."[10]

Tito viewed Kardelj's "theories" with skepticism, especially as he feared that they "would ruin the economy," as he said at the Second Congress of Self-Managers in Sarajevo in 1971.[11] Burdened by the struggles and dramatic events of the previous years, he resigned himself to accepting the new constitution, although not without another clash with Kardelj that definitively ruined their relations.[12] Tito was aging and at this stage he was much more interested in concentrating on his role as a world statesman than on the issues at home. According to Josip Kopinič, he was active and responsible for his deeds until the mid-sixties. From that time on, he progressively lost control of the domestic situation, allowing Kardelj and Bakarić to shape policy.[13] Before giving his blessing to the constitution, he asserted that the text must include a series of guarantees that would preserve the regime's fundamental characteristics as he had formulated them. He demanded, first of all, that the role of the party and the army should be precisely defined as guarantors of the independence of the country, and that he would attain the presidency for life, for which Kardelj promised to assure his support. Thus Tito's power became absolute from a formal point of view as well. Kardelj tried to excuse himself: "I know that the proclamation of a life president cannot be a point of honor for a democratic country, but I had to do it to make this work. In the past, the most important officials were hindered in their work because Tito suspected all of them, seeing in everybody a possible rival. I was under this pressure, as was Dolanc and Ljubičić. Jovanka nourished such suspicions and assumptions with her fantasies."[14]

Tito announced the new constitution on 23 April 1973 with a solemn speech at the Federal Assembly. On that occasion, the British ambassador wrote that he was looking all right, but that it was difficult to avoid the impression that he was reading, without enthusiasm, words written by somebody else. His speech was limited in time, lasting just one hour. Then the Assembly remained in session for five minutes, probably on the orders of Tito's doctors.[15]

The brevity of the session was not only due to medical considerations. Tito was not at all enthused about the constitution, because he believed that giving too much autonomy to republics and provinces undermined Yugoslavia. He considered the right granted to every republic to secede from the federation without the assent of the others and without a national referendum to be the most dangerous, and accepted it only because he found himself in the minority in the constitutional commission and because his age rendered him unable to fight harder. He considered it his duty to emphasize that in three, or at most four years, it would be evident that his doubts were well-founded. To show his disappointment, he refused to sign the constitutional charter when it was voted in on 21 February 1974. With the excuse of being ill, he delegated the task to Mika Špiljak, the president of the Nationality Chamber in the Federal Assembly.[16]

Kardelj began formulating the ideas for this fourth constitution in the sixties, when he presented a report entitled "Critical Analysis of the Functioning of the Self-Managed Political System." When distributed, it provoked a lively discussion in the party organs, since it touched on basic problems, most of them addressed during the following years in the constitutional amendments of 1971. After the fall of the liberals in Zagreb, Belgrade, and Ljubljana, the "party theologian," as he was called scornfully, did not cease his ideological research,[17] believing that his efforts would be an important step toward the realization of Marx's vision of the "republic of associated labor," where the working people would exercise power without mediators (i.e., without party bureaucracy). He aimed to create a society "where the individual will be increasingly less a citizen, which means subject to the state, and more an equal member of a self-managed society." To this end, self-management should also be introduced into activities that were not linked directly to production, becoming a global system able to oppose every attempt to resurrect the "bureaucratic monopoly" typical of the Soviet Union, while the state would become a "simple instrument of power for the working class."[18]

According to Kardelj, to reach this goal "basic organizations of associated labor" should be established, able to function autonomously and to collaborate according to their interests. The policy should not meddle in self-management but should only plan the socioeconomic system and how it should run. To include "the basic organizations of associated labor" in the political structure as much as possible, Kardelj thought it necessary to replace traditional parliamentary representation with delegates who would fulfill a role that did not exist in any other part of the world—they would not be professional politicians but rather representatives of whatever collective they worked in. He imagined a complex structure of councils and assemblies in factories and enterprises, in local and municipal communities, and in the autonomous provinces and republics, up to the federal level. Every "basic organization of associated labor" should elect a delegation that was tasked with sending a "corporative delegate" to the municipal, republican, or federal assembly. These delegates would maintain their normal work obligations in order not to lose touch with their constituencies. In this way, a direct democracy would be created, closely linked to the self-managed organizations that could not be exploited by external forces interested in monopolizing power. This new social structure would guarantee the working people the immediate realization of their political and economic interests, and the ability to fully control the instruments and results of their labor.[19] This was the implementation of an old dream of Kardelj's: a "non-party democracy able to guarantee incomparably more freedom than that guaranteed by the multiparty system." In reality, he had created a frightening administrative machine, in which about a million people were involved as delegates, administrators, and so on by 1975.

The constitution, one of the longest and most complex in the world, with its 406 articles, contained a series of elements to strengthen the socialist basis of Yugoslavia: a new specific form of the dictatorship of the proletariat within the framework of a harmonious state structure, where the republics and the provinces would enjoy special autonomies. Only defense, internal security, foreign policy, and the common market would be handled by the federal government.[20] "According to this constitution," said Kardelj, "Yugoslavia will not be a federation or a classical confederation, but a union of people, able to introduce a new category into international relations. In such a union, national independence can develop better than in traditional federal or confederal systems."[21] Tito was much more circumspect. When he gave the constitutional draft to his old friend Fitzroy Maclean, he asked: "Do you think it will function?"

"I don't see why it shouldn't," answered Maclean politely.

"I hope so," said the marshal, not without a hint of skepticism.[22]

Actually, the constitution did not function, as a Serb politician observed: "The shrewd Slovene has fooled Tito terribly. . . . Instead of a monolithic party, which was his ideal, eight parties were created. Instead of a strong state, the 1974 constitution created a confederation of eight states. Instead of a common economy, we had eight economies, all debt-ridden. The clever Slovene had no doubt calculated the laws of nature, believing that he would survive Tito and be able to manipulate the constitution in such a way as to oblige everybody to obey him."[23]

Serbia was most stubborn about accepting the new charter, seeing in it a further attack against its central role in the federation and an attempt on its territorial integrity. "Under the mask of 'democratization and decentralization,' separatism and the destruction of Yugoslavia are legitimized," noted Dobrica Ćosić.[24] And one of his friends, a prominent scholar, added: "We understood the constitution of 1974 as the necrology of the Partisan revolution, of the Partisan Yugoslav bias, which meant the end of Yugoslavia."[25] As Serbia was being poorly represented at the top of the power structure, having lost its best politicians after 1972, it had to accept the charter, although not without an animated discussion in which Tito himself was involved. He refrained, however, from supporting either those who wanted more autonomy for the two provinces, Vojvodina and Kosovo, or their adversaries, leaving it to Kardelj to implement his ideas.[26] Convinced by that time that it would be possible to save Yugoslavia after Tito's death only if its different ethnic components preserved a political equilibrium among themselves, Kardelj hoped that the "nations and nationalities" of the country would be mature and disciplined enough to guard against the dangers of fragmentation of the existing state, even without the presence of a charismatic personality at its center.[27] He formulated a text that posed a grave threat to those supporting a Greater Serbia, since it abolished the federal state as it had been created by the Second AVNOJ, further weakening Belgrade's protection of the Serb population in Bosnia-Herzegovina, Croatia, and both provinces. Kardelj made the provinces practically equal to the republics, recognizing a series of rights for the "new" state entities that confirmed the near confederal character of the whole. The members of the SFRY presidency were not elected by the Federal Assembly but by local assemblies. They were equipped with veto power, while the right to self-determination and secession was reaffirmed for individual republics.[28]

Kardelj was intelligent enough to have no illusions about the short-term efficacy of his work, although he hoped for its eventual success. During a confidential meeting in Ljubljana, he explained to friends the constitution's innovations, confessing that this was his last attempt to save Yugoslavia.[29] In spite of his high-minded words, in the end the charter was nothing other than an experiment, constructed in such a way as to untie the many political, social, economic, and national knots of the country, through an articulated administrative system. In reality, it guaranteed the survival of the only structures that, after the general fragmentation, still had a strong internal organization: the armed forces and the police. In this sense, the "Law of National Defense" (1974), which strengthened the control of the army over territorial defense, and the "Law of State Defense and Its Socialist Order" (1975), which stiffened penalties for the "enemies of the people," were significant. In this latter law, the infamous Article 133, in clear Leninist style, spoke of "hostile propaganda" and "counterrevolutionary activity," including in this definition all criticism of the regime. The law was formulated in such a generic manner that it allowed the authorities to act against anyone daring enough to defend fundamental human rights. "The police interrogate, arrest, threaten, invite to cooperate," wrote Dobrica Ćosić to denounce the actual situation.[30] The latter phrase, "invite to cooperate," was a euphemism for spying on one's friends.

The Law on Associated Labor and the Destruction of the Yugoslav Economy

In this period of busy legislative activity, the most significant law was the Law of Associated Labor, voted in on 25 November 1976 after a public discussion of five months in which Tito did not take part. This "mammoth" law of 671 articles, rightly described as the "small constitution," aimed to "strengthen, regulate and make more efficient self-management in the conditions of a socialist market economy." Kardelj asserted that it would defend the economy from both the Stalinist and the centralist dangers present in the system, but also from the "anarchy" that the market constantly created, although unlike Bakarić, he knew little about economics. "He always looked at economics," said Stane Kavčič, "from an ideological perspective, trying to find means and measures to direct the economy through this lens." Bakarić thought of the economy as a wild horse that could not be fully tamed. Kardelj, on the contrary, thought that it was possible to tame it with the help of will, science, and communist consciousness.[31] In the name of the "agreed economy," as its critics scornfully called the consciously non-competitive economy, and in the name of self-managing agreements, he rejected not just the traditional laws of the market economy but also every attempt at rational planning.[32] The Bolshevik slogan "factories to the workers" was supplemented by "all earnings to the workers," in the conviction that, in this way, political power would be guaranteed to "free producers." This assumption was based on the belief that Yugoslavia had reached a stage of social development in which products were not exchanged according to their market value but according to the amount of work invested in them. The law introduced the Grassroots Organizations of Associated Labor (Osnovna Organizacija Udruženohg Rada) and the Complex Organizations of Associated Labor (Složena

Organizacija Udruženog Rada), inaugurating an enormous bureaucratic body that reached macroscopic dimensions: it has been calculated, wrote Bilandžić, that more than a million norms were implemented, most of which were never put into practice.[33] In order to respect these norms, at least in part, a business of five thousand employees wasted, by reckoning, more than a million working hours per year. The result of this legislative inflation and of administrative superstructures was the paralysis of the economy: over the following decade, the annual growth rate collapsed from 13 percent to zero. At the end of 1977, a survey by the federal government showed that "one third of all organizations of associated labor failed to create a penny of profit."[34] The worst effects of this situation were temporarily forestalled thanks to massive foreign loans, which were easy to get since Western banks bubbled with "petrodollars" that were distributed left, right, and center, without any serious control. The republics and the provinces squandered money, and the federal government suggested that a lot of it probably "wound up in the Swiss banks." This was confirmed by the Swiss finance minister, who revealed that Yugoslav citizens had squirrelled away nearly $13 billion in interest-free Helvetic accounts.[35]

In formulating his concept of "integral self-management," Kardelj could not ignore the challenge of the Italian and Spanish communist parties, which had renounced the dogma of proletarian dictatorship in the mid-seventies, recognizing political pluralism and parliamentary democracy as essential premises of a healthy society.[36] Kardelj hailed "Eurocommunism" as a positive phenomenon within the framework of the international workers movement, stressing especially its critical attitude toward Brezhnev-style hegemony. He considered the new variant of Marxism appropriate only for specific Western conditions, and not a "recipe" or a model Yugoslavia should adhere to. According to him, at the stage of mature socialism his country had achieved, political pluralism would mean a step backward. The results of these considerations were summarized by Kardelj in his essay "Developing Trends of the Socio-Political System," published in November 1977, as a starting point for the Eleventh Congress of the LCY.[37] He tried to square the circle, combining the ruling socialism in Yugoslavia with pluralism—not political pluralism, but pluralism of "self-managed interests."

According to Kavčič:

> Kardelj attempted to make his vision of socialism as democratic as possible. In this vision there is one political subject, the party, organized according to the model of the Bolshevik party. He was not able to overcome these limits and did not believe it was possible to do so as he believed socialism should be determined by Marxism-Leninism. In his view, Marxism was not just an ideology, but a science. He overcame the bonds of the Comintern on a tactical level, but not on a philosophical

> one. He was not coherent as to why, and was not able to clearly explain the relationship between democracy and socialism. He wanted to give citizens as much space as possible, asking them, however, to stay under the political umbrella of an all-knowing leadership.[38]

The "inflation of norms" in terms of regulations, prescriptions, and laws that Kardelj produced (due to his constant dissatisfaction with the results achieved), sounded like a broken record to his own comrades in the presidency of the LCY. Between words and practice, between the "reform of the reform" and the moral and economic crisis that gripped Yugoslav society, there was too wide a gap not to be noticed. In conservative circles of the party, it was not-so-secretly whispered that "Djilas's ideas" had been revived.[39] Kardelj was not criticized openly, since everyone believed that he would succeed Tito, but nobody valued his theories any longer. "It is the general opinion," commented Dušan Bilandžić in December 1978, "that the old ideas are worn out. New solutions, new trends, new policy cannot be formulated while Tito is alive. Everybody is waiting for D-Day."[40]

The sad truth was that behind the utopia preached by Kardelj, Tito's autocracy was hidden, the last bulwark of the failed Yugoslav experiment.[41] The entire government structure, at the federal and republican levels, was incompetent and marked by dilettantism: from 1972 until the end of the decade it spent more than $40 billion on different development projects without any tangible results.[42] Meanwhile, it became heavily indebted abroad, following the example of the federal finance secretary, Petar Kostić, who took out a billion-dollar loan to save the iron foundry at Smederevo without informing his government.[43] It seems that no one in Yugoslavia was aware that, as a consequence of the petrol crisis in 1973, the Soviet model of quick industrialization, to which Tito and his comrades remained faithful, became unsustainable for a country with poor energy resources. After the 1974 constitution, the level of foreign debt grew substantially, since the republics, being "sovereign," did not need Belgrade's permission to take out new loans. By the mid-seventies Yugoslavia had a foreign debt of $4.6 billion, which rose to $16 billion by the end of the decade. Combined with internal difficulties economic growth ground to a halt as a result of the world economic crisis, which was caused by a steep increase in petroleum prices. The Yugoslavs were not used to economic stagnation, and the republics reacted with self-sufficiency, further stressing the inability of the federal government to create a common market and to carry out the plan for the "associated labor" that the regime's propaganda endorsed. Although within the framework of the five-year plan of 1971–75 the developed north gave some $3 billion to the south and promised to increase this sum in the period to follow, the gap between the two geographic areas of the country seemed impossible to bridge.[44]

Kardelj was aware just how precarious the Yugoslav situation was. From 1974 onward he criticized current economic and political trends at every party session. In February 1977, when he already knew that he was terminally ill, he said during a meeting of high officials: "Do not count on me anymore. . . . When I read the newspapers and listen to speeches I am frightened. . . . In a year or two, we will have galloping inflation, a situation similar to Chile [where, in 1973, there was a coup against the left-wing president, Salvador Allende]."[45] Even more bitter was his observation, confided to Bogdan Maglić, a Yugoslav researcher who worked in the US, that "our system is terrible and wrong. Practically nothing can be done. And no improvement is possible."[46] In the end, he recognized his defeat with one of his most sincere and pregnant sentences: "A human being cannot find happiness from a state, or a regime, or a party: he can create happiness only by himself."[47]

Kardelj's Death

During his twilight years, Tito took part ever more rarely in sessions, conferences, and meetings, preferring to summon the representatives of various administrative branches to his residences to give him reports and to be given instructions. The Executive Bureau of the LCY worked through Stane Dolanc, who transmitted Tito's and Kardelj's directives to its members, who were simply obliged to accept them. "This trinity," said Jure Bilić, the secretary of the Croat CC, "wishes to maintain power. It is not interested in anything else."[48] In the atmosphere of late "Titoism," which was celebrated in Yugoslavia with much propagandistic zeal, its protagonist was divinized as a tool for those on top to safeguard their positions. Kardelj was aware of it to the point that he said, without denying the marshal's historical importance, that "Yugoslavia could not afford another Tito."[49] At the sixth session of the LCY presidency, convened at Brdo Castle on 9 October 1978, he envisaged the problem of the party's structure after Tito's passing. He mentioned the candidates for succession, who toured Yugoslavia presenting themselves as "small Titos," poised to step into his shoes but without his charisma and capabilities. "Surely, in the future," he said, "we will not seek another Tito, since there is no one like him nor will there be for a long time." For this reason, he proposed the creation of a new collective body to govern the LCY in a truly democratic way, although he had no illusions that it would be easy, considering the backwardness of Yugoslav society. "This would need to destroy the force of hierarchy and of a hierarchical principle that is still pretty strong," he noted.[50]

Did he include his protégé among the "small Titos," fifty-two-year-old Stane Dolanc, the operative of the LCY, whom many predicted would be the marshal's successor? In those years, a strong propaganda machine churned behind him, aided by the confidence that the beefy Slovene enjoyed with Tito and by his close contacts with military and intelligence circles.[51] At the Eleventh Congress of the LCY, in June 1978, he was nominated for a new office—secretary of the Presidium of the LCY—which confirmed his preeminent role among Tito's closest collaborators. According to a CIA report, he was even angling to become secretary of defense and engaging in a "dirty" campaign against the other candidate, Admiral Branko Mamula. Many, however, disliked his rise and the increasingly aggressive expansion of his influence. Dobrica Ćosić said that he was the strong man of the Brioni monarchy, its iron fist for nearly fifteen years. He wrote: "To the reign of Tito, debilitated by old age, he gave the energy of an alpinist and the cruelty of a small game hunter. Dolanc supplied the strength Tito was lacking. Without him, his despotism could not have functioned."[52] As evidence of this, it is worth quoting the rumor circulating in the mid-seventies that it was not safe to go hunting bears with Dolanc. "It was not said with much animosity," wrote the British ambassador, "but the fact itself that it was said by a politician, close to the real inner circle, confirms my conviction that you cannot be Tito's tool for recentralization, without creating a lot of enemies regarding the future after Tito."[53]

While party officials waited for the "rotation" of leaders due in 1976, a large hostile front formed against Dolanc, with Jure Bilić, a member of the party executive committee, at its fore.[54] CIA analysts suspected that this anti-Dolanc group was nourished by the Soviets, who disliked him because he did not hide his critical attitude toward their hegemonic ambitions. In Washington they were convinced, however, that the "highly pragmatic and organized" Dolanc would be able to consolidate his position while awaiting D-Day. At the same time, they did not exclude the possibility of his fall in the case of unforeseen events, noting that "the pivotal factor is likely to be Tito himself. His personal reaction to the squabbling in the leadership currently appears to be to let the contest run its course. He can thereby influence the selection of the first-among-equals, without appearing to force his own wishes on those who survive him."[55]

The atmosphere of intrigue that characterized the last years of Tito's life is exemplified by the fate of Džemal Bijedić, a capable Bosnian Muslim who was called to the presidency of the federal government in July 1971. During his mandate, he was in two airplane crashes, losing his life in the second one, on 18 January 1977. The general opinion was that he was killed by those who disliked a "Muslim nation" being recognized in the heart of Yugoslavia, and that he was an architect of that recognition and of the alliance of the smaller Yugoslav nations against Belgrade.[56]

When in July 1978 Dolanc proposed a reduction of the forty-seven-man Presidium of the LCY by half and the establishment of a seven-man "political bureau" with himself at the head, the "old guard," with Vladimir Bakarić in the lead, reacted immediately. It seems that the Croat politician told him that party elders knew perfectly well how Stalin had come to power after Lenin's death, and that they had no intention of repeating the experience. In the internal conflicts that followed, mutual rivalries and jealousies grew stronger, provoking a paralysis of the decision-making processes in political life. At the top of the party the wait for D-Day created an oppressive atmosphere. A British general commented that "the last great favor Tito could do for his country is to die as soon as possible."[57]

Since he was not ready to allow any of his colleagues to grow too strong, it is probably no coincidence that only eleven days after Kardelj's speech on "small Titos," the marshal proposed, without warning the members of the LCY Presidium, that this institution be transformed into a collective body similar to the state presidency of the federation. It was therefore decided that a new chairman should be nominated every year, according to an established rotation mechanism. Fifty-year-old Branko Mikulić, an ally of Bakarić's known for being a ruthless courtier, was chosen first. Stane Dolanc remained the secretary of the renewed twenty-four-member Presidium, therefore a diarchy was created at the top of the party. This was designed so that the two would control each other, but in fact it resulted in Dolanc's withdrawal. On 15 May 1979, a day before he was to travel to Moscow in Tito's entourage, Dolanc declared, to general surprise, that he was resigning his office, having filled some of Kardelj's duties.[58] Kardelj had died the previous February, unable to protest against Tito's policy from beyond the grave in any way other than refusing a state funeral at the federal level and opting for a markedly Slovenian ceremony. The marshal took part in the funeral service without being able to hide his animosity toward his deceased comrade.[59]

The inclusion of Stane Dolanc in the delegation accompanying Tito to Moscow suggested to Western observers that he was back in the running as a possible successor to Tito. His sudden resignation, which also meant that he would not accompany the president after all, said something quite different. Although he remained in the Presidium as a representative of Slovenia, and received the highest Yugoslav decoration, he lost his key role at the top of the party at a critical moment, less than a year before Tito's death. He had dominated the Executive Bureau for nearly a decade, although the mandate for this office, according to the rotation rules, should have lasted just one year. He was the last of the eminent personalities that Tito removed from power during his long life. (It did not even help that he entertained him with dirty jokes and played cards with him, knowing that it was a better strategy to lose.[60]) Dolanc's dismissal confirmed Tito's ruling style: keep his potential successors uncertain of their status and play them against each other. His comment when Stalin died could be applied to himself too: "Stalin never built up a successor."[61]

After Kardelj's burial, Tito rid himself of both his beliefs and his followers. Faithful to the maxim "divide et impera," he disavowed the reformism of the Slovenes, favoring a group of conservatives, whose eminent representative was Dušan Dragosavac, a member of the Serb minority in Croatia, called now to be the new secretary of the LCY. Meanwhile, there was also a change at the top of the army: the Slovenian general Stane Potočar, chief of the General Staff, had to give way to Admiral Branko Mamula, a Dalmatian Serb. Other Serbs, originally from the former Habsburg provinces, came to power with the clear assignment of keeping Slovenes and Croats in check, but also monitoring their own compatriots in Belgrade.[62]

The Changing Relations between Washington and Belgrade

The fall of the Serb, Slovene, and Macedonian liberals in 1972 was welcomed by the Soviets, who saw it as a restoration of party centralism. The diplomats of the Eastern bloc in Belgrade noted with favor that the Yugoslav officials once again began "to speak our language" in their fight against nationalism and liberalism.[63] Tito did not, however, revive the old *nomenklatura* system, which Ranković had used with such ability, but assigned the administration of the party to his trustees in different republics, reserving for himself the appointments to key positions at the federal level and making sure that the strong Serb and Macedonian influence of the past would not be restored. In the years after 1971–72, the party's grip on society was strengthened: in the publishing houses, universities, factories, and administrative institutions of every kind "collectives" reappeared (groups of engaged communists, or people who pretended to be), which became an important instrument for the restoration of political orthodoxy.[64] The press removed the term "Stalinist" from its lexicon and avoided any criticism of Soviet reality. The leitmotif of the new trend was the danger coming from the West. It was championed by Tito himself, who mentioned at the Third Conference of the LCY in Belgrade on 3 December 1972 the three hundred thousand reserve soldiers who were "temporarily" working in Western Europe. These reservists were enough to man three armies. In saying this he wondered if, in "case of a conflict," the Western governments would allow these reservists to return home, and asserted that "the party has until now been too careful of hard currency and too insensitive of the consequences of the exodus of so many young and capable people."[65]

In this he was supported by Stane Dolanc, who stressed in an interview on New Year's Eve 1973 that in some Western European countries the hostile propaganda against Yugoslavia was directed against progressive forces in general, even in their own backyards. Although influenced by tense relations with Italy and Austria because of the border question between Zones A and B of the former Free Territory of Trieste (still not recognized by Rome), and because of the Slovenian minority in Carinthia, these reflections were above all aimed at creating a feeling of public alarm to be used as a safety valve that would relieve the dissatisfaction of the popular masses regarding the difficult domestic situation.[66]

When a new war between the Arabs and the Israelis started on 8 October 1973, Tito had no doubts about with whom to side: he immediately promised "all-round" support to the Arabs to shore up his waning authority in the nonaligned movement. While the fight was going on, Yugoslav journalists were given the directive to write "as if we were at war with Israel." They did so against their feelings.[67] The marshal granted fly-over rights for the Soviet airlift supplying arms to Egyptian and Syrian units and, when these were heavily defeated, he went so far as to suggest to Anwar Sadat, Nasser's successor, that he bomb Tel Aviv. This advice, intercepted by American intelligence, provoked a wave of indignation in Washington. The United States accused Tito of having decisively contributed to the outbreak of hostilities in the Middle East and definitively abandoned the hope of using him as a mediator in that region. The relations between Belgrade and Washington deteriorated so much that, for a certain period, they were nearly interrupted altogether. Henry Kissinger broke off contacts with the Yugoslav ambassador and the following autumn refused to receive the Yugoslav foreign secretary during his stay in New York for the UN General Assembly.[68] Nahum Goldmann, founder of the Jewish World Congress, took a different attitude; he invited his old friend Tito to resume his mediation between the warring parties. The marshal did so, but without success.[69]

The cooling of relations between Belgrade and Washington was welcomed by Yugoslav military chiefs who believed that the "aggressive and imperialist powers were offensive everywhere in the world: first in Vietnam and Cambodia, then in Chile, Panama, Puerto Rico and in Middle East. This offensive, aimed at gaining new positions, went very far—"to the limits of a Third World War."[70] In the government and in economic and intellectual circles, by contrast, Tito's pro-Arab policy caused bewilderment. It was widely said that he had sacrificed the interest of the country to his ambition to play an important role on the world stage. He was heavily criticized—but obviously without any consequences—and he stubbornly persevered in his pro-Arab policy, which was in perfect agreement with the Soviets. They were so delighted with his attitude that they invited him to meet with Brezhnev in Kiev. When he went there in November 1973, allegedly for a hunting trip, the Western newspapers were full of cynical commentaries: "Just good friends? Why do the Russians and the Yugoslavs go on meeting like this?" asked the *Economist*, with suspicion.[71] The press release at the end of the meeting seemed to suggest that they were not just friends but allies as well. To describe the spirit of their conversations, the two leaders used the word "trust" for the first time and forgot to mention the Belgrade and Moscow declarations, as if they were obsolete. Tito did not hide his critical attitude toward the American "gangsters" and their policies in the Middle and Far East or in the Mediterranean, convinced that he was besieged by capitalist states such as Italy, Greece, and Austria. He asked for and received military supplies from Brezhnev, including SAM rockets like those recently used on the Israeli-Egyptian front. A mutual sympathy was created between the two statesmen, demonstrated by Tito's emotion when Brezhnev gifted him a collection of his writings published in Russian.[72]

"Leninist discipline" was confirmed at the Tenth Congress of the LCY in 1974, which hosted a Soviet delegation for the first time since 1964. *Pravda*, in its commentary, praised Tito's firmness in fighting the "enemies of socialism." The marshal was convinced that he deserved these sorts of encomia, as testified by the self-aggrandizing expressions he used without restraint at this "Victory Congress," where he was confirmed as president for life of the LCY. "We have defeated all our opponents," he claimed on that occasion, which was, in his opinion, the "best congress of our party" and "a congress that has illuminated the entire world like a torch." At the same time, he condemned the entire political experience of recent years, stressing that the "worst enemies of socialism and self-management were technocracy and bureaucracy, especially if ideologically supported by nationalism, liberalism and dogmatism."[73]

This return to Soviet-style orthodoxy troubled not just Belgrade's relations with Washington but also the European Economic Community. When the Arab States decided to raise the price of petroleum as a reaction to the Israeli victory in the Yom Kippur War, the Yugoslavs hailed this step enthusiastically, ignoring their own economic interests. The admonitions of Foreign Secretary Miko Tepavac went unheard: he advised that the country should follow a neutral course, similar to that of the Swiss, rather than persist in its pro-Arab attitude. "Our policy," Kavčič confided with resignation in his diary, "sees a more important ally in every Arab sheikh, black chieftain or Asian despot than in developed and civilized Europe."[74] In his opinion, this attitude contained something of Stalin's distrust of the West, as well as his sectarianism and

"Asiatic" mentality. He was wrong, however, to speak of "our" policy; this was actually Tito's own personal policy, as over the years he had become increasingly prone to identify Yugoslavia with himself and to be easily swayed by adulation. During the Fourth Non-Aligned Conference in Algiers in 1975, Jean-Bedel Bokassa, the ruler of the Central African Republic, addressed him thus: "Mister President—what Alexander the Great, Caesar, Napoleon and Wilhelm II were unable to achieve, to unite the majority of humanity with force of arms, you have achieved with the force of ideas. You have united small and mid-sized states of the contemporary world, representing two-thirds of humanity, and with reason proclaiming themselves its conscience."[75]

It is clear that, after such compliments, the relations between Yugoslavia and the Central African Republic (later Empire) were marked by a maximum of cordiality. Foreign Secretary Miko Tepavac, already weakened by the fall of his liberal friends and confronted with a policy he could not agree with, decided he could not stay in office. On 1 November 1972 he resigned and was replaced by Miloš Minić, known for his conservative ideas. Minić had been in disgrace for some time, but at the moment he was considered "Tito's man," given that he favored close collaboration with Moscow. The price for the recovered friendship with the Soviets was paid by the "Praxis" group of philosophers, including illustrious professors from the Universities of Belgrade and Ljubljana. Because of the influence these "Trotskyists" exercised on intellectual and student circles, they were removed from their chairs and their magazine was closed. "Yugoslavia," said the vice-president of the federal Presidium, speaking with the Czechoslovak defense minister, Martin Dzúr, "feels part of the socialist world. In case of tensions, it will fight with it against imperialists."[76] In the name of such friendly relations, or even an informal alliance, Tito allowed the Soviets, at the beginning of 1974, to use the Dalmatian ports for the repair of their fleet: an important concession considering the increasing Soviet presence in the Mediterranean.

The Cominformist Emigration

Just at the moment when it seemed that there were no stumbling blocks between Moscow and Belgrade—although economic collaboration still needed improvement—an unexpected incident happened that was connected to the Cominform emigration (those who followed Stalin rather than Tito when the two split in 1948). After the exclusion of the CPY, the Cominform had developed virulent propaganda against Tito with the help of the press and radio stations broadcasting from the socialist countries and the Soviet Union.[77] It also sponsored espionage and armed groups that continually provoked incidents on the frontier, trying to sabotage production and to destabilize Yugoslavian society. The Soviet military authorities even created an air force in the Urals region that was transferred to Moscow at the beginning of the fifties to be on hand in case of an attack against Yugoslavia.

During the dramatic years of the struggle with Stalin, the émigrés were considered "healthy forces," true Marxists, destined to be the nucleus of the future new CPY. Their representatives took part in every party congress of the socialist "camp" and when Stalin died they placed a wreath on his coffin with the dedication: "To the greatest friend and defender of Yugoslav peoples." After 1954, when the "normalization" between Khrushchev and Tito took root, their organizations were closed, although only formally, and their press and radio stations were silenced. The problem of the Cominform diaspora was not solved until after 1956 when, on the occasion of Tito's visit to the Soviet Union, Khrushchev asked him to meet a delegation of émigrés in Kiev. It was then that an agreement was signed between the two governments that aimed to guarantee amnesty to the Cominformists and to allow those who wished to return home to Yugoslavia from the USSR and other bloc countries to do so.[78]

Although Tito tried to resolve this delicate issue, groups of émigrés continued to plot against his regime. When amnesty was proclaimed about 1,300 of them made use of it and left the "camp." However, the Soviet secret services prevented a significant number of émigrés from being informed about the amnesty (nearly all those who lived outside Moscow). Consequently, the majority accepted Soviet citizenship, a decision welcomed by the authorities, who now had at their disposal a group of people they could manipulate at will.[79] Their anti-Tito activities were not completely interrupted: they continued to meet in the "patriotic clubs" that became active when relations between Moscow and Belgrade returned to a heightened state of tension. In 1956 they sent a letter to the Twentieth Congress of the CPSU that was not read to the delegates because of Khrushchev's decision to demolish Stalin's myth. But at the end of the fifties, when Kardelj's "revisionist" party program rekindled the struggle between the CPSU and the LCY, they reappeared with a message to the Twenty-First Extraordinary Congress of the CPSU, which was included in its official documents.[80] In subsequent years they split into two streams: an extremist one led by Mile Perović, and another more moderate group headed by Vlado Dapčević. The latter was a much more interesting personality than Perović (who was just an aging fanatic) and had an adventurous past worth remembering. He was a half-brother of the legendary General Peko Dapčević and a close collaborator of Arso Jovanović. Together with Jovanović he had tried to expatriate to Romania in August 1948 but had been arrested and sentenced to prison. After the amnesty in 1956 he was banished to his native village near Cetinje in Montenegro from where, three years later, after the Seventh Congress of the LCY, he escaped to Albania with eight prison mates who were opposed to Kardelj's "revisionism."

From there he traveled to the Soviet Union and then went to Brussels in 1967, more or less in agreement with the Soviet authorities (who were not orthodox enough for his tastes) to engage in anti-Tito propaganda with the guest workers in Western Europe.[81]

During his conversations with Tito after Khrushchev's fall, Brezhnev admitted that secret contacts between some émigrés and those circles in Moscow that were hostile to the Yugoslav regime may have occurred. But he categorically denied that they were supported by the Soviet authorities: "For us, this does not exist. Something similar can be speculated only by our enemies."[82] In reality, however, even in May 1971 the émigrés could "celebrate" Tito's birthday in Moscow with two conferences attacking him personally. Consequently, polemics flared up between Belgrade's newspaper *Politika* and the Russian daily, *Izvestiia*, accompanied by an official note of protest from the Yugoslav foreign secretary. The following September, during their meeting in Karadjordjevo, Tito and Brezhnev discussed the Cominformist machinations and the Soviet leader assured him again that he did not support hostile activity against Yugoslavia. In fact, the Moscow government had banished the Cominformists from its territory but with some advice: "If you wish to do something, do it abroad."[83]

1974: The New Yugoslav Communist Party

On 6 April 1974, at a time when Tito was loudly proclaiming that the Soviet Union did not present any danger to Yugoslavia and was protesting against Western attempts to use it as a scarecrow, a congress of a "renewed" Yugoslav Communist Party was convened in the Montenegrin port of Bar. It came in response to Kardelj's constitution, which provoked a wave of criticism in Moscow because it "lacked not just Marxist analysis, but even the most elementary class approach."[84] Among the organizers of the meeting, which happened while the preparations for the Tenth Congress were underway, was Dušan Brkić, a former prisoner on Goli Otok who had apparently learned no lessons from his time there. Under his chairmanship, the participants voted on a program and a statute diametrically opposed to the policy implemented by Tito and his comrades from 1948 onward. They declared the "disbandment of the LCY" and proclaimed the constitution of a "new CPY" that would restore the Stalinist regime and recognize the Brezhnev "doctrine" of "limited sovereignty" in order to align the country with the Soviet Union. Tito was dismissed from his office as secretary general and replaced by the old Cominformist, Mile Perović, all in absentia and purely theoretically, of course.[85]

The Yugoslav authorities certainly did not learn about the clandestine congress by chance, since they had their own informant in the "Kiev group." When it was clear that the material needed for the Bar gathering would be smuggled from Budapest in a diplomatic car, they arranged an accident near the border. The son of a diplomat from the Soviet Embassy in Belgrade was implicated in the smuggling. In his baggage the police found leaflets the young man was bringing to Bar. The authorities acted immediately, arresting the participants in the congress and sentencing them to jail for two to fourteen years.[86]

This event was a heavy blow for Tito and his comrades, who had to acknowledge that the leaders of the Soviet Union, in spite of their declared friendship, had not renounced their "hegemonic plans" and must have been behind this ploy. In case of internal troubles, caused for instance by the marshal's death, they could presumably exploit the expedient that had proven so useful during the Hungarian and Czechoslovak crises and invade the country after an "appeal" from the "legitimate" CPY to "restore order."[87] That would have come from this "Kiev group," had their subversive activities not been foiled. As Vladimir Bakarić said to the Danish journalist Gunnar Nissen, the conviction was spread in Moscow that only Tito was "trustworthy," whereas his colleagues were not.[88]

In spite of the assurances that the discovery of the anti-party group would not influence relations with the Soviet Union, a notable chill entered the air, since the Yugoslavs could not free themselves from the suspicion that the subversives were controlled by the Russians.[89] General Jan Šejna, a former chief of the political office of the Czechoslovak army who had defected to the United States in 1968, reinforced this conviction. In February 1974, he published an interview in the Vienna magazine *Profil* revealing a Warsaw Pact military plan: in case of a crisis, the troops of the Soviet bloc would invade Yugoslavia, passing through Austrian territory.[90]

In the past, the Yugoslavs had not hidden their suspicions about subversive Soviet activities, denouncing them from time to time and claiming that they were remarkably widespread. Privately they accused the Soviets of being involved in the Kosovo uprising in 1968 and in subsequent emigrant intrigues of all ideological shades. In January 1970 Tito had a harsh discussion with the Soviet ambassador, Ivan A. Benediktov, but to no avail.[91] Even during the most cordial periods between the marshal and Brezhnev, the Soviet secret services did not give up the idea of creating a fifth column in Yugoslavia, as evidenced by the June 1973 decision by KGB director Yuri V. Andropov to warn Dobrica Ćosić, through his agent, to beware top personalities (obviously Tito himself). The Soviets evidently saw a possible ally in the famous writer, considered at that time to be the standard-bearer of Serb nationalistic opposition.[92]

Although according to Yugoslav intelligence only twelve people took part in the Bar congress, Tito did not take the matter lightly: he ordered an inquiry that ended with the arrest of thirty-two Cominformists, mostly Montenegrins, and the confiscation of a large amount of material printed in the Soviet Union.

Rumors about the congress began circulating in the spring, but Tito prohibited anyone from writing about it publicly before he could clear things up with Brezhnev. The Executive Bureau of the LCY sent a note to the Politburo of the CPSU on 25 July 1974 recalling that subversive Cominformist activity had been discussed at the highest level during meetings between Yugoslav and Soviet representatives. It read in part: "The Bureau is therefore convinced that the anti-Yugoslav activity of the Cominformist emigration is not unknown to the competent Soviet organs. These organs did not take any efficient measure against them."[93]

After the exchange of two diplomatic notes that did not yield any results, and after Stane Dolanc had held several conversations with the Soviet chargé d'affaires and with the Hungarian and Czechoslovak ambassadors, Kardelj went to the Soviet Union at the beginning of September, officially "on vacation" but actually to ask questions. The result of this trip was not positive: the Kremlin leaders denied, as in the past, any involvement in the affair, stressing that the most important Cominformists who remained in the Soviet Union after 1956 had been ordered long ago to emigrate to the West. They also tried to mollify Tito with shipments of modern arms and energetic reassurances of good will. They reaffirmed, however, their critical attitude toward self-management and non-alignment. To their way of thinking, the Yugoslavs ignored the reality of the modern world, which was split into two blocs, reproaching them not just for "deifying" Tito but also his policy, so that it became impossible to make any critical observation.[94]

This swinging between denying responsibility for the Cominformists and criticizing his regime convinced Tito that the Soviets had not given up either their hostile attitude toward his "revisionism" or their proposal to be rid of it and to pull Yugoslavia into their orbit.[95] Meanwhile, since the *Washington Post* had revealed the Bar plot, there was no reason to remain silent about it. Two days after Kardelj's return from Kiev, on 12 September 1974, Tito denounced the discovery of the conspiracy against the LCY in a speech to the workers of the Jesenice steel mill. A different message was sent to Moscow two days later with the sentencing of thirty-three Cominformists, who were condemned collectively to more than two hundred years in jail. At the same time, the security services carried out an extensive witch hunt against their alleged sympathizers. In the following days the press was full of news about the Cominform émigrés, 725 persons in all, mostly Serbs by nationality.[96]

This helped sour even further relations with the Soviets, who replied in their typically perfidious and oblique manner. In the spring of 1975, on the thirtieth anniversary of the victory of the Second World War, Marshal Ivan I. Iakubovskii and his colleague, Andrei A. Grechko, published two articles in Prague newspapers affirming that the Red Army had liberated all of East and Central Europe between 1944 and 1945, Yugoslavia included, thus contributing to the affirmation of socialism in the area. According to them, Tito's Partisans had a marginal role in the war effort against the "Fascists."[97] As if this were not enough, the Bulgarians adopted the stance that the CPY had reached power in a similar way to other East European parties, thanks to Soviet troops, as they were ready to exalt in their media the contribution of their own army to the liberation of Serbia in autumn 1944.

This affront to the liberation struggle, which indirectly denied the importance of the Yugoslav revolution and the legitimacy of the CPY, was the subject of furious commentary by Tito on 2 April in Skopje and the following day in Kosovo. Later he spoke about it, although less violently, in a long TV interview in which he presented his version of the Second World War in the Balkans.[98] With this he opened the dam to a flood of declarations by veterans' associations, who did not tire of repeating his words: "We have allied with the Soviet Union from the very beginning. I would like to know who else, among those who today deny our sacrifices, has done the same."[99] The Russians, starting with Brezhnev, tried to excuse themselves, but the rancor of the Yugoslavs died hard, and they continued to nourish an underlying distrust. Kardelj eloquently stressed his disapproval by refusing the invitation to take part in the celebrations of the bicentenary of the Soviet Academy of Arts and Sciences.[100]

The Americans hurried to exploit the situation. President Gerald Ford came to Belgrade on 3–4 August 1975 and signed an agreement to provide $600 million for the construction of a nuclear plant in Slovenia.[101] Tito accepted the offer, hoping to heal relations with the US, which had deteriorated after 1973 over divergent opinions about the Arab-Israeli war. The process of rapprochement, however, was not easy, since there was no lack of new tensions and arguments. At the beginning of 1976, for instance, the marshal interrupted the discussions with Washington on acquiring TOW anti-tank missiles, which he badly needed, as a sign of protest against the activity of Ustaša and Chetnik émigrés in the United States who, according the Yugoslav press, were supported by local "hostile elements."[102] In October of the same year, he was furious again when the presidential candidate for the Democratic Party, Jimmy Carter, who was inexperienced in foreign policy, declared in a debate with his adversary Gerald Ford that a Soviet invasion of Yugoslavia, in the event of Tito's death, was improbable. He went further, stating that even if it did happen, he would not employ troops in defense of the Balkan country, since such an event would not threaten the security of the United States. Consequently, when Carter entered the White House, the relations between Washington and Belgrade reached their lowest point since the early postwar years. In 1978 Carter tried to atone, inviting Tito to visit the United States for the third time. On that occasion he changed his stance completely, promising to take severe measures against the extremist émigrés and guaranteeing all his support for the independence, territorial integrity, and unity of Yugoslavia.[103] The discussion between the two presidents was quite frank. At one point Carter asked Tito to explain why the Russians hated the Americans so much. The latter replied bluntly: "Because you have encircled them with your military bases and are trying to ruin them economically, endangering them with a neutron bomb and compelling them to engage in an arms race."[104] This frankness impressed Carter's national security adviser, Zbigniew Brzezinski, very much and moved him to declare later that, together with the United States and the Soviet Union, Yugoslavia was "the only protagonist in the global arena."[105] The resumption of weapons deliveries by the American army to Yugoslavia was one of Tito's few foreign policy successes during his final years.[106]

In spite of the Soviet press's repeated affirmations that Moscow had nothing to do with the subversive activity against Yugoslavia and that these were "slanders of Western circles," 1975 concluded with new arguments about the Cominformists, against whom the Belgrade authorities did not hesitate to take unorthodox measures.[107] On 26 December they gave notice of the trial of Vlado Dapčević, which had been held behind closed doors after he had disappeared from his Bucharest hotel under mysterious circumstances on the night of 8–9 August 1975. He had gone to the Romanian capital trusting in his Soviet patrons, but without taking into account the excellent relations between Tito and the "*conducator*," Nicolae Ceaușescu, and between the UDBA and the local Securitate. After a daring kidnapping he was transported to Belgrade, where he was sentenced to death—a penalty changed later to twenty years in jail—for having illegally crossed the border and having acted against the country by supporting the secession of Kosovo and Macedonia and attempting to unite them with Albania. *Pravda* declared these accusations to be groundless, but no one in Yugoslavia believed these Soviet reassurances.[108]

In order to improve the efficiency of the secret services, Tito gave them unknown "specific tasks," which did not bode well: the threat of a crackdown was growing. In the entire country a state of "vigilance" was building that developed into paranoia.[109] The campaign against domestic and foreign enemies, murder not excluded, reached such dimensions in the mid-seventies that the German magazine *Der Spiegel* wrote about a "political mafia" in the Balkans. The mysterious death of two Yugoslav émigrés in Paris and Nice led the French president, Valéry Giscard d'Estaing, to postpone his planned visit with Tito. When, in August 1976, the Belgrade authorities accused an American tourist of Yugoslav origins of being a spy and arrested him, apparently without due cause, a similar split happened with Washington. The US ambassador, Lawrence Silberman, reacted to the behavior of the Belgrade government harshly, which angered Tito, who accused him of meddling in Yugoslavia's domestic affairs. The diplomat was proclaimed persona non grata and put in a sort of quarantine, boycotted by everybody who was anybody in town, which prompted him to resign. Silberman took revenge by publishing a caustic article in the magazine *Foreign Policy* about Yugoslavia swinging between East and West and comparing the country to "the Fiddler on the Roof."[110]

At the end of the sixties Yugoslavia had very few political prisoners. After the purge of the liberals in Croatia and Serbia, the situation changed dramatically, compelling Tito to admit during a visit to Sweden in 1976 that there were probably more "politicals" in his cells than in any other East European country except the Soviet Union. He tried to recover by clumsily—and falsely—asserting that those in prison were all Soviet sympathizers.[111] The secretary of the Swedish section of Amnesty International observed that the number was about a thousand, if not more. This public accusation struck the marshal profoundly, especially as it came on the eve of a conference on security and cooperation in Europe, planned for June 1976 in Belgrade as a supplement to the Helsinki talks.[112] This important event was meant to consolidate the détente reached a year earlier in the Finnish capital and to be a model for further such meetings. The fact that the conference was impending moved Tito to proclaim a rather generous amnesty. Aware of just how much the human rights violation had harmed Yugoslavia's prestige, he proposed striking so-called "verbal delict" from the penal code. It seems that a special session of the CC of the LCY was planned to implement this, but it never took place.[113]

The Final Crisis in Relations with Moscow

In Tito's final years, Yugoslavia had two faces: on the one hand it wanted to demonstrate its democratic "respectability" to the West, but on the other it wanted the East to see its socialist orthodoxy and its will to independence so it could escape from the embrace of the Soviet bear. This was exemplified by an incident in mid-November 1976, during Brezhnev's official visit to Belgrade. At the start of the conversation, the secretary general of the CPSU said that he would not speak in the presence of Stane Dolanc, since he had "sold himself to the imperialists." Tito reacted violently. He ripped the cigarette from Brezhnev's mouth, crushed it on the carpet and yelled: "You ox! We are not in Czechoslovakia here, and I am not called Dubček!"[114] The conversation went on, but the atmosphere was frosty. Brezhnev asked again for naval bases on the Dalmatian coast, military overflight rights, and closer political and economic relations between their countries. He also mentioned an opportunity for the LCY to take part in a meeting of Soviet bloc leaders and asked Tito to engage in favor of Moscow among the non-aligned countries and to stop the "unfriendly" propaganda of the Yugoslav media against the Soviet Union. Tito listened to him, apparently calm, but then lit a cigar, closed his notebook, and said: "It is late. It is better to go to dinner. We will resume the discussion tomorrow." He left without waiting to see how the surprised Russians would react.[115]

When alone with his colleagues, he commented irritably on the requests proposed by Brezhnev and immediately appointed a task force to find the right answers. The group worked through the night and came up with a plan: the following day, the marshal flatly rejected all Soviet requests. In doing so, he stressed that he was not speaking in his own name, but that he was interpreting the opinion of all the present Yugoslav leaders, and certainly of the entire LCY and of the Yugoslav people.[116] This firm attitude did not prevent Brezhnev from proposing his demands again the following August, when the two met in Moscow. Tito turned a deaf ear this time, too.[117] The Soviet "ultimatum," as it was labeled by Western journalists once the American agency UPI (United Press International) had revealed the "eight requests of Brezhnev's and the eight *nos* from Tito," alarmed the Yugoslavs, who interpreted it as further proof that Moscow was not willing to renounce its hegemonic pretensions. In this context, they were especially worried by the assertion of the CPSU ideologue, Mikhail Suslov, that Soviet foreign policy had been 100 percent blameless from 1917 onward, including during the Stalinist era.[118] Because of such assertions, Kardelj sent Tito a special message through Stane Dolanc during the last days of his life, in which he predicted that escaping the Soviet threat would be the main task, not just of present but also of future generations.[119]

Tito's hostile attitude toward the Soviet Union emerged at the end of 1976, during the visit of French president Giscard d'Estaing to Belgrade. During a private discussion the marshal confessed that he was skeptical about the idea of general disarmament, although it was supported with much clamor by a number of states at the United Nations as well as by Yugoslavia. It was, in his opinion, pure propaganda. As Henry Kissinger affirmed during a meeting at the White House with French, British, and West German top officials, the Yugoslavs "have prepared very carefully what they'll do if the Soviets do one, two or three." And his French colleague, Louis de Guiringaud, referring to his recent trip to Belgrade, added: "They made it clear several times that they're determined to resist the Russians. I have never heard Tito say this before. This time, we heard him for one or two hours. It was clear that they would defend very strongly their independence, their integrity."[120]

Jovanka and the Others

Tito was a man of great appetites, of greedy rapacity in everything: drinking, eating, loving, and hating. "Tito knows fully how to savor life," wrote Dobrica Ćosić, who observed him up close in 1961. "This man does not renounce any pleasure. In nothing is he ascetic."[121] Especially in his quest for power.

In interpersonal relations he was casual, in particular with his comrades on private occasions. "He was impulsive," wrote Vladimir Dedijer. "He knew how to speak in a down-to-earth way, with a vernacular studded with all the typical words of our language."[122] But he lost his temper only in the most stressful moments, and only for a short time. He was also compassionate, as demonstrated by a speech in the early fifties in which he invited the population to "hold tight to your chests" the orphans of the collaborationists who fought with the Germans against the Partisans and lost their lives during the war and after it. And he knew what empathy was: after Ranković's demise, the post of secretary of internal affairs, which was responsible for the suppression of opposition, was offered to Anton Vratuša, who declined, saying in an interview with him that, as a boy, when a pig was slaughtered at the family farm, he would run away so as not to hear its cries. Tito was moved and did not insist.[123]

He liked to entertain, often hosting social events, receptions, lunches, dinners, or film screenings as an entrée to the most important political and strategic decisions. Unlike Stalin, he did not force his guests to drink excessively or to misbehave.[124] In his old age, he would frequently enjoy a glass of whiskey with a twist of lemon after dinner (but also during the day), claiming that Churchill had taught him how to drink. The alcohol loosened his tongue, his joviality, and his wit, which were part of his natural charm.[125] He had inherited a nice voice from his mother and liked to sing popular songs. He had also learned how to cook from her, refining this art during his underground life working illegally before the Second World War.[126] He loved political jokes and when they sprouted up like mushrooms during the sixties he tasked his personal secretary with collecting them and referring them to him. He generally enjoyed them very much, even if he was frequently the main victim.[127] He was able to joke about himself. In July 1944 the writer Evelyn Waugh, who came to Vis with Randolph Churchill, son of the British prime minister, began spreading rumors that Tito was a "she" and a lesbian. Waugh repeated this "joke" for years, referring to Tito as a "she" in his correspondence with Randolph Churchill. An editor once refused to publish an article by Waugh, claiming it was offensive to a head of state that had diplomatic relations with Great Britain. When Tito by chance met him on the beach, wearing just a bathing suit, he asked: "Captain Waugh, what makes you think I am a woman?"[128] Another memorable moment came in the seventies, when he returned from abroad on his plane. On landing at Belgrade airport he noticed Stevan Doronjski from the window, a representative of the Presidium of the LCY, waiting to receive him. Tito joked drily: "OK, they are here. The regime is still strong, we can disembark."[129] He was not so in love with himself as to accept every scrap of flattery and to deny every false step. For instance, he could not bear the popular song that compared him to a "white violet," and he was ashamed of his first photo with Churchill during their meeting in Naples, where he appears stiff in a pompous uniform that had been sent him by Stalin. "I am in a pose, as if I'd just hiked down from a mountain," he said.[130]

Tito knew how to fascinate even those who were not under the influence of his charisma. In 1973, during a visit to Kiev, at the intermission of an opera, Brezhnev began reciting a Russian ballad. To everyone's surprise, Tito also began to recite Pushkin, poem after poem, for at least twenty minutes. The Russians were stupefied and enthusiastic. Brezhnev, already tipsy and prone to emotion, cried the entire time.[131]

Tito loved women "more than Suleiman the Magnificent," to quote his last wife, and was a sexual enthusiast, even during the most rigidly clandestine life, the heaviest Partisan struggle, and into his old age. He liked to remember a countess from Styria who was so fond of young revolutionaries that she gave them shelter in her Viennese home. Her male protégés, not at all grateful, called her *Parteistrohsack*, the "party's straw mattress," for her favoritism of lovers. "You know how we were, we illegals . . . ," Tito told Jovanka, not without merry self-complacency. "Surely we were not monks."[132] He claimed to have learned etiquette during the sub-officer course in the Austro-Hungarian Imperial Army, but it is quite probable that the noblewoman from Graz was also his teacher.

Tito married three times, but had two partners with whom he lived out of wedlock.

His first wife was Pelagiia Denisova Belousova, "Polka," whom he married in a church in 1918 and in a civil ceremony two years later, since the Bolsheviks did not recognize religious weddings.[133] Pelagiia was the daughter of a Saint Petersburg worker exiled to Siberia at the time of the tsar because of his leftist leanings. In Omsk he found a job as a master builder in a railway workshop, as Tito later did. And it seems that he learned the first rudiments of Marxism from his future father-in-law. When she married young Josip, Pelagiia was only fourteen, much younger than he, and a beautiful girl.[134]

Tito's women ran the gamut from beautiful to pretty, but were also quite aggressive. He once confessed: "Every one of my wives was a virgin when I knew them, and a naive little lamb. During the marriage they all became lionesses, whose personality I respected and appreciated. But when the lionesses started to bite, I was forced to tame them, which was not easy and caused a lot of misunderstandings."[135] When, in 1920, he returned home from his time as a prisoner in Russia, he brought Pelagiia with him. They had five children but only one, their son Žarko, survived childhood. The marriage began to crumble in the mid-twenties, but Tito never revealed the motive. Evidently the memory of that failure was painful for him. In any case, after he was sentenced to many years in prison in 1928, Pelagiia returned home in Russia to avoid being banished to her husband's village (a common punishment for a spouse) or arrested. She was convinced that she would lose her life in Yugoslavia and that Josip would be killed if he persevered in his ideas and activities.[136]

When settled in Moscow, she enrolled in the KUNMZ and sent Žarko to a home for children of Comintern agents, being unable or unwilling to keep him with her and her new partner. When Tito appeared in Moscow in 1935, she could not even tell him where the eleven-year-old boy was, having lost track of him. This unmotherly disinterest moved Tito to tears when he told the story to his friend, Kopinič. Probably for this reason, after a short attempt to live together again in April 1936, he decided to divorce Pelagiia. "I guess she was not Tito's great love," opined Zdenka Kidrič, who was a friend during their time in Moscow.[137]

There is, however, another story about this episode, as told by the Croat, Ante Ciliga, who later argued and broke with the Communist Party after living in Moscow in the mid-thirties. After her return from Zagreb, Pelagiia consorted with a group of Yugoslavs who were critical of Stalin's dictatorship. For this reason she was arrested as a "Trotskyist." This happened during the night, at the Hotel Lux, in the presence of Tito, who did nothing to help her. Because of his connection to her, he was in a life-threatening situation, as he was likewise suspected of Trotskyism. Pelagiia was expelled from the party and exiled for ten years to Central Asia. In Moscow the rumor circulated that she had died in jail.[138] It seems that Tito believed it, considering that he mentioned the death of his first wife when conversing with Louis Adamic in 1949.[139] Actually, "Polka" returned to Moscow from exile before the war but was sentenced again to ten years' banishment when the split between Stalin and Tito happened, although by that time she had another family. The KGB made her a deal: she could leave for Yugoslavia as an agent, but Polka refused this offer, even though she was told that Tito had killed Žarko, suspecting him of being a Stalinist. In 1956, once rehabilitated, she moved to Istra, a small town near Moscow, where she lived very modestly as a primary school teacher. There she was discovered by a Croatian historian, Ivan Očak, who told her the truth about her son and helped her to renew contact with him.[140]

Pelagiia died in 1968, before Žarko managed to bring her to Yugoslavia. Tito, who took care to assure her a modest pension for her party work before the war, asked his ambassador to send a wreath to her grave. Otherwise, he erased her from his life and did not try to get in touch with her in the fifties and sixties when he began visiting Moscow again, even forbidding any mention of her. Before the beginning of the war, Kardelj advised Djilas never to ask about her, as she was an unpleasant and hurtful topic for Tito. Nevertheless, when he died, a photo of Pelagiia was found in his usual daily briefcase.[141]

Tito nurtured sentiments of affection for his son Žarko, who, thanks partially to his bizarre character and partially due to repressive Soviet pedagogical methods, became an absolute hooligan and caused his father a great deal of trouble after they reconnected. Until the beginning of the war, Tito had little to do with him, since the boy continued to live in various children's homes or with tutors, in quite difficult financial conditions. They were so difficult that the secretary general of the Comintern, Dimitrov, was moved to assign him a monthly allowance of an additional 100 rubles, since the 250 that he got was not enough.[142] During the war, Tito thought of his son often and was very proud when informed that Žarko, who at seventeen had volunteered for the Red Army, was proclaimed a hero of the Soviet Union when he lost a hand during the Battle of Moscow. This was not exactly accurate: he was awarded only a medal for defense of the country, but this did not diminish Tito's love for him.[143]

At the end of the war, the boy returned to Yugoslavia and began to cause his father a great deal of trouble. He drank too much and behaved licentiously. Žarko and a Russian officer engaged in a duel over a ballerina, provoking a scandal. The following day, when Tito's secretary Gustav Vlahov (whom Tito had assigned to watch over his son) told him about the incident, Tito exclaimed with outrage: "You should have shot him!"[144] Žarko ended up under house arrest but did not come to his senses. Shortly afterward, he wounded himself "by accident" in the center of Belgrade so seriously that Stalin decided that given the complexity of the surgery, he would send him his personal doctor. But this was not the last of Žarko's wicked deeds. In 1966 he nearly killed Lazar Koliševski, the Macedonian politician, who was taking a walk at Brioni with his wife and daughter. Žarko was attempting to shoot crows from the window of his apartment and narrowly missed his father's guests. When Koliševski, upset over the incident, hurried to Tito to complain about him, the marshal replied in a resigned tone: "Go on, what happened, happened. You know what kind of guy Žarko is."[145]

Elsa Johanna König/Lucia Bauer

On 13 October 1936, Tito married a twenty-two-year-old German woman, Elsa Johanna König, who lived under the name Lucia Bauer and worked as a radio operator at the Comintern. She lived in the Hotel Lux, as he did. Their relationship was a short one, because Tito left Moscow three days after the wedding and did not return until the middle of 1938. In September 1937, when he commuted between Zagreb and Paris, the NKVD accused the young woman of being a Gestapo spy and, according to one version of the story, executed her the following December.[146] According to another, she escaped this fate and lived in Moscow until the end of the century, at one point having been given a generous amount of money by Tito.[147] From the four extant letters that he sent to Lucia, it seems that their relationship was not without strong sentimental and sexual involvement. According to the testimony of Zdenka Kidrič, the "German girl" suffered a lot because she rarely heard from her husband, so much so that in a fit of jealousy and wrath she scratched his eyes out of a photograph.[148] When Broz was informed about her arrest, he immediately distanced himself from her. In order to explain his connection to her, he said he had married her to provide a surrogate mother for his son Žarko.[149] In any case, Tito engaged in his obligatory self-criticism: "I guess that, in this case, I was not prudent enough. It is a big stain on my career."[150] He was once again saved from the situation by his old friend Kopinič, who called the attention of the inquisitors to how reliable Elsa had seemed, since she lived for a long time under the same roof as many high Cominform officials and was never suspected of treason.[151]

Herta Haas and "Zdenka"

Tito's third partner was Herta Haas, a student of economics originally from Maribor who was born in 1914. She was the daughter of a well-off Austrian lawyer and was therefore seen as bourgeois by the Slovenian "comrades." She was an attractive young lady, intelligent and elegant, with an irreproachable dedication to the party. The photos of her in her youth show a happy smiling girl with wonderful eyes à la Bette Davis.[152] Since her mother tongue was German, and she was fluent in other languages, she was used before the war as an international courier for important party missions. "I was a master in clandestine work and in camouflage," she recalled.[153] After the war, during which her relationship with Tito had come to an end, she lived in Belgrade, where she married and had two children. She maintained a detached but respectful attitude toward Tito, without forgetting that he was father to her first-born son, Aleksandar, better known as Miša.[154]

The break between Herta and Tito, which began in 1941, was final by 1943. Before the beginning of the war a Serbian student, Davorjanka Paunović, appeared in Zagreb. She was called "Zdenka," a typically Croatian nickname, given to her by Tito himself: "I called her that because she reminded me of a brook, a perpetual spring of clear and fresh water, a spring that gushes from beneath a stone and enhances the view, just with its appearance. Zdenka was an infinite source for my ideas, intellectual, revolutionary, and political. She inspired me and gave me physical pleasure. And until the end of her short life she was a strong source of spiritual support for me."[155]

In Zagreb, Zdenka took a radiotelegraphy course to be able to communicate with Moscow, where she was connected to the Russian secret service. She met Tito in the home of Stella and Josip Kopinič. By the time he had decided to go with the Politburo members to Belgrade, they were already intimately connected. They lived together during the war, while Zdenka worked as Tito's secretary, although she was not particularly suited to this job. She was nervous, frequently neurotic, and disliked by all but Tito, who was madly in love with her. She was beautiful, slim, bronzed, with extraordinary green eyes. "She had a smile, a glance I cannot forget," recalled Josip Kapičić, her first boyfriend.[156]

When Tito and Zdenka arrived in Belgrade in 1941, the party was practicing a strict puritanism as preached by Djilas and Ranković. Tito adapted to this, hiding their romantic relationship. The comrades became aware of it only in the spring of 1942 when Zdenka wanted to be treated as a wife, leading to a very tense atmosphere at the Supreme Staff meetings. Consequently, everybody tried to avoid her, wondering how it was possible that she was able to seduce a man like Tito. Marjan Stilinović, secretary of the party cell at the Supreme Staff, decided at a certain point to say openly what he and his comrades thought about Zdenka. "I know Marjan," said Tito, "and I am ashamed, but I cannot live without this woman. Not a moment."[157]

Apparently, in the spring of 1942 Zdenka had a child who was given to foster parents. It was then that the situation became extremely critical. A session was convened at Foča with just one order of the day: Tito's relationship with Zdenka Paunović. One of the comrades threatened the secretary general with expulsion for immoral conduct. But Tito was firm: "I cannot live without her. Do what you wish!"[158] He was not the only one to have a mistress during the war, however. Other members of the Supreme Staff had them too. "Step by step, I understood how things were," Dedijer wrote. "In the Partisan group, all those who surrendered to the lure of sex were severely punished. But not those who had established those punishments."[159]

As for Tito, everyone in his circle hoped that he would renew his relationship with Herta Haas. She was arrested in 1943 by the Germans and imprisoned in an Ustaša concentration camp. Some months later she was freed thanks to an exchange of prisoners, and at the end of this tragic experience, which pushed her to attempt suicide, she came to the Supreme Staff, which was located in a wood near Sarajevo, accompanied by Djilas. It was a rainy day when Herta entered the cabin where Tito and his "secretary" lived. Tito was shaving, since he wanted to appear neat even in the most difficult moments.[160] "What is this woman doing here?" Herta asked. "What you are doing here?" replied Zdenka. "Her or me," said Herta. "No, I will go," replied Tito.[161] Herta, obliged to confront the sad reality of having been abandoned, began to cry in Djilas's arms, though she accepted the separation with dignity. She courageously survived Operation Schwarz and returned to Slovenia in the summer of 1943, where she fought with the local Partisans, without a bad word to say against Tito. Zdenka, on the contrary, had continuous hysterical breakdowns during the offensive, provoking ironic comments among the members of the Supreme Staff. "She behaved," observed Djilas sarcastically, "as if the main aim of the Germans was to kill her personally."[162] When, during one of her usual outbursts, Tito asked the commander of his bodyguard, more in jest than earnest, what he should do, he replied drily: "If I were you, comrade, I would shoot her."[163]

At the end of the war, Zdenka fell ill with tuberculosis, which she had probably nursed for a time and which might partially explain her tantrums, her fears, and her strange behavior. In July 1944 she was sent to a hospital in the Soviet Union but without result as she was not ready to follow medical advice. When Tito came to Moscow in autumn, Zdenka obliged him to take her home even though she was gravely ill. Her life was in danger and much depended on her discipline, but the patient, as Gustav Vlahov wrote, was far from understanding the seriousness of her condition.[164] After her return, she was rarely seen. She appeared with a painful smile on her face, Djilas said, as if she wanted to excuse herself. Meanwhile, she was preoccupied in a maniacal way with Tito's well-being, and nearly pathologically jealous. She never forgave his aide, Moma Djurić, for having permitted Herta Hass to visit her son Miša, who at the time lived with his father.[165]

Zdenka died on 1 May 1946, in the Golnik Sanatorium in Slovenia, where Tito had sent her in hopes of saving her from tuberculosis. She was only twenty-seven years old. According to her wishes, she was buried in the garden of the White Palace in order to always be near Tito, who was intensely struck by her loss. He shut himself away and did not inform anybody of what had happened, not even inviting his comrades to the funeral. Nobody apart from himself mourned her.[166] In this sorrowful situation he wrote a long letter to Herta, asking her to return. The reply was laconic: "My dear, Herta Haas kneels down before a man only once."[167] After that, he also considered Cana Babović, a Serb communist with whom he had had a short affair ten years earlier in Moscow, but abandoned the idea quickly, following Ranković's advice, as he had disliked her. It seems that Cana, a party heroine, bore a grudge against "Comrade Marko" and her influence within Tito's entourage contributed to his downfall in 1966.[168] Pepca Kardelj told Dedijer that, after Zdenka's death, Tito proposed a "menage à trois" to her and her husband, but her husband had refused. Their common friend, Zdenka Kidrič, commented caustically that this was pure fantasy: "Pepca dreamt of being the Yugoslav first lady."[169]

Tito got over Zdenka's loss quickly, falling in love with Zinka Kunc, alias Milanov, a famous singer who returned home from New York after the war, where she had been a star of the Metropolitan Opera. She was a majestic woman, breathtakingly beautiful and with a regal manner. She refused him, preferring to marry General Ljubomir Ilić, who had become famous during the Spanish Civil War and later during the French Resistance. Although the chatter of the women in his circle, who were hostile to newcomers in their elite group and especially to opera singers, had no influence on him, Tito still did not insist on his courtship, obviously because he could not do this to one of his generals.[170]

Later, in 1946, he met one of the most popular Soviet film stars, Tat'iana Okunevskaia, called the Russian Greta Garbo. It seems he told her that he was unable to marry her immediately, but that he was ready to open all the Yugoslav theaters and studios to her. It was useless. In spite of her refusal, Tat'iana paid dearly for Tito's courtship; when he was excluded from the Cominform, she found herself banished for years to a Siberian gulag because of her association with him.[171]

Jovanka Budisavljević

It was a captain in the People's Army, Jovanka Budisavljević, who would become Tito's last wife. She was a Serb, originally from Lika, an extremely poor Croatian region. In 1942, at only seventeen years old, she joined the local female Partisan unit and was wounded twice during the struggle, although not seriously. She came from a modest peasant family and managed to complete primary school, a rarity for country girls. At the end of the war she was a commissioner at the hospital in Drvar, then in the same capacity in the surgery hospital of the First Army. After the victory, as a trusted cadre, she worked at the General Staff headquarters in Belgrade and later in the Serbian town of Niš. She was finally chosen by the OZNA to be a housekeeper in the marshal's residence at the end of 1945 or beginning of 1946, which meant that she worked for the secret service. She had some experience with household chores, as she had once worked in a guest house owned by a relative, but her most important qualification was Partisan militancy—she had been awarded several medals—and her total dedication to the party and its leader. She came into direct contact with the marshal as a member of his personal guard, created by NKVD agents, similar to that of Stalin, but also that of King Aleksandar Karadjordjević. She came to work in uniform, heavy boots and with a cap on her head, à la Tito.[172]

Jovanka had allegedly been chosen for this job by Ranković himself, hoping that "nature would take its course."[173] It is more probable, however, that she was included in Tito's entourage by the NKVD collaborator, Ivan Krajačić (Stevo), who was interested in strengthening his influence at court and was convinced that he could easily manipulate this ignorant young woman. Josip Kopinič, a former Comintern agent in Zagreb, confided later to Vladimir Dedijer that Jovanka was sent to a "cadre" school in Moscow in mid-1945 founded by Lenin's spymaster, Feliks E. Dzerzhinskii, where Soviet and satellite secret agents were trained. "When she turned, Stevo put her in Tito's house," probably obeying his Russian superiors, who wanted to have trusted people near the marshal.[174] (Both Jovanka and Krajačić denied this assertion.)

With flowing, silky black hair and a pale complexion, Jovanka was strikingly beautiful. She was devoid of coquetry, but not without a reserved femininity, which Djilas said called to mind nuns or unmarried peasants. The tight uniform highlighted her charms and the slenderness of her young body. She had a gentle face and big brown eyes that reflected patience, respect, and dedication. The only small imperfection was her querulous voice, which at the time was not a grave defect since she spoke little. She was only twenty-three, whereas Tito was fifty-five. His comrades were quickly aware that the two had established an intimate relationship and were not at all scandalized. "Why not?" said Koča Popović. "It is perfectly natural."[175] As Gustav Vlahov, Tito's secretary, related: "Once, when we were in the big hall near the piano, Jovanka Budisavljević ascended the stairs to the first floor to check if everything was alright there. Tito looked at me, commenting: 'Jovanka is a really cool girl.' It was a signal to me that he was attracted to her."[176]

Their relationship, which for a time they tried to hide, got off on the wrong foot. For six years, Jovanka's role at Tito's side was not clear to his entourage as she was both part of the staff and his lover. She had practically no private life, so during important meetings she remained waiting in the anteroom with the bodyguards until Tito appeared. She had an extremely deferential attitude toward members of the Politburo, almost not daring to say a word.[177] This was a situation that exposed her to humiliations and all kinds of harassment, to the point of being obliged to taste the food that she herself had prepared for the marshal to make sure it was not poisoned. In love as she was with her hero, she bore all this willingly. She saw Tito as an idol and he was just as captivated by her. When she went to the Golnik Sanatorium because of a pulmonary infection for a period during 1946 and 1947, he sent her red roses and love letters daily. It is not clear why he decided to marry her after more than five years of cohabitation, but it is probable that he had (well-founded) doubts about her ability to show up in public as his wife. At Golnik, the female patients who had met both Zdenka and Jovanka noted that there was no comparison between them. Whereas the first, in the shadow of death, became silent and melancholic, the second behaved aggressively and haughtily.[178] In 1948 she took part in the Fifth Congress of the CPY as one of the representatives of the Ministry of Defense, taking a place usually reserved for high officers and Spanish Civil War veterans. Seated in the first row, she behaved like a cheerleader during Tito's inaugural speech, leaping up at every moment to applaud and forcing the other two thousand delegates to follow suit. When Jovanka went to Koper in 1949 with Ranković's wife, where she got a fake passport to go incognito to Trieste "to go shopping," she did not make a good impression on the local policemen. "Who is this goose?" asked one of them. "Shut up, she's Tito's future wife!" said the other.[179]

Tito's decision to make his relationship with Jovanka official was heavily influenced by the puritan Ranković, according to whom the top cadres should be an example to others, even in their private lives.[180] On 15 April 1952 their marriage was celebrated without fuss and pomp; the wedding dinner was served at an estate on the Danube among vineyards and woods. Jovanka was twenty-eight, while her husband was more than twice her age. The guests, Tito's closest collaborators, had not completely shed the popular and rather primitive habits of their youth. As Slavka, Ranković's wife, related, they made toast after toast, everything degenerating into a state of collective drunkenness.[181] The ever present Ivan Krajačić (Stevo) welcomed Tito into the "henpecked husbands' club," where he would shortly be joined by other eminent bachelors who obeyed the marshal's council to follow his example. In Belgrade, there was an epidemic of weddings, which prompted the wife of the French ambassador to make the amused comment: "In other countries we go to funerals, here we go to weddings."[182]

Jovanka appeared for the first time in public as Tito's consort on 10 September 1952, when the British foreign minister, Anthony Eden, visited Yugoslavia. It was not a routine meeting, but an occasion for important discussions regarding the Trieste question. It was also the first official visit of a foreign dignitary after Tito's split with Stalin. The meeting took place at Lake Bled, where Tito used the occasion to introduce his wife to the public. The photo of the three sitting on a sofa went around the world: on one side sat the marshal, portly but still youthful, on the other the aristocratic Eden, in the middle Jovanka with short hair, slim as a mannequin, with a marvelous Hollywood smile that would shortly be proclaimed "the best Yugoslav smile." (Later, Belgrade students would mock her as "Holy Jovanka of the smile.")[183] The harmonious impression of the photo, however, hides Eden's outrage at not having been informed of Tito's marriage by the Yugoslavs. Convinced he was a bachelor, Eden had left his young, recently wedded wife at home out of kindness.[184] Not to mention the embarrassed Jovanka, who seemed like a fledgling fallen from the nest. According to Djilas she was so frightened that she trembled like a debutante from a Russian novel at her first court ball.[185] Her fears overcame her some months later, in the spring of 1953, when Tito visited a Western country for the first time: he went to London, to Queen Elizabeth's court. Jovanka was not with him, probably unsure as to whether she could rise to the occasion. She came from a modest family, was semiliterate, and knew how to handle a gun better than wield a fork at an elegant table. Before her wedding she had been sent to Rome for two weeks as a guest of Ambassador Vlatko Velebit and his wife, Vera, to receive instruction on etiquette.[186] But evidently it was not enough. The Velebits asserted the contrary, but they were among the few in Tito's circle to have a friendly attitude toward Jovanka. Her bad temper, which became evident after the wedding, did not improve others' opinions of her. She was especially frowned upon by the wives of the political elite. When Pepca Kardelj criticized her overly generous cleavage at a reception in 1954, Jovanka responded sharply: "*I* have something to show." She took her revenge, banishing Kardelj's wife from the court receptions for eight years.[187]

However, Jovanka—"Jole" or "my comrade" as Tito sometimes called her—was intelligent and quickly learned how to behave, so much so that according to foreign diplomats she represented Yugoslavia with dignity. Nevertheless she was not able to overcome her deep-seated insecurity, although she did eventually pass gymnasium exams (a high school or O-level equivalent).[188] Perhaps to hide her discomfort she began dressing extravagantly, wearing jewelry not suitable for the wife of a revolutionary and head of a socialist state. This was particularly evident in 1974 during Tito's official visit to Bangladesh. In Dhaka he was greeted by a million-person crowd who saw in him a spokesman for their hope for a better life. As he later told a colleague, he had only ever been greeted in this way in Mexico and Egypt. A description of the event relates that "in the Bangladeshi parliament, a solemn session was organized. In that country, the poorest in the world, even the parliament building is modest, as are the clothes of the local population. Jovanka came to the ceremony, at which Tito was going to give a speech, in an elaborate white dress, with heavy diamond earrings and necklace. In that tropical heat she looked like a sad Christmas tree. Everyone in the hall looked at her with a touch of contempt and indignation. Meanwhile, Tito spoke of poverty and misery."[189] Stress led Jovanka to seek comfort in food, and she became dependent. Marija and Joža Vilfan, who were in Tito's circle in the fifties, related that during her stays at Brdo Castle Jovanka would wake at night and go to the kitchen to eat cakes from the fridge.[190] This, along with drinking too much, led her to become obese and she became the stereotype of the Balkan matron, though in photographs she managed to retain her appeal. In real life she was unbearable, full of herself, and often cruel: she behaved tyrannically with the personnel at Tito's residences, sacking waiters, cooks, maids, and gardeners, creating an atmosphere of tension and unease. It is alleged that over time she fired more than a thousand people.[191] Leo Mates, who succeeded Joža Vilfan as Tito's secretary in 1958, said: "Jovanka was so malicious with the staff of the White Palace that she deserved a life sentence."[192]

She was rude and sometimes aggressive even toward the president's most eminent collaborators, who took their revenge by describing her in a rather critical way in their memoirs. During the handover from Joža Vilfan to Leo Mates, the former warned the latter: "Try to collaborate with the first lady, since her opinion is more important than Tito's."[193] Apart from Vilfan, who was the first to treat her according to her rank, Jovanka quarreled with all Tito's secretaries, even with Vladimir Popović, a member of his inner circle who was sent into exile to London where he died shortly thereafter following a battle with cancer. On his deathbed, he exclaimed with indignation: "I was hunted like a dog," and warned those who were at his bedside that Tito had long been Jovanka's prisoner.[194] A similar fate befell Bogdan Crnobrnja, who Jovanka said should be "hanged from a lamppost." The first lady did not stop persecuting him even when Tito got rid of him by appointing him ambassador to Washington. In September 1971, on the eve of the marshal's visit to the United States, which Crnobrnja had organized with care, Jovanka argued that he should be removed from that assignment (he had dared to suggest that she dress as simply as Nixon's wife). When Foreign Secretary Tepavac got this order, he could not help but ask Tito why it had to be done in such a hurry. "Have you ever had a quarrel with your wife?" Tito answered candidly. "Jovanka is stronger than me. What could I do but go along with her for a quiet home life?"[195]

Jovanka had become unbearable by the end of the fifties. As the memoirs of Milan Žeželj, commander of the guard, show, during the grand Afro-Asian tour of 1959 she began protesting the protocol, complaining of being relegated to the background and creating a tense atmosphere on their flagship, the *Galeb*.[196] Things deteriorated during the second important journey, in 1961, when Tito visited Africa. Jovanka was accompanied on this occasion by a team of seamstresses, and not just one or two, but dozens to fit her for each visit to each country. In all she had about 150 dresses. "There was a fashion atelier on the ship," said Leo Mates.[197] Jovanka demanded that a special plane bring her a cut of silk she had forgotten at home. Tito did not agree and a violent quarrel arose, during which she reproached him venomously: "And you, what did you do yesterday? You took advantage of the calm to go on the escort vessel to admire the sea lion that you got in Ghana. But you told everyone that you wanted to visit the sailors and see how they fared." These words, spoken in the presence of his entourage, sent Tito into a rage: "As soon as the plane comes, you will return home immediately." Jovanka burst into tears. They retired to their cabin and did not come out again for two days.[198]

During Tito's last years, Jovanka, steeped in myths of Serb greatness and her family's tradition, began to nurture political ambitions, weaving intrigue after intrigue. She started with Ranković. She said that she did not want to go the way of Queen Draga, who, together with her husband, Aleksandar Obrenović, was atrociously murdered in 1903 by a group of officers. She demanded the removal of "Leka." According to Kardelj's testimony, she expressed herself in an even more radical way, arguing that he should be killed and buried three meters underground, like a vampire.[199] It also seems that she collaborated with Krajačić and his technicians to reveal "bugs" under Tito's bed. Later she boasted that the Brioni plenum that had sanctioned Ranković's removal was her work. The result was so satisfying that she rewarded herself by taking a private plane to Paris to stock her summer wardrobe.[200]

After Tito's death, his notes and other documents related to Ranković's fall were discovered in a washing machine where they had allegedly been hidden by Jovanka. While she was at court, she had the keys to all of her husband's safes.[201] When "Comrade Marko" was liquidated, Jovanka began to manifest her political ambitions more openly. She said that she wanted to free her elderly husband from too many obligations and posed as his guardian: "Tito is blind. They are plotting around him, but he does not notice anything. I am here alone, a hen attentive to her chicks. Only I can save him."[202] To this end, she began to choose who could contact him and check his telephone conversations, helping to create a siege mentality within which the pair enclosed themselves. It is hard to say which of them was most responsible for this state of paranoia.[203]

When they came to power, the Zagreb liberals tried to woo "Comrade Jovanka," going so far as to propose her as a representative of Croatia in the collective presidency then in formation. When Savka Dabčević-Kučar mentioned this idea to Tito, he remained silent for a moment and then, after finishing his glass of whisky, said: "Let's go."[204] With that, the proposal was quashed, but not Jovanka's role in the drama that was looming. Some months later, in the heated atmosphere of the worsening Croat *maspok* crisis, she was spontaneously chosen by the Serbs in Croatia as their protector and advocate. They overwhelmed her with letters (at one point two thousand per day) to convince her of the existence of a "genocidal Ustaša" policy on the part of the Zagreb leaders, which was so threatening that it prevented them from sleeping in their homes and forced them to install guards around their villages.[205] "Madame

Broz plays behind the scenes a more and more pronounced role, which is not always useful," the British ambassador wrote with understatement in his dispatch to the Foreign Office.[206]

In October 1971, during a lunch for her birthday, Jovanka claimed in the presence of Dolanc that the 1941 massacre in Croatia would happen again if the army did not intervene. "This time, I hope that the Serbs will not be so naïve and reckless as to be slaughtered like sheep," she said.[207] She told Dolanc that she was convinced that even Tito was "a poisonous nationalist snake," as she overwhelmed her husband "day and night" with the information received from Croatia, the Ustaša were at work in the republic, but he did nothing.[208] Savka Dabčević-Kučar gave this eloquent description of Jovanka's role in the last chapter of the Croat drama, in November 1971, when Tito decided to overthrow the Zagreb liberals: "When we came to Karadjordjevo, I remember her as in a picture by a Spanish master: she is there, superb, her head raised, her face hard, barely polite. She is there, the sovereign, and looks at us from above with satisfaction, and her eyes seem like those of an octopus."[209]

For the status she had earned in the fight against the Croatian nationalists, and for the commitment with which she had collaborated on the nonalignment policy, Jovanka aspired to be included in the CC of the LCY, hoping to succeed Tito after his death. In the late sixties and early seventies she exercised great influence on Tito, who allowed her to read telegrams for his eyes only.[210] In her memoirs, Savka Dabčević-Kučar affirms that it was not possible to speak with the marshal about the excessive power of the Serbs in the army in Jovanka's presence.[211]

Jovanka made many enemies with her behavior, among them Bakarić and Kardelj, both of whom had a low opinion of her. Although for the sake of prudence they did not make it known openly, she could feel their hostility and privately reciprocated it.[212] Fearing for her life and that of her husband, she tried to build about her a bulwark of trusted people, encouraging their rise to the top of the state and party. During the first years of their marriage, Tito often said to her: "It is enough that you smile!" As her power grew, however, said Slavka Ranković, Jovanka smiled less and less, until she stopped completely and began to take on a rather grim expression.[213] At that point the situation became tragic. Toward the end of his life Tito was physically afraid of her, so much so that he would lock himself in the bathroom at night to keep her away from him.[214] As he told his confidantes, Jovanka could have been a supervisor in the South African gold mines, where the workers were treated with the whip.[215]

One episode in July 1972 testifies to the change in their relationship. On the eve of Tito's departure for the Soviet Union she claimed that Lieutenant Colonel Slavko Popović, the marshal's military attendant, should stay at home, since she accused him of being a Russian spy. After a memorable quarrel, Tito gave in, but on his return ordered an investigation that proved Popović innocent.[216] This was the turning point. Instead of maintaining her composure, Jovanka became more and more aggressive, establishing an atmosphere of absolute terror at court. Being an old conspirator, Tito could not explain his wife's behavior, unless it was the result of a plot inspired by internal opposition or by foreign secret services. He instructed Ivan Mišković, who at that moment seemed omnipotent since he served as Tito's special security adviser, to keep Jovanka under strict surveillance to find out why she took his documents and to whom she passed them.[217] Mišković discovered her daily contacts with Zagreb, including with Ivan Krajačić (Stevo) and Miroslav Krleža, as well as her relationships with several generals, in service and retired, and prominent politicians. He also discovered her habit of hiding behind a curtain in the Belgrade residence, one that separated the marshal's office and library from his private apartments, to listen to his conversations. (Bakarić claimed later that she did it systematically, betrayed only by the poodles that continuously ran from Tito to the curtain and back again.)[218] In his memoir, Czechoslovak party leader Antonín Novotný relates that during his visit in October 1967, Tito interrupted their confidential conversation from time to time to see whether somebody was listening behind the door: "And this happened in his own palace."[219]

At the end of January 1974, a special commission was established to investigate all those with whom Jovanka was in contact and to determine what influence they exerted on her. Tito wanted to know who was "ruining" his wife, causing her "to create an atmosphere of tension around him."[220] After a violent quarrel with the leader of the commission, Ratko Dugonjić, one of the vice-presidents of the federal Presidium, Jovanka began complaining that the UDBA was controlling her and Tito. She claimed to be in possession of documents that seriously incriminated General Mišković, but she was not disposed to show them to anyone. The members of the commission did not believe her, but agreed that Jovanka wanted to seize power, starting with the Foreign Office and the army. According to them, from 1958 the president's wife followed foreign policy with particular attention, read diplomatic dispatches and intelligence reports sent to her husband, and collaborated not just in organizing his travels but also in selecting the most important state and party cadres.[221] At a common session of the commission and the Executive Bureau, Kardelj declared outspokenly: "She is a sick person. So sick as to be dangerous to Tito. We need to think seriously about how to isolate her." Stane Dolanc agreed: "If something happens, it will be our fault." At a later session, which was attended by Tito and, at his request, also by Jovanka, the marshal reproached his wife: "I have been building this party for forty years and will not allow you to destroy it, Jovanka. Where do we go from here?" On 9 March, during another meeting of the Executive Bureau, Kardelj suggested that in future all the officials of importance should report only to Tito and take orders only from him. He and Dolanc informed Jovanka about this, but during the conversation she fell apart completely, the meeting was halted, and the confrontation was not resolved.[222] The only victim of this affair was Mišković himself, against whom Jovanka waged an absolute psychological war. He was abruptly removed from all his offices in July 1973, ostensibly for "health reasons."[223]

Despite his advanced age, Tito did not lose interest in the fairer sex. Two masseuses appeared at court, sisters Darijana and Radojka Grbić, with whom Jovanka engaged in a fight without quarter, but a fruitless one. From the beginning of her relationship with Tito, she indulged in bouts of jealousy, which continued to torment her, although she knew well that the marshal could at most bestow "pats on the butt."[224] His intimate contact with the two young women, which lasted every day for hours and was necessary for his damaged leg, sent her flying off the handle. She insisted that the massages should be strictly regulated and should be carried out in presence of the doctor, which Tito refused, being infatuated with the two women. He did not know, or preferred not to know, that after every session they informed his attending officer what was discussed during the treatment. If the information was interesting, they reported it to the secretary of defense, Nikola Ljubičić.[225]

In February 1975, a series of quarrels arose between Mr. and Mrs. Broz at Igalo, a Montenegrin spa. Jovanka behaved in such a violent way that she seriously worried the president's personal doctor and his attendant, General Marko Rapo. They feared that in the midst of a nervous breakdown she might shoot or strike her husband. Petar Stambolić, the head of his cabinet and the vice-president of the SFRY, summoned Stane Dolanc, the president of the Federal Council, Džemal Bijedić, and Nikola Ljubičić to Igalo. During a secret meeting aboard the *Galeb*, Tito confessed that he was in anguish: he would have to relinquish all his duties if he could not appease Jovanka. The Yugoslav Xanthippe was taken into custody and transported to Belgrade to be examined by a special "medical and political" commission. After a series of meetings with her, the commission established that she was not involved in any plot; she was simply paranoid. The best solution would be a divorce. Tito could not go that far, and instead he reconciled with his wife and allowed her to take revenge on her "enemies."[226] He did, however, accept the restructuring of his cabinet, which strongly limited Jovanka's influence in favor of Dolanc, Bakarić, and Kardelj. (In spite of his serious illness, the latter obviously thought he would live longer than Tito.) According to an order simply called "Kardelj's rule," the marshal was insulated from politics as much as possible, with the excuse that because of his age he should not be disturbed.[227]

At the Tenth Congress of the LCY in 1974, Jovanka had hoped to be elected to the CC, believing this to be her last chance to consolidate her position before Tito's death. She expected the support of the regime's top men—Dolanc, Bakarić, and Kardelj—but once they understood that Tito did not approve of this, they were happy to let her down. When she realized at the final session of the congress that she had been betrayed, Jovanka indulged in a bout of tears, which the deputies interpreted as sign of joy for the umpteenth confirmation of her husband to the presidency of the League. Later, in the hall where the elders of the party had gathered, she raged hysterically, attacking Bakarić and others "guilty" of causing her defeat and kicking her husband's chair.[228] She did not forgive her opponents any insult and tried to convince Tito how dangerous they were and how urgent was the need to "liquidate" them. To calm her down, he decided to award her the highest Yugoslav decoration, at Kardelj's and Bakarić's suggestion. Afraid to be seen as similar to Ceaușescu and Mao Zedong, who promoted their wives' careers, he did not want to deliver it personally and delegated Bakarić to do it. Jovanka refused it and boycotted the ceremony, which was planned for 11 December 1975, because she did not want to make peace with the Croat politician: her hatreds were as sudden as they were implacable.[229]

The conflict between Tito and Jovanka flared up again in August 1976, during a trip to Sri Lanka where a non-aligned summit (largely paid for by the Yugoslavs) had been organized. When Jovanka learned that the masseuse, Darijana, was also in Tito's suite, she had one of her hysterical attacks. The dispute ended with Tito slapping her. Later he tried to apologize, entrusting her to receive foreign dignitaries who came to greet him on the *Galeb* at the end of the conference.[230] Although flattered, she was not appeased. Feeling more and more besieged, in March 1977, she sponsored the printing of a richly illustrated book in Florence, entitled *Their Days*, which was meant to demonstrate their domestic harmony. According to many, the publication hid another more recondite message. In the numerous photos in the book, Tito is shown as an old man needing care while Jovanka, who was not yet fifty, was a fountain of energy.[231]

In August of the same year, Tito went to the Soviet Union, North Korea, and China, where he was invited by the new leadership, after the deaths of Mao and Zhou Enlai. It was a source of great satisfaction for him to be the first foreign statesman to meet Hua Guofeng and his collaborators. In fact, he reckoned on creating a dialogue with Mao's successors that could be useful in the context of his struggle with the Soviet Union. He went on the long trip without his wife, who insisted on the exclusion of the masseuse Darijana, the aide Tihomir Vilović, and Stane Dolanc from his suite. Tito refused these terms.[232] On the eve of his departure, a new furious quarrel burst out between the spouses, during which Jovanka accused her husband of being crazy and depraved, while he proclaimed her a paranoid liar.[233] On returning from China, where he had experienced a real triumph and succeeded in reestablishing both state and party relations with Chairman Hua Guofeng,[234] Jovanka disappeared from public life. To Lazar Koliševski, president of yet another commission tasked with her "affair," Tito said: "A revolutionary should never marry."[235] The split was, however, very painful for him. When the most influential people in his entourage lobbied him to divorce, he remained silent for so long that it embarrassed those present, and then he replied that he could not follow their advice: "I've been living with Jovanka for more than thirty years. I loved her very much and still have a strong affection for her. We will live separately, but will not divorce."[236]

The news of the first lady's fall from grace came like a bolt from the blue. No one expected it, as evidenced by the good wishes sent for New Year's 1978 to both Tito and Jovanka, signed by their most intimate colleagues, comrades, and friends.[237] Inevitably rumors sprang up that Jovanka's disgrace had a political basis and that Tito had discovered that she was a Soviet spy.[238] According to the diaries of Dobrica Ćosić, who as president of Yugoslavia (or what remained of it) in 1993 was able to see the records related to "the Jovanka affair," the highest authorities discussed her case in fifty-nine meetings between 1974 and 1988—hence long after Tito's death. He wrote: "For two decades, Jovanka really shook Yugoslavia."[239] Considering the notes of those commissions, one gets the impression that Tito was more distressed by his marital troubles than by the political, moral, and economic agony of his country. He continued to send bouquets of red roses to his wife, but Jovanka never forgave him for abandoning her. When he invited her to his penultimate New Year's party, she refused, saying that her human dignity had been insulted.[240]

When he began to court her, Tito said: "I feel that with you I could finally find tranquility and happiness." He had commited an enormous error. "Tito," said Dobrica Ćosić, "was a communist Napoleon, whose Waterloo was his double bed."[241]

6

Tito's Death and His Political Legacy

1980

The Cult of Personality

To avoid thinking abut Tito's seemingly imminent death, the late sixties and seventies saw an increase in his cult of personality. It was a copy of Stalin's cult, but although it elevated the marshal to the level of the "Boss," it stressed the exceptionality of his experience. Tito's physicality contributed to his legendary status. He was a handsome man of medium height, robust build, ash blond hair, and a fair face, more noble of bearing than his peasant origins might have suggested. The artist Antun Augustinčić, who had sculpted Tito's bust before the Second AVNOJ, said half-jokingly: "He must be of aristocratic origin. Who has ever seen such a type in Zagorje?"[1] Twenty years later, Dobrica Ćosić agreed: "He has the head and the face of a condottiere. The head is made especially for busts, the profile for gold coins. The head and the face of this man have something classical, Roman."[2]

The cult of Tito started even before the war, in restricted communist circles, but developed further during the liberation struggle. Ranković related that in autumn 1942 he was chatting with Tito, Kardelj, and Djilas under a beech tree. Djilas stressed that Tito was not popular enough as a personality. "We too should have a chief, a man for whom the masses feel an affinity. A leader. A party secretary. As the Russians have in Stalin."[3] In a patriarchal environment, where the folk poetry had deep roots, this idea found fertile ground. With the poem "Tito, Violet White," the simple fighters compared him to a small flower to stress his exceptional rarity. The most famous poem in his honor ended with a collective promise: "Comrade Tito, we swear never to depart from your road."[4] The same thought was expressed, if more challengingly, by the Montenegrin poet Radovan Zogović with some "constructivist" verses: "Tito has been born with rage / in a collective effort / by a Titan / the people / and by the struggle, the mother / Tito, are we all / all / the army, the country and the mountain."[5] Vladimir Nazor, the Croat writer, added in a more colloquial manner: "With Tito and Stalin / two heroic sons / even hell cannot devour us."[6] As prominent Slovene communist Lado Kozak explained, the cult of Tito had been institutionalized by the Second AVNOJ: "Glowing uniform, applause, raucous cheers, pomp, attitude like a monarch."[7] He became a "total" leader, as Djilas had wanted.[8]

The arrival of the Soviet mission in Drvar in spring 1944 gave additional momentum to the cult of personality. Its members suggested that Tito should take the Soviet archetype as a model. The Russians affirmed that Tito should be addressed with *vi* (second person plural, the formal form) and not with *ti* (second personal singular, or informal) as had been usual until then. This was immediately approved by Ranković, who sent instructions to the commanders of all the army corps on how to communicate with the head of the Supreme Staff in their dealings with him. The Soviet mission also encouraged the abolition of Partisan egalitarianism with regard to food and clothing, a step accepted gladly by the chiefs, starting with Tito, who already enjoyed such privileges.[9] In June 1944, when he arrived on the island of Vis, his cult was already so rooted in the consciousness of the masses that when the group of exiles disembarked from the British ship several hundred people on the quay were dumbstruck when someone said that this was Tito. As Louis Adamic tells it: "Then, after a minute's complete silence, some of the crowd broke into wild cheering, others wept for joy, embraced one another, and fell on their knees in thanksgiving."[10]

After the war, Tito's photo appeared in all barracks, offices, factories, businesses, banks, and even in restaurants, coffee shops, and pubs. This became a constant of Yugoslav daily life. The name TITO was also inscribed on all possible surfaces: walls, airplane wings, mountain slopes. When Adamic returned from the Unites States to the "old country" in 1949, he was assured that "Tito is everything to us. *Everything*!"[11] At the Second Congress of the Serb CP, in which the writer took part, the ovations at the inaugural session would not stop: rhythmic applause, thunderous shouts of "Hero Tito! Hero Tito! Hero Tito! Hero Tito!" And so on.[12]

After the split with Stalin, the cult of Tito, "our chief and teacher," acquired new dimensions, since he no longer had a competitor in Yugoslavia atop the communist Olympus. When the illusion dissipated that the Muscovite Boss would recognize the injustice done to the CPY, photos of Stalin disappeared from the empty shop windows of Belgrade, Zagreb, Ljubljana, and other more or less important centers, replaced by burnished plaster busts of the marshal.[13]

Djilas said: "The cult of Tito, which in some aspects aped that of Stalin, gave Yugoslavia the opportunity to rebel and defend its independence. Only with

Soviet methods was it possible to reject Soviet claims."[14] During demonstrations in favor of the CPY at the end of 1949, the Belgrade students sang an atrocious and mocking refrain, playing on the name of Stalin, the "steel man" par excellence: "Comrade Tito, you are of steel, with you is the whole of America. We are young members of SKOJ and do not drink wine, but we are thirsty for the blood of mustachioed Stalin."[15] When, however, the power elite went to New York for the General Assembly of the United Nations and *Life* magazine published a photo of the marshal and his circle, Aleš Bebler observed that Tito resembled a Latin American dictator. Back home, at a session where the results of the mission were discussed, Djilas mentioned this, embarrassing Tito, although he was not moved to adjust his lifestyle accordingly. The authorities sometimes tolerated some criticism, but it was rare. In 1962, for instance, a group of students took part in the May Day parade, carrying an enormous mirror. When they passed by the stands where Tito and other grandees of the regime were sitting, the students turned toward them so they could see themselves in the mirror.[16] Ten years later, when the painter Mića Popović opened an exhibition in which he showed two pictures, *The President of the Republic Visits the Dutch Royal Couple* and *Trains That Transport Workers to Germany*, the exhibition was immediately shut down "for political reasons."[17] It was in that period, as Koča Popović correctly noted, that the cult of personality became one of the inhibiting factors of Yugoslav society.[18]

The more Tito aged, the more dependent he was on this cult, which acquired pharaonic dimensions. "On our planet," lamented Dobrica Ćosić, "only Yugoslavia has the 'baton'" (carried around the country by young people in a relay, to be given to the marshal on his birthday on 25 May). It was also the only country to use the salutation "dearest guest," as he was ritually declared in the republics or towns he visited.[19] "He was really convinced," added Savka Dabčević-Kučar, "that he was the army! He was the party! He was the state! Certainly he did not suffer the sickness called modesty."[20] He received compliments from crowned heads as well as from his subjects. The parade of royal highnesses at his court was headed by the emperor of Ethiopia, Haile Selassie, when he visited Yugoslavia in July 1954, at the most intense moment of the diplomatic struggle with Italy. This was not without symbolic significance, since both countries had been victims of Mussolini's imperialism in the past and both had unresolved issues with Rome. The event was significant also because Haile Selassie was the first head of state to come to Yugoslavia after the split with Stalin. For that occasion, the protocol department sent the "comrades" a circular on how to dress for the various meetings with the descendant of King Solomon and the Queen of Sheba. The men were advised as to what kind of jacket or tuxedo they had to wear for this or that occasion, while the women were asked to come to the evening receptions in long dresses. In addition, "At no time are sports wear or sandals allowed."[21] The care taken to dress properly became grotesque in subsequent years: when Tito visited a foreign country, the protocol department procured a set of new clothes for the members of the delegation in attendance and up to twenty different dresses for their wives, each tailored in Paris.[22]

Tito loved medals and was delighted by his honorary degrees and memberships in the various academies of science and arts.[23] He possessed thirteen gold swords, bestowed upon him on various occasions by friendly governments, a dozen gold and diamond collars of different orders, sixteen Yugoslav and ninety-nine foreign decorations, some of them prestigious, such as the Knight Grand Cross of the Order of the Bath, bestowed upon him by Queen Elizabeth II in 1972, or the Danish Order of the Elephant, received in 1974. Not to mention the socialist honors: the Order of Lenin (Soviet Union, 1972) or the Hero of the Republic of North Korea—but also exotic ones, such as the Grand Collar of the Queen of Sheba (Ethiopia, 1952), the Collar of the National Order of the Aztec Eagle (Mexico, 1963), the Grand Cordon of the Supreme Order of the Chrysanthemum (Japan, 1968), or the Grand Cross of the Order of Mono (Togo, 1976). The absurdity came to a head when the Serb Socialist Alliance of Working People proposed shortly before his death that he should be awarded, for the fourth time, the title of "People's Hero," after having emerged successfully from his amputation surgery. The initiative was dropped when his condition worsened.[24]

Tito felt at ease among royals. He loved to tell of how Queen Frederica of Greece, niece of the last kaiser, assured him during a visit to Brioni that she would surely have joined the party had she been born in Yugoslavia. Her gift, a couple of white poodles that he held dear, started a canine dynasty at the court.[25] For his eightieth birthday, the British ambassador suggested that the queen gift him with some silver object. He advised that "local knowledge and taste are such that late Victorian would be more appropriate than earlier and more distinguished."[26] Instead of silver or Chivas Regal whiskey, as was also suggested, the monarch celebrated Tito's jubilee with an official visit to Yugoslavia "while the Marshal was still in the saddle." It was her first journey to a socialist country.[27] After having hosted Princess Margaret and the queen of the Netherlands, Tito's court knew well how to handle the scions of the old European dynasties. Elizabeth II was so enthusiastic about all the attention she was given in October 1972, just as Tito was demolishing the Serb liberal leadership, that on her return she sent him a silver cup, along with a flattering appraisal. Allegedly she said: "If this man is a mechanic, I am not the Queen of England." Tito reached the height of his social status when he invited Her Majesty to waltz during a soirée at Brioni.[28]

The cult of personality could have been crowned by a Nobel Peace Prize, and Tito's name was put forward by Pierre Grégoire, the president of the parliament of Luxembourg. When the unofficial confirmation came from Oslo that Tito had been included on the short list of candidates, a special task force was formed to assure him the necessary national and international support. The Yugoslav ambassadors abroad were asked to recruit prestigious supporters to his cause.[29] About a hundred statesmen of rank—among them Willy Brandt, Indira Gandhi, Haile Selassie, U Thant, Urho Kekkonen, Habib Bourguiba, and Nahum Goldmann—but also writers and famous artists—Ivo Andrić, Fitzroy Maclean, and Charlie Chaplin—supported the three-hundred-page proposal supporting his candidacy, written by Vladimir Dedijer and the Slovenian sociologist Rudi Rizman. The Yugoslav diplomats considered it appropriate to ask for the support of the Holy See. The papal secretary of state, Cardinal Agostino Casaroli, had no objection, nor did the Zagreb cardinal Franjo Kuharić (although he asked for the rehabilitation of Alojzije Stepinac in return, affirming that this was necessary to keep the conservatives in the Vatican and the Yugoslav episcopal conference quiet).[30] The Holy Synod of the Serb Orthodox Church was more reserved, preferring not to weigh in on the candidacy.[31]

The Supreme Soviet of the USSR, which supported his candidature with a special, published declaration, wound up doing Tito a disservice, because this had a negative effect in the West.[32] It seems that his candidacy was unsuccessful because of opposition from the United States and the "Jewish lobby," who had not forgotten his pro-Arab policy, and also because of the protests of Yugoslav émigrés, starting with Ljubo Sirc, a Slovenian economist who was sentenced to death after the war but managed to escape to Great Britain, where he made a name as specialist for Eastern Europe. In his lengthy memorandum, he convincingly enumerated all of Tito's sins.[33] The king of Norway allegedly tried to save his candidature, counseling the marshal to make amends, at least for Goli Otok. "If I should ask the forgiveness of anybody," he replied, offended, "it would be to those who died there without guilt. To Cominformists, I do not intend to apologize."[34]

The unofficial explanation by the Nobel Prize Committee for his rejection was naturally different. Tito was a military man and as such he could not get a peace prize.[35] Considering the role he had played on the world stage and that Yugoslavia, thanks almost exclusively to his efforts, was held as one of the ten most influential countries in the international arena, the decision might be thought unjust.[36] That year the prize was shared by the Vietnamese diplomat and general, Le Duc Tho, and the American secretary of state, Henry Kissinger, who had brought the Vietnam War to an end but had also been responsible for the bombardments of Hanoi and for the overthrow of the Chilean president,

Salvador Allende. By way of consolation, Tito got the Nehru Peace Prize, awarded by the Indian president, Varahagiri Venkata Giri. It was a balm that could not heal the wound inflicted on his pride.[37]

Tito's Health

Diplomatic circles began speaking about Tito's renunciation of power, or his death, as early as the fifties. From then on the marshal was the object of careful observation, recorded in numerous dispatches by ambassadors in Belgrade or by their colleagues in the countries he visited. In 1964, the rumor spread that he intended to retire from active political life and settle for the post of president of the state. His friend Krajačić, who was a megalomaniac—his swimming pool was filled with salt water transported daily from Dalmatia—began work on an enormous residence for him where he could sojourn once retired.[38] Allegedly, he modeled it on palaces he had seen in India, financing "Villa Zagorje" on the outskirts of Zagreb partially with public funds and partially with illicit traffic in cigarettes, of which Tito was aware. The villa boasted a game reserve and an antinuclear bunker and cost 27 billion dinars. Tito did not like it and reacted angrily when he saw it—"You have built it for you, not for me"—living there for just a few days in total, at least at first. Later he became accustomed to the place and started to dwell there regularly, agreeing with those who knew his tastes for luxury, in spite of his initial protests.[39] It was not the only building Krajačić erected for the marshal in Croatia. He boasted that he also constructed residences at Dubrovnik, Split, Brioni, Samobor, and Kumrovec, not to mention the numerous hunting chalets that were built for Tito where he never stayed.[40]

Whereas in the sixties the diplomatic dispatches spoke mainly about Tito's good health, in the early seventies there were ever more frequent hints of his physical decline, which indeed at times he was aware of. Still, in July 1969, during the delivery of letters of accreditation by the American and West German ambassadors, Tito gave the impression of "a healthy man, more in his sixties than in his seventies: he was mobile, agile in speech and full of spontaneous humor."[41] Two years later, in November 1971, the German ambassador in Canada, where Tito had stopped during his return trip from the United States, reported that he appeared fresh and energetic at the start of the official ceremonies, but soon it was possible to notice his increasing fatigue.[42]

In mid-June 1971, President Richard Nixon asked the National Security Council to prepare a study on possible scenarios related to Yugoslavia after Tito's "departure."[43] In early March a joint Anglo-American Intelligence Committee had convened in London with the same task. The British even prepared a telegram of condolences that the queen would send to Tito's widow.[44] It was not just protocol: in fact, the question arose about Italy's possible reaction if

Yugoslavia became "communist" (that is, if it were occupied by the Soviet Union). In such a case, might NATO's entire strategy in the Mediterranean be disrupted?[45] Between the end of September and October 1972, the Americans and the British conducted further talks about what to do if Yugoslavia was invaded by the Soviets after Tito's death.[46] Similar conversations were held in the following years, spurred by the news that Tito was taking medical advice seriously for the first time.[47] In Washington, a paper prepared by the National Security Council Interdepartmental Ad Hoc Group for Yugoslavia from September 1971 suggested that if the Soviets occupied Serbia, Macedonia, and Montenegro, the United States would ask the UN to send the "blue helmets" to Slovenia and Croatia, "trying to force this action by making it clear that in the absence of a UN effort the US and NATO would have no recourse but to take steps to guarantee the continued independence and Western orientation of Croatia and Slovenia. In the absence of UN action, we would move into the two northern republics."[48]

From the spring of 1973 through the summer, Tito was ill, although this was covered up with the announcement that he was preparing for the Tenth Congress of the LCY.[49] In April of that year the French ambassador reported that he was better, but that his voice "was now that of an old man."[50] Shortly thereafter, for health reasons not fully explained, his visit to Serbia was interrupted. In fact, he had had a stroke, to which he was prone.[51] The following year, after a challenging trip in India, Bangladesh, Nepal, and Syria, he contracted a flu that lasted six weeks and did not allow him to attend the proclamation of the new constitution (if, indeed, the reasons for his absence were not political). In Western military circles they whispered that his hour had come.[52] In May 1974, the National Intelligence Organization, which dealt with the Soviet Union and East Europe, organized a conference of experts in Washington to discuss what would happen in the first six months after Tito's death.[53]

In 1975 Tito suffered a painful bout of sciatica, which he had experienced a number of times before, so much so that he had to defer the date of János Kádár's visit and take a painkilling injection in order to attend the parade celebrating the thirtieth anniversary of the victory of the Second World War. When he was finally able to receive the Hungarian leader, he tried to deny rumors about his declining health: "In the West, they like to speculate. How many times have they said that I am dying? Look at me, do you have the impression that I am finished?"[54] He could not have imagined that his entourage spoke of the "fossilization" of Tito, mocking his speeches at banquets or visits to factories. In the last ten years, they said, he had always closed his meetings with them in the same way: "Comrades, only brotherhood and unity will save us, will boost our self-managed socialism, only brotherhood and unity. . . . We all should keep this in mind."[55] Those who derided him did not realize that this was his "last battle cry," as his interpreter, Ivan Ivanji said, aware as Tito was of the collapse that Yugoslavia would face.[56]

The most vivid description of Tito's physical decline was given by a friend from his youth, Rodoljub Čolaković, who was tasked by the federal council to go to Brioni in 1978 as a member of the delegation that would congratulate Tito on his eighty-sixth birthday. He said, "I would prefer not to go. The old man is dilapidated, he moves with fatigue, he speaks with fatigue, but in spite of this, he sports his white uniform and his decorations, which look sad. But the party went on, as if he were well and healthy. Actually, he is seriously ill with diabetes, his legs are failing him, but he thinks that this is sciatica. . . . The old man's right hand is trembling, his lower lip is drooping, but he continuously clenches his teeth, conscious that his mouth is slackening."[57]

The awareness that his days were numbered mainly influenced relations with Italy. The government in Rome reached the conclusion that the still unresolved border question between Zones A and B of the former Free Territory of Trieste should be dealt with while Tito was still alive, because if not, then Russian tanks could appear on the streets of Trieste. After years of tension, which the Yugoslavs interpreted as imperialist pressure dictated by Washington, the two governments engaged in secret negotiations that concluded on 10 November 1975 with the signing of the Osimo Treaty. Apart from modest tweaks to the border, the division of the contested territory was confirmed as enshrined in the 1954 London Memorandum. Tito, who was directly involved in the diplomacy, considered the treaty his personal success, likely without realizing how Italian willingness to solve the longstanding issue was the result of Washington's influence.[58]

In spite of his health troubles, the marshal did not cancel his journeys to Latin America, Sweden, Greece, Portugal, Turkey, or Finland. He played an important role at the Conference on Security and Cooperation in Europe, held in Helsinki in July 1975, trying to overcome the tensions that still lacerated the continent, knowing better than the other statesmen present of "the terrible Calvary of Fascism and war."[59] Since Yugoslavia was surrounded by seven states, two of which were members of NATO and three of the Warsaw Pact, it was in his interest to contribute to collective security and play mediator. To this end, he favored strengthening the contacts between the four neutral European states (Austria, Finland, Sweden, and Switzerland) and creating the "N-N group" (neutrals and non-aligned). The latter group supported the détente between the blocs reached in Helsinki and tried to add a military dimension to the agreements as well.[60] The following year he took part in the Congress of European Communist Parties in East Berlin on 29 and 30 June 1976, which their delegations had carefully prepared for during the preceding eighteen months. Tito's attendance was uncertain up to the last moment, given that in spite of "long and frank negotiations," the Yugoslavs were not able to find a common language with the Soviets.[61] In the end, he decided to go to the East German capital, surprising everyone since it was the first time he had participated in such a gathering as a party and state president. For Brezhnev, his presence was very important, as can be inferred by the attention reserved for him. They met before the opening day and at the inaugural session of the congress he greeted him at the entrance to the hall, installing him at the banquet in a place of honor between himself and Erich Honecker, the host. Aleksandar Grličkov, who led the Yugoslav delegation at the preparatory meetings, affirmed that Tito came to the congress "on a white horse," since on that occasion a declaration on the right of every party to follow its own road to socialism was adopted—something for which he had fought for over thirty years.[62] He commented to his closest collaborators: "We have settled accounts for 1948."[63]

At the end of his life, Tito was as concerned about the domestic situation as he was about international matters, doubling his efforts to make improvements. On the internal front he lamented the slowdown in industrial growth but feared nationalism most, as it could undermine the relations between the republics and the provinces. In threatening tones he declared that in the event of trouble the army—a force that he considered the best in Europe—would be required to step in; only it could guarantee state unity. The military was ready to pander to him, asking for and receiving stronger security laws, described as "social self-defense," which were meant to ensure the regime's stability.[64] Tito was worried by the spread of fundamentalism among the four million Sunni Muslims in Bosnia-Herzegovina, but most of all by the situation in Kosovo, where he forecast an Albanian "national revolt" if the authorities were not able to prevent it in time. "The first explosion will happen there," he predicted in 1976 to the journalist Dara Janeković. He was convinced that the Tirana government was sending its agents throughout the province, and that with the support of local politicians they were smuggling gold, drugs, and weapons to the Albanian émigrés and foreign secret services.[65]

Tito also feared the "Shiptars" (Albanians) because, in league with the Ustaša, they had planned the most recent of many attempts against his life—somewhere between the twenty-first or twenty-fifth.[66] The assassination attempt was to have taken place in Zagreb in 1975, where Tito was set to confer the title of "People's Hero" on some Croatian leaders at the International Trade Fair. The Yugoslavs were alerted to the conspiracy by Soviet agents and the schedule was changed at the last minute. The bombs placed at the square where he would have stopped did explode, but only blew out the windows of the nearby

Bank of Zagreb. The press did not mention what had happened, but the authorities were deeply concerned, fearing a plot to attack Yugoslavia after Tito's death on the part of various exile groups. "The boldness of recent terrorist actions," a CIA document notes, "has led Belgrade to redouble its security effort at home and to make representations to foreign governments with jurisdictions over potential terrorists."[67] But it was useless, since Kosovar nationalism could not be bridled. Tito experienced this in relation to his own person when, in October 1979, he visited the hostile province for what would be the last time. On the eve of his arrival his photos at the faculty of humanities of the University of Priština were torn down and ripped.[68]

On an international level, Tito wanted to complete his plans to put things in order while he still could, and once and for all cement relations with the Soviet Union. In November 1976 he met Leonid Brezhnev, who returned to Belgrade on an official visit after a five-year absence. This took place some weeks after major military maneuvers known as "Goliath" occurred in Bosnia-Herzegovina, Montenegro, and Serbia, which rehearsed an initial tank clash on the plains of the Hungarian and Romanian border, and a long Partisan struggle in the core of the country. Although it was not openly stated, it was evident that according to the Yugoslav strategists the peril came from Russia.

Brezhnev, who had a string of frank and heated discussions with Tito, Kardelj, and Dolanc, tried to dissipate these fears. At the gala dinner he said jokingly during a toast that Yugoslavia was certainly not a Little Red Riding Hood in danger of being eaten by the Big Bad Russian Wolf, as the Western press had written. His assurances, however, did not convince the Yugoslavs. In the press release published at the end of the visit there was a passage on the independence of the LCY that had not appeared in previous joint declarations. But the word "trust," included in the declaration of 1972, was missing. In short, after the "Cominform affair" the Yugoslavs no longer believed the Soviets and were certain they were vulnerable to treachery at the most delicate moment: Tito's death.[69] When the Soviet press tried to present the summit in the context of a "collective discussion on the strategy and tactics of the socialist countries," the Yugoslav commentators reacted firmly—obviously on orders from above—stressing that a return of Yugoslavia to the "socialist community" was out of the question.[70]

Tito and his comrades were especially susceptible to allegations that they were ready to return to the "camp" because they had the impression that the West accepted the idea of their dependence on the Warsaw Pact. This was the gist of what Helmut Sonnenfeldt, the chief of the Eastern European desk at the State Department, said at a meeting in London of the American ambassadors to the communist countries. He had developed the theory that the latent conflict between the Soviet Union and its satellites was more dangerous to world peace than the tension between the blocs. It was in the interest of the West to contribute to the establishment of "more natural and organic" relations in the Soviet geopolitical sphere since Moscow had rights that should be respected in this area.[71] When the "Sonnenfeldt doctrine" went public, it was accepted in Belgrade with considerable apprehension as the US diplomat included Yugoslavia in his reflections, asserting its leaders should understand that "our interest in their independence is not superior to theirs, and hence they cannot allow themselves whatever foreign policy they would like."[72] These words were interpreted by the Yugoslav media as an attempt to revive the spirit of Yalta, that is to say the division of Europe between the two superpowers, and therefore an attempt on the sovereignty and non-alignment of their country. Tito was convinced of the existence of a gentlemen's agreement between Moscow and Washington whereby the Americans and the Russians should be allowed "to hunt freely on their [own] game reserve."[73] Clearly, the idea that Yugoslavia was part of the Soviet game reserve was unacceptable to the marshal.

Tito and the Freedom Fighters of the Third World

Tito remained a guerrilla fighter until his last breath, contributing to the development of liberation struggles in a decisive manner with his aid, counsel, and prestige, particularly in certain African countries. While in the fifties he was very much engaged in supporting the Algerian National Liberation Front, and in the sixties the Viet Cong, in the following decade he devoted his attention not only to the Palestinians but also to the liberation struggles in the Portuguese colonies of Angola, Mozambique, and Guinea Bissau.

As he said in 1974 at the Tenth Congress of the LCY, these movements were an important part of the progressive forces in the contemporary world; fighting for national independence, they contributed to the struggle against imperialism and colonialism. Offering aid was the duty of all socialist and democratic countries.[74] Dimče Belovski, an eminent Macedonian diplomat, affirmed in an article in 1974 that Yugoslavia had used the international prestige that it had acquired due to its resistance in order to assist the colonial peoples in Asia and Africa. "There is no movement of national liberation that we, according to our possibilities, would not support morally, politically and materially," he wrote.[75] Tito, however, was not just interested in national liberation struggles. When a border dispute broke out between Reza Shah Pahlavi's Iran and Saddam Hussein's Iraq in the mid-seventies, he did everything possible to convince the two states, both members of the Non-Aligned Movement, to reach a peace settlement. The peace was, in any case, provisional.[76] After a short truce the war recommenced in 1980.

After the passage of the constitution of 1974, Yugoslavia organized a special solidarity fund for non-aligned and developing countries. It was grafted onto the aid program that already existed in the form of loans and technical assistance and instruction offered to the youth of the Third World by Yugoslav high schools and universities. The aim of the new fund was to offer coordinated aid to the national liberation movements under the supervision of the Socialist Alliance of Working People. In a period when the Palestine Liberation Organization (PLO) was isolated internationally, Tito was one of the first to support it. He even went so far as to indirectly approve some terrorist actions by its members, stressing that subjugated peoples had the right to use every means in the fight for their liberty. It is no wonder that, in the last decade of Tito's life, Yasser Arafat, the leader of the PLO, was his guest at least once a year. He met even more frequently with the leader of the Angolan guerrillas, Agostinho Neto, since Yugoslavia organized training courses for the People's Movement for the Liberation of Angola (MPLA), as well as for similar groups in Guinea Bissau and Mozambique, providing them with weapons, food, and medicine.

In November 1975 when Angola's independence was proclaimed, the troops of the South African Union, a part of Zaire's regular army, as well as some dissident Angolan movements attacked from all sides in an attempt to occupy the capital, Luanda, and to suffocate the MPLA. Tito ordered military assistance for the MPLA, sending two ships of the Yugoslav Navy to Angola, which intervened in a decisive manner. As local leaders later affirmed, the independence struggle that culminated in the Luanda battle was won thanks to Yugoslav help.[77]

Tito was on good terms with the rebellious leader of Rhodesia (later Zimbabwe), Robert Mugabe, although Yugoslavia did not discriminate against the other liberation movement, headed by Joshua Nkomo. Generally, however, it followed the norm of having regular relations only with the movements recognized by the Organization of African Unity and by the non-aligned. The Polisario Front, the national liberation movement of Western Sahara, was not included among these. When Tito died, however, members of this movement also attended his funeral—unannounced. The protocol officers at first thought they belonged to the vanguard of the Algerian president, only to find out later they were mistaken. To explain their presence a tall, raven-haired young man said: "We are Tito's sons. We have to pay him our last respects."[78] Obviously they were accepted despite the Moroccan protests.

The Independence of the Non-Aligned

In the years of his decline, Tito was preoccupied with the independence of the Non-Aligned Movement. In that period he visited Kuwait to strengthen the unity of the Arab world, and was also involved in the conflict between Ethiopia and Somalia. He also attempted to convince the Soviets and the Cubans to recall their troops from the Horn of Africa.[79] His commitment, however, was primarily to the conference of the non-aligned. In September 1979 he went to a meeting in Havana in the name of the "original principles" he had established, to prevent its collapse. Immediately after the summit in Algiers in September 1973, it seemed that the Third World would be able to carry more weight on the international stage, since the higher oil prices imposed by the Arabs after the Israeli-Egyptian war in October of that year proved to what extent the nations referred to generally as the "South" were able to influence the wealthy "North." Tito's ideas on the need to set a common policy to prevent the "rich becoming increasingly rich and the poor increasingly poor," which he reiterated on that occasion, appeared more relevant than ever. Although the sharp rise in the price of oil and its derivatives damaged Yugoslavia, Tito proclaimed in an interview with the German chancellor Helmut Schmidt that the lesson the Arabs had taught to the West was "probably the most important event in the history of mankind."[80] He expected that the developed countries would be forced to initiate a new dialogue with those that were less developed but rich in raw materials. He lobbied the UN secretary general to dedicate the next General Assembly mainly to the problem of bridging the North-South gap. In September 1973 a special session was organized in which these issues were discussed for the first time in the history of the UN. It ended with a Declaration of the Establishment of a New International Economic Order and a program of action, which was considered a great success by the non-aligned.[81]

The idea of a more equitable economic order, which became the battle cry of the Third World countries at the summit in Algiers, was not realized in practice. On the contrary, following internal conflicts between its members the Non-Aligned Movement experienced an identity crisis in the second half of the seventies that weakened its influence at the UN. Tito was convinced that the Americans were mainly responsible for this, because of their "imperialist strategy of fragmentation," which was designed to break up the united front of the non-aligned countries with the help of "mercenary regimes." He tried to overcome the crisis by becoming a mediator in different regional conflicts and a spokesman of common values, including the disarmament of the great powers and the establishment of a new economic order more attentive to developing countries. This policy was not without consequences for Yugoslavia. The marshal's support of various liberation movements aroused considerable dismay in the West and involved the country in a series of controversies, which nevertheless did not escalate beyond verbal skirmishes. The situation was eloquently summed up by Henry Kissinger in a discussion about Tito's foreign policy with his most important Western colleagues in December 1976: "Officially Washington understands that Yugoslavia must follow an independent line, for its own security, which won't always please us. But we have to shoot one across their bow when they get too enthusiastic, as they did on Puerto Rico. But at the same time, I understand what they're up to."[82]

In this international context, Cuba and fifteen other countries began contesting the equidistance between the blocs, saying that, in the fight against imperialism, the "natural" ally of the non-aligned should be the Soviet Union. This theory was discussed at the congress in Havana, convened in early September 1979. The Cuban stance, which had already appeared at the Algiers congress in 1973, was accompanied by a more or less blatant attempt to remove Tito from the leadership of the movement, something unacceptable to the Yugoslavs. According to them, this was a dangerous, essentially reactionary policy, since it would undermine the unity of the non-aligned, weakening their role and harming the further development of socialism as a "world process."[83] Tito had no great sympathy for Fidel Castro who, in his pro-Soviet enthusiasm, had tried to boycott the Belgrade Non-Aligned Conference in the early sixties and had even dared to assert that "the LCY is neither a party nor communist." The piqued Yugoslav diplomats assured the Americans that they would not allow the Cubans to use the Non-Aligned Movement as a means of advancing an anti-Western, pro-Soviet policy.[84] In the following years Tito opposed Castro's attempts to develop subversive activity in Latin America and Africa, and supported the policy of friendship with all the Third World countries, regardless of their regimes, unlike the *líder máximo*, who would ally only with the socialists.[85]

Although extremely critical of American imperialism, in 1979 Tito was still of the opinion that Soviet hegemony should not be underestimated. He decided to oppose the radicalism of the Cuban dictator, believing himself to be the only one capable of preventing the non-aligned from becoming Soviet dependents. Firmly convinced that it was a question of "to be or not to be for our movement," he visited seven African and Asian countries in six months to get their support. He even contemplated convening a counter-conference in Belgrade because "Cuban behavior is really absurd. According to many, Cuba does not have the credentials to host the summit."[86]

At the Havana Congress, which was the sixth conference of the non-aligned, ninety-five members and twenty-one observers took part. At this world gathering, the largest summit of heads of state in all of history, Tito played his role of leader and teacher for the last time, trying to convince the non-aligned not to be misled by those who wanted to engage them in "interests alien to the movement."[87] It was his personal triumph: at the opening session, he was greeted by cheers. The president of Guinea, Ahmed Sékou Touré, proclaimed him "the great statesman of the poor of the world."[88] However, his efforts to isolate Castro were not successful. After dramatic discussions, the congress ended with a declaration that differed from the draft prepared by the Cubans who, with their allies, were nevertheless given the task of leading the Organizational Bureau of the movement for the next five years. Although aware of their isolation, the Yugoslavs preferred to ignore the fact that their primacy was waning and that this was a mirror image of the profound crisis of their regime. To reinvigorate the Non-Aligned Movement they would have to roundly condemn Soviet socialism, which would bring their own legitimacy into question. "But here flows the Rubicon," wrote Stane Kavčič, "that the current leadership, with Tito at the head, does not want to and cannot cross."[89] Tito lost his last battle with the Soviets because he was too close to them, too similar.

In assessing the struggle with the Soviets, it should not be overlooked that Yugoslavia was more and more economically linked to the Soviet Union. In 1979 it reached the same level of trade it had enjoyed before the split with Stalin, not to mention the armaments received, mostly of Soviet origin, in spite of the development of a domestic military industry.[90] The disagreement between the Yugoslavs and Soviets over how to implement socialism continued to smolder. Tito discussed it one last time with Brezhnev during his "friendly and unofficial" visit to Moscow in May 1979, a visit that was marked by Ceaușescu's recent, urgent, and top secret communication to Tito warning him that Romanian intelligence had learned of Russian strategic plans to invade Yugoslavia.[91] Against this background, the marshal and his host were not able to reach any agreement on the most important questions—relations with China and Southeast Asia, the Horn of Africa, Bulgarian irredentist ambitions in Macedonia, and the Non-Aligned Movement. The only point of understanding was the mutual commitment to put a damper on the controversies in the press in their respective countries, and a five-year plan for commercial exchange.[92] But as soon as Tito left—not without the traditional kisses—Radio Moscow broadcast a comment that sounded dangerously ambiguous, since it confirmed Brezhnev's doctrine about the limited sovereignty of the socialist countries: it stated that the Soviet Union was ready to cultivate equal relations with Yugoslavia, taking into account, however, "not just national interests, but international too."[93]

"Nothing Should Surprise Us"

At the end of the seventies, Tito was even more concerned about Southeast Asia than about Cuba. He saw Vietnam's intervention in Cambodia on 25 December

1978 as an aggression that had been suggested by the Soviet Union in the name of "fraternal aid," regardless of world public opinion. The assertion that Cambodia under Pol Pot's murderous regime could not be considered socialist was, according to him, just an excuse with which the aggressors justified the evident violation of international law. No one had the right to criticize the social character of any state, said the marshal, except the population and its leaders. Those who asserted that the crimes of Pol Pot's regime indicated its foreignness to socialism had a poor knowledge of history. Under Stalin's rule in the Soviet Union there were millions of deaths, but nobody dared to conclude that its socialist character was lost. According to Tito, Vietnam's attack on Cambodia created an extremely dangerous precedent, not just in the Southeast Asia but around the world. It must be asked in all seriousness where this would lead. The LCY thoroughly discussed what had happened in Indo-China, reaching two conclusions: firstly, that Kardelj's prophecy about the possibility of future wars between socialist states had come true; secondly, that Yugoslavia should be ready for anything, exposed as it was to repeated Soviet interference and to Bulgarian irredentism. Preparations for defense had to embrace all sectors of social, political, economic, and military life. In Tito's opinion, the mass media in the Soviet Union were creating an atmosphere hostile to Yugoslavia, while Bulgaria was amassing its troops at the border. At the meeting he declared: "Today we have a situation that we have not had since the war. At the end of the war we said that we would work as if we had a hundred years of peace ahead of us, but that we would prepare as if war could break out tomorrow. I think we are there. We need to work by reinforcing internal unity, as if war really were going to break out tomorrow. The complexity of international relations is such that it is impossible to predict the immediate future."[94] A comprehensive "campaign of vigilance" was implemented, under the slogan "nothing should surprise us," an attempt to involve the entire population in the defense against an eventual invader, purposely creating a psychological state of fear and danger, as if the entire world were conspiring against Yugoslavia.[95] It aimed mainly to strengthen the regime and overcome the economic and political tensions that were accumulating daily. After the fall of the Croatian, Serbian, and Slovenian liberals, the party recovered its central role in Yugoslav life, restoring its supreme authority. Despite the proclamations about the "completeness of self-management," the levers of power remained in the hands of Tito's inner circle, who still believed in the validity of democratic centralism. The Eleventh Congress of the LCY in 1978 reinforced the concept of the "dictatorship of the proletariat" and its vanguard, which did not intend to renounce control of the regime's key organs: the secret services, the army, and the diplomatic apparatus.[96] The situation can be summed up by an episode that occurred during the drafting of

Tito's report for the Eleventh Congress. Based on his directions, the text was written by a team of experts who worked through the night so the next morning the marshal could read and edit it. So he did, meeting the experts again in the late afternoon and giving them notes. At the end of the discussion, in a relaxed mood, they all went to dinner and one of them took the liberty of suggesting that the draft, or at least the part of it that dealt with international relations, should be sent to the foreign secretary. Tito drummed his fingers, paused a moment, then said: "Yes, of course, we could also send it." Then he grimaced, beat his fist on the table and hissed furiously: "But we will not send it. I know these things better than anyone else in Yugoslavia."[97]

Everything Passes. Yugoslavia, Too

In autumn 1979, at the end of his hundred and seventeenth trip abroad, to Romania, which of all Eastern countries was closest to him, Tito's health worsened rapidly. The main culprit was diabetes and, consequently, circulatory difficulties in his left foot that could not be overcome even with intensive therapy.

During the war Tito and his comrades faced death every day, accepting it as the price of victory. When in power their attitude toward death changed, since it was not the rule anymore, but a bitter exception. The 1953 loss of Boris Kidrič, who had coauthored the reforms after the split with Stalin, was extremely painful for them, since he was the first member of their inner circle to die. Tito went to Ljubljana for the funeral and returned to Belgrade on the "blue train," inherited after the war from King Aleksandar but refurbished with the help of Soviet experts, since it had not been sufficiently luxurious or safe enough. During the journey, a discussion developed on life's transiency, with Djilas affirming that humans were just matter and life after death was an illusion. Tito reproached him with a smile: "Do not speak about this now. Who knows, who may know?"[98]

Tito was conscious of leaving a void behind him and it seems this may have been his intention.[99] When, at the tenth anniversary of the Second AVNOJ in November 1953, Djilas proposed minting a special "marshal" decoration that would pass to his successor after his death, he opposed the idea, saying: "Yes, certainly, so that any coward will wear it."[100] In the last years of his life, Yugoslavia experienced a rapid economic and political decline and the 1974 constitution remained largely unimplemented, as it was not possible to transform the state into a confederation nor was it possible to go from a one-party system to democratic pluralism. The shift of power in favor of the republics seriously hindered the central government's ability to formulate an efficient economic strategy and prevented the LCY from controlling the local political centers.

Stane Dolanc summarized the situation, declaring: "Democratic centralism stops at the borders of the republics."[101]

Miroslav Krleža, who knew as much about Yugoslavia under the monarchy as he did about its socialist reality, recognized what this would lead to. In the early seventies, he had already understood that the federation, as had been modeled by Tito, could not survive him, noting that "the old gentleman has made a tailored suit, but does not realize that it is falling apart."[102] It is unlikely that Tito was unaware of this. In an interview with the Italian writer Alberto Moravia, Tito affirmed that the First World War had taught him the transience of everything: no state is eternal, every empire is ephemeral.[103] Before his death he was forced to recognize that his country was, too. In May 1978, at the Eleventh Congress of the LCY, he declared, "We communists have honored, as always, our debt toward the working class, toward our nations and nationalities, toward all the progressive and democratic forces of the world. . . . Therefore, we look to the future with fresh optimism."[104] But he no longer believed. In October 1967, meeting his Czechoslovak colleague Antonín Novotný in a confidential discussion, he expressed his doubts about the strength of the Yugoslav federation: "They all hate each other. Every session of our CC is a general massacre."[105] And only a month after the maneuvers of "Freedom 1971," when he hurriedly returned from Bucharest in November to settle accounts with the Croat liberals, he said to his attendants: "If you knew how I see the future of Yugoslavia, you would be horrified."[106]

Near the end of his days he was visited by his old comrade, Svetozar Vukmanović (Tempo), who asked: "What is happening to Yugoslavia?"

Tito answered dryly: "Yugoslavia does not exist anymore."

"What is happening to the party?"

"The party does not exist anymore."[107]

He was right. Nevertheless he could look to his legacy with some pride: during the years of his rule, the quality of life of the popular masses had improved decisively, police pressure decreased, and the gap between the privileges of those in power and the common citizens diminished. One in four households had a car, to say nothing of "weekend" houses that sprouted like mushrooms—a sign of reasonable affluence. Yugoslavia was one of the most open countries in the world, as much for foreign tourists as for its citizens, who could travel without visas to forty-four countries. Yugoslavs enjoyed every freedom, apart from the freedom of thought and speech. But in this was hidden the germ of collapse: since there was no freedom of opinion, it was not possible to discuss a post-Tito era freely.[108] It was clear that after his death Yugoslavia would not be the same anymore. "As a national patriarch, savior, and political entrepreneur, Tito is truly irreplaceable," wrote the American intelligence analysts in 1967, in a paper on the "Yugoslav Experiment." "For nearly a quarter of a century, he has stood as a symbol of national unity and as Yugoslavia's supreme arbiter. Arranging an orderly succession to his office is the greatest problem the Yugoslav party—and Tito himself—face. Though Tito is not blind to the problem his departure will create, this is one area of potential dissension in which his genius for compromise and improvisation cannot be brought fully to bear. It is possible for a man to arrange for his own funeral, but is difficult for him to play a very active role in it."[109]

Because of the oppressive atmosphere, those who were able to think feared Tito's death and at the same time desired it, conscious that nothing would change until it happened. "His death is waited for as the last hope and salvation," wrote Dobrica Ćosić in early January 1978.[110]

In private life during his last years, Tito was without a wife (they had separated, though not divorced) and without comrades. He was so lonely that even the British ambassador thought it important to mention this emotional state in his yearly report for 1978.[111] This was especially evident at the thirty-fifth anniversary of the battle on the Neretva. None of his closest fellow soldiers participated in the grand celebration apart from the functionaries of his entourage: Koča Popović was disgraced and Peko Dapčević, the legendary commander of the Second Proletarian Division, was absent. In the middle of his inaugural speech Tito asked loudly: "How is it that Peko Dapčević is not here? Send him a helicopter immediately." It was done, but Peko declined to come, since he had not been invited earlier.[112] Things got worse: during his speech Tito completely lost his sense of proportion, describing his role in the famous battle without any restraint, and far from historical truth. As Lazar Koliševski commented acidly, "He convinced himself that he was a great man."[113]

Tito's Death

The marshal celebrated New Year's Eve 1980 at Karadjordjevo with his sons and close collaborators, while all Yugoslavia could see on television that he used a walking stick and remained seated while he received greetings.[114] On 1 January he took part in the traditional lunch with the most important political leaders of the country, expressing on that occasion the hope to celebrate "together again next year." He pretended to be in good spirits and tried to hide his physical troubles.[115] In fact, before the holidays he had been struck by a thrombosis in his left leg that could not be cured with anticoagulants. Two days later he was rushed by helicopter to the Ljubljana Clinical Center for a "routine checkup." One of his last political decisions before going to the hospital was to prohibit the devaluation of the dinar by 30 percent, as proposed by the president of the federal government, the finance secretary, and the governor of the national bank. He was aware that doing so would signal to the world that the economic situation in Yugoslavia was disastrous.[116] The country's debt stood at about $21 billion and a good part of the GNP went toward repayment. About 6.5 percent of the population was jobless, despite the security valve of mass emigration of the most enterprising young people to the West.

After the visit Tito was released from the Clinical Center even though doctors considered surgery necessary. After a further hospitalization, on the advice of the famous American specialist Michael De Bakey and the Russian Marat Kniazhev, the doctors decided to try a bypass of the femoral artery of the left leg. The operation did not have a favorable outcome and only a week later the news came that the leg would have to be amputated to avoid gangrene. When he was informed about this after waking from anesthesia, Tito was so stricken that he threatened suicide with the pistol that he had kept under his pillow, from his clandestine years on.[117] He tried to refuse surgical treatment, claiming that he was fed up with life. He was born with two legs and was not ready to die a cripple, but at last, in extremis, he agreed to surgery.[118]

It was evident that he was fighting his last battle and political leaders began to prepare for his funeral as early as mid-February. The international situation was anything but favorable, since on 27 December 1979 the Soviet Union had invaded Afghanistan to safeguard its interests there. This move against a member of the Non-Aligned Movement confirmed the conviction that Yugoslavs, too, were in danger, considering their strategic position in the Mediterranean and their unrepentant "revisionism." "Today in Afghanistan, tomorrow in your house," sang the Zagreb students, which the authorities stopped with the help of police.[119] It was evident that the Soviets were ready to use arms to achieve their foreign policy aims, and not just in Central Asia. "It is a shame," said Tito. "There are no guarantees that they will not invade another country in the same way. Us too."[120] This fear was also shared by the White House, prompting President Jimmy Carter to send a personal letter in support of Tito.[121] For her part, British prime minister Margaret Thatcher, in wishing Tito a speedy recovery, declared in the House of Commons: "We will do everything possible to assure the independence of Yugoslavia."[122] This assurance was very much appreciated by the Yugoslavs, who counted first of all "on our friends in the West," as Secretary of Defense Ljubičić said to the chief of the British Air Force.[123] Meanwhile, a panicked atmosphere spread throughout the country: people looted shops, many decided to withdraw savings from the banks, some even emigrated to the West. The army was put in a partial state of alert, while tanks and cannons were dispatched around Belgrade and other major cities.[124] According to CIA information, some high-ranking politicians even spoke, as they had in the fifties, of a preventive strike against Albania, which would cover their backs and help them to avoid being caught in the grip of the enemy.[125] "Yugoslavia will not give anybody the chance to 'take care' of it. It is able to take care of itself alone." This was the slogan of the moment. Meanwhile, behind the scenes, a power struggle began between Bakarić's group, which called for his election to the party chairmanship, and the Serbs, led by Petar Stambolić and Miloš Minić, who opposed him.[126]

In order to make the transition as secure as possible, it was necessary to prolong Tito's agony. During a meeting between the members of the presidency and his doctors, Dolanc informed them that in Bulgaria a column of tanks had moved toward the Yugoslav border that same day. It had stopped a few meters from the border and then, after some time, turned back. "Because of this," said Dolanc, "every day, every hour of the president's life is precious, considering the enormous work we have to do."[127] Tito underwent intensive medical care, which dragged on for several weeks.

"For an unbelievable amount of time" the doctors succeeded in conveying blood to vital organs, although they were not able to prevent continuous arterial occlusions. There were also other collateral effects that forced them to connect Tito to a dialysis machine. To quote the autopsy report, the clinical situation was so complex as to be "almost unknown in medical practice." "Long before death," there were breathing difficulties, prompting doctors to make use of an artificial lung, on which the patient remained dependent "for an extremely long time." Copious bleeding occurred, especially in the stomach, and liver complications caused a pronounced jaundice. Death came after weeks of coma, which had been induced because of the collapse of the peripheral vascular system and cardiac arrest. During the autopsy a tumor was found in Tito's stomach, probably benign, but as big as an egg. The report notes that because of his long illness, many alterations in the vital organs occurred that "are rarely observed in other patients."[128]

Josip Broz died on Sunday 4 May 1980 at 3:05 p.m. at the age of 88. The supreme state and party authorities were informed with the coded phrase: "The match is cancelled."[129] Three hours later, an official announcement was broadcast that the "great heart" of Comrade Tito had stopped beating. After his death, "the greatest man of the past, of the present and of the future" returned to Belgrade aboard his armored blue train. Tito, who was protected during his life as Stalin had been, had, like the Boss, a pharaonic funeral—even more majestic, since heads of state and leaders from nearly every country in the world attended. It was, according to the British ambassador, a "probably unique assembly."[130] The Italian communist leader, Giancarlo Pajetta, wrote in his memoirs: "An enormous crowd waited, day and night, to see the coffin. I remember the march of the heroic First Proletarian Brigade, with its red flag and the ribbon with

Yugoslav colors at the head of the procession. Together with the great of the world, there were communists, socialists, representatives of liberation movements from everywhere. I remember the roar of machine guns, with which the workers' militia fired blanks, to pay their last respects, and the rising to their feet of kings and emirs, Thatcher and Brezhnev, the Chinese representative, heads of every state, ministers, generals from every army. All stood listening to [proletarian anthem] the *Internationale*."[131]

Like Stalin, Tito, too, was buried in a mausoleum, although not as gloomy as the one that the Boss shared with Lenin before his body was expelled from it. As the place of his final rest, Tito chose the "House of Flowers" at Dedinje, built after his separation from Jovanka. During one of his last meetings with General Ljubičić, he said: "When I die, I wish to be buried there . . . from there, there is a beautiful view of Belgrade."[132] In contrast to Lenin and Stalin, he was not embalmed, since he abhorred the practice. If the testimony of an old UDBA member, Marko Lopušina, is to be believed, there was a plan for his corpse to be preserved in this way against his wishes but because of the therapy he had to endure his body decomposed rapidly. For hygienic reasons, Dolanc and others who supervised the burial ceremony decided that the coffin should be empty during the ceremony.[133] These allegations have been authoritatively refuted, however, by Ivan Dolničar, secretary general of the presidency at the time, who was in charge of the funeral. He adds that before his death Tito requested in writing to be buried with his diamond ring, to which many moments of his life were connected, and so it was done.[134]

In spite of thirty-five years of dictatorship, it would be unjust to finish Tito's story by saying that he was merely a tyrant, as Stalin was. On the contrary, because he rebelled against the Stalinist terror, establishing in Yugoslavia self-managed socialism with its human face, Tito remained in the memory of many of his "subjects" as a man to whom they should be grateful. The Yugoslavia that he left at his death was decidedly different from that of 1945. It had passed from a centralized totalitarian regime to "market socialism" and had known rapid industrialization, thanks to which the popular masses had experienced a constant increase in their standard of living—although this was mostly due to foreign aid or international loans. Even though power was in the hands of the LCY, the self-managed system allowed citizens, at least on the local level, to exercise some influence on political life. Opposition of every kind was prohibited, but intellectual life and literature were not subjected to preventive censorship and, more important, the borders were wide open, not only to the passage of people but also to the passage of ideas.

Without Tito, the split with Stalin would not have occurred. "That was his own doing," Kardelj and Bakarić affirmed.[135] His epic rebellion against Hitler and Mussolini, which assured to Yugoslavia the victory over Fascism, will never be forgotten. Nor will the fact that in the early fifties he was able to resist the siren song of the West, instead putting himself at the head of the "humiliated" and "offended" of the Third World. In the international field, Yugoslavia moved from the frightening isolation of 1948 to a multilateral policy that, within the framework of the Non-Aligned Movement, gave it an influence and prestige utterly disproportionate to its economic and military weight. As bearer of a special form of socialism, and mediator between West and East, North and South, it acquired vast influence in the international context.

Nevertheless, it is impossible to ignore the initial hardships of Tito's dictatorship, the postwar massacres, the appalling Goli Otok concentration camp, and the failure of his regime to carry on without his cohesive presence and to develop the self-managing experiment into a modern and pluralist democracy. The economic crisis of the seventies brought a series of problems that the system was unable to manage: a median inflation of 17 percent, a large trade imbalance with other countries, and more and more evident differences between the "developed" and the "undeveloped" republics and autonomous provinces of the federation, which nourished ethnic conflicts. "The early 1980s," wrote CIA experts in September 1979, in a paper entitled "Prospects for Post-Tito Yugoslavia," "will probably be a time of troubles in Yugoslavia. The precipitant will be the incapacitation or death of President Josip Broz Tito, whose role in the creation and preservation of contemporary Yugoslavia has been so large that one cannot be confident it will prove dispensable."[136] They were right. Only ten years after his death, Yugoslavia collapsed like a house of cards, and many of its people experienced a bloody fate. What then should be said about Tito's life? Perhaps it could be summarized with a popular saying that he preferred above all others: "Although I was in the mosque, I never bowed down."[137]

Notes

Abbreviations

AAB—Arbeiderbevegelsens Arkiv og Bibliotek, Oslo (Labor Movement Archives and Library)
AJ—Arhiv Jugoslavije, Belgrade (Archive of Yugoslavia)
AM—Arhiv Ministerstva Inostranih Poslova, Belgrade (Archive of the Ministry of Foreign Affairs)
AMZV—Archiv ministerstva zahraničních věcí, Prague (Archive of the Ministry of Foreign Afffairs)
AS—Arhiv Republike Slovenije, Ljubljana (Archive of the Republic of Slovenia)
ASME—Archivio Storico Diplomatico Ministero degli Esteri, Rome (Diplomatic Historical Archive, Ministry of Foreign Affairs)
BA—Bundesarchiv, Berlin
BBC—British Broadcasting Corporation
CAB—Cabinet Office
FCO—Foreign and Commonwealth Office
FO—Foreign Office
GWU—Gelvan Library, George Washington University
HS—Special Operations Executive
HW—Government Code and Cypher School
JFK—John F. Kennedy Library, Boston
NARA—National Archives and Records Administration, Washington
NIE—National Intelligence Estimate
NSC—National Security Council
NSK—Nacionalna i sveučilišna knjižnica, Zagreb (National and University Library)
ORE—Office of Reports and Estimates
PA—Politisches Archiv des Auswärtigen Amtes, Berlin (Political Archive of the Foreign Office)
RG—Record Group
RGASPI—Rossiiski gosudarstvennyi arkhiv sotsial'no-politicheskoi istorii, Moscow (Russian State Archive of Social and Political History)
SNIE—Special National Intelligence Estimate

t. e.—tehnična enota (technic unit)
TNA—The National Archives, London
WO—War Office

Foreword

1. Among this early wave of biographies, see Phyllis Auty, *Tito: A Biography* (New York: McGraw-Hill, 1970); Louis Adamic, *The Eagle and the Roots* (Garden City, NY: Doubleday, 1952); Vladimir Dedijer, *Tito* (New York: Simon and Schuster, 1953).

2. Tony Judt, "The Past Is Another Country: Myth and Memory in Postwar Europe," *Daedalus* 121, no. 4 (1992): 83–118.

3. Among the earliest examples of Partisan hero stories, see M. Sotra, *Naši Heroji: Sinovi i kćeri Bosne i Hercegovine—narodni heroji Jugoslavije* (Sarajevo: Zadruga, 1946) and *Narodni Heroji Srbije* (Belgrade: Narodni univerzitet, 1951).

4. Milovan Djilas addresses this in several of his books, notably *Tito: The Story from Inside* (New York: Harcourt Brace Jovanovich, 1980); *Conversations with Stalin* (New York: Houghton Mifflin Harcourt, 1962); and *Land without Justice* (New York: Harcourt, Brace, 1958). Additionally there is an extensive émigré literature that presented an alternative story, such as Radoslav Kostić-Katunac, *Pogledaj, Gospode, na drugu stranu! Jugoslavenski Gulag* (New York: Naša reč, 1978), and Joseph Hećimović, *In Tito's Death Marches and Extermination Camps* (New York: Carlton, 1962).

5. An overview of this process can be found in Oskar Gruenwald, "Yugoslav Camp Literature: Rediscovering the Ghost of a Nation's Past-Present-Future," *Slavic Review* 46, nos. 3–4 (1987): 513–28. For examples of specific texts, see Vojislav Koštunica and Kosta Čavoski, *Stranački pluralizam ili monizam: Društveni pokreti i politički sistem u Jugoslaviji 1944–1949* (Belgrade: Centar za filozofiju i društvenu teoriju, 1983); Nikola Milovanović, *Kroz tajni arhiv Udbe*, vol. 1 (Belgrade: Sloboda, 1986); Veselin Djuretić, *Saveznici jugoslovenska ratna drama* (Belgrade: Balkanološki Institut SANU, 1985).

6. Vladimir Dedijer, *Novi prilozi za biografiju Josipa Broza Tita*, vol. 2 (Zagreb: Mladost, 1981).

7. On the larger role of human rights activism in the eighties, see Sarah B. Snyder, *Human Rights Activism and the End of the Cold War: A Transnational History of the Helsinki Network* (New York: Cambridge University Press, 2011).

8. Sabrina Ramet, *Nationalism and Federalism in Yugoslavia, 1963–1983* (Bloomington: Indiana University Press, 1984); Dennison I. Rusinow, *The Yugoslav Experiment 1948–1974* (Berkeley: University of California Press, 1978).

9. Ivo Banac, *With Stalin against Tito: Cominformist Splits in Yugoslav Communism* (Ithaca, NY: Cornell University Press, 1988).

10. Stevan K. Pavlowitch, *Tito—Yugoslavia's Great Dictator: A Reassessment* (Columbus: Ohio State University Press, 1992).

11. See for example Richard West, *Tito and the Rise and Fall of Yugoslavia* (New York: Carroll and Graf, 1995); Jasper Ridley, *Tito: A Biography* (London: Constable, 1994); Lorraine Lees, *Keeping Tito Afloat: The United States, Yugoslavia, and the Cold War* (University Park: Pennsylvania State University Press, 1997).

12. For example, *Zločini i terror u Dalmaciji, 1943–1948: Dokumenti* (Split, 2011); Zdravko Dizdar et al., eds., *Partizanska i komunistička represija i zločini u Hrvatskoj 1944–1946: Dokumenti* (Slavonski Brod: Hrvatski Institut za Povijest, 2005); Srđan Cvetković, "Žrtve komunističkog revolucionarnog terora u Srbiji posle 12. septembra

1944 (Istraživanja Državne komisije za tajne grobnice)," *HERETICUS-Časopis za preispitivanje prošlosti* 1–2 (2011): 9–36.

13. There is an extensive English-language scholarship on historical revisionism and nationalist reframings in ex-Yugoslavia. For examples from different parts of the region, see Sabrina P. Ramet, "Memory and Identity in the Yugoslav Successor States," *Nationalities Papers* 41, no. 6 (2013): 876, and Ramet, "The Denial Syndrome and Its Consequences: Serbian Political Culture since 2000," *Communist and Post-Communist Studies* 40, no. 1 (2007): 41–58; Oto Luthar, "Forgetting Does (Not) Hurt: Historical Revisionism in Post-Socialist Slovenia," *Nationalities Papers* 41, no. 6 (2013): 882–92; Vjeran Pavlaković, "Symbols and the Culture of Memory in Republika Srpska Krajina," *Nationalities Papers* 41, no. 6 (2013): 893–909; Tea Sindbaek, "The Fall and Rise of a National Hero: Interpretations of Draža Mihailović and the Chetniks in Yugoslavia and Serbia since 1945," *Journal of Contemporary European Studies* 17, no. 1 (2009): 47–59; Nebojša Čagorović, "Anti-fascism and Montenegrin Identity since 1990," *History* 97, no. 398 (2012): 578–90.

14. A useful overview of this process in Croatia and Serbia can be found in Srdjan Cvijić, "Swinging the Pendulum: World War II History, Politics, National Identity and Difficulties of Reconciliation in Croatia and Serbia," *Nationalities Papers* 36, no. 4 (2008): 713–40. Timothy Garton Ash discusses this phenomenon in a broader East European context in the opening section of "Trials, Purges and History Lessons: Treating a Difficult Past in Post-Communist Europe," in *Memory and Power in Post-war Europe*, ed. Jan-Werner Müller (New York: Cambridge University Press, 2002), 266.

15. Critiques of the parallel can be found in Jelena Subotić, "The Mythologizing of Communist Violence," in *Post-Communist Transitional Justice: Lessons from 25 Years of Experience*, ed. Lavinia Stan and Nadya Nedelsky (New York: Cambridge University Press, 2015), 188–209, and Slavko Goldstein and Ivo Goldstein, *Jasenovac i Bleiburg nisu isto* (Zagreb: Novi Liber, 2011).

16. Pirjevec did so through analysis of the Vidovdan holiday over the course of the Yugoslav twentieth century. See Jože Pirjevec, *Il Giorno di san Vito. Jugoslavia 1918–1992: Storia di una tragedia* (Turin: Nuova Eri, 1993). English-language overviews of Yugoslavia include John B. Allcock, *Explaining Yugoslavia* (New York: Columbia University Press, 2000); John R. Lampe, *Yugoslavia as History: Twice There Was a Country* (New York: Cambridge University Press, 2000); Sabrina P. Ramet, *The Three Yugoslavias: State-Building and Legitimation, 1918–2005* (Bloomington: Indiana University Press, 2006).

17. On interwar Yugoslavia, see Christian Axboe Nielsen, *Making Yugoslavs: Identity in King Aleksandar's Yugoslavia* (Toronto: University of Toronto Press, 2014), and Dejan Djokić, *Elusive Compromise: A History of Interwar Yugoslavia* (New York: Columbia University Press, 2007). On World War II, see Jelena Batinić, *Women and Yugoslav Partisans: A History of World War II Resistance* (New York: Cambridge University Press, 2015); Max Bergholz, *Violence as a Generative Force: Identity, Nationalism, and Memory in a Balkan Community* (Ithaca, NY: Cornell University Press, 2016); Marko Attila Hoare, *Genocide and Resistance in Hitler's Bosnia: The Partisans and the Chetniks, 1941–1943* (Oxford: Oxford University Press/British Academy, 2006); Emily Greble, *Sarajevo, 1941–1945: Muslims, Christians, and Jews in Hitler's Europe* (Ithaca, NY: Cornell University Press, 2011). On the early socialist era, see Melissa Katherine Bokovoy, *Peasants and Communists: Politics and Ideology in the Yugoslav Countryside, 1941–1953* (Pittsburgh, PA: University of Pittsburgh Press, 1998).

18. On everyday life and culture in Yugoslavia, see Patrick Hyder Patterson, *Bought and Sold: Living and Losing the Good Life in Socialist Yugoslavia* (Ithaca, NY: Cornell University Press, 2011), and Madigan Fichter, "Yugoslav Protest: Student Rebellion in Belgrade, Zagreb, and Sarajevo in 1968," *Slavic Review* 75, no. 1 (2016): 99–121. On the ways Yugoslavia is being reframed in international history, see, for example: Vladimir Kulić, "Building the Non-Aligned Babel: Babylon Hotel in Baghdad and Mobile Design in the Global Cold War," in "Socialist Networks," special issue of *ABE Journal* 6 (2014), and Vladimir Petrović, "Josip Broz Tito's Summit Diplomacy in International Relations of Socialist Yugoslavia," *Annales: Series historia et sociologia* 24, no. 4 (2014): 577–92.

19. For an overview of how Tito's legacy began to transform in the region, see Tamara Pavasović Trošt, "A Personality Cult Transformed: The Evolution of Tito's Image in Serbian and Croatian Textbooks, 1974–2010," *Studies in Ethnicity and Nationalism* 14, no. 1 (2014): 146–70. Among the first historians seeking to demystify Tito was Pero Simić. His first study, *Tito-agent kominterne* (Belgrade: ABC Product, 1990), was eventually expanded with more archival documentation into the more comprehensive *Tito: Fenomen 20. veka* (Belgrade: Službeni glasnik, 2011). Similarly committed to demystifying Tito in other national contexts was Miro Simčič, *Tito bez maske* (Ljubljana: Mladinska knjiga, 2008), and Zvonimir Despot, *Tito—tajne vladara: Najnoviji prilozi za biografiju Josipa Broza* (Zagreb: Večernji list, 2009). In English, Geoffrey Swain's political biography, published in 2010, introduced important new material on Tito's political journey and his relationship with the Soviet Union; but the biography was unambiguously sympathetic to the communist project and did not integrate available archival sources or published primary sources that could challenge some of the established narratives. See Geoffrey Swain, *Tito: A Biography* (New York: I. B. Taurus, 2010).

20. On the cult of personality in East European communist states, see Balázs Apor et al., eds., *The Leader Cult in Communist Dictatorships: Stalin and the Eastern Bloc* (New York: Palgrave Macmillan, 2004). On Yugoslavia specifically, see the essay in this volume by Stanislav Sretenović and Artan Puto, "Leader Cults in the Western Balkans (1945–90): Josip Broz Tito and Enver Hoxha," 208–23. Mitja Velikonja also addresses this in his superb study of Tito nostalgia: Mitja Velikonja, *Titostalgija: Študija nostalgije po Josipu Brozu* (Ljubljana: Mirovni inštitut, 2009).

21. The most exhaustive study on Tito in Croatian is the 911-page study by Ivo and Slavko Goldstein, *Tito* (Zagreb: Profil, 2015); analytically, the 860-page volume edited by Olga Manojlović Pintar provides a range of historical interpretations: *Tito: Vidjenja i tumačenja*, Biblioteka Zbornici Radova 8 (Belgrade: Institut za noviju istoriju Srbije, 2011). An analysis of Tito's international position can be found in Vladimir Petrović, *Titova lična diplomatija: Studije i dokumentarni prilozi* (Belgrade: Institut za savremenu istoriju, 2010). For an example of the less academic, more nationalist framing of Tito's legacy, see William Klinger and Denis Kuljiš, *Tito: Neispričane priče; Tajni imperij Josipa Broza Tita* (Banja Luka: Nezavisne novine, 2013). Tito still has his defenders as well, including from the Museum of Yugoslavia in Belgrade, which oversees its own publications, such as Predrag Marković, *Tito: Kratka biografija* (Belgrade: Muzej istorije Jugoslavije, 2015).

Introduction

1. K. Marx, review of "Les Conspirateurs" by A. Chenu, *Neue Rheinische Zeitung: Politisch-ökonomische Revue* 4 (April 1850): 30–48; reprinted in *Marx & Engels Collected Works* (London: Lawrence and Wishart, 1978), 10:311.

2. Vladimir Dedijer, *Novi prilozi za biografiju Josipa Broza Tita* (Zagreb: Mladost, 1980), 1:164; J. Marković, "Titova komunikaciona strategija kao publicistički činilac," in *Tito: Vidjenja i tumačenja*, Biblioteka Zbornici Radova 8, ed. Olga Manojlović Pintar (Belgrade: Institut za Noviju Istoriju Srbije, 2011), 650.

3. Milovan Krleža, "Titov povratak 1937," *Večernji list* (newspaper), 25 May 1972; Louis Adamic, *The Eagle and the Roots* (Garden City, NY: Doubleday, 1952), 395–99.

4. Dedijer, *Novi prilozi*, 1:233.

5. Gojko Nikoliš, *Korijen, stablo, pavetina: Memoari* (Zagreb: Liber, 1980), 335.

6. Fitzroy Maclean, *Josip Broz Tito: A Pictorial Biography* (New York: McGraw Hill, 1980), 76–80.

7. Politisches Archiv, Berlin (Political Archive, hereafter PA), B 11, Bd. 263, I, p. 41.

8. Dobrica Ćosić, *Piščevi zapisi* (Belgrade: Višnjić, 2001), 1:175.

9. The National Archives, London (hereafter TNA), FCO 28/1641/ENU 3/312/I.

10. Adamic, *Eagle and the Roots*, 104, 413.

11. Henry Kissinger, *The White House Years* (London: Weidenfeld and Nicolson, 1979), 928.

12. Veljko Vlahović, *Strogo pov., 1955–1958: Neobjavljeni rukopis* (Belgrade: Stručna knjiga, 1998), 58.

13. Ćosić, *Piščevi zapisi*, 1:177.

Chapter 1. The Young Broz

1. Vladimir Dedijer, *Novi prilozi za biografiju Josipa Broza Tita* (Rijeka: Liburnija, 1981), 2:136, 137.

2. Louis Adamic, *The Eagle and the Roots* (Garden City, NY: Doubleday, 1952), 285, 286.

3. Dedijer, *Novi prilozi*, 2:136, 221, 226.

4. Adamic, *Eagle and the Roots*, 280.

5. Arhiv Jugoslavije, Belgrade (Archive of Yugoslavia, hereafter AJ), 837, KPR, IV-5-b, K 49.

6. Adamic, *Eagle and the Roots*, 263.

7. Dedijer, *Novi prilozi*, 2:219–31.

8. William Klinger and Denis Kuljiš, *Tito: Neispričane priče* (Zagreb: Paragon, 2013), 22.

9. Miroslav Krleža, "Moji susreti s Titom," *Večernji list* (newspaper), 23 May 1972, 4.

10. Jasper Ridley, *Tito: A Biography* (London: Constable, 1994), 59.

11. Milovan Djilas, *Tito: Eine kritische Biographie* (Vienna: Molden, 1980), 234.

12. A term meaning a southern (*Jugo*) Slavic (*Slavija*) state.

13. Djilas, *Tito*, 251.

14. Savka Dabčević-Kučar, *'71: Hrvatski snovi i stvarnost* (Zagreb: Interpublic, 1997), 2:666.

15. Dedijer, *Novi prilozi*, 1:60.

16. Ibid., 3:61.

17. Dobrica Ćosić, *Piščevi zapisi* (Belgrade: Višnjić, 2001), 1:200.

18. Iurii Girenko, *Stalin-Tito* (Moscow: Izdatel'stvo politicheskoi literatury, 1991), 18.

19. Dedijer, *Novi prilozi*, 1:63, 64.

20. Vladimir Dedijer, *Novi prilozi za biografiju Josipa Broza Tita* (Belgrade: Izdavačka radna organizacija "Rad," 1984), 3:609.

21. Ibid., 1:65–66.

22. Ridley, *Tito*, 320; Josip Broz Tito, *Intervjui* (Belgrade: August Cesarec, 1980), 112.
23. Dedijer, *Novi prilozi*, 3:50.
24. Tito, *Intervjui*, 91.
25. Dedijer, *Novi prilozi*, 1:75.
26. Ibid., 1:67, 3:50.
27. Arhiv Slovenije, Ljubljana (Archive of Slovenia, hereafter AS), Dedijer, t. e. 262.
28. AJ, 837, KPR, IV-5-a, K 38.
29. Adamic, *Eagle and the Roots*, 309.
30. Krleža, "Moji susreti s Titom," 4.
31. AS, Dedijer, t. e. 274.
32. Ibid.
33. Miro Simčič, *Ženske v Titovi senci: Tito brez maske 2* (Ilirska Bistrica: Samozal., 2010), 131; Klinger and Kuljiš, *Tito*, 14, 51.
34. Dedijer, *Novi prilozi*, 1:75.
35. Dušan Bilandžić, *Povijest izbliza: Memoarski zapisi 1945–2005* (Zagreb: Prometej, 2005), 502.
36. Dedijer, *Novi prilozi*, 2:173, 267, 268.
37. Ridley, *Tito*, 78.
38. AS, Dedijer, t. e. 111.
39. Nacionalna i Sveučilišna Knjižnica, Zagreb (National and University Library, hereafter NSK), M. Krleža, "A," 210.
40. Aleksandr Bajt, *Bermanov dosje* (Ljubljana: Mladinska knjiga, 1999), 782, 783.
41. Rossiiski gosudarstvennyi arkhiv sotsial'no-politicheskoi istorii (Russian State Archive of Social and Political History, hereafter RGASPI), f. 575, op. 1, d. 413; AS, Dedijer, t. e. 7.
42. AS, Dedijer, t. e. 111.
43. Djilas, *Tito*, 99.
44. AJ, 838, LF, III-11/8.
45. Dedijer, *Novi prilozi*, 2:232.
46. Ibid., 1:153.
47. NSK, Arhiv Bakarić, Kutija 10; Dedijer, *Novi prilozi*, 2:279.
48. AJ, 837, KPR, IV-5-a, K 38.
49. Dedijer, *Novi prilozi*, 2:267, 268; N. Kisić-Kolanović, *Andrija Hebrang: Iluzije i iztrežnjenja* (Zagreb: Institut za suvremenu povijest, 1996), 29.
50. NSK, Arhiv Bakarić, Kutija 22.
51. Marijan F. Kranjc, *Zarote in atentati na Tita* (Grosuplje: Graphis Trade, 2004), 127.
52. Ridley, *Tito*, 102.
53. Adamic, *Eagle and the Roots*, 343.
54. Ibid., 340.
55. AJ, 838, LF III-11/12.
56. Adamic, *Eagle and the Roots*, 335.
57. Ibid., 357.
58. RGASPI, f. 495, op. 73, d. 161.
59. AS, Dedijer, t. e. 261.
60. Adamic, *Eagle and the Roots*, 354.
61. Girenko, *Stalin-Tito*, 38.
62. Adamic, *Eagle and the Roots*, 368.
63. AS, Dedijer, t. e. 111.

64. Dedijer, *Novi prilozi*, 1:211–15.
65. Silvin Eiletz, *Titova skrivnostna leta v Moskvi 1935–1940* (Celovec: Mohorjeva, 2008), 29, 43, 44.
66. Adamic, *Eagle and the Roots*, 351.
67. Pero Simić, *Svetac i magle: Tito i njegovo vreme u novim dokumentima Moskve i Beograda* (Belgrade: Službeni list SCG, 2005), 57, 58.
68. Adamic, *Eagle and the Roots*, 370.
69. Ibid., 373.
70. Dedijer, *Novi prilozi*, 1:218.
71. Ibid., 219.
72. Ruth von Mayenburg, *Hotel Lux* (Munich: Bertelsmann, 1978), 18.
73. RGASPI, f. 495, op. 277, d. 21.
74. Dedijer, *Novi prilozi*, 3:56.
75. Nikita Bondarev, *Misterija Tito: Moskovske godine* (Belgrade: Čigoja štampa, 2013), 84, 85.
76. Eiletz, *Titova skrivnostna*, 32, 99.
77. Pero Simić, *Tito: Skrivnost stoletja* (Ljubljana: Orbis, 2009), 62.
78. TNA, FCO 28/2118.
79. RGASPI, f. 575, op. 1, d. 413.
80. Djilas, *Tito*, 74.
81. Dedijer, *Novi prilozi*, 3:53.
82. "Spomini tovariša Tita na slavno preteklost," *Slovenski poročevalec*, 17 April 1959.
83. Mayenburg, *Hotel Lux*, 200.
84. Calling someone a Trotskyist was akin to condemning him as an outcast. Lev Trotsky was one of Lenin's closest collaborators but, after Lenin's early death, Trotsky clashed with Stalin and lost. In 1927 he was expelled from the party and in 1929 exiled from the Soviet Union. From Mexico, where he found shelter, he continued to oppose Stalin's bureaucratic regime in the name of pristine revolutionary values. Hence in Moscow he was seen as the archenemy, so much so that even his name was banned from public use. Only the term "Trotskyism" or "Trotskyist" was allowed, to indicate the worst ideological heresy and its adherents.
85. Djilas, *Tito*, 85.
86. Eiletz, *Titova skrivnostna*, 33.
87. Dabčević-Kučar, *'71: Hrvatski snovi*, 2:863.
88. National Archives and Record Administration, Washington (hereafter NARA), CIA, CREST, "Tito Throws Down the Gauntlet," *Bi-Weekly Propaganda Guidance*, 11 May 1959.
89. Miro Poč, ed., *Edvard Kardelj: Skica za monografijo* (Ljubljana: Delo, 1979), 15; AS, Dedijer, t. e. 7.
90. AS, Dedijer, t. e. 242.
91. AS, Dedijer, t. e. 111.
92. Bajt, *Bermanov dosje*, 784, 870–74.
93. Vjenceslav Cenčić, *Titova poslednja ispovijest* (Belgrade: Orfelin, 2001), 73.
94. Adamic, *Eagle and the Roots*, 379.
95. "Spomini tovariša Tita na slavno preteklost."
96. G. R. Swain, "Tito: The Formation of a Disloyal Bolshevik," *International Review of Social History* 34, no. 2 (1989): 250, 251.

97. Dedijer, *Novi prilozi*, 1:223, 224; 3:53, 189.
98. RGASPI, f. 575, op. 1, d. 413; f. 539, op. 3, d. 1390; f. 495, op. 74, d. 584.
99. Ivan Očak, *Gorkić: Život, rad i pogibija* (Zagreb: Globus, 1988), 244.
100. RGASPI, f. 495, op. 18, d. 1109.
101. Swain, "Tito," 251.
102. Anton Bebler, Letter to the Editor, *Mladina* 26 (2009).
103. Adamic, *Eagle and the Roots*, 382.
104. RGASPI, f. 495, op. 18, d. 1135; Georgi Dimitrov, *Diario: Gli anni di Mosca (1934–1945)* (Turin: Einaudi, 2002), 48.
105. RGASPI, f. 495, op. 18, d. 1134.
106. RGASPI, f. 495. op. 18, d. 1134; Dedijer, *Novi prilozi*, 1:228, 229.
107. Simić, *Tito*, 87.
108. AS, Dedijer, t. e. 3; t. e. 236.
109. Eiletz, *Titova skrivnostna*, 63; RGASPI, f. 575, op. 1, d. 411.
110. Očak, *Gorkić*, 250.
111. Swain, "Tito," 252; AS, Dedijer, t. e. 242.
112. "Spomini tovariša Tita na slavno preteklost."
113. Adamic, *Eagle and the Roots*, 387; Dedijer, *Novi prilozi*, 1:231.
114. "Spomini tovariša Tita na slavno preteklost."
115. Adamic, *Eagle and the Roots*, 389; AS, Dedijer, t. e. 242.
116. "Spomini tovariša Tita na slavno preteklost"; Dedijer, *Novi prilozi*, 1:237, 238.
117. Fitzroy Maclean, *Disputed Barricade: The Life and Times of Josip Broz-Tito, Marshal of Yugoslavia* (London: Jonathan Cape, 1957), 103, 104.
118. Djilas, *Tito*, 75.
119. Milo Gligorijević, *Rat i mir Vladimira Dedijera: Sećanja i razgovori* (Belgrade: Narodna knjiga, 1986), 44; Vladimir Dedijer, "My Two Comrades," *Cross Currents* 4 (1985): 398.
120. Adamic, *Eagle and the Roots*, 344, 345.
121. "Is Yugoslav President Tito Really a Yugoslav?," http://www.nsa.gov/-info/-files.
122. Andreas Razumovsky, *Ein Kampf um Belgrad: Tito und die jugoslawische Wirklichkeit* (Berlin: Ullstein, 1980), 245, 246.
123. Tomislav Badinovac, ed., *Zagreb i Hrvatska u Titovo doba* (Zagreb: Savez društva "Josip Broz Tito" Hrvatske, 2004), 52.
124. Djilas, *Tito*, 261.
125. AS, Dedijer, t. e. 242.
126. Gojko Nikoliš, *Zapisi pod pritiskom* (Belgrade: NIRO, Književne novine, 1998), 410, 411.
127. Momčilo Stefanović, *Podpis: Tito: "Bila sva Titova šifranta"; Pripoved Branke in Pavleta Savića* (Zagreb: Globus, 1980), 18.
128. Badinovac, *Zagreb i Hrvatska*, 51.
129. Dedijer, *Novi prilozi*, 1:233, 234.
130. Ibid., 3:317.
131. Mira Šuvar, *Vladimir Velebit: Svjedok istorije* (Zagreb: Razlog, 2001), 57, 463; Simčič, *Ženske v Titovi senci*, 167.
132. Ridley, *Tito*, 123.
133. Vjenceslav Cenčić, *Enigma Kopinič* (Belgrade: Rad, 1983), 2:106, 197.

134. Milovan Djilas, *Memoir of a Revolutionary* (New York: Harcourt Brace Jovanovich, 1973), 175.

135. AS, Dedijer, t. e. 223.

136. Djilas, *Memoir of a Revolutionary*, 181.

137. Ivo Banac, *Sa Staljinom protiv Tita* (Zagreb: Globus, 1990), 74.

138. Eiletz, *Titova skrivnostna*, 51.

139. Dedijer, *Novi prilozi*, 1:235.

140. Dejan Jović, *Yugoslavia: A State That Withered Away* (West Lafayette, IN: Purdue University Press, 2009), 56.

141. Bilandžić, *Povijest izbliza*, 39, 247, 295; RGASPI, f. 495, op. 69, d. 272.

142. AS, Dedijer, t. e. 75; t. e. 274.

143. Badinovac, *Zagreb i Hrvatska*, 52, 55; AJ, 837, KPR, IV-5-b, K 49.

144. AJ, 837, KPR, IV-5-b, K 49.

145. "Spomini tovariša Tita na slavno preteklost."

146. Očak, *Gorkić*, 307, 319; RGASPI, f. 485, op. 585, d. 74; AJ, 837, KPR, IV-5-b, K 49.

147. Adamic, *Eagle and the Roots*, 389; Simić, *Tito*, 98.

148. "Spomini tovariša Tita na slavno preteklost."

149. AS, Dedijer, t. e. 242.

150. Rodoljub Čolaković, *Kazivanje o jednom pokoljenju* (Sarajevo: Svetlost, 1972), 3:139, 140, 151.

151. Pero Simić and Zvonimir Despot, *Strogo poverljivo: Arhivski dokumenti* (Belgrade: Službeni glasnik, 2008), 81.

152. Djilas, *Tito*, 85.

153. Girenko, *Stalin-Tito*, 57.

154. Adamic, *Eagle and the Roots*, 355; Kosta Čavoški, *Tito: Tehnologija vlasti* (Belgrade: Dosije, 1990), 83.

155. AS, Dedijer, t. e. 143; t. e. 188; t. e. 235; t. e. 236.

156. Adamic, *Eagle and the Roots*, 388; Gusti Stridsberg, *Mojih pet življenj* (Maribor: Obzorja, 1971), 413, 414.

157. Simić and Despot, *Tito*, 70, 71.

158. Adamic, *The Eagle and the Roots*, 387.

159. "Tito's Sojourn in Spain," *The South Slav Journal* 18, no. 4 (1982–1983): 47, 48.

160. Fred Copeman, *Reason in Revolt* (London: Blandford Press, 1948); Santiago Carrillo, *Mi testamento politico* (Barcelona: Galaxia Gutenberg, 2012), 193.

161. Simić, *Tito*, 92.

162. AS, Dedijer, t. e. 261; t. e. 298.

163. Marko Lopušina, *Ubij bližnjeg svog: Jugoslovenska tajna policija 1945–1995* (Belgrade: Biblioteka "Revija 92," 1996), 1:22.

164. Adamic, *Eagle and the Roots*, 388; Simić, *Tito*, 93.

165. AS, Dedijer, t. e. 271.

166. AS, Dedijer, t. e. 236.

167. Stridsberg, *Mojih pet življenj*, 411.

168. Swain, "Tito," 253, 254.

169. Djilas, *Tito*, 81; RGASPI, f. 575, op. 1, d. 411; f. 495, op. 74, d. 588; Simić, *Tito*, 99, 100.

170. Dedijer, *Novi prilozi*, 2:332–43, 3:105; AS, Dedijer, t. e. 274.

171. Josip Broz Tito, *Zbrana dela* (Ljubljana: Komunist, Borec, 1979), 4:14–17.

172. AS, Dedijer, t. e. 212.
173. Eiletz, *Titova skrivnostna*, 50, 52; RGASPI, f. 575, op. 1, d. 411.
174. Kisić-Kolanović, *Andrija Hebrang*, 35.
175. RGASPI, f. 575, op. 1, d. 411.
176. Ibid.
177. Zdravko Antonić, *Rodoljub Čolaković u svetlu svog dnevnika* (Belgrade: IP Knjiga, 1991), 422.
178. Tito, *Zbrana dela*, 4:31. (By "democracy," Tito meant the direct rule of the people without bourgeois parties acting as intermediaries.)
179. Ridley, *Tito*, 136; Swain, "Tito," 257; AS, Dedijer, t. e. 111.
180. Badinovac, *Zagreb i Hrvatska*, 50.
181. Djilas, *Memoir of a Revolutionary*, 279, 280.
182. AS, Dedijer, t. e. 188.
183. RGASPI, f. 575, op. 1, d. 411.
184. RGASPI, f. 495, op. 18, d. 1232.
185. RGASPI, f. 495, op. 74, d. 587.
186. Dedijer, "My Two Comrades," 399.
187. RGASPI, f. 575, op. 1, d. 411; f. 496, op. 74, d. 587.
188. RGASPI, f. 495, op. 18, d. 1256.
189. Swain, "Tito," 52; Čolaković, *Kazivanje o jednom pokoljenju*.
190. Cenčić, *Enigma*, 1:30; AS, Dedijer, t. e. 229; Igor Grdina, "Josip Kopinić," in *Tvorci slovenske pomorske identitete*, ed. Paulina Bobič (Ljubljana: Založba ZRC, 2010), 111, 136.
191. Šuvar, *Vladimir Velebit*, 62, 63.
192. Josip Kopinič, "Zgodovinske enigme," *Mladina* (25 October 1985): 9.
193. Eiletz, *Titova skrivnostna*, 97.
194. Ibid.
195. Ibid., 97–99; AS, Dedijer, t. e. 236.
196. Dedijer, *Novi prilozi*, 3:52, 54.
197. AJ, 837, KPR, IV-5-b, K 49.
198. Dedijer, *Novi prilozi*, 2:333.
199. Eiletz, *Titova skrivnostna*, 92, 93; "Spomini tovariša Tita na slavno preteklost"; AS, Dedijer, t. e. 236.
200. Simić, *Tito*, 105–8.
201. Silvin Eiletz, *Pred sodbo zgodovine: Stalin, Tito in jugoslovanski komunisti v Moskvi* (Celovec: Mohorjeva, 2010), 154.
202. Eiletz, *Titova skrivnostna*, 93.
203. Dedijer, *Novi prilozi*, 1:240; 3:327.
204. RGASPI, f. 495, op. 18, d. 1256; Tito, *Zbrana dela*, 4:109–18.
205. Dimitrov, *Diario*, 117.
206. Adamic, *Eagle and the Roots*, 400; AS, Dedijer, t. e. 74; t. e., 242.
207. Dedijer, *Novi prilozi*, 3:56.
208. RGASPI, f. 495, op. 74, d. 590; AS, Dedijer t. e. 223; t. e. 236; Eiletz, *Pred sodbo zgodovine*, 137.
209. Cenčić, *Enigma*, 1:103, 195, 106; AS, Dedijer, t. e. 199; t. e. 236.
210. Gligorijević, *Rat i mir*, 219, 220.
211. Eiletz, *Titova skrivnostna*, 101; Simčič, *Ženske v Titovi senci*, 158.

212. AS, Dedijer, t. e., 111.
213. RGASPI, f. 495, op. 74, d. 587.
214. Eiletz, *Titova skrivnostna*, 73.
215. Dimitrov, *Diario*, 151.
216. Dedijer, *Novi prilozi*, 3:56.
217. Dedijer, *Novi prilozi*, 1:240.
218. Adamic, *Eagle and the Roots*, 391.
219. RGASPI, f. 495, op. 18, d. 1296; Tito, *Zbrana dela*, 4:144–51.
220. RGASPI, f. 575, op. 1, d. 411; AS, Dedijer, t. e. 274.
221. RGASPI, f. 575, op. 1, d. 411.
222. Dimitrov, *Diario*, 140; AS, Dedijer, t. e. 236.
223. AS, Dedijer, t. e. 111.
224. Djilas, *Tito*, 74–76.
225. Simić, *Tito*, 156.
226. Čolaković, *Kazivanje o jednom pokoljenju*, 3:439.
227. AS, Dedijer, t. e. 111.
228. RGASPI, f. 575, op. 1, d. 411.
229. AS, Dedijer, t. e. 111.
230. Dedijer, *Novi prilozi*, 2:326; RGASPI, f. 575, op. 1, d. 411; f. 495, op. 11, d. 371.
231. Djilas, *Tito*, 86.
232. AS, Dedijer, t. e., 242.
233. Djilas, *Tito*, 87.
234. Dedijer, *Novi prilozi*, 2:362.
235. F. W. Deakin, "The British Image of Yugoslav Communism (1921–1941)," in *Yugoslavia, 1941–1945* (an unpublished manuscript provided by Bogo Gorjan), 21.
236. Dedijer, *Novi prilozi*, 2:936.
237. Bilandžić, *Povijest izbliza*, 299.
238. RGASPI, f. 575, op. 1, d. 411; AS, Dedijer, t. e., 111.
239. Eiletz, *Titova skrivnostna*, 74–76.
240. RGASPI, f. 495, op. 74, d. 591.
241. Dedijer, *Novi prilozi*, 3:56.
242. Eiletz, *Titova skrivnostna*, 55; AS, Dedijer, t. e. 197; t. e. 223.
243. AS, Dedijer, t. e. 111.
244. Eiletz, *Titova skrivnostna*, 106; AS, Dedijer, t. e. 236.
245. Dedijer, *Novi prilozi*, 3:56; "Spomini tovariša Tita na slavno preteklost"; AS, Dedijer, t. e. 223.
246. Cenčić, *Enigma*, 1:95.
247. AJ, 837, KPR, IV-5-b, K 49.

Chapter 2. World War Two and the Partisan Struggle

1. Arhiv Slovenije, Ljubljana (Archive of Slovenia, hereafter AS), Dedijer, t. e. 7.
2. G. R. Swain, "The Comintern and Southern Europe," in *Resistance and Revolution in Mediterranean Europe 1939–1948*, ed. Tony Judt, 8th ed. (New York: Routledge, 1989), 34.
3. Vladimir Dedijer, *Novi prilozi za biografiju Josipa Broza Tita* (Rijeka: Liburnija, 1981), 2:360.
4. AS, Dedijer, t. e. 111.

5. Aleksandr Bajt, *Bermanov dosje* (Ljubljana: Mladinska knjiga, 1999), 745.

6. Ibid.

7. F. W. Deakin, "The British Image of Yugoslav Communism (1921–1941)," in *Yugoslavia, 1941–1945* (an unpublished manuscript provided by Bogo Gorjan), 23.

8. Ibid., 18, 25; The National Archives, London (hereafter TNA), Fo 371/25029/R 2176/G.

9. Rodoljub Čolaković, *Kazivanje o jednom pokoljenju* (Sarajevo: Svetlost, 1972), 3:430.

10. Ivan Očak, *Gorkić: Život, rad i pogibija* (Zagreb: Globus, 1988), 249.

11. Dobrica Ćosić, *Piščevi zapisi* (Belgrade: Višnjić, 2001), 1:176.

12. Josip Broz Tito, *Zbrana dela* (Ljubljana: Komunist, Borec, 1979), 5:18.

13. G. R. Swain, "Tito: The Formation of a Disloyal Bolshevik," *International Review of Social History* 34, no. 2 (1989): 361.

14. Louis Adamic, *The Eagle and the Roots* (Garden City, NY: Doubleday, 1952), 401.

15. AS, Dedijer, t. e. 3.

16. Mira Šuvar, *Vladimir Velebit: Svjedok istorije* (Zagreb: Razlog, 2001), 59; Arhiv Jugoslavije, Belgrade (Archive of Yugoslavia, hereafter AJ), 838, LF III-10/2.

17. AS, Dedijer, t. e. 261; t. e. 262.

18. AS, Dedijer, t. e. 292.

19. Marijan F. Kranjc, *Zarote in atentati na Tita* (Grosuplje: Graphis Trade, 2004), 298.

20. Stephen Clissold, *Djilas: The Progress of a Revolutionary* (Hounslow: Maurice Temple Smith, 1983), 34.

21. Adamic, *Eagle and the Roots*, 402; AS, Dedijer, t. e. 111.

22. AS, Dedijer, t. e. 242.

23. Tomislav Badinovac, ed., *Zagreb i Hrvatska u Titovo doba* (Zagreb: Savez društva "Josip Broz Tito" Hrvatske, 2004), 54.

24. Dedijer, *Novi prilozi*, 3:217.

25. Očak, *Gorkić*, 251.

26. Dedijer, *Novi prilozi*, 3:18.

27. Nacionalna i Sveučilišna Knjižnica, Zagreb (National and University Library, hereafter NSK), M. Krleža, "A" 169.

28. AS, Dedijer, t. e. 242.

29. Pero Simić, *Tito: Skrivnost stoletja* (Ljubljana: Orbis, 2009), 139.

30. Tito, *Zbrana dela*, 6:15.

31. Rossiiski gosudarstvennyi arkhiv sotsial'no-politicheskoi istorii (Russian State Archive of Social and Political History, hereafter RGASPI), f. 575, op. 1, d. 411; f. 495, op. 74, d. 65.

32. Bajt, *Bermanov dosje*, 745–49; 766.

33. RGASPI, f. 495, op. 74, d. 592.

34. Swain, "Tito," 262, 263.

35. Dedijer, *Novi prilozi*, 3:170.

36. RGASPI, f. 495, op. 18, d. 1325.

37. Dušan Bilandžić, *Hrvatska moderna povijest* (Zagreb: Golden Marketing, 1999), 126.

38. RGASPI, f. 575, op. 1, d. 411; Tito, *Zbrana dela*, 6:196–99.

39. AS, Dedijer, t. e. 111.

40. Dedijer, *Novi prilozi*, 3:27.

41. Badinovac, *Zagreb i Hrvatska*, 54, 55.
42. Ćosić, *Piščevi zapisi*, 1:178.
43. Dedijer, *Novi prilozi*, 3:147.
44. Badinovac, *Zagreb i Hrvatska*, 54, 55.
45. Nada Kisić-Kolanović, *Andrija Hebrang: Iluzije i otrežnjenja* (Zagreb: Institut za suvremenu povijest, 1996), 46.
46. Tito, *Zbrana dela*, 6:50.
47. Dedijer, *Novi prilozi*, 3:215.
48. Aleksandar Ranković, *Dnevničke zabeleške* (Belgrade: Jugoslovenska knjiga, 2001), 130–34.
49. AS, Dedijer, t. e. 242.
50. Adamic, *Eagle and the Roots*, 366, 367; Dedijer, *Novi prilozi*, 3:317.
51. AS, Dedijer, t. e. 111.
52. AS, Dedijer, 188.
53. AS, Dedijer, 242.
54. Vjenceslav Cenčić, *Enigma Kopinič* (Belgrade: Rad, 1983), 1:137.
55. Tito, *Zbrana dela*, 6:149–77.
56. G. R. Swain, "Tito and the Twilight of the Comintern," in *International Communism and the Communist International, 1919–43*, ed. Tim Rees and Andrew Thorpe (Manchester: Manchester University Press, 1998), 214.
57. William M. Leary, *Fueling the Fires of Resistance: Army Air Forces Special Operations in the Balkans during World War II* (Washington, DC: Air Force History and Museums Program, 1995), 1.
58. Iurii Girenko, *Stalin-Tito* (Moscow: Izdatel'stvo politicheskoi literatury, 1991), 85.
59. AS, Dedijer, t. e. 242.
60. TNA, HS 3/151.
61. Dedijer, *Novi prilozi*, 1:264.
62. Momčilo Stefanović, *Podpis: Tito: "Bila sva Titova šifranta"; Pripoved Branke in Pavleta Savića* (Zagreb: Globus, 1980), 177, 178.
63. Dimitrov, *Diario*, 291.
64. RGASPI, f. 495, op. 74, d. 594.
65. Dedijer, *Novi prilozi*, 2:375.
66. AS, Dedijer, t. e. 7.
67. F. W. Deakin, "The Setting (1941)," in *Yugoslavia, 1941–1945*, 12.
68. National Archives and Record Administration, Washington (hereafter NARA), CIA, CREST, "The Role of the Military in the Yugoslav System," *Weekly Summary*, 20 May 1969.
69. Deakin, "The Setting," 2, 3.
70. Šuvar, *Vladimir Velebit*, 59, 61, 62.
71. Simić, *Tito*, 192; Cenčić, *Enigma*, 1:195; 2:100.
72. Ćosić, *Piščevi zapisi*, 2:242, 243.
73. RGASPI, f. 495, op. 74, d. 607; AS, Dedijer, t. e. 242.
74. RGASPI, f. 495, op. 74, d. 607.
75. Milovan Djilas, *Tito: Eine kritische Biographie* (Vienna: Molden, 1980), 19.
76. Dedijer, *Novi prilozi*, 2:382; Bajt, *Bermanov dosje*, 782.
77. RGASPI, f. 495, op. 74, d. 607; Šuvar, *Vladimir Velebit*, 69.
78. Bilandžić, *Hrvatska moderna povijest*, 127.

79. AS, Dedijer, t. e. 111.
80. AS, Dedijer, t. e. 7.
81. Badinovac, *Zagreb i Hrvatska*, 44.
82. Djilas, *Tito*, 20; AS, Dedijer, t. e. 242; I. V. Buharkin et al., eds., *Otnoshenija Rossii (SSSR) s Jugoslaviej, 1941–1945 gg.* (Moscow: Terra-Knizhnyj klub), 1:37.
83. Djilas, *Tito*, 22; Dušan Bilandžić, *Povijest izbliza: Memoarski zapisi 1945–2005* (Zagreb: Prometej, 2005), 610.
84. Bilandžić, *Povijest izbliza*, 188.
85. Šuvar, *Vladimir Velebit*, 69, 241, 242.
86. Dedijer, *Novi prilozi*, 1:272.
87. AS, Dedijer, t. e., 271; Bajt, *Bermanov dosje*, 576.
88. Šuvar, *Vladimir Velebit*, 70.
89. M. F. Kranjc, *Zarote in atentati*, 132; Marko Lopušina, *Ubij bližnjeg svog: Jugoslovenska tajna policija 1945–1995* (Belgrade: "Revija 92," 1996), 1:30, 31.
90. Tito, *Zbrana dela*, 7:26, 27.
91. Girenko, *Stalin-Tito*, 92.
92. AS, Djilas, t. e. 242.
93. Dedijer, *Novi prilozi*, 1:273; 2:383; RGASPI, f. 495, op. 74, d. 607.
94. Girenko, *Stalin-Tito*, 91.
95. Tito, *Zbrana dela*, 7:12–15.
96. NSK, Arhiv Bakarić, Kutija 116.
97. RGASPI, f. 495, op. 74, d. 593.
98. Aleksandar Nenadović, *Razgovori s Kočom* (Zagreb: Globus, 1989), 132.
99. Bilandžić, *Povijest izbliza*, 88.
100. RGASPI, f. 495, op. 74, d. 602.
101. Tito, *Zbrana dela*, 7:42–45.
102. Ćosić, *Piščevi zapisi*, 1:69.
103. Ibid., 2:243.
104. AS, Dedijer, t. e. 261.
105. Tito, *Zbrana dela*, 7:46.
106. Dedijer, *Novi prilozi*, 1:274; 2:996; Dimitrov, *Diario*, 320, 325; Stephen Clissold, *Yugoslavia and the Soviet Union, 1939–1973: A Documentary Survey* (New York: Oxford University Press, 1975), 128.
107. AS, Dedijer, t. e. 51.
108. Dedijer, *Novi prilozi*, 1:276, 2:389.
109. AS, Dedijer, t. e. 111.
110. Girenko, *Stalin-Tito*, 107.
111. Bilandžić, *Povijest izbliza*, 13.
112. RGASPI, f. 575, op. 1, d. 413; Dedijer, *Novi prilozi*, 3:344, 345.
113. AS, Dedijer, t. e. 8; t. e. 197; t. e. 261.
114. Dimitrov, *Diario*, 326.
115. Bilandžić, *Povijest izbliza*, 318.
116. Kisić-Kolanović, *Andrija Hebrang*, 59; AS, Dedijer, t. e. 215.
117. Tito, *Zbrana dela*, 7:61–63, 75.
118. Clissold, *Djilas*, 53.
119. Ivo Banac, *Sa Staljinom protiv Tita* (Zagreb: Globus, 1990), 88.
120. Dedijer, *Novi prilozi*, 3:131; AS, Dedijer, t. e. 201.
121. Dedijer, *Novi prilozi*, 3:131, 132; Girenko, *Stalin-Tito*, 111.

122. Lucien Karchmar, *Draža Mihailović and the Rise of the Četnik Movement 1941–1942* (New York: Garland, 1987), 2:201.
123. Girenko, *Stalin-Tito*, 109.
124. Predrag Lalević, *S Titom po svetu* (Belgrade: Službeni glasnik, 2012), 52.
125. Banac, *Sa Staljinom protiv Tita*, 21.
126. Nenadović, *Razgovori s Kočom*, 128.
127. Interview with Koča Popović, *Danas*, 7 February 1989, 25.
128. RGASPI, f. 495, op. 74, d. 602.
129. Edvard Kardelj, *Spomini: Boj za priznanje in neodvisnost nove Jugoslavije, 1944–1957* (Ljubljana: Državna založba Slovenije, 1980), 27, 162.
130. Lalević, *S Titom po svetu*, 53.
131. Bajt, *Bermanov dosje*, 337, 338.
132. Ćosić, *Piščevi zapisi*, 2:243.
133. AS, Dedijer, t. e. 7.
134. Girenko, *Stalin-Tito*, 110.
135. Djilas, *Tito*, 26.
136. AS, Dedijer, t. e. 236.
137. Djilas, *Tito*, 183.
138. AS, Dedijer, t. e. 111.
139. Djilas, *Tito*, 46.
140. Ibid., 30.
141. AS, Dedijer, t. e. 111.
142. AS, Dedijer, t. e. 201; t. e. 215.
143. L. Ia. Gibianskii, *Sovetskii Soiuz i Novaia Iugoslaviia, 1941–1947* (Moscow: Nauka, 1987), 31, 41; Cenčič, *Enigma*, 1:199.
144. TNA, HS 3/151.
145. Vojmir Kljaković, "Velika Britanija, Sovjetski savez i ustanak u Jugoslaviji 1941. godine," *Vojnoistorijski glasnik* 2 (1970): 71, 72.
146. TNA, CAB 121/576/11.
147. Elizabeth Barker, "British Wartime Policy towards Yugoslavia," *The South Slav Journal* 2 (April 1979): 4.
148. TNA, HS 3/126; Dedijer, *Novi prilozi*, 1:308.
149. TNA, HS 3/198.
150. Ranković, *Dnevničke zabeleške*, 204, 225.
151. F. W. Deakin, "Partisan Suspicions of the British," in *Yugoslavia, 1941–1945*, 2.
152. Jasper Ridley, *Tito: A Biography* (London: Constable, 1994), 179.
153. Banac, *Sa Staljinom protiv Tita*, 25.
154. Dedijer, *Novi prilozi*, 1:307, 308.
155. Milovan Djilas, *Wartime* (London: Harcourt Brace Jovanovich, 1977), 88.
156. Vladimir Dedijer, *Dnevnik, 1941–1944* (Zagreb: Mladost, 1981), 1:52.
157. Dedijer, *Novi prilozi*, 3:148, 220.
158. RGASPI, f. 495, op. 74, d. 607.
159. Ranković, *Dnevničke zabeleške*, 204, 205.
160. Ridley, *Tito*, 182.
161. Girenko, *Stalin-Tito*, 113.
162. Deakin, "Partisan Suspicions," 18.
163. Dedijer, *Novi prilozi*, 2:392.

164. Bajt, *Bermanov dosje*, 373, 374.
165. Bilandžić, *Povijest izbliza*, 40.
166. Tito, *Zbrana dela*, 8:67, 68.
167. Josip Broz Tito, "Vojni memoari," *Front*, 5 May 1972.
168. Bilandžić, *Povijest izbliza*, 434.
169. Bilandžić, *Hrvatska moderna povijest*, 138.
170. Ćosić, *Piščevi zapisi*, 1:244.
171. Dedijer, *Novi prilozi*, 2:55, 3:472.
172. Bajt, *Bermanov dosje*, 372.
173. RGASPI, f. 495, op. 73, d. 112.
174. AS, Dedijer, t. e. 7.
175. Ćosić, *Piščevi zapisi*, 1:244.
176. Dedijer, *Novi prilozi*, 1:314–16; Bilandžić, *Hrvatska moderna povijest*, 138.
177. AS, Dedijer, t. e. 7.
178. Girenko, *Stalin-Tito*, 128.
179. Dedijer, *Novi prilozi*, 2:394; Bundesarchiv, Berlin (hereafter BA), DY 30 IV 2/20/127.
180. AS, Dedijer, t. e. 7.
181. Dedijer, *Novi prilozi*, 3:471.
182. Ćosić, *Piščevi zapisi*, 1:201.
183. Ibid., 1:244, 245.
184. Nenadović, *Razgovori s Kočom*, 51, 52; A. S. Anikeev, *Kak Tito ot Stalina ushel: Iugoslaviia, SSSR i SSHA v nachal'nyi period "kholodnoi voiny" (1945–1957)* (Moscow: Institut Slavianovedeniia RAN, 2002), 26, 27.
185. NSK, Arhiv Bakarić, Kutija 46.
186. Bilandžić, *Povijest izbliza*, 593; Dedijer, *Novi prilozi*, 2:145; Blažo Mandić, *S Titom: Četvrt veka u Kabinetu* (Belgrade: Dan Graf, 2012), 28; Stefanović, *Podpis*, 62.
187. Bajt, *Bermanov dosje*, 373.
188. Cenčić, *Enigma*, 2:12.
189. Dedijer, *Novi prilozi*, 1:320.
190. Tito, *Zbrana dela*, 9:65; Gibianskii, *Sovetskii Soiuz*, 44.
191. Adamic, *Eagle and the Roots*, 479.
192. Aleksandr E. Golovanov, *Dal'naia bombardirovochnaia* (Moscow: Del'ta NB, 2004), 133, 134.
193. Bajt, *Bermanov dosje*, 887; Dedijer, *Novi prilozi*, 1:322–24.
194. Girenko, *Stalin-Tito*, 130.
195. Clissold, *Yugoslavia*, 145, 146.
196. Ibid., 23, 146, 147.
197. Adamic, *Eagle and the Roots*, 473, 474; Dedijer, *Novi prilozi*, 3:220; Dimitrov, *Diario*, 355–57.
198. Girenko, *Stalin-Tito*, 132, 133; Tito, *Zbrana dela*, 9:135.
199. Djilas, *Tito*, 27; Dimitrov, *Diario*, 320, 322, 382, 383, 427.
200. Milovan Djilas, *Der Krieg der Partisanen: Memoiren, 1941–1945* (Vienna: Molden, 1977), 192.
201. Šuvar, *Vladimir Velebit*, 84, 87, 90.
202. Bilandžić, *Hrvatska moderna povijest*, 137, 138.
203. Kisić-Kolanović, *Andrija Hebrang*, 75.

204. Zdenko Čepič, Ferdo Gestrin, et al., *Zgodovina Slovencev* (Ljubljana: Cankarjeva založba, 1979), 764.
205. Adamic, *Eagle and the Roots*, 508, 509; AJ, 837, KPR, IV-5-a, K 38.
206. Ćosić, *Piščevi zapisi*, 2:243.
207. AS, Dedijer, t. e. 298.
208. Dedijer, *Novi prilozi*, 1:334.
209. Adamic, *Eagle and the Roots*, 478; Dimitrov, *Diario*, 451.
210. Cenčić, *Enigma*, 2:23–27; AS, Dedijer, t. e. 8; t. e. 261.
211. F. W. Deakin, "Broz alias Tito: The First 'Revelations' (February–June 1942)," in *Yugoslavia, 1941–1945*; Šuvar, *Vladimir Velebit*, 246.
212. Kranjc, *Zarote in atentati*, 179, 180.
213. Cenčić, *Enigma*, 2:50.
214. Ibid., 1:181; 2:55, 56; AS, Dedijer, t. e. 199; t. e. 271.
215. AS, Dedijer, t. e. 68; t. e. 264; AJ, 837, KPR, IV, K 19.
216. Dedijer, *Novi prilozi*, 3:341.
217. Girenko, *Stalin-Tito*, 296.
218. Dimitrov, *Diario*, 458, 472.
219. Adamic, *Eagle and the Roots*, 479, 480; Ridley, *Tito*, 192, 193.
220. Dimitrov, *Diario*, 486, 488.
221. Elizabeth Barker, *Britanska politika prema jugoistočnoj Evropi u Drugom svjetskom ratu* (Zagreb: Globus, 1978), 275.
222. Dedijer, *Novi prilozi*, 1:337; AS, Dedijer, t. e. 284.
223. TNA, HS 3/170.
224. Dedijer, *Novi prilozi*, 2:606.
225. Ibid., 3:130; Dimitrov, *Diario*, 494, 495, 528, 540, 541.
226. AS, Dedijer, t. e. 111; t. e. 201.
227. Kardelj, *Spomini*, 19; Šuvar, *Vladimir Velebit*, 295.
228. Stefanović, *Podpis*, 77.
229. Girenko, *Stalin-Tito*, 144.
230. Ridley, *Tito*, 194, 195.
231. Kisić-Kolanović, *Andrija Hebrang*, 76.
232. Stefanović, *Podpis*, 74.
233. Adamic, *Eagle and the Roots*, 513.
234. Dušan Biber to the author.
235. F. W. Deakin, "The German and Allied Plans for a Balkan Landing," in *Yugoslavia, 1941–1945*, 4.
236. Ibid., 5.
237. Ibid., 6; Dedijer, *Novi prilozi*, 1:339, 340.
238. F. W. Deakin, "The German Planning of Operation 'Schwarz' (January–March 1943)," in *Yugoslavia, 1941–1945*.
239. Gojko Nikoliš, *Korijen, stablo, pavetina: Memoari* (Zagreb: Liber, 1981), 467–69.
240. Šuvar, *Vladimir Velebit*, 99; Dedijer, *Novi prilozi*, 2:25.
241. Nikoliš, *Korijen, stablo, pavetina*, 467.
242. Vasilije Kalezić, *Djilas, miljenik in otpadnik komunizma: Kontroverze pisca i ideologa* (Belgrade: Zodne, 1988), 144; Dedijer, *Novi prilozi*, 2:25.
243. Djilas, *Tito*, 50.
244. Interview with Koča Popović, *Danas*, 7 February 1989, 26.

245. L. Rendulic, *Soldat in stürzenden Reichen* (Munich: Damm Verlag, 1965), 332.
246. Ranković, *Dnevničke zabeleške*, 219; AS, Dedijer t. e. 143.
247. Dedijer, *Novi prilozi*, 1:344; Ćosić, *Piščevi zapisi*, 2:236, 245.
248. Dedijer, *Novi prilozi*, 2:802; AS, Dedijer, t. e., 45; t. e. 201.
249. F. W. Deakin, "The German First Mountain Division and Operation 'Schwarz,'" in *Yugoslavia, 1941–1945*, 6.
250. Deakin, "German Planning," 17.
251. Ibid.
252. Djilas, *Tito*, 26, 56.
253. Ibid., 48.
254. F. W. Deakin, "German-Partisan Negotiations and the Case of Mr. Ott (March to December 1943)," in *Yugoslavia, 1941–1945*, 2; Dedijer, *Novi prilozi*, 2:804, 805.
255. Girenko, *Stalin-Tito*, 153.
256. Dedijer, *Novi prilozi*, 2:804, 805; Nenadović, *Razgovori s Kočom*, 72, 73.
257. Girenko, *Stalin-Tito*, 154, 155; AS, Dedijer, t. e. 189.
258. Deakin, "German-Partisan Negotiations," 3, 4.
259. Ibid.
260. Ibid.; Ridley, *Tito*, 205–7.
261. Clissold, *Djilas*, 106.
262. Deakin, "German-Partisan Negotiations," 10–13; F. W. Deakin, "'The Livno Affair' (September 1942)," in *Yugoslavia, 1941–1945*.
263. Nenadović, *Razgovori s Kočom*, 72, 75, 77; Šuvar, *Vladimir Velebit*, 279–89.
264. Dimitrov, *Diario*, 594, 595; Girenko, *Stalin-Tito*, 156.
265. Clissold, *Djilas*, 102; Ćosić, *Piščevi zapisi*, 1:184.
266. Girenko, *Stalin-Tito*, 158.
267. Barker, "British Wartime Policy," 5.
268. F. W. Deakin, "Mihailovic and/or Tito: Summit Considerations (February–April 1943)," in *Yugoslavia, 1941–1945*, 1 and further.
269. Deakin, "German and Allied Plans," 7.
270. Deakin, "German Planning," 11.
271. Deakin, "German First Mountain Division," 2.
272. F. W. Deakin, "The German Appreciation of 'Schwarz,'" in *Yugoslavia, 1941–1945*, 2–4.
273. AS, Dedijer, t. e. 8.
274. Nikoliš, *Korijen, stablo, pavetina*, 38.
275. F. W. Deakin, *The Embattled Mountain* (New York: Oxford University Press, 1971).
276. AS, Dedijer, t. e. 215.
277. Nikoliš, *Korijen, stablo, pavetina*, 525, 526.
278. Adamic, *Eagle and the Roots*, 440.
279. AS, Dedijer, t. e. 220.
280. Adamic, *Eagle and the Roots*, 106, 107.
281. Stefanović, *Podpis*, 193; Ćosić, *Piščevi zapisi*, 1:193.
282. AS, Dedijer, t. e. 220.
283. Edvard Kocbek, *Dnevnik 1949* (Ljubljana: Cankarjeva založba, 1999), 241, 242.
284. AS, Dedijer, t. e., 220.
285. Nenadović, *Razgovori s Kočom*, 79–87.

286. Ćosić, *Piščevi zapisi*, 2:242.
287. Deakin, "German Appreciation of 'Schwarz,'" 5, 6.
288. Šuvar, *Vladimir Velebit*, 303.
289. Ridley, *Tito*, 211.
290. Nikoliš, *Korijen, stablo, pavetina*, 536.
291. Gibianskii, *Sovetskii Soiuz*, 103.
292. F. W. Deakin, "Tito and/or Mihailovic (May–June 1943)," in *Yugoslavia, 1941–1945*, 9.
293. Adamic, *Eagle and the Roots*, 468.
294. Djilas, *Tito*, 106.
295. Deakin, "German and Allied Plans," 10.
296. Nikoliš, *Korijen, stablo, pavetina*, 555.
297. BA, DY 30/IV B2/20/134; Dedijer, *Novi prilozi*, 2:857, 858.
298. Nikoliš, *Korijen, stablo, pavetina*, 561.
299. AS, Dedijer, t. e. 284; Gorazd Bajc, *Operacija Julijska Krajina: Severovzhodna meja Italije in zavezniške obveščevalne službe (1943–1945)* (Koper: Založba Annales, 2006), 71, 72.
300. TNA, HS 3/120: HS/5 969.
301. Fitzroy Maclean, *Eastern Approaches* (London: Jonathan Cape, 1949), 308.
302. Dušan Biber, *Tito-Churchill: Strogo tajno* (Zagreb: Globus, 1981), 37.
303. Ibid., 29–37; TNA, HW 1/1451.
304. Antony Beevor, *The Second World War* (London: Weidenfeld & Nicolson, 2012), 512; Bajt, *Bermanov dosje*, 503, 504; Dedijer, *Novi prilozi*, 2:857.
305. Svetozar Vukmanović-Tempo, *Revolucija teče dalje: Memoari* (Ljubljana: Mladinska knjiga, 1972), 1:315.
306. Bilandžić, *Povijest izbliza*, 684.
307. AS, Dedijer, t. e. 7.
308. Bilandžić, *Povijest izbliza*, 274.
309. Dedijer, *Novi prilozi*, 3:144.
310. Ivan Matović, *Vojskovodja s oreolom mučenika* (Belgrade: Vojska, 2001), 301–10.
311. AS, Dedijer, t. e. 111.
312. Kisić-Kolanović, *Andrija Hebrang*, 50.
313. Jože Pirjevec, *Jugoslavija 1918–1992: Nastanek, razvoj ter razpad Karadjordjevićeve in Titove Jugoslavije* (Koper: Lipa, 1995), 138, 139.
314. Šuvar, *Vladimir Velebit*, 101.
315. Anikeev, *Kak Tito ot Stalina ushel*, 49.
316. Bilandžić, *Povijest izbliza*, 38.
317. Tito, *Zbrana dela*, 17:xi.
318. Ibid., 6, 7; Anikeev, *Kak Tito ot Stalina ushel*, 30.
319. Tito, *Zbrana dela*, 17:167.
320. Girenko, *Stalin-Tito*, 167.
321. Ibid., 170.
322. Dedijer, *Novi prilozi*, 1:353–56.
323. Simić, *Tito*, 197.
324. Djilas, *Der Krieg der Partisanen*, 469.
325. AJ, 838, LF, III-10/2.
326. AS, Dedijer, t. e. 7.
327. Simić, *Tito*, 173.

328. Djilas, *Der Krieg der Partisanen*, 461.
329. Tito, *Zbrana dela*, 17:152.
330. AS, Dedijer, t. e. 7.
331. Bilandžić, *Hrvatska moderna povijest*, 156.
332. AJ, 838, LF III-11/14.
333. Novica Veljanovski, "Titove dileme o AVNOJU i ustavnom uredjenju Jugoslavije 1943–1946," in *Tito: Vidjenja i tumačenja*, Biblioteka Zbornici Radova 8, ed. Olga Manojlović Pintar (Belgrade: Institut za Noviju Istoriju Srbije, 2011), 292, 293.
334. Šuvar, *Vladimir Velebit*, 109–11.
335. Stefanović, *Podpis*, 132.
336. AS, Djilas, t. e. 261.
337. AS, Dedijer, t. e. 7.
338. Ibid., 664; Dedijer, *Novi prilozi*, 1:358, 359.
339. AS, Dedijer, t. e. 7.
340. Ćosić, *Piščevi zapisi*, 1:202.
341. Branko Miljuš, *La Révolution yougoslave* (Lausanne: L'Age d'homme, 1982), 160, 161.
342. F. W. Deakin, "The Prime Minister in Cairo (2–10 Dec. 1943)," in *Yugoslavia, 1941–1945*, 4; HW 1/1451.
343. Barker, *Britanska politika*, 343.
344. Nikoliš, *Korijen, stablo, pavetina*, 575, 576.
345. Biber, *Tito-Churchill*, 128.
346. Djilas, *Tito*, 60.
347. Gibianskii, *Sovetskii Soiuz*, 91, 92.
348. Djilas, *Tito*, 72, 73; TNA, HW 17/51.
349. Gibianskii, *Sovetskii Soiuz*, 84.
350. TNA, WO 202/138.
351. Kardelj, *Spomini*, 25.
352. Golovanov, *Dal'naia bombardirovochnaia*, 490–93.
353. Anikeev, *Kak Tito ot Stalina ushel*, 32.
354. Girenko, *Stalin-Tito*, 182, 183.
355. Anikeev, *Kak Tito ot Stalina ushel*, 33.
356. TNA, HW 17/51.
357. Ibid.
358. Bajt, *Bermanov dosje*, 620.
359. TNA, WO 202/337.
360. Ćosić, *Piščevi zapisi*, 1:200.
361. Gibianskii, *Sovetskii Soiuz*, 83, 84.
362. Ibid., 85–90.
363. Dedijer, *Novi prilozi*, 1:363.
364. Djilas, *Tito*, 62.
365. Kisić-Kolanović, *Andrija Hebrang*, 102.
366. Bilandžić, *Hrvatska moderna povijest*, 163.
367. Elizabeth Barker, *Churchill in Eden v vojni* (Zagreb: Globus, 1980), 232, 233.
368. Biber, *Tito-Churchill*, 144 and further.
369. Šuvar, *Vladimir Velebit*, 129.
370. Biber, *Tito-Churchill*, 119.

371. Girenko, *Stalin-Tito*, 192, 193.
372. Dedijer, *Novi prilozi*, 1:365.
373. Gibianskii, *Sovetskii Soiuz*, 87, 90, 94.
374. Tito, *Zbrana dela*, 20:30.
375. AJ, KMJ 1–3 h/574 D.
376. Nikoliš, *Korijen, stablo, pavetina*, 596.
377. Dedijer, *Novi prilozi*, 2:137.
378. David Greentree, *Knight's Move: The Hunt for Marshal Tito 1944* (Oxford: Osprey Publishing, 2012), 32–36.
379. TNA, WO 106/3283; Cenčić, *Enigma*, 2:91, 92.
380. AS, Dedijer, t. e. 227.
381. Kranjc, *Zarote in atentati*, 193–98.
382. Greentree, *Knight's Move*, 22 and further.
383. AS, Dedijer, t. e. 262.
384. Miro Simčič, *Ženske v Titovi senci: Tito brez maske 2* (Ilirska Bistrica: Samozal., 2010), 202; Girenko, *Stalin-Tito*, 197, 198.
385. Ćosić, *Piščevi zapisi*, 2:239.
386. AS, Dedijer, t. e. 227.
387. Ćosić, *Piščevi zapisi*, 2:240.
388. AS, Dedijer, t. e. 7.
389. Ladislava Becele Ranković, *Življenje z Leko: Spomini slovenske partizanke* (Grosuplje: Grafis Trade, 2002), 67–70.
390. Adamic, *Eagle and the Roots*, 503; Dedijer, *Novi prilozi*, 1:367–69.
391. Nikoliš, *Korijen, stablo, pavetina*, 598–603.
392. AJ, 837, KPR, IV-5-b, K 49.
393. NARA, German Archives, T 120, 1080.
394. Ridley, *Tito*, 236.
395. AS, Djilas, t. e. 603.
396. Nikoliš, *Korijen, stablo, pavetina*, 603.
397. Golovanov, *Dal'naia bombardirovochnaia*, 490–94.
398. Dedijer, *Novi prilozi*, 2:864.
399. Golovanov, *Dal'naia bombardirovochnaia*, 490–94.
400. Adamic, *Eagle and the Roots*, 459.
401. Djilas, *Tito*, 236.
402. Šuvar, *Vladimir Velebit*, 131; Frank McLynn, *Fitzroy Maclean* (London: John Murray, 1992), 204, 205.
403. Kranjc, *Zarote in atentati*, 207, 211.
404. Leary, *Fueling the Fires*, 17.
405. Kardelj, *Spomini*, 21.
406. AS, Dedijer, t. e. 7.
407. Biber, *Tito-Churchill*, 182; TNA, PREM 3/514, 19, 20.
408. Dedijer, *Novi prilozi*, 1:373, 376.
409. Gibianskii, *Sovetskii Soiuz*, 90.
410. Two Partisan personalities were also involved, but as private citizens and not as representatives of the National Liberation Committee.
411. Dedijer, *Novi prilozi*, 2:867.
412. E. Waught, "Salut für Tito," *Rainischer Merkur*, 27 February 1952.

413. Biber, *Tito-Churchill*, 243.
414. Šuvar, *Vladimir Velebit*, 327.
415. Girenko, *Stalin-Tito*, 210.
416. Šuvar, *Vladimir Velebit*, 135–38, 350.
417. Nikoliš, *Korijen, stablo, pavetina*, 611.
418. Šuvar, *Vladimir Velebit*, 144.
419. Robert Murphy, *Diplomat among Warriors* (Garden City, NY: Doubleday, 1964), 223.
420. AS, Dedijer, t. e. 7.
421. AJ, KMJ I-1/! D; KPR, IV-5-a, K 38.
422. AS, Dedijer, t. e. 92; t. e. 198.
423. Winston Churchill, *The Tide of Victory*, vol. 11 of *The Second World War* (London: Cassell, 1964), 80.
424. Ćosić, *Piščevi zapisi*, 1:202.; Djilas, *Wartime*, 401.
425. Jože Smole, *Pripoved komunista novinarja 1945–1980* (Ljubljana: ČZP Enotnost, 1994), 145; Ćosić, *Piščevi zapisi*, 1:202.
426. Tito, *Zbrana dela*, 22:42.
427. Girenko, *Stalin-Tito*, 219.
428. Kisić-Kolanović, *Andrija Hebrang*, 73.
429. Nikoliš, *Korijen, stablo, pavetina*, 613.
430. Stefanović, *Podpis*, 158.
431. Girenko, *Stalin-Tito*, 222.
432. Kermit Roosevelt, *War Report of the OSS (Office of Strategic Services)* (New York: Walker, 1976), 1:127; NARA, CREST, W. J. Donovan, 14 January 1951.
433. Roosevelt, *War Report*, 1:132.
434. Dušan Biber, "Failure of a Mission: Robert McDowell in Yugoslavia," in *The Secrets War: The Office of Strategic Services in World War II*, ed. George C. Chalou (Washington, DC: National Archives and Records Administration, 2002), 194–217.
435. Roosevelt, *War Report*, 132.
436. AS, Dedijer, t. e. 201.
437. AS, Dedijer, t. e. 220; NARA, CREST, Memorandum to Secretary of Defense James W. Forrestal on Subversive Warfare from William J. Donovan, 1 January 1945.
438. Simić, *Tito*, 182; Stefanović, *Podpis*, 160.
439. Kisić-Kolanović, *Andrija Hebrang*, 102.
440. AJ, 837, KPR, IV-5-a, K. 38.
441. Ridley, *Tito*, 247.
442. Stefanović, *Podpis*, 161.
443. Ćosić, *Piščevi zapisi*, 1:177, 184.
444. Clissold, *Yugoslavia*, 38.
445. Bilandžić, *Hrvatska moderna povijest*, 179.
446. Rodoljub Čolaković, *Zapisi iz oslobodilačkog rata* (Sarajevo: Svjetlost, 1977), 2:807.
447. AS, Dedijer, t. e. 271.
448. Girenko, *Stalin-Tito*, 234, 249.
449. Ibid., 227, 234, 236, 262.
450. Ibid., 237.
451. Clissold, *Yugoslavia*, 42.

452. Ibid., 165; Branko Petranović, "Tito i Stalin (1944–1946)," *Jugoslovenski istorijski časopis* 23, nos. 1–2 (1988): 152, 153; AJ, KMK I-3-b/571.
453. Girenko, *Stalin-Tito*, 257.
454. AS, Dedijer, t. e. 243, OSS, Memorandum for the President, 24 December 1944.
455. AS, Dedijer, t. e. 46.
456. Biber, *Tito-Churchill*, 394.
457. AS, Dedijer, t. e. 252.
458. Dedijer, *Novi prilozi*, 3:132, 133, 171.
459. Ibid., 3:211, 212.
460. Clissold, *Djilas*, 154.
461. Simić, *Tito*, 206.
462. AJ, 836, KMJ I-3-b/572.
463. Bilandžić, *Povijest izbliza*, 239.
464. Nikoliš, *Korijen, stablo, pavetina*, 666.
465. Janko Pleterski, *Senca Ajdovskega gradca: O slovenskih izbirah v razklani Evropi* (Ljubljana: Samozaložba, 1993), 16.
466. Pirjevec, *Jugoslavija*, 148.
467. TNA, CAB 121/677/146.
468. Jože Pirjevec, "The Roots of British, American, and Yugoslav Policy toward Greece in 1944," *Journal of the Hellenic Diaspora* 11, no. 3 (Fall 1984): 86.
469. TNA, CAB 121/677/150, 152.
470. Anikeev, *Kak Tito ot Stalina ushel*, 86
471. Adamic, *Eagle and the Roots*, 118; Vladimir Dedijer, *Izgubljeni boj J. V. Stalina* (Ljubljana: Delo, 1969), 68.
472. Walter R. Roberts, *Tito, Mihailović and the Allies, 1941–1945* (New Brunswick, NJ: Rutgers University Press, 1973), 263, 264.
473. Kardelj, *Spomini*, 62–64.
474. Ibid., 70.
475. Banac, *Sa Staljinom protiv Tita*, 29, 30.
476. AS, Dedijer, t. e. 7.
477. Dedijer, *Novi prilozi*, 2:886.
478. Ibid., 3:318.
479. Biber, *Tito-Churchill*, 406.
480. Bilandžić, *Hrvatska moderna povijest*, 181.
481. Dedijer, *Novi prilozi*, 2:913.
482. Simčič, *Ženske v Titovi senci*, 200.
483. Kardelj, *Spomini*, 62.
484. Girenko, *Stalin-Tito*, 264: Petranović, "Tito i Stalin," 156, 157.
485. Herbert Romerstein, "Aspects of World War Two History Revealed through 'ISCOT' Radio Intercept," *The Journal of Intelligence History* 5, no. 1 (Summer 2005): 17.
486. TNA, CAB 121/678/431; Petranović, "Tito i Stalin," 151–62.
487. Girenko, *Stalin-Tito*, 265, 266.
488. Biber, *Tito-Churchill*, 492.
489. Jože Pirjevec, *"Trst je naš!": Boj Slovencev za morje (1848–1954)* (Ljubljana: Nova revija, 2007), 296–98.
490. Jovo Popović, *Druže Tito, rat je završen* (Belgrade: Četvrti jul, 1985), 193, 194.
491. Dedijer, *Novi prilozi*, 3:156.
492. Adamic, *Eagle and the Roots*, 28.

493. Bilandžić, *Povijest izbliza*, 248.
494. Ibid., 235.
495. Dedijer, *Novi prilozi*, 2:938; 3:138, 139.
496. "Kult Josipa Broza Tita," II, http://www.nrbg.rs/concent/view/blog/134/153, p. 6.
497. Tito, *Zbrana dela*, 4:184.
498. AS, Dedijer, t. e. 264.
499. AJ, 837, KPJ, IV-5-b, K 49.
500. AS, Dedijer, t. e. 298.
501. AJ, 838, LF II-I/78, K 4.
502. "Kult Josipa Broza Tita," 4.
503. AJ, 848, LF, III-10/2.
504. Adamic, *Eagle and the Roots*, 509.
505. AS, Dedijer, t. e. 197.
506. Djilas, *Tito*, 246.
507. AS, Dedijer, t. e. 3.
508. Savka Dabčević-Kučar, *'71: Hrvatski snovi i stvarnost* (Zagreb: Interpublic, 1997), 2:675, 858.
509. Ibid., 2:861.
510. Ćosić, *Piščevi zapisi*, 1:189.
511. Djilas, *Tito*, 213.
512. NARA, Pol. 15–1, Yugo, 25 February 1964.
513. AS, Dedijer, t. e. 111; t. e. 271.
514. Politisches Archiv, Berlin (Political Archive, hereafter PA), B 42, Band 1343.
515. Marko Vrhunec, *Josip Broz Tito: Osebnost—stvaritve—titoizem* (Ljubljana: Društvo piscev zgodovine NOB Slovenije, 2009), 31.
516. TNA, FCO 28/2162.
517. Djilas, *Tito*, 196.
518. Ibid., 186.
519. PA, B. 12, Band 547.

Chapter 3. The Postwar Period

1. Bundesarchiv, Berlin (hereafter BA), DY 30/IV B2/20/134.
2. Mira Šuvar, *Vladimir Velebit: Svjedok istorije* (Zagreb: Razlog, 2001), 350.
3. Vladimir Dedijer, *Novi prilozi za biografiju Josipa Broza Tita* (Belgrade: Izdavačka radna organizacija "Rad," 1984), 3:133, 134.
4. Mitja Ribičič, *Iskanja* (Ljubljana: Društvo piscev zgodovine NOB Slovenije, 1994), 23, 47, 48.
5. Ibid., 50, 52, 53, 60.
6. Arhiv Slovenije, Ljubljana (Archive of Slovenia, hereafter AS), Dedijer, t. e. 223; Zdenko Roter, *Pravi obraz: Neizbrisna znamenja resničnosti* (Ljubljana: Sever & Sever, 2017), 83–86.
7. National Archives and Record Administration, Washington (hereafter NARA), Pol 302, Committee for Investigation of the Bleiburg Tragedy, Postwar Massacres in Communist Yugoslavia, Cleveland, Ohio, 1964; Dušan Bilandžić, *Povijest izbliza: Memoarski zapisi 1945–2005* (Zagreb: Prometej, 2005), 309.
8. Marjan Drnovšek et al., *Slovenska kronika XX. stoletja* (Ljubljana: Nova revija, 1996), 102.
9. AS, Dedijer, t. e. 252.

10. Josip Broz Tito, *Govori i članci* (Zagreb: Naprijed, 1959–1972), 11:220.

11. AS, Dedijer, t. e. 252.

12. Milovan Djilas, *Tito: Eine kritische Biographie* (Vienna: Molden, 1980), 165.

13. NARA, CREST, "Yugoslav Interior Security Troops May Be Disbanded," *Central Intelligence Bulletin*, 28 October 1952.

14. Djilas, *Tito*, 97.

15. Bilandžić, *Povijest izbliza*, 187.

16. Ibid., 649; Dušan Bilandžić, *Hrvatska moderna povijest* (Zagreb: Golden Marketing, 1999), 214.

17. Arhiv Jugoslavije, Belgrade (Archive of Yugoslavia, hereafter AJ), 837, KPR, IV-5-a. K 38.

18. Dedijer, *Novi prilozi*, 3:381.

19. Bilandžić, *Povijest izbliza*, 294.

20. Ibid., 294, 355; Bilandžić, *Hrvatska moderna povijest*, 215.

21. AS, Dedijer, t. e. 111.

22. AJ, 837, KPR, IV-5-a, K 58.

23. Dušan Biber, *Tito-Churchill: Strogo tajno* (Zagreb: Globus, 1981), 470, 471.

24. AS, Dedijer, t. e. 7.

25. Biber, *Tito-Churchill*, 488.

26. Iurii Girenko, *Stalin-Tito* (Moscow: Izdatel'stvo politicheskoi literatury, 1991), 266–68.

27. Georgi Dimitrov, *Diario. Gli anni di Mosca (1934–1945)* (Turin: Einaudi, 2000), 823.

28. Dedijer, *Novi prilozi*, 3:197, 222.

29. Girenko, *Stalin-Tito*, 267, 268; Milovan Djilas, *Conversations with Stalin* (Harmondsworth: Penguin Books, 1963), 112, 113.

30. Tito, *Govori i članci*, 1:253–55.

31. Ribičič, *Iskanja*, 43.

32. Dušan Biber, "Trst, Triest ali Trieste: Geneza in dileme o tržaški krizi," in *Konec druge svetovne vojne v Jugoslaviji* (Ljubljana: Revija Borec, 1986), 678, 677.

33. AS, Dedijer, t. e. 7; t. e. 143.

34. L. Ia. Gibianskii, *Sovetskii Soiuz i Novaia Iugoslaviia, 1941–1947* (Moscow: Nauka, 1987), 179.

35. Dedijer, *Novi prilozi*, 3:95.

36. AS, Dedijer, t. e. 8.

37. AJ, 836, KMJI-3-d/16; Girenko, *Stalin-Tito*, 277.

38. Dedijer, *Novi prilozi*, 2:73, 917.

39. Jože Smole, *Pripoved komunista novinarja 1945–1980* (Ljubljana: ČZP Enotnost, 1994), 68.

40. Jože Pirjevec, *"Trst je naš!": Boj Slovencev za morje (1848–1954)* (Ljubljana: Nova revija, 2007), 317, 318.

41. Jože Pirjevec, "La corsa jugoslava per Trieste," in *La crisi di Trieste: Maggio-giugno 1945; Una revisione storiografica*, ed. Giampaolo Valdevit (Trieste: Istituto regionale per la storia del movimento di liberazione nel Friuli-Venezia Giulia, 1995), 91.

42. AS, Dedijer, t. e. 252; Rossiiski gosudarstvennyi arkhiv sotsial'no-politicheskoi istorii (Russian State Archive of Social and Political History, hereafter RGASPI), f. 575, op. 1, d. 413.

43. Gojko Nikoliš, *Korijen, stablo, pavetina: Memoari* (Zagreb: Liber, 1981), 657.

44. Janko Pleterski, *Senca Ajdovskega gradca: O slovenskih izbirah v razklani Evropi* (Ljubljana: Samozaložba, 1993), 69, 80.

45. Girenko, *Stalin-Tito*, 278, 279.

46. A. S. Anikeev, *Kak Tito ot Stalina ushel: Iugoslaviia, SSSR i SSHA v nachal'nyi period "kholodnoi voiny" (1945–1957)* (Moscow: Institut Slavianovedeniia RAN, 2002), 72; Biber, *Tito-Churchill*, 447.

47. Edvard Kardelj, *Spomini: Boj za priznanje in neodvisnost nove Jugoslavije, 1944–1957* (Ljubljana: Državna založba Slovenije, 1980), 74–76.

48. NARA, CREST, Interview Given by Marshal Josip Broz Tito of Yugoslavia to Sherwood Eddy Group, 29 July 1953.

49. Anikeev, *Kak Tito ot Stalina ushel*, 75.

50. Bilandžić, *Hrvatska moderna povijest*, 219.

51. Dedijer, *Novi prilozi*, 3:393.

52. Edvard Kocbek, *Dnevnik, 1946* (Ljubljana: Cankarjeva založba, 1991), 56.

53. Dedijer, *Novi prilozi*, 3:156–64, 168–170; Communication by Jens Reuter.

54. Šuvar, *Vladimir Velebit*, 149.

55. T. V. Volotkina, ed., *Sovetskii faktor v vostochnoi Evrope 1944–1953: Dokumenty*, vol. 1, *1944–1948* (Moscow: ROSSPEN, 1999), 276.

56. AS, Dedijer, t. e. 7.

57. RGASPI, f. 575, op. 1, d. 413; AS, Dedijer, t. e. 179; t. e. 261.

58. Kocbek, *Dnevnik, 1946*, 22.

59. Politisches Archiv, Berlin (Political Archive, hereafter PA), B 11, Band 125, 1.

60. Tito, *Govori i članci*, 1:282, 283.

61. Dedijer, *Novi prilozi*, 3:36, 95, 96; Aleksa Benigar, *Stepinac: Hrvatski kardinal* (Rome: Ziral, 1974), 506; AS, Dedijer, t. e. 15.

62. Charles R. Gallagher, *Vatican Secret Diplomacy: Joseph P. Hurley and Pope Pius XII* (New Haven, CT: Yale University Press, 2008), 161, 170.

63. Stella Alexander, *Church and State in Yugoslavia since 1945* (Cambridge: Cambridge University Press, 1979), 58–60. See also Sabrina P. Ramet, *The Three Yugoslavias: State-Building and Legitimation, 1918–2005* (Bloomington: Indiana University Press, 2006), and *Balkan Babel: The Disintegration of Yugoslavia from the Death of Tito to the Fall of Milošević*, 4th ed. (Boulder: Westview Press, 2002).

64. Ivo Banac, *Sa Staljinom protiv Tita* (Zagreb: Globus, 1990), 34; Dedijer, *Novi prilozi*, 3:484; AS, Dedijer, t. e. 111; t. e. 271.

65. Aleksandar Nenadović, *Razgovori s Kočom* (Zagreb: Globus, 1989), 106.

66. Djilas, *Tito*, 156.

67. Savka Dabčević-Kučar, *'71: Hrvatski snovi i stvarnost* (Zagreb: Interpublic, 1997), 1:426.

68. The National Archives, London (hereafter TNA), FO 371/67440/R 13091.

69. TNA, FO 934/3.

70. Gibianskii, *Sovetskii Soiuz*, 166.

71. Kardelj, *Spomini*, 84.

72. Lorraine M. Lees, *Keeping Tito Afloat: The United States, Yugoslavia, and the Cold War* (University Park: Pennsylvania State University Press, 1997), 6.

73. AS, Dedijer, t. e. 51.

74. Ribičič, *Iskanja*, 58.

75. Keith Miles, "How Tito Betrayed Slovenia over Trieste," Centre for Research into Post-Communist Economies, Lessons from History, http://www.crce.org.uk/lessons/trieste.php.
76. Gibianskii, *Sovetskii Soiuz*, 175.
77. Kardelj, *Spomini*, 207.
78. AJ 837, KPR, IV-5-a, K 38.
79. Kardelj, *Spomini*, 86, 87.
80. TNA, FO 37159551/R 12345; Dedijer, *Novi prilozi*, 3:263, 264.
81. Gibianskii, *Sovetskii Soiuz*, 186.
82. AS, Dedijer, t. e. 51.
83. Kardelj, *Spomini*, 90.
84. Ibid., 88.
85. Ibid., 181; Roter, *Pravi obraz*, 122.
86. Šuvar, *Vladimir Velebit*, 354.
87. RGASPI, f. 575, a. 1, d. 323.
88. Milovan Djilas, "Vlast kao strast," *Start*, 21 January 1989, 30.
89. PA, B 11, Band 125, 2.
90. Kardelj, *Spomini*, 193.
91. Kosta Nikolić, *Tito govori što narod misli* (Belgrade: Službeni list SCG, 2006), 191.
92. Dedijer, *Novi prilozi*, 3:317.
93. Kardelj, *Spomini*, 196.
94. Dedijer, *Novi prilozi*, 1:415–20; 3:602.
95. Dobrica Ćosić, *Piščevi zapisi* (Belgrade: Višnjić, 2001), 1:185.
96. Dedijer, *Novi prilozi*, 3:223; AS, Dedijer, t. e. 143.
97. Nikolić, *Tito govori*, 175.
98. Pero Simić, *Tito: Skrivnost stoletja* (Ljubljana: Orbis, 2009), 229.
99. Dedijer, *Novi prilozi*, 3:264, 265.
100. Nenadović, *Razgovori s Kočom*, 104.
101. AJ, KMJ I-3-b/616.
102. Dedijer, *Novi prilozi*, 1:426–30; 3:223, 244, 245, 322.
103. Djilas, *Tito*, 93.
104. Christopher Andrew and Vasili Mitrokhin, *The Sword and the Shield: The Mitrokhin Archive and the Secret History of the KGB* (New York: Basic Books, 1999), 356.
105. Marijan F. Kranjc, *Zarote in atentati na Tita* (Grosuplje: Graphis Trade, 2004), 270.
106. Dedijer, *Novi prilozi*, 3:326–28.
107. Smole, *Pripoved komunista novinarja*, 10.
108. Jasper Ridley, *Tito: A Biography* (London: Constable, 1994), 280.
109. Dimitrov, *Diario*, 708, 711, 722–35, 753, 771, 782–89.
110. Ibid., 785; AJ, 836, KMJ I-3-b/586.
111. Dimitrov, *Diario*, 793, 797, 801.
112. Kardelj, *Spomini*, 105.
113. Anikeev, *Kak Tito ot Stalina ushel*, 91–93.
114. Dimitrov, *Diario*, 769; Georgi Dimitrov, *Dnevnik (9 mart 1933–6 fevruari 1949)* (Sofia: Univerzitetsko izdatelstvo Sv. Kliment Ohridski, 1997), 528, 535.
115. Dedijer, *Novi prilozi*, 3:311.
116. RGASPI, f. 575, op. 1, d. 413.
117. Bilandžić, *Povijest izbliza*, 647.
118. Girenko, *Stalin-Tito*, 325, 326.

119. Ibid.; Dimitrov, *Dnevnik*, 590; Blažo Mandić, *Tito u dialogu s svijetom* (Novi Sad: Agencija Mir, 2005), 16.

120. NARA, CREST, Yugoslavia/USSR, "Break between Tito and the Soviet Union," 6 November 1948.

121. Girenko, *Stalin-Tito*, 351, 352.

122. RGASPI, f. 575, op. 1, d. 413.

123. Dimitrov, *Diario*, 823.

124. RGASPI, f. 575, op. 1, d. 413.

125. Geoffrey R. Swain, "The Cominform: Tito's International?," *Historical Journal* 35, no. 3 (1992): 656.

126. Giuliano Procacci, ed., *The Cominform: Minutes of the Three Conferences 1947/1948/1949* (Milan: Feltrinelli, 1994), 217–51.

127. Dimitrov, *Dnevnik*, 574.

128. RGASPI, f. 575, op. 1, d. 413.

129. Ibid.

130. Girenko, *Stalin-Tito*, 289, 290.

131. Swain, "The Cominform," 658.

132. RGASPI, f. 575, op. 1, d. 413.

133. Dedijer, *Novi prilozi*, 3:304, 307.

134. RGASPI, f. 575, op. 1, d. 413.

135. Ibid.

136. Dedijer, *Novi prilozi*, 3:127, 207.

137. RGASPI, f. 575, op. 1, d. 413; Jeronim Perović, "The Tito-Stalin Split: A Reassessment in Light of New Evidence," *Journal of Cold War Studies* 9, no. 2 (Spring 2007): 45, 46.

138. Jože Pirjevec, *Tito, Stalin in Zahod* (Ljubljana: Delavska enotnost, 1987), 45.

139. Dedijer, *Novi prilozi*, 1:459.

140. Dimitrov, *Dnevnik*, 595.

141. Dedijer, *Novi prilozi*, 3:309; Girenko, *Stalin-Tito*, 334.

142. Kranjc, *Zarote in atentati*, 235.

143. Dedijer, *Novi prilozi*, 3:304.

144. J. Perović, "The Tito-Stalin Split," 49.

145. Girenko, *Stalin-Tito*, 334–38.

146. Miladin Adamović, *Brozovi strahovi: Kako je čuvan Tito i pokušaji atentata* (Belgrade: M. Adamović, 2004), 32; G. Vlahov, "Život u Belom dvoru," *Duga* 402 (22 July 1989): 83, 64.

147. Dedijer, *Novi prilozi*, 3:206.

148. AJ, 838, LF-1/78, K 4.

149. AS, Dedijer, t. e. 4.

150. AS, Dedijer, t. e. 179.

151. Dedijer, *Novi prilozi*, 1:460–467.

152. Girenko, *Stalin-Tito*, 340; Dimitrov, *Dnevnik*, 596–603.

153. AS, Dedijer, t. e. 143.

154. Kardelj, *Spomini*, 119; AS, Dedijer, t. e. 201.

155. Dimitrov, *Dnevnik*, 599, 603.

156. Girenko, *Stalin-Tito*, 342; Kardelj, *Spomini*, 118.

157. Pirjevec, *Tito*, 62; AS, Dedijer, t. e. 143.

158. Andrei B. Edemskii, *Ot konflikta k normalizatsii: Sovetsko-iugoslavskie otnosheniia v 1953–1956 godakh* (Moscow: Nauka, 2008), 20.
159. J. Perović, "The Tito-Stalin Split," 45, 55–57.
160. Kardelj, *Spomini*, 216.
161. Dedijer, *Novi prilozi*, 3:303–6.
162. RGASPI, f. 575, op. 1, d. 413.
163. Dedijer, *Novi prilozi*, 3:307, 308.
164. Djilas, *Tito*, 239.
165. Girenko, *Stalin-Tito*, 348–53.
166. Ibid., 354.
167. Ibid., 354, 355.
168. Ibid., 356.
169. AS, Dedijer, t. e. 51.
170. Dedijer, *Novi prilozi*, 1:413; 3:226, 311, 373, 375, 600.
171. Girenko, *Stalin-Tito*, 358, 359.
172. Dedijer, *Novi prilozi*, 1:475.
173. Girenko, *Stalin-Tito*, 360–62.
174. Pirjevec, *Tito*, 68, 69; Vladimir Dedijer, *Dokumenti 1948* (Belgrade: Rad, 1979), 1:234.
175. AS, Dedijer, t. e. 7.
176. Šuvar, *Vladimir Velebit*, 163, 164.
177. Dedijer, *Dokumenti 1948*, 1:239, 240.
178. Ibid., 249–51.
179. Milovan Djilas, *Jahre der Macht: Kräftespiel hinter dem Eisernen Vorhang: Memoiren 1945–1966* (Munich: Molden-S. Seewald, 1983), 206.
180. Vladimir Dedijer, *Izgubljeni boj J. V. Stalina 1948–1955* (Ljubljana: Delo, 1969), 231.
181. Djilas, *Tito*, 184, 185.
182. Girenko, *Stalin-Tito*, 362, 363.
183. Dedijer, *Novi prilozi*, 1:480; 3:369–83.
184. Stephen Clissold, *Djilas: The Progress of a Revolutionary* (Hounslow: Maurice Temple Smith, 1983), 194.
185. Edemskii, *Ot konflikta k normalizatsii*, 24.
186. Djilas, *Tito*, 248.
187. Nada Kisić-Kolanović, *Andrija Hebrang: Iluzije i otrežnjenja* (Zagreb: Institut za suvremenu povijest, 1996), 195.
188. Girenko, *Stalin-Tito*, 366.
189. RGASPI, f. 495, op. 277, d. 88.
190. Dedijer, *Novi prilozi*, 3:383–85.
191. Dedijer, *Dokumenti 1948*, 1:249.
192. Pirjevec, *Tito*, 76.
193. Dedijer, *Izgubljeni boj*, 132.
194. Girenko, *Stalin-Tito*, 369; Dedijer, *Novi prilozi*, 3:137.
195. Dedijer, *Novi prilozi*, 3:340.
196. Kardelj, *Spomini*, 129.
197. Dedijer, *Novi prilozi*, 3:235; Pirjevec, *Tito*, 92.
198. AS, Dedijer, t. e. 8.
199. Djilas, *Tito*, 172, 173, 237.

200. TNA, FO 371/72578/R 6862/G.
201. Kardelj, *Spomini*, 129.
202. Borislav Mihajlović Mihiz, *Autobiografija—o drugima* (Belgrade: Evro-Giunti, 2008), 422, 423.
203. Dedijer, *Novi prilozi*, 3:311, 390.
204. RGASPI, f. 575, op. 1, d. 413.
205. Dedijer, *Novi prilozi*, 3:347.
206. Ibid.
207. Ibid., 80; RGASPI, f. 575, op. 1, d. 413.
208. Kisić-Kolanović, *Andrija Hebrang*, 300: AS, Dedijer, t. e. 236.
209. AS, Dedijer, t. e. 8; Vjenceslav Cenčić, *Titova poslednja ispovijest* (Belgrade: Orfelin, 2001), 34, 57, 202, 375.
210. Randolph Churchill, "Tito's Story of Gestapo's Operation: Hebrang, Communist Leader Turned German Spy," *Daily Telegraph*, 21 May 1952.
211. Kisić-Kolanović, *Andrija Hebrang*, 204.
212. Girenko, *Stalin-Tito*, 374, 375.
213. RGASPI, f. 575, op. 1, d. 413.
214. Stephen Clissold, *Yugoslavia and the Soviet Union, 1939–1973: A Documentary Survey* (New York: Oxford University Press, 1975), 187.
215. Dedijer, *Dokumenti 1948*, 1:280.
216. Massimo Caprara, *Quando le Botteghe erano oscure, 1944–1969: Uomini e storie del comunismo italiano* (Milan: Il Saggiatore, 2000), 137.
217. Dimitrov, *Dnevnik*, 611; AS, Dedijer, t. e. 143.
218. RGASPI, f. 575, op. 1, d. 413.
219. Girenko, *Stalin-Tito*, 378.
220. Dedijer, *Novi prilozi*, 1:495, 496.
221. Dedijer, *Dokumenti 1948*, 1:295.
222. Ibid., 295, 296–98.
223. Djilas, *Jahre der Macht*, 229.
224. Procacci, *The Cominform*, 610–17.
225. Girenko, *Stalin-Tito*, 385, 386.
226. Pirjevec, *Tito*, 133; AJ, KPR, IV-5-a, K 48, 365.
227. Dedijer, *Novi prilozi*, 3:334; Edemskii, *Ot konflikta k normalizatsii*, 18, 32, 503.
228. RGASPI, f. 575, op. 1, d. 413.
229. Clissold, *Djilas*, 198.
230. TNA, FO 371/72581/R 7867/R 8797.
231. TNA, FO 371/72579/R 7715.
232. Wolfgang Leonhard, *Child of the Revolution* (London: Collins, 1957), 387–90.
233. TNA, FO 371/72185/R 5456.
234. Dedijer, *Dokumenti 1948*, 1:368–376.
235. Dedijer, *Novi prilozi*, 3:295, 361.
236. Aleš Bebler, *Čez drn in strn: Spomini* (Koper: Založba Lipa, 1981), 187.
237. Dedijer, *Novi prilozi*, 3:460.
238. Andrew and Mitrokhin, *The Sword and the Shield*, 357.
239. Dedijer, *Novi prilozi*, 3:406.
240. Girenko, *Stalin-Tito*, 391, 392.
241. AS, Dedijer, t. e. 244.

242. Banac, *Sa Staljinom protiv Tita*, 130; Geoffrey R. Swain, *Tito: A Biography* (New York: I. B. Tauris, 2011), 96.
243. Nikoliš, *Korijen, stablo, pavetina*, 397, 398.
244. Dedijer, *Novi prilozi*, 3:350; AS, Dedijer, t. e. 7; Ivan Matović, *Vojskovodja s oreolom mučenika* (Belgrade: Vojska, 2001), 635–38.
245. AS, Dedijer, t. e. 252; Matović, *Vojskovodja s oreolom mučenika*, 797.
246. Pirjevec, *Tito*, 179.
247. Dedijer, *Novi prilozi*, 3:461; Matović, *Vojskovodja s oreolom mučenika*, 809.
248. NARA, 860H.00/8–2148.
249. TNA, FO 371/72588/R 10129.
250. TNA, FO 371/72608/R 10240; FO 371/72608/R 10454.
251. Djilas, *Tito*, 174; Dedijer, *Novi prilozi*, 3:464; Bilandžić, *Povijest izbliza*, 219.
252. Djilas, *Tito*, 169, 170, 171.
253. Simić, *Tito*, 240.
254. Dedijer, *Novi prilozi*, 3:464.
255. Slavko Ćuruvija and Vlado Dapčević, *Ibeovac: Ja, Vlado Dapčević* (Belgrade: Filip Višnjić, 1990), 262.
256. NARA, CREST, CIA, *Current Intelligence Digest*, 27 March 1952.
257. Nikolić, *Tito govori*, 281.
258. Kardelj, *Spomini*, 199.
259. Dedijer, *Novi prilozi*, 3:243.
260. Ćosić, *Piščevi zapisi*, 1:122.
261. Dedijer, *Novi prilozi*, 3:233, 234.
262. Ibid., 210.
263. AS, Dedijer, t. e. 188.
264. Dedijer, *Novi prilozi*, 3:358.
265. Ibid., 364, 517, 518.
266. Djilas, *Tito*, 167.
267. PA, B 11, Band 123, 1.
268. Dedijer, *Novi prilozi*, 3:612.
269. Ibid., 518; Simić, *Tito*, 239.
270. Bilandžić, *Povijest izbliza*, 32, 33, 79.
271. Cenčić, *Titova poslednja ispovijest*, 519; Dedijer, *Novi prilozi*, 3:519.
272. BA, IV A 2/20/238; Bestand Ulbricht, Walter, NL 182/1235.
273. Girenko, *Stalin-Tito*, 388.
274. Ibid., 394, 395.
275. TNA, FO 371/72588/R 10439.
276. Archivio Storico Diplomatico Ministero degli Esteri, Rome (hereafter, ASME), Jugoslavia, Busta 33, fasc. 1.
277. US Department of State, *Foreign Relations of the United States, 1948*, vol. 4, *Eastern Europe; The Soviet Union* (Washington, DC: US Government Printing Office, 1974), 1109.
278. TNA, FO 371/78680/R 649.
279. NARA, 800.00B CI/9–2348; TNA, FO, 371/72589/R 10964.
280. Djilas, *Jahre der Macht*, 288.
281. Pirjevec, *Tito*, 207.
282. NARA, 860H.00/10–1448.

283. Djilas, *Jahre der Macht*, 286–88.

284. TNA, FO 371, 72589/R 11692.

285. "NIE-7, the Current Situation in Yugoslavia, 21 November 1950," in *Yugoslavia: From "National Communism" to National Collapse; US Intelligence Community Estimative Products on Yugoslavia*, ed. Thomas Fingar (Pittsburgh, PA: GPO, 2006), 85, 92, 93.

286. Djilas, *Tito*, 240.

287. Ridley, *Tito*, 296.

288. Svetozar Rajak, "In Search of a Life outside the Two Blocks, Yugoslavia's Road to Non-Alignment," in *Great Powers and Small Countries in Cold War 1945–1955: Issue of Ex-Yugoslavia*, ed. Ljubodrag Dimić (Belgrade: University of Belgrade, Archives of Serbia and Montenegro and SD Public, 2005), 7.

289. TNA, FO 371/72744/UN 2612.

290. TNA, FO 371/72589/R 11501.

291. TNA, FO 371/72589/R 11666; 72990/R 12041; ASME, Jugoslavia, Busta 53, fasc. 1.

292. TNA, FO 371/72576/R 12455; R 11209.

293. Anikeev, *Kak Tito ot Stalina ushel*, 140.

294. NARA 760H-61/7-2249/R 5577; 760H.61/6-449; TNA, FO 371/78708/R 5682; ASME, Jugoslavia, Busta 50.

295. AJ, 838, LF II-1/78.

296. Kardelj, *Spomini*, 132, 142.

297. Anikeev, *Kak Tito ot Stalina ushel*, 142, 143.

298. TNA, FO 371/78716/ R 5235; R 4691; 4734/G.

299. "NIE-7," 89; Anikeev, *Kak Tito ot Stalina ushel*, 147–49.

300. Jože Pirjevec, *Il gran rifiuto: Guerra fredda e calda tra Tito, Stalin e l'Occidente* (Trieste: Editoriale Stampa Triestina, 1990), 356, 357.

301. Dedijer, *Novi prilozi*, 3:481; Girenko, *Stalin-Tito*, 396; Anikeev, *Kak Tito ot Stalina ushel*, 166.

302. Pirjevec, *Il gran rifiuto*, 360.

303. Nenadović, *Razgovori s Kočom*, 107, 109.

304. "ORE 16-49, the Yugoslav Dilemma, 10 February 1949," in *Yugoslavia: From "National Communism" to National Collapse; US Intelligence Estimative Products on Yugoslavia*, ed. Thomas Fingar (Pittsburgh, PA: GPO, 2006),16; AS, Dedijer, t. e. 252.

305. Bogdan Osolnik, *Med svetom in domovino: Spomini 1945–1981* (Maribor: Obzorja, 1992), 198.

306. Dedijer, *Novi prilozi*, 3:462, 463.

307. Ladislava Becele Ranković, *Življenje z Leko: Spomini slovenske partizanke* (Grosuplje: Grafis Trade, 2002), 123, 124.

308. Kardelj, *Spomini*, 142, 246–50.

309. Anikeev, *Kak Tito ot Stalina ushel*, 172.

310. Louis Adamic, *The Eagle and the Roots* (Garden City, NY: Doubleday, 1952), 511.

311. Anton Kolendić, *Staljinova smrt: Od Staljinove do Berijine smrti* (Belgrade: Altera, 1989), 264–67; NARA, CREST, Information Report, Hungary, "Background of the Rajk Case," 23 May 1956.

312. Girenko, *Stalin-Tito*, 397.

313. Clissold, *Djilas*, 206.

314. "ORE 8-50, Evolution of Soviet-Yugoslav Relations (1950), 11 May 1950," in *Yugoslavia: From "National Communism" to National Collapse; US Intelligence Estimative Products on Yugoslavia*, ed. Thomas Fingar (Pittsburgh, PA: GPO, 2006), 41.

315. Dedijer, *Novi prilozi*, 3:461.
316. AS, Dedijer, t. e. 244.
317. Pirjevec, *Il gran rifiuto*, 386, 387.
318. Coleman Armstrong Mehta, "'A Rat Hole to be Watched?' CIA Analyses of the Tito-Stalin Split, 1948–1950" (PhD diss., North Carolina State University, 2005), 9; Jak Koprivc, *Generalov let: Spomini generala Ivana Dolničarja* (Ljubljana: Modrijan, 2005), 103.
319. Gojko Berić, *Zbogom XX. stoljeće: Sjećanja Ive Vejvode* (Zagreb: Profil knjiga, 2013), 123; Stefano Terra, *Tre anni con Tito* (Trieste: MGS Press, 2004), 89.
320. Ranko Petković, *Subjektivna istorija jugoslovenske diplomatije* (Belgrade: Službeni list SRJ, 1995), 143.
321. AS, Dedijer, t. e. 197; t. e. 223; t. e. 298; Edemskii, *Ot konflikta k normalizatsii*, 350, 360, 367.
322. AJ, 836, KMJ I-8/2 I-6/2.
323. Ridley, *Tito*, 304, 305.
324. Tito, *Govori i članci*, 5:17; AS, Dedijer, t. e. 198.
325. Moše Pijade, *About the Legend That the Yugoslav Uprising Owed Its Existence to Soviet Assistance* (London: Yugoslav Embassy, 1950); Adamic, *Eagle and the Roots*, 477.
326. Ridley, *Tito*, 306, 307.
327. NARA, CREST, Untitled, June 1950.
328. "NIE-7," 90; Gelvan Library, George Washington University (hereafter GWU), "A Report to the National Security Council by the Executive Secretary," 29 July 1950, 8.
329. Dedijer, *Novi prilozi*, 3:427, 428.
330. NARA, CIA, CREST, Information from Foreign Documents or Radio Broadcasts, 7 February 1951.
331. Djilas, *Tito*, 240.
332. Ridley, *Tito*, 308; Anikeev, *Kak Tito ot Stalina ushel*, 188.
333. NARA, CREST, CIA, Information Report, 8 May 1951.
334. NARA, CREST, "Yugoslavia Charges USSR with Applying Military Pressure," *Central Intelligence Bulletin*, 20 March 1951.
335. Ćosić, *Piščevi zapisi*, 1:18, 19; GWU, "A Report to the NSC: The Position of the US with Respect to Yugoslavia," 2 March 1951.
336. Tvrtko Jakovina, *Američki komunistčki saveznik: Hrvati, Titova Jugoslavija i Sjedinjene Američke Države, 1945–1955* (Zagreb: Profil, 2003), 328–30.
337. "NIE 15-61, Outlook for Yugoslavia, 23 May 1961," in *Yugoslavia: From "National Communism" to National Collapse; US Intelligence Community Estimative Products on Yugoslavia*, ed. Thomas Fingar (Pittsburgh, PA: GPO, 2006), 264.
338. NARA, 768.5.-MSP/10–1854.
339. Tito, *Govori i članci*, 4:73–75.
340. NARA, CREST, *Central Intelligence Bulletin*, 28 June 1951.
341. NARA, CREST, "Tito Evidences Pro-American Sentiment," *Central Intelligence Bulletin*, 8 June 1951; "Yugoslav Chief of Staff Concerned over West's Strategic Plans," 17 October 1951; "Tito Considers Danger of Soviet Aggression Lessening," 3 January 1952.
342. Anikeev, *Kak Tito ot Stalina ushel*, 202; Darko Bekić, *Jugoslavija u hladnom ratu: Odnosi s velikim silama, 1949–1955* (Zagreb: Globus, 1988), 415, 416.
343. Anikeev, *Kak Tito ot Stalina ushel*, 216.

344. NARA, 768.5-MSP/11-1352.

345. TNA, WO 106/6087; Jakovina, *Američki komunistčki saveznik*, 337, 338, 346.

346. NARA, CREST, "Yugoslavia: Tito Desires to Remain Aloof from West," *Central Intelligence Bulletin*, 19 February 1951.

347. Rajak, "In Search of a Life," 11.

348. AS, Dedijer, t. e. 3; Predrag Simić, *Tito i NATO: Uspon i pad druge Jugoslavije* (Belgrade: Novisti, 2008), 73.

349. NARA, 768.5-MSP/I-1053; CREST, CIA, Office of Current Intelligence Daily Digest, "Yugoslav Demarche to Greece," 6 April 1951; "Greece: Reported Greek Proposal to Partition Albania Clarified," 16 April 1951.

350. Anikeev, *Kak Tito ot Stalina ushel*, 232–46.

351. Dedijer, *Novi prilozi*, 3:438.

352. Ibid., 627, 628.

353. Pirjevec, *"Trst je naš!,"* 433.

354. TNA, FO 482/7.

355. TNA, FO 371/112734 WE 1015/254.

356. J. Pirjevec, *"Trst je naš!,"* 440.

357. Ibid., 441; NARA, CREST, CIA, "Yugoslav Reaction to the American-British Announcement on Trieste," *Current Intelligence Weekly*, 16 October 1953; Memorandum for the Record, Conversation between Congressman John Blatnik and the DCI, 12 November 1955.

358. TNA, FO 371/107387; NARA, CREST, "Yugoslav Relation to the American-British Announcement on Trieste," *Current Intelligence Weekly*, 16 October 1953.

359. Šuvar, *Vladimir Velebit*, 186–89.

360. Nacionalna i Sveučilišna Knjižnica, Zagreb (National and University Library, hereafter NSK), Arhiv Bakarić, Kutija 8, Bilten 691, 15 October 1954, 1.

361. John Creighton Campbell, *Successful Negotiation: Trieste 1954—An Appraisal by the Five Participants* (Princeton, NJ: Princeton University Press, 2016), 18, 168, 169.

362. TNA, FO 371/112742 WE 1015/482.

363. Ćosić, *Piščevi zapisi*, 1:202; NARA, CREST, "Murphy Makes Significant Trieste Concession," *Central Intelligence Bulletin*, 21 September 1954.

364. Svetozar Vukmanović-Tempo, *Revolucija teče dalje: Memoari* (Ljubljana: Mladinska knjiga, 1972), 2:185–93.

365. Ridley, *Tito*, 315; AS, Dedijer, t. e. 126; t. e. 244.

366. NARA, CREST, Comment on FBI Report, 10 February 1953.

367. Andrew and Mitrokhin, *The Sword and the Shield*, 357–58; Ken Alibek and Stephen Handelman, *Biohazard* (New York: Delta, 2000), 29–49.

368. Pavel Sudoplatov, *Razvedka i Kreml'* (Moscow: Gea, 1996), 390–94.

369. Roy A. Medvedev and Zhores A. Medvedev, *The Unknown Stalin: His Life, Death and Legacy* (Woodstock, NY: Overlook Press, 2004), 60–70.

370. Caprara, *Quando le Botteghe erano oscure*, 140–141; Gian Carlo Pajetta, *Le crisi che ho vissuto* (Rome: Editori Riuniti, 1982), 29–49.

371. Melvyn Bragg, *The Life of Richard Burton* (London. Hodder and Sloughton, 1988), 368; Dedijer, *Novi prilozi*, III, 582.

372. Kolendić, *Staljinova smrt*, 26; Dmitrii A. Volkogonov, *Stalin: Politicheskii portret* (Moscow: Novosti, 1996), 2:598, 599.

373. Ćosić, *Piščevi zapisi*, 1:197.

374. Edemskii, *Ot konflikta k normalizatsii*, 59, 60.

375. Svetozar Rajak, *Yugoslavia and the Soviet Union in the Early Cold War: Reconciliation, Comradeship, Confrontation, 1953–1957* (New York: Routledge, 2011), 44, 45.

376. Svetozar Rajak, "New Evidence from the Former Yugoslav Archives: The Tito-Khrushchev Correspondence 1954," *Cold War History Project Bulletin*, nos. 12–13 (Fall–Winter 2001): 315.

377. AS, Dedijer, t. e. 244.

378. Edemskii, *Ot konflikta k normalizatsii*, 107.

379. Ibid., 112–14.

380. Ibid., 122.

381. Ridley, *Tito*, 318.

382. PA, 12, Band 585/7.

383. AJ, 837, KPR, IV-5-b, K 49.

384. Jelka Kušar, ed., *Viharno stoletje: Pogovori z Janezom Stanovnikom* (Ljubljana: Ustanova Franc Rozman-Stane, 2013), 168.

385. Clissold, *Yugoslavia*, 181.

386. AS, Dedijer, t. e. 7.

387. Dedijer, *Novi prilozi*, 3:30.

388. Edemskii, *Ot konflikta k normalizatsii*, 253–55.

389. Ibid., 260, 261.

390. Ibid., 296, 308.

391. Rajak, "New Evidence," 319–23.

392. Ćosić, *Piščevi zapisi*, 1:66.

393. Girenko, *Stalin-Tito*, 403.

394. Ibid.

395. Edemskii, *Ot konflikta k normalizatsii*, 441.

396. Dedijer, *Novi prilozi*, 3:30.

397. Ibid., 571.

398. Kardelj, *Spomini*, 146; NARA, CREST, Perspectives, "Brezhnev in Yugoslavia," 4 November 1971.

399. RGASPI, f. 575, op. 1, d. 413.

400. AS, Dedijer, t. e. 7.

401. Djilas, "Vlast kao strast," 30.

402. Kardelj, *Spomini*, 136, 235; "Milovan Djilas and George Urban in Conversation," *Encounter* 71, no. 3 (September–October 1988): 19; Djilas, *Tito*, 105.

403. AS, Dedijer, t. e. 7.

404. Kardelj, *Spomini*, 223, 235.

405. Dedijer, *Novi prilozi*, 3:512; Dedijer, *Dokumenti 1948*, 3:83–107.

406. Ćosić, *Piščevi zapisi*, 1:67.

407. Nenadović, *Razgovori s Kočom*, 169.

408. Cenčić, *Titova poslednja ispovijest*, 49.

409. "NIE-7," 85, 91, 92.

410. Dragan Bogetić, *Nova strategija spoljne politike Jugoslavije 1950–1961* (Belgrade: Institut za savremenu istoriju, 2006), 30, 31.

411. "NIE-7," 89.

412. Dedijer, *Novi prilozi*, 3:522, 523.

413. Djilas, *Tito*, 105.

414. NSK, Arhiv Bakarić, K 22, Informativni bilten, Broj 8, Izdanje Sekretariata Komisije CK KPJ za medjunarodna pitanja, Beograd, 15 December 1952.
415. Ibid.
416. Ćosić, *Piščevi zapisi*, 1:28.
417. Dedijer, *Novi prilozi*, 3:513.
418. Veljko Vlahović, *Strogo pov.: 1955–1958* (Belgrade: Stručna knjiga, 1998), 75.
419. Bilandžić, *Povijest izbliza*, 132, 698.
420. PA, B 11, Band 181, 1.
421. Dedijer, *Novi prilozi*, 3:527.
422. Zdenko Čepič, "Jugoslovanske reforme v šestdesetih letih," in *Slovenija-Jugoslavija: Krize in reforme 1968/1988* (Ljubljana: Inštitut za novejšo zgodovino, 2010), 48.
423. NARA, CIA, "Highlights of Tito-Churchill Discussions," *Central Intelligence Bulletin*, 28 March 1953.
424. TNA, FO 371/107835/WY 10754/84/G; WY 1054/93; WY 1054/102/G; Dedijer, *Novi prilozi*, 3:441.
425. Djilas, *Tito*, 93, 102.
426. Ibid., 131.
427. Dedijer, *Novi prilozi*, 3:610, 611.
428. BA, NY 4090/480; Šuvar, *Vladimir Velebit*, 171.
429. NARA, 768.5-MSP/7-753; "NIE-93, Probable Developments in Yugoslavia, 26 June 1953," in *Yugoslavia: From "National Communism" to National Collapse; US Intelligence Community Estimative Products on Yugoslavia*, ed. Thomas Fingar (Pittsburgh, PA: GPO, 2006), 145.
430. PA, B. 12, Band 621.
431. Dedijer, *Novi prilozi*, 3:620.
432. Djilas, *Tito*, 291.
433. RGASPI, f. 575, op. 1, d. 323; Simić, *Tito*, 250.
434. RGASPI, f. 575, op. 1, d. 323.
435. Ibid.; "NIE-31-55, Yugoslavia and Its Future Orientation, 23 February 1955," in *Yugoslavia: From "National Communism" to National Collapse; US Intelligence Community Estimative Products on Yugoslavia*, ed. Thomas Fingar (Pittsburgh, PA: GPO, 2006), 169.
436. Djilas, *Tito*, 135, 204.
437. NSK, M. Krleža, "A," 169.
438. Djilas, *Tito*, 11.
439. "Diskurzija izmedju Stanovnika, Kristla i Djilasa: Klasa ili kasta," *Komunist* 6, nos. 3–4 (May–August 1952): 39–47.
440. Djilas, *Tito*, 197.
441. Girenko, *Stalin-Tito*, 293.
442. Djilas, *Tito*, 111.
443. AJ, 873, KPR II-4-a K 164, 165; AS, Dedijer, t. e. 111.
444. Dedijer, *Novi prilozi*, 3:626.
445. Djilas, "Nove sadržine," *Borba*, 11 October 1953, 3.
446. Djilas, "Bez zaključka," *Borba*, 29 November 1953, 3.
447. Djilas, "Subjektivne snage," *Borba*, 27 December 1953, 3.
448. Djilas, "Objektivne snage," *Borba*, 29 December 1953, 3.
449. Djilas, "Odgovor," *Borba*, 27 December 1953, 3.
450. Djilas, "Savez ili partija?" *Borba*, 4 January 1954, 2, 4.

451. Ibid.
452. Djilas, *Tito*, 383.
453. Fitzroy Maclean, *Josip Broz Tito: A Pictorial Biography* (New York: McGraw-Hill, 1980), 415; AS, Dedijer, t. e. 201; NARA, CREST, Information Report, Background of Djilas Removal, 30 March 1956.
454. Djilas, "Odgovor," *Borba*, 24 December 1953, 3.
455. Dedijer, *Novi prilozi*, 3:532.
456. Djilas, *Tito*, 284; AS, Dedijer, t. e. 201.
457. PA, B 11, Band 126, 1; Djilas, "Nove ideje," *Borba*, 1, 2, 3 January 1954; "Savez ili Partija," *Borba*, 4 January 1954, 2.
458. Ćosić, *Piščevi zapisi*, 1:37.
459. AS, Dedijer, t. e. 188.
460. Aleksandar Ranković, *Dnevničke zabeleške* (Belgrade: Jugoslovenska knjiga, 2001), 153.
461. Clissold, *Djilas*, 244.
462. Dedijer, *Novi prilozi*, 3:532; "NIE 15-61, Outlook for Yugoslavia, 23 May 1961," in *Yugoslavia: From "National Communism" to National Collapse; US Intelligence Community Estimative Products on Yugoslavia*, ed. Thomas Fingar (Pittsburgh, PA: GPO, 2006), 256.
463. Djilas, *Tito*, 103.
464. Ibid., 286.
465. *Borba*, 10 January 1954.
466. Vladimir Dedijer, "My Two Comrades," *Cross Currents* 4 (1985): 416, 417.
467. AJ, 838, LF, II-1.
468. Djilas, *Tito*, 279.
469. Ćosić, *Piščevi zapisi*, 1:39, 43.
470. V. Glišić, "Šef partije preti Sibirom!," *Večernje novosti*, 4 August 2014.
471. Dedijer, "My Two Comrades," 422.
472. Dedijer, *Novi prilozi*, 3:533.
473. Ibid., 3:534, 535.
474. Djilas, *Tito*, 274; Vlahović, *Strogo pov.*, 71.
475. AS, Dedijer, t. e. 111.
476. AS, Dedijer, t. e. 7.
477. Dedijer, *Novi prilozi*, 3:129, 536.
478. Djilas, "Vlast kao strast," 30.
479. Dedijer, *Novi prilozi*, 3:537, 538; AS, Dedijer, t. e. 165.
480. Ibid., 539; Djilas "Vlast kao strast," 30.
481. Djilas, *Tito*, 109, 135.
482. Ibid., 285.
483. Dabčević-Kučar, *'71: Hrvatski snovi*, 1:371.
484. Clissold, *Djilas*, 254.
485. Ćosić, *Piščevi zapisi*, 1:55; Dedijer, "My Two Comrades," 438.
486. PA, B 11, Band 126.
487. Ćosić, *Piščevi zapisi*, 1:38–40, 50, 54.
488. Bilandžić, *Povijest izbliza*, 26.
489. Djilas, *Tito*, 287–89.
490. PA, B 11, Band 123, 3; Djilas, "Vlast kao strast," 30.
491. AS, Dedijer, t. e. 111.

492. Testimony given to the author by Jernej Vilfan.

493. Maclean, *Josip Broz Tito*, 430, 431.

494. Dedijer, *Novi prilozi*, 3:557–59; AS, Dedijer, t. e. 244; PA, B 12, Band 546.

495. AJ, 837, KPR, II-4-a, K 163; Dejan Djokić, "Britain and Dissent in Tito's Yugoslavia: The Djilas Affair," *European History Quarterly* 36, no. 3 (2006): 347; NARA, CREST, "Possible Reopening in Yugoslavia of the Djilas Case," *Current Intelligence Bulletin*, 27 May 1956.

496. Thomas M. Troy Jr., "The Cultural Cold War: The CIA and the World of Arts and Letters," *Central Intelligence Agency Library*, 14 April 2008, https://www.cia.gov.library/center-for-the-study-of-intelligence; Zdravko Antonić, *Rodoljub Čolaković u svetlu svog dnevnika* (Belgrade: IP Knjiga, 1991), 153.

497. Margaret Thatcher, *The Path to Power* (London: HarperCollins, 1995), 370, 371.

498. Arbeiderbevegelsens Arkiv og Bibliotek, Oslo (AAB), Aake Anker-Ording, Box 57, Jugoslavia 3.

Chapter 4. The Presidential Years

1. Politisches Archiv, Berlin (Political Archive, hereafter PA), B 11, Band 420, 2.

2. Rossiiski gosudarstvennyi arkhiv sotsial'no-politicheskoi istorii (Russian State Archive of Social and Political History, hereafter RGASPI), f. 495, op. 277, ed. hr. 15. 1. 136.

3. Veljko Vlahović, *Strogo pov.: 1955–1958* (Belgrade: Stručna knjiga, 1998), 42, 49.

4. PA, B 11, Band 1195, 1.

5. Andrei B. Edemskii, *Ot konflikta k normalizatsii: Sovetsko-iugoslavskie otnosheniia v 1953–1956 godakh* (Moscow: Nauka, 2008), 456, 457; Vladimir Dedijer, *Novi prilozi za biografiju J. Broza Tita* (unpublished), 4:6.

6. Edemskii, *Ot konflikta k normalizatsii*, 456, 457.

7. Galina Vishnevskaya, *Galina: A Russian Story* (London: Hodder and Stoughton, 1984), 146, 147.

8. National Archives and Records Administration, Washington (hereafter NARA), CREST, *Current Intelligence Bulletin*, 11 June 1955; British Comments on Belgrade Meeting, 11 June 1955.

9. NARA, CREST, Staff Memorandum No. 29-55, "Ambassador Riddleberger's Views on Yugoslavia," 21 June 1955; "Ambassador Riddleberger Believes Conference May Have Widened Gap between Yugoslavia and USSR," *Current Intelligence Bulletin*, 7 June 1955.

10. Edemskii, *Ot konflikta k normalizatsii*, 463; Bogdan Osolnik, *Med svetom in domovino: Spomini 1945–1981* (Maribor: Obzorja, 1992), 192.

11. Arhiv Slovenije, Ljubljana (Archive of Slovenia, hereafter AS), Dedijer, t. e. 111.

12. Jože Pirjevec, "Tito, Nehru and Slovenes," in *Indian Studies: Slovenian Contributions*, ed. Lenart Škof (Calcutta: Sampark, 2008), 17, 18.

13. Arhiv Ministerstva Inostranih Poslova, Belgrade (hereafter AM), PA 1950, 34. 4. 414645.

14. AS, Dedijer, t. e. 3; t. e. 244.

15. AS, Dedijer, t. e. 96; Rinna Elina Kullaa, "From the Tito-Stalin Split to Yugoslavia's Finnish Connection: Neutralism before Non-Alignment, 1948–1958" (PhD diss., University of Maryland, 2008), 15, 129.

16. Dušan Bilandžić, *Povijest izbliza: Memoarski zapisi 1945–2005* (Zagreb: Prometej, 2005), 189.

17. Svetozar Rajak, "In Search of a Life outside the Two Blocks, Yugoslavia's Road to Non-Alignment," in *Great Powers and Small Countries in Cold War 1945–1955: Issue of Ex-Yugoslavia*, ed. Ljubodrag Dimić (Belgrade: University of Belgrade, Archives of Serbia and Montenegro and SD Public, 2005), 17; Milovan Djilas, *Tito: Eine kritische Biographie* (Vienna: Molden, 1980), 106.

18. H. W. Brands, *The Specter of Neutralism: The United States and the Emergence of the Third World, 1947–1960* (New York: Columbia University Press, 1989), 195.

19. AM, PA, 1953, 37, 3, 410445.

20. Rajak, "In Search of a Life," 19.

21. Dobrica Ćosić, *Piščevi zapisi* (Belgrade: Višnjić, 2001), 1:201.

22. PA, B 11, Band 1238, 1.

23. Josip Broz Tito, *Govori i članci* (Zagreb: Naprijed, 1959–1972), 10:28.

24. Rajak, "In Search of a Life," 35; Blažo Mandić, *Tito izbliza* (Belgrade: Vuk Karadžić Jugoslovenska revija, 1981), 112.

25. PA, B 11, Band 1236, 1.

26. Brands, *The Specter of Neutralism*, 196.

27. Dedijer, *Novi prilozi*, 3:555.

28. PA, B. 12, Band 583/7.

29. A. S. Anikeev, *Kak Tito ot Stalina ushel: Iugoslaviia, SSSR i SSHA v nachal'nyi period "kholodnoi voiny" (1945–1957)* (Moscow: Institut Slavianovedeniia RAN, 2002), 266.

30. Edemskii, *Ot konflikta k normalizatsii*, 177–79.

31. Dedijer, *Novi prilozi*, 2:20; NARA, CREST, "Tito's Message to Soviet Party Congress," *Current Intelligence Bulletin*, 21 February 1956.

32. PA, B 12, Band 582; B 12, Band 617.

33. PA, B 12, Band 621; NARA, CREST, "Yugoslav Reaction to Developments in the USSR," *Current Intelligence Weekly Summary*, 29 March 1956.

34. NARA, CREST, "Tito's Message to Soviet Party Congress," *Current Intelligence Bulletin*, 21 February 1956.

35. "NIE 31-2-55, Yugoslavia's International Position, 7 September 1955," in *Yugoslavia: From "National Communism" to National Collapse; US Intelligence Community Estimative Products on Yugoslavia*, ed. Thomas Fingar (Pittsburgh, PA: GPO, 2006), 205; "NIE 31-56, Yugoslavia's International Position, 24, 7 (1955)," ibid., 218.

36. Iurii Girenko, *Stalin-Tito* (Moscow: Izdatel'stvo politicheskoi literatury, 1991), 410, 411.

37. Edemskii, *Ot konflikta k normalizatsii*, 556.

38. Ibid., 546.

39. L. Gibianskij, "Pobuna u sovjetskom bloku 1956. godine, Jugoslavia i Kremelj," in *Jugoslavija v hladni vojni—Yugoslavia in the Cold War*, ed. Jasna Fischer (Ljubljana: Inštitut za novejšo zgodovino, 2004), 229–47; Edemskii, *Ot konflikta k normalizatsii*, 5.

40. PA, B 12, Band 585.

41. NARA, CREST, "Of Immediate Interest," *Current Intelligence Weekly Summary*, 21 June 1956.

42. PA, B 12, Band 638.

43. Veljko Mićunović, *Moskovske godine, 1956–1958* (Zagreb: Liber, 1977), 77, 100.

44. Svetozar Rajak, *Yugoslavia and the Soviet Union in the Early Cold War: Reconciliation, Comradeship, Confrontation, 1953–1957* (New York: Routledge, 2011), 400.

45. Edemskii, *Ot konflikta k normalizatsii*, 572, 573; NARA, CREST, "Brezhnev in Yugoslavia," *Perspectives*, 4 November 1971.

46. Mićunović, *Moskovske godine*, 93.

47. Ibid.

48. "NIE 31-56," 220.

49. PA, B 12, Band 587.

50. Dragan Bogetić, *Nova strategija spoljne politike Jugoslavije 1950–1961* (Belgrade: Institut za savremenu istoriju, 2006), 102, 103.

51. NARA, CREST, "Tito Comments on His Moscow Visit," *Current Intelligence Bulletin*, 1 July 1956.

52. Anikeev, *Kak Tito ot Stalina ushel*, 297.

53. PA, B 12, Band 618.

54. Vlahović, *Strogo pov.*, 165; Edemskii, *Ot konflikta k normalizatsii*, 575, 576.

55. Jože Smole, *Pripoved komunista novinarja 1945–1980* (Ljubljana: ČZP Enotnost, 1994), 96; AS, Dedijer, t. e. 298.

56. Rajak, *Yugoslavia and the Soviet Union*, 400; NARA, CREST, "Background and Appreciation of the Yalta Talks," *Current Intelligence Bulletin*, October 1956.

57. Mićunović, *Moskovske godine*, 130; NARA, CREST, "Yugoslav-Soviet Differences Unchanged by Tito-Khrushchev Talks," *Current Intelligence Bulletin*, 13 October 1956.

58. AS, Dedijer, t. e., 126.

59. Vlahović, *Strogo pov.*, 93.

60. Anikeev, *Kak Tito ot Stalina ushel*, 274; NARA, CIA, "Status and Prospects of International Communism," 16 September 1957.

61. Miodrag Marović, *Sumrak staljinizma* (Belgrade: Sloboda, 1978), 1:118, 119.

62. Vladimir Dedijer, *Dokumenti 1948* (Belgrade: Rad, 1979), 3:646, 647; NARA, CREST, "Tito Urges Hungarians to Support Nagy," *Current Intelligence Bulletin*, 31 October 1966.

63. Rajak, *Yugoslavia and the Soviet Union*, 173.

64. Mićunović, *Moskovske godine*, 210–16.

65. Jasper Ridley, *Tito: A Biography* (London: Constable, 1994), 338.

66. Mićunović, *Moskovske godine*, 159.

67. AS, Dedijer, t. e. 298.

68. PA, B 12, Band 582; B 12, Band 618.

69. Mićunović, *Moskovske godine*, 183–93.

70. Ridley, *Tito*, 126.

71. Rajak, *Yugoslavia and the Soviet Union*, 181.

72. Stephen Clissold, *Yugoslavia and the Soviet Union, 1939–1973: A Documentary Survey* (New York: Oxford University Press, 1975), 264.

73. Dedijer, *Novi prilozi*, 4:52.

74. NARA, CREST, "Moscow-Belgrade Propaganda Fight Developed," *Current Intelligence Bulletin*, 22 November 1956; *Pravda* Editorial Justifies Position against Tito, 24 November 1956.

75. Ćosić, *Piščevi zapisi*, 1:121; Anikeev, *Kak Tito ot Stalina ushel*, 297.

76. AS, Dedijer, t. e. 126.

77. Marović, *Sumrak staljinizma*, 1:128.

78. NARA, CREST, "Yugoslav Arrest of Djilas," *Current Intelligence Bulletin*, 21 November 1956; "*Pravda* Answers Yugoslav Analysis on Hungary," 19 December 1956.

79. Ćosić, *Piščevi zapisi*, 1:122, 123.

80. Marović, *Sumrak staljinizma*, 1:131.

81. "NIE 31-57, Yugoslavia's Policies and Prospects, 11 June 1957," in *Yugoslavia: From "National Communism" to National Collapse; US Intelligence Community Estimative Products on Yugoslavia*, ed. Thomas Fingar (Pittsburgh, PA: GPO, 2006), 231.

82. Anton Stipanič, *Od pastirja do direktorja* (Ankaran: Samozal., 2012), 59.

83. "NIE 31-57," 231, 232; NARA, CREST, "Yugoslav Defense Minister to Visit Moscow," *Current Intelligence Bulletin*, 25 May 1957; "Patterns and Perspectives, Soviet-Yugoslav Relations," *Current Intelligence Weekly Summary*, 10 October 1957.

84. The National Archives, London (hereafter TNA), FO 975/149/PR 117/86/G.

85. Girenko, *Stalin-Tito*, 302, 303.

86. Vlahović, *Strogo pov.*, 135, 149.

87. "SNIE 31/1-57, Yugoslavia's International Position, 19 November 1957," in *Yugoslavia: From "National Communism" to National Collapse; US Intelligence Community Estimative Products on Yugoslavia*, ed. Thomas Fingar (Pittsburgh, PA: GPO, 2006), 243.

88. Ibid.

89. PA, B 12, Band 621.

90. PA, B 12, Band 97.

91. Bundesarchiv, Berlin (hereafter BA), DY 30/IV 2/20/128; NY 4090/480.

92. NARA, CREST, "Tito May Rise German Confederation Scheme on Moscow," *Current Intelligence Bulletin*, 5 June 1956; "Yugoslavia Disclaim Any Immediate Intention to Recognize East Germany," 8 July 1956; Dušan Nečak, *Hallsteinova doktrina in Jugoslavija: Tito med Zvezno republiko Nemčijo in Nemško demokratično republiko* (Ljubljana: Znanstveni inštitut Filozofske fakultete, 2002).

93. Gelvan Library, George Washington University (hereafter GWU), Memorandum of Conversation, Views of West German Foreign Office Official on Reunification, 762.00/10-2758.

94. NARA, CREST, CIA, "Tito Encourages UAR and India to Oppose Bloc," *Current Intelligence Weekly Summary*, 7 May 1959; Jože Pirjevec and Jure Ramšak, eds., *Od Mašuna do New Yorka: 20. stoletje skozi pričevanja štirih slovenskih diplomatov* (Koper: Univerzitetna založba Annales, 2014), 173. http://www.zrs.upr.si/monografije/single/od-masuna-do-new-yorka-20-stoletje-skozi-pricevanja-stirih-slovenskih-diplomatov-1885.

95. Anikeev, *Kak Tito ot Stalina ushel*, 280, 281, 288–91; GWU, NSC, U.S. Policy toward Yugoslavia, 28 February 1958.

96. Dragan Bogetić, *Nova strategija spoljne politike Jugoslavije* (Belgrade: Institut za suvremenu istoriju, 2006), 111.

97. Vlahović, *Strogo pov.*, 146, 176.

98. Dedijer, *Novi prilozi*, 3:443, 583; Ćosić, *Piščevi zapisi*, 1:138, 139; Vladimir Naumov et al., eds., *Georgii Zhukov: Stenogramma oktiabr'skogo plenuma TsK, KPSS i drugie dokumenty* (Moscow: Mezhdunarodnyi fond Demokratiia, 2001), 175, 634, 635.

99. "SNIE 31/1-57," 243.

100. PA, B 12, Band 621.

101. Edvard Kardelj, *Spomini: Boj za priznanje in neodvisnost nove Jugoslavije, 1944–1957* (Belgrade: Državna založba Slovenije, 1980), 149.

102. Dedijer, *Novi prilozi*, 3:34.

103. Vlahović, *Strogo pov.*, 165.

104. BA, DY IV 2/20/127; PA 12, Band 821.

105. Vlahović, *Strogo pov.*, 166, 197.
106. BA, DY IV 2/20/127, PA, B 12, Band 621.
107. Bilandžić, *Povijest izbliza*, 222.
108. Ćosić, *Piščevi zapisi*, 1:64.
109. Svetozar Vukmanović-Tempo, *Revolucija teče dalje: Memoari* (Ljubljana: Mladinska knjiga, 1972), 2:276; AS, Dedijer, t. e. 298.
110. Mateja Režek, "Odmev madžarske vstaje leta 1956 v Sloveniji in Jugoslaviji," *Prispevki za novejšo zgodovino* 46, no. 2 (2006): 102, 103.
111. AS, Dedijer, t. e. 7.
112. AS, Dedijer, t. e. 188.
113. Dušan Bilandžić, *Hrvatska moderna povijest* (Zagreb: Golden Marketing, 1999), 403.
114. Ćosić, *Piščevi zapisi*, 1:56.
115. PA, B 12, Band 542, 2.
116. Ćosić, *Piščevi zapisi*, 1:143.
117. Dedijer, *Novi prilozi*, 3:618.
118. Bilandžić, *Povijest izbliza*, 81.
119. Testimony by Anton Vratuša.
120. Mićunović, *Moskovske godine*, 431.
121. AS, Dedijer, t. e. 96; Dedijer, *Novi prilozi*, 4:65.
122. PA, B 12, Band 542, 2.
123. NARA, CREST, "Yugoslav-Soviet Rift Widens," *Central Intelligence Bulletin*, 24 April 1958.
124. Smole, *Pripoved komunista novinarja*, 109.
125. PA, B 12, Band 542.
126. PA, B 12, Band 542, 2.
127. PA, B 12, Band 542.
128. AS, Dedijer, t. e. 274.
129. Vlahović, *Strogo pov.*, 71.
130. PA, B 12, Band 621.
131. PA, B 12, Band 226; NARA, CREST, "Daily Brief: The Communist Bloc," *Central Intelligence Bulletin*, 30 April 1958; "Yugoslavs Branded Anti-Marxist-Leninist," *Central Intelligence Weekly Summary*, 8 May 1958; 21 August 1958.
132. Ridley, *Tito*, 349.
133. Ćosić, *Piščevi zapisi*, 1:148, 149; NARA, CREST, "Execution of Nagy," *Intelligence Bulletin*, 17 June 1958.
134. Sergei N. Khrushchev, *Rozhdenie sverkhderzhavy* (Moscow: Vremia, 2000), 180.
135. PA, B 12, Band 336.
136. BA, DY 30/IV 2/20/131.
137. BA, DY 30/1/IV 2/201128.
138. NARA, CREST, "Tito May Delegate Some of His Responsibilities," *Central Intelligence Weekly Summary*, 26 December 1957; National Security Council Briefing, Background Piece on Yugoslavia, 1 April 1958.
139. PA, B 12, Band 547; TNA, FO 371/95496/ RY 1076/1 G.
140. PA, B 12, Band 547.
141. PA, B 12, Band 620; "NIE 15-61, Outlook for Yugoslavia, 23 May 1961," in *Yugoslavia: From "National Communism" to National Collapse; US Intelligence Community*

Estimative Products on Yugoslavia, ed. Thomas Fingar (Pittsburgh, PA: GPO, 2006), 262; NARA, CREST, "Soviet-Yugoslav Conflict May Be Easing," *Central Intelligence Bulletin*, 15 October 1958.

142. PA, B 12, Band 336.

143. AS, Dedijer, t. e. 111; Dedijer, *Novi prilozi*, 3:72.

144. Ibid., 3:556; Mira Šuvar, *Vladimir Velebit: Svjedok istorije* (Zagreb: Razlog, 2001), 201.

145. Zhihua Shen and Yafend Xia, "Hidden Currents during the Honeymoon: Mao, Khrushchev, and the 1957 Conference," *Journal of Cold War Studies* 11, no. 4 (2009): 74–117.

146. Kardelj, *Spomini*, 154.

147. Fondazione Basaglia, Venezia, Fondo Dedijer, Kinezi, 1956, 1957.

148. PA, B 12, Band 336; B 12, Band 556.

149. PA, B 12, Band 618.

150. BA, DY 30/1/IV 2/20/131; NARA, CREST, "Yugoslav-Bloc Dispute," *Central Intelligence Bulletin*, 27 June 1958.

151. Kardelj, *Spomini*, 156.

152. NARA, CREST, CIA, Staff Memorandum, "Yugoslavia and the Non-U Countries," 1 June 1960.

153. BA, NY 4090/480; NARA, CREST, "China and Albania Reaffirm Solidarity of Ideological Views," *Central Intelligence Bulletin*, 6 October 1969; "Daily Brief: Sino-Soviet Dispute," 8 October 1960.

154. BA, DY, 30/1/IV 2/20/128; "NIE, Authority and Control in the Communist Movement, 8 August 1961," in *Yugoslavia: From "National Communism" to National Collapse; US Intelligence Community Estimative Products on Yugoslavia*, ed. Thomas Fingar (Pittsburgh, PA: GPO, 2006), 278.

155. BA, DY 30/IV 2/20, 313.

156. NARA, CREST, "Communist Revisionism and Dissidence (2)," 28 June 1960, 17.

157. Ibid.

158. Smole, *Pripoved komunista novinarja*, 110; AS, Dedijer, t. e. 111.

159. NARA, CREST, "Communist Revisionism and Dissidence (2)," 26 June 1960, 21.

160. NARA, CREST, "Daily Brief: The Communist Bloc," *Central Intelligence Bulletin*, 30 September 1960; ibid., "China and Albania Reaffirm Solidarity of Ideological Views," 8 October 1960.

161. NARA, CREST, "Khrushchev Tito Meeting Will Affront Chinese," 30 September 1960.

162. TNA, FO 975/149/PR 117/86/G.

163. BA, DY 30/IV 2/20/131.

164. NARA, CREST, "Yugoslav Role in Detente," *Bi-Weekly Propaganda Guidance*, 15 February 1980.

165. PA, B 12, Band 605.

166. PA, B 12, Band 336; B 12, Band 638.

167. Ćosić, *Piščevi zapisi*, 1:155.

168. PA, B 12, Band 618; B. 12, Band 620; NARA, CREST, "Tito's Travels and the Bloc's Reaction," *Current Intelligence Weekly Summary*, 8 January 1959; "Yugoslavia's International Position," 8 March 1959.

169. Miladin Adamović, *Brozovi strahovi: Kako je čuvan Tito i pokušaji atentata* (Belgrade: M. Adamović, 2004), 235, 241; Marijan F. Kranjc, *Zarote in atentati na Tita*

(Grosuplje: Graphis Trade, 2004), 289; NARA, CIA, "The Communist Bloc," *Central Intelligence Bulletin*, 20 January 1958.

170. BA, Bestand Ulbricht, Walter, NI 182/1235.

171. BA, DY 30/IV 2/20/239; "NIE 15-61," 253.

172. BA, DY 30/IV 2/20/132.

173. PA, B 12, Band 604 A.

174. PA, B 12, Band 547.

175. Bilandžić, *Hrvatska moderna povijest*, 406, 407.

176. BA, DY 30/IV 2/20/132.

177. Savka Dabčević-Kučar, *'71: Hrvatski snovi i stvarnost* (Zagreb: Interpublic, 1997), 2:780, 181, 877.

178. NARA, CREST, "Yugoslavia on Eve of Seventh Party Congress," *Current Intelligence Weekly Summary*, 10 January 1958.

179. PA, B 12, Band 547.

180. Dabčević-Kučar, *'71: Hrvatski snovi*, 2:603.

181. PA, B 12, Band 547.

182. PA, B 12, Band 547.

183. "Memo: The Yugoslav Succession Problem, 10 March 1969," in *Yugoslavia: From "National Communism" to National Collapse; US Intelligence Community Estimative Products on Yugoslavia*, ed. Thomas Fingar (Pittsburgh, PA: GPO, 2006), 330.

184. Ibid.; "NIE 15-61," 258.

185. PA, B 12, Band 604 A.

186. Ibid.

187. BA, Bestand Ulbricht, Walter, NI 182/1235; NARA, CREST, CIA, Staff Memorandum No. 29-60, "Yugoslavia and the Non-U Countries," 1960.

188. Bilandžić, *Hrvatska moderna povijest*, 407.

189. TNA, FO 371/163932/C Y 1102/5; PA, B 12, Band 643; Aleksander Lorenčič, "Gospodarske razmere v Jugoslaviji v obdobju 1968–1988: Na poti v razpad," in *Slovenija-Jugoslavija: Krize in reforme 1968/1988*, ed. Zdenko Čepič (Ljubljana: Inštitut za novejšo zgodovino, 2010), 261.

190. BA, IV A 2/20/239.

191. PA, B 12, Band 605.

192. PA, B 12, Band 604 A.

193. Ćosić, *Piščevi zapisi*, 1:170.

194. PA, B 12, Band 605.

195. TNA, FO 371/163932/CY 1102/13.

196. Bilandžić, *Povijest izbliza*, 32, 46, 188.

197. AS, Dedijer, t. e. 215.

198. Bilandžić, *Hrvatska moderna povijest*, 419.

199. Dabčević-Kučar, *'71: Hrvatski snovi*, 2:815.

200. NARA, CREST, CIA, Staff Memorandum No. 29, 60, "Yugoslavia and the Non-U Countries," 1 June 1960.

201. BA, DY 30/IV 2/29, 132.

202. PA, B 12, Band 547.

203. Smole, *Pripoved komunista novinarja*, 117–19.

204. Archiv ministerstva zahraničních věcí, Prague (hereafter AMZV), Zprávy ZÚ, Bělehrad 1961–1962, 020239.

205. Ćosić, *Piščevi zapisi*, 1:169, 175, 192.
206. Ibid., 175, 203.
207. PA, B 12, Band 640.
208. Ćosić, *Piščevi zapisi*, 1:210.
209. Zdravko Antonić, *Rodoljub Čolaković u svetlu svog dnevnika* (Belgrade: IP Knjiga, 1991), 30.
210. Aleksandar Ranković, *Dnevničke zabeleške* (Belgrade: Jugoslovenska knjiga, 2001), 167.
211. AS, Dedijer, t. e. 68; t. e. 215; t. e. 244.
212. PA, B 12, Band 640.
213. Ranković, *Dnevničke zabeleške*, 167; AS, Dedijer, t. e. 197; t. e. 264.
214. Aleksandar Matunović, *Titova sovladarica* (Ljubljana: Mladinska knjiga, 2008), 107; Dedijer, *Novi prilozi*, 2:45, 55; Ćosić, *Piščevi zapisi*, 1:213, 214.
215. Ćosić, *Piščevi zapisi*, 1:213, 214.
216. Ranković, *Dnevničke zabeleške*, 166, 167; AS, Dedijer, t. e. 197; t. e. 264.
217. Todor Kuljić, *Tito: Sociološkoistorijska studija* (Zrenjanin: Gradska narodna biblioteka Žarko Zrenjanin, 2005), 81.
218. AMZV, Zprávy ZÚ, Bělehrad 1961–1964, 01253/61.
219. Ridley, *Tito*, 358.
220. NARA, CREST, CIA, Memorandum for the Director, "Yugoslavia's Foreign Policy Position," 5 October 1961.
221. Mladin Milošević, V. P. Tarasov, and N. G. Tomilina, *Vstrechi i peregovory na vysshem urovne rukovoditel'ei SSSR i Iugoslavii v 1946–1980 gg.*, vol. 1, *1946–1964* (Moscow: Mezhdunarodnyi fond Demokratiia, 2014), 328, 329.
222. AS, Dedijer, t. e. 298.
223. NARA, CREST, CIA, Memorandum for the Director, "Yugoslavia's Foreign Policy Position," 5 October 1961.
224. John F. Kennedy Library, Boston (hereafter JFK), National Security Files Box 252A; BA, Bestand Ulbricht, Walter, NL 181/1235.
225. PA, 702/84/04.
226. AS, Dedijer, t. e. 68; t. e. 215.
227. Ranković, *Dnevničke zabeleške*, 289.
228. BA, Bestand Ulbricht, Walter, NL 182/1235.
229. Arbeiderbevegelsens Arkiv og Bibliotek, Oslo (hereafter AAB), Arkiv Stoltenberg, Thorvald, "The Outlook for Yugoslavia 1960–1974," DA-L0014; Antonić, *Rodoljub Čolaković*, 464.
230. NARA, CREST, CIA, Memorandum for the Director: "Yugoslavia's Foreign Policy Position," 5 October 1961.
231. Ćosić, *Piščevi zapisi*, 1:183, 191.
232. Dedijer, *Novi prilozi*, 3:316.
233. Arhiv Jugoslavije, Belgrade (Archive of Yugoslavia, hereafter AJ), 838, LF II-1/78, K 4.
234. AS, t. e. 111; t. e. 298.
235. AS, Dedijer, t. e. 143.
236. Dedijer, *Novi prilozi*, 3:549; Kardelj, *Spomini*, 120–23.
237. Ibid., 147.
238. AS, Dedijer, t. e. 298.

239. Aleksandar Nenadović, *Razgovori s Kočom* (Zagreb: Globus, 1989), 21; PA, B 12, N and 587; B 12, Band 621.

240. Ćosić, *Piščevi zapisi*, 1:291; AS, Dedijer, t. e. 271.

241. Ćosić, *Piščevi zapisi*, 1:291.

242. Ranković, *Dnevničke zabeleške*, 125, 126.

243. NARA, CREST, "Belgrade May Adopt Attitude of Soviet Bloc," *Current Intelligence Bulletin*, 30 September 1956; *Current Intelligence Weekly Summary*, *Yugoslav-Soviet Relations* 19, no. 9 (1957); "SNIE 31/1-57," 245.

244. AS, Dedijer, t. e. 68.

245. AJ, KPR, IV-5-b, K 49; AS, Dedijer, t. e. 68.

246. Ćosić, *Piščevi zapisi*, 1:123.

247. Ibid., 1:291.

248. Latinka Perović, "Kako su se izražavali različiti politički interesi u Jugoslaviji: Polemika izmedju Dobrice Ćosića i Dušana Pirjevca 1961/1962. godine," in *Dominantna i neželjena elita: Beleške o intelektualnoj i političkoj eliti u Srbiji (XX–XXI vek)* (Belgrade: Dan Graf, 2015), 69–78; Antonić, *Rodoljub Čolaković*, 37.

249. Jože Prinčič, "Vlada Staneta Kavčiča in njena gospodarska politika," in *Slovenija-Jugoslavija: Krize in reforme 1968/1988*, ed. Zdenko Čepič (Ljubljana: Inštitut za novejšo zgodovino, 2010), 122.

250. AS, Dedijer, t. e. 68; t. e. 215; t. e. 264; t. e. 271, t. e. 298.

251. PA, B 12, Band 440.

252. AS, Dedijer, t. e. 271; Kranjc, *Zarote in atentati*, 304.

253. Bilandžić, *Povijest izbliza*, 105; AS, Dedijer, t. e. 68; t. e. 215.

254. *Delo*, 23 August 1961; AS, Dedijer, t. e. 298.

255. AS, Dedijer, t. e. 261.

256. AS, Dedijer, t. e. 283.

257. Neven Borak, "Jugoslavija med integracijo in dezintegracijo," in *Slovenija-Jugoslavija: Krize in reforme 1968/1988*, ed. Zdenko Čepič (Ljubljana: Inštitut za novejšo zgodovino, 2010), 30.

258. Ćosić, *Piščevi zapisi*, 1:291.

259. Bilandžić, *Hrvatska moderna povijest*, 417.

260. Bože Repe, "Utrinki iz bližnjega leta 1962," *Teorija in praksa* 26, nos. 11–12 (1989): 1505, 1506.

261. Bilandžić, *Hrvatska moderna povijest*, 423.

262. Interview with Miko Tripalo, *Vjesnik u Srijedu*, 7 September 1966; Zdenko Čepič, "Jugoslovanske reforme v šestdesetih letih," in *Slovenija-Jugoslavija: Krize in reforme 1968/1988* (Ljubljana: Inštitut za novejšo zgodovino, 2010), 10.

263. AS, Dedijer, t. e. 298.

264. Pero Simić, *Tito: Skrivnost stoletja* (Ljubljana: Orbis, 2009), 333.

265. France Perovšek, *Moja resnica: Spominski utrinki iz delovanja po letu 1945 na Primorskem in v Ljubljani* (Ljubljana: Društvo Piscev zgodovine NOB Slovenija, 1995), 283–88.

266. Ćosić, *Piščevi zapisi*, 1:292.

267. NARA, Pol 15–1 Yugo, Zagreb, 18 March 1964.

268. Marjan Drnovšek et al., *Slovenska kronika XX. stoletja* (Ljubljana: Nova revija, 1995–96), 2:261.

269. Bilandžić, *Hrvatska moderna povijest*, 431.

270. AS, Dedijer, t. e. 3; t. e. 68.

271. Vjenceslav Cenčić, *Titova poslednja ispovijest* (Belgrade: Orfelin, 2001), 39, 48, 154, 170, 178, 297.
272. Ranković, *Dnevničke zabeleške*, 124, 125.
273. TNA, FO 371/163932/C Y 1102.
274. BA, DY 30J IV 2/2 A-1.277 Bd. 2.
275. Niko Kavčič, *Pot v osamosvojitev* (Ljubljana: Samozaložba, 1996), 269.
276. AS, Dedijer, t. e. 197.
277. Interview with Koča Popović, *Danas*, 7 February 1989, 26.
278. JFK, National Security Files, Box 210 A.
279. AS, Dedijer, t. e. 5.
280. AS, Dedijer, t. e. 261; t. e. 284; t. e. 298.
281. AS, Dedijer, t. e. 96; t. e. 143; t. e. 215.
282. Slobodan Stanković, "Tito Will Have to Make His Position Clear," *Open Society Archives*, 11 February 1963, http://catalog.osaarchivum.org/catalog/osa:46654231-b7be-43bc-931f-83b6e54d14be.
283. Ibid.; Slobodan Stanković, "Favorable Yugoslav Reaction to Pravda Article," *Open Society Archives*, 14 February 1963, http://catalog.osaarchivum.org/catalog/osa:2c33ef5a-78b9-4802-b2d9-d2bf4630c0f8.
284. Stanković, "Favorable Yugoslav"; Stanković, "Tito."
285. Ranković, *Dnevničke zabeleške*, 91.
286. Dejan Jović, *Yugoslavia: A State That Withered Away* (West Lafayette, IN: Purdue University Press, 2009), 109.
287. AS, Dedijer, t. e. 5.
288. Ćosić, *Piščevi zapisi*, 1:217.
289. AS, Dedijer, t. e. 187; t. e. 274.
290. "Memo for the Director, Yugoslavia and the Soviet Bloc, 18 July 1983," in *Yugoslavia: From "National Communism" to National Collapse; US Intelligence Community Estimative Products on Yugoslavia*, ed. Thomas Fingar (Pittsburgh, PA: GPO, 2006), 292.
291. Matunović, *Titova sovladarica*, 161.
292. Dedijer, *Novi prilozi*, 3:106; Kranjc, *Zarote in atentati*, 255, 256, 316.
293. Ranković, *Dnevničke zabeleške*, 251; Z. Skušek Močnik, Interview with Vojin Lukić, *Mladina*, 17 April 1987.
294. "Memo for the Director," 292.
295. Vladimir Bakarić, "Močneje se moramo zavzeti za socialistična načela," *Delo*, 22 September 1964.
296. NARA, Pol 15 Yugo, Belgrade, 5 February 1964.
297. AS, Dedijer, t. e. 233.
298. Nacionalna i Sveučilišna Knjižnica, Zagreb (National and University Library, hereafter NSK), Arhiv Bakarić, Kutija 24.
299. Ćosić, *Piščevi zapisi*, 1:287.
300. Ibid., 292–94.
301. Čepič, "Jugoslovanske reforme," 56.
302. NARA, Pol 12-3, Belgrade, 8 December 1964.
303. Ćosić, *Piščevi zapisi*, 1:288.
304. Branko Petranović and Momčilo Zečević, eds., *Jugoslavija 1918–1988: Tematska zbirka dokumenata* (Belgrade: Rad, 1988), 928–33.
305. Ćosić, *Piščevi zapisi*, 1:290.
306. BA, DY 30/IV A 2/201158; BA, IV A 2/20/237.

307. TNA, 371/182839/NU 1015/1; NU 15/13.
308. NARA, Pol 12, Yugo, Belgrade, 8 January 1965.
309. BA, IV A 2/20/240.
310. Bilandžić, *Povijest izbliza*, 56.
311. PA, Zwischenarchiv 651; NARA, CREST, Intelligence Memorandum, "Yugoslavia: Power to the Center," 9 February 1973.
312. Money in communist countries had a fixed value that bore no connection to what its actual value would be on the free market in the West. The Soviets, for instance, never recognized the true international value of the ruble, keeping it exclusively and fixedly within the Soviet context.
313. An official authorization appended to a passport, permitting entry into and travel within a particular country or region.
314. TNA, FO 371/182857/NU 1102/22.
315. TNA, FO 371/182866/NU 113145/6.
316. BA, IV A 2/20/239.
317. Bilandžić, *Hrvatska moderna povijest*, 481.
318. PA, MFA, A 5433, 3.
319. Ibid.
320. AS, Dedijer, t. e. 68; t. e. 215.
321. Ranković, *Dnevničke zabeleške*, 57, 62.
322. AS, Dedijer, t. e. 3.
323. Ćosić, *Piščevi zapisi*, 1:298.
324. Borislav Mihajlović Mihiz, *Autobiografija—o drugima* (Belgrade: Evro-Giunti, 2008), 550.
325. Ćosić, *Piščevi zapisi*, 1:298; Kranjc, *Zarote in atentati*, 257; AS, Dedijer, t. e. 298.
326. AS, Dedijer, t. e. 3.
327. NARA, Pol 12 Yugo, Zagreb, 21 September 1965.
328. Božo Repe, "Oris obravnave nacionalne problematike in nacionalnih programov v Sloveniji od konca druge svetovne vojne do začetka osemdesetih let," *Borec* 44, nos. 3–5 (1992): 290, 291.
329. Bilandžić, *Hrvatska moderna povijest*, 486.
330. NARA, W 1 Yugo, XR Pol 15-1, Washington, 4 November 1965.
331. AS, Dedijer, t. e. 7.
332. NARA, Pol 15-1 Yugo, Belgrade, 27 July 1966.
333. TNA, FO 371/182839/NU 1015/18.
334. NARA, Pol 12, Yugo, Belgrade, 7 July 1966.
335. NARA, Pol 13-8 Yugo, Belgrade, 16 December 1966; Bilandžić, *Povijest izbliza*, 217.
336. AS, Dedijer, t. e. 111.
337. NARA, Pol 12-3 Yugo, Belgrade, 3 July 1966; Pol 12 Yugo, Zagreb, 13 September 1966.
338. PA, MFA, A 5434, 2; NARA, Pol 12 Yugo, 7 July 1966.
339. PA, MFA, A 5434, 3.
340. NARA, Pol 23 Yugo, Belgrade, 6 June 1964.
341. NARA, Pol 12 Yugo, Zagreb, 9 March 1966.
342. Ladislava Becele Ranković, *Življenje z Leko: Spomini Slovenske partizanke* (Grosuplje: Grafis Trade, 2002), 176.

343. Ranković, *Dnevničke zabeleške*, 151.
344. NARA, CREST, "Special Report, Yugoslavia: The Fall of Ranković," *Current Intelligence Weekly*, 5 August 1966; Bilandžić, *Povijest izbliza*, 202.
345. Ćosić, *Piščevi zapisi*, 1:293.
346. Josip Broz Tito, *Zbrana dela* (Ljubljana: Komunist, Borec, 1979), 12:186, 187.
347. Cenčić, *Titova poslednja ispovijest*, 191, 270.
348. Dabčević-Kučar, *'71: Hrvatski snovi*, 1:475.
349. Becele Ranković, *Življenje z Leko*, 174, 175, 277.
350. Franc Šetinc, *Zbogom, Jugoslavija* (Ljubljana: DZS, 1993), 185.
351. NARA, Pol 15-2 Yugo, Zagreb, 14 May 1966.
352. NARA, Pol 15 Yugo, Belgrade, 26 January 1966; AMZV, Zprávy ZÚ, Bělehrad 1966–1967, 825.328/SM.
353. NARA, Pol 12, Yugo, Belgrade, 26 April 1966.
354. NARA, Pol 12-3 Yugo, Belgrade, 4 October 1966.
355. NARA, Pol 12-6 Yugo, Belgrade, 3 August 1966; Pol 15-1 Yugo, 28 January 1966; AS, Dedijer, t. e. 215.
356. Nenad Prokić, "Jugoslovenski Tezej," *Danas*, 23 August 2013.
357. Ranković, *Dnevničke zabeleške*, 36, 49, 50, 268, 275.
358. Becele Ranković, *Življenje z Leko*, 155, 156, 181.
359. Bilandžić, *Hrvatska moderna povijest*, 491.
360. Ranković, *Dnevničke zabeleške*, 287.
361. Ibid., 252–55.
362. Becele Ranković, *Življenje z Leko*, 156.
363. AS, Dedijer, t. e. 233.
364. Ibid.
365. Nenadović, *Razgovori s Kočom*, 139.
366. Ranković, *Dnevničke zabeleške*, 41, 152, 153.
367. Ćosić, *Piščevi zapisi*, 1:293.
368. AS, Dedijer, t. e. 264.
369. Ranković, *Dnevničke zabeleške*, 52, 259; Becele Ranković, *Življenje z Leko*, 166.
370. NARA, Pol 12-6 Yugo, Belgrade, 12 July 1966.
371. Marko Vrhunec, *Šest let s Titom (1967–1973)* (Ljubljana: LaserPrint, 2001), 16; AS Dedijer, t. e. 3.
372. AJ, 838, LF, II-1/78.
373. AS, Dedijer, t. e. 5.
374. Becele Ranković, *Življenje z Leko*, 195.
375. Ranković, *Dnevničke zabeleške*, 262.
376. Nenadović, *Razgovori s Kočom*, 146.
377. Ranković, *Dnevničke zabeleške*, 89, 90.
378. NARA, Pol 12-3 Yugo, Belgrade 3 July 1966; Pol 15-1 Yugo, Belgrade, 13 September 1966; AS, Dedijer, t. e. 68.
379. Cenčić, *Titova poslednja ispovijest*, 58.
380. AS, Dedijer, t. e., 58.
381. NARA, Pol 12 Yugo, Zagreb, 1 July 1966.
382. Dabčević-Kučar, *'71: Hrvatski snovi*, 1:83.
383. Latinka Perović, "Na tragu srpske liberalne tradicije," in *Srpska krhka vertikala*, ed. Marko Nikezić (Belgrade: Helsinški odbor za ljudska prava u Srbiji, 2003), 17.
384. Ćosić, *Piščevi zapisi*, 1:248–54, 256, 262; L. Perović, "Kako su se izražavali," 55.

385. PA, MFA, A-5435, 1.

386. Ćosić, *Piščevi zapisi*, 1:270.

387. NARA, Pol 12 Yugo, Zagreb, 17 October 1966; Pol 12 Yugo, Belgrade, 6 October 1966.

388. NARA, Pol 12-3, Yugo, Zagreb, 27 September 1966; Zdenko Roter, *Padle maske: Od partizanskih sanj do novih dni* (Ljubljana: Sever & Sever, 2013), 248, 249.

389. Z. Skušek Močnik, Interview with Vojin Lukić, *Mladina*, 17 April 1987, 24.

390. Roter, *Padle maske*, 252.

391. AJ 838, LF/1&78, K. 4; Ćosić, *Piščevi zapisi*, 1:382: AS, Dedijer, t. e. 197; Antonić, *Rodoljub Čolaković*, 254.

392. NARA, Pol 23-3 Yugo, Belgrade, 20 July 1966.

393. Dabčević-Kučar, *'71: Hrvatski snovi*, 1:404, 405.

394. NARA, Pol 14 Yugo, Belgrade, 7 June 1966; Pol 23-3 Yugo, Belgrade, 18 July 1966.

395. NARA, Pol 12-3 Yugo, Belgrade, 3 October 1966.

396. NARA, Pol 12 Yugo, Belgrade, 8 September 1966; L. Perović, "Kako su se izražavali," 142.

397. NARA, Pol 12-3 Yugo, Belgrade, 6 October 1966, 8 October 1966; BA, Bestand Ulbricht, Walter, NL 182/1237.

398. Nenadović, *Razgovori s Kočom*, 217.

399. Ranković, *Dnevničke zabeleške*, 181, 265.

400. NARA, Pol 29 Yugo, Belgrade, 12 December 1968.

401. Ranković, *Dnevničke zabeleške*, 185.

402. Ćosić, *Piščevi zapisi*, 2:234, 235.

403. Dabčević-Kučar, *'71: Hrvatski snovi*, 2:870.

404. AS, Dedijer, t. e. 111; Nenadović, *Razgovori s Kočom*, 125.

405. Bilandžić, *Povijest izbliza*, 296; Interview with K. Popović, *Danas*, 7 February 1989, 25.

406. Ćosić, *Piščevi zapisi*, 1:311.

407. Bilandžić, *Hrvatska moderna povijest*, 513.

408. BA, Bestand Ulbricht, Walter, NL 182/1238.

409. Ibid.

410. Ibid.

411. Bilandžić, *Povijest izbliza*, 53, 54.

412. Matunović, *Titova sovladarica*, 122.

413. Bilandžić, *Povijest izbliza*, 66; AS, Dedijer, t. e. 233.

414. NARA, Pol 12 Yugo, 7 July 1966; Belgrade, 7 July 1966.

415. "NIE 15-67, The Yugoslav Experiment, 13 April 1967," in *Yugoslavia: From "National Communism" to National Collapse; US Intelligence Community Estimative Products on Yugoslavia*, ed. Thomas Fingar (Pittsburgh, PA: GPO, 2006), 308.

416. Bilandžić, *Povijest izbliza*, 125.

417. AS, Dedijer, t. e. 188.

418. Ibid.

419. NARA, Pol 12-3 Yugo, Zagreb, 27 September 1966.

420. Dabčević-Kučar, *'71: Hrvatski snovi*, 1:57, 58.

421. Ibid., 1:71.

422. L. Perović, "Na tragu srpske liberalne tradicije," 30–32.

423. NARA, CREST, CIA, "Yugoslavia: An Intelligence Appraisal," 27 July 1971.

424. Peter Vodopivec, "Od poskusov demokratizacije (1968–1972) do agonije in karastrofe (1988–1991)," in *Slovenija-Jugoslavija: Krize in reforme 1968/1988*, ed. Zdenko Čepič (Ljubljana: Inštitut za novejšo zgodovino, 2010), 14; Bože Repe, "Slovenski 'liberalizem' šestdesetih let in vloga Staneta Kavčiča," in *Slovenija-Jugoslavija: Krize in reforme 1968/1988*, ed. Zdenko Čepič (Ljubljana: Inštitut za novejšo zgodovino, 2010), 110.

425. NARA, CREST, CIA, "Yugoslavia: An Intelligence Appraisal," 27 July 1971.

426. BA, DY 30/IV A 2/20/1158.

427. Dedijer, *Dokumenti 1948*, 3:685–712.

428. BA, DY 30/IV 2/20/132; AMZV, Zprávy ZÚ, Bělehrad 1961–1962, 022857/62-2.

429. JFK, National Security Files, Box 210, G. Kennan to Llewellyn E. Thompson, February 9, 1962.

430. TNA, FO 371/169614/CY 100/1; AMZV, Zprávy ZÚ, Bělehrad 1961–1962, 025122/62-2.

431. Nenadović, *Razgovori s Kočom*, 6.

432. TNA, FO 371/163907/CY 1022/16.

433. TNA, FO 371/169617/CY 1022/13.

434. TNA, FO 371/177760/NU 1011/1.

435. "Memo for the Director," 294.

436. GWU, Incoming Telegram, Department of State, Zagreb, 13 November 1962.

437. NARA, CREST, CIA, "Special Report: Yugoslav Interest in Latin America," 12 April 1963, CIA, Weekly Summary, 11 October 1963.

438. Dedijer, *Novi prilozi*, 3:37; NARA, CREST, CIA, Current Intelligence Memorandum, "Reaction of Tito and His Entourage to His US Visit," 4 November 1963.

439. Adamović, *Brozovi strahovi*, 353–62.

440. NARA, CREST, CIA, Office of Current Intelligence, "Reaction of Tito and his Entourage to his US Visit," 4 November 1963.

441. JFK, Oral Histories, William A. Crawford, 12 March 1971, 26.

442. BA, Bestand Ulbricht, Walter, NI 182/1235.

443. NARA, Pol 151 Yugo, Belgrade, 21 June 1965; Pol 15-1 Yugo, Belgrade, 11 May 1965.

444. TNA, FO 371/182850/NU 103170/8.

445. NARA, Pol 15-1 Yugo, Belgrade, 11 May 1965; 3 June 1965.

446. NSK, Arhiv Bakarić, Kutija 31.

447. NARA, Pol 15-1 US-Yugoslavia, Washington 2.9 (1965); GWU, Notes on Telcon with the President, 01673, 28 December 1965.

448. AS, Dedijer, t. e. 120.

449. PA, B 42, Band 989; TNA, FCO 28/512/NU 1/3.

450. BA, Bestand Ulbricht, Walter, NI 182/1238.

451. AJ, KPR I-1/1340; Blažo Mandić, *S Titom: Četvrt veka u kabinetu* (Belgrade: Dan Graf, 2012), 167.

452. NARA, CREST, CIA, "Special Report: The Yugoslav Power Structure under Revision," *Weekly Summary*, 21 February 1968.

453. Geoffrey R. Swain, *Tito: A Biography* (New York: I. B. Tauris, 2011), 157.

454. Boris Kanzleiter, *Die "Rote Universität": Studentenbewegung und Linksopposition in Belgrad 1962–1975* (Hamburg: VSA, 2011), 189–300; Antonić, *Rodoljub Čolaković*, 185–88.

455. NSK, Arhiv Bakarić, Kutija 25; AS, Dedijer, t. e. 233.

456. Bilandžić, *Povijest izbliza*, 270; Bilandžić, *Hrvatska moderna povijest*, 519.

457. TNA, FCO 28/37.

458. Zdravko Vuković, *Od deformacije SDB do Maspoka i liberalizma: Moji stenografski zapisi 1966–1972. godine* (Belgrade: Narodna knjiga, 1989), 178, 179.

459. BA, DY 30/IV A 2/20/1158.

460. PA, B 12, Band 547.

461. Ćosić, *Piščevi zapisi*, 1:344.

462. NARA, Pol 15-I Yugo, Belgrade, 26 May 1965; TNA, FO 371/177767/NY 105/11.

463. Marović, *Sumrak staljinizma*, 1:269; Blažo Mandić, *Titu u dialogu s svijetom* (Novi Sad: Agencija Mir, 2005), 212–24.

464. TNA, FO 371/182846/NU 138/6.

465. TNA, FO 371/182864/NU 113138/5.

466. NSK, Arhiv Bakarić, Kutija 12.

467. TNA, FCO 28/1635/ENU 3/303/1.

468. Girenko, *Stalin-Tito*, 420; AS, Dedijer, t. e. 126.

469. PA, B 42, Band 1348.

470. BA, DY 30/IV A2/20/1175.

471. BA, DY 30/J IV 2/2 A-1.331.

472. Dabčević-Kučar, *'71: Hrvatski snovi*, 2:600.

473. AS, Dedijer, t. e. 126; Jurij Hadalin, "Tito in praška pomlad v jugoslovanskih diplomatskih virih," in *Slovenija-Jugoslavija: Krize in reforme 1968/1988*, ed. Zdenko Čepič (Ljubljana: Inštitut za novejšo zgodovino, 2010), 161, 162; Mateja Režek, "Odmev praške pomladi in njenega zloma v Sloveniji in v Jugoslaviji," ibid., 169.

474. Dedijer, *Dokumenti 1948*, 724.

475. NSK, Arhiv Bakarić, Kutija 33.

476. AS, Dedijer, t. e. 111.

477. Režek, "Odmev praške pomladi," 175, 176.

478. BA, DY 30/J IV "/2 A-1.331.

479. AS, Dedijer, t. e. 126; Miodrag Marović, *Sumrak staljinizma* (Belgrade: Sloboda, 1978), 2:53.

480. PA, B. 42, Band 1348.

481. Djoko Tripković, "Pisma koja je Josip Broz Tito razmenio sa Leonidom Brežnjevim i Lindonom Džonsonom povodom dogadjaja u Čehoslovačkoj u jesen 1968," *Istorija 20. Veka* 28, no. 2 (2010): 176, 182; Gojko Berić, *Zbogom XX. stoljeće: Sjećanja Ive Vejvode* (Zagreb: Profil knjiga, 2013), 159, 160.

482. NARA, CREST, CIA, "Yugoslavia: An Intelligence Appraisal," 27 July 1971; "NIE 15-73, Yugoslavia after Tito, 5 July 1973," in *Yugoslavia: From "National Communism" to National Collapse; US Intelligence Community Estimative Products on Yugoslavia*, ed. Thomas Fingar (Pittsburgh, PA: GPO, 2006), 519.

483. PA, B 42, Band 1348; NSK, Arhiv Bakarić, Kutija 33.

484. PA, B 42, Band 1348; BA, Bestand Ulbricht, Walter, NI, 182/4238.

485. Girenko, *Stalin-Tito*, 421.

486. NSK, Arhiv Bakarić, Kutija 33.

487. Damijan Guštin, "Teritorialna obramba—vojaška potreba in politični projekt 1968–1988," in *Slovenija-Jugoslavija: Krize in reforme 1968/1988*, ed. Zdenko Čepič (Ljubljana: Inštitut za novejšo zgodovino, 2010), 279.

488. PA, B 12, Band 1341; NARA, CREST, CIA, "Yugoslavia: An Intelligence Appraisal," 27 July 1971; "IIM 76-040C, the Yugoslav Armed Forces, 1 October 1976," in *Yugoslavia: From "National Communism" to National Collapse; US Intelligence Community*

Estimative Products on Yugoslavia, ed. Thomas Fingar (Pittsburgh, PA: GPO, 2006), 530; AS, Dedijer, t. e. 111.

489. Guštin, "Teritorialna obramba," 281.

490. Bilandžić, *Hrvatska moderna povijest*, 527.

491. Jože Smole, *Pred usodnimi odločitvami* (Ljubljana: Založba ČZP Enotnost, 1992), 46, 47.

492. TNA, FCO 28/1647; "NIE 15-79, Prospects for Post-Tito Yugoslavia, Vol. II—Annexes, 25 September 1979," in *Yugoslavia: From "National Communism" to National Collapse; US Intelligence Community Estimative Products on Yugoslavia*, ed. Thomas Fingar (Pittsburgh, PA: GPO, 2006), 607.

493. Nenadović, *Razgovori s Kočom*, 145.

494. AS, Dedijer, t. e. 68; t. e. 261; t. e. 264.

495. Mile Bjelajac, "JLA v šestdesetih in v prvi polovici sedemdesetih," in *Slovenija-Jugoslavija: Krize in reforme 1968/1988*, ed. Zdenko Čepič (Ljubljana: Inštitut za novejšo zgodovino, 2010), 93, 94; Guštin, "Teritorialna obramba," 283; NARA, CREST, "The Role of the Military in the Yugoslav System," *Weekly Summary Special Report*, 20 June 1989.

496. NARA, Pol 15-8 Yugo, Belgrade, 8 November 1966.

497. BA, DY 30/IV 2/21/8077.

498. Dabčević-Kučar, *'71: Hrvatski snovi*, 1:452.

499. Ridley, *Tito*, 383.

500. PA, B 12, Band 547.

501. Languages were particularly important because they defined national identity they were a way to be patriotic about one's ethnicity within the Yugoslav context.

502. AS, Dedijer, t. e. 188.

503. AJ, KPR II-4-a, K 163; Radina Vučetić, *Monopol na istinu: Partija, kultura i cenzura u Srbiji šezdesetih i sedamdesetih godina XX veka* (Belgrade: CLIO, 2016), 154–69.

504. NSK, Arhiv Bakarić, Kutija 47.

505. AJ, 836, LF, II-1/78; Dabčević-Kučar, *'71: Hrvatski snovi*, 2:822.

506. Matunović, *Titova sovladarica*, 121; Bilandžić, *Povijest izbliza*, 191, 246.

507. AJ, KPR II-4-a, K 166; NARA, CREST, "Yugoslavia: The Kosovo Problem; A Research Paper," 21 April 1979.

508. AJ, KPR II-4-b, K 169.

509. AJ, KPR, II-4-b, K 169; Bilandžić, *Povijest izbliza*, 68. Kosovo had been a part of the medieval Serbian Kingdom until it was conquered by the Turks. It was only reconquered by Serbia in 1913. Serbs considered the region to be the cradle of their nation, despite the fact that the majority living there were Albanian.

510. Ćosić, *Piščevi zapisi*, 2:10, 11, 202, 203, 275.

511. NARA, CREST, CIA, "Yugoslavia. An Intelligence Appraisal," 27 July 1971.

512. Serbo-Croatian, Slovenian, Macedonian, Hungarian, Italian, Slovakian, Romanian, Albanian, Turkish, Rusyn, Bulgarian.

513. AJ 837, KPR, II-a, K 168; Swain, *Tito*, 149–51.

514. AAB, Arkiv Stoltenberg, Thorvald, "The Outlook for Yugoslavia 1969–1947."

515. PA, B 42, Band 1327; AS, Dedijer, t. e. 215.

516. Bilandžić, *Povijest izbliza*, 78; Bilandžić, *Hrvatska moderna povijest*, 536.

517. Latinka Perović, *Zatvaranje kruga: Ishod razcepa* (Sarajevo: Svjetlost, 1991), 90; Olivera Milosavljević, *Činjenice i tumačenja* (Belgrade: Helsinški odbor za ljudska prava u Srbiji, 2010), 62.

518. PA, B 42, Band 1343.

519. It stated that if a nation recognized East Germany, then it could not have diplomatic relations with West Germany.

520. BA, DY 30/1 IV 2/2 A-1.277; Dušan Nečak, "'Ostpolitik' Willyja Brandta in Jugoslavija (1966–1974): Ponovna vzpostavitev diplomatskih stikov," in *Slovenija-Jugoslavija: Krize in reforme 1968/1988*, ed. Zdenko Čepič (Ljubljana: Inštitut za novejšo zgodovino, 2010), 221–23.

521. Willy Brandt, *Erinnerungen* (Berlin: Ullstein, 2003), 42.

522. Ibid., 237.

523. NSK, Arhiv Bakarić, Kutija 20.

524. Ljubograd Dimić, "Josip Broz Tito, Yugoslav Policy and the Formation of the Concept of European Security, 1968–1975," in *From Helsinki to Belgrade: The First CSCE Follow-Up Meeting and the Crisis of Détente*, ed. Vladimir Bilandžić, Dittmar Dahlmann, and Milan Kosanović (Bonn: Bonn University Press, 2014), 69.

525. Kavčič, *Pot v osamosvojitev*, 274, 275.

526. Božo Repe and Jože Prinčič, *Pred časom: Portret Staneta Kavčiča* (Ljubljana: Modrijan, 2009), 135–65.

527. Smole, *Pripoved komunista novinarja*, 140, 141.

528. Stane Kavčič, *Dnevnik in spomini: 1972–1987* (Ljubljana: Časopis za kritiko znanosti, 1988), 430.

529. Franc Šetinc, *Vzpon in sestop* (Ljubljana: Cankarjeva založba, 1989), 67.

530. AS, Dedijer, t. e. 233.

531. Dabčević-Kučar, *'71: Hrvatski snovi*, 1:117, 118, 137, 363.

532. Ibid., 1:431.

533. Ibid., 2:788, 794.

534. Bilandžić, *Povijest izbliza*, 76.

535. AJ, KPR, II-4-a, K 166.

536. Dabčević-Kučar, *'71: Hrvatski snovi*, 1:119, 120.

537. Matunović, *Titova sovladarica*, 551.

538. Dabčević-Kučar, *'71: Hrvatski snovi*, 1:123, 147, 156; 2:808, 827.

539. Ćosić, *Piščevi zapisi*, 2:27.

540. Milosavljević, *Činjenice i tumačenja*, 101.

541. Ridley, *Tito*, 391.

542. Kavčič, *Pot v osamosvojitev*, 225.

543. PA, B 12, Band 547.

544. Dabčević-Kučar, *'71: Hrvatski snovi*, 2:803.

545. Bilandžić, *Povijest izbliza*, 94.

546. TNA, FCO 28/1629/ENU 175.

547. PA, B 12, Band 547.

548. AS, Dedijer, t. e. 233.

549. Dabčević-Kučar, *'71: Hrvatski snovi*, 2:754.

550. TNA, FCO 28/1630/ENU 1/1.

551. TNA, FCO 28/1627/ENU 1/3.

552. Kardelj, *Spomini*, 243.

553. L. Perović, "Kako su se izražavali."

554. Trying to mimic Piedmont's feat of unifying Italy under its own king in the mid-nineteenthth century.

555. PA, B 12, Band 547; Nenadović, *Razgovori s Kočom*, 155.
556. TNA, FCO 28/1628.
557. Dabčević-Kučar, *'71: Hrvatski snovi*, 1:488, 506, 514, 515, 540, 577.
558. NARA, CREST, CIA, "Yugoslavia: An Intelligence Appraisal," 27 July 1971; AS, Dedijer, t. e. 233; Kranjc, *Zarote in atentati*, 35.
559. Swain, *Tito: A Biography*, 169.
560. Dabčević-Kučar, *'71: Hrvatski snovi*, 1:504, 506, 507; Marko Lopušina, *Ubij bližnjeg svog: Jugoslovenska tajna policija 1945–1995* (Belgrade: Biblioteka "Revija 92," 1996), 1:192, 193.
561. TNA, FCO 28/1630; Dabčević-Kučar, *'71: Hrvatski snovi*, 1:521–23.
562. PA, B 12, Band 547; Dabčević-Kučar, *'71: Hrvatski snovi*, 1:522; Matunović, *Titova sovladarica*, 122.
563. AS, Dedijer, t. e. 233.
564. NARA, CREST, "Yugoslavia: An Intelligence Appraisal," 27 July 1971; Dabčević-Kučar, *'71: Hrvatski snovi*, 1:560–62; Milorad Lazić, "The Soviet Intervention That Never Happened," 4 December 2017, https://www.wilsoncenter.org/blog-post/the-soviet-intervention, 1–4.
565. Bilandžić, *Hrvatska moderna povijest*, 593.
566. Miko Tripalo, *Hrvatsko proljeće* (Zagreb: Nakladni zavod Matice Hrvatske, 2001), 150, 151; PA, B I342, Band 1327.
567. Dabčević-Kučar, *'71: Hrvatski snovi*,1:552.
568. AS, Dedijer, t. e. 233.
569. PA, B. 12, Band 547; Bilandžić, *Povijest izbliza*, 258.
570. Dabčević-Kučar, *'71: Hrvatski snovi*, 1:548; AS, Dedijer, t. e. 233.
571. Nada Kisić-Kolanović, *Andrija Hebrang: Iluzije i otrežnjenja* (Zagreb: Institut za suvremenu povijest, 1996), 142.
572. AJ, KPR, II-4-a, K 167.
573. Ćosić, *Piščevi zapisi*, 1:293.
574. Dabčević-Kučar, *'71: Hrvatski snovi*, 2:602, 603; Kranjc, *Zarote in atentati*, 120, 121; Milosavljević, *Činjenice i tumačenja*, 107.
575. Vrhunec, *Šest let s Titom*, 221, 252; AS, Dedijer, t. e. 68; Kranjc, *Zarote in atentati*, 250.
576. Milosavljević, *Činjenice i tumačenja*, 240, 241.
577. Ćosić, *Piščevi zapisi*, 1:293; AS, Dedijer, t. e. 68; t. e. 184.
578. PA, B 12, Band 547.
579. Ridley, *Tito*, 394; AS, Dedijer, t. e. 233.
580. Vrhunec, *Šest let s Titom*, 258; AS, Dedijer, t. e. 233.
581. Dabčević-Kučar, *'71: Hrvatski snovi*, 2:661.
582. TNA, FCO 28/2115/ENU 1/1.
583. Marko Vrhunec, *Josip Broz Tito: Osebnost—stvaritve—titoizem* (Ljubljana: Društvo piscev zgodovine NOB Slovenije, 2009), 97.
584. Bilandžić, *Hrvatska moderna povijest*, 545–551.
585. Vrhunec, *Josip Broz Tito*, 102.
586. TNA, FCO 28/1628/A 20; FCO 28/2118.
587. Bilandžić, *Povijest izbliza*, 265.
588. Vrhunec, *Šest let s Titom*, 265.
589. Dabčević-Kučar, *'71: Hrvatski snovi*, 2:695, 696–99.
590. PA, B 12, Band 547.
591. AS, Dedijer, t. e. 233.

592. Dabčević-Kučar, *'71: Hrvatski snovi*, 2:683.
593. Bilandžić, *Povijest izbliza*, 109.
594. Dabčević-Kučar, *'71: Hrvatski snovi*, 2:683, 684.
595. Bilandžić, *Povijest izbliza*, 174.
596. Ibid., 111, 112, 174.
597. AS, Dedijer, t. e. 233; Roter, *Padle maske*, 294.
598. BA, Bestand Ulbricht, Walter, NI/1238.
599. Milosavljević, *Činjenice i tumačenja*, 241.
600. Dedijer, *Novi prilozi*, 3:76.
601. PA, B 42, Band 1348; Dragan Bogetić, "Tito i nesvrstani," in *Tito: Vidjenja i tumačenja*, Biblioteka Zbornici Radova 8, ed. Olga Manojlović Pintar (Belgrade: Institut za Noviju Istoriju Srbije, 2011), 410, 411; NARA, CREST, "Yugoslavia: An Intelligence Appraisal," 27 July 1971.
602. PA, B 42, Band 1348; NARA, CREST, CIA, "Yugoslavia. An Intelligence Appraisal," 27 July 1971.
603. AS, Dedijer, t. e. 68.
604. Dabčević-Kučar, *'71: Hrvatski snovi*, 2:604–8.
605. GWU, 00735, "US Policy and Post-Tito Yugoslavia," Prepared by NSC Interdepartmental ad hoc Group for Yugoslavia, 13 September 1971, 1–5.
606. Oral testimony by Marko Bulc.
607. NARA, CREST, CIA, "Yugoslavia: An Intelligence Appraisal," 27 July 1971.
608. PA, B 42, Band 1348.
609. TNA, FCO 28/1640/ENU 3/311/1; Gorazd Bajc, "Dietro le quinte della visita di Tito a Roma nel 1971: Il contesto locale e internazionale letto dalla diplomazia britannica," *Annales, Series historia et socilogia* 24, no. 4 (2014): 714–28.
610. NARA, CIA, *Central Intelligence Bulletin*, 18 December 1953.
611. NARA, Pol. Vat-Yugo, Rome, 2 February 1965; AMZV, Zprávy ZÚ, Bělehrad 1966–1967, 323–25; BA, B 26, Bestand 457; Milan Terzić, "Odnos Josipa Broza Tita prema Rimskokatoličkoj crkvi 1945–1952," *Vojnoistorički glasnik* 1 (1966); Roter, *Padle maske*, 185, 186, 227, 238; Antonić, *Rodoljub Čolaković*, 491, 492.
612. TNA, FO 371/182879/NU 1781/8.
613. PA, B 42, Band 1350.
614. D. Stuparić, *Diplomati izvan protokola: Ambasadori Titove Jugoslavije* (Zagreb: Centar za kulturno djelatnost Saveza socijalističke omladine Zagreba, 1978), 338–40.
615. NARA, CREST, CIA, "Yugoslavia: An Intelligence Appraisal," 27 July 1971; NNA, FCO 28/1628/ENU 1/4.
616. Dabčević-Kučar, *'71: Hrvatski snovi*, 2:681.
617. NARA, CREST, CIA, "Yugoslavia, An Intelligence Appraisal," 27 July 1971.
618. Ibid.
619. Dabčević-Kučar, *'71: Hrvatski snovi*, 2:603.
620. Vrhunec, *Šest let s Titom*, 99–102; TNA, FCO 28/1636/ENU 3/303/1; FCO 28/1635/ENU/ 3/303/1.
621. Osolnik, *Med svetom in domovino*, 121, 122; "Memo, Tito's Time of Troubles, 17 November 1972," in *Yugoslavia: From "National Communism" to National Collapse; US Intelligence Community Estimative Products on Yugoslavia*, ed. Thomas Fingar (Pittsburgh, PA: GPO, 2006), 494; AS, Dedijer, t. e. 111.
622. Dabčević-Kučar, *'71: Hrvatski snovi*, 2:603.

623. PA, B 42, Band 1348.
624. Mandić, *Titu u dialogu*, 369.
625. PA, B 42, Band, 1350.
626. Vrhunec, *Šest let s Titom*, 121, 122.
627. "IIM 76-040C, the Yugoslav Armed Forces, 1 October 1976," in *Yugoslavia: From "National Communism" to National Collapse; US Intelligence Community Estimative Products on Yugoslavia*, ed. Thomas Fingar (Pittsburgh, PA: GPO, 2006), 546.
628. Dabčević-Kučar, *'71: Hrvatski snovi*, 2:888; Kranjc, *Zarote in atentati*, 351.
629. Frane Barbieri, "Uvodnik: Frontovi," *Nedeljne informativne novine* (*NIN*), 14 November 1971, 7.
630. PA, B 12, Band 547; TNA, FCO 28/2113/ENU 1/3; AJ, KPR-II-4-a, K 167.
631. Dabčević-Kučar, *'71: Hrvatski snovi*, 2:819.
632. Dušan Dragosavac, *Zbivanja i svjedočenja* (Zagreb: Globus, 1985), 73.
633. Swain, *Tito*, 175.
634. TNA, FCO 28/1630/ENU 1/7; AJ, KPR, II-4-a, K 167; NARA, CREST, Office of National Estimates, Memorandum: "The Crisis in Croatia," 5 January 1972.
635. Ćosić, *Piščevi zapisi*, 1:289.
636. AS, Dedijer, t. e. 233.
637. Dabčević-Kučar, *'71: Hrvatski snovi*, 2:931.
638. NSK, Arhiv Bakarić, Kutija 33.
639. PA, B 12, Band 557; Dabčević-Kučar, *'71: Hrvatski snovi*, 2:940–49.
640. Bilandžić, *Povijest izbliza*, 220.
641. Simić, *Tito*, 305–7; Dragoslav Draža Marković, *Život i politika, 1967–1978* (Belgrade: RAD, 1987), 2:283, 284; Milosavljević, *Činjenice i tumačenja*, 106.
642. Vrhunec, *Šest let s Titom*, 268.
643. AS, Dedijer, t. e. 233; Milosavljević, *Činjenice i tumačenja*, 105.
644. Dabčević-Kučar, *'71: Hrvatski snovi*, 2:798.
645. NARA, CREST, Soviet Union-Eastern Europe, "Cominformists in Croatia," 5 August 1975; "Political Turmoil Continues in Croatia," *Central Intelligence Bulletin*,15 December 1971.
646. PA, B 12, Band 547.
647. NARA, CREST, CIA, Yugoslavia, *Central Intelligence Bulletin*, 23 December 1971; Memorandum: "The Crisis in Croatia," 5 January 1972.
648. AJ, KPR, II-4-a, K 167.
649. Dabčević-Kučar, *'71: Hrvatski snovi*, 2:992, 996; PA, B12, Band 547.
650. PA, Zwischenarchiv 112617, 13 March 1973.
651. PA, B 42, Band 1341.
652. Ibid.
653. BA, DY 30/IV A 2/20/1158.
654. NARA, CREST, Office of National Estimates, Memorandum: "The Crisis in Croatia," 5 January 1972.
655. Bilandžić, *Povijest izbliza*, 125; TNA, FCO 28/2117; NARA, CREST, "The Yugoslav Experiment Challenged," *Propaganda Perspectives*, March 1972.
656. Dušan Bilandžić et al., *Zgodovina Socialistične Federativne Republike Jugoslavije* (Ljubljana: Partizanska knjiga, 1980), 422; Vrhunec, *Šest let s Titom*, 179, 180.
657. NARA, CREST, CIA, Memorandum: "Tito's Time of Troubles," 17 November 1972.

658. TNA, FCO 28/2407/ENU 1/1.
659. TNA, FCO 28/2115/ENU 1/4.
660. PA, Zwischenarchiv 112618, 28 March 1972.
661. TNA, FCO 28/2117/ENU 1/5.
662. Jože Pirjevec, "Yugoslav Political Emigration to Australia after World War II," *Annales, Series historia et sociologia* 16, no. 1 (January 2006): 1–6.
663. NSK, Arhiv Bakarić, Kutija 33; Kranjc, *Zarote in atentati*, 355.
664. Stipanič, *Od pastirja do direktorja*, 112; Ivo Goldstein and Slavko Goldstein, *Tito* (Zagreb: Profil, 2015), 737.
665. Vrhunec, *Šest let s Titom*, 187, 307.
666. Vrhunec, *Josip Broz Tito*, 27.
667. NSK, Arhiv Bakarić, Kutija 34; AJ, KPR, II-4-a, K 167.
668. NARA, CREST, Memorandum, "Yugoslavia: The Ustashi and the Croatian Separatist Problem," 27 September 1972.
669. NSK, Arhiv Bakarić, Kutija 33.
670. L. Perović, "Na tragu srpske liberalne tradicije," 12.
671. TNA, FCO 28/2114 1/1; Milosavljević, *Činjenice i tumačenja*, 108.
672. Fabio Amodeo and Mario Cereghino, *Tito spiato dagli inglesi: I rapporti segreti sulla Jugoslavia, 1968–1980* (Trieste: MGS, 2014), 86.
673. AJ, KPR II-4-a, K 167.
674. Ćosić, *Piščevi zapisi*, 2:118–21.
675. TNA, FCO 28/2116/ENU 1/4; FCO 28/2407/ENU 1/1.
676. L. Perović, "Na tragu srpske liberalne tradicije," 42; Milosavljević, *Činjenice i tumačenja*, 49–51.
677. Pero Simić and Zvonimir Despot, *Tito: Strogo poverljivo; Arhivski dokumenti* (Belgrade: Službeni glasnik, 2008), 271; Milosavljević, *Činjenice i tumačenja*, 106.
678. TNA, FCO 28/2116//ENU 1/4.
679. Vrhunec, *Šest let s Titom*, 191.
680. AMZV, Zprávy ZÚ, Bělehrad 1973–1975, 01169.
681. TNA, FCO 28/2117/ENU 3/303/1.
682. TNA, FCO 29/2122/ENU 3/303/1; Petranović and Zečević, *Jugoslavija 1918–1988*, 992, 993.
683. L. Perović, "Na tragu srpske liberalne tradicije," 43; TNA, FCO 28/2118/16; Petranović and Zečević, *Jugoslavija 1918–1988*, 993, 994.
684. Bilandžić, *Povijest izbliza*, 192.
685. Ibid., 126; Simić, *Tito*, 308; Simić and Despot, *Tito*, 332; Ćosić, *Piščevi zapisi*, 2:90, 91.
686. Ivan Ivanji, *Titov prevajalec* (Ljubljana: Karantanija, 2007), 167.
687. Stefano Terra, *Tre anni con Tito* (Trieste: MGS Press, 2004), 21.
688. Djilas, *Tito*, 14, 134, 135.
689. Petranović and Zečević, *Jugoslavija 1918–1988*, 995–1003.
690. Ibid.
691. L. Perović, "Kako su se izražavali," 132.
692. "Memorandum, Tito's Time of Troubles, 17 November 1972," in *Yugoslavia: From "National Communism" to National Collapse; US Intelligence Community Estimative Products on Yugoslavia*, ed. Thomas Fingar (Pittsburgh, PA: GPO, 2006), 484, 488.
693. L. Perović, "Kako su se izražavali," 236.

694. Vuković, *Od deformacije SDB*, 735.
695. Marković, *Život i politika*, 1:414.
696. Bilandžić, *Povijest izbliza*, 128; Bilandžić, *Hrvatska moderna povijest*, 664; Drnovšek, *Slovenska kronika XX. stoletja*, 2:334, 335.
697. Kavčič, *Dnevnik in spomini*, 236.
698. AS, Dedijer, t. e. 7.
699. Bilandžić, *Povijest izbliza*, 122.
700. Ćosić, *Piščevi zapisi*, 2:313, 314.
701. Vuković, *Od deformacije SDB*, 681.
702. Bilandžić, *Povijest izbliza*, 132.
703. Ranković, *Dnevničke zabeleške*, 223.

Chapter 5. The Later Years

1. Arhiv Slovenije, Ljubljana (Archive of Slovenia, hereafter AS), Dedijer, t. e. 7.
2. Edvard Kardelj, *Spomini: Boj za priznanje in neodvisnost nove Jugoslavije, 1944–1957* (Belgrade: Državna založba Slovenije, 1980), 244; Archiv ministerstva zahraničních věcí, Prague (hereafter AMZV), Zprávy ZÚ, Bělehrad 1973–1975, 0171/74.
3. AS, Dedijer, t. e. 188.
4. Dušan Bilandžić, *Povijest izbliza: Memoarski zapisi 1945–2005* (Zagreb: Prometej, 2005), 134, 282.
5. Niko Kavčič, *Pot v osamosvojitev* (Lubljana: Samozaložba, 1996), 318, 319.
6. Milovan Djilas, *Tito: Eine kritische Biographie* (Vienna: Molden, 1980), 312; Danilo Udovički, *Treći juni 1968: Od kritike svega postojećeg, do uništenja svega postignutog* (Novi Sad: Prometej, 2008), 67.
7. Politisches Archiv, Berlin (Political Archive, hereafter PA), B 42, Band 1343.
8. Savka Dabčević-Kučar, *'71: Hrvatski snovi i stvarnost* (Zagreb: Interpublic, 1997), 1:548.
9. AMZV, Zprávy ZÚ, Bělehrad 1973–1975, 0171/74.
10. The National Archives, London (hereafter TNA), FCO 28/2118.
11. Vjenceslav Cenčić, *Titova poslednja ispovijest* (Belgrade: Orfelin, 2001), 178.
12. AS, Šentjurc, t. e. 40.
13. AS, Dedijer, t. e. 215.
14. Aleksandar Matunović, *Titova sovladarica* (Ljubljana: Mladinska knjiga, 2008), 186.
15. TNA, FCO 28/2407/W/35.
16. Cenčić, *Titova poslednja ispovijest*, 13,23, 39, 175; AMZV, Zprávy ZÚ, Bělehrad 1973–1975, 0318/74.
17. Dabčević-Kučar, *'71: Hrvatski snovi*, 1:360.
18. TNA, FCO 28/24411/ENU 1/4.
19. Bundesarchiv, Berlin (hereafter BA), DY 30/J IV 2/2-J/5258; AS, Dedijer, t. e. 7; Mitja Žagar, "Ustava SFRJ in ustavni sistem 1974: Povzročitelj krize ali mehanizem za njeno razreševanje?," in *Slovenija-Jugoslavija: Krize in reforme 1968/1988*, ed. Zdenko Čepič (Ljubljana: Inštitut za novejšo zgodovino, 2010), 233.
20. BA, DY 30/IV B2/20130.
21. Cenčić, *Titova poslednja ispovijest*, 290.
22. Jasper Ridley, *Tito: A Biography* (London: Constable, 1994), 393; Fitzroy Maclean, *Josip Broz Tito: A Pictorial Biography* (New York: McGraw-Hill, 1980), 108.

23. AS, Dedijer, t. e. 298.

24. Dobrica Ćosić, *Piščevi zapisi* (Belgrade: Višnjić, 2001), 2:217, 218.

25. Latinka Perović, "Kako su se izražavali različiti politički interesi u Jugoslaviji: Polemika izmedju Dobrice Ćosića i Dušana Pirjevca 1961/1962. godine," in *Dominantna i neželjena elita: Beleške o intelektualnoj i političkoj eliti u Srbiji (XX–XXI vek)* (Belgrade: Dan Graf, 2015), 46.

26. AMZV, Zprávy ZÚ, Bělehrad 1973–1975, 0341/74.

27. National Archives and Record Administration, Washington (hereafter NARA), Pol 15 Yugo, Belgrade, 22 January 1964.

28. Bilandžić, *Povijest izbliza*, 147; AS, Dedijer, t. e. 244.

29. Written testimony by Aleksander Lucu, Ljubljana, 2010.

30. Ćosić, *Piščevi zapisi*, 2:263.

31. AS, Dedijer, t. e. 188; t. e., 233.

32. Nacionalna i Sveučilišna Knjižnica, Zagreb (National and University Library, hereafter NSK), Arhiv Bakarić, Kutija 6; BA, DY 30/J IV 2/2-J/7179.

33. Dušan Bilandžić, *Hrvatska moderna povijest* (Zagreb: Golden Marketing, 1999), 680.

34. Pero Simić, *Tito: Skrivnost stoletja* (Ljubljana: Orbis, 2009), 279, 316.

35. NARA, CREST, National Intelligence Daily Cable, 13 December 1978; J. Kopinič, "Če državo vodijo šuštarji in peki . . . ," *Nedeljski Dnevnik*, 2 July 1989.

36. NARA, CREST, Soviet Union-Eastern Europe, "Yugoslavs Fire a Salvo at Zarodov," 18 September 1975, 2.

37. Bilandžić, *Hrvatska moderna povijest*, 686, 687.

38. AS, Dedijer, t. e. 188.

39. Bilandžić, *Povijest izbliza*, 686, 687.

40. Ibid., 181, 699.

41. Aleksandar Nenadović, *Razgovori s Kočom* (Zagreb: Globus, 1989), 170.

42. Bilandžić, *Povijest izbliza*, 223.

43. Bilandžić, *Hrvatska moderna povijest*, 684.

44. "NIE 15-79, Prospects for Post Tito Yugoslavia, Vol. II—The Annexes, 25 September 1979," in *Yugoslavia: From "National Communism" to National Collapse; US Intelligence Community Estimative Products on Yugoslavia*, ed. Thomas Fingar (Pittsburgh, PA: GPO, 2006), 590, 601, 602.

45. Bilandžić, *Hrvatska moderna povijest*, 685.

46. Simić, *Tito*, 316.

47. Edvard Kardelj, *Smeri razvoja političnega sistema socialističnega samoupravljanja* (Ljubljana: Komunist, 1983), 196, 197.

48. Bilandžić, *Povijest izbliza*, 171.

49. Matunović, *Titova sovladarica*, 158, 159.

50. NSK, Arhiv Bakarić, Kutija 121.

51. "NIE 15-73, Yugoslavia after Tito, 5 July 1973," in *Yugoslavia: From "National Communism" to National Collapse; US Intelligence Community Estimative Products on Yugoslavia*, ed. Thomas Fingar (Pittsburgh, PA: GPO, 2006), 511, 514.

52. Marko Lopušina, *Ubij bližnjeg svog: Jugoslovenska tajna policija 1945–2002* (Belgrade: Narodna knjiga, 2002), 4:152.

53. TNA, FCO 28/2622/ENU 1/4/80.

54. NARA, CREST, Memorandum, "Yugoslavia: Tensions on the Top," 10 December 1976.

55. Ibid.

56. Ante Ciliga, *Il labirinto jugoslavo: Passato e futuro delle nazioni balcaniche* (Milan: Jaca Book, 1983), 85, 131, 132; Ivan Ivanji, *Titov prevajalec* (Ljubljana: Karantanija, 2007), 131.

57. TNA, FCO 28/3909/ENU 010/3; FCO 28/3907/ENU 010/1.

58. Bilandžić, *Povijest izbliza*, 251; AS, Dedijer, t. e. 252.

59. Ciliga, *Il labirinto jugoslavo*, 132; Lado Ambrožič, *Novljanovo stoletje, 1908–2004* (Ljubljana: Modrijan, 2006), 473–78.

60. Bilandžić, *Povijest izbliza*, 251; AS, Dedijer, t. e. 252.

61. NARA, CREST, "Yugoslavia: Rivalries Continue," National Intelligence Daily Cable, 25 January 1979.

62. Ciliga, *Il labirinto jugoslavo*, 122; Dušan Dragosavac, *Zbivanja i svjedočenja* (Zagreb: Globus, 1985), 184, 185.

63. AMZV, Zprávy ZÚ, Bělehrad 1973–1975, 622461.

64. "NIE 15-79," 585, 587, 599, 600.

65. Politisches Archiv, Berlin (Political Archive, hereafter PA), Zwischenarchiv, 112619, 12 December 1972.

66. PA, Zwischenarchiv, 112618, 12 March 1973; TNA, FCO 28//2407/5.

67. Stane Kavčič, *Dnevnik in spomini: 1972–1987* (Ljubljana: Časopis za kritiko znanosti, 1988), 615; NARA, CREST, *Central Intelligence Bulletin*, 13 December 1973.

68. NSK, Arhiv Bakarić, Kutija 34; TNA, FCO 28/2803/ENU 3/304/1; AS, Dedijer, t. e. 120.

69. NSK, Arhiv Bakarić, Kutija 34; Marko Vrhunec, *Šest let s Titom (1967–1973)* (Ljubljana: LaserPrint, 2001), 59; TNA, FCO, 28/1645/NU 3//548/5.

70. Mile Bjelajac, "JLA v šestdesetih in v prvi polovici sedemdesetih," in *Slovenija-Jugoslavija: Krize in reforme 1968/1988*, ed. Zdenko Čepič (Ljubljana: Inštitut za novejšo zgodovino, 2010), 82.

71. *The Economist*, 24 November 1973, 37.

72. AMZV, Zprávy ZÚ, Bělehrad 1973–1975, 01504/73; NARA, CREST, "Yugoslav-Soviet Relations," *Central Intelligence Bulletin*, 13 December 1973; Pero Simić and Zvonimir Despot, *Tito: Strogo poverljivo; Arhivski dokumenti* (Belgrade: Službeni glasnik, 2008), 344.

73. Simić, *Tito*, 315; Žagar, "Ustava SFRJ," 239.

74. Kavčič, *Dnevnik in spomini*, 132.

75. Dragan Vlahović and Nataša Marković, *Jovanka Broz: Život na dvoru* (Belgrade: Akvarius, 1990), 139.

76. AMZV, Zprávy ZÚ, Bělehrad, 020-285/73-2.

77. O. Vojtěchovský, "Informbirovska emigracija u jugoslovansko-čehoslovačkim odnosima," in *Spoljna politika Jugoslavije 1950–1961*, ed. Slobodan Selinić (Belgrade: Institut za noviju istoriju Srbije, 2008), 207–30.

78. S. Khrushchev, *Nikita Khrushchev and the Creation of a Superpower* (University Park: Pennsylvania State University Press, 2003), 147.

79. AJ KPJ II-9-b, K 267; AS, Dedijer, t. e., 244.

80. AS, Dedijer, t. e. 111.

81. Miodrag Marović, *Sumrak staljinizma* (Belgrade: Sloboda, 1978), 2:141.

82. Ibid., 2:124, 125.

83. Jože Smole, *Pripoved komunista novinarja 1945–1980* (Ljubljana: ČZP Enotnost, 1994), 182, 183; Marović, *Sumrak staljinizma*, 2: 143, 155.

84. Arhiv Jugoslavije, Belgrade (Archive of Yugoslavia, hereafter AJ), 837, KPR, II-4-a, K 168.

85. Vladimir Dedijer, *Novi prilozi za biografiju Josipa Broza Tita* (Belgade: Izdavačka Radna Organizacija "Rad," 1984), 3:459; Vladimir Dedijer, *Novi prilozi za biografiju Josipa Broza Tita* (unpublished), 4:106, 197.

86. AS, Dedijer, t. e. 298.

87. NARA, CREST, Yugoslavia, *National Intelligence Bulletin*, 18 July 1975.

88. NSK, Arhiv Bakarić, Kutija 10.

89. AMZV, Zprávy ZÚ, Bělehrad 1973–1975, 01019/74; "IIM 76-040C, the Yugoslav Armed Forces, 1 October 1976," in *Yugoslavia: From "National Communism" to National Collapse; US Intelligence Community Estimative Products on Yugoslavia*, ed. Thomas Fingar (Pittsburgh, PA: GPO, 2006), 534.

90. PA, Zwischenarchiv, 112620, 25 February 1974.

91. NARA, CREST, CIA, "Yugoslavia: An Intelligence Appraisal," 27 July 1971.

92. Ćosić, *Piščevi zapisi*, 1:117; 2:123, 124.

93. AJ, KPR, II-4-a, K 168.

94. AMZV, Zprávy ZÚ, Bělehrad 1973, 622461; NARA, Soviet Union-Eastern Europe, Staff Note, Soviet-Yugoslav Relations, 12 November 1975.

95. Smole, *Pripoved komunista novinarja*, 182, 183.

96. AJ, KPR, II-4-a, K 168.

97. TNA, FCO 28/2809/ENU 3/303/1; FCO 28/2801/ENU 3/303/1.

98. TNA, FCO 28/2816/ENU 18/4.

99. Bojana Popovska, "Mi smo se leta 1941 edini uprli fašističnim vojskam," *Delo*, 3 April 1975, 1.

100. TNA, FCO 28/2816/ENU 18/4; AMZV, Zprávy ZÚ, Bělehrad 1973–75, 0345/75.

101. NARA, CREST, Soviet Union-Eastern Europe, Tito-Ford Talks, Atmospherics, 1 August 1975.

102. NARA, CREST, National Intelligence Daily Cable, 9 February 1978.

103. Blažo Mandić, *Titu u dialogu s svijetom* (Novi Sad: Agencija Mir, 2005), 583–99.

104. AJ, F. 837, KPR, E, P-2/741.

105. Josip Močnik, "United States-Yugoslav Relations, 1961–80: The Twilight of Tito's Era and the Role of Ambassadorial Diplomacy in the Making of America's Yugoslav Policy" (PhD diss., Bowling Green State University, 2008), 182–91; Tvrtko Jakovina, "Tito's Yugoslavia as the Pivotal State of the Non-Aligned," in *Tito: Vidjenja i tumačenja*, Biblioteka Zbornici Radova 8, ed. Olga Manojlović Pintar (Belgrade: Institut za Noviju Istoriju Srbije, 2011), 398.

106. NARA, CREST, Memorandum, "Talking Themes for Secretary's Brown's Visit to Yugoslavia."

107. NARA, CREST, Soviet Union-Eastern Europe, Staff Notes, USSR-Yugoslavia, "The Kremlin Innocents," 28 November 1975; Lopušina, *Ubij bližnjeg svog*, 4:148–52.

108. NARA, CREST, Yugoslavia, "The Kosovo Problem: A Research Paper," 21 April 1975; Simić and Despot, *Tito*, 388–90.

109. NARA, CREST, Soviet Union-Eastern Europe, Staff Notes, "Yugoslavia: Crackdown Nears," 21 October 1975; "Yugoslav Vigilance Campaign," 11 November 1975; National Intelligence Bulletin, Yugoslavia-USSR, 10 October 1975.

110. Jože Pirjevec, *Jugoslavija 1918–1992: Nastanek, razvoj ter razpad Karadjordjevićeve in Titove Jugoslavije* (Koper: Lipa, 1995), 327. L. Silberman, "Yugoslavia's 'Old' Communism," *Foreign Policy* (Spring 1977): 3–27.

111. Djilas, *Tito*, 327; Stephen Clissold, *Djilas: The Progress of a Revolutionary* (Hounslow: Maurice Temple Smith, 1983), 309; NARA, CREST, National Intelligence Daily Cable, Yugoslavia, 23 June 1976; "Possible Amnesty," 30 April 1977.

112. Vladimir Bilandžić, Dittmar Dahlmann, and Milan Kosanović, *From Helsinki to Belgrade: The First CSCE Follow-Up Meeting and the Crisis of Détente* (Bonn: Bonn University Press, 2014), 14–15.

113. Dedijer, *Novi prilozi*, 3:115; NARA, CREST, "May Day Amnesty," 30 April 1977.

114. Andreas Razumovsky, *Ein Kampf um Belgrad: Tito und die jugoslawische Wirklichkeit* (Berlin: Ullstein, 1980), 135, 136.

115. AS, Dedijer, t. e., 111.

116. Ibid.

117. "NIE 15-79," 609; NARA, CREST, National Intelligence Daily, 17 May 1979.

118. Smole, *Pripoved komunista novinarja*, 183; Anton Kolendić, *Staljinova smrt: Od Staljinove do Berijine smrti* (Belgrade: Altera, 1989), 268.

119. AS, Dedijer, t. e. 111; t. e. 220; t. e. 244.

120. Gelvan Library, George Washington University (hereafter GWU), 02141, The White House, Memorandum of Conversation, 12 August 1976.

121. Ćosić, *Piščevi zapisi*, 1:194.

122. AS, Dedijer, t. e. 298.

123. Jože Pirjevec and Jure Ramšak, eds., *Od Mašuna do New Yorka: 20 stoletje skozi pričevanja štirih slovenskih diplomatov* (Koper: Univerzitetna založba Annales, 2014), 105.

124. Dabčević-Kučar, *'71: Hrvatski snovi*, 2:869, 870; AS, Dedijer, t. e. 274.

125. Dabčević-Kučar, *'71: Hrvatski snovi*, 2:873, 887; Vrhunec, *Šest let s Titom*, 39.

126. AS, Dedijer, t. e. 68.

127. Marko Vrhunec, *Josip Broz Tito: Osebnost—stvaritve—titoizem* (Ljublijana: Duštvo piscev zgodovine NOB Slovenije, 2009), 12.

128. *The Diaries of Evelyn Waugh* (London: Weidenfeld & Nicolson, 1976), 572; R. West, *Tito and the Rise and Fall of Yugoslavia* (London: Sinclair-Stevenson, 1994), 185.

129. AS, Dedijer, t. e. 68.

130. Ivanji, *Titov prevajalec*, 38; Blažo Mandić, *Tito izbliza* (Belgrade: Vuk Karadžić, Jugoslovenska revija, 1981), 101.

131. Matunović, *Titova sovladarica*, 130.

132. Franc Šetinc, *Zbogom, Jugoslavija* (Ljubljana: DZS, 1993), 190.

133. Dedijer, *Novi prilozi*, 2:308, 309; Iurii Girenko, *Stalin-Tito* (Moscow: Izdatel'stvo politicheskoi literatury, 1991), 19.

134. Ante Ciliga, "Come Tito si impadronì del Partito comunista Jugoslavo," *Quaderni del centro studi Pietro Tasso* 12 (1989): 13.

135. Matunović, *Titova sovladarica*, 17; Simić and Despot, *Tito*, 43.

136. Louis Adamic, *The Eagle and the Roots* (Garden City, NY: Doubleday, 1952), 347; AJ, LF IIO-11/13.

137. AS, Dedijer, t. e. 271.

138. Ciliga, "Come Tito si impadronì," 12.

139. Adamic, *Eagle and the Roots*, 394.

140. Miro Simčič, *Ženske v Titovi senci: Tito brez maske 2* (Ilirska Bistrica: Samozal., 2010), 141, 144; Ridley, *Tito*, 144.

141. AS, Dedijer, t. e., 271; Simčič, *Ženske v Titovi senci*, 141–47.

142. Dedijer, *Novi prilozi*, 2:315; AS, Dedijer, t. e. 201; t. e. 261; t. e. 262; t. e. 271; Rossiiski gosudarstvennyi arkhiv sotsial'no-politicheskoi istorii (Russian State Archive of Social and Political History, hereafter RGASPI), f. 495, op. 74, d. 594.

143. Djilas, *Tito*, 255, 256; AS, Dedijer, t. e. 262.

144. G. Vlahov, "Život u Belom dvoru," *Duga* 400 (24 June 1989): 86.

145. AS, Dedijer, t. e.; 264; t. e. 271.

146. Simčič, *Ženske v Titovi senci*, 155; RGASPI, f. 495, op. 74, d. 587.

147. Ridley, *Tito*, 344.

148. Simić, *Tito*, 81–84; AS, Dedijer, t. e. 262.

149. Simić and Despot, *Tito*, 91, 92.

150. Simić, *Tito*, 108.

151. AS, Dedijer, t. e. 252.

152. Dedijer, *Novi prilozi*, 2:952.

153. D. Bisenić, "Život bez rukavica," *Danas*, 30 December 2009.

154. B. A. Novak, "Herta Haas (1914–2010)," *Delo*, 18 March 2010.

155. Matunović, *Titova sovladarica*, 19.

156. AS, Dedijer, t. e. 5.

157. Mira Šuvar, *Vladimir Velebit: Svjedok istorije* (Zagreb: Razlog, 2001), 82; Simčič, *Ženske v Titovi senci*, 194.

158. Matunović, *Titova sovladarica*, 19, 20; Marijan F. Kranjc, *Zarote in atentati na Tita* (Grosuplje: Graphis Trade, 2004), 156, 157.

159. Milo Gligorijević, *Rat i mir Vladimira Dedijera: Sećanja i razgovori* (Belgrade: Narodna knjiga, 1986), 61.

160. Šuvar, *Vladimir Velebit*, 464.

161. Testimony by Lučka Čehovin.

162. Clissold, *Djilas*, 91.

163. Ibid.

164. Simčič, *Ženske v Titovi senci*, 203; Vlahov, "Život u Belom dvoru," 83.

165. Djilas, *Tito*, 261.

166. Dedijer, *Novi prilozi*, 2:955; AS, Dedijer, t. e. 262.

167. Simčič, *Ženske v Titovi senci*, 180.

168. AS, Dedijer, t. e. 264.

169. AS, Dedijer, t. e. 271.

170. Djilas, *Tito*, 262.

171. Tat'iana Okunevskaia, *Tat'ianin den'* (Moscow: Vagrius, 1998), 302; E. Franceschini, "Gli stupri di Beria," *La Repubblica*, 29 June 1993.

172. Miladin Adamović, *Brozovi strahovi: Kako je čuvan Tito i pokušaji atentata* (Belgrade: M. Adamović, 2004), 14, 15; AS, Dedijer, t. e. 298.

173. Djilas, *Tito*, 264.

174. AS, Dedijer, t. e. 271; t. e. 274; Kranjc, *Zarote in atentati*, 371; Dedijer, *Novi prilozi*, 3:99, 100; Simčič, *Ženske v Titovi senci*, 183, 227, 238, 249.

175. Djilas, *Tito*, 263, 264.

176. Vlahov, "Život u Belom dvoru," 85.

177. Djilas, *Tito*, 265.

178. Testimony by Mara Samsa.
179. Ladislava Becele Ranković, *Življenje z Leko: Spomini Slovenske partizanke* (Grosuplje: Grafis Trade, 2002), 126.
180. AS, Dedijer, t. e. 3.
181. Becele Ranković, *Življenje z Leko*, 127–29.
182. Djilas, *Tito*, 268.
183. Udovički, *Treći juni 1968*, 74.
184. Ridley, *Tito*, 315.
185. Djilas, *Tito*, 268.
186. Šuvar, *Vladimir Velebit*, 181; AS, Dedijer, t. e. 261.
187. AS, Dedijer, t. e. 3; t. e. 271.
188. Djilas, *Tito*, 270.
189. AS, Dedijer, t. e. 3.
190. Testimony by Marija and Joža Vilfan.
191. Matunović, *Titova sovladarica*, 71; Vrhunec, *Šest let s Titom*, 32, 35, 106, 296, 297; Ćosić, *Piščevi zapisi*, 1:156; Kranjc, *Zarote in atentati*, 106.
192. Bilandžić, *Povijest izbliza*, 272.
193. Ibid., 189.
194. AS, Dedijer, t. e. 3.
195. AS, Dedijer, t. e. 398; Adamović, *Brozovi strahovi*, 590.
196. Adamović, *Brozovi strahovi*, 266–68, 270, 286, 288–90.
197. AS, Dedijer, t. e. 3; t. e. 271.
198. Ibid.
199. Matunović, *Titova sovladarica*, 164, 166; Bilandžić, *Povijest izbliza*, 193, 194.
200. Bilandžić, *Povijest izbliza*, 149, 271; Ćosić, *Piščevi zapisi*, 1:262.
201. Dedijer, *Novi prilozi*, 2:61, 47; Adamović, *Brozovi strahovi*, 125.
202. AS, Dedijer, t. e. 261.
203. AS, Dedijer, t. e. 298.
204. Vrhunec, *Šest let s Titom*, 167.
205. Dabčević-Kučar, *'71: Hrvatski snovi*, 1:345; 2:627, 687.
206. Fabio Amodeo and Mario Cereghino, *Tito spiato dagli inglesi: I rapporti segreti sulla Jugoslavia, 1968–1980* (Trieste: MGS, 2014), 15.
207. Matunović, *Titova sovladarica*, 141.
208. Ibid., 141.
209. Dabčević-Kučar, *'71: Hrvatski snovi*, 2:935.
210. Bilandžić, *Povijest izbliza*, 179.
211. Dabčević-Kučar, *'71: Hrvatski snovi*, 1:431.
212. Ibid., 2:796.
213. Becele Ranković, *Življenje z Leko*, 127.
214. Simčič, *Ženske v Titovi senci*, 320.
215. Andrija Čolak, *Peklenska rezidenca Brozovih* (Mengeš: Ciceron, 2014), 101.
216. Kranjc, *Zarote in atentati*, 372.
217. Simčič, *Ženske v Titovi senci*, 30.
218. Ibid., 254, 255; AS, Dedijer, t. e. 3.
219. Karel Kaplan, *Antonín Novotný: Vzestup a pád "lidového" aparátčika* (Brno: Barrister & Principal, 2011), 202.
220. Ćosić, *Piščevi zapisi*, 2:297.

221. Ibid., 2:298.
222. Ibid., 2:298, 299; Čolak, *Peklenska rezidenca Brozovih*, 54–61.
223. Čolak, *Peklenska rezidenca Brozovih*, 32–41; Razumovsky, *Ein Kampf um Belgrad*, 331, 332.
224. Testimony by Stane Dolanc; Jovanka Broz and Ž. Jokanović, *Moj život, moja istina* (Belgrade: Ringier Axel Springer, 2013), 75.
225. Matunović, *Titova sovladarica*, 235.
226. Ibid.; Simčič, *Ženske v Titovi senci*, 289–91.
227. Ćosić, *Piščevi zapisi*, 2:300, 301; AS, Dedijer, t. e. 143.
228. Matunović, *Titova sovladarica*, 173–76; AS, Dedijer, t. e. 271.
229. Ćosić, *Piščevi zapisi*, 2:301; Kranjc, *Zarote in atentati*, 376.
230. Ibid., 110–14, 252–60.
231. Simčič, *Ženske v Titovi senci*, 305.
232. AS, Dedijer, t. e. 3.
233. Simčič, *Ženske v Titovi senci*, 323–25.
234. AS, Dedijer, t. e. 271; NARA, CREST, National Intelligence Daily Cable, 31 August 1977; 6 September 1977; Marović *Sumrak staljinizma*, 2:283–86.
235. Simčič, *Ženske v Titovi senci*, 31, 259.
236. Ćosić, *Piščevi zapisi*, 2:302.
237. AJ, LF, II-I, A-J.
238. Smole, *Pripoved komunista novinarja*, 205, 206.
239. Ćosić, *Piščevi zapisi*, 2:302.
240. Ibid., 2:301; Kranjc, *Zarote in atentati*, 376.
241. J. Broz and Ž. Jokanović, *Moj život, moja istina*, 45; Ćosić, *Piščevi zapisi*, 2:303.

Chapter 6. Tito's Death and His Political Legacy

1. Milovan Djilas, *Tito: Eine kritische Biographie* (Vienna: Molden, 1980), 220.
2. Dobrica Ćosić, *Piščevi zapisi* (Belgrade: Višnjić, 2001), 1:174.
3. Ibid., 2:238; Milovan Djilas, "Kako je stvorena Titova karizma," *Slobodna Dalmacija*, 22 October 1989.
4. Louis Adamic, *The Eagle and the Roots* (Garden City, NY: Doubleday, 1952), 37.
5. Vladimir Dedijer, *Novi prilozi za biografiju Josipa Broza Tita* (Rijeka: Liburnija, 1981), 2:30.
6. Ibid., 2:831; Marc Halder, *Der Titokult: Charismatische Herrschaft im sozialistischen Jugoslawien* (Munich: Oldenbourg, 2013), 147–52.
7. Arhiv Slovenije, Ljubljana (Archive of Slovenia, hereafter AS), Dedijer, t. e. 179.
8. Djilas, "Kako je stvorena."
9. Dedijer, *Novi prilozi*, 2:973; 3:216, 217.
10. Adamic, *Eagle and the Roots*, 465.
11. Ibid., 23.
12. Ibid., 98.
13. Stefano Terra, *Tre anni con Tito* (Trieste: MGS Press, 2004), 139.
14. Iurii Girenko, *Stalin-Tito* (Moscow: Izdatel'stvo politicheskoi literatury, 1991), 392.
15. Jože Pirjevec, *Il gran rifiuto: Guerra fredda e calda tra Tito, Stalin e l'Occidente* (Trieste: Editoriale Stampa Triestina, 1990), 398.
16. Politisches Archiv, Berlin (Political Archive, hereafter PA), B 42, Band 243.

17. Arhiv Jugoslavije, Belgrade (Archive of Yugoslavia, hereafter AJ), KPR II-4-a, K 168; Ćosić, *Piščevi zapisi*, 1:159–64; Radina Vučetić, *Monopol na istinu: Partija, kultura i cenzura u Srbiji šezdesetih i sedamdesetih godina XX veka* (Belgrade: CLIO, 2016), 228–41.

18. Interview with Koča Popović, *Danas*, 7 February 1989, 26.

19. Ćosić, *Piščevi zapisi*, 1:308; 2:247; Halder, *Der Titokult*, 193–200.

20. Savka Dabčević-Kučar, *'71: Hrvatski snovi i stvarnost* (Zagreb: Interpublic, 1997), 2:844.

21. Nacionalna i Sveučilišna Knjižnica, Zagreb (National and University Library, hereafter NSK), Arhiv Bakarić, Kutija 7; Kutija 12.

22. AS, Dedijer, t. e. 3.

23. Dragomir Bondžić, "Titove titule: Josip Broz i naučne ustanove," in *Tito: Vidjenja i tumačenja*, Biblioteka Zbornici Radova 8, ed. Olga Manojlović Pintar (Belgrade: Institut za Noviju Istoriju Srbije, 2011), 377–78; AS, Dedijer, t. e. 244.

24. Djilas, *Tito*, 209.

25. Dedijer, *Novi prilozi*, 2:85; AS, Dedijer, t. e. 271.

26. The National Archives, London (hereafter TNA), FCO 28/2155/5.

27. TNA, FCO 28/2167/ENU 26/1; 28/2155; *The Economist*, "King Tito at Home to the Queen," 14 October 1972.

28. Marko Vrhunec, *Šest let s Titom (1967–1973)* (Ljubljana: LaserPrint, 2001), 140, 141; Dedijer, *Novi prilozi*, 2:237.

29. Zdravko Antonić, *Rodoljub Čolaković u svetlu svog dnevnika* (Belgrade: IP Knjiga, 1991), 332; Ranko Đukić, *"Topli zec" u Oslu. Neuspeli pohod J. B. Tita na Nobelovu nagradu za mir 1973. godine* (Belgrade: Građevinska knjiga, 2004).

30. NSK, Arhiv Bakarić, Kutija 10; TNA, FCO 28/2156/ENU 18/9.

31. Radmila Radić, "Josip Broz Tito i patrijarsi Srpske pravoslavne crkve (Gavrilo, Vikentije i German)," in *Tito: Vidjenja i tumačenja*, Biblioteka Zbornici Radova 8, ed. Olga Manojlović Pintar (Belgrade: Institut za Noviju Istoriju Srbije, 2011), 133.

32. AS, Dedijer, t. e. 3.

33. L. Sirc, "Nobelova nagrada za predsednika Tita? Odprto pismo, avgust 1973," *Ampak*, February 2008, 31.

34. AS, Dedijer, t. e. 3.

35. Marko Vrhunec, *Josip Broz Tito: Osebnost—stvaritve—titoizem* (Ljubljana: Duštvo piscev zgodovine NOB Slovenije, 2009), 42.

36. Ibid., 130.

37. AS, Dedijer, t. e. 3.

38. National Archives and Record Administration, Washington (hereafter NARA), PO, 15-1 Yugo, Zagreb, 25 February 1964; 4 October 1965.

39. Blažo Mandić, *S Titom: Četvrt veka u kabinetu* (Belgrade: Dan Graf, 2012), 161, 162; Niko Kavčič, *Pot v osamosvojitev* (Ljubljana: Samozaložba, 1996), 203; Dabčević-Kučar, *'71: Hrvatski snovi*, 2:848.

40. Ibid., 2:849; AS, Dedijer, t. e. 68.

41. PA, B 42, Band 1343.

42. PA, B 42, Band 1349.

43. Gelvan Library, George Washington University (hereafter GWU), 00733 National Security Study Memorandum 129, "US Policy and Post-Tito Yugoslavia," 15 June 1971.

44. TNA, FCO 28/2119/ENU 1/7; FCO 28/2408/46.

45. TNA, FCO 28/2119/UD of S (RAF)/V 23/72/7/538; FCO 28/2119/ENU 1/7.

46. TNA, FCO 28/2119/ENU 1/7.

47. NARA, CREST, Memorandum for the Record, "NIO Sponsored Seminar on Yugoslav Affairs," 21 May 1974.

48. GWU, "US Policy and Post-Tito Yugoslavia," 13 September 1971, 63.

49. Archiv ministerstva zahraničníh věcí, Prague (hereafter AMZV), Zprávy ZÚ, Bělehrad 1973–1975, 0279.

50. TNA, FCO 28/2407/29.

51. Pero Simić, *Tito: Skrivnost stoletja* (Ljubljana: Orbis, 2009), 353.

52. TNA, FCO 28/2621/ENU 1/4/36.

53. TNA, FCO 28/1625/ENU 1/1; NARA, Memorandum for the Record, "NIO Sponsored Seminar on Yugoslav Affairs," 21 May 1974; NSK, Arhiv Bakarić, Kutija 34.

54. AMZV, Zprávy ZÚ, Bělehrad 1973–1975, 0481.

55. AS, Dedijer, t. e. 261.

56. Ivan Ivanji, *Titov prevajalec* (Ljubljana: Karantanija, 2007), 135.

57. Antonić, *Rodoljub Čolaković*, 437.

58. NSK, Arhiv Bakarić, Kutija 34; Kutija 35; TNA, FCO 28/2804/ENU 3/311/1; AMZV, Zprávy ZÚ, Bělehrad 1973–1975, 0341; AS, Dedijer, t. e. 298.

59. AS, Dedijer, t. e. 123.

60. Vladimir Bilandžić, Dittmar Dahlmann, and Milan Kosanović, eds., *From Helsinki to Belgrade: The First CSCE Follow-Up Meeting and the Crisis of Détente* (Bonn: Bonn University Press, 2014), 10–14.

61. AS, Dedijer, t. e. 271; NARA, CREST, Soviet Union-Eastern Europe, "Yugoslav Security Concerns Outlined," 25 September 1975.

62. NARA, CREST, National Intelligence Daily Cable, "European Communist Meeting," 8 June 1976; Marović, *Sumrak staljinizma*, 2:223–41.

63. Blažo Mandić, *Titu u dialogu s svijetom* (Novi Sad: Agencija Mir, 2005), 451.

64. "IIM 76-040C, the Yugoslav Armed Forces, 1 October 1976," in *Yugoslavia: From "National Communism" to National Collapse; US Intelligence Community Estimative Products on Yugoslavia*, ed. Thomas Fingar (Pittsburgh, PA: GPO, 2006), 534.

65. NARA, CREST, Yugoslavia, "The Kosovo Problem: A Research Paper," 21 April 1979.

66. Živorad Mihajlović-Šilja, *Atentati: Hteli su da ubiju Tita* (Belgrade: Medicinska knjiga, 1989).

67. NARA, CREST, Soviet Union-Eastern Europe, "Explosion on Tito's Travel Route in Zagreb," 18 September 1975; "Yugoslav Security Concerns Outlined," 25 September 1975.

68. Mandić, *S Titom*, 176.

69. NARA, CREST, *Weekly Summary*, 19 November 1976.

70. AS, Dedijer, t. e. 123.

71. Marović, *Sumrak staljinizma*, 2:58; Douglas Martin, "Helmut Sonnenfeldt, Expert on Soviet and European Affair, Is Dead at 86," *New York Times*, 21 November 2012.

72. AS, Dedijer, t. e. 123.

73. Ibid.

74. AS, Dedijer, t. e. 220.

75. Andreas Razumovsky, *Ein Kampf um Belgrad: Tito und die jugoslawische Wirklichkeit* (Berlin: Ullstein, 1980), 405, 406.

76. AS, Dedijer, t. e. 252.

77. Jože Božič, *Jug Afrike in narodnoosvobodilni boj* (Ljubljana: Zavod SR Slovenije za šolstvo, 1978), 130.

78. AS, Dedijer, t. e., 220.

79. NARA, CREST, National Intelligence Daily Cable, 16 January 1979.

80. PA, Zwischenarchiv, 1126118, 26 June 1974.

81. Dragan Bogetić, "Tito i nesvrstani," in *Tito: Vidjenja i tumačenja*, Biblioteka Zbornici Radova 8, ed. Olga Manojlović Pintar (Belgrade: Institut za Noviju Istoriju Srbije, 2011), 411, 412.

82. NARA, CREST, Memorandum of Conversation, 12 August 1976.

83. BA, DY 30/IV B/130; Pero Simić and Zvonimir Despot, *Tito: Strogo poverljivo: Arhivski dokumenti* (Belgrade: Službeni glasnik, 2008), 416.

84. PA, 70284/04.

85. V. Petrović, "Havana 1979: Labudova pesma Titove lične diplomacije," in *Tito: Vidjenja i tumačenja*, Biblioteka Zbornici Radova 8, ed. Olga Manojlović Pintar (Belgrade: Institut za Noviju Istoriju Srbije, 2011), 418, 419.

86. NSK, Arhiv Bakarić, Kutija 11; Vjenceslav Cenčić, *Enigma Kopinič* (Belgrade: Rad, 1983), 2:147.

87. AS, Dedijer, t. e. 3.

88. NARA, CREST, "The Nonaligned Movement: Dynamics and Prospects, An Intelligence Assessment," 30 March 1979.

89. Stane Kavčič, *Dnevnik in spomini: 1972–1987* (Ljubljana: Časopis za kritiko znanosti, 1988), 313.

90. Simić, *Tito*, 335.

91. J. Koprivc, "Prezgodaj je razkrival nevarne ideje," *Večer*, 16 December 1999.

92. TNA, FCO 28/1647; "NIE, Prospects for Post-Tito Yugoslavia, Vol. II—The Annexes, 25 September 1979," in *Yugoslavia: From "National Communism" to National Collapse; US Intelligence Community Estimative Products on Yugoslavia*, ed. Thomas Fingar (Pittsburgh, PA: GPO, 2006), 610; NARA, CREST, National Intelligence Daily Cable, 17 May 1979; Mandić, *Titu u dialogu*, 632–42.

93. Razumovsky, *Ein Kampf um Belgrad*, 452.

94. NSK, Arhiv Bakarić, Kutija 11.

95. Ibid.

96. BA, DY 30/IV B 12/20/129.

97. AS, Dedijer, t. e. 298.

98. Djilas, *Tito*, 251.

99. NARA, CREST, "Outside Official Reaction to Stalin's Death," 11 March 1953.

100. Djilas, *Tito*, 299.

101. TNA, FCO 28/3909 ENU 010/3.

102. Dabčević-Kučar, *'71: Hrvatski snovi*, 2:820.

103. Dedijer, *Novi prilozi*, 2:262.

104. Simić, *Tito*, 331.

105. Karel Kaplan, *Antonín Novotný: Vzestup a pád "lidového" aparátčika* (Brno: Barrister & Principal, 2011), 202, 203.

106. Dejan Jović, *Yugoslavia: A State That Withered Away* (West Lafayette, IN: Purdue University Press, 2009), 139.

107. Dušan Bilandžić, *Hrvatska moderna povijest* (Zagreb: Golden Marketing, 1999), 693.

108. TNA, FCO 28/2798/ENU 1/1.

109. "NIE 15-67, The Yugoslav Experiment, 13 April 1967," in *Yugoslavia: From "National Communism" to National Collapse; US Intelligence Community Estimative Products on Yugoslavia*, ed. Thomas Fingar (Pittsburgh, PA: GPO, 2006), 316.

110. Ćosić, *Piščevi zapisi*, 2:295.

111. TNA, FCO 28/3909/ENU 010/3.

112. AS, Dedijer, t. e. 68.

113. AS, Dedijer, t. e. 197.

114. Ćosić, *Piščevi zapisi*, 2:355.

115. Ibid.; Vladimir Dimitrijević, *Tito i Srbi. knjiga druga: Kako sahraniti Broza* (Belgrade: Catena Mundi, 2013), 251, 252.

116. Dušan Bilandžić, *Povijest izbliza: Memoarski zapisi 1945–2005* (Zagreb: Prometej, 2005), 204, 251; Marović, *Sumrak staljinizma*, 2:255-58.

117. Miro Simčič, *Ženske v Titovi senci: Tito brez maske 2* (Ilirska Bistrica: Samozal., 2010), 289.

118. Ćosić, *Piščevi zapisi*, 2:356.

119. AS, Dedijer, t. e. 68; t. e. 298.

120. Mandić, *S Titom*, 192.

121. NARA, CREST, "Worldwide Reaction to the Soviet Invasion of Afghanistan," An Intelligence Memorandum; GWU, NIE, 15-79, Prospects for Post-Tito Yugoslavia, 1 February 1980.

122. TNA, FCO 28/4229.

123. Fabio Amodeo and Mario Cereghino, *Tito spiato dagli inglesi: I rapporti segreti sulla Jugoslavia, 1968–1980* (Trieste: MGS, 2014), 19.

124. Ćosić, *Piščevi zapisi*, 2:364.

125. NARA, CREST, National Intelligence Daily, "Yugoslavia-Romania: Reaction to Afghanistan," 3 January 1980; "Yugoslavia: Tito's Illness," 8 January 1980; Memorandum for the Record, Staff Meeting Minutes, 18 February 1980; "Worldwide Reaction to the Soviet Invasion of Afghanistan," An Intelligence Memorandum, 18 January 1980.

126. NARA, CREST, National Intelligence Daily, "Yugoslavia: Contest for Party Position," 10 April 198.

127. Predrag Lalević, *S Titom po svetu* (Belgrade: Službeni glasnik, 2012), 160, 170.

128. Stefano Lusa, *La dissoluzione del potere: Il partito comunista sloveno e il processo di democratizzazione della repubblica* (Udine: Kappa VU, 2007), 19–21; AS, Dedijer, t. e. 36.

129. Franc Šetinc, *Zbogom, Jugoslavija* (Ljubljana: DZS, 1993), 222.

130. TNA, FCO, 28/4229.

131. Gian Carlo Pajetta, *Le crisi che ho vissuto* (Rome: Editori Riuniti, 1982), 49.

132. Djilas, *Tito*, 198.

133. Marko Lopušina, *Ubij bližnjeg svog: Jugoslovenska tajna policija 1945–1995* (Belgrade: Biblioteka "Revija 92," 1996), 1:210.

134. Jak Koprivc, *Generalov let: Spomini generala Ivana Dolničarja* (Ljubljana: Modrijan, 2005), 191.

135. AS, Dedijer, t. e. 261.

136. NARA, CREST, "Prospects for Post-Tito Yugoslavia," National Intelligence Estimate, 25 September 1979; see also *Yugoslavia: From "National Communism" to National Collapse*, 570.

137. AS, Dedijer, t. e. 220; t. e. 298.

Index

Page references in italics indicate an illustration.